HIGH COURT CASE SUMMARIES

TORTS

Keyed to [Prosser, Wade,] Schwartz, Kelly, and
Partlett's Casebook on Torts,
11th Edition

THOMSON

WEST

Mat #40421537

© 2005 Thomson/West
      610 Opperman Drive
      P.O. Box 64526
      St. Paul, MN 55164–0526
      1–800–328–9352
Printed in the United States of America

ISBN 0–314–16382–4

TEXT IS PRINTED ON 10% POST CONSUMER RECYCLED PAPER

Table of Contents

Alphabetical Table of Cases

CHAPTER ONE

Development of Liability Based Upon Fault

Anonymous

Instant Facts: In this case Brian, the arguing counsel, is describing the state of law as it existed in 1466.

Black Letter Rule: A man, whose actions directly cause an injury to another, is liable to the injured person even though his action was not unlawful.

Weaver v. Ward

Instant Facts: Weaver (P) and Ward (D) were engaged in military exercises when Weaver (P) was injured as a result of Ward (D) firing his gun. Weaver (P) sued Ward (D) in an action of trespass for assault and battery.

Black Letter Rule: A defendant is liable for all his actions causing injury unless the injury was caused utterly without his fault.

Brown v. Kendall

Instant Facts: In an attempt to separate his own dog from Brown's (P) dog, Kendall (D) hits Brown (P) in the eye and injures him.

Black Letter Rule: An individual, who during the commission of a lawful act uses ordinary care, is not liable for injuries caused to another party as a result of his act.

Cohen v. Petty

Instant Facts: Cohen (P), a passenger in Petty's (D) car, suffers injuries when Petty (D) loses consciousness and his car hits a tree.

Black Letter Rule: A party is not liable in negligence for injury caused by his unforeseeable and involuntary actions.

Spano v. Perini Corp.

Instant Facts: Spano (P) suffered property damage as a result of blasting caused by Perini Corp (D). Perini (D) was not negligent in conducting the blasting

Black Letter Rule: An individual who has sustained property damage caused by blasting may recover for his damages without a showing of negligence by the defendant.

Anonymous

King's Bench, 1466, Y.B. 5 Edw. IV, folio 7, placitum 18

UNDER EARLY COMMON LAW, WHERE ONE WAS THE DIRECT CAUSE OF INJURY TO ANOTHER, THE FORMER WAS LIABLE REGARDLESS OF HIS LACK OF INTENT OR NEGLIGENCE

■ **INSTANT FACTS** In this case Brian, the arguing counsel, is describing the state of law as it existed in 1466.

■ **BLACK LETTER RULE** A man, whose actions directly cause an injury to another, is liable to the injured person even though his action was not unlawful.

■ **PROCEDURAL BASIS**

Counsel establishing a point of law in British Court.

■ **FACTS**

Counsel in this case (Brian) is arguing that an individual is liable for his/her actions regardless of the lawfulness of his conduct. Additionally, an individual is liable for the direct results of his actions even if his actions where done in good conscience.

■ **ISSUE**

Is a man, whose actions directly cause an injury to another, liable to the injured person even though his action was not unlawful?

■ **DECISION AND RATIONALE**

(Brian, arguing counsel) Yes. A man, whose actions directly cause an injury to another, is liable to the injured person even though his action was not unlawful. This is so even though the individual's action was lawful and he did not have the intent to cause any injury to another party.

Analysis:

This case illustrates the traditional Common Law view of Tort law. Under this view, an individual was basically strictly liable for the consequences of his actions, however lawful these actions may have been. Thus, as the case illustrates, if an individual, in defending himself, hits a third party by accident, he will be held liable for the injuries caused to the third party even though he did not have the intent to injure that party. The same results would be reached if the individual was not in the slightest bit negligent in his actions. Thus, this case is the earliest example of imposition of strict liability where the state of mind of the defendant is irrelevant. Note that in early Common Law, where plaintiff's injury was directly caused by the actions of the defendant, the plaintiff had an action in trespass. However, where the plaintiff's injuries were an indirect result of the defendant's actions, the plaintiff had an action in trespass on the case. Under the latter, parties would have to show either intent to cause the injury or negligence in bringing about the plaintiff's injury.

■ CASE VOCABULARY

ACTION: A suit or judicial proceeding.

ASSAULT: An attempt or threat, with unlawful force, to inflict bodily injury upon another, accompanied by the apparent present ability to give effect to the attempt if not prevented.

Weaver v. Ward

(Battered Soldier) v. *(Tortfeasor Soldier)*
Hobart 134, 80 Eng.Rep. 284 (King's Bench, 1616)

IN EARLY TORT CASES, DEFENDANT HAD THE BURDEN OF PROVING THAT HE WAS NOT AT FAULT FOR THE INJURY INFLICTED UPON THE PLAINTIFF

■ **INSTANT FACTS** Weaver (P) and Ward (D) were engaged in military exercises when Weaver (P) was injured as a result of Ward (D) firing his gun.

■ **BLACK LETTER RULE** A defendant is liable for all his actions causing injury unless the injury was caused utterly without his fault.

■ **PROCEDURAL BASIS**

Action in trespass for personal injury in English Court.

■ **FACTS**

While Ward (D) was engaged in military exercises with Weaver (P), Ward (D) accidentally shot and wounded Weaver (P). Weaver (P) brought an action of trespass for assault and battery against Ward (D), and won on demurrer.

■ **ISSUE**

Is a defendant liable for all his actions which directly cause an injury to a third party if the injury was caused utterly without his fault?

■ **DECISION AND RATIONALE**

No. A defendant is liable for all his actions causing injury unless the injury was caused utterly without his fault. Although a man who hurts another unintentionally and without felonious intent is not guilty of a felony, he is guilty in trespass. Trespass gives damages to the injured party on the basis of the party's loss. Thus, for an action in trespass the defendant need not have the intent to cause the injury, and he is liable unless the injury was caused utterly without his doing, such as where the plaintiff runs in front of the defendant's gun when he is firing his gun.

Analysis:

As mentioned earlier, traditional tort law allocated liability on the basis of injury and not on the basis of individual's fault. Thus, if an individual's actions directly caused an injury to a third party, he will be liable, regardless of the level of his intent. This case is a loosening of the earlier strict liability standard in cases of trespass. Here, the court indicates that if the injury to the plaintiff occurred truly without the defendant's fault (i.e., a man took the defendant's hand and forced him to strike the plaintiff), then the defendant may not be found liable. Notice in this case, that the burden of proof is on the defendant to prove that he is not at fault. Later cases will show a shift in the burden of proof from the defendant to the plaintiff.

■ CASE VOCABULARY

ACTION OF TRESPASS: In early common law, provided a remedy against injury to the person or property directly resulting from the conduct of the defendant.

BATTERY: The unlawful application of force to the person of another.

DEMURRER: To stop, stay or rest; in pleading, a formal objection attacking the legal sufficiency of the opponent's pleadings; an assertion made, without disputing the facts, that the pleading does not state a cause of action.

FORMS OF ACTION: Various classes of personal action at common law.

NEGLIGENT BATTERY: Absence of care in physical violence on a human being.

TILT: Attack, clash, duel.

TRESPASS ON THE CASE: In early common law, trespass on the case or "case," afforded remedy against injury to the person or property indirectly resulting from the conduct of the defendant.

TURNEY: Tournament, competition.

Herrin v. Sutherland

(*Landowner*) v. (*Trespasser*)

74 Mont. 587, 241 P. 328 (1925)

UNDER THE COMMON LAW A LANDOWNER/POSSESSOR OWNED ALL THE SPACE UPWARDS AND DOWNWARDS FROM THE LAND TO AN INDEFINITE EXTENT

■ **INSTANT FACTS** Herrin (P) sued Sutherland (D) in trespass for shooting a gun over the space above Herrin's (P) land.

■ **BLACK LETTER RULE** It is trespass to pass over, or cause an object to pass over, the land of another, even if there has been no touching of the soil.

■ **PROCEDURAL BASIS**

Appeal from action in trespass.

■ **FACTS**

Sutherland (D), while standing on the land of another and hunting ducks, was constantly firing his gun at the birds above Herrin's (P) land. Herrin (P) sued Sutherland (D) for trespass to his land and asked for nominal damages in the amount of $10. The trial court granted a judgement in favor of Herrin (P) for $1. Sutherland (D) appeals.

■ **ISSUE**

Is it trespass to pass over, or cause an object to pass over the land of another, even if there has been no touching of the soil?

■ **DECISION AND RATIONALE**

(Callaway, C.J.) Yes. It is trespass to pass over, or cause an object to pass over, the land of another, even if there has been no touching of the soil. It is the consensus that airspace, at least the airspace near the ground, is almost as inviolable as the soil itself. In this case, although the plaintiff has suffered no physical damages to his person or property, he has, at least, a claim for nominal damages. (Affirmed.)

Analysis:

Under early Common Law, one owned all the air space above and below his land. This view became a little extreme in modern times and the courts and Congress (as we will see in *City of Newark v. Eastern Airlines*) limited the definition of land to the area above and below the property that was safe and the landowner could make use of. Note that this case also stands for the proposition that an individual need not touch the soil of another in order to be held liable in trespass. It is enough that he cause an object to fly into or over the landowner's land.

■ CASE VOCABULARY

INVIOLABLE: Not to be violated; sacred.

MAXIM: A concise rule of conduct.

NOMINAL DAMAGES: A trivial sum of damages awarded; this sum is frequently $1, and it is given as a recognition that a legal injury was sustained, though slight.

Brown v. Kendall

(Battery Victim) v. *(Dog Owner)*
60 Mass. (6 Cush.) 292 (1850)

AN INDIVIDUAL ATTEMPTING TO RECOVER FROM ANOTHER MUST PROVE THAT THE LATTER WAS NEGLIGENT IN HIS ACTIONS

■ **INSTANT FACTS** In an attempt to separate his own dog from Brown's (P) dog, Kendall (D) hits Brown (P) in the eye and injures him.

■ **BLACK LETTER RULE** An individual, who during the commission of a lawful act uses ordinary care, is not liable for injuries caused to another party as a result of his act.

■ **PROCEDURAL BASIS**

Appeal from action in personal injury

■ **FACTS**

Kendall (D) and Brown (P) had dogs who were fighting with one another. In attempting to separate the dogs from one another, Kendall (D) unintentionally hit Brown (P) in the eye and injured him. Contrary to Kendall's (D) request, the trial court instructed the jury that if Kendall's (D) act in separating the dog was an act which he was under a duty to perform, Kendall (D) need only have used ordinary care. However, if the act was one that he was not under an obligation to perform, he should have used extraordinary care in performing it. Kendall (D) appeals on the ground that the instructions given to the jury were erroneous.

■ **ISSUE**

Is an individual, who during the commission of a lawful act, uses ordinary care, liable for injuries caused to another party as a result of his act.

■ **DECISION AND RATIONALE**

(Shaw, C.J.) No. An individual, who during the commission of a lawful act, uses ordinary care is not liable for injuries caused to another party as a result of his act. There is no authority for the holding that damage received by a direct act from another will be a sufficient basis of liability, whether the individual's act was lawful, or unlawful, and when it is neither intentional nor careless. The plaintiff in such cases must show that either the defendant's intention was unlawful or that the defendant was at fault. If the injury to the plaintiff was unavoidable, the defendant is not liable. Thus, the trial court should have instructed the jury that if the defendant in this case was using ordinary care, he is not liable for the plaintiff's injuries. It is the plaintiff who must prove either that the defendant's act was unlawful or that defendant failed to exercise due care. The burden of proof is on the plaintiff and not on the defendant. (New trial ordered.)

Analysis:

The significance of this case is two-fold. In the first place, it is moving away from the concept of strict liability. In this case, defendant is not liable if his act was not intentional, unlawful, or if it is done with due care necessary under the circumstances. Secondly, this case shifts the burden of proof for establishing lack of due care to the plaintiff. It is important to note that it is no longer enough that the plaintiff's injury resulted directly from the defendant's actions. It is the plaintiff here, who must prove that not only did the defendant cause his injuries, but he also did so negligently or intentionally.

■ CASE VOCABULARY

ASSAULT AND BATTERY: A violent attack with physical violence.

CIRCUMSPECTION: Caution; looking on all sides.

DICTA: Opinions of a judge which do not determine a case.

EXIGENCY: Demand or need arising suddenly; calling for immediate action.

WANT OF PRUDENCE: Lack of care or good judgment.

Cohen v. Petty

(Passenger) v. *(Driver)*
62 App.D.C. 187, 65 F.2d 820 (App.D.C.1933)

A PERSON IS ONLY LIABLE FOR HIS VOLUNTARY ACTIONS WHICH ARE WITHIN HIS CONTROL

■ **INSTANT FACTS** Cohen (P), a passenger in Petty's (D) car, suffers injuries when Petty (D) loses consciousness and his car hits a tree.

■ **BLACK LETTER RULE** A party is not liable in negligence for injury caused by his unforeseeable and involuntary actions.

■ **PROCEDURAL BASIS**

Appeal in personal injury action.

■ **FACTS**

Cohen (P) was a passenger in Petty's (D) car. Other passengers in the car and several witnesses indicated that Petty (D) lost consciousness while driving his car and hit a tree. Petty (D) claims that he has had no history of losing consciousness and that he did not anticipate it. The trial court rendered a decision in favor of Petty (D), stating that no action lies on negligence where the act leading to the injury was involuntary and outside of Petty's (D) control. Cohen (P) appeals.

■ **ISSUE**

Is a party is liable in negligence for injury caused by his unforeseeable and involuntary actions?

■ **DECISION AND RATIONALE**

No. (Groner, Ass. J.) A party is not liable in negligence for injury caused by his unforeseeable and involuntary actions. The evidence is uncontroverted that Petty (D) fainted right before the collision which gave rise to Cohen's (P) injury. Also, the evidence indicates that Petty (D) has no history of fainting and did not anticipate it. Under these circumstances, defendant is not chargeable with negligence and the trial court was correct for taking the case from the jury. Petty (D) did not have any reason to know that he would have fainted. Thus, negligence can not be based on his recklessness for driving the car as it would if he knew or should have known of his condition. (Affirmed.)

Analysis:

This case defines negligence as the failure to exercise reasonable care. In this case, the defendant was not negligent in driving the car. Neither did he know or should he have had any reason to know that he would faint. As such, he did not fail to exercise reasonable care, and will not be liable for his involuntary and unanticipated actions. Note also, that the defendant in this case received a directed verdict because the plaintiff failed to carry its burden of production of enough evidence to prove the prima facie case of negligence.

■ CASE VOCABULARY

NEGLIGENCE: The failure to exercise that degree of care which a person of ordinary prudence (a reasonable person) would exercise under the same circumstances; also, the conduct which fails below the standard established by law for the protection of others against unreasonable risk of harm.

Spano v. Perini Corp.

(Garage Owner) v. *(Dynamite Corp.)*

25 N.Y.2d 11, 250 N.E.2d 31, on remand, 33 A.D.2d 516 (1969)

AN INDIVIDUAL MAY RECOVER IN STRICT LIABILITY FOR DAMAGES SUSTAINED AS A RESULT OF A DEFENDANT'S ULTRAHAZARDOUS ACTIVITIES

■ **INSTANT FACTS** Spano (P) suffered property damage as a result of blasting caused by Perini Corp (D). Perini (D) was not negligent in conducting the blasting

■ **BLACK LETTER RULE** An individual who has sustained property damage caused by blasting may recover for his damages without a showing of negligence by the defendant.

■ **PROCEDURAL BASIS**

Appeal from an action for recovery for property damage.

■ **FACTS**

Spano (P), an owner of a garage, suffered property damage when Perini Corp. (D) set off 194 sticks of dynamite a little more than a 100 feet away form Spano's (P) garage. Spano (P) who had claimed negligence as the basis for liability, had failed to show a lack of due care on the part of Perini (D). The lower court decided in the favor of Spano (P). The appellate division reversed. Spano (P) appeals, requesting the court to change the status of the law regarding blasting.

■ **ISSUE**

May an individual who has sustained property damage caused by blasting recover for his damages without a showing of negligence by the defendant?

■ **DECISION AND RATIONALE**

(Fuld, C.J.) Yes. An individual who has sustained property damage caused by blasting may recover for his damages without a showing of negligence by the defendant. Traditional law requires that in order to recover for property damage the plaintiff must make a showing of negligence in blasting cases, unless there is physical invasion of the plaintiff's property. The defendant stores explosives which are highly dangerous and likely to cause injury and property damages in their vicinity. Such damage may not be guarded against even with the highest degree of care. The question in this case is not whether the actions of the defendant were lawful or not. However, the question is who bears the loss when injury occurs as a result of blasting: the person who has engaged in the dangerous activity or the innocent neighbor. (Reversed.)

Analysis:

Once again this case takes us back to strict liability as a standard of recovery in Tort law. In this case, the court has drawn its decision partly on policy reasons. Where a party has engaged in a lawful, but dangerous activity, who should bear the cost of any losses occurring as a result of the activity: the innocent party or the party who has chosen to commit the lawful, yet dangerous act. Clearly, between the two, the latter should bear the cost. Note that in this case, the defendants were not negligent. Thus, without strict liability as a theory for recovery, the plaintiff would have never recovered for his damages in negligence.

■ **CASE VOCABULARY**

ABSOLUTE LIABILITY: Unconditional responsibility.

EXTINGUISHMENT OF THE RIGHT: Cancellation of a right.

GRANTING LEAVE TO APPEAL: Allowing the right to appeal without interference.

JUDICIAL "TREND": A current judicial tendency.

STRICT LIABILITY: In tort law, liability, if one engages in an activity that has an inherent risk of injury such as those classified as ultra-hazardous activities, for all injuries proximately caused by his/her enterprise, even without a showing of negligence; in tort and criminal law, refers to liability without fault.

CHAPTER TWO

Intentional Interference With Person or Property

Garratt v. Dailey

Instant Facts: Garratt (P) suffered injuries when Dailey (D), a five-year old boy, pulled a chair from underneath her.

Black Letter Rule: A party is liable for battery when he is substantially certain that his act will result in harmful or offensive touching.

Spivey v. Battaglia

Instant Facts: After Battaglia (D) intentionally puts his arms around Spivey (P) she suffers severe neck and back pains and becomes paralyzed.

Black Letter Rule: A party who acts with knowledge and substantial certainty that a particular result will follow is liable for all results flowing from his act regardless of how unforeseeable or unreasonable.

Ranson v. Kitner

Instant Facts: Kitner (D), when hunting, shot Ranson's (P) dog, thinking that it is a wolf.

Black Letter Rule: Good faith mistake is not a defense to intentional torts where the defendant intended the consequence of his act.

McGuire v. Almy

Instant Facts: McGuire (P), Almy's (D) care-taker, brought an action against the latter, an insane person, for injuries suffered when Almy (P) hit her with a chair.

Black Letter Rule: An insane individual who is capable of forming the intent to strike another and acts upon that intent is liable to that individual for the injuries suffered.

Talmage v. Smith

Instant Facts: Smith (D), intending to scare away two boys who were on his property aims, throws a stick at one boy but instead hits Talmage (P), the other boy, and injures him.

Black Letter Rule: An individual who intends an act or consequence against one party and instead injures a third party is liable to the third party for the injuries suffered.

Cole v. Turner

Instant Facts: (No facts are given in this case.)

Black Letter Rule: Intentional touching of another in an unreasonable and violent manner is considered battery.

Wallace v. Rosen

Instant Facts: During a school fire drill, Rosen (D) placed her hand on Wallace's (P) back, causing her to fall down the stairs.

Black Letter Rule: A battery is the knowing or intentional touching of one person by another in a rude, insolent, or angry manner.

Fisher v. Carrousel Motor Hotel, Inc.

Instant Facts: Fisher (P) sued Carrousel Motor Hotel (D) for battery and assault by Carrousel's (D) employees who snatched a plate from his hands and yelled offensive words at him.

Black Letter Rule: The snatching or knocking of an object closely attached to an individual constitutes battery even though there was no actual physical contact to the individual's body.

I de S et Ux v. W de S

Instant Facts: W de S (D), while in front of the house belonging to I de S (P) and his wife (P), threw a hatchet at the wife (P) which missed her.

Black Letter Rule: A defendant may be liable in assault of a plaintiff, even though there has been no actual physical invasion of the plaintiff by the defendant.

Western Union Telegraph Co. v. Hill

Instant Facts: Hill (P) instituted an action in assault against Western Union Telegraph Co. (D) after one of the latter's employees made improper advances towards Hill (P) who was standing across the counter from the employee.

Black Letter Rule: The actual ability of the defendant to cause harmful or offensive touching is not a requirement for actionable assault.

Big Town Nursing Home, Inc. v. Newman

Instant Facts: Newman (P), a resident of Big Town Nursing Home (D), who had entered the nursing home on his own, was kept in the nursing home against his will after having attempted to leave several times.

Black Letter Rule: A defendant is liable for false imprisonment when the defendant has prevented the plaintiff from leaving a certain limited area without legal justification.

Parvi v. City Of Kingston

Instant Facts: Parvi (P) sued the City of Kingston (D) for false imprisonment because the police had taken him to the outskirts of the city against his will. At trial, he testified that he could not recall anything that happened at the time in question.

Black Letter Rule: A defendant is not liable for falsely imprisoning the plaintiff when the latter was not aware of the confinement at the time it occurs.

Hardy v. Labelle's Distributing Co.

Instant Facts: Hardy (P) who was falsely accused of stealing from the store where she was employed, sues her employer, Labelle's Distributing Co. (D) for false imprisonment.

Black Letter Rule: A person can not maintain an action for false imprisonment when no threat of force was used to compel that person to stay against his/her will.

Enright v. Groves

Instant Facts: Enright (P) instituted an action in false imprisonment because she was arrested by Gorves (D) upon her refusal to hand him her driver's license.

Black Letter Rule: A police officer is liable for false arrest when he arrests an individual without a warrant or probable cause that an offense has been committed by the individual.

Whittaker v. Sandford

Instant Facts: Sandford (P) sued Whittaker (D) for false imprisonment because of the latter's refusal to provide Sandford (P) a means of getting from Whittaker's (D) boat to the shore.

Black Letter Rule: Confinement of an individual to a bounded area, without means of egress, can result in false imprisonment even if there is no actual physical restraint used upon the individual.

State Rubbish Collectors Ass'n v. Siliznoff

Instant Facts: State Rubbish Collectors Ass'n (D) sued Siliznoff (P) to collect on a debt that he owed. Siliznoff (P) countersued State Rubbish (D) for causing him duress and distress.

Black Letter Rule:

One who causes severe emotional distress to another is liable for such emotional distress and for bodily harm resulting from it.

Slocum v. Food Fair Stores Of Florida

Instant Facts: While a customer at Food Fair Stores of Florida (D), Slocum (P) was severely insulted by an employee which caused her to suffer a heart attack.

Black Letter Rule: Conduct that causes mere emotional distress is not severe enough to allow recovery based on an independent cause of action.

Harris v. Jones

Instant Facts: Harris (P), claiming that his supervisor, Jones (D) constantly ridiculed his stuttering, sought recovery from Jones (D), under the tort of intentional infliction of emotional distress.

Black Letter Rule: An individual must suffer a severely disabling emotional response to the tortfeasor's conduct in order to recover damages for intentional infliction of emotional distress.

Taylor v. Vallelunga

Instant Facts: Taylor (P), who saw Vallelunga (D) severely beat her father, sued Vallelunga (D) for damages for intentional infliction of emotional distress.

Black Letter Rule: A third party may not recover damages for intentional infliction of emotional distress when the defendant was not aware of the third party's presence at the time that defendant's conduct was taking place and the third party did not suffer any physical injury.

Dougherty v. Stepp

Instant Facts: Dougherty (P) sued Stepp (D) for unauthorized and unlawful entry onto his land.

Black Letter Rule: In order to maintain an action in trespass, it is not necessary that there be actual physical injury to the land.

Bradley v. American Smelting and Refining Co.

Instant Facts: Bradley (P), who owns property 4 miles away from American Smeltering and Refining Co. (D), sued the latter in trespass for emitting various gases onto Bradley's (P) property.

Black Letter Rule: A landowner/possessor must show actual physical damages for recovery in trespass by intangible objects or substances?

Herrin v. Sutherland

Instant Facts: Herrin (P) sued Sutherland (D) in trespass for shooting a gun over the space above Herrin's (P) land.

Black Letter Rule: It is trespass to pass over, or cause an object to pass over, the land of another, even if there has been no touching of the soil.

Rogers v. Board Of Road Com'rs for Kent County

Instant Facts: Rogers (P) sought recovery for the death of her husband whose death she claims to have been caused by Board of Road Com'rs for Kent County, due to their trespass onto Rogers' property.

Black Letter Rule: Trespass may be committed by the continued presence of a structure on land after the landowner has effectively terminated his consent to have the property on his land.

Glidden v. Szybiak

Instant Facts: Glidden (P), bitten by Szybiak's (D) dog, sues to recover for damages. Szybiak contends that Glidden (P) can not recover because her injuries resulted from her trespass to the dog.

Black Letter Rule: An individual may not maintain an action for trespass unless he has suffered actual damages as a result of the trespass.

Compuserve Inc. v. Cyber Promotions Inc.

Instant Facts: A promotions company was sending unsolicited e-mail advertisements to CompuServe Internet service subscribers.

Black Letter Rule: Trespass to chattels is actionable where the value or condition of the chattel is intentionally impaired.

Pearson v. Dodd

Instant Facts: Senator Pearson (P) instituted an action in conversion against Dodd (D), a journalist, for unauthorized photocopying of Pearson's (P) office files.

Black Letter Rule: Photocopying of documents, which contain information not protected by property laws, does not constitute conversion.

Garratt v. Dailey

(Tort Victim) v. *(Tortfeasor)*

46 Wash.2d 197, 279 P.2d 1091 (1955)

INTENT TO CAUSE AN ACT IS SATISFIED WHEN A PARTY INTENDS TO BRING ABOUT THE ACT OR ITS CONSEQUENCE OR WHEN THE PARTY IS SUBSTANTIALLY CERTAIN THAT HIS/HER ACT WILL BRING ABOUT A CERTAIN CONSEQUENCE

■ **INSTANT FACTS** Garratt (P) suffered injuries when Dailey (D), a five-year old boy, pulled a chair from underneath her.

■ **BLACK LETTER RULE** A party is liable for battery when he is substantially certain that his act will result in harmful or offensive touching.

■ **PROCEDURAL BASIS**

Appeal from action in battery

■ **FACTS**

While in the backyard of Garratt's (P) home, Dailey (D) pulled a chair from underneath Garratt (P) before she could sit on it. As a result, Garratt (P) fell to the ground and suffered a fractured hip and other serious injuries. Garratt (P) instituted an action in battery. The trial court dismissed Garratt's (P) action, indicating that she failed to prove that Dailey (D) had moved the chair for the purpose of bringing about Garratt's (P) contact with the ground. Plaintiff appeals.

■ **ISSUE**

Is a party liable for battery when he is substantially certain that his act will result in harmful or offensive touching?

■ **DECISION AND RATIONALE**

(Hill, J.) Yes. A party is liable for battery when he is substantially certain that his act will result in harmful or offensive touching. To maintain an action in battery, it is not enough that the defendant commits the act itself intentionally, even though the act may cause a great risk of harm. The defendant must know or realize to a substantial certainty that his act will bring about the contact or harmful touching. In this case, battery would be established if the defendant knew to a substantial certainty that the plaintiff would sit where the chair had been. However, the absence of intent to injure the plaintiff does not absolve the defendant from liability. If the defendant knew to a substantial certainty that plaintiff would sit where the chair was, he is liable, even if he did not act with the purpose of harming the plaintiff. Thus, it is the task of the trial court to determine whether or not the defendant, possessed such intent. (Remanded for clarification.)

Analysis:

In order to be liable in battery, a defendant must have the intent to bring about harmful or offensive touching. The requisite intent is satisfied if the defendant knows that the contact will occur or is substantially certain that the contact will occur. Note however, that the requisite intent required is not maliciousness. It is not required that the defendant act with the purpose of harming the plaintiff. It is enough that the defendant act with the intent to bring about the harmful or offensive touching.

■ CASE VOCABULARY

APPURTENANT: Apparatus, accessory or equipment.

BATTERY: Physical violence on a human being.

REMAND: To set back, as for further deliberation; to send back a matter to the tribunal or body from which it was appealed or moved. When a judgment is reversed, the appellate court usually remands the matter for a new trial to be carried out consistent with the principles announced in its opinion.

TORT: A civil or private wrong or injury.

VOLITIONAL: A willing act.

Spivey v. Battaglia

(Battery Victim) v. *(Embracing Man)*
258 So.2d 815 (Fla.1972)

KNOWLEDGE AND APPRECIATION OF A RISK, SHORT OF SUBSTANTIAL CERTAINTY, DOES NOT CONSTITUTE THE REQUISITE INTENT FOR INTENTIONAL TORTS

■ **INSTANT FACTS** After Battaglia (D) intentionally puts his arms around Spivey (P) she suffers severe neck and back pains and becomes paralyzed.

■ **BLACK LETTER RULE** A party who acts with knowledge and substantial certainty that a particular result will follow is liable for all results flowing from his act regardless of how unforeseeable or unreasonable.

■ **PROCEDURAL BASIS**

Appeal to from summary judgment dismissing action in negligence.

■ **FACTS**

While in the lunch room at work, Battaglia (D) teasingly puts his arms around Spivey (P) whom he knew to be shy. Immediately after this, Spivey (P) suffered a sharp pain in the back of her neck and ear. As a result, she became paralyzed on the left side of her face. She sued Battaglia (D) in an action for negligence, and assault and battery. However, the trial court dismissed her action in assault and battery on the ground that it was barred by the two-year statute of limitations. The trial court, in a summary judgment motion, dismissed Spivey's (P) action in negligence. Spivey (P) appeals in order to bring an action in negligence.

■ **ISSUE**

Is a party who acts with knowledge and substantial certainty that a particular result will follow liable for all results flowing from his act regardless of how unforeseeable or unreasonable?

■ **DECISION AND RATIONALE**

(Dekle, J.) Yes. A party who acts with knowledge and substantial certainty that a particular result will follow is liable for all results flowing from his act regardless of how unforeseeable or unreasonable. However, knowledge and appreciation of a risk, short of substantial certainty is not the equivalent of intent. Such lesser appreciation of the risk is considered unintentional and it qualifies as negligence. A person who acts with the requisite intent to bring about an act or a consequence is liable for all consequences of the act, whether foreseeable or not. However, a person who acts with a lesser degree of intent, is liable only for those harms that are reasonably foreseeable. The existence of negligence in each case depends on the circumstances surrounding the case. The trial judge in this case committed an error by dismissing the case in favor of the defendant without submitting the case to the jury with appropriate instructions regarding elements of negligence. (Reversed and Remanded.)

Analysis:

This case stands for several propositions. First, a defendant who has the requisite intent for an intentional tort is liable for all injuries or harms that flow from his/her actions. This is true regardless of

---

how remote or unforeseeable the injuries or harms may be. On the contrary, in an action based on negligence, the defendant is only liable for those harms that are reasonably foreseeable. Additionally, this case stands for the proposition that bringing a suit based on one cause of action does not bar a plaintiff from bringing a suit on other causes of actions.

■ CASE VOCABULARY

CERTIORARI: [Latin] An appellate proceeding for re-examination to obtain further information.

INFRA: [Latin] Below in this writing.

NEGLIGENCE: Absence of care.

PETITIONER: Person bringing action.

QUASH: To overthrow or make void.

RESPONDENT: Person responding to action.

SUMMARY: Short, Brief; without a jury.

SUPRA: [Latin] Refers reader to previous portion of this writing.

Ranson v. Kitner

(Battery Victim) v. *(Dog Owner)*

31 Ill.App. 241 (1889)

INTENT TO CAUSE AN INTENTIONAL TORT IS NOT VITIATED BY GOOD FAITH MISTAKE

■ **INSTANT FACTS** Kitner (D), when hunting, shot Ranson's (P) dog, thinking that it was a wolf.

■ **BLACK LETTER RULE** Good faith mistake is not a defense to intentional torts where the defendant intended the consequence of his act.

■ **PROCEDURAL BASIS**

Appeal from an action in battery.

■ **FACTS**

While hunting for wolves, Kitner (D) shot Ranson's (P) dog. At trial, it was established that Kitner (D) was under the mistaken belief that the dog was a wolf. The trial court returned a verdict in favor of Ranson (P) for $50 as the value of his dog. Kitner (D) appeals on the ground that the trial court made an error by not considering his good faith mistake as a defense.

■ **ISSUE**

Is good faith mistake a defense to intentional torts where the defendant intended the consequence of his act?

■ **DECISION AND RATIONALE**

(Conger, J.) No. Good faith mistake is not a defense to intentional torts where the defendant intended the consequence of his act. The defendant is liable for the damage that he has caused to the plaintiff regardless of the fact that his mistake was made in good faith.

Analysis:

The results in this case seem a little harsh. However, given the requisite intent for intentional torts, it makes sense. The defendant in this case intended to shoot. In other words, he intended to bring about a harmful or offensive touching. The requisite intent here is not the specific intent to kill a dog, but to shoot an animal. Thus, despite the fact that he was wrong about who the receiver of his act was, he is liable.

■ **CASE VOCABULARY**

APPELLANT: One who makes an appeal from a lower to a higher court.

APPELLEE: The person in a case against whom an appeal is taken.

McGuire v. Almy

(*Caretaker*) v. (*Insane Person*)

297 Mass. 323, 8 N.E.2d 760 (1937)

INSANE INDIVIDUALS WHO BY THEIR ACT DO INTENTIONAL DAMAGE TO THE PERSON OR PROPERTY OF ANOTHER ARE LIABLE FOR THAT DAMAGE TO THE SAME EXTENT AS A NORMAL PERSON

■ **INSTANT FACTS** McGuire (P), Almy's (D) care-taker, brought an action against the latter, an insane person, for injuries suffered when Almy (P) hit her with a chair.

■ **BLACK LETTER RULE** An insane individual who is capable of forming the intent to strike another and acts upon that intent is liable to that individual for the injuries suffered.

■ **PROCEDURAL BASIS**

Appeal from directed verdict in action for battery.

■ **FACTS**

Almy (D) was an insane person who was being cared for by McGuire (P). On April 19, 1932, Almy (D), while locked in her room became violent and dangerous, crashing and breaking furniture and other items. Upon entering Almy's (D) room, McGuire (P) saw that the former was holding a chair by the leg as if she were going to strike someone. While McGuire (P) was attempting to remove the chair from Almy's (D) hand, the latter struck her with the chair, causing her injuries for which she brought an action against Almy (D) in battery. The trial court directed a verdict in favor of Almy (D). McGuire (P) appeals the trial court's decision on the ground that the directed verdict was erroneous.

■ **ISSUE**

Is an insane individual who is capable of forming the intent to strike another and acts upon that intent liable to that individual for the injuries suffered?

■ **DECISION AND RATIONALE**

(Qua, J.) Yes. An insane individual who is capable of forming the intent to strike another and acts upon that intent is liable to that individual for the injuries suffered. In the broadest sense, the law today almost invariably holds insane persons liable for the torts that they commit. No distinction has been made between the liability of insane individuals for intentional torts and negligent torts. Additionally, insane people must pay for the damage that they may cause to other individuals. While authority may be conflicting as to the role of fault in determining the liability of an insane person, that issue need not be determined in this case. An insane person who by his act does intentional damage to the person or property of another is liable for that damage to the same extent as a normal person would be. In this case, the jury could have found that the defendant was capable of entertaining and did entertain an intent to strike and to injure the plaintiff, and that she acted with that intent. Thus, the defendant is liable. (Judgment for the plaintiff.)

Analysis:

Note, once again, that this case defines the intent that is necessary in order to hold someone liable for intentional torts. The requisite intent does not require that the tortfeasor's purpose be malicious or harmful. So long as the tortfeasor intended the act or consequence he is liable. In this case, whether the insane person had the mental capacity to recognize and appreciate the danger of hitting someone with a chair is irrelevant. It is important that the person had the intent to commit the act, namely, the act of hitting someone with the chair. If the person had this intent, then he/she is liable. Compare the insane person's liability in this case, with a child's liability in *Garratt v. Dailey*. In both cases, regardless of age or mental capacity, the defendants were liable for the acts that they intended to bring about.

■ CASE VOCABULARY

DEFAMATION: Harming of a person's reputation by false and malicious statement(s).

DIRECTED VERDICT: A verdict entered in a jury trial by the court, without consideration by the jury, because the facts elicited during the trial, together with the applicable law, made it dear that the directed verdict was the only one which could have been reasonably returned.

MALICIOUS PROSECUTION: Charges brought without probable cause.

Talmage v. Smith

(Injured Boy) v. *(Landowner)*
101 Mich. 370, 59 N.W. 656 (1894)

UNDER THE DOCTRINE OF TRANSFERRED INTENT, A DEFENDANT WHO POSSESSES THE NECESSARY INTENT TO COMMIT AN ACT AGAINST ONE PARTY IS LIABLE TO ANY OTHER PARTY WHO MAY HAVE SUFFERED THE CONSEQUENCES OF THE DEFENDANT'S INTENTIONAL CONDUCT

■ **INSTANT FACTS** Smith (D), intending to scare away two boys who were on his property aims, throws a stick at one boy but instead hits Talmage (P), the other boy, and injures him.

■ **BLACK LETTER RULE** An individual who intends an act or consequence against one party and instead injures a third party is liable to the third party for the injuries suffered.

■ **PROCEDURAL BASIS**

Appeal in an action for battery and assault.

■ **FACTS**

Six to eight children were playing on a shed located on Smith's (D) property. After a warning by Smith (D) they left the premises. Talmage (P) and another boy remained on another shed. In an attempt to scare the other boy away, Smith (D) threw a stick in the direction of the boy. Instead of hitting the boy, the stick hit Talmage (P) in the eye and caused him to lose his sight. In an action for battery and assault, the trial court decided in favor of Talmage (P). Smith (D) appeals on the ground that he did not see Talmage (P) and did not intend to hit him or scare him away. Instead he was attempting to scare away the other boy.

■ **ISSUE**

Is an individual who intends an act or consequence against one party and instead injures a third party liable to that third party for the injuries suffered?

■ **DECISION AND RATIONALE**

(Montgomery, J.) Yes. An individual who intends an act or consequence against one party and instead injures a third party is liable to that third party for the injuries suffered. The right of Talmage (P) to recover depends upon the intention of Smith (D) to hit somebody, and to inflict an unwarranted injury upon someone. Smith (D) is not relieved of liability simply because he injured someone other than the intended victim. If Smith (D) threw the stick with unreasonable force with the intent of hitting one boy, but instead hit another, he is liable. On the other hand, if Smith (D) threw the stick with the intent merely to frighten either boy, he is not liable. Likewise, if the jury concludes that the throwing of the stick was reasonable under the circumstances, then Talmage (P) could not recover. However, in this case the jury reasonably concluded that Smith (D) intended to inflict an unwarranted injury upon someone. He is liable regardless of whether the person struck was the intended victim. Affirmed.

Analysis:

This case stands for the doctrine of "transferred intent." Transferred intent works between individuals and between torts. In the person-to-person transferred intent, where A throws a rock intending to hit B, but instead hits C, A is liable to C for battery, even though he did not intend to hit C. Under the tort-to-tort transferred intent, the intent to do one tort transfers to the tort that occurs. For example, if A intending to scare B whose back is to A, throws a punch towards B, but instead hits B, A is liable to B for battery, even though he did not intend to hit B or cause any harmful or offensive touching. The tort-to-tort transferred intent applies between the torts that were originally categorized under trespass. These are torts of battery, assault, false imprisonment, intentional infliction of emotional distress, and trespass. Thus, if the intended tort and the resulting tort are both one of these five torts then the doctrine of transferred intent applies to hold defendant liable for the resulting tort.

■ CASE VOCABULARY

TRANSFERRED INTENT: A doctrine in tort law that provides that if a defendant intends to harm A but instead harms B, the "intent" is said to be transferred to the harm befalling the actual victim as far as defendant's liability to B is concerned.

Cole v. Turner

(*Not Stated*) v. (*Not Stated*)

Nisi Prius, 6 Modem Rep. 149, 90 Eng. Rep. 958 (1704)

EARLY ENGLISH CASES DEFINE BATTERY AS AN INTENTIONAL TOUCHING WHICH IS UNREASON-ABLE AND OFFENSIVE

■ **INSTANT FACTS** (No facts are given in this case.)

■ **BLACK LETTER RULE** Intentional touching of another in an unreasonable and violent manner is considered battery.

■ **PROCEDURAL BASIS**

Action in trespass for battery and assault.

■ **FACTS**

(No facts are given in this case.)

■ **ISSUE**

Is the intentional touching of another in an unreasonable and violent manner considered battery?

■ **DECISION AND RATIONALE**

(Holt, C.J.) Yes. Intentional touching of another in an unreasonable and violent manner is considered battery. The touching of another in anger constitutes battery. If there is no violence or intent to touch another person, there is no battery. However, when one uses violence against another, and forces his way in an unreasonable manner, then there is battery.

Analysis:

Battery is defined as the harmful or offensive touching of another person with the intent to bring about the harmful or offensive touching. As discussed before, "intent" may be defined as acting with the purpose of bringing about an act or consequence, or knowing to a substantial certainty that an act or consequence will follow. Note however, that battery does not include just any type of intended contact. The contact must be unreasonable to an average person. Thus, for example, if A is standing in a bus and the bus comes to a sudden stop, and A grabs B slightly to prevent him/her from falling, it is unlikely that there will be battery. Thus, always look at the time, place and circumstances surrounding the contact in order to determine whether it is offensive or harmful. Also, remember that battery may be caused through transferred intent. Note that the more modern definition of battery does not require there to be any anger or violence (as is required by the definition in *Cole v. Turner*). Under a more modern view, intentional contact results in battery if the contact is harmful or offensive to an average reasonable person. Additionally, note that battery may exist even though the plaintiff is not aware of the contact at the moment that it occurs. Imagine a patient who has consented to surgery on his left ear. While in the middle of the operation, the surgeon decides to open up the right ear and take a look inside of it. Although, the patient who is anesthetized throughout the surgery, is unaware of the contact with the right ear, the patient can sue the surgeon in battery.

■ **CASE VOCABULARY**

NISI PRIUS: Court where issues of fact are first tried before a judge and jury.

Wallace v. Rosen

(Student's Mother) v. *(Teacher)*

765 N.E.2d 192 (Ind.Ct.App.2002)

TOUCHING ANOTHER TO GET HER ATTENTION IS NOT BATTERY

■ **INSTANT FACTS** During a school fire drill, Rosen (D) placed her hand on Wallace's (P) back, causing her to fall down the stairs.

■ **BLACK LETTER RULE** A battery is the knowing or intentional touching of one person by another in a rude, insolent, or angry manner

■ **PROCEDURAL BASIS**

Appeal to consider a decision of the trial court in favor of the defendant.

■ **FACTS**

Wallace (P), who was recovering from foot surgery, was delivering homework to her daughter at the top of a stairwell in the daughter's high school when a fire drill occurred. Rosen (D), a teacher at the school, instructed everyone to move down the stairs in order to evacuate. Wallace (P) was unable to hear the instructions over the noise of the students in the hall, so Rosen (D) put her hand on Wallace's (P) back, whereupon Wallace (P) fell down the stairs. At trial, Wallace (P) claimed Rosen (D) pushed her down the stairs, which accusation Rosen (D) denied. At the close of trial, the judge refused to instruct the jury on civil battery. The jury found in favor of the defendant.

■ **ISSUE**

Did the court err in concluding that a casual, intentional touching does not warrant a jury instruction for civil battery?

■ **DECISION AND RATIONALE**

(Kirsch, J.) No. Here, an instruction for civil battery was not appropriate. "A battery is the knowing or intentional touching of one person by another in a rude, insolent, or angry manner." The touching need not be severe, but rather any slight touching may constitute a battery if the requisite intent is established. In determining an actor's intent, a jury may infer that the actor's state of mind was that of a reasonable person under similar circumstances. Battery may be established when one touches with reckless disregard for the consequences of the touching, regardless of whether injury is intended. On the other hand, knowledge of the risks of touching may establish the actor's negligence, but not the requisite intent for civil battery. To manifest the requisite intent, one must intend to bring about a result invasive of another's interests, even if injury is not intended.

Accordingly, in order for a battery instruction to be justified in this case, the evidence must establish both that Rosen (D) intended to touch Wallace (P) and that she did so in a rude, insolent, or angry manner. While the evidence suggests that Rosen (D) intended to touch Wallace (P), the evidence does not support an inference of rudeness, insolence, or anger. Rosen (D) had a responsibility to expedite the evacuation of the building, and Wallace (P) could reasonably expect some physical contact in the crowded stairwell. Because Rosen's (D) touching was for the purpose of getting Wallace's (P) attention, civil battery has not been established. Affirmed.

Analysis:

Because battery is an intentional tort, the intent to touch another is a required element of any claim. For instance, had Wallace (P) fallen down the stairs because she came in contact with a fleeing student in the crowded hallway, a cause of action for battery would not exist. It is Rosen's (D) intentional contact with Wallace (P) that potentially gives rise to a battery claim, but there must also be also be an intent to bring about an invasive result, which was lacking here.

■ CASE VOCABULARY

BATTERY: An intentional and offensive touching of another without lawful justification.

INTENT: The state of mind accompanying an act, especially a forbidden act. While motive is the inducement to do some act, intent is the mental resolution or determination to do it. When the intent to do an act that violates the law exists, motive becomes immaterial.

Fisher v. Carrousel Motor Hotel, Inc.

(Patron) v. *(Motel)*
424 S.W.2d 627 (Tex.1967)

BATTERY RESULTS FROM UNPERMITTED AND INTENTIONAL TOUCHING OF A PERSON OR ANY-
THING SO CONNECTED TO THE PERSON AS TO BE CONSIDERED A PART OF HIM

■ **INSTANT FACTS** Fisher (P) sued Carrousel Motor Hotel (D) for battery and assault by Carrousel's (D) employees who snatched a plate from his hands and yelled offensive words at him.

■ **BLACK LETTER RULE** The snatching or knocking of an object closely attached to an individual constitutes battery even though there was no actual physical contact to the individual's body.

■ **PROCEDURAL BASIS**

Appeal in action for assault and battery.

■ **FACTS**

Fisher (P) was attending a conference at Carrousel Motor Hotel (D). While in line at the buffet of the hotel, he was approached by an employee of Carrousel (D) who snatched the plate from his hand, and shouted that "a Negro could not be served in the club." Although the employee did not make physical contact with Fisher (P) at all, Fisher (P) was highly embarrassed and offended in front of his colleagues. At the trial level, the jury returned a verdict in favor of Fisher (P). The trial judge set aside the jury verdict and decided in favor of Carrousel (D). Fisher appeals.

■ **ISSUE**

Does the snatching or knocking of an object closely attached to an individual constitute battery even though there was no actual physical contact to the individual's body?

■ **DECISION AND RATIONALE**

(Greenhill, J.) Yes. The snatching or knocking of an object closely attached to an individual constitutes battery even though there was no actual physical contact to the individual's body. In this case, the intentional grabbing of the plaintiff's plate is battery. The Restatement (Second) of Torts indicates that the essence of the plaintiff's complaint in a case of battery is the offense to the dignity of the person because of the unpermitted touching. It is not necessary that there be contact with the person's body or actual harm to the person. Intentional and offensive touching of anything that is so closely connected to the body of a person is to be viewed as part of the person. Additionally, in an action in battery, damages for mental suffering are recoverable without a showing of actual physical harm. (Reversed.)

Analysis:

This case stands for two major propositions. First, battery occurs not only as a result of intentional and harmful touching of a person's body, but also as a result of contact with any object that is so closely

---

connected to the person as to be viewed as a part of the person's body. An illustrative example of such an object is one's clothing. In this case, the object in question was a plate in the plaintiff's hand. Thus, one could say that contact with any object that is immediately connected with a person may constitute battery. Secondly, this case illustrates that where intentional battery is involved, the plaintiff, in order to recover damages for mental suffering, need not prove that he/she suffered any physical harm or damage. This is important, especially in cases where there has been no direct bodily contact between the plaintiff and the defendant. So long as the plaintiff establishes the elements of battery, the plaintiff can recover for damages resulting therefrom.

■ CASE VOCABULARY

INVIOLABILITY: Not to be violated, defiled or made impure.

I de S et Ux v. W de S

(Victim and Husband) v. *(Assailant)*

At the Assizes, 1348, Y.B.Lib.Ass. folio 99, placitum 60

A PLAINTIFF CAN RECOVER DAMAGES FOR ASSAULT EVEN THOUGH THERE HAS BEEN NO PHYSICAL CONTACT OR INJURY TO THE PLAINTIFF BY THE DEFENDANT

■ **INSTANT FACTS** W de S (D), while in front of the house belonging to I de S (P) and his wife (P), threw a hatchet at the wife (P) which missed her.

■ **BLACK LETTER RULE** A defendant may be liable in assault of a plaintiff, even though there has been no actual physical invasion of the plaintiff by the defendant.

■ **PROCEDURAL BASIS**

Appeal from action in assault

■ **FACTS**

W de S (hereafter "W") (D) approached the house of I de S and his wife (P) to buy some wine. When W (D) started pounding on the door, the wife (P), sticking her head out of the window, asked W (D) to stop the pounding. At this point, W (D) threw a hatchet at the wife which missed her. I de S and his wife (P) sued W (D) for assault. The lower court dismissed the action on the ground that the wife had not suffered any injury and therefore, could not recover. I de S and his wife (P) appeal.

■ **ISSUE**

May a defendant be liable for assault of a plaintiff even though there has not been an actual physical invasion of the plaintiff by the defendant?

■ **DECISION AND RATIONALE**

(Thorpe, C.J.) Yes. A defendant may be liable for assault of a plaintiff, even though there has been not an actual physical invasion of the plaintiff by the defendant. Although he did no harm to the wife (P), he did commit the tort of assault and thus, he should pay damages. (Reversed.)

Analysis:

This case is one of the first cases where the court found an action in tort without any proof of actual injury to the plaintiff. Today the tort of assault is defined as an intentional act by the defendant which causes imminent apprehension of harmful or offensive touching in the plaintiff. Thus, the defendant must have intended to cause the plaintiff some apprehension. Like battery, the extent to which one has been apprehensive is judged based on what is reasonable to an average person under similar circumstances. Once again, note that in order to have an action in assault, there is no need for the plaintiff to have been actually touched and physically harmed by the defendant. It is enough that the plaintiff has a reasonable fear that he/she would suffer harmful or offensive touching (i.e., at the hands of the defendant). Also, remember the doctrine of transferred intent. If one intends to commit one tort which results in an assault, then an action in assault is appropriate.

■ **CASE VOCABULARY**

ASSAULT: An attempt or threat, with unlawful force, to inflict bodily injury upon another, accompanied by the apparent present ability to give effect to the attempt if not prevented.

INQUEST: Judicial inquiry before a jury.

Western Union Telegraph Co. v. Hill

(Employer of the Assailant) v. *(Woman Assaulted)*

25 Ala.App. 540, 150 So. 709 (1933)

ACTIONABLE ASSAULT IS AN INTENTIONAL ACT BY A PARTY WHICH CREATES AN APPREHENSION OF IMMINENT BATTERY IN THE MIND OF ANOTHER PERSON

■ **INSTANT FACTS** Hill (P) instituted an action in assault against Western Union Telegraph Co. (D) after one of the latter's employees made improper advances towards Hill (P) who was standing across the counter from the employee.

■ **BLACK LETTER RULE** The actual ability of the defendant to cause harmful or offensive touching is not a requirement for actionable assault.

■ **PROCEDURAL BASIS**

Appeal from an action for assault.

■ **FACTS**

After having called Western Union Telegraph Co. (D), Hill (P) went to a Western Union (D) store in order to have her clock fixed. A Western Union (D) employee, Sapp, who was standing across a counter from Hill (P) made improper advances towards her and told her that he would fix her clock if she would allow him to pet her and love her. Then, the employee reached over the counter and attempted to touch her. However, he did not succeed because the counter was too high. Hill (P) instituted an action against Western Union (D) for assault. The trial court returned a verdict in her favor. Western Union (D) appeals on the ground that Sapp did not have the present ability to touch Hill (P) from across the counter.

■ **ISSUE**

Is the actual ability of the defendant to cause harmful or offensive touching a requirement for actionable assault?

■ **DECISION AND RATIONALE**

(Samford, J.) No. The actual ability of the defendant to cause harmful or offensive touching is not a requirement for actionable assault. However, there must be an apparent ability on the part of the defendant to cause the offensive or harmful touching. Western Union (D) presents evidence that the height of the counter was such that Sapp could not have reached Hill (D) even if he tried to. However, there is also testimony that despite the measurements of the counter, Sapp could have reached beyond the counter and touched Hill (P). This is a question for the jury and the trial court's instructing the jury as such was not erroneous. (Reversed on the ground that Sapp was not acting within the scope of his employment.)

Analysis:

Note that in order to have actionable assault, it is not necessary that the defendant have the actual ability to carry out the harmful or offensive touching. It is enough that the defendant has the apparent

---

ability to do so. However, the apparent ability is judged by a reasonable person standard. An example of the distinction between actual and apparent ability is the assault resulting from defendant pointing an unloaded gun at the plaintiff. Although there is no actual ability to injure the plaintiff (the gun is unloaded), there may be assault because the defendant appears to have the ability to fire the gun and cause a battery against the plaintiff. Another important twist under this tort is that the effect of assault can be undone by words. In the gun example, if the defendant tells the plaintiff, "only if this gun had bullets in it," then there is no apparent ability for immediate harmful or offensive touching, thus no tort. Note also that many state laws indicate that words alone do not constitute assault. Under these laws there has to be some conduct on the part of the defendant that adds to the character of the words. Unlike the tort of battery, the plaintiff in an assault case must be aware of the harm occurring because the definition of assault requires the plaintiff to show that plaintiff suffered from apprehension of imminent harmful or offensive touching. Note also that apprehension does not always equate with fear. As long as plaintiff reasonably believes that plaintiff is in danger of immediate battery, he/she has satisfied this requirement.

■ **CASE VOCABULARY**

PER CONTRA: [Latin] To the contrary; on the other hand.

Big Town Nursing Home, Inc. v. Newman

(*Caretaker*) v. (*Nursing Home Resident*)

461 S.W.2d 195 (Tex.Civ.App.1970)

FALSE IMPRISONMENT IS THE DIRECT RESTRAINT OF AN INDIVIDUAL'S PHYSICAL LIBERTY WITHOUT ADEQUATE LEGAL JUSTIFICATION

■ **INSTANT FACTS** Newman (P), a resident of Big Town Nursing Home (D), who had entered the nursing home on his own, was kept in the nursing home against his will after having attempted to leave several times.

■ **BLACK LETTER RULE** A defendant is liable for false imprisonment when the defendant has prevented the plaintiff from leaving a certain limited area without legal justification.

■ **PROCEDURAL BASIS**

Appeal from an action for false imprisonment.

■ **FACTS**

Newman (P), a 67-year-old man, who suffered from Parkinson's disease, heart problems and other ailments, was admitted to Big Town Nursing Home by his nephew who signed the admission papers for him. The papers provided that Newman (P) would not be kept in the nursing home against his will. A few days after his admission, Newman (D) decided to leave the nursing home. Newman was caught by the employees of the home and put in a wing with drug addicts and alcoholics. Although Newman (P) had been treated for alcoholism prior to his admission to the nursing home, he had not been drinking any more. Neither was he using any drugs. Newman (P) attempted to leave the nursing home about six more times, and each time he was caught by the employees and brought back to the nursing home. Additionally, he was prevented from using the phone for 51 days, and he was taped to his bed to prevent him from leaving. Consequently, Newman (P) sued Big Town (D) for false imprisonment. The trial court decided in favor of Newman (P). Big Town (D) appeals on the ground that its employees did not falsely imprison Newman (P).

■ **ISSUE**

Is a defendant liable for false imprisonment when the defendant has prevented the plaintiff from leaving a certain limited area without legal justification?

■ **DECISION AND RATIONALE**

(McDonald, C.J.) Yes. A defendant is liable for false imprisonment when the defendant has prevented the plaintiff from leaving a certain limited area without legal justification. In this case, there is ample evidence to show that the plaintiff was falsely imprisoned. First, he was placed in a wing with drug addicts and alcoholics even though he did not belong there. Additionally, he was tied to his bed and he was not allowed to use the telephone. Defendants, in addition to actual damages, are liable for exemplary damages if they acted intentionally in depriving the plaintiff from his rights. In this case, the defendants disregarded the plaintiff's rights intentionally. Thus, they are liable for actual and exemplary damages. However, the amount awarded to the plaintiff in the trial court was excessive. (Affirmed as to judgment and reduced as to amount of recovery.)

Analysis:

False imprisonment occurs where a party intends to confine another individual against his/her will. In order for the individual to be confined, he/she must be within a definite physical boundary from where he/she is not free to leave. Note however, that if there is a reasonable means of escape of which the individual is aware, then there is no false imprisonment. Do not forget, it is crucial that the individual confined know of the means of escape and that the means be reasonable in that it would not pose a danger to the individual. There is no false imprisonment when an individual is prevented from entering an area or a building. Remember, in order to have confinement, the individual must be limited by clear physical boundaries.

■ CASE VOCABULARY

ACTUAL DAMAGES: The type of damages (also known as compensatory damages) directly referable to the breach or tortious act; the losses which can readily be proven to have been sustained, and for which the injured party should be compensated as a matter of right.

EXEMPLARY DAMAGES: Compensation (also known as punitive damages) in excess of actual damages; a form of punishment to the wrongdoer and excess enhancement to the injured; nominal or actual damages must exist before exemplary damages will be found, and then they will be awarded only in instances of malicious and willful misconduct.

REMITTITUR: Giving back part of awarded damages. In its broadest meaning, the procedural process by which the verdict of a jury is diminished by subtraction; term used to describe generally any reduction made by the court without the consent of the jury.

Parvi v. City of Kingston

(Drunkard) v. *(Police)*

41 N.Y.2d 553, 362 N.E.2d 960, 394 N.Y.S.2d 161 (1977)

THE RESTATEMENT (2D) OF TORTS INDICATES THAT AN INDIVIDUAL HAS NOT SUFFERED FALSE IMPRISONMENT UNLESS HE IS AWARE OF HIS/HER CONFINEMENT OR HAS SUFFERED PHYSICAL INJURY

■ **INSTANT FACTS** Parvi (P) sued the City of Kingston (D) for false imprisonment because the police had taken him to the outskirts of the city against his will. At trial, he testified that he could not recall anything that happened at the time in question.

■ **BLACK LETTER RULE** A defendant is not liable for falsely imprisoning the plaintiff when the latter was not aware of the confinement at the time it occurs.

■ PROCEDURAL BASIS

Appeal from an action for false imprisonment.

■ FACTS

In response to a complaint, the police found two brothers fighting, and Parvi (P) accompanying them. Parvi (P), who had apparently consumed alcohol, told the police that he had no place to go. The police (D) took him to the outskirts of the city and left him there to sober up. Parvi (P) sued the City of Kingston (D) for false imprisonment. At the trial, however, Parvi (P) indicated that he did not recollect the events of the night. The trial court dismissed the action on the ground that in order to bring an action in false imprisonment, the individual must be aware of the confinement. The Appellate Court affirmed. Parvi (P) appeals.

■ ISSUE

Is a defendant liable for falsely imprisoning the plaintiff when the latter was not aware of the confinement at the time that it occurs?

■ DECISION AND RATIONALE

(Fuchsberg, J.) No. A defendant is not liable for falsely imprisoning the plaintiff when the latter was not aware of the confinement at the time that it occurs. False imprisonment is a dignitary tort, and as such it is not suffered unless one is aware of the dignitary invasion. Although the court below applied the correct law in this case, the trial court did not examine the issue of awareness correctly. At his trial the plaintiff mentioned that he had no recollection of what happened on the night in question. However, the court failed to determine whether plaintiff did not recollect due to lapse of memory or whether the plaintiff was not conscious of his confinement at the time that it was occurring. Although the plaintiff was not sober at the time of confinement, it is not clear that he was clearly unaware of his confinement. There is evidence showing that he may have been aware. Examples of such evidence are plaintiff's responses to the police and his conversation with them at the time he was in their car. (Reversed.)

Analysis:

As this case indicates, in order to bring a successful action in false imprisonment, the victim must have been aware of the confinement at the time that it was occurring. This is not to say that the victim must remember the confinement at a later time. However, it means that the victim must have been aware at the time of confinement that he was confined. In some jurisdiction, and under the Restatement (Second) of Torts, this requirement is waived if the victim has suffered physical injury as a result of the confinement.

■ CASE VOCABULARY

DIGNITARY TORT: Tort which is an affront to the dignity of a person.

PRIMA FACIE CASE: A case which is sufficient "on its face," being supported by at least the requisite minimum of evidence, and being free from palpable defects; refers to a state of facts that entitles a party to have the case go to the jury.

SINE QUA NON: [Latin] That without which something cannot be; an indispensable condition.

Hardy v. Labelle's Distributing Co.

(Employee) v. *(Employer)*

203 Mont. 263, 661 P.2d 35 (1983)

AN INDIVIDUAL IS A VICTIM OF FALSE IMPRISONMENT WHEN HE/SHE IS UNLAWFULLY RESTRAINED AGAINST HIS WILL

■ **INSTANT FACTS** Hardy (P) who was falsely accused of stealing from the store where she was employed, sues her employer, Labelle's Distributing Co. (D) for false imprisonment.

■ **BLACK LETTER RULE** A person can not maintain an action for false imprisonment when no threat of force was used to compel that person to stay against his/her will.

■ **PROCEDURAL BASIS**

Appeal from an action in false imprisonment.

■ **FACTS**

Hardy (P), an employee at Labelle Distributing Co. (D), was falsely accused of stealing a watch. Hardy (P) was approached by the assistant manager of the store, who took her to the manager's office under the guise of giving her a tour of the store. Hardy (P) denied having stolen the watch and took a lie detector test that verified the same. Because of the incident, Hardy (P) sued her employer for false imprisonment. The trial court found in favor of Labelle (D) on the ground that Hardy (P) was not retained against her will. Hardy (P) appeals.

■ **ISSUE**

Can a person maintain an action in false imprisonment when no threat of force was used to compel that person to stay against his/her will?

■ **DECISION AND RATIONALE**

(Gulbrandson, J.) No. A person cannot maintain an action in false imprisonment when no threat of force was used to compel that person to stay against his/her will. In this case, there is evidence supporting the fact that Hardy (P) was not falsely imprisoned. Although Hardy (P) testified that she felt compelled to stay, she testified that she also wanted to stay to clarify the matter. She was never told that she could not leave. She also testified that she would have followed the assistant manager into the office voluntarily had she known of the true purpose of the meeting. Under these circumstances, the jury was not wrong in finding that Hardy (P) was not falsely imprisoned.

Analysis:

As this case illustrates, in order to maintain an action for false imprisonment, the plaintiff must prove that she was under restraint to stay against her will and that she had no reasonable means of escape. A mere obligation to stay, or other mental compulsion, such as fear of losing one's job will not be enough of a restraint to qualify as false imprisonment. Additionally, submission to stay somewhere due to persuasion does not reach the level of force required for false imprisonment. Note that "restraint" may

---

come in many forms. It could be by physical force, or by threat of physical force, or by restraining certain objects belonging to the plaintiff. For example, removing an individual's purse is enough of a restraint to constitute false imprisonment.

■ CASE VOCABULARY

FALSE IMPRISONMENT: The unjustified detention of a person; restraint must be total so that it amounts to an imprisonment; mere obstruction, stopping, locking one out of his room, etc., are not enough. No physical force need be used so long as the victim reasonably believes that he is restrained against his will.

Enright v. Groves

(Dog Owner) v. *(Police Officer)*

39 Colo.App. 39, 560 P.2d 851 (1977)

FALSE ARREST, WHICH ARISES WHEN ONE IS TAKEN INTO CUSTODY BY A PERSON WHO CLAIMS BUT DOES NOT HAVE LEGAL AUTHORITY, CAN GIVE RISE TO A CLAIM OF FALSE IMPRISONMENT

■ **INSTANT FACTS** Enright (P) instituted an action in false imrison ment because she was arrested by Gorves (D) upon her refusal to hand him her driver's license.

■ **BLACK LETTER RULE** A police officer is liable for false arrest when he arrests an individual without a warrant or probable cause that an offense has been committed by the individual.

■ **PROCEDURAL BASIS**

Appeal from action for false imprisonment.

■ **FACTS**

Officer Groves (D), while on duty, noticed a dog running loose in the direction of a residence which was owned by Mrs. Enright. Groves (D) then followed the dog which approached a boy, Mrs. Enright's (P) son. The boy, who was ordered to take the dog inside, pointed to his mother, Enright (P), who was next to her car at the curb. Gorves (D) then approached Enright (P) and asked her for her identification which she refused to give him. Groves (D) grabbed Enright's (P) arm and placed her under arrest for her refusal to present her identification. Enright (P) instituted an action against Groves (D) in false imprisonment. The trial court decided in Enright's (P) favor and granted her damages. Groves (D) appeals on the ground that Enright (P) was validly arrested for violation of a city ordinance and as such, her claim for false imprisonment or false arrest was not valid.

■ **ISSUE**

Is a police officer liable for false arrest when he arrests an individual without a warrant or probable cause that an offense has been committed by the individual?

■ **DECISION AND RATIONALE**

(Smith, J.) Yes. A police officer is liable for false arrest when he arrests an individual without a warrant or probable cause that an offense has been committed by the individual. The evidence in this case indicates that Groves (D) arrested Enright (P) not for violation of the city's dog leash law, but for her refusal to produce her identification to Groves (D). In fact, Groves (D) specifically mentioned that she would go to jail if she did not show him her identification. No law requires a citizen to show her identification to a police officer upon demand unless the citizen has committed an offense. Thus, Groves' (D) demand for the driver's license was not a lawful order, and as such Groves (D) could not use force in arresting Enright (P). (Affirmed.)

Analysis:

Note that where there has been a false arrest, such as in the instant case, an action in false imprisonment can be instituted against the arresting party. However, if the person arrested has actually committed the crime, then no action for false imprisonment lies.

■ CASE VOCABULARY

FALSE ARREST: Incident in which one is taken into custody by a person who claims to have, but does not have, proper legal authority.

LIE: To be sustainable.

Whittaker v. Sandford

(Boat Passenger) v. *(Boat Owner)*

110 Me. 77, 85 A. 399 (1912)

FALSE IMPRISONMENT MAY RESULT FROM REFUSING AN INDIVIDUAL A MEANS OF EGRESS

■ **INSTANT FACTS** Sandford (P) sued Whittaker (D) for false imprisonment because of the latter's refusal to provide Sandford (P) a means of getting from Whittaker's (D) boat to the shore.

■ **BLACK LETTER RULE** Confinement of an individual to a bounded area, without means of egress, can result in false imprisonment even if there is no actual physical restraint used upon the individual.

■ **PROCEDURAL BASIS**

Appeal from an order denying motion for a new trial.

■ **FACTS**

Sandford (D), a member of a religious sect of which Whittaker (D) was a leader, decided to leave the sect. The sect was quartered in Jaffa (Tel Aviv). Whittaker (D) offered Sandford (P) his boat so that Sandford (P) could come back to the United States. Upon arrival to the States, Whittaker (D) refused to provide Sandford (P) any means of getting to the shore. Sandford (P) was detained on the boat for nearly one month. Sandford (P) sued Whittaker (D) for false imprisonment. The trial court instructed the jury that for a valid action in false imprisonment a plaintiff must show actual physical restraint. However, the court further instructed the jury that there need not be actual physical force upon the plaintiff herself. In this case, as Sandford (P) was restrained such that she could not leave the boat, the requirement of physical restraint was satisfied. The trial court in deciding in favor of Sandford (P), dismissed Whittaker's (D) motion for a new trial. Whittaker (D) appeals the trial court's decision on the ground that the court's instructions to the jury regarding the requirements of false imprisonment was erroneous.

■ **ISSUE**

Can confinement of an individual to a bounded area, without means of egress, result in false imprisonment even if there is no actual physical restraint used upon the individual?

■ **DECISION AND RATIONALE**

(Savage, J.) Yes. Confinement of an individual to a bounded area, without means of egress, can result in false imprisonment even if there is no actual physical restraint used upon the individual. In this case, Whittaker (D), the owner of the boat, assured Sandford (P) that she could leave the boat. However Whittaker (D) failed to provide Sandford (D) with a row boat, which was the only means of getting to the shore. Thus, Sandford (P) in this case was locked in the boat, the physical barrier, as if she were actually locked in a room without her consent. It is clear that Whittaker's (D) duty was not simply to bring Sandford (P) to the U.S., but to also furnish her with a means of getting to the shore. As such, Whittaker (D) is liable for false imprisonment (Affirmed.)

Analysis:

This case illustrates the fact that failure to provide an individual a means of egress, when there is an obligation to do so, could constitute the physical barrier requirement for false imprisonment. Thus, here it is not the defendant's act that has resulted in false imprisonment, but his failure to release the plaintiff when there is a duty to do so.

■ CASE VOCABULARY

HABEAS CORPUS: A writ requiring that a person be brought before a court to decide legality of his detention.

State Rubbish Collectors Ass'n v. Siliznoff

(*Creditor*) v. (*Debtor*)

38 Cal.2d 330, 240 P.2d 282 (1952)

CALIFORNIA SUPREME COURT RECOGNIZES INTENTIONAL INFLICTION OF EMOTIONAL DISTRESS AS A CAUSE OF ACTION FOR RECOVERY OF DAMAGES

■ **INSTANT FACTS** State Rubbish Collectors Ass'n (D) sued Siliznoff (P) to collect on a debt that he owed. Siliznoff (P) countersued State Rubbish (D) for causing him duress and distress.

■ **BLACK LETTER RULE** One who causes severe emotional distress to another is liable for such emotional distress and for bodily harm resulting from it.

■ **PROCEDURAL BASIS**

Appeal from action for infliction of emotions distress.

■ **FACTS**

Siliznoff (P) owed State Rubbish Collectors (D) on certain notes. The latter had threatened to beat Siliznoff, destroy his truck and put him out of business completely if he did not pay the note. Siliznoff (P) attended a meeting with the president of State Rubbish Collectors and told him that he would pay the note because he was scared. Because of the fear, Siliznoff (P) claimed to have gotten ill and was unable to work for several days. The trial court granted judgment in favor of Siliznoff (P). The Rubbish Collectors (D) appeal on the ground that there was no assault to Siliznoff (P) because the threats were not immediate.

■ **ISSUE**

Is one who causes severe emotional distress to another liable for such emotional distress and for bodily harm resulting from it?

■ **DECISION AND RATIONALE**

(Traynor, J.) Yes. One who causes severe emotional distress to another is liable for such emotional distress and for bodily harm resulting from it. In the past it was frequently stated that the interest in emotional and mental tranquility is not one that the law will protect from invasion. However, often, if the defendant intentionally subjected the plaintiff to such distress and bodily harm resulted, the defendant would be liable for negligently causing the plaintiff bodily harm. This cause of action was based on the right to be free from negligent interference with physical well-being. Today, there are persuasive arguments that support the recognition of the right to be free from serious, intentional invasion of one's mental and emotional tranquility. If such cause of action is established, then damages for mental suffering ensuing from the acts complained of should be given. Although allowing recovery in the absence of physical injury may result in many unfounded claims, the jury is in a better position to determine whether damages should be allowed in each case, even in the absence of physical injury. In this case, the State Rubbish Collectors caused Siliznoff (P) extreme fright which resulted in physical injury. Their liability to the latter is clear. (Affirmed.)

Analysis:

Note that the tort of intentional infliction of emotional distress is a fairly new cause of action. Under this cause of action, a defendant is liable for extreme and outrageous conduct toward the plaintiff which has caused the plaintiff severe emotional distress. Note that as the case illustrates, where there is intentional infliction of the distress, the plaintiff need not prove actual physical injury and can still recover for damages resulting from mental suffering. This tort is different from assault. The latter is described as the intentional conduct which causes an immediate apprehension of harmful or offensive contact with another person. Thus, future threats can not be assault because they are not imminent.

■ CASE VOCABULARY

ACTOR: One who takes action.

ANOMALY: Abnormality; deviation from the common rule.

WANT OF CONSIDERATION: Lack of something of value which should have been given in return for a performance or promise of performance by another.

Slocum v. Food Fair Stores of Florida

(Customer) v. *(Grocery Store)*
100 So.2d 396 (Fla.1958)

THE FLORIDA SUPREME COURT DOES NOT RECOGNIZE INDEPENDENT CAUSE OF ACTION PROTECTING AGAINST MERE EMOTIONAL DISTRESS

■ **INSTANT FACTS** While a customer at Food Fair Stores of Florida (D), Slocum (P) was severely insulted by an employee which caused her to suffer a heart attack.

■ **BLACK LETTER RULE** Conduct that causes mere emotional distress is not severe enough to allow recovery based on an independent cause of action.

■ **PROCEDURAL BASIS**

Appeal from order dismissing complaint for failure to state a cause of action.

■ **FACTS**

Slocum (P) was a customer at Food Fair Stores of Florida (D), when she asked an employee in the store what the price of an item was. The employee responded to her impolitely, telling her that the only way she could find out the price was to "stink" him. Slocum (P) who suffered from pre-existing heart problems, had a heat attack. She sues Food Fair (D) to recover money damages for mental suffering and emotional distress. The trial court dismissed on the ground that she had failed to state a proper cause of action. Slocum (P) appeals.

■ **ISSUE**

Does conduct that causes mere emotional distress enough to allow recovery based on an independent cause of action?

■ **DECISION AND RATIONALE**

(Drew, J.) No. Conduct that causes mere emotional distress is not severe enough to allow recovery based on an independent cause of action. There is strong support in case law for adoption of intentional infliction of emotional distress as a new cause of action. However, even if we adopt such cause of action, the facts in this case do not allow recovery by the plaintiff. The conduct complained of under this theory must be likely to cause severe emotional distress and not mere emotional distress. There is liability for conduct exceeding all bounds which could be tolerated by the society. Whether the conduct in question is actionable or not will be determined based on an objective standard, rather than a subjective one. The act complained of must cause severe emotional distress to a person of ordinary sensibilities. Thus, instances of mere vulgarities do not create severe emotional distress. Although innkeepers and common carriers are held to a stricter standard with respect to their patrons, there is no need to extend this rule to the case at hand. (Affirmed.)

Analysis:

Note that this court is reluctant to extend the scope of intentional infliction of emotional distress as a new cause of action. The modern version of this tort has several elements. In the first place, there

---

must be an intent which is comparable to the intent in other intentional torts such as assault, and battery (knowledge or substantial certainty that a certain result will follow). Under this cause of action, recklessness would also satisfy the intent level. This means that a tortfeasor is liable for the consequence of his act if he knew that there is a high probability that emotional distress would result. Another required element is that the tortfeasor's action must be extreme and outrageous, an act which is outside of bounds of decency. Thus, a mere insult is not enough to create liability. Additionally, the extreme and outrageous nature of the act is determined based on a reasonable person standard (objective). This means that the special sensitivities of the plaintiff do not raise a certain conduct to the level of outrageousness required under this tort. However, remember that if the tortfeasor is aware of the plaintiff's sensitivities, then he made be held liable for an act which is not considered extremely outrageous under the objective standard. Finally, the plaintiff, in order to recover, must have suffered severe emotional distress. Initially, courts were highly reluctant to accept this cause of action because of the difficulty in calculating and proving mental pain and suffering.

■ CASE VOCABULARY

CARRIER DOCTRINE: Rules applying to common carriers and their servants/employees relating to treatment of their customers, the general public.

EQUANIMITY: Composure.

INNOCUOUS: Harmless.

SITUATION AT BAR: Case before the court.

Harris v. Jones

(Employee) v. *(Supervisor)*
281 Md. 560, 380 A.2d 611 (1977)

MERE INSULTS, INDIGNITIES, AND THREATS DO NOT RISE TO THE LEVEL OF EXTREME AND OUTRAGEOUS CONDUCT REQUIRED AS AN ELEMENT OF INTENTIONAL INFLICTION OF EMOTIONAL DISTRESS

■ **INSTANT FACTS** Harris (P), claiming that his supervisor, Jones (D) constantly ridiculed his stuttering, sought recovery from Jones (D), under the tort of intentional infliction of emotional distress.

■ **BLACK LETTER RULE** An individual must suffer a severely disabling emotional response to the tortfeasor's conduct in order to recover damages for intentional infliction of emotional distress.

■ **PROCEDURAL BASIS**

Appeal from action in intentional infliction of emotional distress.

■ **FACTS**

Harris (P) sued his supervisor Jones (D) for intentional infliction of emotional distress. Harris (P) claimed that Jones (D) was aware of Harris' (P) speech impediment and Harris' (P) sensitivity to it. Despite his knowledge, Jones (D) constantly imitated Harris' stuttering and ridiculed him in front of other co-workers. Additionally, Harris (P) claimed that Jones' (D) actions caused him severe nervousness and worsened his speech problem. Based on this evidence, the trial court granted judgment to Harris (P) for both compensatory and punitive damages. The Court of Special Appeals reversed this judgment on the ground that there was no causal connection between Jones' (D) conduct and Harris' (P) emotional distress, and because Harris' (P) emotional distress was not severe enough to allow him recovery. Harris (P) appeals.

■ **ISSUE**

Must an individual suffer a severely disabling emotional response to the tortfeasor's conduct in order to recover damages for intentional infliction of emotional distress?

■ **DECISION AND RATIONALE**

(Murphy, C.J.) Yes. An individual must suffer a severely disabling emotional response to the tortfeasor's conduct in order to recover damages for intentional infliction of emotional distress. Four elements must be present in order to impose liability under the tort of infliction of emotional distress: 1) The conduct must be intentional or reckless, and 2) the conduct must be extreme and outrageous, 3) there must be a causal connection between the wrongful conduct and the emotional distress, and 4) the emotional distress must be severe. Conduct that is extreme and outrageous is one that goes beyond all bounds of decency; conduct that is not tolerated in a civilized community. The nature of the conduct will be determined, not in a sterile setting, but based on the community standards, and based on the facts and circumstances of each particular case. In this case, the conduct in question was intentional. However, the second and the third element need not be dwelled on because there is not sufficient evidence to prove that Harris (P) suffered severe emotional distress. The humiliation suffered

---

by Harris (P) due to Jones' (D) conduct was not, as a matter of law, so intense as to constitute the "severe" emotional distress required for recovery of damages in this tort. (Affirmed.)

Analysis:

Note that as this case illustrates, to satisfy the requirement of "severe emotional distress," the plaintiff must provide clear evidence that he/she suffered certain injury. In the instant case, the court indicated that the mere worsening of the plaintiff's nervous condition was not evidence of severe emotional distress. Remember that whether a defendant's conduct is extreme and outrageous is determined based on an objective, reasonable person standard. However, where the defendant is aware of an individual's special sensitivity, he may be held to a higher standard. For example, in this case, since the defendant knew that the plaintiff had a stuttering problem and was very sensitive to it, the defendant's conduct did qualify as extreme and outrageous. (But the suffering was not severe enough.) This case also illustrates that there has to be a causal connection between the extreme conduct and the emotional distress suffered by the plaintiff. It is not enough that the conduct merely worsens a pre-existing condition.

■ CASE VOCABULARY

ANTEDATED: To come before in time.

Taylor v. Vallelunga

(Witness to Beating) v. *(Batterer)*
171 Cal.App.2d 107, 339 P.2d 910 (1959)

CALIFORNIA COURT DENIES RECOVERY TO A THIRD PARTY UNDER INTENTIONAL INFLICTION OF EMOTIONAL DISTRESS WHERE THE DEFENDANT DOES NOT HAVE KNOWLEDGE OF THE THIRD PARTY'S PRESENCE

■ **INSTANT FACTS** Taylor (P), who saw Vallelunga (D) severely beat her father, sued Vallelunga (D) for damages for intentional infliction of emotional distress.

■ **BLACK LETTER RULE** A third party may not recover damages for intentional infliction of emotional distress when the defendant was not aware of the third party's presence at the time that defendant's conduct was taking place and the third party did not suffer any physical injury.

■ **PROCEDURAL BASIS**

Appeal from a judgment of dismissal.

■ **FACTS**

Taylor's (P) father was beaten and suffered severe bodily injury by Vallelunga (D). Unbeknownst to Vallelunga (D), Taylor (P) was present at the scene and witnessed the beating. Taylor (P) sues Vallelunga (D) for intentional infliction of emotional distress suffered as a result of watching Vallelunga (D) beat her father. Taylor (P) has suffered no actual physical injury. The trial court, sustaining a demurrer by Vallelunga (D), dismissed Taylor's (P) action. Taylor (P) appeals.

■ **ISSUE**

May a third party recover damages for intentional infliction of emotional distress when the defendant was not aware of the third party's presence at the time that defendant's conduct was taking place and the third party did not suffer any physical injury?

■ **DECISION AND RATIONALE**

(O'Donnell, J. Pro tem) No. A third party may not recover damages for intentional infliction of emotional distress when the defendant was not aware of the third party's presence at the time that defendant's conduct was taking place and the third party did not suffer any physical injury. A claim brought under intentional infliction of emotional distress requires a showing of intent to cause severe emotional distress. The defendant must have acted with the purpose of causing severe emotional distress or with knowledge that his conduct is substantially certain to produce such a result. In this case, there is no allegation that the defendant knew that Taylor (P) was present and witnessed the beating of her father. Nor is there an allegation that her father was beaten for the purpose of causing her severe emotional distress, or that such result was substantially certain to follow the defendant's conduct. (Affirmed.)

Analysis:

This case illustrates that in order for a third party to recover damages in intentional infliction of emotional distress, the tortfeasor must have been aware of the third party's presence at the time that the tortfeasor's conduct was taking place. In order to allow recovery to third person's, some court's require not only that the tortfeasor be aware of the third party's presence (such as in this case) but also that the third party suffer actual physical injury. An additional element required by some courts is that the third party be a close relative of the person against whom the defendant has targeted his/her conduct. Note that the doctrine of transferred intent is not applicable to this tort. Some courts reject the application of this doctrine on the ground that the intent necessary to maintain this cause of action is lacking where the defendant is not aware of the third party's presence. Other courts reject it on the ground that the mental effect of the defendant's conduct on the third party is not foreseeable. Other courts have rejected the application of transferred intent on the ground that it would open a wide gate for litigation if all third party's were allowed recovery in such instances. One large exception, adhered to by many courts is in cases of "mishandling of corpses." These courts have allowed recovery to relatives, even though not present at the time of defendant's conduct, for mutilation, disinterment, or interference with proper burial of a person's dead body.

■ **CASE VOCABULARY**

DEMURRER: In pleading, a formal objection attacking the legal sufficiency of the opponent's pleadings; an assertion made, without disputing the facts, that the pleading does not state a cause of action and that the demurring party is entitled to judgment.

PRO TEM: Temporary; for the time being.

Dougherty v. Stepp

(Landowner) v. *(Trespasser)*
18 N.C. 371 (1835)

AN INTENTIONAL AND UNAUTHORIZED ENTRY INTO THE LAND OF ANOTHER CONSTITUTES TRESPASS

■ **INSTANT FACTS** Dougherty (P) sued Stepp (D) for unauthorized and unlawful entry onto his land.

■ **BLACK LETTER RULE** In order to maintain an action in trespass, it is not necessary that there be actual physical injury to the land.

■ **PROCEDURAL BASIS**

Appeal from action in trespass.

■ **FACTS**

In suing Stepp (D) in an action for intentional trespass to land, Dougherty (P) presented evidence that Stepp (D) had entered on Dougherty's (P) unenclosed land, with a surveyor and had actually surveyed a part of it. Stepp (D) did not cut any trees or cause any other major damage to the land. The trial court held that there was no intentional trespass in this case on the ground that there was no injury to the land. Dougherty (P) appeals.

■ **ISSUE**

Must there be actual physical injury to land in order to maintain an action in intentional trespass?

■ **DECISION AND RATIONALE**

(Ruffin, C.J.) No. In order to maintain an action in trespass, it is not necessary that there be actual physical injury to the land. The amount of damages may depend on the nature of the act and the extent of injury to it. However, regardless of the damages, every unauthorized entry on the land of another is trespass and from every such injury the law infers certain damages. (Reversed.)

Analysis:

This case illustrates that trespass is the intentional and unauthorized entry onto the land of another and that such entry is actionable even though there is no injury. Note that the required intent is the intent to enter upon land, not the specific intent to enter upon the land of another. Thus, a trespasser's honest mistake or belief that he was on his own land or on another's with permission does not relieve the trespasser of liability. Note however, that, as in this case, there may be no actual damages as a result of the trespass. In such cases, the court allows the recovery of nominal damages for the commission of the tort itself.

■ **CASE VOCABULARY**

TRESPASS: Wrongful interference with, or disturbance of, the possession of real or personal property of another.

TRESPASS QUARE CLAUSUM FERGIT: Type of trespass whereby the trespasser "broke the close," i.e., entered upon the land of the plaintiff.

Bradley v. American Smelting and Refining Co.

(Landowner) v. *(Trespasser)*

104 Wash.2d 677, 709 P.2d 782 (1985)

TRESPASS IS AN INTENTIONAL INTRUSION WHICH INTERFERES WITH ONE'S RIGHT TO EXCLU-SIVE POSSESSION OF THE PROPERTY WHEREAS NUISANCE IS INTERFERENCE WITH ONE'S USE AND ENJOYMENT OF THE PROPERTY

■ **INSTANT FACTS** Bradley (P), who owns property four miles away from American Smeltering and Refining Co. (D), sued the latter in trespass for emitting various gases onto Bradley's (P) property.

■ **BLACK LETTER RULE** A landowner/possessor must show actual physical damages for recovery in trespass by intangible objects or substances?

■ **PROCEDURAL BASIS**

Appeal in action for trespass.

■ **FACTS**

Bradley (P) owns property which is four miles away from American Smeltering (D). The latter is a smeltering company which smelts copper, a procedure which emits various gases which can not be seen with the human eye. Bradley (P) sued American Smeltering (D) in trespass for emitting the gases onto Bradley's property.

■ **ISSUE**

Must a landowner/possessor show actual physical damages for recovery in trespass by intangible objects or substances?

■ **DECISION AND RATIONALE**

(Callow, J.) Yes. A landowner/possessor must show actual physical damages for recovery in trespass by intangible objects or substances. Liability on the theory of trespass had been recognized where there is a tangible physical invasion of the landowner's property. However, with modern science advancing, this tort theory should apply to intangibles as well. The *Martin* case indicates that in cases of intangible objects separate actions may be brought in nuisance or in trespass. These causes of action are mutually exclusive. Trespass is invasion of the right to exclusive possession, while nuisance is interference with the use and enjoyment of one's property. Under modern law, in order to recover in trespass by intangibles, four elements must be met: 1) an invasion affecting an interest in the exclusive possession of the land, 2) an intentional doing of the act which results in the invasion, 3) reasonable foreseeability that the act done could result in the said invasion, and 4) substantial damages to the property or things on the property. In this case, the plaintiff failed to show any damages to his property and is barred from recovery.

Analysis:

This case simply illustrates that in order to obtain damages in trespass for intangibles, such as gases, the plaintiff must show that there has been substantial damage to his/her property.

■ CASE VOCABULARY

NUISANCE: Any action which interferes with one's property or disturbs one's ordinary use and enjoyment of the property; the defendant's interference with the plaintiff's interests.

STATUTE OF LIMITATIONS: Statute limiting the time for legal action.

SUMMARY JUDGMENT: An immediate resolution without a jury.

Rogers v. Board of Road Com'rs for Kent County

(*Landowner*) v. (*Trespasser*)

319 Mich. 661, 30 N.W.2d 358 (1947)

ONCE AN INDIVIDUAL'S PRIVILEGE TO ENTER UPON THE LAND OF ANOTHER IS EFFECTIVELY TERMINATED, THE INDIVIDUAL'S ENTRY UPON THE LAND CONSTITUTES TRESPASS

■ **INSTANT FACTS** Rogers (P) sought recovery for the death of her husband whose death she claims to have been caused by Board of Road Com'rs for Kent County, due to their trespass onto Rogers' property.

■ **BLACK LETTER RULE** Trespass may be committed by the continued presence of a structure on land after the landowner has effectively terminated his consent to have the property on his land.

■ PROCEDURAL BASIS

Appeal from dismissal of action in trespass.

■ FACTS

The Board of Road Com'rs (D) had obtained a license to place a snow fence in Rogers' (P) and her husband's property. Rogers (P) claims that the Board (D) had agreed to remove the fence and all anchor posts at the end of each winter and it failed to do so. Rogers' (P) husband hit the posts and was killed when his mowing machine struck the posts. Rogers (P) brought an action against the Board (D) in trespass. The trial court dismissed her action on the ground that the basis of liability was in negligence and not in trespass. Rogers (P) appeals.

■ ISSUE

May trespass be committed by the continued presence of a structure on land after the landowner has effectively terminated his consent to have the property on his land?

■ DECISION AND RATIONALE

(Reid, J.) Yes. Trespass may be committed by the continued presence of a structure on land after the landowner has effectively terminated his consent to have the property on his land. In this case, the failure to remove the posts constituted trespass and was the proximate cause of the decedent's death. (Reversed.)

Analysis:

Consent to enter upon someone's land may be limited and if so, once this consent has been effectively terminated, entry upon the land constitutes trespass. The consent in question may be limited to time (as illustrated by the instant case), space and purpose. Where injury has occurred as a result of trespass, some courts do not require a showing of foreseeability of the injury in order to compensate the plaintiffs.

■ **CASE VOCABULARY**

CHATTEL: Property or goods.

DECEDENT: A deceased person.

REMANDED: Sent back.

Glidden v. Szybiak

(Injured Child) v. *(Dog Owner)*
95 N.H. 318, 63 A.2d 233 (1949)

NO ACTION FOR TRESPASS TO CHATTEL MAY BE MAINTAINED IF THE ONLY DAMAGES SUSTAINED BY THE OWNER OF THE CHATTEL ARE NOMINAL DAMAGES

■ **INSTANT FACTS** Glidden (P), bitten by Szybiak's (D) dog, sues to recover for damages. Szybiak contends that Glidden (P) can not recover because her injuries resulted from her trespass to the dog.

■ **BLACK LETTER RULE** An individual may not maintain an action for trespass unless he has suffered actual damages as a result of the trespass.

■ **PROCEDURAL BASIS**

Appeal from action in trespass and personal injuries.

■ **FACTS**

Glidden (P), a four-year-old girl, was playing with Szybiak's (D) dog, climbing on his back and pulling his ears, when the dog bit her and caused her to suffer severe injuries. Szybiak (D) defended on the ground that since Glidden (P) had engaged in trespass to chattel, and her injuries were a result of such trespass, she could not recover from Szybiak (D) for her injuries. The trial court found for the plaintiff on the ground that Glidden (P) was too young to be guilty of contributory negligence and as such also too young to be guilty of an intentional tort. Szybiak (D) appeals.

■ **ISSUE**

May an individual maintain an action for trespass to chattel if he has not suffered actual damages as a result of the trespass?

■ **DECISION AND RATIONALE**

(Branch, C.J.) No. An individual may not maintain an action for trespass unless he has suffered actual damages as a result of the trespass. There is trespass to chattel when one interferes with another's property without the owner's consent. However, unlike trespass to land, such trespass is not actionable unless there is actual injury suffered by the owner. In this case there is no evidence that the dog was in any way harmed as a result of Glidden's (P) actions. Thus, Glidden (P) can recover from the defendants for her injuries. (Affirmed.)

Analysis:

Trespass to chattel is defined as the intentional interference with the use and enjoyment of one's property. Basically, it occurs when someone had dispossessed a rightful owner of the chattel, and his/her use of the chattel. However, an action in trespass to chattel is not actionable unless the owner of the chattel has suffered some kind of harm. An example of harm is that the chattel is damaged. Courts also allow damages where one is deprived of the use of his own chattel. In such cases, most often the measure of actual damages is the rental value of the chattel. Note that the complete destruction of a chattel constitutes conversion and not trespass. The latter can be seen as a little more temporary than conversion. (Please see *Pearson v. Dodd* for further explanation of conversion.)

■ CASE VOCABULARY

ACTIONS AT LAW: Judicial proceeding whereby one party prosecutes another party for a wrongdoing.

CHATTEL: Any tangible, movable thing; personal as opposed to real property.

INVIOLABLE: Not to be violated; sacred.

CompuServe Inc. v. Cyber Promotions, Inc.

(Service Provider) v. *(Promoter)*

962 F.Supp. 1015 (S.D.Ohio 1997)

UNWANTED E-MAILS CAN CONSTITUTE TRESSPASS TO CHATTELS

■ **INSTANT FACTS** A promotions company was sending unsolicited e-mail advertisements to CompuServe Internet service subscribers.

■ **BLACK LETTER RULE** Trespass to chattels is actionable where the value or condition of the chattel is intentionally impaired.

■ **PROCEDURAL BASIS**

Action for a preliminary injunction to extend temporary restraining order based on trespass to chattels.

■ **FACTS**

Cyber Promotions, Inc. (D) sent hundreds of thousands of unsolicited e-mail advertisements known as "spam" to CompuServe (P) subscribers. [Can "spam" recipients dislike it as much as that pink canned meat?] CompuServe (P), a major Internet service provider, asked Cyber Promotions (D) to stop using its computer equipment to process and store the e-mails. Cyber Promotions (D) refused and began sending more e-mails to CompuServe (P) subscribers. CompuServe (P) even attempted to use software to screen out the "spam." However, Cyber Promotions (D) modified their messages to circumvent CompuServe's (P) screening software. CompuServe (P) received numerous complaints from its subscribers who threatened to discontinue their subscriptions unless the annoying e-mails were prohibited. CompuServe (P) subscribers pay for the service in increments of time, thus reading and discarding the advertisements costs them money. CompuServe (P) also complains that the mass mailings place a significant burden on its equipment. CompuServe (P) sought a preliminary injunction.

■ **ISSUE**

Do unwanted and unsolicited e-mail advertisements sent through an Internet service provider's system constitute trespass to chattels?

■ **DECISION AND RATIONALE**

(Graham, J.) Yes. The Restatement (Second) of Torts § 217(b) states that a trespass to chattel may be committed by intentionally using or intermeddling with the chattel of another. Comment(e) to the above section defines "intermeddling" as intentionally bringing about a physical contact with the chattel. Electronic signals sent by computer have been held to be sufficiently tangible to support a trespass action. Cyber Promotions (D) cites Restatement (Second) § 221 for the proposition that physical dispossession or substantial interference with the chattel is required for an actionable trespass to occur. Cyber Promotions (D) argues that it did not physically dispossess the equipment or substantially interfere with it. However, Restatement (Second) § 218 broadens the circumstances under which trespass to chattels may be actionable. This includes where the chattel is impaired as to its condition, quality, and value. Cyber Promotions (D) also asserts that there is no "substantial interference" unless the trespasser actually takes physical custody of the property or damages it. However, case law and Restatement (Second) § 218 show that this is not the case. Cyber Promotion's (D) mass mailings have drained CompuServe's (P) disk space and processing power. As a result, these resources are not available to subscribers. Therefore, the value of CompuServe's (P) equipment has been diminished even though it has not been physically damaged. Finally, Restatement (Second) § 218(d) indicates that recovery can be made for a trespass that harms something in which the possessor has a legally protected interest. In this case, Cyber Promotion's (D) e-mails inconvenienced CompuServe (P) subscribers and caused some to cancel their subscriptions. This harm to goodwill and reputation is actionable. CompuServe's (P) Motion for preliminary injunction is granted and Cyber Promotions (D) is enjoined from sending further advertisements to CompuServe (P) e-mail addresses.

Analysis:

This case is a good example of the courts struggling to apply old law to new technology. Trespass to chattels has been called the "little brother" of conversion. It occurs when there is some interference with the possession of property which is not sufficiently important to be classed as conversion. Cyber Promotions (D) argued for a narrow definition of trespass to chattels and "substantial interference." Cyber Promotions (D) wanted to limit liability to when the alleged trespasser takes physical custody of the property or physically damages it. The court rejected this narrow definition by relying on the list of circumstances in Restatement (Second) § 218 under which trespass to chattels may be actionable. Dispossession is only one circumstance under which trespass to chattels is actionable. Others include impairing the value of the chattel or causing harm to something in which the possessor has a legally protected interest. The court found that both of these circumstances occurred in this case. CompuServe's (P) equipment was harmed by being less able to serve its subscribers, and CompuServe's (P) subscribers were harmed by receiving the unwanted e-mails. CompuServe (P) brought this case as a trespass to chattels action. Are there any other causes of action CompuServe (P) may have brought against Cyber Promotions (D)?

■ CASE VOCABULARY

CHATTEL: Moveable or transferable property; personal property.

PRELIMINARY INJUNCTION: A temporary order preventing an action.

Pearson v. Dodd

(*Senator*) v. (*Journalist*)

410 F.2d 701 (D.C.Cir.1969), cert. denied, 395 U.S. 947, 89 S.Ct. 2021, 23 L.Ed.2d 465 (1969)

THE MEASURE OF DAMAGES IN CONVERSION, A SUBSTANTIAL INTERFERENCE WITH THE POS-SESSORY RIGHTS OF ANOTHER, IS THE FULL VALUE OF THE CHATTEL, WHILE THE MEASURE OF DAMAGES IN TRESPASS TO CHATTEL IS THE ACTUAL DIMINUTION IN THE VALUE OF THE CHATTEL CAUSED BY THE INTERFERENCE TO THE CHATTEL

■ **INSTANT FACTS** Senator Pearson (P) instituted an action in conversion against Dodd (D), a journalist, for unauthorized photocopying of Pearson's (P) office files.

■ **BLACK LETTER RULE** Photocopying of documents, which contain information not protected by property laws, does not constitute conversion.

■ **PROCEDURAL BASIS**

Appeal from action in conversion.

■ **FACTS**

Dodd (D), a journalist, copied files that had been taken from Senator Pearson's (P) office without his authorization. Later, Dodd (D) printed the contents of the documents which contained information about alleged misdeeds of Pearson (D). Pearson (D) sued Dodd (D) on the ground that his photocopying of the information constituted conversion. Pearson (P) moved for a summary judgment that the trial court granted. Dodd (D) appeals.

■ **ISSUE**

Does photocopying of documents, which contain information not protected by property laws, constitute conversion?

■ **DECISION AND RATIONALE**

(Wright, J.) No. Photocopying of documents, which contain information not protected by property laws, does not constitute conversion. This tort requires a complete interference with the chattel of another which substantially deprives the other person of possessory rights in the property. The measure of damages for conversion is the actual value of the property. Additionally, courts allow nominal damages where there has been no actual damage or injury. Trespass to chattel, on the other hand, requires a showing of actual damages. Under this tort, recovery is based on the diminution in value of the property. The facts indicate that there was no conversion of the documents in question. The photocopying was conducted at night, and the files were returned the next day before the office opened. Additionally, the information contained on the documents is not protected as a property right. The documents are neither for sale, nor crucial for commercial reasons. Thus, no action lies on conversion. (Reversed.)

Analysis:

Conversion, unlike trespass to chattel, requires a substantial interference and deprivation of one's possessory rights in a chattel. Under this theory, a plaintiff may recover nominal damages, or if there has been damage may recover the full value of the property converted. Some ways to convert a chattel include stealing, damaging, destroying, and extreme inconvenience caused to the owner of the property.

■ **CASE VOCABULARY**

ACTION FOR TROVER: A way to recover personal property "wrongfully" converted by another for his own use.

CONVERSION: The tortious deprivation of another's property without his/her authorization or justification; requires a wrongful taking, a wrongful detention, an illegal assumption of ownership, or an illegal use of another's property.

INTERLOCUTORY: Provisional or temporary, not final.

POSSESSORY RIGHTS: Rights of possession.

SUBSTANTIVE TORT THEORY: Basis and thinking behind the decisions in the field of tort law.

SUMMARY JUDGMENT: A pre-verdict judgment rendered by the court on the basis of pleadings because no material issue of fact exists, and one party or the other is entitled to judgment as a matter of law.

CHAPTER THREE

Privileges

O'Brien v. Cunard S.S. Co.

Instant Facts: O'Brien (P), a passenger on a Cunard S.S. Co. (D) ship, brings an action in assault and negligence against the latter when the doctor employed by Cunard S.S. (D) vaccinated her on board.

Black Letter Rule: Where consent is not expressed, an individual may rely on the other party's behavior and overt acts in order to determine whether that party has consented to the individual's conduct.

Hackbart v. Cincinnati Bengals, Inc.

Instant Facts: Dale Hackbart (P) sued Cincinnati Bengals (D) when Charles Clark (D), a player for the Bengals (D), struck a blow to the back of Hackbart's (P) head and neck.

Black Letter Rule: An individual is liable for the intentional striking of another during a violent game, where the rules of the sport prohibit such intentional acts.

Mohr v. Williams

Instant Facts: Mohr (P) sued her doctor, Williams (D), in battery and assault for operating on her left ear without her consent, during a consensual operation on her right ear.

Black Letter Rule: A doctor, who has obtained the patient's consent for a specific operation, may not perform another operation on the patient without his/her consent.

De May v. Roberts

Instant Facts: Roberts (P) sued De May (D), her physician, in battery for allowing his friend into Roberts' (P) presence while she was giving birth to her child.

Black Letter Rule: An individual's consent is not valid if the individual would not have consented, but for a mistaken belief about a material aspect of the conduct or transaction in question.

Katko v. Briney

Instant Facts: Katko (P) sued Briney (D) as a result of injuries that he suffered when he trespassed on Briney's (D) property and was shot by a mechanical spring gun placed on the property.

Black Letter Rule: An owner of property may not protect his property from trespassers by use of direct or indirect force which may cause serious bodily injury or death.

Hodgeden v. Hubbard

Instant Facts: Hodgeden (P) sued Hubbard (D) for forcefully removing from Hodgeden (P) a stove that he had bought from Hubbard (D) by misrepresenting his credit.

Black Letter Rule: A person may use reasonable force to recover property which is fraudulently obtained from him.

Bonkowski v. Arlan's Department Store

Instant Facts: Bonkowski (P) sought damages from Arlan's Department Store (D), which had falsely accused her of stealing merchandise from the store.

Black Letter Rule: A merchant, who reasonably believes that an individual has stolen merchandise from his/her store, may detain the individual for a reasonable investigation of the facts.

Surocco v. Geary

Instant Facts: Surocco (P), a homeowner, brings an action against Geary (D) for blowing up and destroying Surocco's (P) property in order to prevent the spread of fire.

Black Letter Rule: An individual who destroys another party's property in good faith, and under apparent necessity of preventing further harm to the community, is not personally liable in an action by the owner of the property destroyed.

Vincent v. Lake Erie Transp. Co.

Instant Facts: Vincent (P) sued Lake Erie Transport Co. (D) for damages caused to his dock when the latter fastened its ship to Vincent's (P) dock during a severe storm.

Black Letter Rule: Appeal from action for recovery of damages.

Sindle v. New York City Transit Authority

Instant Facts: Sindle (P), a teenage passenger on a bus owned by New York City Transit Authority (D), sued the latter for false imprisonment which resulted when an employee of the bus company took the bus and all its passengers to the police station as a result of the passengers' vandalizing the bus.

Black Letter Rule: Restraint or detention, which is reasonable under the circumstances, imposed for the purpose of preventing another from inflicting personal injuries or property damage, is not unlawful.

O'Brien v. Cunard S.S. Co.

(Passenger) v. *(Ship)*

154 Mass. 272, 28 N.E. 266 (1891)

WHERE CONSENT TO AN OTHERWISE TORTIOUS ACT IS NOT EXPRESSED, ONE MUST LOOK AT THE SURROUNDING CIRCUMSTANCES IN ORDER TO DETERMINE WHETHER CONSENT EXISTS

■ **INSTANT FACTS** O'Brien (P), a passenger on a Cunard S.S. Co. (D) ship, brings an action in assault and negligence against the latter when the doctor employed by Cunard S.S. (D) vaccinated her on board.

■ **BLACK LETTER RULE** Where consent is not expressed, an individual may rely on the other party's behavior and overt acts in order to determine whether that party has consented to the individual's conduct.

■ **PROCEDURAL BASIS**

Appeal from action in assault and negligence.

■ **FACTS**

O'Brien (P) was a passenger aboard S.S. Cunard (D), a ship going from Queenstown to Boston. Prior to reaching Boston, a surgeon, employed by Cunard S.S. (D), vaccinated O'Brien (P) pursuant to Boston laws requiring certification of vaccination for small pox. O'Brien (P) held her arm up to be vaccinated and said nothing about the fact that she did not want to be vaccinated. O'Brien (P) sued Cunard S.S. (D) for vaccinating her against her will. The trial court directed a verdict in favor of S.S. Cunard (D). O'Brien (D) appeals.

■ **ISSUE**

Where consent to an act is not explicitly expressed, may an individual rely on the other party's behavior and overt acts in order to determine whether that party has consented to the individual's conduct?

■ **DECISION AND RATIONALE**

(Knowlton, J.) Yes. Where consent is not expressed, an individual may rely on the other party's behavior and overt acts in order to determine whether that party has consented to the individual's conduct. At Boston, there are strict regulations in regard to the examination of immigrants, to see that they are protected from small-pox by vaccination, and only those persons who have a certificate of vaccination from the doctor of the ship may land without detention in the port of Boston. Notices of the requirement of vaccination and the duties of the ship doctor were posted on the ship in many languages. The doctor on the ship had the right to assume that the passengers, including O'Brien (P), understood the importance of vaccination. In this case, the plaintiff held her arm up to the doctor for vaccination and did not tell him that she did not want to be vaccinated, and after the vaccination, she took the certificate given to her. There was nothing in the conduct of the plaintiff to alert the doctor that she did not wish to be vaccinated or to receive the certificate of vaccination. In light of the circumstances, the doctor's conduct was not unlawful. (Affirmed.)

Analysis:

One way to prevent liability for assault and battery and other intentional torts is to obtain the consent of the person upon whom the conduct in question is being committed. Consent may be expressly given or as we have seen in this case it may be implied. Where consent is not expressed, the party claiming that consent existed must show the consent based on the circumstances surrounding the case, and based on the acts of the individual in question. It is, however, up to the finder of fact to determine whether an individual's acts and conduct is within the scope of consent given to that individual. See *Hackbart v. Cincinnati Bengals* [next case], for an illustration of the scope of consent.

■ CASE VOCABULARY

ASSAULT: An attempt or threat, with unlawful force, to inflict bodily injury upon another, accompanied by the apparent present ability to give effect to the attempt if not prevented.

CONSENT: Voluntary agreement; a concurrence of wills; an act of reason, not based on fraud, duress or mistake. Consent is implied in every agreement.

PRIVILEGE: An advantage which is not enjoyed by all; a benefit enjoyed by a person, company or class beyond the common advantages of other citizens; an immunity held beyond the course of the law.

Hackbart v. Cincinnati Bengals, Inc.

(Football Player) v. *(Opposing Team)*

601 F.2d 516 (10th Cir.1979), cert. denied, 444 U.S. 931, 100 S.Ct. 275, 62 L.Ed.2d 188 (1979)

IN PLAYING VIOLENT SPORTS, THE PLAYERS' CONSENT IS LIMITED TO THE RULES OF THE GAME AND GENERAL CUSTOMS REGARDING THE SPORT

■ **INSTANT FACTS** Dale Hackbart (P) sued Cincinnati Bengals (D) when Charles Clark (D), a player for the Bengals (D), struck a blow to the back of Hackbart's (P) head and neck.

■ **BLACK LETTER RULE** An individual is liable for the intentional striking of another during a violent game, where the rules of the sport prohibit such intentional acts.

■ **PROCEDURAL BASIS**

Appeal in action for battery.

■ **FACTS**

Dale Hackbart (P) was injured during the course of a game between the Broncos and the Cincinnati Bengals (D) when the latter's player, Charles Clark, struck Hackbart (P) in the back of his head and his neck. The trial court found that Clark hit Hackbart (P) out of anger and frustration, but without the intent to injure him. The trial court ruled that although Clark's act was intentional, the Bengals (D) were not liable as a matter of law because football is a violent game and the remedy for Hackbart (P) could be sought in the sanctions and penalties provided by the rules of the game. Hackbart (P) appeals.

■ **ISSUE**

Is an individual liable for the intentional striking of another during a violent game, where the rules of the sport prohibit such intentional acts?

■ **DECISION AND RATIONALE**

(Doyle, William E., J.) Yes, An individual is liable for the intentional striking of another during a violent game, where the rules of the sport prohibit such intentional acts. The evidence shows that intentional striking of blows, such as in this case, are clearly prohibited by the rules of football. Additionally, general customs of the game strictly prohibit acts and conduct such as the one in this instant case. The rules of the game and the customs are certainly intended to establish reasonable boundaries so that one player can not intentionally inflict a serious injury to another. In this case, the trial court's ruling as a matter of law was erroneous and the plaintiff was entitled to an assessment of his rights and whether his rights had been violated. (Reversed and Remanded.)

Analysis:

When playing a violent game, the players clearly consent to a certain amount of contact. However, this consent is limited in its scope. Just because a player consents to play a game does not mean that he/she consents to whatever acts are committed upon him during the game. Each sport has its rules and general customs, and most sports, including the ones that are violent, prohibit the intentional hitting or striking of other players. Thus, although a player who plays a violent sport, consents to certain amount of touching and contact, he/she has not consented to being intentionally hit and injured by other players. Thus, as in the instant case, in order to determine whether one's action is within the scope of the consent, we have to look at the rules of the game, in addition to the general customs of the game or sport. Finally, just because a certain act has violated a rule of the game or sport does not in and of itself create liability. The plaintiff must prove that the tortfeasor acted intentionally, or wilfully. Otherwise, no liability lies.

■ CASE VOCABULARY

CONSENT: Voluntary agreement; a concurrence of wills; an act of reason, not based on fraud, duress or mistake. Consent is implied in every agreement.

Mohr v. Williams

(Patient) v. *(Physician)*
90 Minn. 261, 104 N.W. 12 (1905)

A DOCTOR TREATING A NON-EMERGENCY PATIENT WITHOUT HIS/HER CONSENT HAS COMMITTED AN INTENTIONAL TORT EVEN THOUGH THE TREATMENT WAS COMPLETED SUCCESSFULLY

■ **INSTANT FACTS** Mohr (P) sued her doctor, Williams (D), in battery and assault for operating on her left ear without her consent, during a consensual operation on her right ear.

■ **BLACK LETTER RULE** A doctor, who has obtained the patient's consent for a specific operation, may not perform another operation on the patient without his/her consent.

■ **PROCEDURAL BASIS**

Appeal from action for assault and battery.

■ **FACTS**

Mohr (P) consulted Williams (D) about a problem in her right ear. Pursuant to an examination by Williams (D), Mohr (P) consented to a surgery on her right ear in order to remove the problem. While Mohr (P) was anesthetized, Williams (D) found a condition in her left ear, which although not life threatening, needed surgery. Williams (D) performed this surgery skillfully and successfully. Mohr (P) sued Williams (D) for battery. At the trial level, the jury awarded damages in favor of Mohr (P). The trial court however, granted a new trial on the ground that the damages were excessive. Both Mohr (P) and Williams (D) appeal.

■ **ISSUE**

May a doctor, who has obtained the patient's consent for a specific operation, perform another operation on the patient without his/her consent?

■ **DECISION AND RATIONALE**

(Brown, J.) No. A doctor who has obtained the patient's consent for a specific operation may not perform another operation on the patient without his/her consent. Ordinarily, a patient must be consulted and his consent obtained before a doctor can operate on the patient. No rule or principle of law extends to a doctor a free license respecting surgical operations. However, we will not lay down a strict rule which will interfere with a doctor's use of his own discretion in times of emergency when the patient's consent cannot be obtained. In such emergency situations, the patient's consent is implied. In this case, there was no emergency. The diseased condition of the plaintiff's left ear was not discovered in the course of operations on the right ear. It was, however, the result of an independent examination on the left ear. In this case, the surgeon was accompanied by the patient's family physician. The surgeon made the condition of the left ear known to the physician and recommended surgery to which the physician did not object. It does not appear, however, that the physician was present as an agent of the patient. His presence was requested simply to allay the fears of the patient. The question of whether his presence and his failure to object to the operations on the left ear constituted an implied consent on behalf of the plaintiff is a question for the jury to determine. Additionally, Williams' (D) second contention is that his act did not constitute battery because the operation was a success. In other words, Williams (D) claims that the absence of a wrongful intent or negligence should relieve the defendant of liability under battery. We are unable to reach that conclusion. If the act of the defendant was performed without the plaintiff's consent, then it was unlawful and amounted to battery, regardless of the skill with which the defendant performed the surgery. However, the amount that the plaintiff can recover will depend on the character and extent of the injury inflicted upon her, and the beneficial nature of the operation must be taken into consideration, as well as the good faith of the defendant.

Analysis:

This is another case which deals with the scope of consent. Here, just because the plaintiff had consented to a surgery on the right ear does not give the doctor the right to perform a surgery on the left ear, if the patient has not consented, the doctor is liable, technically, for battery. Note that as this case indicates, the amount of the patient's recovery may depend on the nature and extent of the injury, the good faith of the defendant, and the success of the operation. Additionally, this case indicates that the rule of consent does not apply to emergency situations where the plaintiff's condition is life-threatening, and the plaintiff is unable to consent (e.g., the plaintiff is unconscious). In emergency situations the doctor is allowed to exercise his/her discretion more freely. Note that an additional source of liability may arise in negligence if the doctor fails to perform the operation with the skill and knowledge of an ordinary or reasonable doctor. In such cases, the doctor may be liable for both the intentional torts of assault and battery and under negligence. Again, remember that liability in tort for assault and battery does not require a wrongful or malicious intent. It is enough that the touching or the apprehension of the touching be intentional. It is important to know that the physician must not only disclose the specifics of the operation or treatment, but also the risks associated with it. You may already be familiar with the doctrine of informed consent. Under this doctrine, a physician must disclose to the patient the risks of the proposed medical treatment, and if she/he does not do so, he may be liable for the injury that is caused as a result of the treatment.

■ CASE VOCABULARY

ACTUATED: Put in motion.

ASSENT: Consent or agreement.

EXPRESS CONSENT: Permission given directly, either orally or in writing.

PRIVILEGE (DOCTRINE OF): An advantage, benefit, right or power granted to an individual or a few.

De May v. Roberts

(Physician) v. *(Patient)*
46 Mich. 160, 9 N.W. 146 (1881)

IN ORDER TO BE VALID, CONSENT TO AN OTHERWISE TORTIOUS ACT MUST BE KNOWING AND VOLUNTARY

■ **INSTANT FACTS** Roberts (P) sued De May (D), her physician, in battery for allowing his friend into Roberts' (P) presence while she was giving birth to her child.

■ **BLACK LETTER RULE** An individual's consent is not valid if the individual would not have consented, but for a mistaken belief about a material aspect of the conduct or transaction in question.

■ **PROCEDURAL BASIS**

Appeal from action in battery.

■ **FACTS**

Roberts (P) was in labor when her physician, De May (D), and a stranger entered her room. Roberts (P), believing the stranger to be De May's assistant, allowed him to be present at the time of the child's delivery. Additionally, Roberts (P), under the same mistaken belief, allowed the stranger to hold her hand during delivery. Roberts (P) sued De May (D) upon realizing that the stranger, a young, unmarried man, was not De May's assistant and in fact had no knowledge of medicine and was simply accompanying the doctor to carry the necessary equipment for the doctor. The trial court ruled in favor of Roberts (P). De May (D) appeals.

■ **ISSUE**

Is an individual's consent valid, if the individual would not have consented but for a mistaken belief about a material aspect of the conduct or transaction in question?

■ **DECISION AND RATIONALE**

(Martson, C.J.) No. An individual's consent is not valid if the individual would not have consented, but for a mistaken belief about a material aspect of the conduct or transaction in question. In this case, neither Roberts (P) nor her husband were told that the stranger was not the physician's assistant. The occasion in question was a private one for the plaintiff, and no one had the right to intrude upon her unless it were absolutely necessary. The fact that at the time of the incident, Roberts (P), believing the stranger to be the physician's assistant, gave her consent, does not preclude her from bringing an action against the defendant. The physician in this case is liable for failing to disclose the true character of the stranger. (Affirmed.)

Analysis:

This case illustrates that consent must be voluntary and knowing. Thus, consent, even though express, which has been obtained through trickery, or fraud, or even a mistake as to a material fact, is not truly "consent." When obtaining consent, it is important to reveal material facts which are critical to giving of the consent. For example, it is clear in the case at hand, that had Roberts been aware that the stranger was not an assistant physician, she would not have consented to his presence. Thus, although she consented, the consent was under a mistaken belief of a material fact and as such, is null and void.

■ **CASE VOCABULARY**

EXTREMITY: Highest degree of distress.

PAROXYSM (OF PAIN): A sudden attack.

PARTURITION: Act of bringing forth (as in childbirth).

Katko v. Briney

(Trespasser) (Property Owner)
183 N.W.2d 657 (Iowa 1971)

AN INDIVIDUAL MAY NOT USE DEADLY FORCE TO PROTECT HIS/HER PROPERTY

■ **INSTANT FACTS** Katko (P) sued Briney (D) as a result of injuries that he suffered when he trespassed on Briney's (D) property and was shot by a mechanical spring gun placed on the property.

■ **BLACK LETTER RULE** An owner of property may not protect his property from trespassers by use of direct or indirect force which may cause serious bodily injury or death.

■ **PROCEDURAL BASIS**

Appeal from action in battery.

■ **FACTS**

Briney (D), weary of the constant intrusions into the old abandoned house he inherited from his grandparents, had posted "no trespass" signs and had boarded up the doors and the windows of the house. Later, Briney (D) set a "shotgun trap" in one of the bedrooms in the property. The gun, which was rigged to the doorknob, would fire if someone attempted to enter the room. There were no signs warning trespassers of the presence of the gun. Katko (P) was shot in his legs and suffered serious injuries when he was trespassing in the house. As a result, Katko (P) sued Briney (D) for an award of damages for injuries that he sustained. The trial court awarded a judgment in favor of Katko (P). Briney (D) appeals.

■ **ISSUE**

May an owner of property protect his property from trespassers by use of direct or indirect force which may cause serious bodily injury or death?

■ **DECISION AND RATIONALE**

(Moore, C.J.) No. An owner of property may not protect his property from trespassers by use of direct or indirect force which may cause serious bodily injury or death. Thus, a person owning a premise is prohibited from setting spring guns or other dangerous devices which will likely take life or inflict great bodily injury, for the purpose of harming trespassers. The only time that such force could be used is when the trespasser is committing a felony of violence or a felony punishable by death, or where the trespasser is endangering human life by his act. Thus, a type of force which the owner of the premise could not himself use in defending his property cannot be used indirectly through installation of mechanical devices either. (Affirmed.)

■ **DISSENT**

(Larson, J.): The trial judge's instructions failed to tell the jury that it could find that the installation was not made with the intent or purpose of striking or injuring the plaintiff.

Analysis:

Remember that in defending his/her own person, an individual may use reasonable force. Such reasonable force may even included force which may create serious bodily injury or death where under the circumstances such force is necessary. However, one can never use force which may cause serious bodily harm or death when protecting one's property. Such force is never considered reasonable. Thus, whether the force used is direct, by the person himself, or through the use of mechanical devices, it cannot be force which may cause serious bodily injury or death. Note, however, that there is an exception to this rule which is really not an exception: one can use force which causes serious bodily harm or death when the trespasser to the property threatens the life of the owner or other individuals on the owner's property.

■ CASE VOCABULARY

INFRA: Below; later in this writing.

REVERSIBLE ERROR: Also called prejudicial error, an error substantially affecting an appellant's legal rights and obligations which, if uncorrected, would result in a miscarriage of justice and which justifies reversing a judgment in the court below even if the error was not objected to in the lower court.

Hodgeden v. Hubbard

(Buyer) v. *(Store Owner)*

18 Vt. 504, 46 Am. Dec. 167 (1846)

AN INDIVIDUAL WHO IS UNLAWFULLY DISPOSSESSED OF HIS CHATTEL MAY NOT USE DEADLY FORCE TO RECOVER THE CHATTEL

■ **INSTANT FACTS** Hodgeden (P) sued Hubbard (D) for forcefully removing from Hodgeden (P) a stove that he had bought from Hubbard (D) by misrepresenting his credit.

■ **BLACK LETTER RULE** A person may use reasonable force to recover property which is fraudulently obtained from him.

■ **PROCEDURAL BASIS**

Appeal from action in assault and battery and in trespass to chattel.

■ **FACTS**

Hodgeden (P) bought a stove from Hubbard's (D) department store on credit and carried it away. Hubbard (D) at once realized that Hodgeden (P) had misrepresented his credit in buying the stove. Hubbard (D) immediately set out after Hodgeden (P) and caught up with him two miles away. Hodgeden (P) drew a knife and Hubbard (D) had to resort to force to remove the stove. Hodgeden (P) brought an action against Hubbard (D) in assault and battery and for trespass to chattel. The trial court ruled in favor of Hodgeden (P) stating that Hubbard (D) was not justified in using force to remove the property and that his only redress was the legal process. Hubbard (D) appeals.

■ **ISSUE**

May a person use reasonable force to recover property which is fraudulently obtained from him?

■ **DECISION AND RATIONALE**

(Williams, C.J.) Yes. A person may use reasonable force to recover property which is fraudulently obtained from him. In this case, the property did not pass to Hodgeden (P) because although he was in possession of the property, he had obtained possession through fraud and misrepresentation. Thus, his possession was unlawful. In recovery of the property, however, no violence to the person of the plaintiff was necessary unless from his resistance. By drawing the knife, the plaintiff became the aggressor, and it was the right of the defendant to hold him by force and as long as he did not use unnecessary force, defendant was justified. (Reversed.)

Analysis:

Note that one may use reasonable force to recover chattel or property which is unlawfully taken from him. However, this force may not be deadly force. Remember, however, that recovery of chattel is allowed only to the extent that the original possessor's possession of the property is not interrupted. This means that one can only recover his/her chattel right after it has been unlawfully taken. In other words, if someone takes your chattel and you realize this two days later, you cannot recover it by use of reasonable force. However, if you realized that someone is taking your chattel at the time that person takes it, or you realize it shortly thereafter to the extent that your recovery of the chattel can be considered "fresh pursuit," use of reasonable force to recover the chattel is allowed. Otherwise, the remedy is to refer to the proper authorities.

■ **CASE VOCABULARY**

EXCEPTION: An objection to a court ruling, or calling an error to the attention of the court in some manner.

REDRESS: To set right a wrong or grievance.

Bonkowski v. Arlan's Department Store

(Buyer) v. *(Store)*

12 Mich.App. 88, 162 N.W.2d 347 (1968)

A MERCHANT HAS THE RIGHT TO DETAIN FOR REASONABLE INVESTIGATION A PERSON WHOM HE/SHE REASONABLY BELIEVES TO HAVE TAKEN A CHATTEL UNLAWFULLY

■ **INSTANT FACTS** Bonkowski (P) sought damages from Arlan's Department Store (D), which had falsely accused her of stealing merchandise from the store.

■ **BLACK LETTER RULE** A merchant, who reasonably believes that an individual has stolen merchandise from his/her store, may detain the individual for a reasonable investigation of the facts.

■ **PROCEDURAL BASIS**

Appeal from action for damages for false arrest and slander.

■ **FACTS**

On the night of December 18, 1962, when Mrs. Bonkowski (P) and her husband left Arlan's Department Store (D), Reinhardt, a private security officer who was hired by the store, followed the two out of the store, suspecting that they had stolen merchandise from the store. Reinhardt motioned Bonkowski (P) and her husband to stop, telling them that someone had seen them steal jewelry from the store. Bonkowski (P) denied the allegations. However, Reinhardt urged her to empty the contents of her purse. Bonkowski (P) offered sales receipts for all the items that she had purchased, and Reinhardt, content that she had committed no theft, returned to the store. Bonkowski (P) brought action for damages against Arlan's (D) for slander and false arrest, claiming that she suffered nervousness, headaches, depression, and other illnesses as a result of Reinhardt's action. At the trial the jury returned a verdict in favor of Bonkowski (P) and the trial court dismissed Arlan's (D) motion for a new judgment notwithstanding the verdict. Arlan's (D) appeals.

■ **ISSUE**

May a merchant who reasonably believes that an individual has stolen merchandise from his/her store, detain the individual for a reasonable investigation of the facts?

■ **DECISION AND RATIONALE**

(Fitzgerald, Neil E., J.) Yes. A merchant, who reasonably believes that an individual has stolen merchandise from his/her store, may detain the individual for a reasonable investigation of the facts. This privilege is a defense to the common law tort of false arrest. It is a privilege that is necessary for the protection of a shopkeeper against the dilemma of not being able to arrest shoplifters. This court believes that the privilege should be extended to those who have left the store, but as in this case are within the immediate premises of the store. Thus in this case, on remand, it is the duty of the jury to determine whether or not Reinhardt reasonably believed that Bonkowski (P) had unlawfully taken goods from the store. Additionally, the jury must further determine whether the investigation that followed was reasonable under the circumstances of the case. If the facts do not indicate reasonableness of the arrest and the investigation, then Arlan's (D) can not take advantage of the privilege, and it may be liable for false arrest. (Reversed and Remanded.)

Analysis:

Courts have struck a balance between a merchant's right to protect his property and other individual's right to be free from arrest. Thus, they allow merchants and shopkeepers the very limited privilege of detaining an individual whom they *reasonably* believe to have unlawfully taken their property. However, as mentioned, this privilege is very limited in that 1) the merchant must reasonably believe that the individual has taken his/her property unlawfully, and 2) the length and manner of the detention must be reasonable (sufficient for investigatory purposes). If the merchant's actions are not reasonable, he may be liable for false arrest and false imprisonment.

■ CASE VOCABULARY

CAVEAT: A warning or emphasis for caution.

IN DICTUM: In general (a statement, remark or observation).

LARCENY: Theft; the unlawful taking of another's property.

REMAND: To send back.

REMITTITUR: In its broadest meaning, the procedural process by which the verdict of a jury is diminished by subtraction; generally, any reduction made by the court without the consent of the jury.

SLANDER: Words falsely spoken which tend to damage the reputation of another.

TORTIOUS: A private or civil wrong.

Surocco v. Geary

(Homeowner) v. *(Firefighter)*
3 Cal. 69, 58 Am.Dec. 385 (1853)

THE PRIVILEGE OF NECESSITY ALLOWS AN INDIVIDUAL TO HARM AN INNOCENT PARTY'S PROPERTY DUE TO EXIGENT CIRCUMSTANCES IN ORDER TO PREVENT GREATER HARM TO THE COMMUNITY

■ **INSTANT FACTS** Surocco (P), a homeowner, brings an action against Geary (D) for blowing up and destroying Surocco's (P) property in order to prevent the spread of fire.

■ **BLACK LETTER RULE** An individual who destroys another party's property in good faith, and under apparent necessity of preventing further harm to the community, is not personally liable in an action by the owner of the property destroyed.

■ **PROCEDURAL BASIS**

Appeal from action to recover for damage to property.

■ **FACTS**

On December 24, 1849, there was a fire raging in the city of San Francisco. Geary (D), an official of the city, decided that blowing up Surocco's (P) property would help prevent the spread of the fire. So, he blew it up! At the time of destruction of the property, Surocco (P) was removing furnishings and other items that were inside the property, and Surocco (P) claims that had his property not been destroyed, he could have removed more, if not all of his goods from the property. The trial court ruled in favor of Surocco (P) and Geary (D) appeals.

■ **ISSUE**

Is an individual who destroys another party's property in good faith, and under apparent necessity of preventing further harm, personally liable in an action by the owner of the property destroyed?

■ **DECISION AND RATIONALE**

(Murray, C.J.) No. An individual who destroys another party's property in good faith, and under apparent necessity of preventing further harm, is not personally liable in an action by the owner of the property destroyed. The right to destroy someone's property to prevent the spread of conflagration has been traced to the highest law of necessity. It rests in the maxim that "necessity provides a privilege for private rights." The common law has adopted this principle of necessity as a justification for what would otherwise be a tortious act. In these situations private rights of individuals yield to the considerations of general convenience, and the interests of the society. In every case, however, in order to avoid liability, the existence of necessity must be clearly shown. The legislature of each state has the power to regulate this matter by determining how structures may be destroyed and by determining the amount of compensation that must be given to the owners of the property or structure destroyed. In the absence of such legislation the rules of common law will be followed. In this case destruction of Surocco's (P) property was clearly a necessity, and Surocco (P) cannot recover for the value of the property lost in the destruction. (Reversed.)

Analysis:

Under the privilege of necessity, interference with one's real property or chattel must be necessary to prevent a disaster to the community or to a large number of people. If this privilege exists, then the person taking advantage of it is not personally liable for the value of the property that was lost or destroyed. This privilege is also known as public necessity. One who asserts this privilege must prove the existence of exigent circumstances which required the destruction of another person's property for the sake of the community as a whole, and must prove that the act was committed in good faith. Under cases such as the one above, interests of the community outweigh the individual's interests.

■ CASE VOCABULARY

ABATE: To make or become less; to end.

BULWARK: Fortification for defense or security.

CONFLAGRATION: A great destructive fire.

EXIGENCIES: Pressing necessity; emergency.

NECESSITY: The defense of justification which excuses the defendant from liability when he has unavoidably been forced to make a "choice of evils."

OBVIATE: To prevent or avert (a danger).

Vincent v. Lake Erie Transp. Co.

(Dock Owner) v. *(Ship Owner)*

109 Minn. 456, 124 N.W. 221 (1910)

PRIVATE NECESSITY IS A PRIVILEGE WHICH ALLOWS AN INDIVIDUAL TO HARM THE PROPERTY OF ANOTHER TO PREVENT INJURY TO HIS PROPERTY OR TO HIMSELF OR TO THIRD PARTIES IF HARMING THE PROPERTY OF ANOTHER IS THE LEAST HARMFUL SOLUTION

■ **INSTANT FACTS** Vincent (P) sued Lake Erie Transport Co. (D) for damages caused to his dock when the latter fastened its ship to Vincent's (P) dock during a severe storm.

■ **BLACK LETTER RULE** Appeal from action for recovery of damages.

■ **PROCEDURAL BASIS**

An individual who damages the property of another as a result of private necessity is liable for the damage to that individual's property.

■ **FACTS**

Lake Erie Transport Co. (D) had moored its ship to Vincent's (P) dock for the purpose of unloading its cargo. However, at the time of unloading a severe storm developed, which suspended navigation until the next morning. After unloading the ship the crew of the ship fastened the vessel to the dock until the next morning. The storm caused the ship to be constantly lifted and hit against the dock, which in turn caused damage to the dock. Vincent (P) sued Lake Erie Transport (D), owner of the vessel, for damages to the dock. The trial court ruled in favor of Vincent (D), and Lake Erie (D) appeals.

■ **ISSUE**

Is an individual who damages the property of another as a result of private necessity liable for the damage to that individual's property?

■ **DECISION AND RATIONALE**

(O'Brien, J.) Yes. An individual who damages the property of another as a result of private necessity is liable for the damage to that individual's property. The storm in this case was of such nature that it would have been imprudent for the master of the ship to leave the dock on the night in question. Thus, in holding the vessel to the dock, the ship master exercised good judgment and skill. The defendant contends that because of the master's exercise of good judgment, it should not be liable for damages to the plaintiff's dock. In this case, those in charge of the vessel deliberately held the vessel in a position that resulted in damage to the plaintiff's dock. They preserved their ship at the expense of the dock; as such the owners of the ship are liable to the plaintiff for the damages that they caused. Note, however, as in the case of *Ploof v. Putnam* the defendants are not liable in trespass. In *Ploof* a vessel, because of a storm, moored to a private dock without permission. That court, however, found that the owner of that vessel was not liable in trespass, and the dock owner was liable in damages because he unmoored the vessel, causing it to sustain damages. This is not a case of an unavoidable accident, or a situation where because of an act of God infliction of injury was beyond the defendant's control. This is a situation where the defendant prudently availed itself of the plaintiff's property in preserving its own property, and as such the plaintiff is entitled to compensation for the injury to his property.

Analysis:

Private necessity arises when an individual injures or damages the property of another in order to prevent injury to himself or to his own property or that of a third party because in that way a bigger harm will be prevented. Although the law allows individuals this privilege, unlike public necessity the individual who damages the property of another is liable for the damage caused. However, as in the case at hand, the individual is not liable for technical trespass.

■ **CASE VOCABULARY**

APPROPRIATE: To take as one's own.

NECESSITY: The defense of justification which excuses the defendant from liability when he has unavoidably been forced to make a "choice of evils."

Sindle v. New York City Transit Authority

(Bus Passenger) v. *(Bus Company)*

33 N.Y.2d 293, 307 N.E.2d 245, 352 N.Y.S.2d 183 (1973)

A DEFENDANT CLAIMING JUSTIFICATION AS DEFENSE TO FALSE IMPRISONMENT MUST PROVE THAT THE DETENTION OF THE PLAINTIFF WAS REASONABLE UNDER THE CIRCUMSTANCES OF THE CASE

■ **INSTANT FACTS** Sindle (P), a teenage passenger on a bus owned by New York City Transit Authority (D), sued the latter for false imprisonment which resulted when an employee of the bus company took the bus and all its passengers to the police station as a result of the passengers' vandalizing the bus.

■ **BLACK LETTER RULE** Restraint or detention which is reasonable under the circumstances, imposed for the purpose of preventing another from inflicting personal injuries or property damage, is not unlawful.

■ **PROCEDURAL BASIS**

Appeal from action for false imprisonment.

■ **FACTS**

Sindle (P), a fourteen-year-old boy, and many of his classmates took the bus owned by New York City Transit Authority (D) on the last day of school. While on the bus, the students started vandalizing the bus, breaking windows, and tearing off the advertisements inside of the bus. The bus driver admonished the students on at least one occasion, but to no avail. There is no clear evidence that Sindle (P) was engaged in the acts of vandalism. Finally, the bus driver, assessing the damage on the bus, informed the students that he was going directly to the police station. He drove to the police with the students as passengers. Sindle (P) sued New York City Transit Authority (D) for false imprisonment. The trial court ruling in favor of Sindle (P), denied the bus company's motion to amend their answer in order to include the defense of justification. New York City Transit Authority (D) appeals.

■ **ISSUE**

Is restraint or detention which is reasonable under the circumstances, imposed for the purpose of preventing another from inflicting personal injuries or property damage, unlawful?

■ **DECISION AND RATIONALE**

(Jasen, J.) No. Restraint or detention which is reasonable under the circumstances and imposed for the purpose of preventing another from inflicting personal injuries or property damage, is not unlawful. The trial court abused its discretion in denying the defendant its motion to bring evidence of justification. A school bus driver entrusted with the care of his student passengers and the custody of public property has the duty to take reasonable measures for the safety and protection of both. Thus, the reasonableness of the driver's actions under the circumstances should have been determined. (Reversed and remanded for new trial.)

Analysis:

Justification could be used as a defense where a defendant's conduct does not fall squarely within any other defense. Under this defense the circumstances surrounding the defendant's conduct will be looked at and assessed in order to determine whether the defendant acted reasonably in light of the circumstances. Also, the court may look at the defendant's position of authority and the alternatives that the defendant could have chosen in determining the reasonableness of his actions. Like other defenses such as self-defense, defense of property, consent, or necessity, justification is a defense to intentional torts.

■ CASE VOCABULARY

JUSTIFICATION: A just cause or excuse; the just or lawful excuse for an act which may otherwise be illegal; existence of reasonable justification may excuse a defendant of liability for his/her tortious conduct.

CHAPTER FOUR

Negligence

Lubitz v. Wells

Instant Facts: Lubitz (P) sued Wells (D) for injuries that she sustained when the latter's son hit her with Wells' (D) golf club.

Black Letter Rule: An individual cannot be held liable in negligence for risks that are not reasonably known to him.

Blyth v. Birmingham Waterworks Co.

Instant Facts: Blyth (P) sued Birmingham Waterworks Co. (D) in negligence for laying water pipes which exploded in Blyth's (P) home due to the severity of the cold weather.

Black Letter Rule: An individual is not negligent if his/her conduct and precautions conform to the standard followed by a prudent or reasonable person.

Gulf Refining Co. v. Williams

Instant Facts: Williams (P) brought action against Gulf Refining Co. (D) for the injuries that he suffered when attempting to open a can of gasoline that he bought from Gulf Refining Co. (D).

Black Letter Rule: An individual may be liable in negligence even if his/her conduct creates a risk of harm which is highly improbable and unlikely.

Chicago, B. & Q.R. Co. v. Krayenbuhl

Instant Facts: Krayenbuhl (P), brings an action against Chicago, B & Q Railroad company to recover for damages that she sustained when her ankle got stuck in the railroad turntable that the railroad company had failed to lock.

Black Letter Rule: An individual using a socially beneficial yet inherently dangerous instrument, must take reasonable precautions such that the risk of injury posed by the instrument does not outweigh its utility.

Davison v. Snohomish County

Instant Facts: Davison (P) sued Snohomish County (D) for injuries he suffered when his car skidded off the road and into the guard rails which failed to protect him from falling to the ground.

Black Letter Rule: A county is not negligent for failing to build safety railing where the construction of such railing would create an undue burden on the county and prevent construction of other roads.

United States v. Carroll Towing Co.

Instant Facts: United States (P) sued Carroll Towing Co. (D) for its negligence in handling the moorings of the ship owned by the United States (P) which caused the ship to sink.

Black Letter Rule: An individual may be liable for failing to take reasonable precaution against great risk of injury even where the probability of the injury occurring is very little.

Vaughan v. Menlove

Instant Facts: Vaughan (P), a cottage owner, sued Menlove (D) for the damage and destruction of his cottage, caused by a fire, which started in Menlove's (D) hay rick.

Black Letter Rule: The standard of care used to determine negligence is that of the reasonable person in similar circumstances and not the good faith or subjective standard adhered to by the defendant.

Delair v. Mcadoo

Instant Facts: Delair (P) brought an action against McAdoo (D) to recover damages sustained when the tires on McAdoo's (D) car blew up as McAdoo (D) was passing Delair (P).

Black Letter Rule: A reasonable driver of an automobile should be charged with the knowledge that driving with worn tires poses a danger to other individuals on the road.

Trimarco v. Klein

Instant Facts: Trimarco (P), a tenant of Klein (D), sued the latter for injury that Trimarco (P) suffered when the glass shower door in his apartment broke.

Black Letter Rule: Evidence of custom, common usage, and practice, although compelling, may not be used as the conclusive test of negligence.

Cordas v. Peerless Transportation Co.

Instant Facts: Cordas (P), a pedestrian, sued Peerless Transportation (D) for injuries that Cordas (P) sustained when hit by Peerless Transportation's (D) cab from which the driver jumped while a gun was held to his head.

Black Letter Rule: The conduct of an individual who is in an emergency situation is not measured by the standard of care of a reasonable person in a non-emergency situation.

Roberts v. State of Louisiana

Instant Facts: Roberts (P) sued the State of Louisiana (D) for injuries that he sustained when he was bumped into by Burson, a blind employee of the state (D).

Black Letter Rule: In determining the negligence of an individual, the court must take into consideration the physical attributes or shortcomings of the individual.

Robinson v. Lindsay

Instant Facts: A suit was brought on behalf of Kelly Robinson (P), an 11–year-old girl who was injured in a snowmobile which was driven by Billy Anderson (D), a 13–year-old boy.

Black Letter Rule: A minor child engaged in the operation of machinery ordinarily used by adults is held to an adult standard of care.

Breunig v. American Family Ins. Co.

Instant Facts: Breunig (P) brought action against American Family Insurance Co. (D) to recover for injuries he sustained when Mrs. Veith, American Family's (D) insured, was driving on the wrong side of the highway.

Black Letter Rule: Insanity is not a defense to negligent conduct where the defendant had prior warning and knowledge of his/her insanity.

Heath v. Swift Wings, Inc.

Instant Facts: Swift Wings (D) was sued in negligence when a plane flown by its pilot, Fred Heath, crashed causing the death of Fred Heath's wife and children.

Black Letter Rule: A professional's negligence is not determined based on the degree of ordinary care and caution exercised by professionals having the same experience and training.

Hodges v. Carter

Instant Facts: Hodges (P) sued Carter (D), an attorney, in negligence for losses that Hodges (P) suffered due to Carter's (D) failure to properly serve Hodges' (P) insurance carriers.

Black Letter Rule: An attorney who has acted in good faith and in the best interests of his client is not liable in negligence for a mere error in judgment.

Boyce v. Brown

Instant Facts: Boyce (P) brought an action in negligence against her surgeon Brown (D) for his failure to take an x-ray of Boyce's (P) ankle on which Brown (D) had operated seven years before.

Black Letter Rule: In a medical malpractice case, the plaintiff must prove the standard of care in the medical community and that the defendant's conduct departed from this standard.

Morrison v. Macnamara

Instant Facts: Morrison (P) brought a malpractice action against MacNamara (D), a medical laboratory, for injuries that Morrison (P) sustained when he fainted and struck his head on a blood pressure stand.

Black Letter Rule: The conduct of health professionals who are certified through a system of national board certification must be measured against nationally accepted standards of care.

Scott v. Bradford

Instant Facts: Scott (P) brought an action against Bradford (D), Scott's (P) surgeon, on the ground that Bradford (D) had failed to disclose the risks and alternatives of the surgery to Scott (P).

Black Letter Rule: A physician is liable in negligence if he does not inform the patient of his options and its attendant risks before treating the patient.

Moore v. The Regents Of The University Of California

Instant Facts: Moore (P), who has sought medical treatment from Dr. Golde at the UCLA Medical Center, brought an action against the Regents of the University of California for Dr. Golde's failure to disclose his own personal interest in treatment of Moore (P).

Black Letter Rule: In order to satisfy his fiduciary duty to the patient and obtain the patient's consent, a physician who is seeking a patient's consent for a medical procedure must disclose his own personal interests, unrelated to the patient's health, that may affect the patient's decision.

Pokora v. Wabash Ry. Co.

Instant Facts: Pokora (P) brought an action in negligence against Wabash Ry. Co. (D) for injuries that he sustained when his car was struck by Wabash's (D) train.

Black Letter Rule: An automobile driver who is crossing over railroad tracks does not, under all circumstances, have the absolute legal duty to stop the car to look for oncoming trains.

Osborne v. Mcmasters

Instant Facts: Osborne (P), administrator of the estate of the decedent, brought an action against McMasters for death of the decedent due to McMasters' (D) selling poison to the decedent without labeling it as such.

Black Letter Rule: An individual who breaches a duty imposed on him by statute is liable for injuries to those whom the statute is designed to protect if the injuries resulted from his breach.

Stachniewicz v. Mar–Cam Corp.

Instant Facts: Stachniewicz (P) brought action against Mar–Cam Corp. (D), owner of a bar, for injuries that Stachniewicz (P) sustained as a result of a barroom brawl.

Black Letter Rule: A violation of a statute or regulation constitutes negligence per se when the violation results in injury to a member of the class of persons protected by the statute or regulation and when the harm is of the kind which the statute or regulation is designed to prevent.

Ney v. Yellow Cab Co.

Instant Facts: Ney (P) brought action against Yellow Cab Co.(D) for injuries that Ney (P) suffered when the taxicab, stolen by a thief, ran into Ney's (P) vehicle.

Black Letter Rule: A plaintiff who bases his claim for negligence on a defendant's violation of a statute, must prove that his injuries were directly and proximately caused by the defendant's violation of the statute.

Perry v. S.N. and S.N.

Instant Facts: A man witnessed children being abused and failed to report the abuse to authorities as required by statute.

Black Letter Rule: A child abuse reporting statute does not create civil liability for one who fails to report abuse.

Martin v. Herzog

Instant Facts: Martin (P) brought an action against Herzog (D) alleging the death of Martin's (P) husband as a result of Herzog driving on the wrong side of the road.

Black Letter Rule: Proof of negligent conduct, without a showing of causal connection between the conduct and injury suffered, is not enough to impose liability on the party whose conduct was negligent.

Zeni v. Anderson

Instant Facts: Zeni (P), a pedestrian walking on the street with her back to the traffic, sued Anderson (D) for injuries that Zeni (P) suffered when Anderson (D) hit Zeni (P) with her automobile.

Black Letter Rule: The violation of a statute which is found to apply to a particular set of facts creates a presumption which can be rebutted by a showing of an adequate excuse or justification for violation of the statute.

Goddard v. Boston & Maine R.R. Co.

Instant Facts: Goddard (P) brought an action in negligence against Boston & Maine R.R. Co. (D) for injuries he suffered when he fell on a banana peel on the platform at the train station.

Black Letter Rule: In a negligence action, in order to avoid a directed verdict, the plaintiff must provide sufficient evidence from which reasonable jurors could infer that the defendant was engaged in negligent conduct and that his negligence caused the plaintiff's injury.

Anjou v. Boston Elevated Railway Co.

Instant Facts: Anjou (P) brought an action against Boston Elevated Railway Co. (D) for injuries suffered when Anjou (P) fell on a banana peel in Boston Elevated Railway's (D) train station.

Black Letter Rule: A directed verdict in favor of the defendant is not appropriate where the plaintiff has presented evidence sufficient to support an inference of negligence on the part of the defendant.

Joye v. Great Atlantic and Pacific Tea Co.

Instant Facts: A customer who slipped and fell on a banana at a grocery store argued that the store should have known that the banana was on the floor.

Black Letter Rule: Actual or constructive knowledge of a dangerous condition, established through direct or circumstantial evidence, must be proven to impose liability for injuries caused by the condition.

Ortega v. Kmart Corp.

Instant Facts: While shopping in Kmart (D), Ortega (P) slipped and fell in a puddle of milk.

Black Letter Rule: Although a storeowner is not an insurer of the safety of its patrons, the owner does owe them a duty to exercise reasonable care in keeping the premises reasonably safe.

H.E. Butt Groc. Co. v. Resendez

Instant Facts: Resendez (P) slipped and fell near the defendant's grape display designed for public sampling and sued the grocer.

Black Letter Rule: To establish a premises liability claim, the plaintiff must establish that the defendant had actual or constructive notice of a dangerous condition creating an unreasonable risk of harm and the defendant's failure to use reasonable care to minimize the harm, which caused the plaintiff's injuries.

Byrne v. Boadle

Instant Facts: Byrne (P) brought action in negligence against Boadle (D) for injuries suffered when a barrel of flour rolled out of Boadle's (D) shop and fell on Byrne (P).

Black Letter Rule: A plaintiff need not provide evidence of negligence on the part of the defendant when the mere fact of the accident or injury having occurred is evidence of negligence of the defendant.

Mcdougald v. Perry

Instant Facts: A spare tire bounced from under a trailer injuring the driver following the trailer.

Black Letter Rule: Res ipsa loquitur provides an inference of negligence when the accident is the type that does not occur without negligence and the defendant is in control of the circumstances.

Larson v. St. Francis Hotel

Instant Facts: Larson (P) sued St. Francis Hotel (D) for injuries suffered when Larson (P) was struck by an armchair flying out of St. Francis Hotel's (D) window.

Black Letter Rule: The doctrine of res ipsa loquitur does not apply in a case where the plaintiff's injury could be attributable to more than one cause, some of which are not within the exclusive control and management of the defendant.

Ybarra v. Spangard

Instant Facts: Ybarra (P) sued Spangard (D) and others for injuries to his arm, suffered after Spangard (D) and others performed an appendectomy on Ybarra (P).

Black Letter Rule: Res ipsa loquitur may apply to situations where more than one defendant is the cause of the plaintiff's injury and the various instrumentalities which caused the plaintiff's injuries were in control of the defendants in question.

Sullivan v. Crabtree

Instant Facts: The Sullivans (P), parents of the decedent, brought an action against Crabtree (D), the driver of a motor truck, for the death of the decedent while the latter was riding as a passenger in Crabtree's motor truck.

Black Letter Rule: Where a plaintiff establishes the prima facie case for defendant's negligence based on res ipsa loquitur, the court must not always as a matter of law enter a verdict for the plaintiff.

Lubitz v. Wells

(Injured Girl) v. *(Golf Club Owner)*

19 Conn.Sup. 322, 113 A.2d 147 (1955)

AN INDIVIDUAL IS LIABLE IN NEGLIGENCE IF HIS/HER CONDUCT CAUSES AN UNREASONABLE RISK OF HARM TO OTHERS

■ **INSTANT FACTS** Lubitz (P) sued Wells (D) for injuries that she sustained when the latter's son hit her with Wells' (D) golf club.

■ **BLACK LETTER RULE** An individual cannot be held liable in negligence for risks that are not reasonably known to him.

■ **PROCEDURAL BASIS**

Appeal from action for personal injury.

■ **FACTS**

James Wells (D) left his golf club in his back yard for several days. One day, his eleven-year-old son, while playing in the backyard with Lubitz (P), a nine-year-old girl, hit Lubitz (P) in her jaw and her chin and caused her to suffer injuries. Lubitz (P) sues Wells (D) in negligence on the ground that he left the golf club in the backyard knowing that children would be playing there. Wells (D), in a demurrer, challenges the sufficiency of the allegations of the complaint to state a cause of action.

■ **ISSUE**

May an individual be held liable in negligence for risks that are not reasonably known to him?

■ **DECISION AND RATIONALE**

(Troland, J.) No. An individual cannot be held liable in negligence for risks that are not reasonably known to him. It is alleged the Wells (D) was negligent because, although he knew the golf club was on the ground in the backyard and that his children play with it, and that although he knew that the negligent use of the club could result in injury, he did not remove the golf club from the backyard. However, it is hardly good sense to hold that the club was so obviously dangerous that it is negligence to leave it in the backyard. Wells (D) is not liable. (Demurrer sustained.)

Analysis:

Note that in this case, the court finds that the golf club is not by itself so dangerous that the defendant should have known of the risk of injury that it would create. Negligent conduct should be viewed before the occurrence of injury and not after. One must ask at the time of the conduct, was the defendant's conduct such as to create an unreasonable risk of harm to others? In light of such definition of negligence, it does not appear that leaving a golf club in the backyard is the type of conduct that would create unreasonable risk of harm to others.

■ CASE VOCABULARY

DEMURRER: Stop, stay or rest; a formal objection attacking the legal sufficiency of the opponent's pleadings; an assertion made, without disputing the facts, that the pleading does not state a cause of action and that the demurring party is entitled to judgment.

NEGLIGENCE: The failure to exercise that degree of care which a person of ordinary prudence (a reasonable person) would exercise under the same circumstances; conduct which falls below the standard established by law for the protection of others against unreasonable risk of harm.

Blyth v. Birmingham Waterworks Co.

(Homeowner) v. *(Plumbers)*

11 Exch. 781, 156 Eng.Rep. 1047 (1856)

AN INDIVIDUAL IS NEGLIGENT WHEN HIS/HER CONDUCT FALLS BELOW THE STANDARD OF CARE EXPECTED OF THE AVERAGE REASONABLE PERSON UNDER THE CIRCUMSTANCES

■ **INSTANT FACTS** Blyth (P) sued Birmingham Waterworks Co. (D) in negligence for laying water pipes which exploded in Blyth's (P) home due to the severity of the cold weather.

■ **BLACK LETTER RULE** An individual is not negligent if his/her conduct and precautions conform to the standard followed by a prudent or reasonable person.

■ **PROCEDURAL BASIS**

Appeal from action in negligence.

■ **FACTS**

Birmingham Waterworks Co. (D) had installed water mains in the street where Blyth (P) lived. Twenty-five years after the installation of the pipes, one of the plugs on the pipes opposite of Blyth's (P) home sprang a leak due to a severe winter frost. Consequently, a large quantity of water seeped through the plaintiff's house and caused severe damage. Blyth (P) sued Birmingham (D) in negligence. The jury at the trial court ruled in favor of Blyth (P), finding Birmingham negligent. Birmingham appeals.

■ **ISSUE**

Is an individual negligent when his/her conduct and precautions conform to the standard followed by a prudent or reasonable person?

■ **DECISION AND RATIONALE**

(Alderson, J.) No. An individual is not negligent if his/her conduct and precautions conform to the standard followed by a prudent or reasonable person. Negligence is the omission to do something which a reasonable man would do, or doing something which a prudent, reasonable person would not do. The defendant in this case would have been liable if it had done or had failed to take a precaution that a reasonable person in its position would have taken. A reasonable person in the defendant's position would have acted with reference to the average circumstances of temperature in ordinary years. The defendant is not negligent because it failed to take precautions against the effects of the extreme severity of the frost of that winter. Such a state of circumstances constituted a contingency against which no reasonable man can provide. The result was an accident for which the defendant cannot be held liable. (Reversed.)

Analysis:

It is important to keep in mind that the standard of care to which all persons must adhere in order to avoid liability in negligence is the standard of the reasonably prudent person. In this case, for example, if the town had suffered extreme frost and severe winters on many other occasions, then it is reasonable to expect the defendant to provide for a remedy against bursting of the pipes. However, since no reasonable person could foresee the risk of harm that might be caused by a severe winter, the defendant was not held liable. Just remember, the standard of care in negligence is the standard which is adhered to by the average reasonable person under the circumstances. It is an objective standard. This is in contrast with the intentional torts which provided for a subjective state of mind.

■ CASE VOCABULARY

CONTINGENCY: An event that is of possible but uncertain occurrence.

Gulf Refining Co. v. Williams

(Gasoline Distributor) v. *(Injured Party)*
183 Miss. 723, 185 So. 234 (1938)

AN ACT OR OMISSION WHICH CAUSES INJURY MAY BE NEGLIGENT EVEN THOUGH THE PROBABILITY OF THE INJURY OCCURRING AS A RESULT OF THE ACT OR OMISSION MAY BE VERY LOW

■ **INSTANT FACTS** Williams (P) brought action against Gulf Refining Co. (D) for the injuries that he suffered when attempting to open a can of gasoline that he bought from Gulf Refining Co. (D).

■ **BLACK LETTER RULE** An individual may be liable in negligence even if his/her conduct creates a risk of harm which is highly improbable and unlikely.

■ **PROCEDURAL BASIS**

Appeal from action in negligence for recovery of damages.

■ **FACTS**

Gulf Refining Co. (D), distributors of gasoline, sold Williams (P) a drum of gasoline for use in Williams' (P) tractor. Williams (P) attempted to remove the cap of the drum in order to pour the gasoline in his tractor. A spark was produced and caused a fire which burned Williams (P) severely. Williams (P) brings an action against Gulf Refining Co. (D) claiming that the condition of the drum cap gave rise to the spark and fire which caused his injuries. The jury returned a verdict in favor of Williams (P). Gulf Refining Co.(D) appeals.

■ **ISSUE**

May an individual be liable in negligence even if his/her conduct creates a risk of harm which is highly improbable and unlikely?

■ **DECISION AND RATIONALE**

(Griffith, J.) Yes. An individual may be liable in negligence even if his/her conduct creates a risk of harm which is highly improbable and unlikely. The defendant provides evidence that an explosion of fire due to removing the drum cap is an unusual, extraordinary, and improbable occurrence. Additionally, the defendant turns the attention of this court to some cases which indicate that there is no liability when the occurrence in question is unusual and extraordinary. When dealing with the foreseeability of an event or occurrence under negligence, the inquiry rests not on the probability of the occurrence of the event, but on the whether the occurrence is likely to occur. Thus, the test for foreseeability is not the balance of probabilities, but the existence of some real likelihood of some damage. In this case, the likelihood is of such weight as to induce action to avoid the damage on the part of an reasonable person. In this case, the drum having been of standard construction and material, had it been in reasonably good repair, there would have been no liability. However, this drum was not in good repair. It had been in use for nine years and the threads of the cap were broken. The proof in this case is sufficient to show that a person of ordinary prudence in the defendant's position should have known of the condition of the drum and its cap and should reasonably have anticipated that a sudden fire and explosion would be caused by its condition. As such, the defendant is liable for the injuries to Williams (P). (Affirmed.)

Analysis:

Note that the law of negligence does not deal with probabilities, only with possibilities. It is necessary to show that an act or omission of the defendant would be likely to cause injury. It is not necessary to show that the probability of an injury is very likely. The question then becomes whether or not the likelihood of injury would cause a reasonable and prudent person to take measures to avoid the injury.

■ **CASE VOCABULARY**

BUNGHOLE: The stopper hole in a barrel.

Chicago, B. & Q.R. Co. v. Krayenbuhl

(Railroad Co.) v. *(Trespassing Child)*
65 Neb. 889, 91 N.W. 880 (1902)

MACHINERY AND INSTRUMENTS WHICH CANNOT BE RENDERED ABSOLUTELY SAFE MAY BE USED SO LONG AS THE RISK OF UNREASONABLE INJURY POSED BY THEM DOES NOT OUTWEIGH THEIR BENEFICIAL SOCIAL USE

■ **INSTANT FACTS** Krayenbuhl (P), brings an action against Chicago, B & Q Railroad company to recover for damages that she sustained when her ankle got stuck in the railroad turntable that the railroad company had failed to lock.

■ **BLACK LETTER RULE** An individual using a socially beneficial yet inherently dangerous instrument, must take reasonable precautions such that the risk of injury posed by the instrument does not outweigh its utility.

■ **PROCEDURAL BASIS**

Appeal from action for recovery of damages.

■ **FACTS**

A turntable was located between two of Chicago B & Q's (D) railroad tracks. Chicago B & Q (D) required that its employees lock the turntable which they often failed to do. On one such occasion when the turntable was not locked, Krayenbuhl (P), along with other children, was playing along the tracks and on the turntable when the child's ankle got stuck in between the rails and was severed. The trial resulted in a verdict in favor of Krayenbuhl (P). Chicago B & Q (D) appeals.

■ **ISSUE**

Must an individual, using a socially beneficial, yet inherently dangerous instrument, take reasonable precautions such that the risk of injury posed by the instrument does not outweigh its utility?

■ **DECISION AND RATIONALE**

(Albert, J.) Yes. An individual using a socially beneficial, yet inherently dangerous instrument, must take reasonable precautions such that the risk of injury posed by the instrument does not outweigh its utility. The public good demands the use of machinery that cannot be rendered absolutely safe and which at times result in the loss of life and limb. However, when weighed against their utility, the danger from such machinery is insignificant. When the danger begins to outweigh social utility, the public good demands restriction of the use of such machinery. A railroad turntable is such machinery. Although it cannot be rendered absolutely safe, its dangers may be easily lessened by use of a lock. The interference of the lock with the proper use of the turntable is so slight that it is outweighed by the danger to be anticipated from omission to use it. It is this court's opinion that the public good requires the use of the lock. In all cases of negligence such as this one, the determination of the question of negligence must be resolved by taking into consideration 1) the character and location of the premises, 2) the purpose for which they are used, 3) the probability of injury, 4) the precautions necessary to reduce the risk of injury, and 5) the relations between the precautions and their effects on the beneficial use of the premises. Given all these factors, an individual still owes the duty of reasonable care to others. (Reversed for error in instructions to the jury.)

Analysis:

Note that in this case the court admits that in rendering certain instruments absolutely perfect, we may take away from their social utility. Additionally, this court recognizes that certain instruments and machinery are of such use to the society that risk of injury that they pose is insignificant with respect to their utility. Keeping this in mind, the court engages in a sort of a balancing process, where it weighs all the different factors enumerated above to determine what kinds of precautions are necessary and reasonable in such situations. However, given these factors, do not forget that the underlying determination of negligence is that of a reasonable man. In each negligence case the main question is whether the defendant's conduct or precautions fell below the standard of care observed by the average reasonable person under the circumstances. Although this is quite a murky standard, it is one that will get you the points on any negligence question dealing with the standard of care.

Davison v. Snohomish County

(Injured Driver) v. *(County)*

149 Wash. 109, 207 P. 422 (1928)

FINANCIAL ABILITY AND UNDUE BURDEN ARE FACTORS WHICH MUST BE CONSIDERED IN ASSESSING THE REASONABILITY OF PRECAUTIONARY MEASURES IN NEGLIGENCE CASES

■ **INSTANT FACTS** Davison (P) sued Snohomish County (D) for injuries he suffered when his car skidded off the road and into the guard rails which failed to protect him from falling to the ground.

■ **BLACK LETTER RULE** A county is not negligent for failing to build safety railing where the construction of such railing would create an undue burden on the county and prevent construction of other roads.

■ **PROCEDURAL BASIS**

Appeal in action for negligence to recover for personal injuries sustained.

■ **FACTS**

Davison (P), while driving his car toward the city of Snohomish, proceeded to cross a curved bridge at which point he lost control of his car, striking and breaking through the railing. As a result of the accident, Davison (P) fell to the ground and sustained injuries. Davison (P) sued Snohomish County (D) for negligent construction and maintenance of the bridge and its railings. The trial court decided in favor of Davison (P). Snohomish County (D) appeals.

■ **ISSUE**

Is a county negligent for failing to build safety railing where the construction of such railing would create an undue burden on the county and prevent construction of other roads?

■ **DECISION AND RATIONALE**

(Beals, J.) No. A county is not negligent for failing to build safety railing where the construction of such railing would create an undue burden on the county and prevent construction of other roads. The use of the automobile in recent years has caused changes in laws regarding the liability of municipalities with respect to their duty to protect their roads. While railings were very useful in protecting pedestrians, animals and carriages from going off the road, they are not as a practical proposition sufficient to protect cars against falling off roads. As such, municipalities, for all practical purposes, should not be required to install railings along the long stretches of roads to protect vehicles. Such a duty would put on municipalities burdens that they cannot bear, and would prevent the construction of additional roads. The evidence of negligence in this case was not sufficient to take the case to the jury. (Reversed.)

Analysis:

In reading this case, please keep in mind that it is a very old case (from 1928), when the use of automobiles created new questions of liability for counties and municipalities. The technology and engineering of the era did not allow, as a practical matter, construction of railings which would protect cars from going off the road. This case would probably be decided differently given the technological advancement of this era. This reasoning is backed by the case of *Bartlett v. Northern Pacific R. Co.*, where faced with a question similar to the one in *Davison*, the court determined that the parties should be given the opportunity of presenting evidence of the practicality of guardrails to the jury.

■ CASE VOCABULARY

SLOUGH: A hollow, filled with mud.

VIADUCT: A bridge over a valley or river to carry a road or railroad.

United States v. Carroll Towing Co.

(Ship Owner) v. *(Moorings' Handler)*

159 F.2d 169 (2d Cir.1947)

ACCORDING TO JUDGE LEARNED HAND, LIABILITY IN NEGLIGENCE EXISTS WHERE THE BURDEN OF PROVIDING ADEQUATE PRECAUTIONS IS LESS THAN THE PROBABILITY THAT HARM WILL OCCUR MULTIPLIED BY THE SERIOUSNESS OF THE HARM

■ **INSTANT FACTS** United States (P) sued Carroll Towing Co. (D) for its negligence in handling the moorings of the ship owned by the United States (P) which caused the ship to sink.

■ **BLACK LETTER RULE** An individual may be liable for failing to take reasonable precaution against great risk of injury even where the probability of the injury occurring is very little.

■ **PROCEDURAL BASIS**

Appeal in action in negligence for recovery of damages.

■ **FACTS**

Carroll Towing Co. (D) was in charge of handling the mooring lines of a barge owned by the United States (P). The latter sued Carroll Towing (D) when the barge sank, alleging that Carroll Towing (D) was negligent in handling the mooring lines of the barge, and caused the barge to sink. Carroll Towing (D) defended on the ground that the United States (P) was contributorily liable because its employee was not on the barge to prevent the accident from occurring. The trial court divided the damages accordingly. The United States (P) appeals.

■ **ISSUE**

May an individual be liable for failing to take reasonable precaution against great risk of injury even where the probability of the injury occurring is very little?

■ **DECISION AND RATIONALE**

(Hand, J.) Yes. An individual may be liable for failing to take reasonable precaution against great risk of injury even where the probability of the injury occurring is very small. There is no general rule to determine when the absence of a bargee or other attendant will make the owner of the barge liable for injuries to other vessels if the vessel breaks away from the moorings. The vessel or barge owner's duty in such situations is determined by three variables: 1) the probability that the barge will break away, 2) the seriousness of the injury if the barge does break away, and 3) the burden of adequate precautions to prevent the injury. If the burden of adequate precautions is less than the gravity of the injury multiplied by the probability of the injury, then the barge owner is liable in negligence. While the bargee's absence may not always be a cause for liability, in this case the bargee was gone without an excuse for 21 hours. Additionally, it was not beyond expectation that the barge would break away given the full tide of war activity during the time in question. Under such circumstances, it is reasonable to expect that the barge would have a bargee on board and that the barge owner would be partially liable for the damage caused to or by its barge. (Affirmed.)

Analysis:

This case presents the famous formula for liability which is dictated by Judge Learned Hand. The formula goes as follows: If B (the burden of taking precautions) is less than P (the probability of occurrence of injury) multiplied by L (the gravity of the injury which may occur), then an individual is liable in negligence for failure to take precautions. This formula shows that even though the probability of an injury may be small, an individual may still have the duty to take precautions against injury if the gravity of the injury is high. Certainly, there are no magic numbers that can be plugged in to determine liability. All factors and circumstances of each case must be considered in order to determine whether or not liability exists. This method of determining liability has often been compared to an economic view of liability. In simpler terms, it is a cost-benefit analysis: burden v. probability of injury multiplied by the seriousness of the injury. Again remember the big picture: we always look at the standard of conduct of the average reasonable person in the defendant's position. Judge Hand's formula is one way of determining what that average reasonable person would do under different circumstances.

■ **CASE VOCABULARY**

ADMIRALTY: A court relating to acts done at sea.

FLOTILLA: A fleet of ships.

LIBELANT: The party who files a suit in an admiralty case.

Vaughan v. Menlove

(Cottage Owner) v. *(Owner of Hay Rick)*

3 Bing (N.C.) 467, 132 Eng.Rep. 490 (Com.P.1837)

IN ORDER TO AVOID LIABILITY IN NEGLIGENCE, AN INDIVIDUAL MUST ADHERE TO THE STANDARD OF CARE OF AN AVERAGE REASONABLE PERSON OF ORDINARY PRUDENCE UNDER SIMILAR CIRCUMSTANCES

■ **INSTANT FACTS** Vaughan (P), a cottage owner, sued Menlove (D) for the damage and destruction of his cottage, caused by a fire which started in Menlove's (D) hay rick.

■ **BLACK LETTER RULE** The standard of care used to determine negligence is that of the reasonable person in similar circumstances and not the good faith or subjective standard adhered to by the defendant.

■ **PROCEDURAL BASIS**

Appeal in action for recovery of damages.

■ **FACTS**

Menlove (D) built a hay rick near Vaughan's (P) cottage. While building the cottage, Menlove (D) was often warned that the hay rick was likely to catch on fire if he were not careful. Menlove's (D) response on one occasion was that "he would chance it." Finally, the rick caught on fire which spread to Vaughan's (P) cottage. Vaughan (P) sued Menlove (D) for damages to his cottage claiming that Menlove (D) was negligent in maintaining the rick in a dangerous condition. The trial court instructed the jury that they were to determine whether Menlove (D) was grossly negligent based on the standard of care used by a reasonable man under similar circumstances. The jury decided in favor of Vaughan (P). Menlove (D) appeals on the ground that the trial court should have instructed the jury to determine the issue of negligence based on whether Menlove (D) had acted in good faith to the best of his judgment.

■ **ISSUE**

Is the standard of care used to determine negligence that of a reasonable person in similar circumstances?

■ **DECISION AND RATIONALE**

(Tindal, C.J.) Yes. The standard of care to determine negligence is that of a reasonable person in similar circumstances and not the subjective standard requested by the defendant. It is contended that such a rule of liability is extremely uncertain, and that the standard or the instructions to the jury should have been whether the defendant acted honestly and bona fide to the best of his own judgment. However, this court is of the opinion that the care taken by the reasonable prudent man has always been the correct standard. This is the rule which was adhered to at the trial court level. (Affirmed.)

Analysis:

Once again the standard of care in negligence cases is that adhered to by the average reasonable man of ordinary prudence under similar circumstances. These are the golden words to remember in ordinary negligence cases. (We will, however, see variations of this rule in future cases.) It is important to realize that this is a subjective standard. Thus, the good faith of a defendant is immaterial in determining his liability in negligence. Such a subjective element, however, may be an important factor in determining whether or not to award punitive damages to the plaintiff.

■ CASE VOCABULARY

BONA FIDE: Genuine or in good faith.

GROSS NEGLIGENCE: The failure to use even the slightest care.

HAY RICK: A stack of hay in the open.

PRIMAE IMPRESSIONIS: First impression; refers to cases where the court is confronted with a certain issue for the first time.

RULE NISI: A procedure by which one party, through an ex parte application or an order to show cause, calls upon the other to show cause why the relief set forth in the proposed order should not be made final by the court.

Delair v. McAdoo

(Injured Party) v. *(Defective-Car Owner)*
324 Pa. 392, 188 A. 181 (1936)

AN INDIVIDUAL NEED NOT HAVE ACTUAL KNOWLEDGE OF RISK OR DANGER CREATED BY HIS CONDUCT TO BE HELD NEGLIGENT IF THE REASONABLE PERSON IN THAT INDIVIDUAL'S POSITION IS PRESUMED TO POSSESS THAT KNOWLEDGE

■ **INSTANT FACTS** Delair (P) brought an action against McAdoo (D) to recover damages sustained when the tires on McAdoo's (D) car blew up as McAdoo (D) was passing Delair (P).

■ **BLACK LETTER RULE** A reasonable driver of an automobile should be charged with the knowledge that driving with worn tires poses a danger to other individuals on the road.

■ **PROCEDURAL BASIS**

Appeal from action to recover damages to person and property.

■ **FACTS**

As McAdoo (D) was passing Delair (P) on the road, the tire on his car blew up, causing him to swerve into Delair (P). The latter sued McAdoo (D) to recover for damages that he sustained to his person and his property as a result of the accident. There was ample evidence at the trial, indicating that the tires on McAdoo's (D) car were quite worn out. The jury at the trial level found in favor of Delair (P). McAdoo (D) appeals on the ground that the trial court erred in denying his motion for a new trial.

■ **ISSUE**

Should a reasonable driver of an automobile be expected to know that driving with worn tires poses a danger to other individuals on the road?

■ **DECISION AND RATIONALE**

(Kephart, C.J.) Yes. A reasonable driver of an automobile should be expected to know that driving with worn tires poses a danger to other individuals on the road. In this case, it is clear from the testimony of the witnesses that the tires on the defendant's car were worn "pretty well through." Whether the tires were worn or not was a question of fact for the jury. An ordinary individual, whether a car owner or not, knows that when a tire is worn through, its further use is dangerous and it should be replaced. All drivers must be held to knowledge of these facts. An owner or operator cannot escape liability simply because he says he does not know of the danger. The law requires owners and drivers of motor vehicles to know of the condition of the parts of their vehicle which may pose a danger to others. It will be assumed that all such people know of the dangers which could be revealed through reasonable inspection and examination of their vehicles. (Affirmed.)

Analysis:

One more time, we see that the subjective state of mind of an individual is irrelevant. Under the objective standard for negligence, there are certain facts about which all people are held to have knowledge. This is the minimum knowledge required. It is, if you will, common sense. Certainly all people, especially drivers, know or should know that driving with a completely worn tire is dangerous. This is the type of knowledge that the law assumes all ordinary and reasonable individuals in the community possess. Thus, lack of such knowledge, no matter how sincere, is not a defense in negligent cases.

■ **CASE VOCABULARY**

JUDGMENT N.O.V.: This Latin phrase (Non Obstante Verdicto) means "judgment notwithstanding the verdict," a judgment which reverses the determination of the jury, granted when a judge determines that the jury verdict had no reasonable support in fact or was contrary to the law.

Trimarco v. Klein

(Tenant) v. *(Landlord)*

56 N.Y.2d 98, 436 N.E.2d 502, 451 N.Y.S.2d 52 (1982)

EVIDENCE OF FAILURE TO ADHERE TO CERTAIN CUSTOM AND USAGE CAN BE USED AS A FACTOR TO PROVE CONDUCT BELOW THE REASONABLE STANDARD OF CARE

■ **INSTANT FACTS** Trimarco (P), a tenant of Klein (D), sued the latter for injury that Trimarco (P) suffered when the glass shower door in his apartment broke.

■ **BLACK LETTER RULE** Evidence of custom, common usage, and practice, although compelling, may not be used as the conclusive test of negligence.

■ **PROCEDURAL BASIS**

Appeal in action for personal injury.

■ **FACTS**

Trimarco (P) sued Klein (D), his landlord, for injuries that he suffered when the glass shower door in his apartment broke. At the trial it was revealed that Trimarco (P) did not know, nor was he made aware by his landlord, that the shower door was made of ordinary glass, not tempered safety glass. Trimarco (P) also presented evidence of custom and usage to show that ordinary glass doors no longer conformed to accepted safety standards and that they were considered hazardous in locations such as showers. The jury in the trial court returned a judgment in favor of Trimarco (P). The Appellate Division reversed, dismissing the complaint and indicating that even in light of the evidence presented by Trimarco (P), no duty was imposed on Klein (D) to replace the glass shower doors. Trimarco (P) appeals.

■ **ISSUE**

May evidence of custom, common usage, and practice, although compelling, be used as the conclusive test of negligence?

■ **DECISION AND RATIONALE**

(Fuchsberg, J.) No. Evidence of custom, common usage, and practice, although compelling, may not be used as the conclusive test of negligence. Evidence of custom and usage may be used to show that a person who fails to adhere to it may have fallen below the reasonable standard of care. Although courts and scholars are divided on the effect of custom and usage on the question of negligence, all agree on its potency. Custom and usage need not be universal in order to be accepted. However, once its existence is credited, no matter how compelling, it is not evidence of negligence. Before it can be, the jury must be satisfied with its reasonableness. The evidence presented by the plaintiff in this case was enough to send the case to the jury and to sustain the verdict of the trial court. The trial court was correct in instructing the jury to view evidence of custom and usage with all the other evidence presented to determine the reasonableness of the defendant's conduct under the circumstances of the case. Additionally, it was up to the jury, as the trial court correctly indicated, to determine whether or not the custom and usage claimed by the plaintiffs did in fact exist. (Reversed and new trial ordered.)

Analysis:

This case stands for the same simple and repeated proposition: The standard of care in negligence cases is that which is adhered to by the average reasonable person of ordinary prudence in defendant's position. As we have seen in this case, the plaintiff is free to present evidence which might shed a light on what that standard is. Custom and usage is a type of evidence which may clarify the reasonable standard to which individuals in defendant's position should adhere. However, the ultimate test again is whether the defendant's conduct was reasonable. Thus, as this case clearly indicates, evidence of custom and usage, although very potent, is not conclusive on the issue of negligence.

■ CASE VOCABULARY

BOON: A petition, gift or favor.

EXPERT WITNESS: A witness who has special knowledge of the subject about which he/she testifies; the knowledge of the expert must be such as is not normally possessed by the average person.

GENESIS: The beginning, origin.

PRIMA FACIE: Legally sufficient to establish a fact unless disproved.

PROBATIVE POWER: (Latin) Testing; affording proof.

QUINTESSENTIAL: The most typical example of anything.

Cordas v. Peerless Transportation Co.

(Injured Pedestrian) (Cab Company)

27 N.Y.S.2d 198 (City Ct.1941)

AN INDIVIDUAL IN AN EMERGENCY SITUATION IS EXPECTED TO BEHAVE AS AN AVERAGE REASONABLE PERSON WOULD UNDER THE SAME CIRCUMSTANCES

■ **INSTANT FACTS** Cordas (P), a pedestrian, sued Peerless Transportation (D) for injuries that Cordas (P) sustained when hit by Peerless Transportation's (D) cab from which the driver jumped while a gun was held to his head.

■ **BLACK LETTER RULE** The conduct of an individual who is in an emergency situation is not measured by the standard of care of a reasonable person in a non-emergency situation.

■ **PROCEDURAL BASIS**

Appeal from action for personal injury.

■ **FACTS**

A cab driver, an employee of Peerless Transportation (D), was ordered to drive at the point of an assailant's gun. The cab driver, who had a gun pointed to his head, suddenly slammed on his brakes and jumped out of the cab. The cab, which was still in motion, hit Cordas (P), a pedestrian, and injured her. Cordas sued Peerless (D) for the injuries that she sustained. The trial court dismissed the complaint. Cordas (P) appeals.

■ **ISSUE**

Is the conduct of an individual in an emergency situation measured by the standard of care of a reasonable person in a non-emergency situation?

■ **DECISION AND RATIONALE**

(Carlin, J.) No. The conduct of an individual who is in an emergency situation is not measured by the standard of care of a reasonable person in a non-emergency situation. Negligence has commonly been defined as the failure to exercise that reasonable care and caution which a reasonable person would ordinarily exercise under similar conditions and circumstances. Thus, negligence is always relevant to some circumstances of time, place, or person. As the court in *Kolanka v. Erie Railroad* Co. indicates: "The law does not hold one in an emergency to the exercise of mature judgment required of him under circumstances where he has an opportunity for deliberate action." An act which may be negligent under normal conditions may not necessarily be negligent under an emergency situation which is not of the actor's making. This court cannot hold the defendant liable under the facts presented. (Reversed.)

Analysis:

Once again let's return to the magic words: Negligence is determined based on the care taken by an average reasonable person under similar circumstances. This case explores the importance of these last two words. In determining one's negligence, it is important to take into consideration all the circumstances present. Clearly, one's actions under an emergency situation may not be as deliberate and processed as one's actions under ordinary conditions. The law of negligence has recognized this. Thus, in emergency situations one has to consider how an average reasonable person would have acted if placed under the same conditions. Remember, the standard is the same as in normal conditions. So, don't be tricked by questions that state that the reasonable person is held to a lower standard of care under emergency situations. Such situations are only an added consideration in determining how a reasonable person in defendant's shoes would act. Note, however, that this case indicates that the emergency situation must not have been of the defendant's own making. In those situations, the defendant is held to the negligence standard under normal conditions because we can not allow a defendant to benefit from an emergency or peril which the defendant himself/herself has created.

■ CASE VOCABULARY

AD HOMINEM: (Latin) Appealing to a person's feelings or prejudices rather than his intellect.

DENOUEMENT: The outcome of a complex sequence of events.

PROTAGONIST: The main character in a drama.

TRICE: A brief space of time.

Roberts v. State of Louisiana

(Injured Party) v. *(Employer)*

396 So.2d 566 (La.App.1981)

THE STANDARD OF CARE TO WHICH AN INDIVIDUAL WITH A PHYSICAL HANDICAP MUST ADHERE IS THE SAME STANDARD OF CARE WHICH SHOULD BE EXERCISED BY AN AVERAGE REASONABLE PERSON WITH THE SAME HANDICAP

■ **INSTANT FACTS** Roberts (P) sued the State of Louisiana (D) for injuries that he sustained when he was bumped into by Burson, a blind employee of the state (D).

■ **BLACK LETTER RULE** In determining the negligence of an individual, the court must take into consideration the physical attributes or shortcomings of the individual.

■ **PROCEDURAL BASIS**

Appeal from action for recovery of damages for personal injuries.

■ **FACTS**

On September 1, 1977, Mike Burson, who operated a concession stand in the U.S. Post Office in Louisiana, left his stand to go to the restroom. While on his way there, Burson, who was blind, bumped into Roberts (P) who fell and injured his hip. Roberts (P) sued the State of Louisiana in negligence, under the theory of respondeat superior on the ground that Burson's negligence in not using his cane when walking to the bathroom caused his fall and the resulting injury. The trial court dismissed Roberts' (P) complaint. Roberts (P) appeals.

■ **ISSUE**

In determining the negligence of an individual, must the court take into consideration the physical attributes or shortcomings of the individual?

■ **DECISION AND RATIONALE**

(Laborde, J.) Yes. In determining the negligence of an individual, the court must take into consideration the physical attributes or shortcomings of the individual. In order to find the state liable in negligence under the theory of respondeat superior, it is critical that the court first find that Burson himself was negligent in his conduct. As Professor William L. Prosser indicates, a man who is blind cannot be held to the same standard of care as a man who is not. Yet, the conduct of a person with a physical handicap must be reasonable in light of "his knowledge of his infirmity, which is treated merely as one of the circumstances under which he acts." Burson, who is completely blind, admits that on the date of the incident in question he did not use his cane on his way to the restroom. He testified that he relied on his facial sense as an adequate technique for making short trips in familiar settings. The evidence in the case indicates that it is not uncommon for blind people to rely on such techniques when moving around in familiar places. Burson testified that having worked in the same building for three-and-a-half years, he was familiar with his surroundings. Based on the evidence presented, this court is of the opinion that the plaintiff has failed to show that Burson was negligent in his conduct. Neither was Burson negligent in the way that he was walking or paying attention to his surroundings. (Affirmed.)

Analysis:

Physical handicaps of an individual are simply some of the circumstances taken into consideration in determining whether or not an individual has exercised reasonable care in his/her conduct. As this case indicates, an individual with a physical handicap will be judged based on the standard of care expected of an average reasonable person with the same handicap. In other words, we have to ask ourselves how would an average, reasonable blind person conduct himself under the same circumstances. This does not mean that a blind person is free of liability. For example, a blind person who drives a car and injures another party is clearly negligent because an average, reasonable blind person would not drive a car given his/her handicap.

■ CASE VOCABULARY

RESPONDEAT SUPERIOR: Latin for "let the superior reply," invoked when there is a master-servant relationship between two parties; when an employer/master is acting through an employee/servant and tort liability is incurred during the employee's course of this relationship due to some fault of the employee, then the master/employer must accept the liability and responsibility.

Robinson v. Lindsay

(Injured Child) v. *(Parent of Tortfeasor)*

92 Wash.2d 410, 598 P.2d 392 (1979)

MINORS ARE HELD TO THE STANDARD OF CARE OF A MINOR OF LIKE AGE, INTELLIGENCE AND EXPERIENCE UNDER SIMILAR CIRCUMSTANCES UNLESS THEY ARE ENGAGED IN INHERENTLY DANGEROUS OR ADULT ACTIVITIES

■ **INSTANT FACTS** A suit was brought on behalf of Kelly Robinson (P), an 11-year-old girl who was injured in a snowmobile which was driven by Billy Anderson (D), a 13-year-old boy.

■ **BLACK LETTER RULE** A minor child engaged in the operation of machinery ordinarily used by adults is held to an adult standard of care.

■ **PROCEDURAL BASIS**

Appeal in action for personal injuries.

■ **FACTS**

Kelly Robinson (P), an 11-year-old girl, lost full use of her thumb in a snowmobile accident. At the time of the accident, the snowmobile was being driven by Billy Anderson (D), a 13-year-old boy, and Robinson (P) was a passenger in the snowmobile. The trial court instructed the jury that a minor must exercise the same reasonable standard of care as a child of like age, intelligence, and experience. The jury at the trial court returned a verdict in favor of Anderson (D). Robinson (P) appeals on the ground that the instructions given to the jury by the trial court were erroneous.

■ **ISSUE**

Is a minor child held to an adult standard of care when the child is engaged in the operation of machinery ordinarily used by adults?

■ **DECISION AND RATIONALE**

(Utter, C.J.) Yes. A minor child engaged in the operation of machinery ordinarily used by adults is held to an adult standard of care. Exceptions to the reasonable person standard of care have developed when the individual whose conduct is in question has suffered from a physical impairment, such as blindness, deafness, or lameness. Courts have also developed a different standard when dealing with children. A child's conduct has usually been compared to conduct expected of a reasonable child of the same age, experience, intelligence, maturity, and training. However, many courts have applied the adult standard of care when a child is engaged in an activity which is inherently dangerous. Some courts have couched this exception in terms of a child who is engaged in adult activities. The holding of minors to an adult standard of care when they operate motorized vehicles has gained widespread approval from courts and commentators. The operation of a snowmobile, a motorized vehicle, likewise requires adult care and competence. As such, in this case Billy Anderson (D) should be held to conform his conduct to an adult standard. The court's instructions to the jury were therefore erroneous. (Affirming order granting new trial.)

Analysis:

As this case indicates, the usual standard of care for children is the care exercised by reasonable children of like age, intelligence, experience, maturity, and training. However, as in the case above, where children are involved in adult activities, or inherently dangerous activities, they are held to the adult standard of care. Some activities where courts have applied the adult standard of care to minors include the operation of an automobile, a motor scooter, a child playing golf, or a child who is involved in downhill skiing. Note, however, where a child is involved in a minor's activity, he/she will not be held to a higher standard even if he/she demonstrates that he has more experience, or intelligence than other children his age. The standard of care to which children must adhere is the objective standard of other children under the same circumstances.

Breunig v. American Family Ins. Co.

(Injured Driver) v. *(Insurance Company)*
45 Wis.2d 536, 173 N.W.2d 619 (1970)

SOME COURTS HOLD THAT INSANITY IS A DEFENSE TO NEGLIGENT CONDUCT WHERE THE DEFENDANT IS SUDDENLY OVERCOME BY THE INSANITY WITHOUT ANY WARNING OR PRIOR KNOWLEDGE OF THE INSANITY

■ **INSTANT FACTS** Breunig (P) brought action against American Family Insurance Co. (D) to recover for injuries he sustained when Mrs. Veith, American Family's (D) insured, was driving on the wrong side of the highway.

■ **BLACK LETTER RULE** Insanity is not a defense to negligent conduct where the defendant had prior warning and knowledge of his/her insanity.

■ **PROCEDURAL BASIS**

Appeal from action for personal injuries.

■ **FACTS**

Breunig (P) brought action against American Family Insurance Co. (D) to recover for injuries he sustained when Mrs. Veith, American Family's (D) insured, was driving on the wrong side of the highway. The evidence at trial established that while on her way home, Mrs. Veith saw a light in the back of the car ahead of her and followed it. Her psychiatrist testified that Mrs. Veith told him that at the time she was driving, she believed that God was directing her car. She saw Breunig's (P) car and believed that if she stepped on the gas pedal she would be air-borne [like Batman!!!]. At the trial level, the jury returned a verdict in favor of Breunig (P). American Family Ins. Co. (D) appeals.

■ **ISSUE**

Is insanity a defense to negligent conduct where the defendant had prior warning and knowledge of his/her insanity?

■ **DECISION AND RATIONALE**

(Hallows, C.J.) No. Insanity is not a defense to negligent conduct where the defendant had prior warning and knowledge of his/her insanity. In this case, there is no question that Mrs. Veith was subject to an insane delusion at the time of the accident in question. There are certain kinds of insanity which preclude liability based on negligence. The question of liability in all such cases depends on the kind of mental illness and insanity in question. The effect of the illness must be such as to affect the person's ability to understand and appreciate the duty of ordinary care to which he must adhere. Additionally, there must be an absence of notice or forewarning to the person that he may be suddenly subject to such type of insanity or mental illness. In this case, however, Mrs. Veith had prior warning and knowledge that would reasonably lead her to believe that she would have hallucinations which would affect her driving. As such, she should be held to an ordinary standard of care. The jury could have concluded this based on evidence presented which showed Mrs. Veith believing that she had a special relationship with God. This question was one that was properly left to the jury. (Affirmed.)

Analysis:

Certain kinds of mental illnesses vitiate liability for negligent conduct. As this case indicates, most courts hold that these are types of illnesses of which the defendant is not aware. That is, they are so sudden that they may be likened to a heart attack of which one has no prior knowledge. However, if a defendant is aware that he/she may be subject to a mental illness which may cause his/her conduct to fall below the standard of care, the defendant is already forewarned. Based on this knowledge and forewarning, most courts hold such people to the ordinary standard of negligence.

■ CASE VOCABULARY

INVOLUNTARY NONSUIT: When plaintiff neglects to appear after being called or gives no evidence for a jury to find a verdict; when his case is put out of court by an adverse ruling precluding a recovery.

MOVANT: One who "moves" or makes a motion before court.

STATUTORY: Relating to a written, established rule or law.

Heath v. Swift Wings, Inc.

(Administrator of Deceased's Estate) v. *(Airplane Owner)*

40 N.C.App. 158, 252 S.E.2d 526 (1979)

AN INDIVIDUAL WHO ENGAGES IN A BUSINESS, PROFESSION, OR OCCUPATION, MUST EXERCISE DEGREE OF CARE THAT IS COMMONLY POSSESSED BY THE MEMBERS OF THAT BUSINESS, PROFESSION OR OCCUPATION

■ **INSTANT FACTS** Swift Wings (D) was sued in negligence when a plane flown by its pilot, Fred Heath, crashed causing the death of Fred Heath's wife and children.

■ **BLACK LETTER RULE** A professional's negligence is not determined based on the degree of ordinary care and caution exercised by professionals having the same experience and training.

■ **PROCEDURAL BASIS**

Action in negligence for recovery of damages.

■ **FACTS**

Fred Heath, an employee of Swift Wings (D) was flying an airplane which crashed immediately after take-off. The wife and son of Fred Heath, and Fred Heath himself were on the plane, and died as a result of the crash. The administrator of the son and the wife's estate, Heath (P) brought an action against Swift Wings, Inc. (D) alleging that Fred Heath's negligence caused their death. At the trial, Heath (P), the administrator, introduced evidence by an expert testifying that in his opinion, a reasonably prudent pilot should have made a controlled landing after take-off, and had he done so, the passengers would have survived. The trial court instructed the jury that in aviation, negligence could be defined as failure to exercise the degree and care, which an ordinary prudent pilot with the same experience and training as Fred Heath would have used under the circumstances. The jury returned a verdict in favor of Swift Wings (D). Heath (P), the administrator of the estate, appeals on the grounds that the trial court's instructions to the jury were erroneous.

■ **ISSUE**

Is a professional's negligence determined based on the degree of ordinary care and caution exercised by professionals having the same experience and training?

■ **DECISION AND RATIONALE**

(Morris, C.J.) No. A professional's negligence is not determined based on the degree of ordinary care and caution exercised by professionals having the same experience and training. The trial court erred when it introduced this subjective standard of care into the definition of negligence of professionals. This court is in support of authorities which apply a greater standard of care than that of the ordinary man for persons shown to possess special skill in a particular endeavor. Thus, one who engages in a business, profession or occupation must exercise the requisite degree of learning, skill, and ability of that calling with reasonable and ordinary care. A specialist in a particular profession may be held to a higher standard of care. However, the professional standard is an objective standard. In this case, the instructions regarding the pilot's standard of care are erroneous. They allow the jury to consider Fred

Heath's (the pilot's) own training and experience in determining the required standard of care, rather than the minimum standard of care that is applicable to all pilots. (New Trial Ordered.)

Analysis:

One thing to remember in negligence cases is that the standard of care is almost never subjective. You may remember from previous cases that children's standard of negligence is different from that of an ordinary adult. A child is compared to the reasonable child of like age, experience, and intelligence. Note that the standard for professionals is also objective and a little different. A professional is held to the standard of care of the ordinary prudent person with skill and knowledge that is commonly held by the professionals in the community. This is exactly what *Heath v. Swift Wings* stands for. Professionals are held to a higher standard than the ordinary prudent individual because they hold themselves out as having superior knowledge and skill in a particular field. Thus, they are held to a different standard?? that of the ordinary prudent professional in that particular field. Nevertheless, this standard, too, is objective because it does not take into consideration the subjective experience or training of the individual. Rather, it is the standard of care expected of all the members of that professional community. It is also important to remember that specialists in a particular field are held to another standard. This is a higher standard than that of a general practitioner. For example, a brain surgeon is not held to the same standard of care as a general practitioner, but to a higher standard (that of other brain specialists). It is customary for parties to a case, especially plaintiffs, who have the burden of proving negligence, to offer testimony of expert witnesses in order to determine the standard of care applicable to a professional community. Remember, that professional negligence is more commonly known as malpractice.

■ CASE VOCABULARY

PREJUDICIAL ERROR: Reversible error, one which would substantially affect appellant's legal rights, resulting in a miscarriage of justice.

Hodges v. Carter

(Client) v. *(Attorney)*
239 N.C. 517, 80 S.E.2d 144 (1954)

PROFESSIONALS WHO EXERCISE THEIR BEST JUDGMENT AND ADHERE TO THE STANDARD OF CARE REQUIRED IN THEIR PROFESSION ARE NOT SUBJECT TO LIABILITY FOR MERE ERRORS IN JUDGMENT

■ **INSTANT FACTS** Hodges (P) sued Carter (D), an attorney, in negligence for losses that Hodges (P) suffered due to Carter's (D) failure to properly serve Hodges' (P) insurance carriers.

■ **BLACK LETTER RULE** An attorney who has acted in good faith and in the best interests of his client is not liable in negligence for a mere error in judgment.

■ **PROCEDURAL BASIS**

Action in malpractice for recovery of damages.

■ **FACTS**

Hodges (P), whose drug store was destroyed in a fire, sought to recover for his losses from his four insurance carriers, all foreign companies doing business in the state of North Carolina. The latter refused to compensate Hodges (P). Thereafter, Hodges (P) hired attorneys Carter (D) and D.D. Topping (D), now deceased, to institute separate actions against each of the insurance companies. In each case, Carter and Topping (D) filed a summons and complaint with the Commissioner of Insurance of the State of North Carolina. Carter and Topping (D), however, did not serve each insurance company separately. Each of the insurance companies filed a motion to dismiss the case for failure of proper service of process on the ground that the Commissioner did not have authority to accept service on behalf of foreign insurance carriers. The trial court denied the motions. On appeal, the Supreme Court of North Carolina reversed the lower court's ruling and dismissed each of the actions. Hodges (P) sued Carter and Topping (D) alleging that their failure to properly serve the insurance companies constituted negligence. Carter and Topping (D) denied negligence on the ground that they had acted in good faith and in the exercise of their best judgment. The trial court ruled in favor of Carter and Topping (D). Hodges (P) appeals.

■ **ISSUE**

Is an attorney who has acted in good faith and in the best interests of his client liable in negligence for a mere error in judgment?

■ **DECISION AND RATIONALE**

(Barnhill, C.J.) No. An attorney who has acted in good faith and in the best interests of his client is not liable in negligence for a mere error in judgment. An attorney who is acting on behalf of his client impliedly represents that 1) he possesses the requisite learning, skill, and ability necessary to the practice of law; 2) he will use his best judgment in carrying out the action on behalf of his client; and 3) he will exercise reasonable care and diligence in the use of his skill and knowledge in his client's case. Thus, an attorney acting in good faith and in the best interests of his client is not liable for mere errors in judgment or a mistake in an unsettled point of law. However, the attorney is liable for his failure to exercise that degree of knowledge and skill commonly possessed by other attorneys, for his failure to use diligence and ordinary care, and for his failure to exercise good faith and act in the best interest of his client. In this case, Hodges (P) has not presented any evidence to show that Carter and Topping (D) did not adhere to this implicit standard of care. When the defendants in this case served the Commissioner on behalf of the four foreign insurance companies, they were merely following a custom which had been rampant in the state for more than 20 years. Foreign insurance companies have uniformly ratified such procedure by filing their answers or making their defense. The right of the Commissioner to accept service of process on behalf of insurance companies has not yet been tested in the courts. Yet, the Superior Judge in this case had expressly declared in this case that acceptance of the service of process by the Commissioner subjected the insurance companies to the jurisdiction of the court. In light of these facts, the defendants did not serve the insurance companies personally. This court's earlier decision, granting the insurance companies' motion to dismiss, was not meant to indicate that the defendants in this case were negligent in their duties to their client, Hodges (P). (Affirmed.)

Analysis:

Hodges v. Carter is one of those unforgettable cases because here our colleagues, other attorneys, are being sued in negligence. This case stands for a few propositions. In the first place, it shows that an attorney must adhere to the level of skill and knowledge that is commonly possessed by other individuals in the profession. Second, an attorney must be reasonable in the exercise of his judgment. Here you can sigh in relief because an attorney is not liable for mere errors of judgment, especially where it concerns issues of law that are unsettled. Note, however, that an attorney is liable for such errors where reasonable research and diligence would have clearly revealed the error. Third, an attorney should show diligence in pursuing her client's case. This means that an attorney must follow her client's case with zeal and due care in exercise of her skill and knowledge. For example, an attorney is clearly liable for failing to file a client's lawsuit prior to the running of the statute of limitations on the client's case. Another sigh of relief (!) because in a negligence action against an attorney, the plaintiff has to prove that but for the attorney's negligence, the client would have been successful in his/her case. This is a very important requirement because in a negligence cause of action, the plaintiff must show that he/she has suffered some kind of an injury. Consequently, if plaintiff would have lost his/her case regardless of the attorney's negligence, the client is not entitled to recovery in a malpractice suit.

■ CASE VOCABULARY

DICTUM: Statement in a judicial opinion not necessary for the decision of the case.

INVOLUNTARY NONSUIT: When plaintiff neglects to appear after being called or gives no evidence for a jury to find a verdict; when a case is put out of court by an adverse ruling precluding a recovery.

MOVANT: One who "moves" or makes a motion before court.

PROCESS: A formal writing issued by authority of law; any means used by the court to acquire or exercise its jurisdiction over a person or over specified property; method used to compel the attendance of a defendant in court in a civil suit.

STATUTORY: Relating to a written established rule or law.

Boyce v. Brown

(Patient) v. *(Surgeon)*

51 Ariz. 416, 77 P.2d 455 (1938)

IN MEDICAL MALPRACTICE CASES, THE PLAINTIFF MUST PROVE THAT THE DEFENDANT'S CONDUCT FELL BELOW THE ACCEPTED STANDARDS IN THE MEDICAL COMMUNITY

■ **INSTANT FACTS** Boyce (P) brought an action in negligence against her surgeon Brown (D) for his failure to take an x-ray of Boyce's (P) ankle on which Brown (D) had operated seven years before.

■ **BLACK LETTER RULE** In a medical malpractice case, the plaintiff must prove the standard of care in the medical community and that the defendant's conduct departed from this standard.

■ **PROCEDURAL BASIS**

Appeal in action for negligence.

■ **FACTS**

In September of 1927, Nannie Boyce (P) employed the services of Edgar Brown (D), a surgeon, to operate on her broken ankle. Brown (D) operated on her ankle by bringing together the fragments of Boyce's (P) broken bones and affixing them, using a metal screw. In November of 1934, Boyce (P) consulted Brown (D) again because of the pain in her ankle. Although Brown (D) treated the ankle, its condition did not improve. In January of 1936, Boyce (P) went to another surgeon, Dr. Kent, who took an x-ray of Boyce's (P) ankle. The x-ray showing that there was necrosis of the bone around the screw, the doctor operated on Boyce (P) and removed the screw. Boyce's (P) ankle was normal after her recovery from this operation. Boyce (P) sued Brown (D) claiming that his failure to take an x-ray of her ankle constituted negligence. The trial court granted a verdict in favor of Brown (D) on the ground that Boyce (P) had not presented evidence sufficient to charge Brown (D) with malpractice. Boyce (P) appeals, further alleging that Brown's (D) failure to take an x-ray of Boyce's (P) ankle constituted negligence.

■ **ISSUE**

In a medical malpractice case, must the plaintiff prove the standard of care in the medical community and that the defendant's conduct departed from this standard?

■ **DECISION AND RATIONALE**

(Lockwood, J.) Yes. In a medical malpractice case, the plaintiff must prove the standard of care in the medical community and that the defendant's conduct departed from this standard. In each malpractice suit certain rules are always applicable. First, a medical practitioner is presumed to possess the degree of skill and learning possessed by the average member of the medical community in which he practices, and that he applies the skill and learning with ordinary care and prudence. If the doctor does not do so, he is negligent. Second, before a physician is held liable in malpractice, the plaintiff must prove that the doctor's act or omission was such that it deviated from the applicable standard of care. Third, the plaintiff must prove the applicable standard in the community by affirmative evidence. Fourth, negligence on the part of the physician is never presumed, even if the treatment in question was

---

not successful. This means that the plaintiff must prove affirmatively that the physician was in fact negligent in his acts or omissions. Last, the standard of care must be established through the testimony of expert witnesses. The testimony of other physicians establishing that they would have followed a different course of action is not sufficient unless it also appears that the defendant's course of treatment fell below the accepted standard in the community. In this case, the only testimony bearing on the standards of proper treatment was that of Dr. Kent and Dr. Brown (D). The latter testified that he did what was required at the time he examined Boyce (P). Dr. Kent, on the other hand, testified that he was not sure whether Dr. Brown (D) should have removed the screw from the Boyce's (P) ankle prior to Dr. Kent's operation. Dr. Kent, however, never testified that the method of operation followed by Brown (D) deviated from the standard of care in the medical community. Neither did he indicate that Brown's (D) failure to take an x-ray of Boyce's (P) ankle was a deviation from the standards of the medical community. Contrary to Boyce's (P) contention, this court is not of the opinion that a mere failure to take an x-ray in itself constituted negligence on the part of Brown (D). In many cases, an x-ray is costly and of no value to the treatment of the patient. Given Dr. Kent's testimony that Boyce's (P) arthritis would have been his first thought as to the cause of Boyce's (P) pain, this court believes that Brown's (D) failure to take an x-ray of Brown's (P) ankle was not so far a departure from ordinary medical standards as to constitute negligence. (Affirmed.)

Analysis:

As this case illustrates, in medical malpractice cases the plaintiff has the burden of proving the standard of care in the medical community. Additionally, the plaintiff must prove affirmatively that the defendant's conduct deviated from this standard of care. Thus, a plaintiff may not recover unless he/she proves that the defendant's treatment of the plaintiff was not in accord with recognized medical practice. Note that this case also illustrates that it is not enough for the plaintiff's expert to testify as to what he would have done; the expert must also testify that the defendant's practice was not recognized as valid in the medical community.

■ CASE VOCABULARY

MALPRACTICE: Any professional misconduct, unreasonable lack of skill in professional practice.

NECROSIS: Death of part of the living body.

Morrison v. MacNamara

(Patient) v. *(Medical Laboratory)*

407 A.2d 555 (D.C.1979)

THE DISTRICT OF COLUMBIA COURT OF APPEALS HOLDS THAT MEDICAL PROFESSIONALS WHO ARE TRAINED ACCORDING TO NATIONAL STANDARDS SHOULD BE HELD TO A NATIONAL, RATHER THAN LOCAL, STANDARD OF CARE

■ **INSTANT FACTS** Morrison (P) brought a malpractice action against MacNamara (D), a medical laboratory, for injuries that Morrison (P) sustained when he fainted and struck his head on a blood pressure stand.

■ **BLACK LETTER RULE** The conduct of health professionals who are certified through a system of national board certification must be measured against nationally accepted standards of care.

■ **PROCEDURAL BASIS**

Appeal from malpractice action.

■ **FACTS**

Morrison (P) reported to MacNamara (D), a nationally board certified medical laboratory, for a urethral smear test. Morrison's (P) test was administered while he was standing. As a result of the test, Morrison (P) fainted and struck his head on a metal blood pressure stand nearby. Among other injuries, Morrison's (P) fall resulted a permanent loss of his senses of smell and taste. Morrison (P) sued MacNamara (D) on the ground that the latter was negligent in administering Morrison's (P) test while Morrison (P) was standing up. Additionally, at the trial, Morrison (P) presented evidence that the national standard of care requires that the patient sit or lie down during the smear test. MacNamara (D) presented evidence indicating that in the Washington area such tests were administered with the patient standing. The trial court refused to admit Morrison's (P) evidence on the ground that Morrison (P) must present evidence of the standard of care in the same medical community as that of MacNamara (D). Morrison appeals.

■ **ISSUE**

Must the conduct of health professionals who are certified through a system of national board certification be measured against nationally accepted standards of care.

■ **DECISION AND RATIONALE**

(Newman, C.J.) Yes. The conduct of health professionals who are certified through a system of national board certification must be measured against nationally accepted standards of care. In this case, Morrison (P) contends that in view of the national certification of MacNamara (D), the latter had to adhere to nationally accepted standards for administering the urethral smear test. MacNamara (D), on the other hand, argues that it should be held only to the standard of care recognized in the Washington area. Under the locality rule, the conduct of members of the medical profession is to be measured only by the standard of conduct expected of the other members of the medical profession in the same locality or the same community. This rule was designed to protect doctors in rural areas who, because of inadequate training and experience, and the lack of transportation, could not exhibit the care, skill and training of doctors in urban areas. In this case, this rule is irrelevant because Washington, D.C., as the nation's capitol, is not an isolated rural area. Additionally, any disparity between the skill and training of urban doctors and rural doctors has for the most part been eliminated due to the standardization of medical education and improvements in transportation and communications. Some courts have abandoned the limited locality rule, extending it to include same or similar localities. Other courts, however, noting that medical standards have been nationalized through a system of national board certification, have adopted the national standard of care, completely abandoning the locality rule. This court is of the opinion that at least with respect to board certified physicians, hospitals, and medical laboratories, the standard of care is to be measured by the national standard. In this case, MacNamara (D) is a nationally certified medical laboratory, and it holds itself to the public as such. Thus, the trial court's instruction which compares a nationally certified medical professional's conduct with the standard of care in the District of Columbia or a similar locality is erroneous. (Reversed.)

Analysis:

The locality rule, which surprisingly only applies to medical professionals, required that a medical professional's conduct be compared to the standard of care, knowledge and skill of other professionals in good standing in the local community. This rule, which may have been relevant in days when medical education was not standardized, has been abandoned by most courts. Most courts, however, still adhere to a revised version of the locality rule which compares a medical professional's conduct to that of other medical professionals in the same or similar communities. This rule presents another problem: How can the court determine that two communities are the same or similar? The court in *Morrison v. MacNamara* goes a little further to apply a national standard of care to those professionals who are certified through a national system of board certification. This approach creates a uniform standard of care which is required of all medical professionals and does away with the problem of determining the similarity between communities.

■ CASE VOCABULARY

EMPIRICAL: Known by experience only.

INDIGENOUS: Existing naturally in a county or region; native.

Scott v. Bradford

(Patient) v. *(Surgeon)*
606 P.2d 554 (Okl.1979)

A PHYSICIAN MAY BE LIABLE IN NEGLIGENCE FOR FAILING TO GET THE INFORMED CONSENT OF A PATIENT BEFORE OPERATING ON THE PATIENT

■ **INSTANT FACTS** Scott (P) brought an action against Bradford (D), Scott's (P) surgeon, on the ground that Bradford (D) had failed to disclose the risks and alternatives of the surgery to Scott (P).

■ **BLACK LETTER RULE** A physician is liable in negligence if he does not inform the patient of his options and its attendant risks before treating the patient.

■ **PROCEDURAL BASIS**

Appeal in medical malpractice action.

■ **FACTS**

Scott (P), on the advice of her own physician, reported to Bradford (D), a surgeon, to operate on the fibroid tumors on her uterus. Before the surgery Scott (P) signed a routine informed consent form at the hospital. After the surgery, Scott (P) suffered from incontinence and was referred to a urologist, who after three surgeries corrected her problem. Scott (P) brought a negligence action against Bradford (D) on the ground that Bradford (D) had failed to inform her of the risks of the surgery and other available alternatives to surgery. The trial court instructed the jury of a physician's duty to disclose material risks and feasibility of alternatives to the patient. The jury returned a verdict in favor of Bradford (D). Scott (P) appeals.

■ **ISSUE**

Is a physician liable in negligence if he does not inform the patient of his options and their attendant risks before treating the patient?

■ **DECISION AND RATIONALE**

(Doolin, J.) Yes. A physician is liable in negligence if he does not inform the patient of his options and their attendant risks before treating the patient. In order to be effective, consent to a medical treatment should be made based on the patient's understanding of the treatment, available alternatives, and the collateral risks of the treatment. This requirement, known as "informed consent," is a duty on the part of the physician. A physician's failure to abide by this duty could give rise to his liability in negligence. In determining what information should be disclosed to the patient, some courts adhere to the "professional standard of care" which requires a physician to disclose the information which is in conformance with the prevailing medical practice in the community. The court in *Canterbury v. Spence* indicated that the standard measuring performance of the physician's duty to disclose is conduct which is reasonable under the circumstances. Thus, a patient's right to decide whether to undergo treatment or not cannot be delegated to the local medical community or its general customs. This court adheres to the view presented in *Canterbury*. In other words, a physician has the duty to inform the patient of all the material risks associated with the treatment in question. A risk is material if it is likely to affect the patient's decision. The cause of action for lack of informed consent has three elements, all of which must be proved by the plaintiff. First, the plaintiff must prove that the physician has a duty to disclose. Note that there is no duty where the risks are known to the patient or where the risks ought to be known by the patient. Secondly, the plaintiff must prove causation which requires the plaintiff to prove that he would not have undergone the treatment had he been properly informed of the risks and alternatives. The causation element is one that is objective. The court should determine whether a reasonable patient would have undergone the treatment had he been fully informed of the risks and alternatives of the treatment. The third element of the cause of action requires the plaintiff to have suffered actual injury as a result of submitting to the treatment. Absent injury, there is no cause of action in negligence based on informed consent. The trial court in this case instructed the jury that Bradford (D) should have disclosed the material risks associated with the removal of the tumors and the alternatives available to Scott (P). In light of the circumstances, these instructions are sufficient.

Analysis:

In addition to their duty to conduct their profession based on the standard of care expected of a reasonable and prudent medical professional, doctors owe another duty to patients. This is the duty to disclose and inform the patient of all the material risks associated with a treatment and to inform the patients of their alternative options. In other words, a doctor has the duty to get the "informed consent" of the patient before proceeding with the patient's treatment. Failure to adhere to this duty exposes the doctor to possible malpractice liability. Just like other negligence causes of action, the burden of proving the prima facie case for negligence lies on the plaintiff. In informed consent cases, the plaintiff must establish three elements: 1) The plaintiff must prove that the doctor had a duty to disclose. This is important because there are circumstances where the doctor may not have the duty. One example is when the patient is already aware of the risks or ought to be aware of the risks. 2) The plaintiff must prove causation. That is, the plaintiff must prove that had the doctor properly informed the plaintiff, the latter would not have undergone the surgery; this element is determined based on an objective standard. This means that the court will look at whether a reasonable patient in the plaintiff's position would not have undergone the treatment had he/she been properly informed of the risks and alternatives. 3) The plaintiff has to prove that he suffered actual injury as a result of the treatment. If any one of these three elements is lacking from the plaintiff's case, the court will dismiss the action. Note that this is exactly like the ordinary, run-of-the-mill negligence cases, where the plaintiff has the burden of proving the standard of care, the defendant's failure to adhere to the standard, that the defendant's failure was the cause of plaintiff's injury, and that the plaintiff did in fact suffer an injury. Cases which are based on negligence for the lack of consent are different from those in intentional torts. Remember that in *Mohr v. Williams* the patient sued the doctor for operating on her without even telling her. This is an example of a case where the cause of action lies in the intentional tort of battery. In such cases, the plaintiff need not prove that he/she suffered any kind of injury. Thus, the doctor may be liable even though the operation was a complete success. Where the doctor has gotten the plaintiff's consent, but the consent is not effective or informed, the patient has a cause of action in negligence, and the plaintiff must prove that he/she has suffered actual injury.

■ CASE VOCABULARY

ARROGATE: To claim without right; to claim on behalf of another.

ARTIFICE: Contrivance or trick.

INCONTINENCE: Unable to control natural discharges from the body.

INFORMED CONSENT: Consent accompanied by full notice as to that which is being consented to. In tort law, a patient must be informed of the nature and risks of a medical procedure before the physician can validly claim exemption from liability in battery or negligence.

PRIMA FACIE: Self-evident; legally sufficient to establish a fact unless disproved.

PURDURABLE: Long-lasting; forever.

Moore v. The Regents of the University of California

(Patient) v. *(Treating Institution)*

51 Cal.3d 120, 793 P.2d 479, 271 Cal.Rptr. 146 (1990)

THE DOCTRINE OF INFORMED CONSENT REQUIRES A PHYSICIAN TO DISCLOSE TO THE PATIENT ALL MATERIAL INFORMATION REGARDING THE PHYSICIAN'S OWN PERSONAL INTERESTS IN TREATING THE PATIENT

■ **INSTANT FACTS** Moore (P), who has sought medical treatment from Dr. Golde at the UCLA Medical Center, brought an action against the Regents of the University of California for Dr. Golde's failure to disclose his own personal interest in treatment of Moore (P).

■ **BLACK LETTER RULE** In order to satisfy his fiduciary duty to the patient and obtain the patient's consent, a physician who is seeking a patient's consent for a medical procedure must disclose his own personal interests, unrelated to the patient's health, that may affect the patient's decision.

■ **PROCEDURAL BASIS**

Appeal in action for conversion and negligence.

■ **FACTS**

John Moore (P) was diagnosed with leukemia by Dr. Golde, a physician at the UCLA Medical Center. Dr. Golde recommended removal of Moore's (P) spleen to slow down the progress of the disease. Moore (P) consented to this operation. Unbeknownst to Moore (P), Dr. Golde used Moore's (P) spleen for research which was unrelated to Moore's (P) condition. Dr. Golde had found that Moore's (P) cells were useful in the genetic research that he was performing. Pursuant to his research, Dr. Golde developed a cell line from Moore's (P) cells which he licensed to a pharmaceutical company for commercial development. Moore (P) brought several actions against the Regents of the University of California (D) in conversion and also in negligence, on the ground that Dr. Golde had failed to inform Moore (P) that his cells were being used for Dr. Golde's own personal research and eventual financial interest. The trial court dismissed all of Moore's (P) actions. The Court of Appeal reversed on the conversion count, holding that Moore (P) had stated a cause of action, and dismissed the negligence count based on informed consent. Moore (P) appeals.

■ **ISSUE**

In order to satisfy his fiduciary duty to the patient and obtain the patient's consent, must a physician, who is seeking a patient's consent for a medical procedure, disclose his own personal interests unrelated to the patient's health that may affect the patient's decision?

■ **DECISION AND RATIONALE**

(Panelli, J.) Yes. In order to satisfy his fiduciary duty to the patient and obtain the patient's consent, a physician who is seeking a patient's consent for a medical procedure must disclose his own personal interests, unrelated to the patient's health, that may affect the patient's decision. A reasonable patient would want to know whether a physician has an economic interest that might affect the physician's professional judgment. The law does not prohibit physicians from conducting research in the field in which they practice. Such physicians, however, may have potentially conflicting loyalties. The possibility that an interest other than the patient's health has affected the physician's judgment is information that a reasonable patient would want to know before consenting to treatment. Golde contends that since the spleen has already been removed, Moore (P) no longer has a medical interest. This argument would be correct if the physician has no interest in conducting research on the patient's cells at the time that he is recommending the medical treatment. The argument, however, is not correct if the physician has an interest in the patient's cells before the procedure because the physician may take that pre-existing interest into consideration in recommending the procedure. In this instance, the physician's interest should be disclosed to the patient because it is material in the patient's decision to undergo the treatment. This court does not, however, require a physician to disclose remote risks or interests that are not central to the decision to undergo the treatment. In this case, Dr. Golde's removal of the tissue took place when he had an undisclosed financial interest in Moore's (P) cells. Also, in Moore's (P) later visits to the hospital, post-operative taking of tissue were done again without proper disclosure of Dr. Golde's personal interests to Moore (P). In these instances Moore (P) has a valid cause of action. However, Moore's (P) actions in conversion are not covered by the traditional common law of conversion and should be dismissed. (Affirmed in part and reversed in part.)

Analysis:

So far we have seen that a physician has a duty of care to the patient. A physician, under the doctrine of informed consent, also has the duty to disclose to the patient all material information regarding the risks and alternatives to a course of treatment in order to allow the patient to decide whether or not to undergo a certain treatment. This case imposes another duty on the physician based on the doctrine of informed consent. As this case illustrates, a physician is required to disclose to the patient information regarding his own personal interests, financial or other interests, which are material in the patient's decision. In determining what is material, we will rely on the reasonable patient standard, that is, the information likely to affect a reasonable patient's decision regarding the treatment in question.

■ CASE VOCABULARY

CONVERSION: Wrongful taking or detention of another's property without his authorization or justification.

FIDUCIARY: A person having a legal duty, created by his/her undertaking, to act primarily for the benefit of another in matters connected with his/her undertaking.

INFORMED CONSENT: Consent accompanied by full notice to that which is being consented to; in tort law, a patient must be informed of the nature and risks of medical procedure before the physician can validly claim exemption from liability in battery or negligence.

INTER ALIA: Among other things.

Pokora v. Wabash Ry. Co.

(Truck Driver) v. *(Railroad Co.)*

292 U.S. 98, 54 S.Ct. 580, 78 L.Ed. 1149 (1934)

THE SUPREME COURT OF THE UNITED STATES WARNS AGAINST FRAMING STANDARDS OF BEHAVIOR WHICH AMOUNT TO RULES OF LAW

■ **INSTANT FACTS** Pokora (P) brought an action in negligence against Wabash Ry. Co. (D) for injuries that he sustained when his car was struck by Wabash's (D) train.

■ **BLACK LETTER RULE** An automobile driver who is crossing over railroad tracks does not, under all circumstances, have the absolute legal duty to stop the car to look for oncoming trains.

■ **PROCEDURAL BASIS**

Appeal in action for personal injury.

■ **FACTS**

Pokora (P) was driving his automobile across tracks owned by Wabash Ry. Co. (D). A box car covering the first track had obstructed Pokora's (P) view of the other tracks. When crossing the tracks, Pokora (P) drove slowly, stopped and listened for trains, and when he did not see any, he proceeded. Pokora (P) was then struck by a Wabash (D) train. Pokora (P) brought action against Wabash (D) for injuries that he suffered as a result of the accident. The trial court directed a verdict in favor of Wabash (D) on the ground that Pokora (P) was contributorily negligent as a matter of law. The court of appeals affirmed, and the Supreme Court of the United States granted certiorari.

■ **ISSUE**

Does an automobile driver who is crossing over railroad tracks have the absolute legal duty, under all circumstances, to stop his car to look for oncoming trains?

■ **DECISION AND RATIONALE**

(Cardozo, J.) No. An automobile driver who is crossing over railroad tracks does not, under all circumstances, have the absolute legal duty to stop to look for oncoming trains. In *B. & O.R. Co. v. Goodman* this court stated in dicta that a driver who is not sure whether a train is dangerously close must stop and get out of his vehicle, although most often he will not be required to do more than just stop and look. This decision has created confusion in the lower courts. Some courts have imposed this duty to stop and look on all drivers regardless of how clear the railroad crossing may be. Other courts have stated that the traveler must look and listen, however whether he has to stop or not will be dependent on the circumstances of the case and the judgment of the jury. In none of its opinions has this court suggested that in each and every situation the duty to stop is absolute. The duty to stop and look is conditioned upon the presence of other circumstances whereby sight and hearing alone are not adequate for the protection of the traveler. In this case Pokora (P) did stop before he entered the tracks. The evidence at trial permits the conclusion that a stop after passing the box cars would not have helped Pokora (P) in preventing the accident. Thus this case is in the province of the jury unless the court finds that Pokora's (P) negligence was so obvious that one conclusion alone is permissible for rational minds. Under such circumstances there is no need to frame standards of behavior that amount to rules of law. An individual's behavior may vary depending on the circumstances of each case. Extraordinary situations may not be fairly subjected to tests or regulations that are fair under normal circumstances. (Reversed and remanded.)

Analysis:

This case stands for a very simple proposition: When it comes to negligence, it is not always right to make standards which rise to the same level as rules of law. This is so because the behavior of individuals varies based on the exigencies of each situation or conditions surrounding each case. While it may be prudent to act a certain way under normal conditions, it may be negligent to act the same way under emergency conditions. The U.S. Supreme Court is basically affirming that the question of negligence is one that should be left to the jury unless the conduct or behavior in question is so negligent that rational and reasonable minds can not reach another decision or draw other conclusions.

■ CASE VOCABULARY

CERTIORARI: Latin meaning to be informed of a means of gaining appellate review; a common law writ issued from a superior court to one of inferior jurisdiction, commanding the latter to certify and return to the former the record in the particular case. In the U.S. Supreme Court the writ is discretionary with the Court and will be issued to any court in the land to review a federal question if at least 4 out of 9 justices vote to hear the case.

RECONNOITRE: To make a reconnaissance or "check things out."

Osborne v. McMasters

(Administrator of Deceased's Estate) v. *(Drugstore Owner)*
40 Minn. 103, 41 N.W. 543 (1889)

WHERE A LEGISLATIVE STATUTE IMPOSES THE STANDARD OF CARE IN CERTAIN SITUATIONS, THE VIOLATION OF THE STATUTE CONSTITUTES NEGLIGENCE PER SE

■ **INSTANT FACTS** Osborne (P), administrator of the estate of the decedent, brought an action against McMasters for death of the decedent due to McMasters' (D) selling poison to the decedent without labeling it as such.

■ **BLACK LETTER RULE** An individual who breaches a duty imposed on him by statute is liable for injuries to those whom the statute is designed to protect if the injuries resulted from his breach.

■ **PROCEDURAL BASIS**

Appeal in action for negligence.

■ **FACTS**

Osborne (P), administrator of the estate of the deceased, brought an action in negligence against McMasters (D). A clerk at McMasters' (D) drugstore sold a deadly poison to the administrator's intestate without having labeled it as poison, as was required by statute. Consequently, the decedent ingested the poison and died. The trial court returned a verdict in favor of Osborne (P). McMasters (D) appeals.

■ **ISSUE**

Where an individual breaches a duty imposed on him by a statute, is he liable for injuries to those whom the statute is designed to protect if the injuries were caused by his breach?

■ **DECISION AND RATIONALE**

(Mitchell, J.) Yes. An individual who breaches a duty imposed on him by statute is liable for injuries to those whom the statute is designed to protect if the injuries resulted from his breach. It is immaterial whether the duty is imposed by the rules of common law requiring the exercise of ordinary care, or by a statute designed for the protection of others. In the latter case, the measure of legal duty is fixed by statute, and need not be determined based on common law principles. Thus, violation of the statute constitutes negligence per se. The statute simply imposes a fixed standard of conduct. The action itself is still based on negligence. (Affirmed.)

Analysis:

This case is a simple illustration of the concept of negligence per se. Remember that in an ordinary action in negligence the plaintiff has to prove four elements: 1) there is a certain standard of care; 2) the defendant's conduct has fallen below this standard (defendant's conduct was negligent); 3) the defendant's negligent conduct was the cause of the plaintiff's injury (causation); and 4) the plaintiff did in fact sustain actual injury. Thus, it is up to the plaintiff to show the required level of care and to show that the defendant's conduct fell below it. In many states and local governments the legislatures have made the plaintiff's burden easier. They have created statutes which establish a fixed standard of care. Such statutes are designed to protect certain individuals from certain injuries. Where a plaintiff is within the class protected by such statutes, plaintiff can show that defendant has fallen below the required standard of care by showing that the defendant has violated the statute. Thus, a statute which imposes a fixed standard of care relieves the plaintiff from proving the first two elements in a negligence case. This is often known as negligence per se. To take advantage of this doctrine, the plaintiff simply needs to show that he/she is within the class that the statute is aimed at protecting, and that the defendant has violated the statute. The plaintiff, however, still has the burden of establishing causation and injury. Thus, it is important to remember that negligence per se does not mean that the defendant who violates a statute is automatically liable to the plaintiff. Negligence per se does not impose strict liability on defendants. The plaintiff still has the burden of proving causation and injury.

■ CASE VOCABULARY

INTESTATE: Having no will or dying without a will.

NEGLIGENCE PER SE: Negligence as a matter of law; a violation of a specific requirement of law or ordinance; an act or omission that is recognized as negligent, either because it is contrary to the requirements of law or because it is so contrary to the dictates of common prudence that one could say without hesitation that no careful person would have committed the act or omission.

Stachniewicz v. Mar–Cam Corp.

(Patron) v. *(Bar)*

259 Or. 583, 488 P.2d 436 (1971)

JURY MUST DETERMINE WHETHER STATUTE APPLIES TO CIVIL ACTION IN ORDER TO IMPOSE NEGLIGENCE PER SE LIABILITY

■ **INSTANT FACTS** Stachniewicz (P) brought action against Mar-Cam Corp. (D), owner of a bar, for injuries that Stachniewicz (P) sustained as a result of a barroom brawl.

■ **BLACK LETTER RULE** A violation of a statute or regulation constitutes negligence per se when the violation results in injury to a member of the class of persons protected by the statute or regulation and when the harm is of the kind which the statute or regulation is designed to prevent

■ **PROCEDURAL BASIS**

Appeal in action for personal injury.

■ **FACTS**

A fight erupted in a bar among some of the bar's patrons, including those patrons sitting next to Stachniewicz's (P) booth. Soon after, one of the Stachniewicz's (P) friends who was sitting at Stachniewicz's (P) booth got involved in the fight. Later, the friend found Stachniewicz (P) lying injured just outside the bar. Stachniewicz (P), due to his head injuries, suffered from amnesia and could not remember any of the events that had taken place at the bar. Stachniewicz (P) sued Mar-Cam (D) (the bar owner) for the injuries suffered, contending that Mar-Cam (D) was negligent per se because it had violated an Oregon statute and a regulation which prohibited bar owners from the sale of liquor to patrons who were visibly intoxicated and from allowing loud noises and disorderly conduct in their bars, respectively. The trial court returned a verdict in favor of Mar-Cam (D), indicating that neither the violation of the statute nor the regulation constituted negligence per se. Stachniewicz (P) appeals.

■ **ISSUE**

Does a violation of a statute or regulation constitute negligence per se when the violation results in injury to a member of the class of persons protected by the statute or regulation and when the harm is of the kind which the statute or regulation is designed to prevent?

■ **DECISION AND RATIONALE**

(Holman, J.) Yes. A violation of a statute or regulation constitutes negligence per se when the violation results in injury to a member of the class of persons protected by the statute or regulation and when the harm is of the kind which the statute or regulation is designed to prevent. However, it is for the court to examine preliminarily the appropriateness of the standard of the statute or regulation as a measure of care for civil litigation under the circumstances presented. In this case, the Oregon statute preventing sale of liquor to a visibly intoxicated individual has a standard which is not appropriate for awarding civil damages. It is impossible to determine whether a third party's injuries, as a matter of law, were caused by the already inebriated person. The regulation, on the other hand, concerns matters which have a direct relation to physical disturbances in bars, which in turn create the likelihood of injury to others. It is reasonable to assume that the regulation was promulgated to prevent such injuries and to ensure the safety of patrons of bars as well as the general peace and welfare of the community. The plaintiff in this case was within the class of persons intended to be protected by the regulation, and the harm caused to him was the type of harm that the regulation sought to prevent. In this case, it is fair for the jury to infer that plaintiff's injuries resulted from the brawl and that he would not have been injured except for Mar-Cam's (D) violation of the regulation. (Reversed and remanded.)

Analysis:

Application of the doctrine of negligence per se is simple where the statute or regulation in question clearly states that its violation will give rise to civil liability. However, where a penal statute does not explicitly state this, it is the function of the court to determine whether or not the standard of care promulgated by the criminal statute should apply in civil liability cases. In negligence per se cases, where a criminal statute is involved, a majority of courts look to two requirements to determine whether or not to apply the statute in civil litigation. The first requirement is that the plaintiff must be within the class that the statute is intended to protect. The second requirement is that the plaintiff must have suffered the same injury that the statute is seeking to prevent. As the case above illustrates, the court could not find these two requirements in the statute which prevented sale of liquor to inebriated individuals. However, the court did find that the regulation did satisfy these two requirements.

Ney v. Yellow Cab Co.

(Injured Person) v. *(Cab Company)*

2 Ill.2d 74, 117 N.E.2d 74 (1954)

VIOLATION OF A STATUE IMPOSES LIABILITY ON A DEFENDANT ONLY IF THE PLAINTIFF'S INJURY WAS PROXIMATELY CAUSED BY THE DEFENDANT'S VIOLATION OF THE STATUTE

■ **INSTANT FACTS** Ney (P) brought action against Yellow Cab Co. (D) for injuries that Ney (P) suffered when the taxicab, stolen by a thief, ran into Ney's (P) vehicle.

■ **BLACK LETTER RULE** A plaintiff who bases his claim for negligence on a defendant's violation of a statute, must prove that his injuries were directly and proximately caused by the defendant's violation of the statute.

■ PROCEDURAL BASIS

Appeal in action for personal injury.

■ FACTS

An employee of Yellow Cab Co. (D) had left his taxicab unattended without stopping its engine or removing the key from the ignition. A thief stole the taxicab, and while in flight hit Ney's (P) vehicle, injuring him. The employee's conduct of leaving the taxicab unattended was a violation of the Uniform Traffic Act which prohibited individuals from leaving their vehicles unattended without first stopping the engine, locking the ignition, and removing the key. Ney (P) brought an action against Yellow Cab (D) for the injuries that Ney (P) suffered, claiming that the employee's violation of the statute was negligence and was the proximate cause of the damage that Ney (P) suffered. The trial court judged in favor of Ney (P), and the Appellate Court affirmed. Yellow Cab (D) appeals on the ground that the statute in question was not an anti-theft measure and that no liability could be imposed on Yellow Cab (D) for the misconduct of a thief.

■ ISSUE

Must a plaintiff who bases his claim for negligence on a defendant's violation of a statute, prove that his injuries were directly and proximately caused by the defendant's violation of the statute?

■ DECISION AND RATIONALE

(Maxwell, J.) Yes. A plaintiff who bases his claim for negligence on a defendant's violation of a statute, must prove that his injuries were directly and proximately caused by the defendant's violation of the statute. In this case, Ney (P) contends that the statute in question is a safety measure for the benefit of the public and that its violation is prima facie evidence of negligence. Yellow Cab (D), on the other hand, contends that the statute is an anti-theft measure and as such, its violation does not impose any liability on Yellow Cab (D). In order to determine whether Yellow Cab (D) is liable or not, the court must determine the legislative intent in enacting the statute. This court concludes that the entire statute is a public safety measure. The next question is the type of harm that the legislature was intending to prevent. Clearly, a motor vehicle alone with the key in its engine could do no harm. The motivation of the statute in question seems to be protection of life, limb, and property by prevention of recognized hazards which may result in leaving an unattended vehicle running. While the violation of the statute in itself is prima facie evidence of negligence, this in itself creates no liability. The injury caused to Ney (P) must have a direct and proximate connection with the violation of the statute in order to make Yellow Cab's (D) negligence actionable. A further problem is presented when an independent agency intervenes and the acts of the agency are illegal or criminal. Wrongful acts of independent third parties, not actually intended by the defendant, are not regarded by the law as the natural consequence of his wrong, and the defendant is not bound to anticipate the general probability of such acts. However, if the intervening criminal act might reasonably have been foreseeable, the causal chain is not broken by the intervention of such act. Under the circumstances surrounding this case, there is no compelling reason to hold, as a matter of law, that no actionable negligence can exist. Questions of due care, negligence, and proximate cause, such as those presented in this case, are ordinarily left to the jury. Therefore, it is the opinion of this court that the Appellate Court was correct in affirming the judgment of the trial court. (Affirmed.)

■ DISSENT

(Hershey, J.) The decision of the majority is contradictory. The court found that the statute in question is a public safety measure and not an anti-theft statute. Yet, the court concludes that the statute was designed to prevent accidents caused by a thief in stealing the vehicle. Thus, the court by its decision is in fact finding that the statute is an anti-theft measure. In this case, but for the intervention of the thief, the failure to remove the key from the ignition could not have caused the injury to the plaintiff.

Analysis:

In this case it is significant to determine the type of harm that the statute is intending to prevent and whether the violation of the statute is indeed the proximate cause of the harm. Here, although the court indicates that the statute is not an anti-theft measure, it concludes that the statute was designed to prevent the harm that may arise when an unattended car is stolen by a thief and the thief causes an injury. If this connection seems a little attenuated, you should not be baffled. Generally, courts are liberal in construction of statutes and read the statute as intending to prevent a variety of harms. There is one element in this case that we will come across again. That is the existence of independent intervening acts which may break the chain of causation. Remember that in order for a defendant's negligence to be actionable, the plaintiff has to prove that his/her injury was caused by the defendant's misconduct. In this case, the court determines that the question of causation is one for the jury to decide. Thus, since the jury at trial level had determined that the act of the thief was not the type of intervening act which broke the chain of causation, this court upheld the trial court's decision in finding the defendant liable for the damages to the plaintiff.

■ CASE VOCABULARY

INTERVENING CAUSE: Also known as "supervening," that cause which comes into active operation in producing the result after the negligence of the defendant; "intervening" is used as a time sense, referring to later events.

PRIMA FACIE: A case which is sufficient on its face, being supported by at least the requisite minimum of evidence, and being free from palpable defects; refers to a state of facts that entitles a party to have the case go to the jury.

PROXIMATE CAUSE: The type of cause which in natural and continuous sequence unbroken by any new independent cause produces an event, and without which the injury would not have occurred.

Perry v. S.N. and S.N.

(Witness) v. *(Parents)*

973 S.W.2d 301 (Tex.1998)

A COURT MAY FIND THAT VIOLATION OF A STATUTE IS NOT PRIMA FACIA NEGLIGENCE IF IT WOULD BE AGAINST PUBLIC POLICY TO DO SO

■ **INSTANT FACTS** A man witnessed children being abused and failed to report the abuse to authorities as required by statute.

■ **BLACK LETTER RULE** A child abuse reporting statute does not create civil liability for one who fails to report abuse.

■ **PROCEDURAL BASIS**

Appeal from reversal and remand for trial on negligence per se claim.

■ **FACTS**

Mr. and Mrs. S.N. (P) sued on behalf of their children whom they alleged Perry (D) observed being abused at a day care center. The Texas Family Code requires any person having cause to believe a child is being abused to report the abuse to state authorities. The statute makes failure to report the abuse a misdemeanor. Mr. and Mrs. S.N. (P) alleged that Perry (D) was told by the wife of the alleged abuser, Mrs. Keller, that her husband had "abusive habits toward children." Mr. and Mrs. S.N. (P) also allege that Perry (D) actually witnessed on one occasion Mr. Keller sexually abusing children at the day care center. Perry (D) did not report the abuse to any authorities.

■ **ISSUE**

Does a child abuse reporting statute impose civil liability under the doctrine of negligence per se on one who fails to report abuse?

■ **DECISION AND RATIONALE**

(Phillips, J.) No. (Mr. and Mrs. S.N.'s (P) common law negligence claim has not been preserved on appeal, therefore, we do not decide whether there should be a common law duty to report abuse.) We focus only on the negligence per se claim. The threshold questions in every negligence per se case are whether the plaintiff belongs to the class that the statute was intended to protect and whether the plaintiff's injury is the type that the statute as designed to prevent. Here, Mr. and Mrs. S.N.'s (P) children are clearly within the protected class, and they also suffered the type of injury the statute was intended to prevent. The purpose of the statute is to protect children from abuse. However, this does not end our inquiry. We must also decide if it would be fair and wise to impose civil tort liability for a violation of the statute. We consider a number of factors when making this decision; no single factor is determinative, nor is the issue resolved by merely counting how many factors lean each way. One factor we consider is that the common law imposes to such duty to report. At common law there is generally no duty to protect another from the criminal acts of a third-party. In contrast, in most negligence per se cases there is a preexisting common law duty to act reasonably under the circumstances. The criminal statute merely defines more precisely what conduct breaches that duty. Applying negligence per se in this case would create a new type of tort liability that did not exist before. A second factor to consider is whether the criminal statute gives adequate notice by clearly defining

---

what is required. It is unclear what circumstances give one "cause to believe" that abuse "may be" taking place. Actually witnessing the abuse is clearly enough to cause one to believe abuse is taking place. There are many instances, however, where the abuse may be less clear. Another factor to consider is whether applying negligence per se to the reporting statute would create liability without fault. In this case, it would not because the statute criminalizes only the "knowing" failure to report. This factor weighs in favor of imposing civil liability. The next consideration is whether negligence per se would impose ruinous liability disproportionate to the seriousness of the defendant's conduct. The large penalty imposed on the actual abuser compared to the relatively small penalty imposed on the person who fails to report it, shows that failing to report is viewed as a relatively minor offense. Therefore, it would be unfair to impose severe liability on one who is only a collateral wrongdoer. Finally, we also look at whether the injury resulted directly or indirectly from the violation of the statute. In this case, the injury was not a direct result of Perry's (D) failure to report the abuse. Because of these factors, we conclude that it is not appropriate to adopt the reporting statute as establishing a tort duty. We reverse the lower court's judgment and find that plaintiffs take nothing.

Analysis:

This case adds an additional layer of analysis to a negligence per se claim. The plaintiff must show that he or she is a member of the class of persons that the statute was designed to protect, and that he or she suffered the type of injury the statute was meant to prevent. In addition, the plaintiff must convince the court that it would be fair and wise to impose civil tort liability for a violation of a criminal statute. This is essentially a public policy argument. Would it be in the best interests of the public to impose liability? The court considers several factors in answering this question. Note that no single factor is most important. The factors are merely meant as a guide for courts to follow when deciding whether to apply negligence per se. One factor the court considers is whether the statute gives adequate notice as to what conduct is required or prohibited. In this case, the court found the statute was too vague in that it is unclear what circumstances would give one "cause to believe" that abuse "may be" taking place. If the statute is too vague to impose civil liability, isn't the statute also too vague to impose criminal liability? In other words, perhaps the statute is unconstitutionally vague. Overall, this case presents a good analysis of when a criminal statute can be used to establish a civil duty. The factors the court considers are not clear-cut and simple. They are open to interpretation and leave a great deal to the discretion of the court applying them.

Martin v. Herzog

(Deceased's Wife) v. *(Driver)*

228 N.Y. 164, 126 N.E. 814 (1920)

A DEFENDANT'S NEGLIGENT CONDUCT IS NOT ACTIONABLE UNLESS IT IS PROVEN TO BE THE CAUSE OF THE PLAINTIFF'S INJURIES

■ **INSTANT FACTS** Martin (P) brought an action against Herzog (D) alleging the death of Martin's (P) husband as a result of Herzog driving on the wrong side of the road.

■ **BLACK LETTER RULE** Proof of negligent conduct, without a showing of causal connection between the conduct and injury suffered, is not enough to impose liability on the party whose conduct was negligent.

■ **PROCEDURAL BASIS**

Appeal in action to recover for injuries resulting in death.

■ **FACTS**

Martin (P) and her husband were riding in a wagon when they collided with Herzog's (D) automobile which was coming from the opposite direction. Martin's (P) husband died as a result of the collision. Martin (P) brought an action in negligence against Herzog (D), alleging that Herzog (D) was driving his automobile on the wrong side of the road. Herzog (D), on the other hand, claimed that Martin (P) and her husband were contributorily negligent for failing to drive without headlights as required by the law. The trial court instructed the jury to treat Martin (P) and her husband's failure to use headlights as lightly or as gravely as they saw fit. The trial court entered a verdict in favor of Martin (P). The appellate court reversed and ordered a new trial. Martin (P) appeals.

■ **ISSUE**

Is proof of negligent conduct, without a showing of causal connection between the conduct and injury suffered, enough to impose liability on the party whose conduct was negligent?

■ **DECISION AND RATIONALE**

(Cardozo, J.) No. Proof of negligent conduct, without a showing of causal connection between the conduct and injury suffered, is not enough to impose liability on the party whose conduct was negligent. This court is of the opinion that the failure of the plaintiff's husband to use his headlights in accordance with the law is negligent conduct in itself. The omission of safeguards prescribed by the law for the protection of another's life or limb, is to fall below the standard of diligence prescribed by the law. In this case, however, the trial court instructed the jury to treat the plaintiff's behavior as culpable or as innocent, any way that they chose. Jurors, however, do not have the discretion to relax the duty that the law imposes on individuals. The plaintiff's failure to conform to the law was negligent and the jurors had no discretion to treat it differently. Nevertheless, there has to be a causal connection between negligence of the plaintiff and her husband and the injury suffered. An individual who travels without lights on the roads does not have to pay for his damages unless the damages were caused by his failure to travel with his lights on. Thus, to say that conduct shows negligence does not mean that it is always contributory negligence. In this case, however, evidence of a collision at night between an

---

automobile and an unseen wagon which did not have its lights on is evidence from which a causal connection may be inferred. If no other evidence is offered to break this causal connection, then there is a case of negligence which contributed to the injury. (Affirmed.)

Analysis:

Once again this case illustrates that there is a difference between negligent conduct and actionable negligence. While one's conduct toward another individual may be negligent, the latter may not recover for his/her damages or injuries unless it is proven that the negligent conduct was the cause of the damages or injuries suffered. The same is true in cases where negligence arises from violation of a statute. One who violates a statute imposing a standard of care has fallen below that standard, and is therefore negligent. However, for this negligence to be actionable a plaintiff who has suffered an injury because of the violation must prove that his/her injury was caused by the violation. This rule applies where a plaintiff claims negligence on the part of a defendant, or where as in this case the defendant claims contributory negligence on the part of the plaintiff. Additionally, this case indicates that where a party has fallen below the standard of care prescribed by a statute, he/she has committed negligence as a matter of law, or negligence per se.

■ CASE VOCABULARY

ATTENUATED: To lessen or weaken.

CONTRIBUTORY NEGLIGENCE: Conduct on the part of the plaintiff which falls below the standard to which he should conform for his own protection, and which is a legally contributing cause in addition to the negligence of the defendant in bringing about the plaintiff's harm.

CULPABLE: Deserving of blame.

PRIMA FACIE: A case which is sufficient on its face, being supported by at least the requisite minimum of evidence, and being free from palpable defects; refers to a state of facts that entitle a party to have the case go to the jury.

Zeni v. Anderson

(Pedestrian) v. (Driver)

397 Mich. 117, 243 N.W.2d 270 (1976)

WHERE THERE IS SUFFICIENT EXCUSE OR JUSTIFICATION FOR A PARTY'S VIOLATION OF A STATUTORY STANDARD OF CARE, THE STATUTORY STANDARD IS INAPPLICABLE

■ **INSTANT FACTS** Zeni (P), a pedestrian walking on the street with her back to the traffic, sued Anderson (D) for injuries that Zeni (P) suffered when Anderson (D) hit Zeni (P) with her automobile.

■ **BLACK LETTER RULE** The violation of a statute which is found to apply to a particular set of facts creates a presumption which can be rebutted by a showing of an adequate excuse or justification for violation of the statute.

■ **PROCEDURAL BASIS**

Appeal in action for personal injury.

■ **FACTS**

On a snowy morning, when the sidewalks were covered with snow, Zeni (P) walked on the side of the street with her back to the traffic, in order to get to her work. When walking on the street, Zeni (P) was hit and injured by Anderson (D) who was driving her automobile in the street. Zeni (P) sued Anderson (D) for the injuries that she suffered. Anderson (D) defended on the ground that Zeni (P) was walking in the street in violation of a statute requiring pedestrians to use sidewalks. At the trial, contrary to Anderson's (D) testimony, an eyewitness testified that Anderson's (D) windows were fogged at the time that Anderson (D) hit Zeni (P). Zeni (P) suffering from amnesia, had no recollection that Anderson's (D) car was behind her. Additionally, there was testimony at the trial indicating that it was safer for pedestrians to use the roadway instead of the sidewalk during winter. The trial court entered a verdict in favor of Zeni (P). The court of appeals reversed on other grounds (which grounds were not discussed in this case). Zeni (P) appeals.

■ **ISSUE**

Does the violation of a statute which is found to apply to a particular set of facts create a presumption which can be rebutted by a showing of an adequate excuse or justification for violation of the statute?

■ **DECISION AND RATIONALE**

(Williams, J.) Yes. The violation of a statute which is found to apply to a particular set of facts creates a presumption which can be rebutted by a showing of an adequate excuse or justification for violation of the statute. This court adheres to the decision in *Lucas v. Carson*, which indicates that evidence required to rebut the presumption of negligence per se should be positive, unequivocal, strong, and credible. It would be unreasonable to follow an automatic rule of negligence where observance of a statute would create a danger which may be avoided by disregarding the statute. If violation of a statute is viewed as negligence per se, without regard to an individual's exercise of due care or reasonable excuses for violation of the statute, the rule will be one of strict liability and not negligence. This treatment of statutes in civil litigation is a gross perversion of the legislative intent in enacting penal statutes. To deal with this problem a minority of courts have chosen to view the violation of penal

---

statutes as evidence of negligence in civil litigation. This approach will not be taken by this court. In view of the fairness and ease with which the rebuttable presumption standard can be applied, litigants will be better served if this approach is followed. An accurate statement of law adopted by this court, therefore, is that when a penal statute is adopted as the standard of care in a civil action for negligence, violation of the statute establishes a prima facie case of negligence. It is then up to the jury to determine whether the party who has violated the statute has established a legally sufficient excuse or justification for violating the statute. If such an excuse does exist, then the standard of care becomes that which is established by common law. (Reversed.)

Analysis:

What is the effect of a reasonable excuse or justification for violation of a penal statute which imposes a standard of care in civil actions? As this case indicates, there are three possible approaches. One approach is to view the violation of the statute as negligence per se without regard to any excuses or justifications. This is almost like a rule of strict liability, which does not take into consideration the circumstances surrounding each case. The second approach is to view the violation of the statute as merely evidence of negligence, therefore allowing the jury to find whether the person violating the statute did indeed fall below the acceptable standard of care. The third approach, and one which is adopted by the court in the instant case, is to view a violation of a statute as a rebuttable presumption of negligence, which is overcome only by positive and unequivocal evidence of reasonable excuse or justification. This approach is stricter than the second approach, but more lenient that the first, and allows the person accused of violating a statute to offer excuses and justifications for his/her violation. The question then goes to the jury as to whether the excuse is credible. If it is, then the statute is set aside and the jury must decide the issue of negligence based on common law standards of care.

■ CASE VOCABULARY

LAST CLEAR CHANCE: A defendant may be liable for injuries to a plaintiff (who is guilty of contributory negligence) even if defendant could have avoided injury by exercising ordinary care.

REBUTTABLE PRESUMPTION: An ordinary presumption which must, as a matter of law, be made once certain facts have been proved, and which is thus said to prove a prima facie conclusion; it may be rebutted or overcome through introduction of contrary evidence, but if it is not, it becomes conclusive.

Goddard v. Boston & Maine R.R. Co.

(Passenger) v. *(Railroad Company)*

179 Mass. 52, 60 N.E. 486 (1901)

IN AN ACTION IN NEGLIGENCE, THE PLAINTIFF HAS THE BURDEN OF ESTABLISHING SUFFICIENT FACTS THAT DEFENDANT HAS ENGAGED IN CONDUCT THAT IS NEGLIGENT

■ **INSTANT FACTS** Goddard (P) brought an action in negligence against Boston & Maine R.R. Co. (D) for injuries he suffered when he fell on a banana peel on the platform at the train station.

■ **BLACK LETTER RULE** In a negligence action, in order to avoid a directed verdict, the plaintiff must provide sufficient evidence from which reasonable jurors could infer that the defendant was engaged in negligent conduct and that his negligence caused the plaintiff's injury.

■ **PROCEDURAL BASIS**

Appeal in action in negligence for personal injuries.

■ **FACTS**

When stepping out of a train owned by Boston & Maine R.R. Co. (D), Goddard (P) slipped and fell on a banana peel that was on the platform. Goddard (P) sued Boston & Maine R.R. (D) for the injuries that he sustained as a result of his fall. The trial court directed a verdict in favor of Boston & Maine R.R. (D). Goddard (P) appeals.

■ **ISSUE**

In a negligence action, in order to prevent a directed verdict, must the plaintiff provide sufficient evidence from which reasonable jurors could infer that the defendant was engaged in negligent conduct and that his negligence caused the plaintiff's injury?

■ **DECISION AND RATIONALE**

(Holmes, C.J.) Yes. In a negligence action, in order to avoid a directed verdict, the plaintiff must provide sufficient evidence from which reasonable jurors could infer that the defendant was engaged in negligent conduct and that his negligence caused the plaintiff's injury. In this case, the banana skin upon which the plaintiff slipped may have been dropped within a minute by one of the passengers who was leaving the train. (Affirmed.)

Analysis:

Note that in the instant case the plaintiff simply stated that there was a banana peel on the platform. The plaintiff, however, presented no evidence as to how long the banana peel was there, who had dropped it there, and whether the defendants were aware of its presence. In fact, the plaintiff did not provide any evidence to support his claim that the defendants had engaged in conduct which is negligent. This case, as short as it may be, stands for an important proposition: in a negligence case, the plaintiff, at the outset of the case, has the burden of producing enough evidence to allow reasonable jurors to infer that the defendant was negligent and that his negligence resulted in the plaintiff's injury. The evidence sufficient to avoid a directed verdict is evidence which simply supports the plaintiff's position and is weighed by the jury; the evidence need not compel a certain conclusion or decision in favor of the plaintiff.

■ **CASE VOCABULARY**

CIRCUMSTANTIAL EVIDENCE: Evidence which is indirect; secondary fact(s) by which a principal fact may be rationally inferred.

Anjou v. Boston Elevated Railway Co.

(Passenger) v. *(Railroad Company)*
208 Mass. 273, 94 N.E. 386 (1911)

WHERE THE PLAINTIFF IN A NEGLIGENCE ACTION HAS INTRODUCED EVIDENCE SUFFICIENT TO SUPPORT AN INFERENCE OF NEGLIGENCE ON THE PART OF THE DEFENDANT, THE TRIAL COURT MAY NOT DIRECT A VERDICT IN FAVOR OF THE DEFENDANT

■ **INSTANT FACTS** Anjou (P) brought an action against Boston Elevated Railway Co. (D) for injuries suffered when Anjou (P) fell on a banana peel in Boston Elevated Railway's (D) train station.

■ **BLACK LETTER RULE** A directed verdict in favor of the defendant is not appropriate where the plaintiff has presented evidence sufficient to support an inference of negligence on the part of the defendant.

■ **PROCEDURAL BASIS**

Appeal in action for personal injury.

■ **FACTS**

Anjou (P), a passenger who had just gotten off one of Boston Elevated Railways Co.'s (D) cars, asked one of the railroad employees for directions to another car. While following the employee on a stairway, Anjou (P) slipped and fell on a banana peel and injured herself. Anjou (P) sued Boston Elevated Railway (D) in negligence. The banana peel on which Anjou (P) had fallen was described by several people as dry, black and dirty, as if "trampled over a good deal." Additionally, it was settled that it was the duty of the employees at the train station to remove objects on the platform that would interfere with the safety of the passengers. The trial court directed a verdict in favor of Boston Elevated Railway (D). Anjou (P) appeals.

■ **ISSUE**

Is a directed verdict in favor of the defendant appropriate where the plaintiff has presented evidence sufficient to support an inference of negligence on the part of the defendant?

■ **DECISION AND RATIONALE**

(Rugg, J.) No. A directed verdict in favor of the defendant is not appropriate where the plaintiff has presented evidence sufficient to support an inference of negligence on the part of the defendant. In this case, the inference might have been drawn from the appearance and condition of the banana peel that it had been on the platform for a long period of time, where it could have been seen and removed by a reasonably careful employee of the railroad. Thus, one can draw the conclusion that it was not dropped on the platform a moment before the passenger fell on it. Since it was the obligation of the defendant to ensure the safety of the passengers, and the condition of the platform did not seem safe, one can conclude that there was evidence of negligence on the part of the defendant. Thus, the evidence should have been submitted to the jury. (Judgment for plaintiff.)

Analysis:

Note that this case is a little different from *Goddard v. Boston & Maine R.R. Co.* In the latter case, the plaintiff simply introduced evidence that there was a banana peel on the platform owned by the defendants, and that he fell on it and injured himself. In the instant case, the plaintiff presented evidence that the banana peel on which she fell and injured himself was old, black and dirty, therefore, allowing the inference that it had been on the platform for a long time. Additionally, plaintiff presented evidence that the railroad employees had the duty of ensuring the safety of the passengers by keeping the platform in a safe condition. This evidence allows the inference that the defendant was negligent in not removing the banana peel which had been sitting on the platform. Thus, the appellate court is correct in ruling that a directed verdict in favor of the defendant was not appropriate. Also note that none of the evidence presented by the plaintiff is direct evidence. That is, the plaintiff has no direct evidence that the banana peel was sitting on the platform for a long time, or that the employees were negligent because they, in fact, did not see the banana peel. All this is inferred from circumstantial evidence: the fact that the peel was black and dirty implies that it was there for a long time; and the fact that the defendant's employees did not remove it implies that they were negligent.

■ CASE VOCABULARY

CIRCUMSTANTIAL EVIDENCE: Evidence which is indirect; secondary facts by which a principal fact may be rationally inferred.

Joye v. Great Atlantic and Pacific Tea Co.

(Customer) v. *(Supermarket Owner)*

405 F.2d 464 (4th Cir.1968)

IN A SLIP-AND-FALL CASE, CIRCUMSTANTIAL EVIDENCE MAY IMPOSE CONSTRUCTIVE KNOWL-
EDGE OF DANGEROUS CONDITIONS

■ **INSTANT FACTS** A customer who slipped and fell on a banana at a grocery store argued that the store should have known that the banana was on the floor.

■ **BLACK LETTER RULE** Actual or constructive knowledge of a dangerous condition, established through direct or circumstantial evidence, must be proven to impose liability for injuries caused by the condition.

■ **PROCEDURAL BASIS**

Appeal of denial of motion for judgment n.o.v. following verdict for damages resulting from dangerous condition.

■ **FACTS**

Willard Joye (P) slipped and fell on a banana in a supermarket owned by Great Atlantic and Pacific Tea Co. (A&P) (D). At trial Joye (P) offered no direct evidence as to how long the banana had been on the floor before the accident. The circumstantial evidence showed that the floor may not have been swept for as long as 35 minutes. Apparently no one saw the banana until after Joye (P) fell, at which time it was described as dark brown and dirty. The district court found that A&P (D) had constructive notice that the banana was on the floor, and that A&P (D) was negligent in leaving the banana on the floor. Thus, a verdict was reached in favor of Joye (P), and the court denied A&P's (D) motion for a judgment n.o.v. A&P (D) appealed.

■ **ISSUE**

Must a plaintiff present direct or circumstantial evidence of the defendant's knowledge of a dangerous condition in order to prove negligence?

■ **DECISION AND RATIONALE**

(Craven, J.) Yes. A plaintiff must present direct or circumstantial evidence to show the defendant's knowledge of a dangerous condition in order to prove negligence. In the instant action, Joye (P) presented no direct evidence as to how long the banana had been on the floor. There was no evidence that A&P (D) put the banana on the floor or had actual notice of its presence. Thus, Joye (P) should have shown through circumstantial evidence that A&P (D) had constructive knowledge of the banana. However, the circumstantial evidence was insufficient to allow a jury to determine whether the banana had been on the floor for 30 seconds or 3 days. Based on these uncertain facts, the jury could not have imposed constructive notice on A&P (D). Reversed and remanded.

Analysis:

This is one of three "banana peel" cases, all of which involve a defendant's knowledge of a dangerous condition. In the instant action, the evidence apparently was insufficient to establish that the banana had been on the floor for any particular period of time. Implicit in the opinion is that A&P (D) would not be liable if the banana had recently fallen on the floor. This makes a good deal of sense. The store owner should be liable only if, through the exercise of reasonable diligence, it could have discovered the fallen banana. Interestingly, however, the banana was dark brown and dirty, as in *Anjou.* In addition, the evidence showed that the floor had not been swept for as long as 35 minutes. It could be argued that A&P (D) failed to sweep or inspect the floor for a long period of time. A&P (D) certainly had a duty to inspect the floor, and perhaps the breach of this duty would be sufficient to prove negligence. Remember that the key to all of the cases is the concept of notice. A party must have actual or constructive notice of a dangerous condition in order to be liable for injuries caused by the condition.

■ CASE VOCABULARY

JUDGMENT N.O.V. A judgment notwithstanding the verdict; in other words, a judgment entered by the court that is contrary to the original verdict.

Ortega v. Kmart Corp.

(Customer) v. *(Retail Store)*

114 Cal.Rptr.2d 470, 26 Cal.4th 1200, 36 P.3d 11 (2001)

FAILURE TO INSPECT MAY CONSTITUTE CONSTRUCTIVE NOTICE OF A DANGEROUS CONDITION

Cha-ching!

stus.com

■ **INSTANT FACTS** While shopping in Kmart (D), Ortega (P) slipped and fell in a puddle of milk.

■ **BLACK LETTER RULE** Although a storeowner is not an insurer of the safety of its patrons, the owner does owe them a duty to exercise reasonable care in keeping the premises reasonably safe.

■ **PROCEDURAL BASIS**

Appeal to review a jury verdict for the plaintiff.

■ **FACTS**

Ortega (P) slipped on a puddle of milk while shopping at Kmart (D) and injured his knee. At the personal injury trial, Ortega (P) testified he did notice the puddle before he slipped but could not determine how long it had existed. Ortega (P) claimed that because Kmart (D) had failed to reasonably inspect the area, the jury could infer the puddle had existed for long enough for a Kmart (D) employee to discover it. Kmart (D) offered evidence that it trains all employees to look for and clean up any spills, usually every fifteen to thirty minutes. However, Kmart's (D) former store manager conceded that the puddle could have existed for up to two hours, because the store maintained no written inspection records. On the evidence, the jury returned a verdict for the plaintiff.

■ **ISSUE**

Does a plaintiff establish constructive notice of a dangerous condition by proving the owner's failure to reasonably inspect the premises, even though the exact duration of the condition is not known?

■ **DECISION AND RATIONALE**

(Chin, J.) Yes. "[A]lthough a store owner is not an insurer of the safety of its patrons, the owner does owe them a duty to exercise reasonable care in keeping the premises reasonably safe." An owner exercises ordinary care when it reasonably inspects areas open to the public with the care necessary in light of the risks. A court may not infer negligence by the existence of a dangerous condition and a resulting injury. However, actual notice of the condition is not required. Instead, where the evidence suggests that the condition existed for a sufficient time in which the owner should have reasonably noticed the condition, the owner has constructive notice of the condition. At all times, however, the plaintiff bears the burden of producing evidence to demonstrate the owner's constructive notice. When the evidence shows that an area was not inspected within a reasonable time, the plaintiff carries his burden and an inference of notice is permitted. Because the jury inferred Kmart's (D) constructive notice and failure to remedy the puddle, the verdict is affirmed.

Analysis:

A landowner's duties to the public extend beyond remedying known dangerous conditions. The notion of constructive notice places a duty upon landowners not only to correct those hazards known to exist, but to reasonably inspect the premises to discover such hazards. The concept of reasonableness does not require landowners to keep constant watch over every corner of their premises in all circumstances, so long as reasonable actions are taken to determine any dangers that may exist.

■ CASE VOCABULARY

ACTUAL NOTICE: Notice given directly to, or received personally by, a party.

CONSTRUCTIVE NOTICE: Notice arising by presumption of law from the existence of facts and circumstances that a party had a duty to take notice of, such as a registered deed or a pending lawsuit; notice presumed by law to have been acquired by a person and thus imputed to that person.

SLIP–AND–FALL CASE: A lawsuit brought by a plaintiff for injuries sustained in slipping and falling, usually on the defendant's property.

Jasko v. F.W. Woolworth Co.

(Patron) v. (Pizza Shop)

177 Colo. 418, 494 P.2d 839 (1972)

THE SUPREME COURT OF COLORADO HOLDS THAT WHERE THE EXISTENCE OF DANGEROUS CONDITIONS ON THE DEFENDANT'S PREMISES ARE EASILY FORESEEABLE, THE PLAINTIFF NEED NOT PROVE THAT THE DEFENDANT HAD NOTICE OF THE CONDITIONS

■ **INSTANT FACTS** Jasko (P) brought an action against F.W. Woolworth Co. (D) when she fell on a piece of pizza on the floor of the store owned by F.W. Woolworth (D) and injured herself.

■ **BLACK LETTER RULE** A plaintiff need not prove defendant's notice of the dangerous condition which has caused her injuries, when the dangerous condition is one which is continuous and easily foreseeable.

■ **PROCEDURAL BASIS**

Appeal in action for personal injury.

■ **FACTS**

Jasko (P) was injured when she slipped on a piece of pizza that was on the floor of F.W. Woolworth (D). Jasko (P) brought an action in negligence against Woolworth (D) to recover for her injuries. The trial court entered a judgment in favor of Woolworth (D) on the ground that Jasko (P) had failed to show that Woolworth had actual or constructive notice of the pizza on the floor of the store. Jasko (P) appeals contending that Woolworth's (D) method of selling pizza was one which created a dangerous situation, thus not requiring Jasko (P) to prove that Woolworth (D) was on notice of the condition.

■ **ISSUE**

Does a plaintiff have to prove defendant's notice of the dangerous condition which has caused her injuries when the dangerous condition is one which is continuous or easily foreseeable?

■ **DECISION AND RATIONALE**

(Groves, J.) No. A plaintiff need not prove defendant's notice of the dangerous condition which has caused her injuries when the dangerous condition is one which is continuous and easily foreseeable. The dangerous condition in this case was created by the defendant's method of sale, and the fact that the floors were constantly cleaned shows that the defendant knew of the condition. The defendant's method of selling pizza on wax paper created the reasonable probability that food will drop to the floor, thereby creating a dangerous condition. Therefore, in such a case the plaintiff need not prove that the defendant had notice of the condition. Proof of notice is required where the dangerous condition is out of the ordinary. In such cases the store owner is allowed reasonable time to discover and correct the condition. In this case, however, the dangerous conditions were continuous and easily foreseeable. Therefore, proof of notice on the part of the defendant was not necessary. (Reversed.)

Analysis:

This case is a deviation from the cases which we have already read and analyzed regarding the notice requirement. According to this case, certain businesses should be on constant notice of the dangerous

---

conditions which are inherent in the business itself. In such cases, the plaintiff need not prove actual or constructive notice of the dangerous conditions on the part of the defendant. According to this court, proof of dangerous conditions is required only when the condition is one that is out of the ordinary and seldom associated with the business.

■ **CASE VOCABULARY**

ACTUAL NOTICE: The direct, positive knowledge of a fact in question or information sufficient to put a prudent person on inquiry as to such fact (which includes those things of which one has express information and which reasonably diligent inquiry would have disclosed).

CIRCUMSTANTIAL EVIDENCE: Evidence which is indirect; secondary facts by which a principal fact may be rationally inferred.

CONSTRUCTIVE NOTICE: That notice which is presumed by law to have been acquired.

H.E. Butt Groc. Co. v. Resendez

(Grocery Store Owner) v. *(Customer)*
988 S.W.2d 218 (Tex.1999)

A GRAPE SAMPLE DISPLAY DOES NOT CREATE AN UNREASONABLE RISK OF HARM

DANGER! GRAPES!

stus.com

■ **INSTANT FACTS** Resendez (P) slipped and fell near the defendant's grape display designed for public sampling and sued the grocer.

■ **BLACK LETTER RULE** To establish a premises liability claim, the plaintiff must establish that the defendant had actual or constructive notice of a dangerous condition creating an unreasonable risk of harm and the defendant's failure to use reasonable care to minimize the harm, which caused the plaintiff's injuries.

■ **PROCEDURAL BASIS**

Appeal to review a decision of the Texas Court of Appeals affirming a jury verdict for the plaintiff.

■ **FACTS**

Resendez (P) slipped and fell near two grape displays while shopping in an H.E. Butt Grocery Co. (D) store. Resendez (P) sued, claiming that the displays themselves created an unreasonable risk of harm to customers. The jury agreed, returning a verdict for Resendez (P). On appeal, the Texas Court of Appeals affirmed.

■ **ISSUE**

Does the mere display of produce for customer sampling constitute an unreasonable risk of harm to customers?

■ **DECISION AND RATIONALE**

(Per curiam.) No. To establish her claim, Resendez (P) must establish that the defendant had actual or constructive notice of a dangerous condition creating an unreasonable risk of harm and the defendant's failure to use reasonable care to minimize the harm, which caused her injuries. The mere display of produce, however, for customer sampling, does not create an unreasonable risk of harm to customers. One grape display contained wrapped grapes for customer purchase, while the other contained loose grapes for customer sampling, with a three-inch railing. Floor mats were placed below the displays for customer safety, and cones were used to alert customers of the displays. There was no evidence that the manner of the display created an unreasonable risk of harm. Reversed.

Analysis:

Under different circumstances, the defendant may have been liable for the plaintiff's injuries in this case. The court's holding merely establishes that the display did not per se create an unreasonable risk of harm to the public. Had the display been constructed in such a way that customers were placed at risk and not warned of the potential danger, the defendant would likely have been liable.

■ CASE VOCABULARY

PREMISES LIABILITY: A landowner's or landholder's tort liability for conditions or activities on the premises.

Byrne v. Boadle

(Injured Pedestrian) v. *(Flour Shop)*
2 H. & C. 722, 159 Eng.Rep. 299 (Ex.1863)

UNDER THE DOCTRINE OF RES IPSA LOQUITUR, WHERE A PLAINTIFF'S INJURY WOULD NOT HAVE OCCURRED BUT FOR SOMEONE'S NEGLIGENCE AND THE INSTRUMENTALITY WHICH CAUSED THE INJURY WAS IN DEFENDANT'S CONTROL, NEGLIGENCE ON THE PART OF THE DEFENDANT IS PRESUMED

■ **INSTANT FACTS** Byrne (P) brought action in negligence against Boadle (D) for injuries suffered when a barrel of flour rolled out of Boadle's (D) shop and fell on Byrne (P).

■ **BLACK LETTER RULE** A plaintiff need not provide evidence of negligence on the part of the defendant when the mere fact of the accident or injury having occurred is evidence of negligence of the defendant.

■ **PROCEDURAL BASIS**

Appeal in action for negligence.

■ **FACTS**

Byrne (P) was walking in a public street past Boadle's (D) shop when a barrel of flour fell upon him from a window above the shop and seriously injured Byrne (P). The latter did not present any other evidence to show that Boadle (D) or his employees were negligent. The trial court declared a non-suit. Byrne (P) appeals.

■ **ISSUE**

Does a plaintiff need to provide evidence of negligence on the part of the defendant when the mere fact of the accident or injury having occurred is evidence of negligence of the defendant?

■ **DECISION AND RATIONALE**

(Pollock, J.) No. A plaintiff need not provide evidence of negligence on the part of the defendant when the mere fact of the accident or injury having occurred is evidence of negligence of the defendant. It is wrong to lay down a rule that in no case can a presumption of negligence arise from the fact of the accident. A barrel could not fall out of a warehouse without some negligence. In this case, it is apparent that the barrel of flour was in the custody of the defendant who occupied the premises, and who is liable for the acts of his employees. It is this court's opinion that the falling of the barrel itself is prima facie evidence of negligence. However, if there are facts inconsistent with the presumption of negligence, it is up to the defendant to prove them.

Analysis:

This case is the first illustration of the doctrine of Res Ipsa Loquitur (RIL). Translated literally, RIL means "the thing speaks for itself." There are circumstances where it is nearly impossible for a plaintiff to prove that his/her injuries are a result of the defendant's negligence. In such cases, the plaintiff may succeed in taking his/her case to the jury by showing that 1) the injury would not have occurred, but for someone's negligence, 2) the instrumentality causing the injury was in control of the defendant, and 3) the plaintiff was not contributorily negligent in bringing about the injury (this aspect of RIL is not explored in the instant case). In other words, RIL stands for the proposition that the mere occurrence of certain accidents or injuries is evidence of the defendant's negligence. In such cases, the plaintiff need not prove directly that the defendant was in fact negligent in his/her conduct. Negligence of the defendant is presumed (given that the other two elements are satisfied). After the plaintiff establishes the three elements of RIL, it is up to the defendant to prove that he was not negligent. It is important to remember that RIL is another way of relieving the plaintiff of the burden of directly proving that the defendant's conduct fell below the accepted standard of care. The other method which we explored was in situations where the defendant's conduct was in violation of a statute which imposed a fixed standard of care on individuals. Note that RIL may not be used when direct evidence of negligence exists.

■ CASE VOCABULARY

NONSUITED: Termination of a case which does not adjudicate issues on the merits (i.e., plaintiff cannot prove a case).

RES IPSA LOQUITUR: Directly translated, "the thing speaks for itself," a rule whereby the negligence of the alleged wrongdoer may be inferred from the mere fact that the accident happened, provided: 1) the occurrence is the kind of thing that ordinarily does not happen without negligence; 2) the occurrence must have been caused by an agency or instrumentality within the exclusive control of the defendant; and 3) the occurrence was not due to contribution or voluntary action by the plaintiff.

McDougald v. Perry

(Injured) v. *(Trailer Puller)*
716 So.2d 783 (Fla.1998)

THE DOCTRINE OF RES IPSA LOQUITOR IS ALIVE AND WELL

■ **INSTANT FACTS** A spare tire bounced from under a trailer injuring the driver following the trailer.

■ **BLACK LETTER RULE** Res ipsa loquitur provides an inference of negligence when the accident is the type that does not occur without negligence and the defendant is in control of the circumstances.

■ **PROCEDURAL BASIS**

Appeal from reversal of trial court's instruction on res ipsa loquitur.

■ **FACTS**

McDougald (P) was driving behind a tractor-trailer driven by Perry (D). As Perry (D) drove over some railroad tracks, a large spare tire came out of its cradle underneath the trailer and fell to the ground. As the trailer drove over the spare tire, it bounced up and into the windshield of McDougald's (P) Jeep. The spare tire was secured in its cradle by a chain wrapped around the tire. The chain was attached to the body of the trailer by a nut and bolt. Perry (D) testified at trial that he inspected the chain, but admitted he did not check every link in the chain.

■ **ISSUE**

Is it proper to assert that a particular accident could not have occurred in the absence of some negligence?

■ **DECISION AND RATIONALE**

(Wells, J.) Yes. The trial court correctly instructed the jury on the doctrine of res ipsa loquitur. Res ipsa loquitur is a Latin phrase meaning "the thing speaks for itself." It is a rule of evidence that permits, but does not require, an inference of negligence in certain circumstances. It can provide an injured plaintiff with an inference of negligence where there is no direct proof of negligence. Here, McDougald (P) must show that the instrumentality causing the injury was under Perry's (D) exclusive control, and that the accident is one that would not ordinarily occur without the negligence of the one in control. An injury alone does not ordinarily indicate negligence. There are many types of accidents which occur without the fault of anyone. However, in rare instances, an injury can be such that it would not occur without negligence. Expert testimony is not necessary to establish that this is the type of accident that does not occur absent some negligence. In many cases, common knowledge is sufficient to make this showing. Furthermore, McDougald (P) does not have to eliminate all other possible causes of the accident. He merely has to show that on the whole it is more likely than not that there was negligence associated with the cause of the accident. Therefore, we conclude that the spare tire escaping from the trailer is the type of accident, as a matter of general knowledge, that would not occur but for the lack of reasonable care by the person who had control of the tire. Reversed and remanded with directions to reinstate the jury's verdict in favor of McDougald (P).

■ CONCURRENCE

(Anstead, J.) I write separately to note that an old appellate opinion written in 1863 is still useful today. The case of Byrne v. Boadle involved a barrel falling from a window of the defendant's flour business and striking plaintiff. The court applied res ipsa loquitur and found that such an accident does not occur without negligence. The court noted that it would be impossible for the plaintiff to ascertain the exact cause of the accident. The fact of the barrel falling is prima facie evidence of negligence, and it is for the defendant to prove otherwise. We cannot improve upon this explanation today. The common law tradition is alive and well.

Analysis:

Res ipsa loquitur is a useful tool for plaintiffs to allow an inference of negligence where they cannot prove exactly what caused the accident. Another type of case where res ipsa loquitur is used is airplane accidents in good weather. In the present case, note that Perry (D) argued res ipsa loquitur was not proper because McDougald (P) failed to produce any expert testimony that this was the type of accident that does not occur without negligence. The court rejected this finding that it was a matter of common knowledge. Is this really the case? What other causes, besides Perry's (D) negligence, might have caused the accident. What about a manufacturing defect in the chain or a design defect of the tire cradle? It probably would not be fair to McDougald (P) to require him to rule out all of these other possible causes. Is it really more likely that the accident was caused by Perry's (D) negligence rather than some other cause? It seems that expert testimony might be useful on this point. However, if an expert is involved, it could be argued that it is not really res ipsa loquitur anymore because the "thing" is not "speaking for itself."

Larson v. St. Francis Hotel

(Injured Pedestrian) v. *(Hotel)*

83 Cal.App.2d 210, 188 P.2d 513 (1948)

IN A CASE OF NEGLIGENCE BASED ON RES IPSA LOQUITUR, IN DECIDING A NONSUIT VERDICT IN FAVOR OF THE DEFENDANT THE COURT MUST CONSTRUE THE EVIDENCE IN THE LIGHT MOST FAVORABLE TO THE PLAINTIFF AND MOST STRONGLY AGAINST THE DEFENDANT

■ **INSTANT FACTS** Larson (P) sued St. Francis Hotel (D) for injuries suffered when Larson (P) was struck by an armchair flying out of St. Francis Hotel's (D) window.

■ **BLACK LETTER RULE** The doctrine of res ipsa loquitur does not apply in a case where the plaintiff's injury could be attributable to more than one cause, some of which are not within the exclusive control and management of the defendant.

■ **PROCEDURAL BASIS**

Appeal in action for recovery of damages for personal injury.

■ **FACTS**

Larson (P), while walking past St. Francis Hotel (D), was struck by a heavy armchair and received injuries for which she brought an action against owners of St. Francis Hotel (D). No one saw the chair before it hit Larson (P), and there was no identification on the chair as belonging to St. Francis (D). Larson (P), after presenting the above facts and evidence regarding the extent of injuries, rested her case, relying on the doctrine of res ipsa loquitur. The trial court entered a nonsuit verdict in favor of St. Francis (D). Larson (P) appeals.

■ **ISSUE**

Does the doctrine of res ipsa loquitur apply in a case where the plaintiff's injury could be attributable to more than one cause, some of which are not within the exclusive control and management of the defendant?

■ **DECISION AND RATIONALE**

(Bray, J.) No. The doctrine of res ipsa loquitur does not apply in a case where the plaintiff's injury could be attributable to more than one cause, some of which are not within the exclusive control and management of the defendant. According to *Gerhart v. Southern California Gas Co.*, in order to rely on the doctrine of res ipsa loquitur the plaintiff must prove 1) that there was an accident; 2) that the instrumentality causing the accident was under the exclusive control and management of the defendant; 3) that the accident was such that it would not happen absent negligence on the part of the defendant. Thus, the doctrine only applies where the cause of injury is under the exclusive control of the defendant, not where the accident may have been attributable to one of several causes, for some of which the defendant is not responsible. Where it appears that the accident resulting in the injury was caused by one of two causes for which the defendant is responsible for one but not for the other, the plaintiff must fail, if the evidence does not show that the injury was the result of the former cause. Applying this reasoning, this court concludes the doctrine does not apply in this case. A hotel does not have exclusive control, actual or potential, of its furniture. Guests of the hotel have at least partial control.

Additionally, one cannot conclude that the accident would not have occurred absent negligence on the part of the defendant. On the contrary, the accident could have been the fault of a hotel guest. This is an accident which could happen despite the fact that the defendants used reasonable care and were completely free of negligence. (Affirmed.)

Analysis:

The doctrine of res ipsa loquitur, a natural extension of the tort of negligence, is based on circumstantial evidence. The doctrine allows an inference of negligence from the fact that an injury occurred, provided certain conditions are met. First, the injury must be the type that would not have occurred unless *someone* was negligent. This element was met in the instant case, since an injury certainly occurred and since chairs do not normally fall from the sky absent some negligent conduct. In addition, the injured party must not have contributed to causing the injury. This element is also met, as Larson (P) was simply walking on the street near the hotel. However, in order to hold the Hotel (D) liable, Larson (P) must also prove that only the Hotel (D) could have caused the injury. This element makes logical sense. It would be unfair to hold the Hotel (D) liable simply because that party *could* have caused the injury. But perhaps this final element is overly strict. Shouldn't it be enough for Larson (P) to prove that it was more probable than not that the Hotel (D) controlled the chair which caused the injury? On the other hand, perhaps the rationale for the strict application of this element makes sense, given the generous inferences allowed by the other elements of the doctrine. And remember that Larson (P) could still prevail under a basic negligence analysis, provided Larson (P) could show that the Hotel (D) breached its duty of reasonable care, e.g., by installing windows that could be opened wide enough to hurl a chair out of the window. Of course, based on the language of this opinion, the success of this approach seems doubtful.

■ CASE VOCABULARY

RES IPSA LOQUITUR: Latin, meaning "the thing speaks for itself," a rule whereby the negligence of the alleged wrongdoer may be inferred from the mere fact that the accident happened, provided 1) the occurrence is the type of thing which ordinarily does not occur without negligence; 2) the occurrence must have been caused by an agency or instrumentality within the exclusive control of the defendant; and 3) the occurrence was not due to contribution or voluntary action by the plaintiff.

Ybarra v. Spangard

(Patient) v. *(Physician)*

25 Cal.2d 486, 154 P.2d 687 (1944)

THE DOCTRINE OF RES IPSA LOQUITUR MAY APPLY WHERE MORE THAN ONE DEFENDANT HAS CAUSED THE PLAINTIFF'S INJURY

■ **INSTANT FACTS** Ybarra (P) sued Spangard (D) and others for injuries to his arm, suffered after Spangard (D) and others performed an appendectomy on Ybarra (P).

■ **BLACK LETTER RULE** Res ipsa loquitur may apply to situations where more than one defendant is the cause of the plaintiff's injury and the various instrumentalities which caused the plaintiff's injuries were in control of the defendants in question.

■ **PROCEDURAL BASIS**

Appeal from judgment of nonsuit.

■ **FACTS**

Ybarra (P) was diagnosed with appendicitis by Dr. Tilley (D), who made arrangements for an appendectomy to be performed by Dr. Spangard (D) at Dr. Swift's (D) hospital. Ybarra (P) was anesthetized by an employee of Dr. Swift (D) before the operation. After the surgery, Ybarra (P) felt pain in his right arm and shoulder which did not exist before the surgery. Ybarra (P) received treatment from Dr. Tilley (D), but the condition did not improve. Ybarra (P) sued Spangard (D) and the other doctors, claiming that the evidence presented was sufficient to establish negligence on the basis of res ipsa loquitur. The trial court entered judgments of nonsuit on behalf of Spangard (D) and the other doctors. Ybarra (P) appeals. Spangard (D) and others defend on the ground that there are several defendants in the case and there is a division of responsibility, and that since the injury could have resulted from the actions of any of the defendants, the doctrine could not be properly applied. Additionally, Spangard (D) and others defend on the ground that there are several instrumentalities that may have caused the injury and no showing is made as to which caused the injury.

■ **ISSUE**

May res ipsa loquitur be applied to situations where more than one defendant is the cause of the plaintiff's injury and the various instrumentalities which caused the plaintiff's injuries were in control of the defendants in question?

■ **DECISION AND RATIONALE**

(Gibson, C.J.) Yes. Res ipsa loquitur may apply to situations where more than one defendant is the cause of the plaintiff's injury and the various instrumentalities which caused the plaintiff's injuries were in the control of the defendants in question. In this case, the condition that the injury must not be due to the plaintiff's actions is fully satisfied based on the evidence in question. Also, this is a condition that would not occur ordinarily absent someone's negligence. This is not a case of negligent mistreatment, but one where a healthy part of the plaintiff's body is injured. Under such circumstances, the inference of negligence is raised and it is up to the defendant to explain the unusual result. Defendants here claim that the plaintiff has not shown an injury caused by an instrumentality under a defendant's control because he has not shown which of the several instrumentalities with which he came into contact caused his injury, and because he has not shown exclusive control by any defendant over any particular instrumentality which caused his injury. Also, the defendants claim that some of them were not employees of other defendants and did not stand in any relationship from which liability in tort would follow. This court is of the opinion that neither the number nor the relationship among the defendants alone determines the application of res ipsa loquitur. Any defendant who negligently injured the plaintiff would be liable; the employers would be liable for the negligence of the employees and the doctor in charge of the operation would be liable for the negligence of his temporary employees. In this case, the patient was anesthetized during the entire operation. Therefore, it is unreasonable for the defendants to insist that the plaintiff identify the person who did the negligent act which caused his injury. The number of persons in whose care the patient is left is not a reason for denying him an opportunity for recovery for his injuries. Thus, where a plaintiff receives injuries while unconscious and in the course of medical treatment, all those defendants who had control over instrumentalities which may have caused the injury meet the inference of negligence. (Reversed.)

Analysis:

Although quite fair in its result, this case seems to put the burden of proof on the defendant. Here, as we have seen, there were several defendants and several instrumentalities which could have caused the plaintiff's injuries. The plaintiff did not present evidence that the defendants were in exclusive control of the instrumentalities that caused his injury. However, the court indicated that this is not necessary where the court can be certain that at some point each defendant was in exclusive control of the instrumentality that caused the plaintiff's injury (although the plaintiff cannot prove which defendant and at which point because the plaintiff was unconscious). Thus, it appears that the court in this case departs from the "exclusive control" requirement of res ipsa loquitur and applies a broader view where all the defendants were in control at some time. As long as the plaintiff can prove that each defendant controlled the instrumentality causing his negligence at some point, it is up to the defendants to prove that they were not liable. Note that this interpretation of the rule applies where there are multiple defendants and they are preferably in a legal or professional relationship with one another. In such situations, it seems that the plaintiff's burden of proof is much lighter. However, note that the result may not be unfair, because under circumstances, such as the one in the instant case where the plaintiff is unconscious during the course of the operation, it is nearly impossible for him to determine exactly which doctor was in charge of what.

■ CASE VOCABULARY

EN MASSE: As a whole group.

NEGLIGENCE: Failure to exercise that degree of care which a person of ordinary prudence (a reasonable person) would exercise under the same circumstances; conduct which falls below the standard established by law for the protection of others against unreasonable risk of harm.

NONSUIT: Judgment rendered against a plaintiff who fails to proceed to trial or is unable to prove his case. Since the adjudication is made when the plaintiff has simply failed to provide evidence sufficient to make out a case, it does not decide the merits of the plaintiff's case.

Sullivan v. Crabtree

(Parents of Decedent) v. *(Driver)*
36 Tenn.App. 469, 258 S.W.2d 782 (1953)

COURT OF APPEALS OF TENNESSEE HOLDS THAT WHERE EVIDENCE OF NEGLIGENCE IS NOT EXTREMELY STRONG, RES IPSA LOQUITUR MERELY PERMITS THE JURY TO CHOOSE THE INFERENCE OF THE DEFENDANT'S NEGLIGENCE IN PREFERENCE TO OTHER INFERENCES

■ **INSTANT FACTS** The Sullivans (P), parents of the decedent, brought an action against Crabtree (D), the driver of a motor truck, for the death of the decedent while the latter was riding as a passenger in Crabtree's motor truck.

■ **BLACK LETTER RULE** Where a plaintiff establishes the prima facie case for defendant's negligence based on res ipsa loquitur, the court must not always as a matter of law enter a verdict for the plaintiff.

■ **PROCEDURAL BASIS**

Appeal in action for recovery of damages.

■ **FACTS**

The Sullivans (P) brought an action against Crabtree (D) for the death of their son, a passenger in Crabtree's (D) truck who was killed when the truck swerved off the highway and overturned. The evidence at trial suggested that Crabtree's (D) truck suddenly swerved when it was passed by another truck. It overturned down a steep cliff and crushed the decedent to death. Crabtree (D) testified that there was some loose gravel on the road, that he may have lost control of the truck when the other vehicle passed him, and that his brakes or other mechanical devices on the truck may have broken down, causing him to lose control. The jury at the trial court entered a verdict in Crabtree's (D) favor. The Sullivans (P) appeal and, relying on the doctrine of res ipsa loquitur, claim that the defendant's negligence was, as a matter of law, the cause of the decedent's death and that there was no evidence supporting a verdict for Crabtree (D).

■ **ISSUE**

Where a plaintiff establishes the prima facie case for defendant's negligence based on res ipsa loquitur, must the court always, as a matter of law, enter a verdict for the plaintiff?

■ **DECISION AND RATIONALE**

(Felts, J.) No. Where a plaintiff establishes the prima facie case for defendant's negligence based on res ipsa loquitur, the court must not always, as a matter of law, enter a verdict for the plaintiff. In this case, the plaintiffs insist that the facts of this case brought it within the rule of res ipsa loquitur requiring a finding of negligence in the absence of an explanation disproving negligence. A case of res ipsa loquitur does not differ from an ordinary case of circumstantial evidence; it is a common sense appraisal of the probative value of the evidence. While the doctrine does not generally apply to motor vehicle accidents, it applies to this case where the circumstances causing the accident were within the driver's control and the accident was such as does not ordinarily occur without negligence. Thus, in such cases where a vehicle for no apparent cause goes off the road, the normal inference is that the driver was negligent. However, while the evidence presented made a case of res ipsa loquitur, this court is not of the opinion that the jury was required to make an inference of negligence. The application of res ipsa loquitur could give rise to three procedural possibilities: 1) It warrants an inference of negligence which the jury may or may not choose to draw; or 2) it raises a presumption of negligence which requires the jury to find negligence if the defendant does not produce evidence sufficient to rebut the presumption; or 3) it raises a presumption of negligence and shifts the burden of proof to the defendant, requiring him to prove by a preponderance of evidence that the injury was not caused by his negligence. The procedural effect of the doctrine varies depending on the facts and evidence in each case. In exceptional cases, the inference of negligence may be so strong as to require a verdict for the plaintiff. In ordinary cases such as the instant case, however, the doctrine simply makes a case for the jury to choose a reasonable inference. In this case the jury could reasonably conclude that the cause of the accident was from the brakes of the truck giving away, and due to no fault of the defendant. (Affirmed.)

Analysis:

Note that this case deals with the procedural effects of the doctrine of res ipsa loquitur (RIL). So far we have dealt with the elements of RIL and the type of cases in which RIL applies; now we deal with the effect of RIL on the procedural posture of the case. As the instant case suggests, where a plaintiff attempts to impose liability on a defendant based on the RIL three procedural results are possible: 1) RIL simply creates an inference of negligence which the jury may or may not choose to draw; or 2) RIL raises a presumption of negligence, requiring a finding o?? negligence if the defendant does not produce evidence sufficient to rebut the presumption; or 3) RIL raises the presumption of negligence and shifts the burden of proof on the defendant to prove that his/her negligence did not cause the plaintiff's injury. The first view is the view that is held by most courts. It simply shows that the plaintiff has met its burden of production of evidence and allows the case to go to the jury. Some courts adhere to the second view. Under this view, the application of RIL raises a presumption of negligence, shifting the burden of production onto the defendant. Thus, after the plaintiff has established the elements of RIL, it is up to the defendant to produce evidence rebutting the presumption of negligence. Otherwise the defendant will lose. Sometimes the evidence presented by the plaintiff is so strong that it requires a verdict in favor of the plaintiff as a matter of law; this means that reasonable minds could not come to any other result in light of the evidence produced by the plaintiff. This is the third procedural effect of RIL. In such cases, the defendant has the burden of not only producing evidence to rebut plaintiff's evidence, but also to prove that the defendant was not negligent, or that the defendant's negligence did not cause the plaintiff's injury. This means that the application of RIL shifts the burden of proof on the defendant. Note that a minority of courts hold that the procedural effect of RIL is to shift the burden of proof to the defendant.

■ CASE VOCABULARY

COGENCY: Convincing power.

INFERENCE: A deduction from the facts given which is usually less certain but which may be sufficient to support a finding of fact; a process of reasoning by which a fact or proposition sought to be established is deduced as a logical consequence from other facts, or a state of facts already proved or admitted.

PRESUMPTION: A rule of law which requires the assumption of a fact from another fact or set of facts; term which indicates that certain weight is accorded by law to a given evidentiary fact, which weight is heavy enough to require the production of further evidence to overcome the assumption thereby established.

CHAPTER FIVE

Causation in Fact

Perkins v. Texas and New Orleans R. Co.

Instant Facts: Perkins (P), widow of the decedent, sought damages for the death of her husband caused when the Texas and New Orleans R. Co.'s (D) train struck the car in which the decedent was riding.

Black Letter Rule: Negligence is the cause in fact of injury to another if it is a substantial factor in causing the harm.

Reynolds v. Texas & Pac. Ry. Co.

Instant Facts: Reynolds (P) and his wife sought damages against Texas & Pac. Ry. Co. (D) for injuries suffered when the wife (P) fell down the stairs at the railroad station.

Black Letter Rule: Where the negligence of a defendant greatly increases the chances of an accident giving rise to the plaintiff's injury, the possibility that the accident could have happened without the negligence does not break the chain of causation.

Gentry v. Douglas Hereford Ranch, Inc.

Instant Facts: A man at a ranch stumbled and fell while carrying a rifle. The fall caused the rifle to fire and shoot a woman in the head.

Black Letter Rule: Evidence that defendant's conduct was a cause in fact of the accident must be offered to make a negligence case.

Kramer Service, Inc. v. Wilkins

Instant Facts: Wilkins (P) brought an action against Kramer Services (D) for injuries suffered when a piece of glass from a door in Kramer Services' (D) hotel fell on Wilkins' (P) forehead.

Black Letter Rule: In order to impose liability on a defendant, it is not sufficient that the plaintiff prove that the defendant's negligence and the plaintiff's injury co-existed or that the injury came after the negligent conduct of the defendant.

Herskovits v. Group Health Cooperative of Puget Sound

Instant Facts: The estate of Herskovits (P) brought an action in professional negligence against Group Health Cooperative of Puget Sound (D) ("Puget") as a result of which the decedent's chance of survival was reduced by 14%.

Black Letter Rule: An action in negligence can be maintained where probable reduction in the decedent's chance for survival can be proven, even though the decedent would not have lived to normal life expectancy.

Daubert v. Merrell Dow Pharmaceuticals, Inc.

Instant Facts: Daubert (P) and Schuller (P) sued Merrell Dow Pharmaceuticals, Inc. (D) ("Dow") alleging that their birth defects had been caused by their mothers' ingestion of a drug marketed by Dow (D).

Black Letter Rule: The Federal Rules of Evidence do not require "general acceptance" of a scientific technique in the scientific community as an absolute prerequisite to admissibility of expert witness testimony.

Hill v. Edmonds

Instant Facts: Hill (P), a passenger in Edmonds' (D) car, brought an action in negligence against Edmonds (D) and Bragoli (D) for injuries suffered when Edmonds' (D) car collided with Bragoli's (D) truck, which was parked in the road.

Black Letter Rule: Where separate acts of negligence combine to produce a single injury, each tortfeasor is liable for the entire result even though his act alone may not have caused the result.

Anderson v. Minneapolis, St. P. & S. St. M. Ry. Co.

Instant Facts: Anderson (P), a property owner, sued Minneapolis, St. P. & S. St. M. Ry. Co. (D) ("Railroad") for causing a fire which burned and damaged Anderson's (P) property.

Black Letter Rule: Where a plaintiff is injured by the negligent conduct of more than one tortfeasor, each is independently liable if it was a substantial factor in bringing about the plaintiff's injury.

Summers v. Tice

Instant Facts: Summers (P) sued Tice (D) and Simonson (D) for injuries sustained by a bullet negligently shot from Tice (D) or Simonson (D).

Black Letter Rule: Where two defendants are negligent toward the plaintiff, but only one defendant's negligence has caused the plaintiff's injury, the plaintiff may recover from both defendants even though the plaintiff is unable to show which defendant actually caused the plaintiff's injury.

Sindell v. Abbott Laboratories

Instant Facts: Sindell (P) sued Abbot Laboratories (D) and four other drug manufacturers, alleging that Sindell's (P) cancer was the result of Sindell's (P) mother's consumption during pregnancy of a drug manufactured by Abbot (D) and the other laboratories.

Black Letter Rule: Where more than two defendants have negligently produced a drug causing the plaintiff's injury, the latter may recover from the defendants even though the plaintiff does not prove which defendant's drug was the direct cause of the plaintiff's injury.

Perkins v. Texas and New Orleans R. Co.

(Decedent's Widow) v. *(Train)*

243 La. 829, 147 So.2d 646 (1962)

NEGLIGENCE IS NOT ACTIONABLE UNLESS IT IS THE CAUSE IN FACT OF THE HARM FOR WHICH RECOVERY IS SOUGHT

■ **INSTANT FACTS** Perkins (P), widow of the decedent, sought damages for the death of her husband caused when the Texas and New Orleans Ry. Co.'s (D) train struck the car in which the decedent was riding.

■ **BLACK LETTER RULE** Negligence is the cause in fact of injury to another if it is a substantial factor in causing the harm.

■ **PROCEDURAL BASIS**

Appeal in action for recovery of damages.

■ **FACTS**

Perkins (P), widow of the decedent, sought damages for the death of her husband, caused when the Texas and New Orleans R. Co.'s (D) train crashed into the car in which the decedent was riding. The train stuck the car at the railroad crossing. The evidence suggests that the railroad company had installed a swinging red light and a bell at the railroad crossing in order to warn the public of the approaching train. It was also established that the speed of the train was 37 miles per hour which is 12 miles in excess of the permitted speed limit for the train, and that violation of the speed limit was in itself evidence of negligence. The trial court ruled in favor of Perkins (P). The Court of Appeals affirmed. The railroad company appeals.

■ **ISSUE**

Is negligence the cause in fact of injury to another if it is a substantial factor in causing the harm?

■ **DECISION AND RATIONALE**

(Sanders, J.) Yes. Negligence is the cause in fact of injury to another if it is a substantial factor in causing the harm. In this case, the question is whether the excessive speed of the train was the cause in fact of the decedent's death. The excessive speed would be a substantial factor if the collision would not have occurred without it. On the other hand, if the collision would have occurred regardless of the speed of the train, then it was not a substantial factor. In this case, the testimony of the train engineer and other corroborating evidence suggests that even if the train was going at 25 miles per hour, which was the permitted speed, he would not have been able to stop the train in time to avoid the accident. Additionally, it is important to determine the speed of the car and the distance that it would have had to travel to clear the tracks. However, the evidence here is in hopeless conflict. The plaintiff, however, contends that had the train been going more slowly, the collision might not have occurred. This line of reasoning, however, is not supported by the evidence in the case, and the record does not contain any facts from which a reasonable inference of causation can be drawn based on the plaintiff's theory. On the contrary, it appears that based on the evidence, the accident would have occurred regardless of the excessive speed of the train. Therefore, the speed of the train was not a substantial factor in bringing about the death of the decedent. (Reversed.)

Analysis:

In order to prove a case in negligence, the plaintiff has the burden of proving all the elements of negligence. So far, we have seen two of the elements: 1) duty owed by the defendant to the plaintiff, and 2) breach of the duty by act or omission of the defendant (i.e., negligent conduct). The third element that the plaintiff needs to prove is causation. There are two types of causation: 1) cause in fact and 2) legal cause. This case deals with causation in fact. Simply stated, causation in fact is "but for" causation. That is, but for the defendant's negligent conduct, the harm to plaintiff would not have occurred. The defendant's conduct must be, in fact, the cause of the plaintiff's injury. Note that the negligent conduct of the defendant need not be the only cause of the injury, but it must be a substantial factor in bringing about the injury. Thus, it is not enough to prove that the defendant's conduct was negligent. The plaintiff must also prove that the defendant's negligent conduct was the cause of the plaintiff's injury.

■ CASE VOCABULARY

PROXIMATE: Immediate, as in a chain of events, causes or effects.

SINE QUA NON: That without which the thing cannot be; in tort law, this phrase refers to the act of the defendant without which there would be no injury to the plaintiff.

Reynolds v. Texas & Pac. Ry. Co.

(Injured Passenger) v. *(Railroad Co.)*
37 La.Ann.694 (1885)

THE CHAIN OF CAUSATION BETWEEN THE PLAINTIFF'S INJURY AND THE DEFENDANT'S NEGLI-GENCE IS NOT BROKEN BY THE MERE POSSIBILITY THAT AN ACCIDENT WITHOUT THE DEFEN-DANT'S NEGLIGENCE COULD HAVE LED TO THE SAME RESULT

■ **INSTANT FACTS** Reynolds (P) and his wife sought damages against Texas & Pac. Ry. Co. (D) for injuries suffered when the wife (P) fell down the stairs at the railroad station.

■ **BLACK LETTER RULE** Where the negligence of a defendant greatly increases the chances of an accident giving rise to the plaintiff's injury, the possibility that the accident could have happened without the negligence does not break the chain of causation.

■ PROCEDURAL BASIS

Appeal in tort action for damages.

■ FACTS

Mrs. Reynolds (P), while rushing to get to the train, fell down the unlit steps at Texas & Pac. Ry. Co's (D) station and suffered serious injuries. Reynolds (P) and her husband brought an action against the railroad company for the injuries suffered. The trial court, without a jury, granted a verdict in favor of the Reynolds (P). The railroad company (D) appeals alleging that while not lighting the steps constituted negligent conduct, Reynolds (P) might well have fallen without the negligence of the railroad.

■ ISSUE

Where the negligence of the defendant greatly increases the chances of an accident giving rise to the plaintiff's injury, does the possibility that the accident could have happened without the negligence break the chain of causation?

■ DECISION AND RATIONALE

(Fenner, J.) No. Where the negligence of a defendant greatly increases the chances of an accident giving rise to the plaintiff's injury, the possibility that the accident could have happened without the negligence does not break the chain of causation. It is possible that Mrs. Reynolds' fall could have occurred without the railroad's negligence. However, where, as in this case, the negligence of the defendant greatly multiplies the chances of accident to the plaintiff, the mere possibility that it might have happened without the negligence is not sufficient to break the chain of causation. Courts in such matters consider the natural and ordinary course of events, and do not indulge in suppositions. The evidence in this case connects the injury with the defendant's negligence.

Analysis:

Cause in fact does not require the plaintiff to prove that the accident giving rise to the plaintiff's injury could not have occurred at all, even in the absence of the defendant's negligence. We should always look at the natural consequence of negligence when considering a question regarding causation in fact. Then ask, given all the conditions of the case, would the injury to the plaintiff have occurred without the defendant's negligence? While, as in this case, it is possible that one may fail off stairs without the defendant's negligence, we should not question possibilities unless the plaintiff himself/herself was negligent in his/her own actions. Thus, forget about mere possibilities; just ask, "But for the defendant's negligence would the injury to the plaintiff have occurred?"

■ CASE VOCABULARY

POST HOC ERGO PROPTER HOC: This phrase directly translated means: after this, therefore because of this; a maxim setting forth the false logic that because one event occurs after another event, it was caused by the prior event.

Gentry v. Douglas Hereford Ranch, Inc.

(Widower) v. *(Ranch Company)*

290 Mont. 126, 962 P.2d 1205 (1998)

DEFENDANT'S CONDUCT MUST BE A CAUSE IN FACT OF THE INCIDENT TO MAKE OUT A NEGLIGENCE CLAIM

■ **INSTANT FACTS** A man at a ranch stumbled and fell while carrying a rifle. The fall caused the rifle to fire and shoot a woman in the head.

■ **BLACK LETTER RULE** Evidence that defendant's conduct was a cause in fact of the accident must be offered to make a negligence case.

■ **PROCEDURAL BASIS**

Appeal from summary judgment in favor of ranch company on wrongful death and survival actions.

■ **FACTS**

Gentry's (P) wife, Barbara Gentry, was accidentally shot and killed by Bacon. Bacon was planning to hunt deer on his relative's ranch, the Douglas Hereford Ranch, Inc. (D) ("Ranch Company"). Bacon went to get a rifle from his truck. As he was returning to a house on the Ranch Company (D) property with his rifle, he stumbled near some wooden stairs and the rifle discharged hitting Barbara Gentry in the head. Gentry (P) brought a wrongful death and survival action against Bacon and the Ranch Company (D). Gentry alleged Bacon was negligent in handling the rifle and the Ranch Company (D) was negligent in maintaining the stairs in a dangerous condition that caused the accident. Bacon filed bankruptcy and was dismissed from the case leaving only the Ranch Company (D) as defendant. The Ranch Company (D) moved for summary judgment.

■ **ISSUE**

Must sufficient evidence that the defendant's conduct was a cause in fact of the accident be offered to make out a negligence case?

■ **DECISION AND RATIONALE**

(J.) Yes. A negligence action requires proof of a duty, a breach of that duty, causation, and damages. The causation element requires proof of both cause in fact and proximate cause. A party's conduct is a cause in fact of an event if the event would not have occurred *but for* that conduct. Gentry (P) alleges that the Ranch Company (D) failed to maintain the stairs in a reasonably safe condition. Specifically, Gentry (P) alleges that the bottom stair was unstable and that the area was cluttered with debris such as a drain pipe, wires, and rocks. Bacon testified that he did not remember what caused him to stumble. In an interview, however, Bacon testified that "I think it was the step" that may have caused him to stumble. Gentry (P) contends that this isolated statement is enough to allow a finder of fact to infer that the step caused Bacon to stumble. However, on several other occasions, Bacon stated that he does not remember what caused him to stumble. Bacon's statement can raise only a suspicion or speculation that the stairs caused him to stumble. However, neither a suspicion or speculation is enough to defeat a motion for summary judgment. Gentry (P) has offered no substantial evidence that any condition on the property owned by the Ranch Company (D) caused Bacon to stumble and fall. Therefore, we conclude that cause in fact cannot be proven as a matter of law. We also conclude that the Ranch Company (D) is not vicariously liable for Bacon's negligence because Bacon is not an employee or agent of the Ranch Company (D). Affirmed.

Analysis:

A plaintiff must prove all four elements of negligence: duty, breach, cause, and damage. If the plaintiff fails to offer proof on any one of these elements, the action fails and summary judgment is proper in favor of the defendant. Here, the court found that Gentry (P) failed to prove cause in fact. We use the "but for" test to determine cause in fact. You must ask the question, but for defendant's conduct, would the accident have occurred? Remember, here we are talking about the alleged negligence of the Ranch Company (D) in failing to maintain the stairs. Thus, can it be said that, but for the debris on the stairs, the accident would not have occurred? The court here found that there was no substantial evidence that the Ranch Company (D) had failed to maintain the stairs in a reasonably safe condition. However, isn't the fact that the area was littered with a drain pipe, electric wires, and rocks enough? It seems reasonable that Bacon stumbled over one of these items even though there is no direct evidence that he did. For this court, however, that was not enough. Bacon, the court reasoned, could have stumbled due to his own clumsiness and not on anything negligently left out by the Ranch Company (D).

Kramer Service, Inc. v. Wilkins

(Hotel) v. (iInjured Guest)

184 Miss. 483, 186 So. 625 (1939)

IT IS NOT SUFFICIENT THAT THE PLAINTIFF PROVE THAT THE PLAINTIFF'S INJURY AND THE DEFENDANT'S NEGLIGENCE CO-EXISTED

■ **INSTANT FACTS** Wilkins (P) brought an action against Kramer Services (D) for injuries suffered when a piece of glass from a door in Kramer Services' (D) hotel fell on Wilkins' (P) forehead.

■ **BLACK LETTER RULE** In order to impose liability on a defendant, it is not sufficient that the plaintiff prove that the defendant's negligence and the plaintiff's injury co-existed or that the injury came after the negligent conduct of the defendant.

■ **PROCEDURAL BASIS**

Appeal from jury verdict in tort action for recovery of damages.

■ **FACTS**

Wilkins (P), a guest at a hotel operated by Kramer Services (D), was injured when a piece of glass fell on his forehead as he was opening a door at Kramer's (D) hotel. Two years after the injury, when the injury still had not healed, Wilkins (P) was informed by a skin specialist that Wilkins (P) had developed skin cancer in the injured area. At trial, two medical experts were introduced, one of whom testified that the probability of Wilkins' (P) injury resulting in skin cancer was one out of every one hundred cases. The other expert testified that there was no causal connection between the cancer and the injury. Additionally, Kramer's (D) request that the cancer or prolongation of the injury should not be taken into consideration by the jury was refused. The jury entered a verdict in favor of Wilkins (P). Kramer (D) appeals.

■ **ISSUE**

In order to impose liability on a defendant, is it sufficient that the plaintiff prove that the defendant's negligence and the plaintiff's injury co-existed or that the injury came after the negligent conduct of the defendant?

■ **DECISION AND RATIONALE**

(Griffith, J.) No. In order to impose liability on a defendant, it is not sufficient that the plaintiff prove that the defendant's negligence and the plaintiff's injury co-existed or that the injury came after the negligent conduct of the defendant. The proof that a past event possibly happened or that a certain result was possibly caused by a past event is not sufficient, in probative force, to take the question to the jury. It is not sufficient that the negligence of one person and injury to another co-existed. The injury must have been caused by the negligence. Also, it is not sufficient for the plaintiff to show a possibility that the injury complained of was caused by the negligence. Possibilities are not enough to sustain a verdict. Taking the medical testimony in this case into consideration, there is a possibility that skin cancer could be caused by an injury such as the one that the plaintiff suffered. However, the probability of such a result is nonexistent. The testimony is undisputed that the cause of cancer remains unknown. Such undisputed testimony should be accepted as any other undisputed evidence. (Affirmed as to liability; reversed and remanded on the amount of damages.)

Analysis:

This case illustrates the rule that a plaintiff seeking recovery for an injury must prove that the injury was caused by the defendant's negligence. Note that in previous cases we discovered that it is enough for the plaintiff to show that the defendant's negligence was a substantial factor in bringing about the plaintiff's injury, or that the negligence greatly multiplied the chances of the plaintiff getting injured (*Reynolds v. Texas and Pacific Ry. Co.*). However, a mere possibility that the injury could have been caused by the negligence of the defendant is not enough. Additionally, temporal connection between the negligence of the defendant and the plaintiff's injury is not enough. There has to be a causal connection. However, this case is quite strange when one tries to comprehend the chances of the plaintiff developing cancer in the same exact spot where he was previously injured.

■ CASE VOCABULARY

HYDRAHEADED: Difficult to root out, a persistent problem.

Herskovits v. Group Health Cooperative of Puget Sound

(Estate of Decedent) v. *(Hospital)*

99 Wash.2d 609, 664 P.2d 474 (1983)

IN CASES DEALING WITH REDUCTION IN CHANCE OF SURVIVAL, THE PLAINTIFF NEED ONLY SHOW THAT THE DEFENDANT'S ACTS OR OMISSIONS INCREASED THE RISK OF THE DECEDENT'S DEATH

■ **INSTANT FACTS** The estate of Herskovits (P) brought an action in professional negligence against Group Health Cooperative of Puget Sound (D) ("Puget") as a result of which the decedent's chance of survival was reduced by 14%.

■ **BLACK LETTER RULE** An action in negligence can be maintained where probable reduction in the decedent's chance for survival can be proven, even though the decedent would not have lived to normal life expectancy.

■ PROCEDURAL BASIS

Appeal in tort action from trial court's granting motion for summary judgment.

■ FACTS

The estate of Herskovits (P) brought an action in professional negligence against Group Health Cooperative of Puget Sound (D) ("Puget"). Both counsel for Herskovits (P) and Puget (D) conceded that the latter was negligent in failing to diagnose the decedent's cancer on the first visit which caused a 14% reduction in the decedent's chances of survival. Additionally, the evidence undisputedly indicated that the decedent had less than 50% chance of survival at all times. The trial court granted a summary judgment motion in favor of Puget (D) on the ground that Herskovits' estate (P) failed to prove that the decedent probably would have had a 51% chance of survival if Puget (D) had not been negligent. The estate of Herskovits (P) appeals.

■ ISSUE

Can an action in negligence be maintained where the probable reduction in the decedent's lifespan can be proven, even though the decedent would not have lived to normal life expectancy?

■ DECISION AND RATIONALE

(Dore, J.) Yes. An action in negligence can be maintained where probable reduction in the decedent's lifespan can be proven, even though the decedent would not have lived to normal life expectancy. This court will rely on the reasoning of *Hamil v. Bashline* even though in that case the decedent's chance of recovery exceeded 50%. In that case medical experts testified that the decedent's chance of survival, which was 75%, was substantially reduced as a result of the defendant hospital's failure to provide prompt treatment. The *Hamil* court indicated that in an ordinary negligence action the plaintiff must prove that damages or death would not have occurred but for the negligent conduct of the defendant. However in *Hamil*, as in this case, the defendants failed in their duty to protect the decedent against harm from another source. In such cases which elude certainty by their very nature, the issue should go to the jury on a less than normal threshold of proof. Thus, as held in *Hamil*, once the plaintiff establishes that the defendant's acts or omissions have increased the risk of harm to another, the evidence should go to the jury to determine whether the increased risk caused by the defendant was a substantial factor in bringing about the harm. Thus, in this case medical testimony of reduction of chance of survival from 39% to 25% is sufficient evidence to allow the issue of causation to go to the jury. In such cases, however, damages should be awarded based only on damages caused directly by the premature death, such as lost earnings and additional medical expenses. (Reversed; cause of action reinstated.)

Analysis:

You may have already noticed that there is a difference between this case and the other ones that we have encountered so far. In other cases the plaintiff's have all tried to establish that the defendant's negligence caused their injury or harm. In this case the plaintiff (or I should say the decedent) is already harmed. The defendant is not the cause of the decedent's death. The decedent would have died without reaching normal life expectancy. However, in such cases, the defendant's negligence is the cause of a reduction in the decedent's chance of survival. For example, in this case the decedent originally had a 39% chance of survival. However, the defendant's negligent diagnosis reduced this chance of survival to 25%. In such cases most courts hold that the plaintiff need not prove by a preponderance of evidence that the decedent would have survived. The plaintiff merely needs to present evidence and testimony by experts which shows that the defendant's conduct decreased the decedent's chance of survival by a certain percentage. Upon such showing the evidence will go to the jury, who will decide whether the defendant's action was a substantial factor in bringing about the early death of the decedent.

■ CASE VOCABULARY

SUMMARY JUDGMENT: A pre-verdict judgment by the court on the basis of pleadings because no material issue of fact exists, and one party or the other is entitled to judgment as a matter of law; either party may move for summary judgment at any time after all pleadings have been filed.

Daubert v. Merrell Dow Pharmaceuticals, Inc.

(Child with Birth Defect) v. *(Drug Company)*

509 U.S. 579, 113 S.Ct. 2786, 125 L.Ed.2d 469 (1993)

THE SUPREME COURT DECLARES THAT THE *FRYE* TEST IS NOT A PRE-CONDITION TO ADMISSIBILITY OF SCIENTIFIC EVIDENCE

■ **INSTANT FACTS** Daubert (P) and Schuller (P) sued Merrell Dow Pharmaceuticals, Inc. (D) ("Dow") alleging that their birth defects had been caused by their mothers' ingestion of a drug marketed by Dow (D).

■ **BLACK LETTER RULE** The Federal Rules of Evidence do not require "general acceptance" of a scientific technique in the scientific community as an absolute prerequisite to admissibility of expert witness testimony.

■ PROCEDURAL BASIS

Appeal in tort action by grant of writ of certiorari by the Supreme Court of the United States.

■ FACTS

Daubert (P) and Schuller (P), two minor children, suffer from severe birth defects. In an action against Merrell Dow Pharmaceuticals, Inc. (D) ("Dow"), Daubert (P) and Schuller (P) allege that the defects were caused when their mothers ingested Bendectin, an anti-nausea drug manufactured by Dow (D). The suit, initiated in state court, was removed to a federal court on diversity grounds. Dow (D) submitted a motion for summary judgment on the ground that no study shows that Bendectin causes defects in humans. Their conclusions were based on human statistical evidence. Daubert (P) and Schuller (P) opposed the motion by introducing their own experts who testified that after test tube (in vitro) and live (in vivo) testing on animals, they concluded that the drug does cause birth defects. The trial court granted Dow's (D) summary judgment motion on the ground that, pursuant to *Frye v. United States*, scientific evidence should only be admitted if it has general acceptance in the field to which it belongs and that Daubert (P) and Schuller's (P) evidence did not meet this standard. The Ninth Circuit Court of Appeals, also relying on the test promulgated in *Frye v. United States*, affirmed on the ground that expert opinion based on scientific technique is inadmissible unless the technique is "generally accepted" in the scientific community and scientific technique which diverges from accepted procedures in the field cannot be shown to be accepted as a reliable technique. The court of appeals also concluded that the evidence provided by Daubert (P) and Schuller (P) being insufficient, the latter did not satisfy the burden of proving causation at trial. Daubert (P) and Schuller (P) appeal.

■ ISSUE

Do the Federal Rules of Evidence require "general acceptance" of a scientific technique in the scientific community as an absolute prerequisite to admissibility of expert witness testimony?

■ DECISION AND RATIONALE

(Blackmun, J.) No. The Federal Rules of Evidence do not require "general acceptance" of a scientific technique in the scientific community as an absolute prerequisite to admissibility of expert witness testimony. Under the test in *Frye v. United States*, scientific testimony is not admissible unless the thing from which the expert's deduction is made is sufficiently established to have general acceptance in the particular scientific field in which it belongs. However, the Federal Rules of Evidence, specifically Rule 702, has replaced the *Frye* test, and nothing in the text of the rule establishes "general acceptance" as an absolute prerequisite to admission of expert testimony. However, under the Federal Rules of Evidence the trial judge has the duty to ensure that all scientific testimony or evidence admitted is reliable and relevant. The trial judge must ensure that the evidence in question is "scientific" and that it assists the jury in understanding the evidence to determine a fact in issue. The trial court however, may take into consideration the "general acceptance" of the scientific technique in order to determine its reliability. Thus, although "general acceptance" may be a factor, it is not a necessary precondition to the admissibility of scientific evidence under the Federal Rules of Evidence. (Reversed and remanded.)

Analysis:

You are probably wondering what this case has to do with the issue of causation in fact. Remember that the plaintiff has the burden of proving causation. In scientific cases it is likely that the plaintiff, such as the one in this case, will rely on scientific evidence and expert testimony to establish causation. For example, in this case the plaintiffs relied on expert testimony to prove that the drug in question did cause birth defects in children. The defendant attempted to dispute their evidence by bringing in their own experts to testify that the drug does not cause birth defects. Now, this case considers that type of scientific evidence that is admissible at a federal trial. The trial court and the court of appeals relied on the *Frye* test which requires general acceptance of a scientific technique before such evidence can be introduced at trial. Both courts determined that the techniques relied on by the plaintiff's expert were inadmissible. This in turn means that the plaintiff failed to present sufficient evidence on the issue of causation, and that the court and not the jury could enter a summary judgment in favor of the defendants without submitting the issue of causation to the jury. On appeal, however, the Supreme Court of the United States decided that the *Frye* test was not a precondition to admissibility of scientific evidence, and that under the Federal Rules of Evidence the trial judge could admit such evidence as long as the trial judge could conclude that the evidence is relevant and reliable. General acceptance, although not a prerequisite, could be used as a factor in determining reliability of the scientific technique in question.

■ CASE VOCABULARY

DISPOSITIVE: Directed toward or effecting settlement of a case.

DIVERSITY (Of Citizenship): Basis of federal jurisdiction which grants federal courts original jurisdiction over cases/controversies between citizens of different states.

GENERAL ACCEPTANCE: Approval by those people who have achieved a recognized level of expertise in an area of knowledge.

INIMICAL: Unfavorable; opposed to.

PROFFER: To offer, usually something intangible.

SINE QUA NON: Without which a thing cannot be; a necessary condition or requisite.

Hill v. Edmonds

(Automobile Passenger) v. *(Driver of Vehicle)*

26 A.D.2d 554, 270 N.Y.S.2d 1020 (1966)

WHERE THE PLAINTIFF'S INJURY WAS CAUSED BY THE SEPARATE NEGLIGENT ACTS OF TWO DEFENDANTS, BOTH OF THE DEFENDANTS ARE CONCURRENTLY LIABLE FOR THE PLAINTIFF'S INJURY

■ **INSTANT FACTS** Hill (P), a passenger in Edmonds' (D) car, brought an action in negligence against Edmonds (D) and Bragoli (D) for injuries suffered when Edmonds' (D) car collided with Bragoli's (D) truck, which was parked in the road.

■ **BLACK LETTER RULE** Where separate acts of negligence combine to produce a single injury, each tortfeasor is liable for the entire result even though his act alone may not have caused the result.

■ **PROCEDURAL BASIS**

Appeal in action for negligence from trial court's dismissal of complaint.

■ **FACTS**

Hill (P), a passenger in Edmonds' (D) car, brought an action for injuries that she suffered against both Edmonds (D) and Bragoli (D), the owner of the truck with which Edmonds (D) collided. The evidence revealed that Bragoli (D) had parked his truck, on a stormy night, in the middle of the road without any lights on. Edmonds (D) collided with the rear of Bragoli's truck. At some point in the trial Edmonds (D) testified to having seen the truck in time to avoid it. At other times, however, Edmonds (D) testified to not knowing exactly what happened at the time of the accident. Based upon Edmonds' (D) testimony, the trial court dismissed the complaint against Bragoli (D). Hill (P) appeals.

■ **ISSUE**

Where separate acts of negligence combine to produce a single injury, is each tortfeasor liable for the entire result even though his act alone may not have caused the result?

■ **DECISION AND RATIONALE**

(Memorandum by the Court) Yes. Where separate acts of negligence combine to produce a single injury, each tortfeasor is liable for the entire result even though his act alone may not have caused the result. Based on Edmonds' (D) testimony, assuming that Edmonds was negligent, the accident would not have occurred had the truck driver not left his truck in the middle of the road without the lights on. Accordingly, the complaint against the truck owner must be reinstated. (New trial.)

Analysis:

This apparently simple opinion contains a number of important and complex concepts. In order for a party to be liable for the tort of negligence, several elements must be proven. First, there must be

---

some conduct which falls below the standard of reasonable care. In the instant action, the conduct of both the truck driver and the driver of the automobile likely met this element. Second, the act or omission must be a "cause in fact" of the injury. In other words, if the injury would not have occurred but for a party's conduct or omission, then no liability attaches. The conduct of the truck driver was most likely a "but for" cause of Hill's (P) injuries. If Bragoli (D) would not have left his truck in the middle of the road, Edmonds (D) probably would not have hit the truck. However, the opinion seems to indicate that Bragoli's (D) act of leaving the truck in the road would not have caused any injury unless a driver like Edmonds (D) was also negligent. A reasonable driver would have seen the abandoned truck and avoided it. Indeed, both negligent acts were required in order to cause Hill's (P) injuries. Is it fair to hold Bragoli (D) liable in this situation? In answering this question in the affirmative, it is important to remember the purpose of tort law, i.e., to compensate the injured party. If either Bragoli (D) or Edmonds (D) were not held liable simply because a separate negligent act was required to cause injury, then Hill (P) could not recover anything. Both Bragoli (D) and Edmonds (D) could escape liability by showing that their negligent acts alone caused no injury. Thus, public policy dictates that both should be liable. It is important to note that a final element needs to be proven. Both Bragoli (D) and Edmonds (D) must be shown to have "proximately" caused the injury. This topic will be addressed in the next chapter.

■ CASE VOCABULARY

ARGUENDO: (Latin) To put in a clear light; for the sake of argument; hypothetically.

Anderson v. Minneapolis, St. P. & S. St. M. Ry. Co.

(Homeowner) v. *(Railway)*
146 Minn. 430, 179 N.W. 45 (1920)

WHERE THERE IS MORE THAN ONE CAUSE FOR A PLAINTIFF'S INJURY, EACH TORTFEASOR IS LIABLE IF EACH IS A SUBSTANTIAL FACTOR IN BRINGING ABOUT THE PLAINTIFF'S INJURY

■ **INSTANT FACTS** Anderson (P), a property owner, sued Minneapolis, St. P. & S. ST. M. Ry. Co. (D) ("Railway") for causing a fire which burned and damaged Anderson's (P) property.

■ **BLACK LETTER RULE** Where a plaintiff is injured by the negligent conduct of more than one tortfeasor, each is independently liable if it was a substantial factor in bringing about the plaintiff's injury.

■ **PROCEDURAL BASIS**

Appeal in negligence action from order denying a motion in the alternative for judgment notwithstanding the verdict or for a new trial.

■ **FACTS**

A fire, started by the negligent conduct of the Railway (D), merged with a fire from another independent source, burning Anderson's (P) property. Anderson (P) sued Minneapolis, St. P. & S. ST. M. R.R. Co. (D) ("Railway") to recover for the damage to the property. The trial court instructed the jury that if it finds that the fire caused by the Railway (D) was a material and substantial factor in damaging Anderson's (P) property, then the Railway (D) was liable. The jury returned a verdict in favor of Anderson (P), and the trial court rejected the Railway's (D) motion for a judgment notwithstanding the verdict, or in the alternative, motion for a new trial. The Railway (D) appeals on the ground that since both fires could have independently destroyed the property, the Railway (D) should not be found liable.

■ **ISSUE**

Where a plaintiff is injured by the negligent conduct of more than one tortfeasor, is each of them independently liable if a substantial factor in bringing about the plaintiff's injury?

■ **DECISION AND RATIONALE**

(Lees, J.) Yes. Where a plaintiff is injured by the negligent conduct of more than one tortfeasor, each is independently liable if they are each a substantial factor in bringing about the plaintiff's injury. The Railway (D) proposes that if Anderson's (P) property was damaged by a number of fires combining, one being the fire caused by the Railway's (D) negligent conduct, and the others being of no responsible origin, but of sufficient source to independently damage the property, then the Railway (D) is not liable. The Railway's (D) proposition is based on the case of *Cook v. Minneapolis, St P. & S.S.M. Ry. Co.* [where two fires merged, the court refused to hold a defendant liable where the other fire was of innocent origin]. This court, however, rejects *Cook* if it absolves the Railway (D) of liability regardless of whether its negligent conduct was a substantial and material factor in causing the Anderson's (D) injury. If a fire set by the Railway's (D) negligence unites with a fire of an independent origin, there is joint and several liability, even though either fire would have independently destroyed the property. (Affirmed.)

Analysis:

This case should be contrasted with *Hill v. Edmonds*. In the latter case, there were two causes for the plaintiff's injury, and neither cause by itself was sufficient to bring about the injury. However, in this case, there are two causes, each of which is independently sufficient to have caused the damages suffered by the plaintiff. In such a case the courts have concluded that it would be unfair to deny the plaintiff liability, simply because the plaintiff can not show that "but for" the negligent conduct of one defendant, the injury to the plaintiff would not have resulted. Instead, the courts rely on the substantial factor test. Under this test the plaintiff may recover from either of the negligent defendants if the plaintiff can show that the defendant's conduct was a substantial factor in causing the injury. The court leaves it up to the defendants to fight out the issue of apportionment of the damages. Thus, one defendant is jointly and severally liable for the damage caused to the plaintiff. This means that the plaintiff may recover for all the damages suffered from one defendant. At that point, the defendant may bring suit against the other defendant in order to apportion the damages or recover a portion of the amount paid from the other plaintiff. This test is an extension of "but for" causation and is used in exceptional cases where each defendant's negligence is sufficient by itself to have caused injury to the plaintiff.

■ CASE VOCABULARY

JOINT AND SEVERAL LIABILITY: Refers to the sharing of liabilities among a group of people collectively and also individually; thus, if defendants are jointly and severally liable, the injured party may sue some or all of the defendants together, or each one separately, and may collect equal or unequal amounts from each in satisfaction of his/her damages.

JUDGMENT NOTWITHSTANDING THE VERDICT (JUDGMENT N.O.V.): A judgment that reverses the determination of the jury, granted when a judge determines that the jury verdict had no reasonable support in fact or was contrary to law.

Summers v. Tice

(Injured Party) v. *(Shooter)*

33 Cal.2d 80, 199 P.2d 1 (1948)

WHERE TWO DEFENDANTS ARE SIMULTANEOUSLY NEGLIGENT TOWARD A PLAINTIFF, BUT ONLY ONE DEFENDANT'S NEGLIGENCE CAUSED PLAINTIFF'S INJURY, PLAINTIFF MAY RECOVER AGAINST EITHER DEFENDANT

■ **INSTANT FACTS** Summers (P) sued Tice (D) and Simonson (D) for injuries sustained by a bullet negligently shot from Tice (D) or Simonson (D).

■ **BLACK LETTER RULE** Where two defendants are negligent toward the plaintiff, but only one defendant's negligence has caused the plaintiff's injury, the plaintiff may recover from both defendants even though the plaintiff is unable to show which defendant actually caused the plaintiff's injury.

■ **PROCEDURAL BASIS**

Appeal in action in negligence for recovery of damages.

■ **FACTS**

Summers (P), Tice (D), and Simonson (D) were hunting when Tice (D) and Simonson (D) both negligently fired their guns in Summers' (P) direction. One bullet shot Summers (P) in the eye. Summers (P) sued both Tice (D) and Simonson (D) for the injury. The trial court granted a verdict in favor of Summers (P). Tice (D) and Simonson (D) appeal on the ground that since Summers (P) could not prove which party's negligence caused the injury, there should be no joint and several liability of Tice (D) and Simonson (D).

■ **ISSUE**

Where two defendants are negligent toward the plaintiff, but only one defendant's negligence has caused the plaintiff's injury, may the plaintiff recover from the defendants even though the plaintiff is unable to show which defendant actually caused the injury?

■ **DECISION AND RATIONALE**

(Carter, J.) Yes. Where two defendants are negligent toward the plaintiff, but only one defendant's negligence has caused the injury, the plaintiff may recover from the defendants even though the plaintiff is unable to show which defendant actually caused the plaintiff's injury. In *Oliver v. Miles* the court, confronted with a similar issue, indicated that each defendant is liable because to hold otherwise would exonerate both defendants from liability even though each was negligent and the plaintiff's injury resulted from their negligence. In this case, both Tice (D) and Simonson (D) were negligent toward Summers (P); the negligence of one caused Summers' (P) injury. Thus, the burden should be on Tice (D) and Simonson (D) to absolve themselves, if they can. The same principles apply for apportionment of damages. When the matter of apportionment is incapable of proof, the innocent party should not be denied his right to recovery. It is up to the wrongdoers to apportion damages between themselves. (Affirmed.)

Analysis:

In this case both defendants are equally negligent toward the plaintiff. Only one defendant's negligence is the cause of the plaintiff's injury, yet the plaintiff is incapable of proving which defendant. The courts in such scenarios have relaxed the requirement of causation and have basically shifted the burden of proof to the defendants. Thus, each defendant may come forward and prove that he/she did not cause the injury. In the absence of such proof, each defendant is jointly and severally liable to the plaintiff. Note, however, that it is crucial for the plaintiff to prove that each defendant was in fact negligent. Otherwise the case would be dismissed and we would never get to the issue of causation. Also, this type of causation, known as alternative liability, is different from that seen in the previous two cases. In those cases, also known as "combined causes," the negligence of each defendant is sufficient to bring about the plaintiff's injury. In alternative liability cases only one defendant's negligence is the cause of the plaintiff's injury. However, because of the circumstances surrounding the case, it is impossible for the plaintiff to prove which defendant was the cause. For example, in the instant case although both defendants negligently shot toward the plaintiff, only one bullet injured the plaintiff.

■ **CASE VOCABULARY**

JOINT AND SEVERAL LIABILITY: Refers to the sharing of liabilities among a group of people collectively and also individually; thus, if defendants are jointly and severally liable, the injured party may sue some or all of the defendants together, or each one separately, and may collect equal or unequal amounts from each in satisfaction of his/her damages.

STIPULATION: Agreement made by opposing attorneys or parties.

TORTFEASOR: A person guilty of a tort or wrongdoing.

Sindell v. Abbott Laboratories

(Injured Consumer) v. *(Drug Manufacturer)*

26 Cal.3d 588, 163 Cal.Rptr. 132, 607 P.2d 924 (1980)

AS BETWEEN AN INNOCENT PLAINTIFF AND NEGLIGENT DEFENDANTS, THE LATTER SHOULD BEAR THE COST OF INJURY TO THE PLAINTIFF

■ **INSTANT FACTS** Sindell (P) sued Abbot Laboratories (D) and four other drug manufacturers, alleging that Sindell's (P) cancer was the result of Sindell's (P) mother's consumption during pregnancy of a drug manufactured by Abbot (D) and the other laboratories.

■ **BLACK LETTER RULE** Where more than two defendants have negligently produced a drug causing the plaintiff's injury, the latter may recover from the defendants even though the plaintiff does not prove which defendant's drug was the direct cause of the plaintiff's injury.

■ **PROCEDURAL BASIS**

Appeal from trial court's dismissal of action in negligence.

■ **FACTS**

Sindell (P) alleges that she developed cancer as a result of a drug ingested by her mother during her pregnancy. The drug, Diethylstilbestrol (DES), was manufactured by Abbott Laboratories (D) and approximately 199 other manufacturers. In an action for recovery of damages, Sindell (P) sued Abbott (D) and four other manufacturers who together produced 90% of the total DES manufactured in the country. Sindell (P), however, could not identify the manufacturer of the DES ingested by her mother. The trial court dismissed the action, holding that the case was not similar to *Summers v. Tice* [both defendants responsible when only one is negligent, but the defendants acted concurrently] because not all of the defendants were in the suit and because there was no concert of action on the part of the defendants. Sindell (P) appeals, advancing enterprise liability theory as the basis for recovery.

■ **ISSUE**

Where more than two defendants have negligently produced a drug causing the plaintiff's injury, may the latter recover from the defendants even though the plaintiff does not prove which defendant's drug was the direct cause of the plaintiff's injury?

■ **DECISION AND RATIONALE**

(Mosk, J.) Yes. Where more than two defendants have negligently produced a drug causing the plaintiff's injury, the latter may recover from the defendants even though the plaintiff does not prove which defendant's drug was the direct cause of the plaintiff's injury. In *Hall v. E.I. Du Pont de Nemours & Co., Inc.*, the court used the enterprise liability theory to allow recovery where the defendants, acting independently, had adhered to an industry-wide standard with regard to safety features, thereby jointly controlling the risk to the plaintiff. The court in that case determined that the theory of liability applied to industries composed of a small number of units. Enterprise liability should not be applied in this case, because at least 200 companies manufactured DES. Additionally, in *Hall* the court affirmed the allegations that the defendant companies involved controlled the risk to the plaintiff. No such

---

conclusions apply in this case. Applying *Hall* would preclude the plaintiff in this case from any recovery. It is impossible for the plaintiff to join all the manufacturers of DES, especially since many of the manufacturers are not in business any more. Yet, advances in technology have allowed production of goods which may harm the consumers and which can not be traced to any specific producer. As between the innocent plaintiff and negligent defendants, the latter should bear the cost of injury to the plaintiff. The plaintiff in this case is not at fault for failing to produce evidence of causation, and although the defendants are not at fault either, their conduct in making a drug, the adverse affects of which became apparent years later, is significant when there is an unavailability of evidence of causation. Additionally, from a policy standpoint, the defendants are in a better position to bear the cost of injury to the plaintiff because the manufacturer is in the best position to discover and guard against defects in its products and warn the consumers of the harmful effects. *Summers v. Tice* cannot apply directly because not all the manufacturers of DES are named as defendants. But, the rationale in the *Summers* case should be extended. It is reasonable to measure the likelihood of each defendants liability based on the percentage of DES that each sold on the market as compared to the total DES sold on the market. This way the plaintiff's damages may also be apportioned based on the total contribution of each manufacturer to the market. (Reversed.)

Analysis:

This case marks the "deep pocket" attitude of many courts. Who can afford to pay for the plaintiff's injury? Big rich companies. Also, the court places the burden of paying for the cost of plaintiff's injuries on the defendants, who are more at fault than the plaintiff, thus forwarding the policy consideration that between the innocent party and the negligent defendant the latter should bear the cost of injury. Another important point on which this case can be distinguished from *Summers* is the extent of liability of each defendant. In *Summers* each defendant is liable for the total sum of damages to the plaintiff (joint and several liability). That is, the plaintiff can recover from any defendant the total amount of judgment in his/her favor. In this case, however, there is several liability. This means that the plaintiff recovers from each defendant only to the extent to which the defendant itself is liable.

■ CASE VOCABULARY

CONCERT OF ACTION (CONCERTED ACTION): Action which has been planned, arranged, adjusted, agreed upon and settled between parties acting together, in pursuance of some design or in accordance with some scheme.

ENTERPRISE LIABILITY: Situation in which several defendants, acting independently, have adhered to an industry-wide standard of care, in which all the defendants jointly controlled the risk of injury from their products.

GRAVAMEN: The essence or most important part of a complaint or accusation.

CHAPTER SIX

Proximate or Legal Cause

Atlantic Coast Line R. Co. v. Daniels

Instant Facts: Facts not given.

Black Letter Rule: Courts should not set rigid limitations in defining proximate cause as a basis of liability.

Ryan v. New York Central R.R. Co.

Instant Facts: Ryan (P) brought action against New York Central R.R. Co. (D) ("Railroad") for the destruction of Ryan's (P) house by a fire started by Railroad (D).

Black Letter Rule: A defendant is only liable for the ordinary and natural results of his negligent conduct.

Bartolone v. Jeckovich

Instant Facts: Bartolone (P) sued Jeckovich (D) for injuries that Bartolone (P) suffered subsequent to an automobile accident with Jeckovich (D) for which the latter was found liable.

Black Letter Rule: A defendant is liable to the plaintiff in damages for the aggravation of plaintiff's pre-existing illness due to the defendant's negligent conduct.

In Re Arbitration Between Polemis and Furness, Withy & Co., Ltd.

Instant Facts: Polemis (P) entered into arbitration with Furness (D) to recover damage to a ship that Furness (D) had chartered from Polemis (P).

Black Letter Rule: Where it is reasonably foreseeable that the defendant's negligent conduct would cause damages to the plaintiff, the defendant is liable even though the exact extent of the damages is not foreseeable.

Overseas Tankship (U.K.) Ltd. v. Morts Dock & Engineering Co., Ltd. ["Wagon Mound No. 1"]

Instant Facts: Morts Dock & Engineering Co., Ltd. (P) ("Morts Dock") sued Overseas Tankship (U.K.) Ltd. (D) ("Overseas) for the fire that destroyed Morts Dock's (P) wharf.

Black Letter Rule: A defendant is not liable for unforeseeable consequences of his negligent conduct, even though they were the direct result of defendant's conduct.

Overseas Tankship (U.K.) Ltd. v. Miller Steamship Co. ["Wagon Mound No. 2"]

Instant Facts: Miller Steamship Co. (P) ("Miller") sued Overseas Tankship (U.K.) Ltd. (D) ("Overseas") for destruction of Miller's (P) ships due to a fire.

Black Letter Rule: The foreseeability of the consequences of a defendant's actions depend on the balancing between the likelihood of risk and the magnitude of damages flowing therefrom.

Palsgraf v. Long Island R.R. Co.

Instant Facts: Palsgraf (P) sued Long Island R.R. Co. (D) ("the railroad") for the injuries sustained when a package fell out of the hand of one of the train passengers and exploded.

Black Letter Rule: A defendant owes a duty of care only to those plaintiffs who are in the reasonably foreseeable zone of danger.

Yun v. Ford Motor Co.

Instant Facts: Yun's (P) father, Chang, was struck and killed by a car when he ran across two busy freeway lanes to retrieve a spare tire which fell off his car.

Black Letter Rule: When the court determines that an injury was not reasonably, foreseeably caused by the defendant, the issue of proximate cause may be taken away from the jury.

Derdiarian v. Felix Contracting Corp.

Instant Facts: Derdiarian (P) sued Felix Contracting Corp. (D) ("Felix") for injuries that he sustained when a car ran over the ditch in which Derdiarian (P) was working.

Black Letter Rule: Where the act of a third party intervenes between the defendant's negligent conduct and the plaintiff's injury, the causal connection is not severed if the intervening act is a normal and foreseeable consequence of the risk created by the defendant's negligent conduct.

Watson v. Kentucky & Indiana Bridge & R.R. Co.

Instant Facts: Watson (P) sued the railroad for injuries sustained when oil spilled from the train caught on fire by a match dropped by Duerr.

Black Letter Rule: A negligent defendant is not liable for the intentional intervening malicious acts of a third party which are not reasonably foreseeable.

Fuller v. Preis

Instant Facts: Dr. Lewis committed suicide after being involved in an accident with Preis (D).

Black Letter Rule: An act of suicide is not, as a matter of law, a superseding cause in negligence law which precludes liability of the original tortfeasor.

Mccoy v. American Suzuki Motor Corp.

Instant Facts: McCoy (P) was struck by a passing car as he was assisting at the scene of a traffic accident.

Black Letter Rule: The rescue doctrine may be invoked in product liability actions and, if it is, the rescuer is required to show the defendant proximately caused his injuries.

Kelly v. Gwinnell

Instant Facts: Kelly sued Gwinnell (D) for injuries Kelly (P) sustained when hit by Gwinnell (D) who in turn seeks recovery from Zak (D).

Black Letter Rule: A host is liable for the negligence of an adult social guest who has become visibly intoxicated at the host's home, and where risk of harm to others is foreseeable.

Enright v. Eli Lily & Co.

Instant Facts: Karen Enright (P) sued Eli Lily & Co. (D) ("Eli") alleging that her grandmother's ingestion of a drug manufactured by Eli (D) led to reproductive abnormalities in Enright's (P) mother, which in turn, caused Enright's (P) cerebral palsy.

Black Letter Rule: An injury to a mother, which results in injuries to a later conceived child, does not establish a cause of action in favor of the child against the original tortfeasors.

Atlantic Coast Line R. Co. v. Daniels

(Railroad) v. *(Injured Party)*
8 Ga.App. 775, 70 S.E. 203 (1911)

PROXIMATE CAUSE SHOULD BE LIMITED TO THE ORDINARY AND NATURAL CONSEQUENCES OF AN ACT

■ **INSTANT FACTS** Facts not given.

■ **BLACK LETTER RULE** Courts should not set rigid limitations in defining proximate cause as a basis of liability.

■ **PROCEDURAL BASIS**

Appeal in action for negligence.

■ **FACTS**

Facts not given.

■ **ISSUE**

Should courts set rigid limitations on defining proximate cause as a basis of liability?

■ **DECISION AND RATIONALE**

(Powell, J.) No. Courts should not set rigid limitations in defining proximate cause as a basis of liability. Courts do not attempt to deal with cause and effect in any absolute degree, but only in a way that is within the scope of human understanding. Thus, words such as "proximate" and "natural" are used to set limits between a certain cause and its effect. While a plaintiff may show that a defendant's act was the cause of plaintiff's injury and without the act there would be no injury, this is not enough as a standard for legal responsibility. This type of reasoning leads to the ultimate and absurd conclusion that had the plaintiff not been born, there would be no injury. Thus, courts should instead ask if the defendant's wrongful act was the proximate cause of the plaintiff's injury.

Analysis:

So far we have seen that in order to recover for injury caused by the negligent acts of a defendant, the plaintiff must prove that the defendant owed a duty to the plaintiff, that the defendant breached this duty (defendant was negligent), and that the breach of this duty was the "but for" cause of the plaintiff's injury. An additional element that needs to be proven by the plaintiff is that the defendant's negligent conduct was the proximate cause of the injury. Proximate cause refers to that which in a natural and continuous sequence unbroken by any new independent cause produces an event, without which the injury would not have occurred. Unlike causation in fact, there is no standard or rigid rule for proximate cause. Instead, the issue of proximate cause is a fact-driven analysis of the relationship between the defendant's negligence and the plaintiff's injury. Simply stated, if the relationship between the two is attenuated (lessened in amount, force or value), there may be no proximate cause. In determining this issue, time and distance are some of the factors that the courts will take into consideration. The best way to deal with the issue of proximate causation is to analyze the facts of the cases that follow in the chapter and to try to develop a feel for what is considered by the courts as the natural and ordinary consequence of a defendant's act. Also, use a lot of common sense in this area. Certainly, proximate causation is not a cut-and-dried area in tort law.

■ CASE VOCABULARY

FINITUDE: Having definable limits.

PROXIMATE CAUSE: That cause which in natural and continuous sequence, unbroken by any new independent cause, produces an event without which the injury would not have occurred.

REDUCTIO AD ABSURDUM: (Latin) "To reduce to the absurd," a method of disproving an argument by showing it leads to an absurd conclusion.

Ryan v. New York Central R.R. Co.

(Homeowner) v. *(Railroad)*

35 N.Y. 210, 91 Am.Dec. 49 (1866)

A DEFENDANT IS LIABLE FOR THE PROXIMATE RESULTS OF HIS CONDUCT BUT IS NOT LIABLE FOR THE REMOTE DAMAGES CAUSED BY HIS CONDUCT

■ **INSTANT FACTS** Ryan (P) brought action against New York Central R.R. Co. (D) ("Railroad") for the destruction of Ryan's (P) house by a fire started by Railroad (D).

■ **BLACK LETTER RULE** A defendant is only liable for the ordinary and natural results of his negligent conduct.

■ **PROCEDURAL BASIS**

Appeal from a non-suit verdict in action for recovery of damages.

■ **FACTS**

New York Central Railroad (D), through its own negligence, set fire to its own woodshed. The fire soon spread, destroying among other houses, Ryan's (P) house which was 135 feet away. Ryan (P) brought action against the Railroad (D) to recover for the value of the house. The trial court non-suited Ryan (P). The latter appeals.

■ **ISSUE**

Is a defendant only liable for the ordinary and natural results of his negligent conduct?

■ **DECISION AND RATIONALE**

(Hunt, J.) Yes. A defendant is only liable for the ordinary and natural results of his negligent conduct. A person is liable in damages for the proximate result of his own acts, but not for remote damages. It is not, however, easy to determine what are proximate damages and what are remote damages at all times. In fire cases a destruction is anticipated the moment the fire in question is communicated to another person's property. The negligent party is liable for the natural and expected results of his conduct. A party, however, has no control over accidental and varying circumstances and is not responsible for their effects. Thus, in this case an action cannot be sustained for the reason that the damages incurred are not the immediate but remote result of the negligence of the defendants. The immediate result was the destruction of the defendant's own woodshed; beyond that, other results were remote. To sustain an action in the instant case could subject a person to liability against which no prudence could guard, and to paying of awards for which no private fortune would be adequate. A man may insure his own property, but he cannot insure the property of another. By obtaining insurance, each man can guard against the hazards of a neighbor's conduct. (Affirmed.)

Analysis:

Once again, proximate cause limits the liability that is imposed on a defendant. This court indicates that a defendant is not liable for damages which are caused by his negligent conduct, but which are too remote to be anticipated at the time the negligence of the defendant is taking place. Although this

---

decision may not make sense as to what is considered "remote," the proposition that it puts forward is correct. A negligent party should only be liable for those injuries which are the proximate and foreseeable result of his/her conduct. What is considered "foreseeable" may depend on the court's view of the circumstances of each case. For example, reported cases indicate that in later decisions, recovery was allowed to the first adjoining landowner whose property was destroyed in a fire caused next door. Other courts have allowed recovery for destruction of properties which were located as much as four miles away from the property originally set on fire.

■ CASE VOCABULARY

INDEMNIFY: To insure against loss, damage, etc., or to repay for same.

NONSUIT: A judgment rendered against a plaintiff who fails to proceed to trial or is unable to prove his case; since the adjudication is made when the plaintiff has simply failed to provide evidence sufficient to make out a case, it does not decide the merits of the plaintiff's case.

REMOTE CAUSE: The type of cause which does not necessarily produce an event without which injury would not occur; cause which is not proximate.

SUBROGATION: The substitution of one person for another with reference to a legal claim (usually for the benefit of insurers).

Bartolone v. Jeckovich

(Injured Driver) v. *(Liable Driver)*

103 A.D.2d 632, 481 N.Y.S.2d 545 (1984)

IN NEGLIGENCE CASES, THE DEFENDANT TAKES THE PLAINTIFF AS HE FINDS HIM

■ **INSTANT FACTS** Bartolone (P) sued Jeckovich (D) for injuries that Bartolone (P) suffered subsequent to an automobile accident with Jeckovich (D) for which the latter was found liable.

■ **BLACK LETTER RULE** A defendant is liable to the plaintiff in damages for the aggravation of plaintiff's pre-existing illness due to the defendant's negligent conduct.

■ **PROCEDURAL BASIS**

Appeal in action in negligence for recovery of damages.

■ **FACTS**

Bartolone (P), a 48-year-old male, was injured in an automobile collision with Jeckovich (D) for which the latter was found liable. As a result of the accident, Bartolone (P) suffered whiplash and minor injury to his lower back, the treatment of which did not require hospitalization. Subsequent to the accident Bartolone (P), who prior to the accident was a carpenter and worked out about 4 hours a day at the YMCA, became delusional, withdrawn, and hostile, refusing to participate in his prior interests. At the trial Bartolone's (P) psychiatrists testified to Bartolone's (P) fear of doctors because of his mother's death due to cancer. They also testified that Bartolone (P) engaged in body building, not only to ward off cancer, but also to cope with his emotional problems. Furthermore, they testified that the accident with Jeckovich (D) rendered Bartolone (P) incapable of his former physical feats, depriving him of the mechanism with which Bartolone (P) coped with his emotional problems, thus resulting in Bartolone's (P) degenerative condition. At the trial, the jury returned a verdict of $500,000 in favor of Bartolone (P). The trial court set aside the judgment on the ground that the jury had no evidence for concluding that Bartolone's (P) mental breakdown was a result of the accident with Jeckovich (D). Bartolone (P) appeals.

■ **ISSUE**

Is a defendant liable to the plaintiff in damages for the aggravation of the plaintiff's pre-existing illness due to the defendant's negligent conduct?

■ **DECISION AND RATIONALE**

(Denman, J.) Yes. A defendant is liable to the plaintiff in damages for the aggravation of plaintiff's pre-existing illness due to the defendant's negligent conduct. In this case the jury's verdict is supported by case law. In *Bonner v. United States* the plaintiff's accident aggravated her pre-existing psychotic illness with which the plaintiff was able to cope prior to her accident. In *Steinhauser v. Hertz Corp.* the Second Circuit Court found that the plaintiff had a predisposition to abnormal behavior which activated into schizophrenia by the emotional trauma of the accident between the plaintiff and the defendant. In both cases, the courts determined that the issue of aggravation of a pre-existing illness was one which should be considered by the jury. These cases illustrate that the defendant must take the plaintiff as the defendant finds him, and thus may be liable in damages for aggravation of pre-existing illnesses. In this case also, there is ample evidence that Bartolone (P), although suffering from a pre-existing condition, was able to function in a normal manner prior to the accident, but that the accident aggravated his condition leaving him completely disabled. (Reversed; jury verdict reinstated.)

Analysis:

This case stands for the unforgettable proposition that the defendant takes the plaintiff as he finds him. This means that the prior sensitivity or pre-existing conditions of the plaintiff will not be taken into consideration in reducing the defendant's damages where the defendant has been found liable. This is true even though the physical injuries suffered by the plaintiff may be unforeseeable. Thus, in negligence causes of action it is not important that the defendant foresee the exact kind of injury that the plaintiff would suffer. This is true as long as the defendant's negligent behavior would create an unreasonable risk of harm to the plaintiff. As long as some injury is foreseeable, the exact nature or extent of it is not relevant and the defendant is liable in damages even for aggravation of a pre-existing condition in the plaintiff. Imagine a plaintiff who is a hemophiliac. The defendant negligently causes a cut on the plaintiff's finger. The plaintiff almost bleeds to death. Obviously, if a non-hemophiliac had been injured, the damages from a small cut would be minimal. However, where the plaintiff is a hemophiliac, the damages resulting from the cut are extensive, and the defendant is liable for all the damages. Once again, the defendant takes the plaintiff as he finds him.

■ CASE VOCABULARY

PATHOLOGY: Branch of medicine dealing with the nature of disease.

QUIESCENT: Dormant; causing no symptoms.

In Re Arbitration Between Polemis and Furness, Withy & Co., Ltd.

(Ship Owners) v. (Charterers)

[1921] 3 K.B. 560

A DEFENDANT MAY BE LIABLE FOR DAMAGES EVEN THOUGH THE EXTENT OR TYPE OF THE DAMAGES CAUSED BY THE DEFENDANT'S NEGLIGENT CONDUCT WAS NOT FORESEEABLE AT THE TIME OF THE CONDUCT

■ **INSTANT FACTS** Polemis (P) entered into arbitration with Furness (D) to recover damage to a ship that Furness (D) had chartered from Polemis (P).

■ **BLACK LETTER RULE** Where it is reasonably foreseeable that the defendant's negligent conduct would cause damages to the plaintiff, the defendant is liable even though the exact extent of the damages is not foreseeable.

■ **PROCEDURAL BASIS**

Appeal from arbitration for determination of defendant's liability for plaintiff's damages.

■ **FACTS**

Furness & Co. (D) chartered a ship from Polemis (P) to carry cargo including petrol or benzene. While the cargo was being discharged, a heavy board fell in the area where the cargo was stored, resulting in an explosion which destroyed the whole ship. Polemis (P) claiming that the explosion was due to the negligence of Furness (D), sought the full value of the ship from Furness (D). Furness (D) on the other hand contended that the damages were too remote. The claim was referred to arbitration, where the arbitrators found that the fire that destroyed the ship was caused by the spark between the falling board and the vapor from the benzene. Additionally, the arbitrators found that while the causing of the spark could not have been reasonably foreseeable, some damage to the ship might have reasonably been anticipated. The case is set for opinion for the court of appeal.

■ **ISSUE**

Where it is reasonably foreseeable that the defendant's negligent conduct would cause damages to the plaintiff, is the defendant liable even though the exact extent of the damages is not foreseeable?

■ **DECISION AND RATIONALE**

(Bankes, L.J, and Scrutton, L.J.) Yes. Where it is reasonably foreseeable that the defendant's negligent conduct would cause damages to the plaintiff, the defendant is liable even though the exact extent of the damages is not foreseeable. In this case, the plank (board) fell due to the negligence of Furness' (D) employees and caused a fire. It is immaterial that the causing of the spark could not have been anticipated. Contrary to Furness' (D) contention, neither the type of damages nor the extent of the damages need to be anticipated by the negligent defendant in order to find the defendant liable. Given that Furness (D) was negligent, and given that the damages were a direct result of Fumess' (D) negligence, the exact anticipation of Furness (D) is irrelevant. Once a defendant's act is negligent, the fact that its exact operation was not foreseeable is immaterial. (Appeal dismissed.)

Analysis:

So far we have seen that in negligence cases where physical injury to the plaintiff is involved, the defendant takes the plaintiff as he finds him. What about where there are damages to the plaintiff's property? For what kind of damages is the defendant liable? Note that the proximate cause element of negligence requires that the plaintiff's injury be a natural consequence of the defendant's negligent conduct. In other words, the defendant is liable only for foreseeable consequences of his/her conduct. The foreseeability requirement is satisfied as long as it is reasonably foreseeable that the defendant's conduct would lead to injury to the plaintiff's person or property. However, under this requirement, the extent or the exact type of damages need not be foreseeable. In this case, the board fell due to defendant's negligent conduct, and it was reasonably foreseeable that such conduct would result in some damage to the ship. However, it was not foreseeable that the falling of the board would result in a fire which would destroy the ship. Nevertheless, the defendants are liable for the full value of the ship, because it was foreseeable that their negligent conduct would result in "some" damage. Remember: extent, type and manner in which damages occur need not be foreseeable in order for the defendant to be liable.

■ CASE VOCABULARY

ARBITRATION: The submission of controversies, by agreement of the parties thereto, to persons chosen by themselves for determination.

ARBITRATOR: An impartial person chosen by the parties to a controversy to solve a dispute between them; the arbitrator is vested with the power to make a final determination concerning the issues in the controversy.

REMOTE CAUSE: The type of cause which does not necessarily produce an event without injury; thus, a cause which is not considered to be "proximate" will be regarded as "remote."

Overseas Tankship (U.K.) Ltd. v. Morts Dock & Engineering Co., Ltd. ["Wagon Mound No. 1"]

(Freighter Owners) v. *(Wharf Operators)*
[1961] A.C. 388 (Privy Council, 1961)

A DEFENDANT IS LIABLE ONLY FOR THOSE CONSEQUENCES OF HIS ACT WHICH ARE REASONABLY FORESEEABLE

■ **INSTANT FACTS** Morts Dock & Engineering Co., Ltd. (P) ("Morts Dock") sued Overseas Tankship (U.K.) Ltd. (D) ("Overseas) for the fire that destroyed Morts Dock's (P) wharf.

■ **BLACK LETTER RULE** A defendant is not liable for unforeseeable consequences of his negligent conduct, even though they were the direct result of defendant's conduct.

■ **PROCEDURAL BASIS**

Appeal from action for negligence for recovery of damages.

■ **FACTS**

Overseas Tankship (D) negligently discharged oil in Morts Dock's (P) wharf. Some cotton waste which was floating on the surface of the oil caught on fire when Morts Dock's (P) employees dropped molten metal in the water. The fire damaged the dock and two ships which were docked at the wharf. Morts Dock (P) sued Overseas (D) for damages. The trial court found that Overseas (D) could not have reasonably known that the oil would catch on fire. However, judgment was entered in favor of Morts Dock (P), and was affirmed by the Supreme Court of New South Wales. Overseas appeals to the Privy Council.

■ **ISSUE**

Is a defendant liable for the unforeseeable consequences of his/her negligent conduct which were a direct result of the defendant's conduct?

■ **DECISION AND RATIONALE**

(Simonds, J.) No. A defendant is not liable for unforeseeable consequences of his negligent conduct, even though they were the direct result of defendant's conduct. A man must be considered liable for the probable consequences of his act. To demand more of him is too harsh a rule. One is liable for the natural, necessary and probable consequences of his actions because he should have reasonably foreseen them. Tortious liability is founded on the consequences of one's act and not the act alone. Thus, a defendant's liability should be determined with respect to the consequences and damages of his act and nothing else. A defendant cannot be found liable unless the damages flowing from his negligent conduct are reasonably foreseeable. (Dismissed, and remanded for nuisance cause of action.)

Analysis:

In the previous case, *Polemis*, the court held that a defendant is liable for all kinds of damages directly flowing from his negligent conduct, however unforeseeable, as long as it was reasonably foreseeable that the defendant's conduct would result in some kind of damage or harm. This case, known as *Wagon Mound No. 1* stands for the proposition that the defendant is liable only for the foreseeable consequences of his actions. Thus, even though a defendant's negligent conduct was a direct result of damages to the plaintiff, a defendant may not be held liable unless the actual damages were reasonably foreseeable at the time of the defendant's conduct. Thus, this case stands in sharp contrast to *Polemis*. In a sense, this case is limiting the liability of defendants only to cases where the actual injury or damage to the plaintiffs are reasonably foreseeable.

■ CASE VOCABULARY

CONSONANT: Consistent with.

COTERMINOUS: Having the same or coincident boundaries; coextensive in scope or duration.

DIRECT CAUSE: Direct cause refers to the active, efficient cause that sets in motion a chain of events that brings about a result without the intervention of any other independent source. "Direct cause" is often used interchangeably with proximate cause.

FORESEEABILITY: A concept used in various areas of law to limit liability of a party for the consequences of his acts to the consequences which are within the scope of a foreseeable risk. A foreseeable risk is a risk whose consequences a person of ordinary prudence would reasonably expect to occur.

VENIAL: Pardonable or excusable.

Overseas Tankship (U.K.) Ltd. v. Miller Steamship Co. ["Wagon Mound No. 2"]

(Freighter Owners) v. *(Other Ship Owners)*
[1967] 1 A.C. 617 (Privy Council, 1966)

A DEFENDANT IS LIABLE FOR DAMAGES WHERE A REASONABLE PERSON IN THE DEFENDANT'S POSITION WOULD HAVE FORESEEN AND PREVENTED THE RISK OF INJURY

■ **INSTANT FACTS** Miller Steamship Co. (P) ("Miller") sued Overseas Tankship (U.K.) Ltd. (D) ("Overseas") for destruction of Miller's (P) ships due to a fire.

■ **BLACK LETTER RULE** The foreseeability of the consequences of a defendant's actions depend on the balancing between the likelihood of risk and the magnitude of damages flowing therefrom.

■ PROCEDURAL BASIS

Appeal in action in negligence for recovery of damages.

■ FACTS

Overseas Tankship (D) negligently discharged oil in a dock where Miller Steamship's (P) ships were moored. Some cotton waste which was floating on the surface of the oil caught on fire when the employees dropped molten metal in the water. The fire damaged the dock and Miller's (P) ships. The latter sued Overseas (D) to recover for the damage to the ships. The trial court found that the occurrence of the damage to Miller's (P) property as a result of the oil spillage was not reasonably foreseeable, and that Overseas (D) was not liable for damages to Miller (P). The Supreme Court of New South Wales affirmed. Miller (P) appeals to the Privy Council.

■ ISSUE

Does the foreseeability of the consequences of a defendant's actions depend on the balancing between the likelihood of risk and the magnitude of damages flowing therefrom?

■ DECISION AND RATIONALE

(Reid, J.) Yes. The foreseeability of the consequences of a defendant's actions depend on the balancing between the likelihood of risk and the magnitude of damages flowing therefrom. In this case, some risk of fire would have been present to a reasonable man in the position of the ship's engineer. With appreciation of that risk, then serious damage to the ship and other property was foreseeable. A reasonable man should only neglect a risk where there is valid justification to do so. In this case, there was no justification for discharging the oil in the water. Thus, from every point of view, it would have been reasonable for the engineer to stop the discharge. Additionally, he ought to have known that it is possible to ignite oil on water. Additionally, he should have known that such ignition would occur only under exceptional circumstances. However, even though the risk is minimal he should not have dismissed it if such a risk is easily prevented. If it is clear that a reasonable man would have realized the risk and prevented it, then it must follow that the defendants are liable in damages.

Analysis:

Note that in *Wagon Mound No. 1*, the court held that the defendant is only liable for the damages that are reasonably foreseeable. That case, as we saw, was in direct conflict with Polemis, which held that a defendant is liable for all damages directly resulting from the defendant's negligent conduct. At first glance, *Wagon Mound No. 2* may seem different from both of these cases. However, it really is not Like *Wagon Mound No. 1*, it limits the liability of the defendant to damages which are reasonably foreseeable. However, this case, unlike *Wagon Mound No. 1* presents a formula for determining foreseeability. In this case, the court requires that the risk of damage be weighed against the magnitude of the damage, and also against the cost of preventing the damage. If a reasonable person in the defendant's position would have prevented the risk of damage, then the damage is considered foreseeable and the defendant is liable for it, even if the probability that the damage would occur is very unlikely.

■ CASE VOCABULARY

FORESEEABILITY: The foreseeability of the consequences of a defendant's actions depend on the balancing between the likelihood of risk and the magnitude of damages flowing therefrom.

NUISANCE: Something that annoys and disturbs someone in possession of his property, making its regular use physically difficult or uncomfortable.

Palsgraf v. Long Island R.R. Co.

(Passenger) v. *(Railroad)*

248 N.Y. 339, 162 N.E. 99 (1928)

A DEFENDANT IS ONLY LIABLE FOR DAMAGES TO A PLAINTIFF TO WHOM THE DEFENDANT FORESEEABLY OWES THE DUTY OF CARE

■ **INSTANT FACTS** Palsgraf (P) sued Long Island R.R. Co. (D) ("the railroad") for the injuries sustained when a package fell out of the hand of one of the train passengers and exploded.

■ **BLACK LETTER RULE** A defendant owes a duty of care only to those plaintiffs who are in the reasonably foreseeable zone of danger.

■ **PROCEDURAL BASIS**

Appeal in action in negligence for recovery of damages.

■ **FACTS**

Palsgraf (P) was standing on the platform of the train station when a man jumped on a already-moving train. The man was being pulled in by an employee of the railroad (D), when an unmarked package containing firecrackers fell out of his hand. When the package fell, the firecrackers within it exploded, and the shock of the explosion threw down scales many feet away from the explosion. The scales fell on Palsgraf (P) injuring her. Palsgraf (P) sued the railroad (D) for her injuries. The trial court and the Appellate Division ruled in favor of Palsgraf (P). The railroad (D) appeals.

■ **ISSUE**

Does a defendant owe a duty of care only to those plaintiffs who are in the reasonably foreseeable zone of danger?

■ **DECISION AND RATIONALE**

(Cardozo, C.J.) Yes. A defendant owes a duty of care only to those plaintiffs who are in the reasonably foreseeable zone of danger. In this case, the conduct of the railroad employee (D) was not negligent at all with respect to Palsgraf (P). No one was on notice that the package contained explosives which could harm a person so far removed. In every negligence case, before negligence of the defendant can be determined, it must be found that the defendant owed a duty to the plaintiff, and that the defendant could have avoided the injury to the plaintiff, had he observed this duty. The plaintiff in a negligence case may sue in her own right only for a wrong personal to her. The orbit of the danger or risk as disclosed to a reasonable person would be the orbit of the duty. Thus, a plaintiff must show a wrong to herself, or a violation of her own rights, but not a "wrong" to anyone. In this case, there is no indication in the facts to suggest to the most cautious mind that the wrapped package would explode in the train station. Even if the guard had thrown the package intentionally, he would not have threatened Palsgraf's (P) safety, so far as appearances could warn him. Thus, liability cannot be greater where the act of the guard was unintentional or inadvertent. (Reversed.)

■ **DISSENT**

(Andrews, J.) Where an act threatens the safety of others, the doer is liable for all its proximate consequences, even when the injury is to one who would generally be thought to be outside of the radius of danger. It is important to inquire only as to the relation between cause and effect. Due care is a duty imposed on each member of the society to protect others in the society from unnecessary danger, and not just to protect A, B, or C. Negligence involves a relationship between a man and his fellows, but not merely a relationship between man and those whom he might reasonably expect his act would injure. Everyone owes to the world at large the duty of refraining from those acts which may unreasonably threaten the safety of others. If such an act occurs, not only has he wronged those to whom harm might reasonably be expected to result, but also those whom he has in fact injured, even if they may be thought of as outside the zone of danger.

Analysis:

This case deals with the question of causation in terms of the plaintiff. In other words, to whom does a defendant owe a duty of care? According to the majority opinion written by Cardozo, the defendant only owes a duty of care to those individuals who are within the foreseeable zone of danger. Thus, according to the majority opinion in this case the plaintiff, who was standing far away from the explosion, is not entitled to damages even though she was injured. According to the dissent, however (the famous Andrews dissent), every plaintiff is a foreseeable plaintiff. Thus, regardless of how far or how near or how unforeseeable, any individual is entitled to recover for his/her damages which resulted from the defendant's negligent conduct. The Cardozo opinion in this case is the theory adhered to by a majority of courts. The Andrews opinion is a minority opinion followed in a few jurisdiction. Note that Cardozo's opinion, like *Wagon Mound No. 1,* is a way to limit liability for tortfeasors based on the foreseeability requirement. Thus, when dealing with the issue of proximate causation, we must not only ask whether the injury to the plaintiff was proximately caused by the defendant's negligence, but also whether the plaintiff was a foreseeable plaintiff to whom the defendant owed a duty of care. Andrews' opinion, on the other hand, is similar to the "direct cause" theory which we saw in *Polemis.*

■ CASE VOCABULARY

ATTENUATE: To lessen or weaken.

CONFLAGRATION: A great destructive burning or fire.

FORESEEABILITY: The foreseeability of the consequences of a defendant's actions depend on the balancing between the likelihood of risk and the magnitude of damages flowing therefrom.

INVASION: An encroachment upon the rights of another.

PROXIMATE CAUSE: The type of cause which in the natural and continuous sequence unbroken by any new independent cause produces an event, and without which the injury would not have occurred.

Yun v. Ford Motor Co.

(Daughter Of Man Killed On Freeway) v. *(Any And All Connected With The Accident)*

276 N.J.Super. 142, 647 A.2d 841 (1994)

QUESTIONS OF PROXIMATE CAUSE SHOULD BE DECIDED BY THE JURY AND SUMMARY JUDGMENT ON THE ISSUE SHOULD RARELY BE GRANTED

■ **INSTANT FACTS** Yun's (P) father, Chang, was struck and killed by a car when he ran across two busy freeway lanes to retrieve a spare tire which fell off his car.

■ **BLACK LETTER RULE** When the court determines that an injury was not reasonably, foreseeably caused by the defendant, the issue of proximate cause may be taken away from the jury.

■ **PROCEDURAL BASIS**

Appeal from the trial court's decision granting summary judgment to all defendants.

■ **FACTS**

Yun (P) was driving her van on the Garden State Parkway near midnight. Her sixty-five year old father, Chang, was a passenger in the van. There was some difference in the evidence as to whether the conditions were "dark and rain-slicked," or "light traffic" and "visibility good." In any event, while they were driving along, the spare tire on the van came loose and fell off, rolling across both lanes of freeway traffic and ultimately coming to rest against the median guardrail. The spare tire assembly on the van had previously been bent as a result of an accident Yun (P) had been involved in. Yun had instructed her mechanic not to fix it, as she was waiting for the other driver's insurance company to handle having it repaired. After the spare tire fell off the van, Yun (P) safely drove the van to the right side of the freeway and stopped on the berm. Chang got out of the van and proceeded to run across two lanes of the freeway to retrieve the spare tire and some other parts. On the way back across the freeway, Chang was struck and killed by another vehicle. Yun (P) sues anybody and everybody, including Ford Motor (D).

■ **ISSUE**

If an injury was not reasonably caused by a defendant, may the issue of proximate cause be taken away from the jury?

■ **DECISION AND RATIONALE**

(Villanueva, J.) Yes. The alleged defect in the spare tire bracket assembly was not the proximate cause of Chang's injury, as his actions constituted highly extraordinary conduct, thereby breaking the chain of causation. Proximate cause is a cause which sets off a foreseeable sequence of consequences, unbroken by any superseding cause, and which is a substantial factor in producing the particular injury. The car Chang was riding in had come safely to rest at the side of the freeway, and the act of running out into busy traffic to retrieve a spare tire could be called nothing short of extraordinarily dangerous. Logic and fairness dictate that liability should not extend to injuries received as a result of Chang's senseless decision to cross the freeway under such dangerous conditions. Common sense should have persuaded Chang to wait for assistance or abandon the bald tire and damaged assembly. The van could have been driven safely home. At most, the presence of the spare tire created a condition upon which the subsequent intervening force acted and, as such, there is no proximate cause relationship between the defective product and the injury. Proximate cause is usually an issue reserved for the jury's determination. In certain cases, however, the issue of proximate cause has been held so intertwined with issues of policy as to be treated as a matter of law for the court to determine. Legal responsibility for the consequences of an act cannot be imposed without limit. The events here transgress the judicial line beyond which liability should not be extended as a matter of fairness or policy. It was not reasonably foreseeable that if the spare wheel assembly was defective, and the driver/owner of the car and Chang refused to have it repaired and later while they were driving on the freeway at night, it fell off but they safely brought the car to a stop on a berm, that Chang would then violate the law by twice crossing the freeway to go to the median to retrieve the parts and be killed by a passing car. Furthermore, reasonable people could not differ that the continued driving with knowledge of the defect and the senseless, and illegal crossing of the freeway were intervening superseding causes of the accident which broke the chain of causation. Affirmed.

■ CONCURRENCE AND DISSENT

(Baime, J.) I agree that the judgment in favor of Ford Motor Company (D) should be affirmed because Yun (P) did not oppose the motion to dismiss, and I also agree that the record does not support a negligence claim against Yun's (P) mechanic. I do not agree, however with the majority as to the remaining defendants. I believe that Yun's (P) submissions relating to proximate cause were sufficient to defeat the motion for summary judgment. Questions of proximate cause and intervening cause are to be left to the jury where there might be reasonable difference of opinion as to the foreseeability of a particular risk or the reasonableness of a defendant's conduct. I am convinced that reasonable persons might differ regarding whether Chang's death was proximately caused by the tire assembly. The issue is reasonably debatable and one that should be submitted to the jury for determination.

Analysis:

In an area of the law which is so controversial, it seems astounding that the court would presume to substitute its opinion for that of "reasonable" people. The court admits that the issues of proximate cause and intervening cause are generally within the jury's domain, yet it goes on to rip the decision-making function away from it. The dissent makes a very good point that the general population does not always think and act the way judges do. It does then make sense to have lay people, not judges, make decisions regarding the choices and mind set of the general population. Indeed, a jury might very well find it acceptable for a person to stop and retrieve equipment that fell off the car. It might seem more reasonable [and certainly more environmentally conscious] to stop and pick up automobile parts which have flown off of a vehicle, rather than just saying "Oh well, I didn't need that pesky wheel anyway!" When faced with having to purchase a new wheel, or simply stopping to pick it up, many may have acted as Chang did. Perhaps then the issue should have been left for the jury to decide. Apparently, the Supreme Court felt that way as well, as it reversed the appellate division for the reasons expressed in Baime's dissent.

■ CASE VOCABULARY

CHAIN OF CAUSATION: Foreseeable sequence of consequences leading to the result complained of.

Derdiarian v. Felix Contracting Corp.

(Injured Employee) v. *(Employer)*

51 N.Y.2d 308, 414 N.E.2d 666, 434 N.Y.S.2d 166 (1980)

INTERVENING ACTS OF THIRD PARTIES BREAK THE CAUSAL CONNECTION BETWEEN THE DEFENDANT'S NEGLIGENCE AND THE PLAINTIFF'S INJURIES IF THEY ARE NOT REASONABLY FORESEEABLE

■ **INSTANT FACTS** Derdiarian (P) sued Felix Contracting Corp. (D) ("Felix") for injuries that he sustained when a car ran over the ditch in which Derdiarian (P) was working.

■ **BLACK LETTER RULE** Where the act of a third party intervenes between the defendant's negligent conduct and the plaintiff's injury, the causal connection is not severed if the intervening act is a normal and foreseeable consequence of the risk created by the defendant's negligent conduct.

■ PROCEDURAL BASIS

Action in negligence for recovery of damages for personal injury.

■ FACTS

Derdiarian (P), working in an excavation as the employee of the subcontractor hired by Felix, was hit by an automobile when the driver of the automobile suffered a seizure and lost control of his car. Hit by the automobile, Derdiarian (P) was thrown in the air, and suffered severe injuries and burns. Derdiarian (P) sued Felix (D) claiming that the latter had negligently failed to take measures to insure the safety of workers at the excavation site. At the trial, Derdiarian's (P) traffic safety expert testified that the usual method of safeguarding workers is to erect barriers around the excavation, and to have two flagmen around the site instead of the one provided by Felix (D). The latter defended on the ground that Derdiarian's (P) injury was caused by the automobile driver's negligence and that, as a matter of law, there was no causal connection between Felix's (D) negligence conduct and Derdiarian's (P) injury.

■ ISSUE

Where the act of a third party intervenes between the defendant's negligent conduct and the plaintiff's injury, is the causal connection severed if the intervening act is a normal and foreseeable consequence of the risk created by the defendant's negligent conduct?

■ DECISION AND RATIONALE

(Cooke, C.J.) No. Where the act of a third party intervenes between the defendant's negligent conduct and the plaintiff's injury, the causal connection is not severed if the intervening act is a normal and foreseeable consequence of the risk created by the defendant's negligent conduct. If the intervening act is extraordinary under the circumstances, not foreseeable in the normal course of events, or independent or far removed from the defendant's conduct, then it may sever the causal link. Additionally, such issues of foreseeability are to be decided by the jury. However, where the independent intervening act operates but does not flow from the original negligence of the defendant, as a matter of law there is not causal link between the defendant's negligence and the plaintiff's injury.

In this case, however, the automobile driver's negligence, does not, as a matter of law, sever the causal link. A prime hazard of Felix's (D) failure to erect barriers around the excavation site is the possibility that a driver will negligently enter the work site and cause injury to the workers. The driver's negligence does not relieve Felix (D) from liability. The jury could have concluded that the foreseeable and normal result of the risk created by Felix (D) was injury of a worker by a car entering the improperly protected area. Additionally, the fact that Felix could not anticipate the precise manner of the accident or the extent of Derdiarian's (P) injury, does not relieve Felix (D) from liability, where the general risk and character of injuries are foreseeable. (Affirmed.)

Analysis:

Thus far, we have only encountered cases where the defendant's negligence directly causes the plaintiff's injury. This case is a little more complicated in that there was an independent intervening act between the plaintiff's injury and the defendant's conduct. So whose act is liable for the plaintiff's injury? Again this is a proximate cause issue. If the independent intervening act is foreseeable, then there is no break in the causal chain between the defendant's negligence and the plaintiff's injury. On the other hand, if the intervening act is not foreseeable, then the causal chain is broken. In the latter scenario, the intervening act is also known as a superseding cause. This means that the intervening act is the real cause of the plaintiff's injury and supersedes the original negligence of the defendant.

■ CASE VOCABULARY

INTERVENING CAUSE: A cause which comes into active operation in producing the result after the negligence of the defendant; "intervening" is used in a time sense; it refers to later events.

NEXUS: A link or connection.

SUPERSEDE: To displace instead of another.

SUPERSEDING CAUSE: An intervening cause which is so substantially responsible for the ultimate injury that it acts to cut off the liability of preceding actors regardless of whether their prior negligence was or was not a substantial factor in bringing about the injury complained of.

Watson v. Kentucky & Indiana Bridge & R.R. Co.

(Injured Bystander) v. *(Railroad)*

137 Ky. 619, 126 S.W. 146 (1910)

GENERALLY, THE INTENTIONAL CRIMINAL INTERVENING ACT OF A THIRD PARTY BREAKS THE CAUSAL CHAIN BETWEEN THE ORIGINAL DEFENDANT'S NEGLIGENCE AND THE PLAINTIFF'S INJURY

■ **INSTANT FACTS** Watson (P) sued the railroad for injuries sustained when oil spilled from the train caught on fire by a match dropped by Duerr.

■ **BLACK LETTER RULE** A negligent defendant is not liable for the intentional intervening malicious acts of a third party which are not reasonably foreseeable.

■ **PROCEDURAL BASIS**

Appeal in action for negligence for recovery of damages.

■ **FACTS**

Kentucky and Indiana Bridge & R.R. Co. ("the railroad") (D) negligently spilled a tank of gasoline on the street. A bystander, Duerr, struck a match which caused an explosion injuring Watson (P). At trial, Duerr testified that he dropped his matches in the gasoline after lighting a cigarette. Other witnesses testified that Duerr deliberately lit a match and threw it in the gasoline in order to set it on fire. The trial court directed a verdict in favor of the railroad (D), finding that Duerr's act was malicious and intentional. Watson (P) appeals.

■ **ISSUE**

Is a negligent defendant liable for the intentional intervening malicious acts of a third party which are not reasonably foreseeable?

■ **DECISION AND RATIONALE**

(Settle, J.) No. A negligent defendant is not liable for the intentional intervening malicious acts of a third party which are not reasonably foreseeable. To begin with, the question of proximate cause is one which should be decided by the jury. Thus, in this case it was for the jury and not for the court to determine from the evidence whether Duerr's lighting of the match was inadvertent or wanton and malicious. In the opinion of this court, escaping of the gasoline due to the railroad's (D) negligence and the probable consequence of it coming in contact with fire and causing an explosion was doubtless. It was most probable that someone would strike a match to light a cigarette, and such action under the circumstances of the case cannot be said to be the efficient cause of the explosion. An explosion could not have occurred without the primary negligence of the railroad. On the contrary, if the action of Duerr in lighting the match was malicious and intentional, then the railroad (D) is relieved of liability. The railroad could not have reasonably foreseen that a person would maliciously light a match for the evil purpose of producing an explosion. Thus, if the intervening agency is so unexpected or extraordinary as that the defendant could not or ought not to have anticipated it, the defendant will not be liable. Certainly, a defendant is not bound to anticipate the criminal acts of others and is not liable for them. (Reversed and remanded.)

Analysis:

This case stands for two separate propositions. In the first place, the question of proximate cause is for the jury, and not for the court to decide. This makes sense because the jury consists of the members of the community who can, based on the evidence and based on their everyday experience, determine whether the negligent conduct of the defendant was the cause of the plaintiff's injury. As mentioned in the opinion in *Derdiarian*, there are certain rare cases where the causal link between the defendant's conduct and the plaintiff's injury is completely superseded by an intervening act. In such cases, the issue of proximate cause is determined by the court as a matter of law. However, for most of the cases that we will encounter, the proximate cause issue is not so cut and dried, and is therefore, one which will be decided by the jury. Secondly, the opinion in this case seems to suggest that intervening intentional criminal acts of others relieve the primary defendant of liability. The basis for this concept is that intentional acts of others are not foreseeable, and as such there is no reason that the defendant should have known about them. Thus, such acts break the causal chain and become superseding causes for the plaintiff's negligence. Not all courts are in agreement with this reasoning. Many courts simply determine the issue based on whether or not the criminal act of the third party was reasonably foreseeable. Most courts, however, are in agreement that where the defendant's negligence is that he/she is increasing the risk of criminal harm to the plaintiff, the intervening criminal act will not break the causal chain.

■ CASE VOCABULARY

DIRECTED VERDICT: A verdict entered in a jury trial by the court, without consideration by the jury, because the facts elicited during the trial, together with the applicable law, made it clear that the directed verdict was the only one which could have been reasonably returned.

WANTON: Arbitrary, careless, cruel, evil or malicious.

Fuller v. Preis

(Executor) v. *(Automobile Driver)*

35 N.Y.2d 425, 322 N.E.2d 263, 363 N.Y.S.2d 568 (1974)

SUICIDE COMMITTED BY AN INJURED PLAINTIFF IS NOT NECESSARILY AN INTERVENING AND SUPERSEDING CAUSE PRECLUDING LIABILITY OF ORIGINAL TORTFEASOR

■ **INSTANT FACTS** Dr. Lewis committed suicide after being involved in an accident with Preis (D).

■ **BLACK LETTER RULE** An act of suicide is not, as a matter of law, a superseding cause in negligence law which precludes liability of the original tortfeasor.

■ **PROCEDURAL BASIS**

Appeal from dismissal of complaint in wrongful death action.

■ **FACTS**

Seven months after getting in to an accident, the decedent, Dr. Lewis, committed suicide. The evidence shows that the decedent was suffering from seizures after the accident, while he had not had any seizures before the accident. On the day of his suicide, the decedent had had three seizures. Fuller (P), executor of the decedent's estate, filed a wrongful death action against Preis (D), claiming that Preis'(D) negligence in the automobile accident was the proximate cause of the decedent's suicide. The jury at the trial level returned a verdict in favor of Fuller (P). The Appellate Division dismissed the complaint. Fuller (P) appeals.

■ **ISSUE**

Is an act of suicide, as a matter of law, a superseding cause in negligence law which precludes liability of the original tortfeasor?

■ **DECISION AND RATIONALE**

(Breitel, C.J.) No. An act of suicide is not, as a matter of law, a superseding cause in negligence law which precludes liability of the original tortfeasor. There is no public policy or precedent limiting recovery for suicide of a tortiously injured person driven "insane" by the consequence of the tortious act. In this case, the jury was instructed upon the theory of liability for a suicide by an accident victim who is suffering from ensuing mental disease, and who was unable to control the "irresistible impulse" to destroy himself. Thus, the only issue to be determined is whether the suicide was an "irresistible impulse" caused by traumatic brain damage. Tort law recognizes that one may retain the power to intend, and yet to have an irresistible impulse to act, and therefore be incapable of voluntary conduct. On the day of the suicide, the decedent suffered from three seizures, and his wife testified that he had locked himself in the bathroom, and was saying "I must do it, I must do it." In this case, the jury found that the decedent knew what he was doing, and intended to do what he did, and yet, he was incapable of controlling the impulse to destroy himself. Where suicide is preceded by a history of trauma, brain damage, epileptic seizures, depression, and despair, the question of whether the suicide was a rational act or a result of an irresistible impulse, was a question of fact for the jury. (Reversed, and new trial ordered.)

Analysis:

Remember that a superseding act is one which breaks the causal chain between the negligent conduct and the injury to the plaintiff. This case deals with whether or not suicide is a superseding cause as a matter of law. The answer is no. Where facts prove that the suicide was an involuntary act, or a product of an irresistible impulse, which has ensued from the original tort, then it is not a superseding act. However, where suicide is a rational act of a sound mind, then it is considered a superseding cause, unrelated to the negligent conduct of the defendant. Most importantly, this is a question for the jury to answer. The question always boils down to the same issue: Is the defendant's conduct the proximate cause of the plaintiff's injury. In cases where the independent acts of third parties are involved, the question is whether the causal chain is broken, and this is done by looking at whether the third party's act was foreseeable or not. All these questions are questions of fact and should be decided by the jury.

■ CASE VOCABULARY

IRRESISTIBLE IMPULSE: In tort law, the recognition that one may retain the power to intend, to know, and yet to have an impulse to act, and therefore be incapable of voluntary conduct.

SUPERSEDING CAUSE: An intervening cause which is so substantially responsible for the ultimate injury that it acts to cut off the liability of preceding actors regardless of whether or not their prior negligence was a substantial factor in bringing about the injury complained of.

McCoy v. American Suzuki Motor Corp.

(Injured Pedestrian) v. *(Manufacturer of Disabled Vehicle)*

136 Wash.2d 350, 961 P.2d 952 (1998)

THE RESCUE DOCTRINE IS A VIABLE THEORY WHICH IS APPLICABLE IN PRODUCT LIABILITY ACTIONS

■ **INSTANT FACTS** McCoy (P) was struck by a passing car as he was assisting at the scene of a traffic accident.

■ **BLACK LETTER RULE** The rescue doctrine may be invoked in product liability actions and, if it is, the rescuer is required to show the defendant proximately caused his injuries.

■ **PROCEDURAL BASIS**

Appeal from the Court of Appeals' reversal of the trial court's granting of summary judgment of dismissal.

■ **FACTS**

One evening, McCoy (P) was driving on the interstate when the car in front of him, a Suzuki Samurai, swerved off the road and overturned. McCoy (P) stopped to render assistance to the driver, who was seriously injured. A state trooper arrived on the scene and asked McCoy (P) to place flares on the interstate to warn approaching vehicles [what, no backup?]. McCoy (P) did this, and he also moved further down the interstate from the accident scene, with lit flares in each hand, to manually direct traffic to the inside lane [fulfilling a childhood dream]. About two hours later, the accident scene was cleared, leaving only the trooper and McCoy (P) on the roadway. McCoy (P) began walking back on the shoulder of the road to his car with a lit flare in his road-side hand. As he approached the scene, the trooper drove away without any acknowledgment to McCoy (P) [the ingrate!]. Moments later, McCoy (P) was struck from behind by a hit-and-run vehicle. McCoy (P) sued Suzuki (D), among others, for its allegedly defective Samurai which allegedly caused the wreck in the first place.

■ **ISSUE**

Does the rescue doctrine apply in product liability actions and, if so, must the plaintiff show proximate causation?

■ **DECISION AND RATIONALE**

(Sanders, J.) Yes. The rescue doctrine may be invoked in product liability actions and, if it is, the rescuer is required to show the defendant proximately caused his injuries. The rescue doctrine allows an injured rescuer to sue the party which caused the danger requiring the rescue in the first place. This doctrine serves to inform tort-feasors that it is foreseeable a rescuer will come to aid the person imperiled by the tort-feasor's actions, and therefore the tort-feasor owes the rescuer a duty similar to the duty he owes the person he imperils. Additionally, the rescue doctrine negates the presumption that the rescuer assumed the risk of injury when he knowingly undertook the dangerous rescue, so long as he does not act rashly or recklessly. To achieve rescuer status, one must demonstrate: (1) the defendant was negligent to the person rescued and that negligence caused the peril or appearance of peril to the person rescued; (2) the peril or appearance of peril was imminent; (3) a reasonably prudent person would have concluded such peril or appearance of peril existed; and (4) the rescuer acted with reasonable care in effectuating the rescue. The Court of Appeals found that McCoy (P) demonstrated sufficient facts to put the issue of whether McCoy (P) is entitled to rescuer status to the jury. We do not question this finding. Suzuki (D) argues the rescue doctrine may not be invoked in product liability actions. We disagree. The rescue doctrine is a reflection of a societal value judgment that rescuers should not be barred from bringing suit for knowingly placing themselves in danger to undertake a rescue. We conceive of no reason why this doctrine should not apply with equal force when a product manufacturer causes the danger. This being so, the rescuer, like any other plaintiff, must still show the defendant proximately caused his injuries. We additionally find the foreseeability that a rescuer such as McCoy (P) would be injured by a third vehicle under these particular facts to be sufficiently close that it should be decided by a jury, not the court. In the present case, if the Suzuki Samurai is found to be defective the jury could find it foreseeable that the vehicle would roll and that an approaching car would cause injury to either those in the Suzuki Samurai or to a rescuer, depending on the specific facts to be proved. The alleged fault of Suzuki (D), if proved, is not so remote from the injuries that its liability should be cut off as a matter of law. Accordingly, we will not dismiss this case for lack of legal causation. Instead we remand the case for trial consistent with this opinion.

Analysis:

As Justice Cardozo so eloquently put it, "danger invites rescue." If a wrongdoer puts a person in danger, he should be liable to a rescuer who puts his own safety in peril to render aid. It is generally agreed that a defendant who caused a danger will be liable to someone who is injured trying to escape from it, therefore the rescue doctrine is a natural extension of this rule. The court succinctly identifies the four requirements one must demonstrate in order to achieve rescuer status, and it very clearly outlines the way to the logical conclusion that the rescue doctrine applies to product liability actions just as it may in ordinary negligence actions. Aligning product liability actions with negligence actions as far as applying the rescue doctrine, the court also made a wise decision in requiring that a rescuer must show the defendant proximately caused his injuries. This is the same burden he would bear in a negligence action, and it is in keeping with general principles of liability. But, the issue of causation in this case seems so remote. A car broke down, and somebody stops to render assistance, but a third person (the driver of the hit-and-run vehicle) is negligent, causing the injury. It is difficult to understand how the liability returns to the manufacturer of the vehicle. Here, there is no privity between the manufacturer and McCoy (P), nor the manufacturer and the hit-and-run vehicle. It appears as if there is no connection at all!

■ CASE VOCABULARY

RESCUE DOCTRINE: A tort-feasor is liable to his victim's rescuer for injuries sustained during a reasonable rescue attempt.

Kelly v. Gwinnell

(Injured Driver) v. *(Drunk Driver)*

96 N.J. 538, 476 A.2d 1219 (1984)

A HOST MAY BE LIABLE FOR THE NEGLIGENCE OF AN ADULT SOCIAL GUEST WHO HAS BECOME VISIBLY INTOXICATED AT THE HOST'S HOME AND IS THEN INVOLVED IN A TRAFFIC ACCIDENT

■ **INSTANT FACTS** Kelly sued Gwinnell (D) for injuries Kelly (P) sustained when hit by Gwinnell (D) who in turn seeks recovery from Zak (D).

■ **BLACK LETTER RULE** A host is liable for the negligence of an adult social guest who has become visibly intoxicated at the host's home, and where risk of harm to others is foreseeable.

■ **PROCEDURAL BASIS**

Appeal in action for recovery of damages.

■ **FACTS**

Gwinnell (D) had a few drinks at Zak's (D) home, and while visibly drunk, left Zak's (D) home. While driving, Gwinnell (D) collided with Kelly (P). Kelly (P) sued Gwinnell (D) for injuries suffered. Gwinnell (D) in turn joined Zak (D) as a defendant. The trial court, granting Zak's (D) motion for summary judgment ruled that a host, as a matter of law is not liable for the negligence of an adult social guest who has become intoxicated at the host's home. The Appellate Division affirmed. Gwinnell (D) appeals.

■ **ISSUE**

Is a host liable for the negligence of an adult social guest who has become visibly intoxicated at the host's home and where the risk of harm to others is reasonably foreseeable?

■ **DECISION AND RATIONALE**

(Wilentz, C.J.) Yes. A host is liable for the negligence of an adult social guest who has become visibly intoxicated at the host's home where the risk of harm to others is foreseeable. When the negligent conduct of a party creates a risk of harm or danger to others, setting off foreseeable consequences that lead to the plaintiff's injury, the negligent conduct is deemed the proximate cause of the injury. In this case, the facts suggest that Zak (D) knew that Gwinnell was visibly intoxicated. A reasonable person in Zak's (D) position could foresee that the providing of alcohol to Gwinnell (D) would make it more likely that Gwinnell (D) would not be able to operate his car carefully, and that Gwinnell (D) was likely to injure someone as a result of negligent operation of his vehicle. In this case, in light of the thousands of deaths that occur due to consumption of alcohol and drunk driving, public policy considerations support extension of liability to social hosts who serve liquor to adult social guests who are already visibly intoxicated. (Reversed and remanded)

■ **DISSENT**

(Garibaldi, J.): In cases such as this, the legislature is better equipped to effectuate the goals of reducing injuries from drunken driving and protecting the interests of the injured without placing such a grave burden on the average citizen. This court is imposing high duties of care on social hosts. While such laws may be suitable for commercial providers of alcoholic beverages, the law is not suitable for social hosts. A social host will find it more difficult to determine levels and different degrees of intoxication. There is a lower level of control over the consumption of liquor than in a commercial establishment. Also, from the court's opinion it is not clear to what lengths the social host must go in order to avoid liability. Additionally, unlike commercial establishments which have insurance, a host may not have insurance.

Analysis:

This case is probably a scary decision to a lot of us. Invite some guests over; they have a couple of drinks; they leave, and on the way home they get into an accident. The liability may be imposed on you as the social host. This court extends the duty of a person to protect others against unreasonable risk of harm to unreasonable lengths. Why? The court reasons that the duty should be imposed because it is reasonable for a host to foresee that a drunken guest will get into a car, and collide with another and cause injury. Additionally, the court's other reason for extension of this duty is the public policy of protection of individuals against drunk drivers. Note that as the dissent insists, the ramifications of this law are mind-boggling. How should a host know if someone is truly drunk? How should a host know how many drinks someone's had? Note, however, that there are states which impose such liability on bar owners and other commercial establishments serving alcohol. The reasoning behind such rules is that such establishments are in a better position and more experienced than a social host to determine whether someone is drunk, have a deeper pocket (insurance), and have better control over how many drinks they serve to their patrons.

■ CASE VOCABULARY

DRAM SHOP ACT: A legislative enactment imposing strict liability upon the seller of intoxicating beverages when the sale results in harm to a third party's person.

LICENSEE: One to whom a license has been granted, one whose presence on the premises is not invited, but tolerated. Thus, a licensee is a person who is neither a customer, nor a servant, nor a trespasser, and does not stand in any contractual relationship with the owner of the premises, and who is permitted expressly or impliedly to go thereon for his own interests, convenience, or gratification.

SUBTERFUGE: Deception by artifice or stratagem in order to escape the force of an argument or action.

TANGENTIAL: Touching lightly; having a common point.

Enright v. Eli Lily & Co.

(Injured Party) v. (Drug Manufacturer)

77 N.Y.2d 377, 570 N.E.2d 198, 568 N.Y.S.2d 550 (1991)

AS A POLICY MATTER, COURTS REFUSE TO EXTEND CAUSATION TO RECOGNIZE MULTIGENERATIONAL CAUSES OF ACTION

■ **INSTANT FACTS** Karen Enright (P) sued Eli Lily & Co. (D) ("Eli") alleging that her grandmother's ingestion of a drug manufactured by Eli (D) led to reproductive abnormalities in Enright's (P) mother, which in turn, caused Enright's (P) cerebral palsy.

■ **BLACK LETTER RULE** An injury to a mother, which results in injuries to a later conceived child, does not establish a cause of action in favor of the child against the original tortfeasors.

■ **PROCEDURAL BASIS**

Appeal from trial court's dismissal of action in negligence.

■ **FACTS**

Karen Enright's (P) grandmother ingested DES during her pregnancy which resulted in the birth of Patricia, Enright's (P) mother. DES is an anti-miscarriage drug manufactured by about 300 companies including Eli Lily & Co.(D) ("Eli"). Enright (P) alleges that the drug caused reproductive abnormalities in her mother, which in turn led to Enright's (P) premature birth and her cerebral palsy. The trial court dismissed Enright's (P) cause of action based on negligence. The appellate division affirmed, but reinstated Enright's (P) cause of action based on strict products liability.

■ **ISSUE**

Does an injury to a mother, which results in injuries to a later conceived child, establish a cause of action in favor of the child against the original tortfeasors?

■ **DECISION AND RATIONALE**

(Wachtler, C.J.) No. An injury to a mother, which results in injuries to a later conceived child, does not establish a cause of action in favor of the child against the original tortfeasors. In the cases dealing with DES, courts have already relaxed traditional tort rules by relaxing the statute of limitations and rules regarding issues of causation. This case resembles *Albala v. City of New York,* which rejects the extension of cause of action in favor of a child for injuries suffered as a result of a preconception tort committed against the child's mother. Enright (P) argues that the cause of action should be extended as a matter of policy in DES cases. However, Enright (P) has not identified any special features of DES litigation that justify the recognition of a multigenerational cause of action, that courts have refused in any other context. The facts of this case do not justify a departure from *Albala.* Additionally, the same rationale should be applied to cases brought not under negligence, but under strict products liability. While it is true that a product manufacturer is in a better position to bear the cost of injury to the plaintiff, and the imposition of such a burden would encourage manufacturers to produce safer products, the countervailing policies remain in effect against extension of the cause of action as requested by the plaintiff. For all we know, the effects of DES may extend for generations, thus the cause of action sought by the plaintiff could not be controlled without drawing of arbitrary and artificial limitations. It is the duty of the courts to confine liability within manageable limits. Limiting liability to those who ingested DES and those who were exposed to it *in utero* will serve this purpose. Such limitation will not deter from the manufacturer's incentive to improve its products because the manufacturer is still subject to liability for injuries sustained by those who have ingested the drug or have been exposed to it. Also, it allows manufacturers the incentive to continue with research and testing of new products without fear of limitless liability. Neither in this case, nor in *Albala* was the plaintiff exposed to the defendant's dangerous product or negligent conduct, rather the plaintiffs in both cases were injured as a result of injuries to the reproductive systems of their mothers.

Analysis:

Proximate cause is a way of limiting the liability of defendants. In this case, the granddaughter of the person who had ingested DES is bringing action against the manufacturers of the drug. The relationship between the cause of injury and its effect on the plaintiff (the granddaughter) seem quite tenuous. In other words, holding the defendants liable would impose a duty on them toward someone who is not yet conceived. Such duty would not only deter the manufacturers from introducing new products, but will also expose them to unlimited liability for an unlimited amount of time. It would impose a duty on defendants for injuries which were not in fact foreseeable at the time of their negligent conduct. Thus, one of the effects of the proximate cause doctrine is to limit the liability of defendants to those injuries which are foreseeable.

■ CASE VOCABULARY

AMENABLE: Easy to lead.

CONSORTIUM: The conjugal relationship of a husband and wife, and the right of each to the company, cooperation and the aid of the other in every conjugal relation.

COUNTERVAIL: To counterbalance or compensate for.

LEGAL CAUSE: Type of cause (more commonly known as proximate cause) which in the natural and continuous sequence, unbroken by any new independent cause, produces an event, without which the injury would not have occurred.

SOLICITUDE: Attentive care and protectiveness.

STATUTE OF LIMITATIONS: Any law which fixes the time within which parties must take judicial action to enforce rights or else be thereafter barred from enforcing them.

STRICT LIABILITY: Refers to the concept of liability without fault; often in tort law one who engages in an activity which has an inherent risk of injury such as those classified as ultra hazardous activities, is liable for all injuries proximately caused by his/her enterprise, even without a showing of negligence.

CHAPTER SEVEN

Joint Tortfeasors

Bierczynski v. Rogers

Instant Facts: Rogers (P) sued Bierczynski (D) and Race (D) for injuries sustained when Race's (D) car collided with Rogers' (P), as Race (D) and Bierczynski (D) were racing their cars.

Black Letter Rule: Two parties who engage in an illegal car race are jointly liable for injuries to a third person regardless of which party directly inflicted the injury or damage upon the third person.

Coney v. J.L.G. Industries, Inc.

Instant Facts: Coney (P), administrator of Jasper's estate, brought a wrongful death action against J.L.G. Industries (D) ("JLG"), the manufacturer of the machine causing the decedent's injury and death.

Black Letter Rule: The doctrine of comparative negligence does not eliminate joint and several liability.

Bartlett v. New Mexico Welding Supply, Inc.

Instant Facts: New Mexico Welding Supply vehicle (D) rear-ended Bartlett (P) while Bartlett braked for an unknown driver.

Black Letter Rule: In a comparative negligence jurisdiction, a concurrent tortfeasor is not jointly and severally liable for the entire amount of the plaintiff's judgment.

Bundt v. Embro

Instant Facts: Bundt (P) and other injured passengers of two cars which collided, sued owners and drivers for injuries sustained. Bundt (P) recovered from the city.

Black Letter Rule: A party who has suffered an indivisible harm by negligence of several parties is not entitled to more than one satisfaction for the same harm.

Cox v. Pearl Investment Co.

Instant Facts: Cox (P) settled with Goodwill and then sued Pearl Investment Co.

Black Letter Rule: A contract between one tortfeasor and the plaintiff, where the parties intend to reserve to the plaintiff the right to sue the co-tortfeasor, does not release the co-tortfeasor from liability.

Elbaor v. Smith

Instant Facts: Smith (P), having been treated by Drs. Syrquin, Stephens and Elbaor (D), sues Elbaor (D) for medical malpractice after entering a Mary Carter agreement with the other doctors.

Black Letter Rule: Mary Carter agreements, where a settling defendant has a stake in the outcome of a case against co-defendants, are violative of public policy.

Knell v. Feltman

Instant Facts: Feltman (D), sued by the passengers in Knell's (Cross–D) car, filed a cross-complaint against Knell (Cross–D), with whom Feltman's (D) cab had collided.

Black Letter Rule: The right to contribution does not exist only between tortfeasors against whom the plaintiff has obtained a judgment.

Yellow Cab Co. of D.C., Inc. v. Dreslin

Instant Facts: A taxicab company sought to require the other negligent driver to contribute to injuries suffered by the driver's wife.

Black Letter Rule: Joint liability is required before any contribution can be ordered.

Slocum v. Donahue

Instant Facts: A drunk man killed a small child with his car, claiming the accident was caused by a floor mat due to a manufacturing defect.

Black Letter Rule: A joint tortfeasor is not entitled to indemnification from a fellow tortfeasor.

Bruckman v. Pena

Instant Facts: Pena (D), having had two collisions within one year, sued Bruckman (P), the truck driver in the first collision, for all the injuries sustained.

Black Letter Rule: A defendant cannot be held liable for a plaintiff's subsequent injury where the plaintiff cannot apportion the damages between the causes of the injuries.

Michie v. Great Lakes Steel Division, Nat'l Steel Corp.

Instant Facts: Michie (P) sued Great Lakes (D) and other corporations jointly and severally in nuisance for pollutants emitted from the corporations' plants.

Black Letter Rule: Where the independent concurring acts of defendants have caused an indivisible harm to the plaintiff, and no reasonable means of apportioning the damages is evident, the court may hold the defendant's jointly and severally liable.

Dillon v. Twin State Gas & Electric Co.

Instant Facts: Dillon (P) sued Twin State (D) in negligence for the wrongful death of a 14-year-old boy who fell from a bridge.

Black Letter Rule: Where a plaintiff, regardless of the defendant's negligence, would have suffered injury, the plaintiff's damages would be measured based on the plaintiff's injured condition.

Bierczynski v. Rogers

(*Negligent Driver*) v. (*Injured driver*)

239 A.2d 218 (Del.1968)

TWO OR MORE DEFENDANTS WHO FAIL TO PERFORM A COMMON DUTY TO THE PLAINTIFF ARE BOTH LIABLE TO THE PLAINTIFF ALTHOUGH ONLY ONE CAUSED THE ACTUAL INJURY

■ **INSTANT FACTS** Rogers (P) sued Bierczynski (D) and Race (D) for injuries sustained when Race's (D) car collided with Rogers'(P), as Race (D) and Bierczynski (D) were racing their cars.

■ **BLACK LETTER RULE** Two parties who engage in an illegal car race are jointly liable for injuries to a third person regardless of which party directly inflicted the injury or damage upon the third person.

■ **PROCEDURAL BASIS**

Appeal from jury verdict in action for negligence.

■ **FACTS**

Race (D) and Bierczynski (D) were racing their cars when, Race's (D) car collided with Rogers' (P), injuring the latter. Bierczynski (D) stopped his car 35 feet from the scene of the accident and did not collide with Rogers' (P) car. At the trial, the jury found both Race (D) and Bierczynski (D) negligent and entered a verdict in favor of Rogers (P) against Race (D) and Bierczynski (D) jointly. Bierczynski (D) appeals.

■ **ISSUE**

Are two parties who engage in a illegal car race jointly liable for injuries to a third person regardless of which party directly inflicted the injury or damage upon the third person?

■ **DECISION AND RATIONALE**

(Herrmann, J.) Yes. Two parties who engage in an illegal car race are jointly liable for injuries to a third person regardless of which party directly inflicted the injury or damage upon the third person. While this state does not have a statute prohibiting car racing on public roads, such speed competition constitutes negligence because a reasonable, prudent person would not engage in such conduct. Additionally, all parties involved in the race are wrongdoers and each participant is liable for harm to a third person arising from the tortious conduct of the other because he has encouraged the tort. Thus, in this case if Bierczynski (D) and Race (D) were involved in a car race, each is liable to Rogers (P) even though Bierczynski (D) was not directly involved in the collision itself. Since the jury found that Race (D) and Bierczynski (D) were racing, Bierczynski (D) is liable.

Analysis:

Joint and several liability means that each of several tortfeasors is liable jointly with the others for the amount of the judgment against them, and that each is also individually liable for the full amount. The plaintiff can recover from any of the tortfeasors or any group of them. Usually joint and several liability occurs in three situations. The first is where the defendants act in concert. The second situation is where the defendants all fail to perform a common duty owed to the plaintiff. A third category where joint and several liability applies is where defendants acted independently to cause an indivisible harm to the plaintiff.

■ CASE VOCABULARY

CONCERT OF ACTION: Action which has been planned, arranged, adjusted, agreed upon, and settled between parties acting together, in pursuance of some design or in accordance with some scheme.

CONCURRENT NEGLIGENCE: The wrongful acts or omissions of two or more persons acting independently but causing the same injury. The independent actions do not have to occur at the same time, but must produce the same result. The actors are all responsible for paying the damages, and can usually be sued together in one lawsuit or individually in separate lawsuits.

JOINT AND SEVERAL LIABILITY: A sharing of rights and liabilities among a group of people collectively and also individually. Thus, if defendants in a negligence suit are jointly and severally liable, the injured party may sue some or all of the injured defendants together, or each one separately, and may collect equal and unequal amounts from each in satisfaction of his damages.

Coney v. J.L.G. Industries, Inc.

(*Administrator of Deceased's Estate*) v. (*Machine Manufacturer*)

97 Ill.2d 104, 454 N.E.2d 197, 73 Ill.Dec. 337 (1983)

SUPREME COURT OF ILLINOIS HOLDS THAT COMPARATIVE NEGLIGENCE DOES NOT COMPEL ELIMINATION OF JOINT AND SEVERAL LIABILITY

■ **INSTANT FACTS** Coney (P), administrator of Jasper's estate, brought a wrongful death action against J.L.G. Industries (D) ("JLG"), the manufacturer of the machine causing the decedent's injury and death.

■ **BLACK LETTER RULE** The doctrine of comparative negligence does not eliminate joint and several liability.

■ **PROCEDURAL BASIS**

Appeal from wrongful death action.

■ **FACTS**

Illinois is a state that has adopted the doctrine of corporate negligence. Jasper died while operating a machine manufactured by JLG Industries ("JLG") (D). Coney (P) brought a wrongful death action against JLG (D) in strict liability. JLG (D) defends on the ground that Jasper committed contributory negligence in operating the machine and that Jasper's employer [potential cross-defendant] also committed contributory negligence by failing to instruct and train Jasper to protect against injury. Coney (P) contends that JLG (D) is responsible for the full amount of damages regardless of any other person's negligence.

■ **ISSUE**

Does the doctrine of comparative negligence eliminate joint and several liability?

■ **DECISION AND RATIONALE**

(Moran, J.) No. The doctrine of comparative negligence does not eliminate joint and several liability. JLG (D) argues that with the adoption of the doctrine of comparative negligence, where damages are apportioned according to each party's fault, it is no longer rational to hold the defendant liable for more than his share of the damages. However, the majority of courts adopting comparative negligence have still retained joint and several liability. There are four reasons for retaining joint and several liability: 1) Apportionment of fault under comparative negligence does not make an indivisible injury divisible; a concurrent tortfeasor is liable for all damages to the plaintiff, and in many instances that tortfeasor's negligence alone is sufficient for causing the plaintiff's entire injury. 2) Additionally, where plaintiff is not negligent, without joint and several liability the plaintiff would be forced to bear the portion of the loss for those defendants who are unable to pay. 3) Even where the plaintiff is negligent, he is not as culpable as the defendant because his negligence is lack of due care for himself and not for others. 4) Also, if joint and several liability is eliminated, plaintiff may not be able to recover adequate damages for his injuries. Under contributory negligence, a plaintiff who is contributorily negligent is barred from any recovery. In *Alvis v. Ribar* this court adopted the doctrine of comparative negligence. Under this doctrine, a plaintiff who is contributorily negligent is allowed recovery, however his damages are reduced according to the percentage of fault attributable to plaintiff. Elimination of joint and several liability will impose the burden of insolvent defendants on the plaintiff and will further reduce plaintiff's damages more than his attributed fault. We find no authority for the proposition that comparative negligence compels elimination of joint and several liability. (Affirmed and Remanded.)

Analysis:

Remember that contributory negligence refers to the situation in which the plaintiff's negligence has contributed to his injuries. Where a plaintiff is contributorily negligent, some courts do not allow any recovery at all to the plaintiff, and the defendant gets off without liability. In other jurisdictions the treatment of contributory negligence of the plaintiff is to reduce the plaintiff's damages based on the percentage of fault attributed to the plaintiff. This is known as comparative negligence. The court in the case above follows the doctrine of comparative negligence. The court in this case further holds that joint and several liability does apply in jurisdictions which have adopted comparative negligence. In such situations, the courts simply reduce the plaintiff's damages by the percentage of fault attributed to the plaintiff and hold all the defendants in the case jointly and severally liable for the rest of the plaintiff's damages.

■ CASE VOCABULARY

COMPARATIVE NEGLIGENCE: The allocation of responsibility for damages incurred between the plaintiff and the defendant, based on the relative negligence of the two; the reduction of damages to be recovered by the negligent plaintiff is in proportion to his fault.

CONTRIBUTORY NEGLIGENCE: The conduct on the part of the plaintiff which falls below the standard to which he should conform for his own protection and which is a legally contributing cause in addition to the negligence of the defendant in bringing about the plaintiff's harm.

QUID PRO QUO: Latin for "what for what," something for something.

Bartlett v. New Mexico Welding Supply, Inc.

(Injured Party) v. (Rear-Ending Vehicle)

98 N.M. 152, 646 P.2d 579 (App.1982), cert. denied, 98 N.M. 336, 648 P.2d 794

ACCORDING TO THE COURT OF APPEALS OF NEW MEXICO, JOINT AND SEVERAL LIABILITY SHOULD NOT BE RETAINED IN A PURE COMPARATIVE NEGLIGENCE STATE

■ **INSTANT FACTS** New Mexico Welding Supply vehicle (D) rearended Bartlett (P) while Bartlett braked for an unknown driver.

■ **BLACK LETTER RULE** In a comparative negligence jurisdiction, a concurrent tortfeasor is not jointly and severally liable for the entire amount of the plaintiff's judgment.

■ PROCEDURAL BASIS

Interlocutory appeal in negligence case.

■ FACTS

Bartlett (P), slamming on her brakes, hit an unknown driver who suddenly backed out of a service station. An employee of New Mexico Welding Supply ("New Mexico") (D), driving behind Bartlett (P), could not brake in time and rear-ended Bartlett (P). The latter sued New Mexico (D) in negligence. New Mexico (D) defended on the ground that the driver of the other automobile, who remained unknown, caused or contributed to the accident. The jury at the trial court determined that Bartlett's (P) injury was $100,000 and that New Mexico's (D) negligence contributed to Bartlett's (P) accident and damages in the amount of 30%, while the unknown driver was 70% at fault. Bartlett (P) moved to recover the entire $100,000 from New Mexico (D), however the motion was denied and a new trial was granted. New Mexico (D) requests interlocutory appeal.

■ ISSUE

In a comparative negligence jurisdiction, is a concurrent tortfeasor jointly and severally liable for the entire amount of the plaintiff's judgment?

■ DECISION AND RATIONALE

(Wood, J.) No. In a comparative negligence jurisdiction, a concurrent tortfeasor is not jointly and severally liable for the entire amount of the plaintiff's judgment. Many comparative negligence jurisdictions have retained joint and several liability for concurrent tortfeasors. Under the common law rule, either the defendant in this case or the unknown driver could be liable for the entire damage caused by their combined negligence. There are two main reasons for retaining joint and several liability. First, just because the percentage of each party's negligence can be defined, it does not mean that the plaintiff's injury is divisible. Under this reasoning, one who is 1% at fault could be liable for 100% of the plaintiff's damages. The concept of one indivisible harm has its roots in common law and is now obsolete and should not be followed. The second reason for retaining joint and several liability is to favor plaintiffs and protect them against insolvent defendants. Where one plaintiff is against one defendant, the plaintiff runs the risk of the defendant's insolvency. There is no reason to shift the burden of insolvency on the defendant when there are more defendants involved in the case. Thus, this case rejects the concept of joint and several liability in cases of comparative negligence. In this case New Mexico is not liable for the entire damages, but only for 30% of it.   (Order for New Trial Reversed.)

Analysis:

In the previous case, *Coney,* the court held that comparative negligence jurisdictions should not eliminate the doctrine of joint and several liability.   In this case, however, the court reaches the opposite result.   Note here that the plaintiff is not contributorily negligent.   The only negligence is that of the unknown driver and the defendant.   The court holds that since the defendant's negligence was 30% of the cause of the accident, the defendant should only be liable for the 30% of the damages, and the plaintiff should bear the risk of a no-show or an insolvent defendant.   All you need to remember is that within jurisdictions that follow comparative negligence, there are those which have retained joint and several liability, and those which have rejected it.   Clearly, those jurisdictions which have retained joint and several liability are pro-plaintiff and make the defendant bear the burden and risk of other defendants which may be insolvent.

■ CASE VOCABULARY

INTERLOCUTORY: Provisional; temporary; not final; an order or judgment is interlocutory if it does not determine the issues at trial but directs some further proceeding preliminary to a final decree.

Bundt v. Embro

(*Passenger*) v. (*Car Owners and Drivers*)
48 Misc.2d 802, 265 N.Y.S.2d 872 (1965)

THE SATISFACTION OF A JUDGMENT AGAINST ONE TORTFEASOR RELEASES THE OTHER TORT-
FEASORS

■ **INSTANT FACTS** Bundt (P) and other injured passengers of two cars which collided, sued owners and drivers for injuries sustained. Bundt (P) recovered from the city.

■ **BLACK LETTER RULE** A party who has suffered an indivisible harm by negligence of several parties is not entitled to more than one satisfaction for the same harm.

■ **PROCEDURAL BASIS**

Motion to amend answer to complaint in negligence action.

■ **FACTS**

Two automobiles were involved in a collision. Bundt (P) and other passengers in the two cars which collided brought a negligence action against the drivers and owners of the two cars for their injuries. Bundt (P) and other passengers also sued a city contractor alleging that the latter had negligently covered up a stop sign at the intersection. Embro (D) and other defendants seek leave to amend their answers on the ground that Bundt (P) and other plaintiffs had already received a judgment and satisfaction against the state of New York for the same injuries.

■ **ISSUE**

May a party who has suffered an indivisible harm by the negligence of several parties be entitled to more than one satisfaction for the same harm?

■ **DECISION AND RATIONALE**

(Groat, J.) No. A party who has suffered an indivisible harm by the negligence of several parties is not entitled to more than one satisfaction for the same harm. A party injured by joint tortfeasors may recover damages against either or all. However, while there may be more than one lawsuit, there may only be one satisfaction for the same indivisible harm. Contrary to Bundt's (P) contention, the satisfaction of the judgment against one joint tortfeasor which discharges the others applies to the state as well. In this case, the state of New York holds the same position as a private defendant under Section 8 of the Court of Claims Act. Thus, if the trial court determines that the state is a joint tortfeasor with Embro (D) and other named defendants, the satisfaction of the judgment against the state discharges the defendants. (Leave to Amend Granted.)

Analysis:

Satisfaction refers to the full payment of damages. In cases which involve more than one wrongdoer causing an indivisible injury to the plaintiff, the latter may bring separate actions against each wrongdoer and win a judgment in the action against each. However, the plaintiff is only entitled to one satisfaction. Full payment of plaintiff's damages by one defendant would prevent further enforcement of the judgment. Imagine a plaintiff who is involved in a car accident. One person has stopped short in front of the plaintiff and the other driver collides with the plaintiff from the back. The plaintiff brings an action only against the party who rear-ends him, and the court finds that the total of the plaintiff's damages are $100,000. Imagine that the plaintiff recovers the full amount from the rear-ender. He cannot in a later action recover another $100,000 from the person who has stopped short before him because he has already been paid the full amount of his judgment. In other words, his judgment has already been satisfied for the harm that he suffered from the negligence of both drivers. Note however that a payment, even if in full, which is not made by or on behalf of a wrongdoer or a joint tortfeasor, does not prevent the plaintiff from later recovery from one or both of the joint tortfeasors. This is known as the collateral source rule. For example, a plaintiff may recover the cost of damage to his car and medical expenses from his own insurance company. This recovery does not preclude the plaintiff from recovering those same expenses from the joint tortfeasors because the plaintiff's insurance company did not pay the plaintiff on behalf of the joint tortfeasors.

■ CASE VOCABULARY

COLLATERAL SOURCE RULE: The payments made to the injured party which were not made by, or on behalf of, the tortfeasors; under these circumstances the tortfeasor(s) are not credited even though the plaintiff may receive double compensation for some losses.

SATISFACTION: Discharge and subsequent release of obligation by the payment thereof.

Cox v. Pearl Investment Co.

(Injured Party) v. *(Property Owner)*

168 Colo. 67, 450 P.2d 60 (1969)

RELEASE OF ONE JOINT TORTFEASOR DOES NOT RELEASE ALL OTHERS WHO MAY BE LIABLE

■ **INSTANT FACTS** Cox (P) settled with Goodwill and then sued Pearl Investment Co.

■ **BLACK LETTER RULE** A contract between one tortfeasor and the plaintiff, where the parties intend to reserve to the plaintiff the right to sue the co-tortfeasor, does not release the co-tortfeasor from liability.

■ PROCEDURAL BASIS

Appeal from summary judgment in negligence action.

■ FACTS

Cox (P) and her husband sought recovery from Pearl Investment Co. ("Pearl") (D) for injuries sustained when Cox (P) fell on Pearl's (D) property. The latter's tenant, Goodwill Industries, had paid Cox (P) $2,500 in consideration for Cox (P) signing a contract called "Covenant Not to Proceed With Suit." The contract expressly reserved to Cox (P) the right to sue any other persons against whom Cox (P) may have a claim for the same injuries. The trial court granted Pearl's (D) summary judgment on the ground that the contract between Cox (P) and Goodwill Industries was a release relieving Pearl (D) of further liability. Cox (P) appeals.

■ ISSUE

Does a contract between one tortfeasor and the plaintiff, where the parties intend to reserve to the plaintiff the right to sue the co-tortfeasor, release the co-tortfeasor from liability?

■ DECISION AND RATIONALE

(Hodges, J.) No. A contract between one tortfeasor and the plaintiff, where the parties intend to reserve to the plaintiff the right to sue the co-tortfeasor, does not release the co-tortfeasor from liability. In granting Pearl's (D) summary judgment, the trial court relied on *Price v. Baker* which indicated that the release of one joint tortfeasor is the release of all. This court no longer upholds the rule in *Price*. The contract in *Price* which is substantially similar to the one involved in this case can not be interpreted as full release of all joint tortfeasors. Instead, the intent of the parties to the contract should be taken onto consideration. Where a contract expressly releases one joint tortfeasor, but reserves to the plaintiff the right to sue the other tortfeasors who may be liable, the contract should not be interpreted otherwise. In this case, the restriction in the contract clearly shows that the plaintiff has not received full compensation and that her right to sue others is not precluded. Such interpretation of the contract would not prejudice other joint tortfeasors because the amount of the judgment against them will be reduced by the amount paid by the co-tortfeasors. This court adheres to the holding in *Matheson v. O'Kane,* which gives effect to the intent of the parties where the consideration paid to the plaintiff was not intended as full compensation for the plaintiff's injury and was intended to preserve liability of other tortfeasors, even though the agreement signed by the plaintiff was in the form of a release. 4 Restatement of Torts, Section 885 follows the same rule providing that a release will be construed as a covenant not to sue where the right to sue other tortfeasors is expressly reserved. (Reversed and Remanded.)

Analysis:

A release is a surrender of the plaintiff's claim. Under common law, a release signed between one joint tortfeasor and the plaintiff relieved all joint tortfeasors of further liability. This case, however, interprets this rule differently. It looks at the substance of the contract signed rather than the form of the contract. Where the release is intended to reserve to the plaintiff the right to sue other tortfeasors for the same claim, the release will not relieve the other tortfeasors. Note that the intent of the parties may be determined from the express language of the agreement, such as in this case, or from the circumstances surrounding the agreement. For example, if the release is only partial compensation for the plaintiff's injuries, the court may interpret that the parties did not intend the agreement as an absolute release. Note, however, that under the Restatement of Torts, only an express reservation will show the intent of the parties.

■ CASE VOCABULARY

IPSO FACTO: Latin for "by the fact itself," in and of itself.

RELEASE: The act or writing by which some claim, right, or interest is given up to the person against whom the claim, right, or interest could have been enforced.

SATISFACTION: Discharge and subsequent release of obligation by the payment thereof.

STARE DECISIS: Latin phrase literally meaning to stand by that which was decided; this is a rule by which common law courts are slow to interfere with principles announced in former decisions and often uphold them even though they would decide otherwise were the question a new one.

Elbaor v. Smith

(Physician) v. *(Patient)*

845 S.W.2d 240 (Tex.1992)

THE SUPREME COURT OF TEXAS DECLARES MARY CARTER AGREEMENTS VOID AS VIOLATIVE OF PUBLIC POLICY

■ **INSTANT FACTS** Smith (P), having been treated by Drs. Syrquin, Stephens and Elbaor (D), sues Elbaor (D) for medical malpractice after entering a Mary Carter agreement with the other doctors.

■ **BLACK LETTER RULE** Mary Carter agreements, where a settling defendant has a stake in the outcome of a case against co-defendants, are violative of public policy.

■ **PROCEDURAL BASIS**

Appeal from malpractice action.

■ **FACTS**

Smith (P), having injured her ankle in a car accident, sought treatment from Dallas/Fort Worth Medical Center ("D/FW"), Arlington Community Hospital ("ACH"), Drs. Elbaor, Stephens, Gatmaitan, and Syrquin. Smith (P) filed malpractice action against all the named caretakers. Prior to the trial, Smith (P) entered into a settlement agreement with D/FW, and later into a Mary Carter agreement with all the remaining doctors, except Dr. Elbaor (D), for $405,010. The Mary Carter agreement provided that the settling doctors would remain as defendants and participate in the trial against Elbaor (D), after which the doctors would be paid back all or part of the settlement amount from Smith's (D) judgment against Elbaor (D). The trial court, troubled by the negative effects of the agreement, took steps to mitigate the harmful effects of it. The jury at the trial level allocated 88% of the liability in the case to Elbaor (D) and 22% to the other doctors. The trial court, deducting credits for settlement, entered judgment against Elbaor (D) for $1,872,848. The Court of Appeals affirmed. Dr. Elbaor (D) appeals on the ground that the Mary Carter agreement between Smith (P) and the other doctors was against public policy.

■ **ISSUE**

Are Mary Carter agreements, where a settling defendant has a stake in the outcome of a case against co-defendants, violative of public policy?

■ **DECISION AND RATIONALE**

(Gonzales, J.) Yes. Mary Carter agreements, where a settling defendant has a stake in the outcome of a case against co-defendants, are violative of public policy. A Mary Carter agreement is one where the plaintiff enters into a settlement agreement with a defendant and goes to trial against other defendant(s). The settling defendant guarantees a minimum payment to the plaintiff which may be offset by an excess judgment recovered against other non-settling defendants at trial. Such agreements provide great incentive for settling defendants to help ensure that the plaintiff receives a large recovery and thus, motivate such defendants to help the plaintiff in the presentation of the case, Such agreements do not promote settlement. In fact, they act to ensure a trial against the non-settling defendant. According to the concurring opinion of Judge Spears in *Smithwick,* Mary Carter agreements present to the jury a sham of adversity between the plaintiff and the non-settling defendants, while the settling defendants are actually helping the plaintiff secure a large judgment and exonerate the settling defendants. Mary Carter agreements allow the plaintiffs to get support from settling defendants and encourage the more culpable defendants to make a deal with the plaintiff and pay little or nothing in damages. Remedial tactics adopted by some courts, such as revealing the nature of the agreements, do not alleviate the ill effects of the agreements including their promotion of litigation, misleading the jury, and the promotion of unethical collusion between adversaries. The public policy favoring fair trials outweighs the policy favoring partial settlement of cases. (Reversed and Remanded.)

■ DISSENT

(Doggett, J., Manzy, J., Gammage, J.) In this case, the trial court mitigated the harmful effects of Mary Carter agreements. The court allowed the parties to explain to the jury about the nature of the agreements and that the settling defendants could, as a result of the agreement, recover part or all of the amount which they paid to the plaintiff. Also, the court warned the jury about witness bias. Most jurisdictions allow Mary Carter agreements with similar safeguards as those provided in this case by the trial court.

Analysis:

Mary Carter agreements, such as the one in this case, allow defendant to settle with the plaintiff so long as they remain in the plaintiff's case against the non-settling defendants. As this case indicates, settling defendants have a great incentive to help the plaintiff prove the negligence of the non-settling defendant because the larger the judgment against the latter, the more likely the settling defendant will be in recovering the amount that they have already paid to the plaintiff. Most jurisdictions allow Mary Carter agreements, given procedural safeguards such as those used by the trial court in this case. There are some jurisdictions which allow these agreements without any safeguards and without allowing the parties to present evidence of them to the jurors. The decision in the case, prohibiting such agreements, is followed by a very small minority of jurisdictions.

■ CASE VOCABULARY

MARY CARTER AGREEMENT: An agreement whereby the plaintiff enters into a settlement with a defendant(s) and goes to trial against the remaining defendant(s); the settling defendant remains a party and guarantees the plaintiff a minimum payment, which may be offset in whole or in part by an excess judgment recovered at trial.

PEREMPTORY CHALLENGE: Challenge which may be made without an specific reason or cause.

Knell v. Feltman

(Automobile Owner) v. *(Taxicab Owner)*

85 U.S.App.D.C. 22, 174 F.2d 662 (1949)

THE RIGHT TO SEEK CONTRIBUTION BELONGS TO A TORTFEASOR WHO HAS BEEN FORCED TO PAY A JUDGMENT AND DOES NOT DEPEND ON THE PLAINTIFF'S CHOICE OF DEFENDANTS

■ **INSTANT FACTS** Feltman (D), sued by the passengers in Knell's (Cross-D) car, filed a cross-complaint against Knell (Cross-D), with whom Feltman's (D) cab had collided.

■ **BLACK LETTER RULE** The right to contribution does not exist only between tortfeasors against whom the plaintiff has obtained a judgment.

■ **PROCEDURAL BASIS**

Appeal in negligence action form trial court's judgment requiring contribution.

■ **FACTS**

The Langlands (P), passengers in Knell's (Cross-D) car, sued Feltman (D), the owner of the taxicab with which Knell (Cross-D) had collided, for injuries sustained as a result of the collision. Feltman (D) filed a third-party complaint against Knell (Cross-D) on the ground that the accident was caused by the contributing or sole negligence of Knell (Cross-D). The jury at the trial level found both Feltman (D) and Knell (Cross-D) negligent, entering judgment against Feltman (D) for $11,500, and against Knell (Cross-D) in favor of Feltman (D) for $5,750. Knell (Cross-D) appeals contending that Feltman (D) did not have a right to contribution because the Langlands (P) did not bring action against Knell (Cross-D).

■ **ISSUE**

Does the right to contribution exist only between tortfeasors against whom the plaintiff has obtained a judgment?

■ **DECISION AND RATIONALE**

(Miller, J.) No. The right to contribution does not exist only between tortfeasors against whom the plaintiff has obtained a judgment. Knell's (Cross-D) contention is unreasonable for two reasons. In the first place, Federal Rule of Civil Procedure 14a provides that a defendant may bring into the action another person who may be liable to the defendant for all or any part of the damages, even if the plaintiff does not seek a judgment against that person. Additionally, the right to seek contribution belongs to the tortfeasor who has been forced to pay and the right cannot depend on the plaintiff's choice of defendants. Otherwise, a plaintiff would have the choice to deliberately attach liability to one party, or collude with one tortfeasor against whom the plaintiff has a cause of action, to only impose liability on a co-tortfeasor. The rule denying contribution to joint tortfeasors stems from *Merryweather v. Nixan*. In that case, however, the tort complained of was willful or intentional. While many courts have incorrectly adhered to the no-contribution rule without determining whether the tort was negligent or intentional, dissatisfaction with the rule has led to statutory changes of the rule in many states, and has led many courts to allow exceptions to the no-contribution rule. This court concludes that where a tort is committed by the concurrent negligence of two or more persons, who are not intentional wrongdoers, contribution should be allowed. A joint judgment is not required to allow this right.

Analysis:

Contribution refers to the right of a party required to compensate a victim for his injury to demand reimbursement from another person who is jointly responsible for the injury. Under the common law, no contribution was allowed as between joint tortfeasors. However, this rule has been changed dramatically. Most states allow contribution through statute, while in other jurisdictions, contribution is judicially allowed. Some courts, however, allow contribution only where a joint judgment has been entered against the joint tortfeasors. This means that where there is more than one defendant, and the plaintiff chooses to sue only one defendant, that defendant does not have the right to seek contribution against the other defendants even if they may be liable for part of the plaintiff's damages. The instant case does away with this requirement. Note, however, that contribution is still not allowed for intentional torts in most states. Still, in jurisdictions allowing contribution, the party seeking contribution must prove that the parties against whom he/she seeks contribution are joint tortfeasors. To make this process easier, rules of civil procedure allow a defendant to implead, or join, other tortfeasors as defendants in the case, even if the plaintiff did not originally include those parties in the action.

■ **CASE VOCABULARY**

CONTRIBUTION: The legal right enjoyed by one required to compensate a victim for his injury to demand reimbursement from another person who is jointly responsible for that injury.

IMPLEADER: The procedure by which a third party is brought into a suit between a plaintiff and defendant, where the third party may be liable, so as to settle all claims in a single action.

Yellow Cab Co. of D.C., Inc. v. Dreslin

(Taxicab Company) v. *(Driver)*

86 U.S.App.D.C. 327, 181 F.2d 626 (D.C.Cir.1950)

COURT DECLINES TO REQUIRE CONTRIBUTION FROM A PARTY WHO IS IMMUNE FROM LIABILITY TO THE INJURED PERSON

■ **INSTANT FACTS** A taxicab company sought to require the other negligent driver to contribute to injuries suffered by the driver's wife.

■ **BLACK LETTER RULE** Joint liability is required before any contribution can be ordered.

■ PROCEDURAL BASIS

Appeal from declaratory judgment finding no right of contribution among spouses.

■ FACTS

Mr. Dreslin (P) and his wife were driving in a car that struck a taxicab owned by Yellow Cab Co. of D.C., Inc. ("Yellow Cab.") (D). Mr. Dreslin (P) and Mrs. Dreslin (P) sued Yellow Cab (D). Yellow Cab (D) asserted as an affirmative defense that Mr. Dreslin (P) was contributorily negligent. Yellow Cab (D) also cross-claimed against Mr. Dreslin (P) for damages to the taxicab and for contribution for any sums recovered by Mrs. Dreslin (P) against Yellow Cab (D). The jury found that both Mr. Dreslin (P) and Yellow Cab (D) were negligent. However, no contribution was required by Mr. Dreslin (P) for the payment from Yellow Cab (D) to Mrs. Dreslin (P). Noting that "the right of contribution arises from a joint liability," the Court held that, since Mr. Dreslin (P) could not be liable in tort to his wife, there was no joint liability and therefore no right of contribution. Yellow Cab (D) appealed.

■ ISSUE

May contribution be obtained from a tortfeasor who has no liability to the injured party?

■ DECISION AND RATIONALE

(Proctor, J.) No. Contribution may not be obtained from a tortfeasor who has no liability to the injured party. Because Mr. Dreslin (P) and Mrs. Dreslin (P) were married, the defense of family immunity precludes Mr. Dreslin (P) from having any liability for Mrs. Dreslin's (P) injuries. In the case of a common obligation, the discharge of the obligation by one obligor without payment from the other is unfair. However, there must be a common obligation for contribution to be obtained. In other words, the injured party must have had a cause of action against the party from whom contribution is sought. Because Mr. Dreslin (P) had no such cause of action against Mrs. Dreslin (P), he cannot be jointly liable with Yellow Cab (D) for her injuries. Although this may be unfair, it is grounded in the sound public policy of the preservation of domestic peace and felicity, upon which the family immunity doctrine is based.

Analysis:

This case concisely summarizes the law of contribution. Where two or more parties are jointly liable for injuries, the party who pays for the injuries may seek contribution against the other liable parties. In the case at bar, the Court found that both Mr. Dreslin (P) and Yellow Cab (D) were responsible for Mrs. Dreslin's (P) injuries. Why should Mr. Dreslin (P) reap the benefit of having his wife compensated for the injuries which he caused? The answer rests in public policy, not in any concept of fairness. Mr. Dreslin (P) cannot be held liable to Mrs. Dreslin (P). Thus, there is no joint liability for her injuries. The holding can be questioned on a number of fronts. First, as noted above, it seems fundamentally unfair for Mr. Dreslin (P) to reap the benefit of payment (to his wife) for injuries which he himself caused. Second, is this holding really necessary to preserve the "domestic peace." While the law wants to promote happy marriages and certainly does not want to allow husbands and wives to sue each other, isn't this case fundamentally different? This case does not involve Mrs. Dreslin (P) suing her husband, but rather only involves diminishing the payments to the Dreslin (P) family based on Mr. Dreslin's (P) liability. According to this Appellate Court, the requirement for joint liability is strict, harsh, and unyielding. Contribution is not possible without joint liability.

■ CASE VOCABULARY

DECLARATORY JUDGMENT: A judgment which states the rights and/or liabilities of the parties.

LOSS OF CONSORTIUM: A cause of action for damages arising from injuries to a spouse.

Slocum v. Donahue

(Parents) v. *(Drunk Driver)*

44 Mass.App.Ct. 937, 693 N.E.2d 179 (1998)

JOINT TORTFEASOR NOT ENTITLED TO INDEMNIFICATION FROM FELLOW TORTFEASOR

■ **INSTANT FACTS** A drunk man killed a small child with his car, claiming the accident was caused by a floor mat due to a manufacturing defect.

■ **BLACK LETTER RULE** A joint tortfeasor is not entitled to indemnification from a fellow tortfeasor.

■ **PROCEDURAL BASIS**

Appeal from dismissal of third-party complaint seeking contribution and indemnification.

■ **FACTS**

Donahue (D) plead guilty to motor vehicle homicide in the death of the Slocum's (P) eighteen month old son. The accident occurred when Donahue (D), who had been drinking, backed his car out of his driveway and the engine began to race. Donahue (D) alleges that he repeatedly stepped on the brakes, but the car continued to accelerate until it hit young Slocum (p). The Slocums (P) thereafter filed a civil action against Donahue (D) alleging negligence and gross negligence. Donahue (D) then filed a third-party complaint against Ford Motor Company seeking contribution and indemnity. Donahue (D) claimed that the floor mat in his car manufactured by Ford was defective in that it interfered with the operation of his brakes causing them to fail. Before trial, Slocum (P) settled with Ford for $150,000, and Slocum (P) released any claims against Ford. Ford then moved for summary judgment on Donahue's (D) claim against it.

■ **ISSUE**

Is a joint tortfeasor entitled to indemnification or contribution from a fellow tortfeasor who obtained a release from the plaintiff?

■ **DECISION AND RATIONALE**

No. Our state statute provides that when a release is given in good faith to one of two or more persons who are liable for the same injury, it will discharge the tortfeasor to whom it is given from all liability for contribution to any other tortfeasor. Donahue (D) argues that the settlement between Ford and Slocum (P) was not made in good faith because it was for less than the value of the case and because Ford allegedly was going to allow Slocum (P) to use its experts at trial. However, we find that the settlement was made in good faith. First, the relatively small amount of the settlement is reasonable given the fact that a jury may have easily found that Ford was not responsible at all for the accident. This is because Donahue (D) admitted that he had been drinking vodka at the time of the accident. There was no collusion, dishonesty, or other wrongful conduct that would indicate a lack of good faith in this settlement. Secondly, the Slocum's (P) use of Ford's expert witnesses is not evidence of collusion. It is merely speculation to argue that the Slocum's (P) settled with Ford because they believed Ford was not responsible for the death of their son. Speculation alone is not enough to require a further hearing on the issue of good faith. As to Donahue's (D) contribution and indemnity claims against Ford, our state statutes provide that contribution is allowed between joint tortfeasors who cause injury to another. Here, contribution is not allowed because Slocum (P) released Ford in good faith. According to our statute, this release discharges Ford from liability for contribution to Donahue (D). Donahue (D) is also not entitled to indemnification from Ford. This is because indemnity allows someone who is without fault, compelled by law to defend himself against the wrongful act of another, to recover from the wrongdoer the amount of his loss. Indemnity is allowed only when the indemnitee did not join in the wrongful act. Indemnity is limited to those cases where the would-be indemnity (Donahue) is derivatively or vicariously liable for the wrongful act of another. Under no circumstances could the jury in this case have found that Donahue (D) was vicariously liable for the conduct of Ford. Donahue's (D) liability is not vicarious and he is not entitled to indemnification from Ford. If Ford had remained in the case, any liability on its part would have been as a joint tortfeasor, and contribution would have been required. Indemnity would still not have been appropriate. Summary judgment in favor of Ford was appropriate. Affirmed.

Analysis:

This case presents the sometimes confusing concepts of indemnification and contribution. The primary distinction between the two concepts in this case is that indemnification is available to one who is vicariously liable for the wrongs of another. For example, an employer is vicariously liable for the torts of her employee. This is true even where the employer is not at fault herself. Therefore, if Alice owns a burger stand and her employee, Ben, negligently injures a customer, Alice is liable to the customer for any damages. Alice, however, has a claim for indemnification against Ben. Contribution, on the other hand, is based on the shared fault of joint tortfeasors. Both actors must be at fault. For example, if Ann and Bob negligently build a home which collapses on the owner, and the owner sues Ann. Ann would have a contribution claim against Bob based on Bob's fault. In the present case, Donahue (D) may have had a contribution claim against Ford if the jury had found Ford to be partially at fault for the accident. However, this was not the case because state statute provided that Slocum's (P) release of Ford extinguished any contribution claims of Donahue (D) against Ford. Does this seem fair? Why should Donahue (D) be bound by an agreement to which it was never a party? The rule is good in that it provides finality to Ford who can pay the settlement and not have to worry about further contribution claims. However, is it fair to Donahue (D) who may only be partially at fault? Comparative negligence statutes, which allow a jury to assign a percentage of fault to each individual involved, might be a more just way to resolve the problem.

■ CASE VOCABULARY

RELEASE: Giving up a right or claim to the person against whom it could have been enforced.

THIRD-PARTY COMPLAINT: A complaint filed by a defendant against a third party, alleging that the third party may be liable for some or all of the damages that the plaintiff is trying to recover from the defendant.

Bruckman v. Pena

(*Truck Driver*) v. (*Injured Party*)
29 Colo.App. 357, 487 P.2d 566 (1971)

INITIAL TORTFEASOR IS NOT JOINTLY AND SEVERALLY LIABLE FOR DISTINCT INTERVENING CAUSE OF INJURY

■ **INSTANT FACTS** Pena (D), having had two collisions within one year, sued Bruckman (P), the truck driver in the first collision, for all the injuries sustained.

■ **BLACK LETTER RULE** A defendant cannot be held liable for a plaintiff's subsequent injury where the plaintiff cannot apportion the damages between the causes of the injuries.

■ **PROCEDURAL BASIS**

Appeal in negligence action seeking reversal based on erroneous jury instructions.

■ **FACTS**

Pena's (D) car collided with Bruckman's (P) truck, resulting in Pena's (D) injuries which were aggravated when Pena (D) got into a second collision approximately one year later. Pena (D) sued Bruckman (P) for all the injuries suffered. The court instructed the jury that if it couldn't apportion the injuries between the first and the second accident, Bruckman (P) would be liable for the entire injury. The jury returned a verdict in favor of Pena (D). Bruckman (P) seeks reversal of the verdict on the ground that the court's instructions to the jury were erroneous.

■ **ISSUE**

May a defendant be held liable for a plaintiff's subsequent injury where the plaintiff cannot apportion the damages between the causes of the injuries?

■ **DECISION AND RATIONALE**

(Dwyer, J.) No. A defendant cannot be held liable for a plaintiff's subsequent injury where the plaintiff cannot apportion the damages between the causes of the injuries. In negligence cases the plaintiff has the burden to establish that his damages were proximately caused by the negligence of the defendant. In this case the instruction is erroneous because it allows the plaintiff to recover damages against the defendant for injuries received subsequent to the negligent conduct of the defendant for which the defendant was not responsible. This instruction puts the burden on the defendant to prove that the plaintiff's damages can be apportioned between the two collisions. Contrary to the plaintiff's contentions, the reasons for *Newbury v. Vogel* do not apply in this case. Under *Newbury* a tortfeasor who injures one suffering from a pre-existing condition is liable for the entire damage to the plaintiff where no apportionment is possible. That case is different from the instant case where a tortfeasor is being held liable, not only for damage that he caused, but also for injuries subsequently suffered by the plaintiff as a result of negligent conduct of another party. (Reversed and Remanded.)

Analysis:

Apportionment refers to a situation where the amount of damages awarded to the plaintiff should be divided based on the causes of the plaintiff's injuries. Note that in this case, the plaintiff had two distinct collisions. The first collision injured the plaintiff, and the second collision aggravated the plaintiff's already existing injuries. However, the plaintiff is suing the first defendant for all of his injuries. In this case, the court indicates that regardless of whether apportionment is possible or not, the defendant cannot be held liable for all of the plaintiff's damages. Had the plaintiff sued the second defendant, he would have probably recovered for all of his damages regardless of apportionment because as you remember, a defendant takes a plaintiff as he finds him. Also, be aware, the two defendants in this case are not joint tortfeasors. There is no question of contribution. We are talking about two distinct and separate injuries which have occurred at two different times and have been caused by two different entities.

■ CASE VOCABULARY

APPORTIONMENT: Dividing fairly or according to the parties' respective interests, proportionally, but not necessarily equally.

Michie v. Great Lakes Steel Division, Nat'l Steel Corp.

(Neighbors) v. *(Polluting Companies)*

495 F.2d 213 (6th Cir.1974)

WHERE A PLAINTIFF'S INJURY IS INDIVISIBLE AND CANNOT BE APPORTIONED AMONG THE TORTFEASORS, THE LATTER ARE JOINTLY AND SEVERALLY LIABLE FOR THE ENTIRE DAMAGES TO THE PLAINTIFF

■ **INSTANT FACTS** Michie (P) sued Great Lakes (D) and other corporations jointly and severally in nuisance for pollutants emitted from the corporations' plants.

■ **BLACK LETTER RULE** Where the independent concurring acts of defendants have caused an indivisible harm to the plaintiff, and no reasonable means of apportioning the damages is evident, the court may hold the defendant's jointly and severally liable.

■ PROCEDURAL BASIS

Appeal from trial court denial of motion to dismiss.

■ FACTS

Michie (P) and 36 other individuals in Canada, sued Great Lakes Steel Division ("Great Lakes"), National Steel Corporation (D) and other corporations in the United States jointly and severally, alleging that noxious pollutants emitted by the latters' plants were carried into Canada, creating a nuisance and causing damages to Michie (P) and other individuals, persons and properties. The action was filed based on diversity, each individual's damages ranging between $11,000 and $35,000 jointly and severally. Great Lakes (D) and the other corporations moved to dismiss the complaint claiming that it did not meet the $10,000 diversity requirement for federal court jurisdiction. The trial court denied the motion. The corporations (D) appeal.

■ ISSUE

Where the independent concurring acts of defendants have caused an indivisible harm to the plaintiff, and no reasonable means of apportioning the damages is evident, may the court hold the defendants jointly and severally liable?

■ DECISION AND RATIONALE

(Edwards, J.) Yes. Where the independent concurring acts of defendants have caused an indivisible harm to the plaintiff, and no reasonable means of apportioning the damages is evident, the court may hold the defendants jointly and severally liable. This court follows the reasoning in *Maddux* which states that it is unfair to impose on the injured party the burden of proving specific shares of harm done by the defendant. Where the injury to the plaintiff is factually or medically separable and liability for the injury or damages may be allocated to the defendant with reasonable certainty, then the triers of fact will be instructed to do so, and the defendants will not be held jointly and severally liable. However, where the division of liability isn't possible, authorities are divided as to the solution. Some courts would dismiss the entire claim. However, such a conclusion is erroneous because in such cases the tortfeasors will be relieved from all liability even though their conduct was negligent and caused injury. Where division of liability is impossible, this means that the injury is indivisible, and that the tortfeasors are jointly and severally liable even though there was no common design amongst them. This reasoning applies to nuisance cases as well. Joint and several liability is imposed in four different scenarios: 1) where the actors knowingly join in the tortious conduct; 2) where the tortfeasors fail to perform a common duty owed to the plaintiff; 3) where there is a special relationship between the parties; and 4) where, although no concerted action between the tortfeasors exist, the harm produced by their actions is indivisible. The instant case falls in the fourth scenario. Thus, in cases of indivisible harm, the court shifts the burden of apportionment from the injured plaintiff to the wrongdoers. (Affirmed.)

Analysis:

Joint and several liability, as we have already seen, refers to the situation where the plaintiff can recover his/her entire judgment against one joint tortfeasor. Joint and several liability occurs normally when the plaintiff proves that the defendants acted in concert or that they failed in performance of a common duty owed to the plaintiff. Note that in this case, however, the joint and several liability arises from a third situation: that is, where the conduct of the wrongdoers is not concerted, and their negligence may have occurred at different times. However, the result of their negligence is one single indivisible harm to the plaintiff. In such situations some courts completely dismiss the plaintiff's complaint because the plaintiff is unable to determine which part of his/her injury is attributable to each defendant's conduct. Some courts, however, such as in the instant case, simply shift the burden of proof to the defendants. That is, where the injury is indivisible, and the plaintiff shows that it is impossible to apportion the damages, the defendants are all jointly and severally liable, unless they can prove which part of the plaintiff's injury is attributable to each one of them.

Dillon v. Twin State Gas & Electric Co.

(Administrator of the Deceased's Estate) v. *(Electric Company)*

85 N.H. 449, 163 A. 111 (1932)

WHERE A PLAINTIFF WOULD HAVE BEEN INJURED REGARDLESS OF THE DEFENDANT'S NEGLIGENCE, DAMAGES ARE MEASURED BASED UPON THE PLAINTIFF'S INJURED CONDITION

■ **INSTANT FACTS** Dillon (P) sued Twin State (D) in negligence for the wrongful death of a 14-year-old boy who fell from a bridge.

■ **BLACK LETTER RULE** Where a plaintiff, regardless of the defendant's negligence, would have suffered injury, the plaintiff's damages would be measured based on the plaintiff's injured condition.

■ **PROCEDURAL BASIS**

Appeal from the trial court's motion for directed verdict in wrongful death action.

■ **FACTS**

Twin States Gas & Electric Co. ("Twin State") (D) maintained electric wires to carry electric current across a public bridge. The wires ran through the vertical and horizontal girders above the bridge and did not often carry current during the day. The decedent, a 14-year-old boy, lost his balance while sitting on top of the bridge girders. He held onto the wires to keep from falling, got electrocuted and died. The jury trial resulted in a disagreement, and Twin State's (D) motion for directed verdict was dismissed. Twin State (D) appeals on the ground that the decedent would have fallen to his death regardless of Twin State's negligence.

■ **ISSUE**

Where a plaintiff, regardless of the defendant's negligence, would suffer injury, should the plaintiff's damages be measured based on the plaintiff's injured condition?

■ **DECISION AND RATIONALE**

(Allen, J.) Yes. Where a plaintiff, regardless of the defendant's negligence would suffer injury, the plaintiff's damages would be measured based on the plaintiff's injured condition. In this case, the defendant's only liability to the decedent was exposing him to the current and not preventing him from falling. Although the decedent was electrocuted, by reason of the loss of his balance he would have fallen and would have been seriously maimed or killed regardless of the electrocution. Thus, his loss of balance did not deprive him of a life of normal expectancy, but of one too short to be given damages, or in the alternative, of a life of limited earning capacity. If it is found that the boy would have fallen to his death regardless of the electrocution, the defendant is not liable, except for any conscious suffering which the boy may have sustained from the electric shock. In that situation, however, the boy's life or his earning capacity has no value, and no damages have been sustained. If, however, it is found that the boy's fall would have resulted in injury, then the loss of life or earning capacity would be measured by its value in this injured condition. (Exception Overruled.)

Analysis:

Note that in this case the court is basically indicating that in order for the plaintiff to collect damages, there has to be some injury to the plaintiff's person or property as a result of the defendant's negligence. In this case the boy was falling off a bridge, and it is likely that he would have died regardless of the current that was running through the girders. Notice that the defendant's negligence is not in failing to protect the boy from falling, but in having exposed him to the current. Thus, it is the court's duty to determine what damages the boy sustained from the defendant's exposure of the boy to the electricity. Assuming that the boy would have fallen and would not have died but would have been seriously injured, then the damages that he could recover would be based on his injured condition. In other words, how much worse was the boy's injury due to the electric shock?

CHAPTER EIGHT

Duty of Care

Winterbottom v. Wright

Instant Facts: Winterbottom (P), a coach driver, sued Wright (P), a coach manufacturer, for injuries sustained when the coach broke down.

Black Letter Rule: A person may not sue another on a non-public contract when he/she is not privy to the contract.

MacPherson v. Buick Motor Co.

Instant Facts: An automobile purchaser sued the manufacturer for negligently failing to inspect a vehicle prior to sale to a distributor.

Black Letter Rule: A manufacturer owes a duty of care to remote purchasers if the product is reasonably certain to cause injury when negligently made.

H.R. Moch Co. v. Rensselaer Water Co.

Instant Facts: Moch (P) sought recovery from Rensselaer Water (D) for the latter's failure to supply water to extinguish the fire that was destroying Moch's (P) warehouse.

Black Letter Rule: A party who is in no contractual or special relationship to another may not be held liable for refusal to aid the other.

Clagett v. Dacy

Instant Facts: Clagett (P), highest bidders in a foreclosure sale, sued Dacy (P), attorney for creditors, for failing to follow proper procedure for the sale.

Black Letter Rule: An attorney may not be held liable to a person who is not intended to benefit by his performance, and with whom the attorney does not have a contractual relationship.

Hegel v. Langsam

Instant Facts: The Hegels (P), parents of a minor child who was a university student, sued Langsam (D), a university official, for failing to prevent the student's association with criminals.

Black Letter Rule: A university does not have the duty to control the private lives of its students.

L.S. Ayres & Co. v. Hicks

Instant Facts: Hicks (P), a six-year-old boy, sought recovery from L.S. Ayres & Co. (D) ("Ayres"), a department store, for injuries sustained when Hicks' (P) hand got stuck in the escalator at Ayres' (D) store.

Black Letter Rule: A store owner or an invitor has the duty to rescue a person in peril if the instrumentality causing the person's injury is in control of the owner or invitor.

J.S. and M.S. v. R.T.H.

Instant Facts: Wife of pedophile was sued for failure to protect the neighbor children from sexual abuse by her husband.

Black Letter Rule: When a spouse has actual knowledge or special reason to know of the likelihood of his or her spouse engaging in sexually abusive behavior against a particular person or persons, a spouse has a duty of care to take reasonable steps to prevent or warn of the harm, and a breach of such a duty constitutes a proximate cause of the resultant injury.

Tarasoff v. Regents Of University Of California

Instant Facts: The Tarasoffs (P) brought action against therapists employed by the Regents of the University of California (D) ("Regents") for failing to warn Tarasoff's (D) deceased daughter of a patient's intentions to kill the daughter.

Black Letter Rule: The relationship between a therapist and a patient supports the duty on the part of the therapist to exercise reasonable care to others against dangers posed by the patient's illness.

State of Louisiana ex rel. Guste v. M/V Testbank

Instant Facts: State of Louisiana ex rel. Guste (P) ("the State") sought recovery from M/V Testbank (D) ("M/V") for pure pecuniary loss suffered when M/V's (D) negligence caused fishing waters to be closed.

Black Letter Rule: A plaintiff may not recover for pure economic loss if the loss resulted from physical damage to property in which the plaintiff had no interest.

Daly v. General Motors Corp.

Instant Facts: A driver who was intoxicated and not wearing a seat belt was killed when an allegedly defective door latch gave way.

Black Letter Rule: Comparative fault principles can be applied to strict products liability actions.

Thing v. La Chusa

Instant Facts: Maria Thing (P) sued James La Chusa (D), the driver whose car collided with Thing's (P) child, for emotional distress suffered when Thing (P) arrived at the scene of the accident.

Black Letter Rule: A parent whose child was struck by a negligent driver may not recover damages for emotional distress where the parent did not witness the accident.

Endresz v. Friedberg

Instant Facts: Endresz (P), who was seven months pregnant at the time of the accident with Friedberg (D), brought a wrongful death action against the latter for the death of her still-born babies.

Black Letter Rule: The parents of a stillborn child may not maintain a wrongful death action for the death of an unborn child.

Procanik By Procanik v. Cillo

Instant Facts: Parents of Peter Procanik (P) brought action on behalf of Peter (P) against Dr. Cillo (D) for negligently failing to diagnose Peter's mother during pregnancy, thereby depriving her from the choice of aborting Peter (P).

Black Letter Rule: An infant may not file a "wrongful life" claim to recover general damages for diminished childhood and pain and suffering.

Winterbottom v. Wright

(Coach Driver) v. *(Manufacturer of Coaches)*
10 M. & W. 109, 152 Eng.Rep. 402 (1842)

A PARTY WHO HAS UNDERTAKEN A PUBLIC DUTY IS LIABLE TO ALL FORESEEABLE PLAINTIFFS EVEN THOUGH INJURIES MAY HAVE ARISEN FROM NEGLIGENCE OF THE PARTY'S SERVANT OR AGENT

■ **INSTANT FACTS** Winterbottom (P), a coach driver, sued Wright (P), a coach manufacturer, for injuries sustained when the coach broke down.

■ **BLACK LETTER RULE** A person may not sue another on a non-public contract when he/she is not privy to the contract.

■ **PROCEDURAL BASIS**

Action in negligence for recovery of damages for personal injury.

■ **FACTS**

Wright (D), manufacturer and repairer of coaches, entered into a contract with the Postmaster General to keep mail coaches in safe condition. Winterbottom (P), a mail coach driver, sued Wright (D) for injuries sustained when the coach broke down, alleging that Wright (D) failed to keep the coach in safe condition according to the contract.

■ **ISSUE**

May a person sue another on a non-public contract to which he/she is not privy?

■ **DECISION AND RATIONALE**

(Abinger, C.B) No. A person may not sue another on a non-public contract when he/she is not privy to the contract. There is no privity of contract between Winterbottom (P) and Wright (D). However, where a party has undertaken a public duty, he is liable, though the injury to others may have arisen from the negligence of his servant. Such is the rule in public duty or public nuisance cases. A contract cannot turn into a tort action unless there has been a public duty undertaken. In this case, there is no tort action, and Winterbottom (P) could not bring an action under the contract because he is not privy to it. (Judgment for the defendant.)

■ **CONCURRENCE**

(Alderson, B.) The right to recover should be limited to those who enter the contract. Winterbottom (P), not being a party to the contract, should not recover.

■ **CONCURRENCE**

(Rolfe, B.) Wright's (D) duty to keep the coaches in safe condition is a duty toward the Postmaster General which arose out of the contract between them. Wright (D) owes no duty to Winterbottom (P).

Analysis:

Note that in this case, the plaintiff is suing the defendant in tort based on the contract between defendant and a third party. The court holds that unless the contract is one in which the defendant has undertaken a public duty, the defendant is not liable to the plaintiff and does not owe a duty to the public in general. This doctrine however, has been repudiated to a certain extent. A person entering into a contract, is liable to a non-party for foreseeable physical injuries. Under the new rule, the plaintiff in this case would have been allowed to recover for his damages.

■ CASE VOCABULARY

PRIVY: Refers to persons connected with one another or having mutual interests in the same action or thing, by some relation other than that of actual contract between them.

MacPherson v. Buick Motor Co.

(Consumer) v. (Automobile Manufacturer)

217 N.Y. 382, 111 N.E. 1050 (1916)

MANUFACTURERS OWE A DUTY TO REMOTE PURCHASERS TO INSPECT PRODUCTS WHICH ARE REASONABLY CERTAIN TO CAUSE INJURY

■ **INSTANT FACTS** An automobile purchaser sued the manufacturer for negligently failing to inspect a vehicle prior to sale to a distributor.

■ **BLACK LETTER RULE** A manufacturer owes a duty of care to remote purchasers if the product is reasonably certain to cause injury when negligently made.

■ **PROCEDURAL BASIS**

Appeal from judgment of New York Supreme Court affirming verdict for negligence for defective product.

■ **FACTS**

Donald C. MacPherson (P) purchased a Buick Model 10 Runabout from a retail dealer. One of the wheels on the car was made of defective wood, and MacPherson (P) was injured when the wheel crumbled and the car collapsed. Although the Buick Motor Company (D) did not manufacture the wheel, MacPherson (P) sued Buick (D) for negligence, claiming that the defect could have been discovered by a reasonable inspection, which Buick (D) failed to perform. The Supreme Court of New York affirmed a judgment for MacPherson (P), and Buick (D) appeals.

■ **ISSUE**

Does a manufacturer owe a duty of care to remote purchasers if the product is reasonably certain to cause injury when negligently made?

■ **DECISION AND RATIONALE**

(Cardozo, J.) Yes. A manufacturer owes a duty of care to remote purchasers if the product is reasonably certain to cause injury when negligently made. Prior products liability holdings are in conflict. Some cases have held that manufacturers owe a duty of care to ultimate purchasers only when the product is inherently dangerous, such as a gun or poison. We feel that the more reasonable approach is to impose a duty of care for manufacturers of products which are reasonably certain to place life and limb in peril when negligently made. The manufacturer must have knowledge of the danger, and must have knowledge that the ultimate purchaser might reasonably encounter the danger. In the case at hand, the danger from a defective wheel was to be expected as reasonably certain. Furthermore, customers such as MacPherson (P) should be reasonably anticipated as ultimate purchasers of the automobiles. Thus, Buick (D) had a duty to vigilantly inspect the wheels. Buick (D) was responsible for the finished product, and it is not absolved from its duty of inspection because it bought the wheels from a reputable dealer. Buick (D) was not at liberty to put the finished product on the market without subjecting the component parts to ordinary and simple tests. Where, as here, the danger from a defective part is probable, there is a great need for caution on the part of the manufacturer. Judgment affirmed.

Analysis:

In this opinion, Justice Cardozo adopts a common-sense approach to products liability based on a negligence theory. Cardozo abandons the "inherently dangerous" product requirement for products liability based on negligence. Products liability law should not turn on whether a product is considered "inherently" or "imminently" dangerous, according to Cardozo. Adopting a reasonable approach, New York's highest court holds that manufacturers owe a duty of vigilant inspection where some danger is reasonably certain to occur. The danger of an automobile accident from a defective wheel is reasonably certain. Buick (D) should have recognized this danger and taken the simple steps of inspecting all parts of its vehicles prior to sale. In addition, Buick (D) should have known that MacPherson (P) and other such consumers would be the ultimate purchasers and users of the automobile. In holding that a manufacturer cannot be absolved from liability by relying on the nature of the manufacturer of a component part, the Court essentially makes a policy determination. Buick (D) could have easily inspected the wheels prior to sale to a distributor; furthermore, justice is not served by placing the risk of loss on the ultimate purchaser, who is not in such a position. Why shouldn't the purchaser be required to sue the parties who had a more direct contact with the purchaser or the wheel, i.e., the dealer or the wheel manufacturer? Perhaps Buick (D) is in a better position than the dealer to inspect for component defects. However, the wheel manufacturer could likely be liable as well, since it surely knew that the wheel would be likely to cause injury if negligently made. But the ultimate responsibility lies on the automobile manufacturer, who should make sure that the car is in good condition prior to sale.

■ **CASE VOCABULARY**

MANUFACTURER: An entity that assembles a product for use by a consumer.

H.R. Moch Co. v. Rensselaer Water Co.

(Water Supplier) v. *(Water Co.)*
247 N.Y. 160, 159 N.E. 896 (1928)

WHERE THERE IS NO SPECIAL OR CONTRACTUAL RELATIONSHIP BETWEEN TWO PARTIES, ONE IS NOT LIABLE IN TORT FOR WITHHOLDING BENEFITS TO THE OTHER

■ **INSTANT FACTS** Moch (P) sought recovery from Rensselaer Water (D) for the latter's failure to supply water to extinguish the fire that was destroying Moch's (P) warehouse.

■ **BLACK LETTER RULE** A party who is in no contractual or special relationship to another may not be held liable for refusal to aid the other.

■ **PROCEDURAL BASIS**

Appeal in negligence action for recovery of damages.

■ **FACTS**

Rensselaer Water Co. ("Water Co.") (D) and the city of Rensselaer entered into a contract through which the Water Co. (D) would furnish water to the city, schools, public buildings, and to private takers. The water to the private takers could not exceed a stated schedule. While the contract was in force, Moch's (P) warehouse caught on fire, and the Water Co. (D) refused to supply the water necessary to extinguish the fire. Moch's (P) building was destroyed, Moch (P) sought recovery for damages suffered, claiming that the Water Co.'s (D) refusal to supply water constituted a failure to fulfill the provision of the contract between the Water Co. (D) and the city. The Water Co.'s (D) motion to dismiss the complaint was denied. The Appellate Division reversed, and Moch (P) appeals.

■ **ISSUE**

May a party who is in no contractual or special relationship to another be held liable for refusal to aid the other?

■ **DECISION AND RATIONALE**

(Cardozo, C.J.) No. A party who is in no contractual or special relationship to another may not be held liable for refusal to aid the other. If one's conduct has gone to a stage that inaction would commonly result, not negatively in withholding a benefit, but positively in working an injury, there exists a relationship out of which a duty arises to go forward. In this case, the plaintiff contends that the defendant, once entering a contract with the city, enters into a relationship with everyone who may be potentially benefited by the supply of water, and that failure to perform the contract results in a tort action. Such view of the contract would indefinitely extend the defendant's zone of duty. Based on the plaintiff's contentions, everyone making a contractual promise, will not only be owed a contractual duty to the promisee, but also to an indefinite number of potential and incidental beneficiaries. However, the law does not "spread its protection so far." (Affirmed.)

Analysis:

In this case the plaintiff is an incidental, or unintended, beneficiary of the contract between the defendant water company and the city. Thus, according to the court the defendant does not owe to the plaintiff any contractual or other duty because the plaintiff was not intended to benefit by the contract. An intended beneficiary, on the other hand, would have a cause of action in contract against the defendant. Simply stated, an intended beneficiary is one for whose benefit the contract is entered into. For example, A promises to paint B's house if B pays C $1,000. C, in this situation, is the intended beneficiary and may sue B for lack of performance. Incidentally, the contract between A and B is a third party beneficiary contract.

■ CASE VOCABULARY

INCIDENTAL BENEFICIARY: A person who may incidentally benefit from the creation of a contract or a trust; such a person has no actual interest in the contract or the trust and can not enforce any right to incidental benefits.

THIRD PARTY BENEFICIARY: Persons who are recognized as having enforceable rights created in them by a contract to which they are not parties and for which they give no consideration.

Clagett v. Dacy

(Bidder) v. *(Attorney for Creditors)*
47 Md.App. 23, 420 A.2d 1285 (1980)

AN ATTORNEY MAY NOT BE LIABLE FOR DAMAGE CAUSED BY HIS NEGLIGENCE TO A PERSON NOT INTENDED TO BENEFIT BY HIS PERFORMANCE

■ **INSTANT FACTS** Clagett (P), highest bidders in a foreclosure sale, sued Dacy (P), attorney for creditors, for failing to follow proper procedure for the sale.

■ **BLACK LETTER RULE** An attorney may not be held liable to a person who is not intended to benefit by his performance, and with whom the attorney does not have a contractual relationship.

■ PROCEDURAL BASIS

Appeal in negligence action from grant of demurrer without leave to amend.

■ FACTS

Clagett (P) was the highest bidder in a trustee sale who lost the sale because, twice, Dacy (D), the attorney for the creditors, failed to follow proper procedure for the sale. Consequently, the debtor redeemed his land, causing Clagett (P) to lose the opportunity to buy the property and resell it at a profit. Clagett (P) sued Dacy (D) to recover the losses, alleging that Dacy (D) owed Clagett (P) the duty to conduct the sale with due diligence. The trial court sustained Dacy's (D) demurrer without leave to amend. Clagett (P) appeals.

■ ISSUE

May an attorney be held liable to a person who is not intended to benefit by his performance, and with whom the attorney does not have a contractual relationship?

■ DECISION AND RATIONALE

(Wilner, J.) No. An attorney may not be held liable to a person who is not intended to benefit by his performance, and with whom the attorney does not have a contractual relationship. A true third party beneficiary may sue an attorney as he could sue any other defaulting party to a contract made for his benefit. However, this rule does not supply a basis for permitting third parties to sue attorneys on pure negligence theory or for violation of some general duty arising in the absence of a contractual attorney-client relationship. Additionally, the duties inherent in an attorney-client relationship do not automatically flow to a third party absent clear facts from which such employment may be fairly inferred. Given these rules, the plaintiff's declaration fails to state a cause of action. In this case, the defendant attorney was representing the creditor (mortgagee), and not the bidders. The mortgagee's goal is to get the highest bid possible while the bidders goal is to pay the smallest. Thus, given the opposite interests involved, the defendant attorney could not lawfully represent both parties. (Affirmed.)

Analysis:

Once again, the court holds that the incidental beneficiary of a contract between two parties does not have an enforceable right for the tortious conduct of the two parties. In this case, however, the contract

---

in question is one that creates a relationship between an attorney and his client. Remember that the obligation and basically, the job of the attorney, is to work in the best interest of his/her client. In this case, the bidders could be viewed as the incidental beneficiaries of the attorney-client contract because they may end up buying the property. However, they stand in no special or contractual relationship with the attorney or the client and cannot seek recovery against the attorney for his negligence. Note that if the plaintiffs were intended beneficiaries of the contract between the attorney and the client, then the plaintiffs could maintain a cause of action against the attorney. However, according to the court, the facts indicating the existence of an intended beneficiary must be very clear and logical. Additionally, the bidders and the client in this case are at cross-purposes. The former wants to pay the lowest price; the latter wants to receive the highest price. Thus, it is logically impossible for the attorney to owe a duty to both parties because their interests are opposed. As an attorney, remember that your obligation and duty is to act in the best interests of the client (not anyone else).

Hegel v. Langsam

(*Parents of College Student*) v. (*University Official*)
29 Ohio Misc. 147, 55 O.O.2d 476, 273 N.E.2d 351 (Com.Pl.1971)

UNIVERSITIES DO NOT OWE STUDENTS THE DUTY TO PREVENT THE STUDENTS FROM ASSOCIATION WITH CRIMINALS

■ **INSTANT FACTS** The Hegels (P), parents of a minor child who was a university student, sued Langsam (D), a university official, for failing to prevent the student's association with criminals.

■ **BLACK LETTER RULE** A university does not have the duty to control the private lives of its students.

■ **PROCEDURAL BASIS**

Appeal from defendant's motion for judgment on pleadings.

■ **FACTS**

The Hegels ("Hegel") (P), the parents of a minor child who was a university student from Chicago, sued Langsam (D), a university official, for allowing the student to associate with criminals, to become a drug user, and for failing to return the student to Hegel's (P) custody.

■ **ISSUE**

Does a university have the duty to control the private lives of its students?

■ **DECISION AND RATIONALE**

(Bettman, J.) No. A university does not have the duty to control the private lives of its students. A university is not a nursing home or a prison, and no one is required to attend. Persons who meet the qualifications of the university are presumed to have sufficient maturity to conduct their own personal affairs. There is no requirement of law which imposes on the university the duty to regulate the private lives of its students, or to control their associations. (Affirmed.)

Analysis:

So far we have seen cases where the negligence of the defendant in committing an act has caused the plaintiff's injury. This case, on the other hand, is one where the plaintiffs claim that the negligence of the defendant arose from its failure to act or to perform a duty owed to the plaintiff. Thus, negligence could not only arise from affirmative actions of a defendant, but also by a failure to act where the defendant has a duty to act. Clearly, like other negligence cases, the plaintiff has to establish that the defendant, indeed, has a duty towards the plaintiff, and that the defendant has failed to fulfill that duty. The plaintiffs in this case did not succeed because the defendant, the university, was under no duty to supervise the private lives of its students or to control their associations.

L.S. Ayres & Co. v. Hicks

(*Department Store*) v. (*Injured Boy*)

220 Ind.86, 40 N.E.2d 334, 356 (1942)

THERE IS NO GENERAL DUTY TO RESCUE A PERSON WHO IS IN PERIL UNLESS A SPECIAL RELATIONSHIP BETWEEN THE PARTIES GIVES RISE TO THE LEGAL DUTY TO RESCUE

■ **INSTANT FACTS** Hicks (P), a six-year-old boy, sought recovery from L.S. Ayres & Co. (D) ("Ayres"), a department store, for injuries sustained when Hicks' (P) hand got stuck in the escalator at Ayres' (D) store.

■ **BLACK LETTER RULE** A store owner or an invitor has the duty to rescue a person in peril if the instrumentality causing the person's injury is in control of the owner or invitor.

■ **PROCEDURAL BASIS**

Appeal in action for negligence.

■ **FACTS**

Hicks (P), a six-year-old boy, was accompanying his mother when he fell in L.S. Ayres & Co.'s ("Ayres'") (D) store and got his fingers stuck in the escalator. Ayres' (D) employees unreasonably delayed stopping the escalator, thus aggravating Hicks' (P) injury. Hicks (P) sued Ayres (D) to recover for injuries sustained. The trial court entered a judgment for Hicks (P). Ayres (D) appeals.

■ **ISSUE**

Does a store owner or an invitor have the duty to rescue a person in peril if the instrumentality causing the person's injury is in the control of the owner or invitor?

■ **DECISION AND RATIONALE**

(Shake, J.) Yes. A store owner or an invitor has the duty to rescue a person in peril if the instrumentality causing the person's injury is in the control of the owner or invitor. There is no general duty under the law to rescue a person who is in peril. However, where there is a special relationship between the parties involved, the failure to render assistance may constitute actionable negligence for aggravating injury even though the original injury may have been caused by the negligence of the injured party. Where a party is injured by an instrumentality which is in the control of another party, the latter or its agents are under a legal duty to render such aid to the injured party as may be reasonably necessary to save his life or to prevent a serious aggravation of his injuries. This duty exists even though the person in control of the instrumentality was not the cause of the original injury. In this case, Hicks (P) was an invitee, and Hicks (P) received his injuries in using an instrumentality provided by Ayres (D) and under its control. Thus, there is a sufficient relationship between the two parties to impose on Ayres (D) the duty to rescue Hicks (P). In this case, however, the duty arose after the initial in jury to Hicks (P). Thus, Ayres (D) cannot be charged with anticipation or prevention of the injury, but only with failure to exercise reasonable care to prevent the aggravation of the injury, and Ayres (D) is only liable for damages which were proximately resulted from aggravation of the injuries. (Reversed.)

Analysis:

When is a party negligent for having failed to render assistance to rescue an injured person? The general rule in tort law is that there is no duty to rescue. A simple example will illustrate this point. You are walking down the street, and see an automobile collide with a person, and flee. The person is bleeding profusely, and is in need of dire help. You can stop next to the person, look at him for a few seconds and then walk away. You have no duty to call 911, or to render personal assistance to the injured person. True, there may be a moral obligation to help, and most of us would help. However, there is no legal obligation, and the injured person can not sue you for failing to assist him/her. The duty to rescue, however, may arise under special circumstances. One of those situations is where the instrumentality which has caused the person's injury was provided by and was in the control of the master or an invitor. An invitor is usually a person who requests the presence of another party on his/her property. The invitee is the person who is on another person's property by invitation. A store and a customer are examples of invitor and invitee, respectively. Another type of special relationship is that between an employer and an employee for acts which may cause injury during the course of employment. Common carriers are also under the legal duty to rescue their passengers. So are innkeepers. Another scenario under which the duty to rescue is triggered is where the person who is in charge of rescue has voluntarily assumed the duty to rescue. In such cases, a failure to rescue constitutes negligence.

■ **CASE VOCABULARY**

RESCUE DOCTRINE: A tort rule holding a tortfeasor liable to his/her victim's rescuer, should the latter injure himself during a reasonable rescue attempt.

J.S. and M.S. v. R.T.H.

(Parents of Molested Children) v. *(Pedophile)*

155 N.J. 330, 714 A.2d 924 (1998)

A WIFE OF A PEDOPHILE HAS A DUTY TO WARN OTHERS OF HER HUSBAND'S PROPENSITIES

■ **INSTANT FACTS** Wife of pedophile was sued for failure to protect the neighbor children from sexual abuse by her husband.

■ **BLACK LETTER RULE** When a spouse has actual knowledge or special reason to know of the likelihood of his or her spouse engaging in sexually abusive behavior against a particular person or persons, a spouse has a duty of care to take reasonable steps to prevent or warn of the harm, and a breach of such a duty constitutes a proximate cause of the resultant injury.

■ **PROCEDURAL BASIS**

Certification motion from the Appellate Division's decision reversing the trial court's granting of summary judgment for the defendant, and remanding of the case for entry of an order granting the plaintiffs extended discovery.

■ **FACTS**

Two young girls (P), ages 12 and 15, spent a great deal of time with their 65-year-old neighbor (called John for litigation purposes), riding and caring for his horses. After a trusting relationship was established, John (D) began to sexually abuse both girls (P). The sexual abuse continued for more than a year. Following John's (D) conviction and imprisonment for these sexual offenses, the girls and their parents (P) brought this action against John (D) and his wife (called Mary for litigation purposes) (D) for damages, arguing that Mary's (D) negligence rendered her, as well as her husband, liable for the injuries to the girls. John (D) conceded liability, however Mary (D) denied that she could be found negligent for the girls' injuries. Mary (D) also filed a cross claim for contribution and indemnification against John (D), alleging that even if the plaintiffs' allegations were proven, John (D) was the sole and primary cause of any injuries to the plaintiffs.

■ **ISSUE**

Does a spouse who suspects or should suspect his or her spouse of actual or prospective sexual abuse against a particular person or persons have a duty of care to prevent such abuse and, if so, does breach of that duty constitute a proximate cause of the harm that results from sexual abuse?

■ **DECISION AND RATIONALE**

(Handler, J.) Yes. When a spouse has actual knowledge or special reason to know of the likelihood of his or her spouse engaging in sexually abusive behavior against a particular person or persons, a spouse has a duty of care to take reasonable steps to prevent or warn of the harm, and a breach of such a duty constitutes a proximate cause of the resultant injury. Foreseeability of the risk of harm is the foundational element in the determination of whether a duty exists, and it is based on the defendant's knowledge of the risk of injury, which is susceptible to objective analysis. That knowledge may be an actual awareness, or a constructive one, where the defendant may be charged with the knowledge if she is in a position to discover the risk of harm. The imposition of a duty requires an evaluation and a balancing of the conflicting interests of the respective parties, and ultimately the determination of the existence of a duty is a question of fairness and public policy. The scope of a duty is determined under the totality of the circumstances, and when the defendant's actions are relatively easily corrected and the harm sought to be prevented is serious, it is fair to impose a duty. Here, Mary's (D) husband sexually assaulted young girls whom he had befriended. The abuse occurred on her own property over an extended period of time. Although conduct involving sexual abuse is often secretive, clandestine, and furtive, there is some empirical support for the conclusion that it is a risk that can be foreseen by a spouse. These considerations warrant a standard of "particularized foreseeability" in this case that is based on "particular knowledge" or "special reason to know" that a "particular plaintiff" would suffer a "particular type" of injury. Foreseeability under that definitional standard is neither unrealistic nor unfair. Turning to the interests of the parties, there can be no doubt about the strong public policy to protect children from sexual abuse, however there is also an interest in protecting the marital relationship. The societal interest in enhancing marital relationships simply cannot outweigh the societal interest In protecting children from sexual abuse. Considerations of foreseeability, the comparative interests of the parties, and public policy and fairness support the recognition of a duty of care, however the issue of proximate causation must also be considered in determining whether any liability may be allowed for the breach of such a duty. It does not seem highly extraordinary that a wife's failure to prevent or warn of her husband's sexual abuse or his propensity for sexual abuse would result in the occurrence or the continuation of such abuse. The harm from the wife's breach of duty is both direct and predictable. Accordingly, we affirm the judgment of the Appellate Division.

Analysis:

While the reasoning the court uses in its decision appear to be well thought out and logical in general, the facts of this case don't seem to support the conclusion that Mary (D) breached her duty of care. The facts as presented simply do not indicate that Mary (D) either had or should have had knowledge of the risk John (D) posed to the girls (P). The court lists several relevant factors when determining the foreseeability of such conduct, including whether the husband had previously committed sexual offenses against children, and the details surrounding those prior offenses; the husband's therapeutic history and regimen, the extent to which the wife encouraged or facilitated unsupervised contact with the victims; the presence of physical evidence in the marital home, such as kiddie porn or children's clothing; and the extent of the victims' making sexual comments or engaging in age-inappropriate behavior in the wife's presence. There was no evidence that *any* of these factors existed, and it seems untenable to believe that Mary (D) should have known John (D) was a pedophile simply because they were married.

■ CASE VOCABULARY

CONTRIBUTION: Sharing of the loss in proportion of fault.

INDEMNIFICATION: Total shifting of the economic loss to the party primarily responsible for the loss.

Tarasoff v. Regents of University of California

(Parents of the Decedent) v. *(Employer of Psychologist)*
17 Cal.3d 425, 551 P.2d 334, 131 Cal.Rptr. 14 (1976)

UNDER THE COMMON LAW, ONE PERSON OWES NO DUTY TO CONTROL THE CONDUCT OF ANOTHER UNLESS THE PERSON STANDS IN SOME SPECIAL RELATIONSHIP TO THE OTHER

■ **INSTANT FACTS** The Tarasoffs (P) brought action against therapists employed by the Regents of the University of California (D) ("Regents") for failing to warn Tarasoff's (D) deceased daughter of a patient's intentions to kill the daughter.

■ **BLACK LETTER RULE** The relationship between a therapist and a patient supports the duty on the part of the therapist to exercise reasonable care to others against dangers posed by the patient's illness.

■ **PROCEDURAL BASIS**

Appeal from wrongful death claim.

■ **FACTS**

During the treatment of a patient, Dr. Moore, a psychologist at the University of California, learned that a patient, Poddar, intended to kill Tarasoff's (P) daughter, Tatiana. Poddar ultimately killed Tatiana. Tatiana's parents, the Tarasoffs (P), brought a wrongful death claim against the Regents of the University of California ("Regents") (D) on the ground that the psychologist failed to warn Tatiana about Poddar's threats. On appeal, the Regents (D) claimed that they owed no duty of care to Tatiana or to the Tarasoffs (P), and that in the absence of such a duty, the doctors were free to act in careless disregard of Tatiana's life and safety.

■ **ISSUE**

Does the relationship between a therapist and a patient support the duty on the part of the therapist to exercise reasonable care to protect others against dangers posed by the patient's illness?

■ **DECISION AND RATIONALE**

(Tobriner, J.) Yes. The relationship between a therapist and a patient supports the duty on the part of the therapist to exercise reasonable care to others against dangers posed by the patient's illness. Under the common law, as a general rule, one owes no duty to control the conduct of another, nor to warn others endangered by such conduct. However, there is an exception to this general rule where the defendant stands in a special relationship to either the person whose conduct needs to be controlled or in a relationship to the foreseeable victim of that conduct. In this case, there is a special relationship between the patient and the therapist which may impose duties on the parts of the therapist for the benefit of third parties. Although in this case, the therapist stands in no relationship to the victim, many jurisdictions hold that the single relationship between the therapist and the patient is sufficient to support the duty to exercise reasonable care for the protection of third parties. The Regents (D), however, contend that imposition of a duty to third parties is not workable because therapists can not accurately predict whether or not a patient will resort to violence. Although therapists are not capable of exact predictions at all times, a therapist need only exercise the reasonable degree of skill, knowledge, and care ordinarily exercised by the members of profession under similar circumstances. In this case the therapist did in fact predict Poddar's violence, however negligently failed to warn the victim. In this court's view once a therapist determines that a patient poses a danger to a third person, he is under a duty to exercise reasonable care to protect the foreseeable victim of that danger. The Regents additionally contend that the possibility of revealing communications between the patients and the therapists right make the patients reluctant to make the full disclosure necessary for the diagnosis and treatment of the patients. Yet, the public interest in supporting effective treatment and privacy of patients should be balanced against the public interest in safety from violent assaults. If the exercise of reasonable care will protect the threatened victim, there is no social interest that would protect and justify concealment of the relevant communication between the patient and the therapist. (Order for amended complaint to state cause of action.)

Analysis:

This case again explores the scenario where a person has a duty towards third parties. Remember that in general one has no duty to control the conduct of another or to protect third parties from danger posed by such conduct. One exception that we saw in the previous case applies to parents of children who know or should know of their children's definite and specific dangerous propensities. In this case, a therapist by virtue of his/her special relationship to the patient has a duty to predict and warn others of the dangers posed by his/her patient's illness. Note, however, that the duty and the reasonableness of a therapists actions are all judged based on the degree of skill and knowledge possessed and exercised by other professionals or therapists in the field.

■ CASE VOCABULARY

AMICUS CURIAE: Latin phrase meaning friend of the court; one who gives information to the court on some matter of law which is in doubt; an Amicus Curiae brief is submitted by one who is not party to the lawsuit to aid the court in gaining the information it needs to make a proper decision or to urge a particular result on behalf of the public or a private interest of third parties who will be affected by the resolution of the dispute.

State of Louisiana ex rel. Guste v. M/V Testbank

(The State) v. *(Damaged Ship)*

752 F.2d 1019 (5th Cir.1985) (en banc)

IN NEGLIGENCE CASES, PHYSICAL DAMAGE TO A PROPRIETARY INTEREST IS A PREREQUISITE TO RECOVERY FOR PECUNIARY LOSS

■ **INSTANT FACTS** State of Louisiana ex. rel. Guste (P) ("the State") sought recovery from M/V Testbank (D) ("M/V") for pure pecuniary loss suffered when M/V's (D) negligence caused fishing waters to be closed.

■ **BLACK LETTER RULE** A plaintiff may not recover for pure economic loss if the loss resulted from physical damage to property in which the plaintiff had no interest.

■ **PROCEDURAL BASIS**

En banc re-examination of grant of summary judgment in negligence action.

■ **FACTS**

M/V Testbank ("M/V") (D), a container ship, collided with another ship which caused packages containing pentachlorophenol, PCP, to fall over board. As a result of the accident, the U.S. Coast Guard closed the water for navigation and temporarily suspended fishing and all other related activities. Many parties sued M/V (D) even though they suffered no physical damage to their property. The District Court granted M/V's (D) motion for summary judgment for all the claimants except commercial oyster men, shrimpers, and fishermen. The Fifth Circuit Court affirmed. The case is re-examined en banc.

■ **ISSUE**

May a plaintiff recover for pure economic loss if the loss resulted from physical damage to property in which the plaintiff had no interest?

■ **DECISION AND RATIONALE**

(Higginbotham, J.) No. A plaintiff may not recover for pure economic loss if the loss resulted from physical damage to property in which the plaintiff had no interest. This is the precedent set by past cases, including *Robins Dry Dock v. Flint.* In *Robins*, the Supreme Court of the United States held that a tort to the person or property of one man does not make the tortfeasor liable to another merely because the injured person has a contract with the other person. The plaintiffs contend that *Robins* should be limited to losses suffered for inability to perform contracts between the plaintiff and others. In other words, they contend that the case applies only to negligent interference with contractual rights of others. However, in this court's opinion if a person who has a contract with the injured party is too remote to sue the defendant, then a person who is not in any contractual relationship is even more remote. *Robins* is a pragmatic limitation imposed by the Court based upon the tort doctrine of foreseeability. Plaintiffs contend that the requirement of physical injury is arbitrary and that the question of remoteness and foreseeability should be left to the jury to decide. However, without a bright line rule no determinable measure of the limit of foreseeability would precede the decision on liability, and judgments would not be the result of determinable rules of law. Plaintiffs further attempt to categorize their losses as public nuisance, claiming that when a defendant unreasonably interferes with public rights by obstructing navigation, he creates a public nuisance for which recovery is available to all who have sustained particular damages. These are damages which are greater than those suffered by the general public as a result of the nuisance. With economic losses such as the ones claimed here, the problem is to determine who has suffered pecuniary loss so great as to distinguish his losses from similar losses suffered by others. In this court's opinion, there is no advantage in allowing this difficult task to skirt the *Robins* rule. (Affirmed.)

■ CONCURRENCE

(Gee, J.; Clark, C.J.) The Court should not extend limits of liability because in a case such as this it may result in destruction of enterprises, loss of employment and productive capacity.

■ DISSENT

(Wisdom, J.) The court's requirement of physical damage conflicts with the tort principles of foreseeability and proximate cause. Although rejection of the requirement would require case-by-case analysis, the results would be fair, and would allow the innocent plaintiff to receive compensation. Additionally, this court has extended *Robins* incorrectly. In that case, the court prevented plaintiffs who were neither proximately nor foreseeably injured from recovery solely on the basis of economic loss. However, the majority of this court believes that plaintiff's lack of any contractual relationship with an injured party, taken with the *Robins* rule, forecloses liability. This would make sense had the plaintiffs suffered no loss but for a contract with the injured party. In this case, however, the collision caused the plaintiffs' losses, and their losses were foreseeable. Instead of relying on the strict rule of *Robins,* the court should rely on the principles of foreseeability and proximate cause. Reliance on these principles would compensate the injured party and impose the cost of damages upon the tortfeasors.

Analysis:

This case supports the principle that a party may not recover for pure economic loss unless the party also suffered physical damage to his person or property. An easy example may help illustrate this point. Bus A collides with Bus B due to Bus A's negligence. Because of the collision, the police close the road, and C, who is driving in his car to work, has to re-route. By the time C gets to work, his boss gets very angry and fires him. Can C sue Bus A for his termination? The answer is no. C has not suffered any physical damages to his person or property.

■ CASE VOCABULARY

IN TERROREM: Latin phrase, meaning in fear.

PUBLIC NUISANCE: An unreasonable interference with a right common to the general public. It is behavior which unreasonably interferes with the health, safety, comfort, peace, or convenience of the general community.

Daley v. LaCroix

(Homeowner) v. *(Driver)*

384 Mich. 4, 179 N.W.2d 390 (1970)

THE MICHIGAN SUPREME COURT OVERRULES THE REQUIREMENT OF PHYSICAL IMPACT UPON THE PLAINTIFF FOR RECOVERY FOR NEGLIGENT INFLICTION OF EMOTIONAL DISTRESS

■ **INSTANT FACTS** Estelle and Timothy Daley (P) ("Daley") sought damages for emotional disturbance caused as a result of LaCroix's (D) negligent driving which led to an explosion on Daley's (P) property.

■ **BLACK LETTER RULE** A plaintiff who has suffered physical injury as a result of emotional distress caused by a defendant's negligence may recover damages, even in the absence of any physical impact upon the plaintiff.

■ FACTS

LaCroix's (D) car went off the road, flying in the air, striking electric power lines, and causing an explosion on Daley's (P) property. The latter sued LaCroix (D) for property damages and emotional disturbance caused as a result of the explosion and the circumstances surrounding the accident. The trial court directed a verdict in LaCroix's (D) favor, and the Court of Appeals affirmed on the ground that Michigan law denies recovery of damages for negligent infliction of emotional distress in the absence of physical impact with the plaintiff's person.

■ ISSUE

May a plaintiff who has suffered physical injury as a result of emotional distress caused by a defendant's negligence recover damages, even in the absence of any physical impact upon the plaintiff?

■ DECISION AND RATIONALE

(Kavanagh, J.) Yes. A plaintiff who has suffered physical injury as a result of emotional distress caused by a defendant's negligence may recover damages, even in the absence of any physical impact upon the plaintiff. Except for rare cases involving telegraphic companies and negligent mishandling of corpses, courts deny recovery for mental disturbance in absence of physical injury. This rule protects against fraudulent or fancied claims and the flood of litigation. Thus, courts have denied recovery for a plaintiff's fright due to the defendant's negligence where there is no personal injury to the plaintiff. This court, however, on the basis of change of circumstances in scientific and factual information available, and other authorities, overrules the impact requirement. This court holds that where there is definite and objective physical injury to the plaintiff, as a result of emotional distress caused by the defendant's negligence the plaintiff may recover damages for such injuries even in the absence of physical impact with the plaintiff's person. A plaintiff's recovery, however, is limited to those reactions to be expected of a normal person, except where the defendant has specific knowledge of the plaintiff's hypersensitivity. Additionally, the plaintiff has the burden of proving that the physical harm is the natural result of the fright caused by the defendant's conduct.

Analysis:

This case illustrates a developing modern approach to recovery for mental disturbance, and it also presents a good summary of the traditional approach. In order to prevent the flood of fraudulent claims, courts have typically denied recovery for mental distress unless it is caused by an actual physical impact. While this traditional approach may have accomplished the goal of limiting such claims, it seems to impose an arbitrary barrier to valid claims. After all, in the case at hand, solid scientific evidence was presented to show that the Daleys (P) actually did suffer significant mental disturbances accompanied by physical symptoms. Perhaps the element of proximate cause may be problematic, since the explosion was caused by LaCroix's (D) car striking a utility pole some distance from the Daleys' (P) home. Regardless, should courts require that LaCroix's (P) automobile actually strike the Daleys (P) in order for them to recover? Alternatively, even under the traditional approach, couldn't the Daleys (P) argue that they were physically "impacted" by the shockwaves from the explosion? The Court does not reach this issue, holding instead that physical impact is not required. In doing so, the Court adopts a reasonable approach by imposing several limitations. For example, there must be a definite and objective physical injury that is the natural result of the fright proximately caused by the defendant's conduct, this injury must be proven by scientific testimony; and the plaintiffs cannot claim for mental distress which is beyond what a "normal" person would suffer.

■ CASE VOCABULARY

PARASITIC DAMAGES: Compensation for certain injuries, such as mental distress, when those injuries accompany other injuries for which recovery is traditionally allowed, such as physical injuries.

SUI GENERIS: Of its own kind or class; peculiar.

■ PROCEDURAL BASIS

Appeal from court's grant of motion for directed verdict.

Thing v. La Chusa

(Mother of Injured Child) v. *(Automobile Driver)*
48 Cal.3d 644, 771 P.2d 814, 257 Cal.Rptr. 865 (1989) (In Bank)

ACCORDING TO THE SUPREME COURT OF CALIFORNIA, A PLAINTIFF MAY RECOVER DAMAGES FOR EMOTIONAL DISTRESS FOR INJURY INFLICTED ON A THIRD PERSON IF THE PLAINTIFF IS CLOSELY RELATED TO THE VICTIM AND IS PRESENT AT THE TIME THAT THE VICTIM IS INJURED

■ **INSTANT FACTS** Maria Thing (P) sued James La Chusa (D), the driver whose car collided with Thing's (P) child, for emotional distress suffered when Thing (P) arrived at the scene of the accident.

■ **BLACK LETTER RULE** A parent whose child was struck by a negligent driver may not recover damages for emotional distress where the parent did not witness the accident.

■ **PROCEDURAL BASIS**

Appeal from the trial court's grant of summary judgment in negligence case.

■ **FACTS**

LaChusa (D), an automobile driver, struck and injured Thing's (P) child. Thing (P), who nether saw nor heard the accident, sued La Chusa (D) for emotional distress that Thing (P) suffered upon arriving at the scene of the accident, and seeing her bloody, unconscious child. The trial court granted La Chusa's (D) motions for summary judgment on the ground that Thing (P) could not establish a claim for negligent infliction of emotional distress because she did not perceive the accident. Thing (P) appeals.

■ **ISSUE**

May a parent whose child was struck by a negligent driver recover damages for emotional distress where the parent did not witness the accident?

■ **DECISION AND RATIONALE**

(Eagleson J.) No. A parent whose child was struck by a negligent driver may not recover damages for emotional distress where the parent did not witness the accident. Initially, in California the right to recover damages for negligent infliction of emotional distress was limited to cases where (1) the victim himself was physically injured and damages for emotional distress were awarded as parasitic damages, or (2) to cases where the plaintiff was within the zone of danger, did not suffer injury as a result of physical impact, but did suffer physical injury as a result of emotional trauma. In *Amaya v. Home Ice, Fuel & Supply Co.* the court refused to extend this cause of action to plaintiffs who were not within the "zone of danger." In *Dillon v. Legg*, however, the court abandoned the "zone of danger" limitation and allowed recovery for emotional distress to a mother who witnessed her child being run over by a negligent automobile driver. The *Dillon* court limited recovery to those persons who were, at the time of the accident, reasonably foreseeable. The arbitrary limitations in *Dillon* were abandoned in *Molien v. Kaiser Foundation Hospitals*, where the court allowed recovery to those victims who were "direct victims" of the defendant's negligence. The *Molien* court ruled that the husband of a patient who was erroneously diagnosed as having syphilis was a reasonably foreseeable victim and that the tortious conduct of the defendant doctors was directed at him as well as the patient. A direct victim is a person whose emotional distress is a reasonably foreseeable consequence of the defendant's negligent conduct. Policy considerations justify restrictions on recovery for emotional distress notwithstanding the sometimes arbitrary result, and the court has an obligation to establish those restrictions. The court must balance the impact of arbitrary lines which deny recovery to some victims with real injuries against that of imposing liability out of proportion to culpability for negligent acts. Greater certainty arises when the recovery for emotional distress is limited to those plaintiffs who have personally and contemporaneously perceive the injury-producing event and its traumatic consequences. For the same reason, recovery should also be limited to those plaintiffs who are closely related by blood or by marriage, since it is more likely that they will suffer a greater degree of emotional distress than a disinterested witness to negligently caused pain and suffering or death. Although these limitations are, in some cases, arbitrary, drawing such lines are unavoidable if courts are to limit liability and establish rules for application of this cause of action. Recovery for emotional distress should be limited to those persons who will suffer emotional impact beyond the impact that can be anticipated whenever one learns that a relative is injured, or the emotion felt by a "disinterested" witness. Where the liability is limited to the class of plaintiffs who will suffer the greatest emotional distress, the liability bears a reasonable relationship to the negligence of the defendant. Thus [according to this court], a plaintiff may recover damages for negligent infliction of emotional distress for injury to a third party, if the plaintiff is 1) a close relative of the injured party, 2) present at the scene of the injury, and aware of the injury occurring, and 3) suffers serious emotional distress. In this case, the plaintiff may not recover damages because she was not present at the scene of the accident and did not observe the event giving rise to injury to her child. (Reversed.)

■ CONCURRENCE

(Kaufman, J.) *Dillon* should be overturned, and recovery should be limited to those within the zone of danger who fear for their own safety.

Analysis:

When covering the intentional torts, we came across the tort of intentional infliction of emotional distress. Under that tort, the plaintiff had to prove that he/she suffered extreme emotional distress, that the conduct of the defendant was extreme and outrageous, and that the conduct of the defendant was intentional or reckless. Remember, however, that where a third party was seeking damages under intentional infliction of emotional distress, for intentional injury to a victim, some courts require the third party to prove that he/she has suffered physical injury. This case illustrates the rule for negligent infliction of emotional distress as a result of conduct by the defendant which is not directed at the plaintiff. In such cases, California courts require that the plaintiff be a close relative of the victim, that the plaintiff suffer extreme emotional distress, more than that suffered or anticipated for a disinterested witness, and that the plaintiff be present at the scene of the event giving rise to the victim's injury. Thus, in the instant case the mother, who was not present at the scene of her child's accident, was denied recovery under negligent infliction of emotional distress. However, had the mother been present at the scene of the accident, she could have recovered damages because all the other requirements are fulfilled: she is a close relative and she suffered extreme emotional distress.

Endresz v. Friedberg

(Pregnant Woman) v. *(Automobile Driver)*
24 N.Y.2d 478, 248 N.E.2d 901, 301 N.Y.S.2d 65 (1969)

NEW YORK COURT OF APPEALS HOLDS THAT THERE CAN BE NO WRONGFUL DEATH ACTION FOR THE DEATH OF AN UNBORN CHILD

■ **INSTANT FACTS** Endresz (P), who was seven months pregnant at the time of the accident with Friedberg (D), brought a wrongful death action against the latter for the death of her still-born babies.

■ **BLACK LETTER RULE** The parents of a still-born child may not maintain a wrongful death action for the death of an unborn child.

■ **PROCEDURAL BASIS**

Appeal from dismissal of wrongful claim.

■ **FACTS**

Endresz (P), who was seven months pregnant with twins, was struck by Friedberg's (D) automobile. Two days after the accident, Endresz (P) delivered two stillborn babies. Endresz (P) and her husband sued Friedberg (D) for the wrongful death of the babies. Additionally, Endresz (P) and her husband brought action for the loss of the babies on their own behalf. The trial court dismissed the wrongful death claims on the ground that such action may not be maintained for children who were stillborn. Endresz (P) appeals.

■ **ISSUE**

May the parents of a stillborn child maintain a wrongful death action for the death of an unborn child?

■ **DECISION AND RATIONALE**

(Fuld, J.) No. The parents of a stillborn child may not maintain a wrongful death action for the death of an unborn child. The personal representative of a decedent may maintain an action to recover damages for a wrongful act which caused the death of the decedent. However, before such action may be maintained, there must be a birth, a person born alive. An unborn child does not fit within this description. Additionally, the mother of a stillborn child may sue for injury which she sustained personally, such as her suffering as a result of the stillbirth; and the father may sue for the loss of the mother's services and consortium. An additional award to the distributees of the fetus would give the parents a windfall and would not constitute compensation to the injured party, but punishment to the wrongdoer. The law has never considered an unborn child as having a judicial existence separate from that of her mother's. Thus, a child must be born first, before there can be a wrongful death action against the wrongdoer. (Affirmed.)

■ **DISSENT**

(Burke, J.) The rule adopted by the majority leads to incongruous results. For example, an unborn child who is badly injured by the negligence of another, but who is born alive, could recover, while an unborn child, who was also badly injured, but who is not born alive, could recover nothing.

Analysis:

According to the instant case, there can be no wrongful death claim on behalf of a child who is stillborn. However, as the case points out, there can be such action on behalf of a child who is born and later dies due to the negligent conduct of another. Note that in early tort law, no duty was recognized towards an unborn child, even if the child were born alive. There were three reasons for denial of recovery in such cases: 1) it was assumed that an unborn child has no separate existence apart from the mother, 2) it was thought that the proof of causation in fact would be nearly impossible, and 3) damages were thought to be too vague and speculative. However, the advancement of science and medical technology has repudiated all three reasons. Thus, today, a majority of jurisdictions allow recovery for prenatal injuries to an unborn child who is subsequently born alive. Nevertheless, there is still a large controversy over allowing recovery for prenatal injuries to an unborn child who is born dead. A majority of states allow wrongful death actions for unborn children. Some states even allow criminal claims on behalf of the child.

■ CASE VOCABULARY

WRONGFUL DEATH STATUTES: Statutes that create a cause of action for any wrongful act, neglect, or default that causes death.

Procanik by Procanik v. Cillo

(Deceased Child) v. *(Doctor)*

97 N.J. 339, 478 A.2d 755 (1984)

THE MAJORITY OF JURISDICTIONS REJECT A CAUSE OF ACTION FOR WRONGFUL LIFE OR FOR IMPAIRED CHILDHOOD

■ **INSTANT FACTS** Parents of Peter Procanik (P) brought action on behalf of Peter (P) against Dr. Cillo (D) for negligently failing to diagnose Peter's mother during pregnancy, thereby depriving her from the choice of aborting Peter (P).

■ **BLACK LETTER RULE** An infant may not file a "wrongful life" claim to recover general damages for diminished childhood and pain and suffering.

■ **FACTS**

Rosemary Procanik, during the first trimester of her pregnancy, was diagnosed by Dr. Cillo (D) as having measles. However, no further tests were administered to determine whether Rosemary had German measles. Rosemary allowed her pregnancy to continue and gave birth to Peter (P), who was suffering from congenital rubella syndrome, and multiple birth defects. Peter's (P) parents brought a wrongful life action against Dr. Cillo (D) on behalf of Peter (P), claiming that Dr. Cillo (D) was negligent in failing to diagnose Rosemary with German measles and for depriving Peter's (P) parents of the choice of terminating the pregnancy. Peter (P) sought damages for pain and suffering for his impaired childhood and inability of the parents to deal with his problems. Peter (P) also sought special damages for the expenses that Peter (P) would incur as an adult for medical and other health care services. The Law Division granted Cillo's (D) motion to dismiss the complaint for failure to state a cause of action and the Appellate Division affirmed. Peter (P) appeals.

■ **ISSUE**

May an infant file a "wrongful life" claim to recover general damages for diminished childhood and pain and suffering?

■ **DECISION AND RATIONALE**

(Pollock J.) No. An infant may not file a "wrongful life" claim to recover general damages for diminished childhood and pain and suffering. However, the infant may recover as special damages the extraordinary medical expenses attributable to his affliction. Originally, as in the case of *Gleitman v. Cosgrove*, if a doctor negligently diagnosed or treated a pregnant woman who was suffering from a condition that might cause her to give birth to a defective child, neither the parents nor the child could maintain a cause of action against the negligent doctor. The *Gleitman* court declared that the value of life with impairments against the value of the nonexistence of life itself was an impossibility. Additionally, that court denied the parents' claim for emotional distress and the cost of caring for the infant because of the impossibility of weighing the joys of parenthood against the parent's emotional distress. Furthermore, the public policy against abortions prevented the court from awarding damages to the mother for not having an abortion. However, 17 years later, in *Berman v. Allan* the court awarded the parents of a Down's Syndrome child expenses of raising the child and allowed recovery for the parents emotional distress because the availability of abortions supported the right of a woman to choose to terminate her pregnancy. That court, however, rejected any cause of action in an infant born with birth defects. In this case, the "wrongful life" cause of action refers to an action brought by or on behalf of the infant who claims that but for the defendant's negligent advice to the parents, the infant would not have been born. Note, however, that at no time are the parents claiming that the negligence of the doctor caused the infant's birth defects. The essence of the complaint is that had it not been for the negligent advice of the defendant, the infant's birth would have been prevented. Although the defendant owed a duty to the infant, and was negligent in treating the mother, policy considerations have led this court to reject a "wrongful life" cause of action. Most courts agree that the measure of general damages in such a case is vague and insurmountable. It is too speculative to permit an infant plaintiff to recover for emotional distress because of birth defects when the plaintiff claims he would be better off if he hadn't been born. However, this court allows an award of damages for extraordinary medical expenses necessary for such children. Recovery of such costs, either by the parents or the child, but not both, is consistent with the principle that the defendant's negligence affected the entire family. (Judgment reversed in part, and remanded.)

Analysis:

In this case the infant who is born with birth defects is suing the doctor. Notice that it was not the doctor's negligence that caused the defects. However, the infant claims that had the doctor correctly diagnosed the mother's illness, the mother would have terminated the pregnancy and the infant would not have been born. Thus, the court is faced with the problem of setting a value on the life of a child with birth defects versus no life at all. In other words the infant is asking the court to recognize a new cause of action, known as "wrongful life." According to this court and a majority of jurisdictions, such general damages are too speculative and impossible to measure. Additionally, the court does not want to advance the policy that no life is better than life with birth defects. However, note that this court does allow the infant or the parents, but not both, recovery for extraordinary medical expenses that the parent and the child will incur in treating the child.

■ CASE VOCABULARY

WRONGFUL BIRTH: The cause of action of parents who claim that negligent advice or treatment deprived them of the choice of avoiding conception or terminating pregnancy.

WRONGFUL LIFE: A tort action concerning childbirth, such as the birth of a child after the negligent performance of an operation to sterilize the parent, or the birth of a child with serious defects due to the doctor's failure to advise the parents properly.

CHAPTER NINE

Owners and Occupiers of Land

Taylor v. Olson

Instant Facts: Taylor (P) sought recovery from Olson (D) for injuries sustained when Taylor's (P) car hit a tree which had fallen on the road from Olson's (D) property.

Black Letter Rule: A landowner is under the duty to use common and reasonable methods to examine conditions on his/her property which may give rise to physical injury.

Salevan v. Wilmington Park, Inc.

Instant Facts: Salevan (P) sought recovery against Wilmington Park (D) ("Wilmington") for injuries suffered when Salevan (P) was struck by a fly-away ball from the park.

Black Letter Rule: A landowner who knows or should know of dangerous conditions on his/her property must take reasonable precautions to prevent injury to others using roadways adjacent to his/her land.

Sheehan v. St. Paul & Duluth Ry. Co.

Instant Facts: Sheehan (P) sued St. Paul & Duluth Ry. Co. (D) ("the railroad") for injuries suffered when a train owned by the railroad (D) ran over Sheehan's (D) foot.

Black Letter Rule: A landowner does not owe a duty of care to a trespasser of whom the landowner has no actual or constructive notice.

Barmore v. Elmore

Instant Facts: Stabbed by Elmore's (D) son, Barmore (P) sued Elmore (D) for injuries sustained.

Black Letter Rule: The owner/occupier of a property has the duty to warn a licensee/social guest of hidden dangers unknown to the latter.

Campbell v. Weathers

Instant Facts: Campbell (P) sued Weathers (D), a store owner, for injuries suffered when in Weathers' store.

Black Letter Rule: An individual, entering a place of business open to the public, need not make a purchase in order to be considered an invitee.

Whelan v. Van Natta

Instant Facts: Whelan (P), a customer at Van Natta's (D) store, sued the latter for injuries sustained when Whelan (P) fell in the stairwell in the back of the store.

Black Letter Rule: An invitee ceases to be an invitee after the expiration of a reasonable time within which to accomplish the purpose for which he is invited to enter or remain.

Rowland v. Christian

Instant Facts: Rowland (P) sued Christian (D) for injuries sustained when the handle of the faucet in Christian's (D) home broke.

Black Letter Rule: An owner/occupier owes the duty to warn others of known dangerous conditions which are known to the owner/occupier or to repair the conditions in order to prevent the risk of unreasonable harm to others.

Borders v. Roseberry

Instant Facts: Borders (P), a guest at the home of one of Roseberry's (D) tenants, fell and sued Roseberry (D) for the injuries suffered.

Black Letter Rule: A landlord does not, as a matter of law, owe a duty of care to a social guest of his tenant to remedy known dangerous conditions.

Palsgraf v. Long Island R.R. Co.

Instant Facts: Palsgraf (P) sued Long Island R.R. Co. (D) ("the railroad") for the injuries sustained when a package fell out of the hand of one of the train passengers and exploded.

Black Letter Rule: A defendant owes a duty of care only to those plaintiffs who are in the reasonably foreseeable zone of danger.

Kline v. 1500 Massachusetts Ave. Apartment Corp.

Instant Facts: Kline (P), criminally assaulted and robbed in the hallway of Kline's (P) residence, sued 1500 Massachusetts Ave. Apartment Corp. (D) ("the landlord") for injuries sustained.

Black Letter Rule: A landlord has the duty to take reasonable precautions to protect tenants from foreseeable criminal acts of third parties.

Taylor v. Olsen

(Driver) v. *(Landowner)*
282 Or. 343, 578 P.2d 779 (1978)

AN OWNER/OCCUPIER OF LAND MUST USE REASONABLE CARE TO PREVENT UNREASONABLE RISK OF HARM TO OTHERS FROM CONDITIONS ON HIS PROPERTY

■ **INSTANT FACTS** Taylor (P) sought recovery from Olson (D) for injuries sustained when Taylor's (P) car hit a tree which had fallen on the road from Olson's (D) property.

■ **BLACK LETTER RULE** A landowner is under the duty to use common and reasonable methods to examine conditions on his/her property which may give rise to physical injury.

■ **PROCEDURAL BASIS**

Appeal in action in negligence from directed verdict.

■ **FACTS**

While driving on a windy January evening, Taylor's (P) car hit a tree which had fallen on the road. Taylor (P) sued Olson (D), the owner of the property on which the tree had been located, for injuries sustained. The trial court directed a verdict in favor of Olson (D). Taylor (P) appeals.

■ **ISSUE**

Is a landowner under the duty to use common and reasonable methods to examine conditions on his/her property which may give rise to physical injury?

■ **DECISION AND RATIONALE**

(Linde, J.) Yes. A landowner is under the duty to use common and reasonable methods to examine conditions on his/her property which may give rise to physical injury. The extent of the landowners responsibility can not be defined by categorizing the land as urban or rural. In this case Olson (D) had bought the land for logging purposes and had, prior to the accident, logged half of the timber on the land, including the trees adjacent to the one which fell into the road. The land was near a public roadway used by 790 vehicles a day. The evidence tends to show that only by chopping the trunk of the tree would there have been a substantial chance of discovering the decay which caused the fall of the tree. Thus, the question is whether the defendant's responsibility extends so far as cutting the trunk. There is no evidence to suggest that chopping the trunk would have been the normal method to examine a standing tree. Neither is there any evidence that the defendant was on notice or should have been on notice that there would be possible decay in the tree. In the absence of such evidence, the defendant is not liable. (Affirmed.)

Analysis:

This case deals with the duty of owners and occupiers of land with respect to the natural conditions on their property and the danger that such conditions pose to individuals that are not on the land. As you read the cases, you will notice that the extent of one's liability depends on three questions: 1) Is the condition natural or artificial? 2) Are the individuals threatened by the risk of harm on/off the property? and 3) What is the status of the individual who is upon the land owners property? In this case, we are dealing with a natural condition which poses a risk to an individual who is off the landowner's premises. Generally, courts have held that a landowner does not owe a duty to protect others outside the premises from the natural conditions on his/her property. Trees, however, are an exception to this rule. Most courts hold that the landowner is liable for negligence if he knows that the tree is defective and fails to take reasonable precautions to avoid unreasonable risk of harm. This case further indicates that the landowner has the reasonable duty to inspect for discovery of defects in trees.

Salevan v. Wilmington Park, Inc.

(Injured Pedestrian) v. *(Landowner)*
45 Del. (6 Terry) 290, 72 A.2d 239 (1950)

LANDOWNERS, WHOSE LAND ABUTS A PUBLIC ROADWAY, MUST USE REASONABLE CARE IN ORDER TO NOT INTERFERE WITH THE RIGHTS OF PERSONS LAWFULLY USING THE ROADS

■ **INSTANT FACTS** Salevan (P) sought recovery against Wilmington Park (D) ("Wilmington") for injuries suffered when Salevan (P) was struck by a fly-away ball from the park.

■ **BLACK LETTER RULE** A landowner who knows or should know of dangerous conditions on his/her property must take reasonable precautions to prevent injury to others using roadways adjacent to his/her land.

■ **PROCEDURAL BASIS**

Action in negligence for recovery of damages for personal injury.

■ **FACTS**

Salevan (P) suffered injuries when a baseball struck him in the head as Salevan (P) was passing by a ballpark owned by Wilmington (D). At the time of the accident, Wilmington (D) was in charge of maintenance and renting of the park. The evidence showed that during the course of a ball game, 2 to 3 foul balls would fly over the fence surrounding the park and into the adjacent street. Salevan (P) sued Wilmington Park ("Wilmington") (D) claiming that the latter had notice of the fly-away balls and that Wilmington's (D) failure to take reasonable precautions against injury to others constituted negligence.

■ **ISSUE**

Must a landowner who knows or should know of dangerous conditions on his/her property take reasonable precautions to prevent injury to others using roadways adjacent to his/her land?

■ **DECISION AND RATIONALE**

(Wolcott, J.) Yes. A landowner who knows or should know of dangerous conditions on his/her property must take reasonable precautions to prevent injury to others using roadways adjacent to his/her land. Clearly, the public has the right to free use of the public roadways, and landowners should take reasonable precautions not to interfere with this right. The precautions that are necessary depend on the nature and circumstances of each case. In this case the required precautions are those necessary based on the nature of the game and its past history in the location in question. In this case, the evidence is uncontradicted that the defendant knew or should have known that the baseballs flew out of the park. Thus, although the defendant took certain precautions, they were not sufficient. Additionally, the defendant knew or should have known that the precautions were insufficient because the balls were still flying out of the park. (Judgment for the plaintiff.)

Analysis:

Note that with a few exceptions (e.g., trees), a landowner does not owe a duty to protect those who are off his property from the dangerous natural conditions on his property. However, once the conditions are altered or are artificial, the duties of the landowner change. Where there are artificial conditions on the property, the owner must exercise reasonable care to protect those who are outside of the premises. Whether a landowner has exercised reasonable care is clearly based on the average prudent person and the circumstances surrounding the case.

Sheehan v. St. Paul & Duluth Ry. Co.

(Trespasser) v. *(Railroad Company)*
76 Fed. 201 (7th Cir.1896)

A LANDOWNER OWES NO DUTY TO TRESPASSERS OF WHOM THE LANDOWNER HAS NO NOTICE

■ **INSTANT FACTS** Sheehan (P) sued St. Paul & Duluth Ry. Co. (D) ("the railroad") for injuries suffered when a train owned by the railroad (D) ran over Sheehan's (D) foot.

■ **BLACK LETTER RULE** A landowner does not owe a duty of care to a trespasser of whom the landowner has no actual or constructive notice.

■ PROCEDURAL BASIS

Appeal from directed verdict in action for damages for personal injury.

■ FACTS

Sheehan (P) while walking on St. Paul & Duluth Ry. Co.'s ("the railroad's") (D) tracks without permission, caught his foot in the tracks. A train, owned by the railroad (D), ran over Sheehan's (D) foot. The train's crew had no notice of Sheehan (P) until the train had already reached Sheehan (P). The latter sued the railroad (D) for his injuries. The trial court directed a verdict in favor of the railroad (D) on the ground that there was no wrongful act on the part of the railroad (D). Sheehan (P) appeals.

■ ISSUE

Does a landowner owe a duty of care to a trespasser of whom the landowner has no actual or constructive notice?

■ DECISION AND RATIONALE

(Seaman, J.) No. A landowner does not owe a duty of care to a trespasser of whom the landowner has no actual or constructive notice. In this case, the plaintiff was not a passenger, nor at a public cross walk, but a trespasser on the defendant's tracks. Courts have held that a trespasser can not be treated as an outlaw and some duty exists on the part of the railroad to exercise some degree of care towards the trespasser. Most cases have held that the railroad should have the right to a free track in areas which are not for public crossing and that a trespasser who enters in such an area assumes all risks of dangerous conditions which may be found there. However, the railroad has the positive duty to exercise strict and constant care at street crossings or other places at which it is presumable that persons may be passing. Thus, it is the notice to the railroad which arises out of the probability and existence of the use of the tracks that imposes the duty of care on the railroad. In the absence of notice, the case of a trespasser in an area which is not open for the public is distinguishable. In such situations, since there is no constructive notice of trespassers, the obligation of the railroad arises at the time of discovery of the trespasser. At that point, unless the crew on the train acted unreasonably in averting the injury, there is no liability on the part of the railroad. (Affirmed.)

Analysis:

This case is the first one which deals with individuals on the landowner's property. Always ask three questions when analyzing the duties of a landowner/occupier with respect to conditions on the premises: 1) Is the condition natural or artificial? 2) Are the individuals threatened by the risk of harm on/off the property? and 3) What is the status of the individual who is upon the land owners property? In this case, the condition of the property is clearly artificial (tracks); the individual is on the landowner's premises; the individual is a trespasser. A landowner owes the least duty of care to a trespasser. As this case indicates, there is no duty of care owed to the trespasser unless the landowner has notice (actual or constructive) of the trespasser. This immunity towards trespassers has eroded in cases of discovered trespassers (as illustrated by this case), where the landowner uses unreasonable force or unreasonably injures the trespassers, and where the dangerous condition is known to the landowner and he/she has not remedied or taken precautions against it. Under these exceptions the landowner must exercise a reasonable degree of care toward the trespasser, otherwise he/she will be held liable.

■ CASE VOCABULARY

CONSTRUCTIVE NOTICE: The type of notice which is presumed by law to have been acquired.

TRESPASSER: One who enters or remains upon the land of another without the owner's permission. The owner of the land has no duty to guard against injury of the trespasser and is not liable if a trespasser injures himself unless an unjustified risk of injury to such person is created, such as by use of spring guns or human traps.

Barmore v. Elmore

(Stabbed Guest) v. *(Homeowner)*

83 Ill.App.3d 1056, 403 N.E.2d 1355, 38 Ill.Dec. 751 (1980)

A LANDOWNER OWES 1) A LICENSEE THE DUTY TO WARN OF KNOWN AND HIDDEN CONDITIONS, AND 2) AN INVITEE THE DUTY TO EXERCISE REASONABLE CARE IN KEEPING THE PROPERTY SAFE

■ **INSTANT FACTS** Stabbed by Elmore's (D) son, Barmore (P) sued Elmore (D) for injuries sustained.

■ **BLACK LETTER RULE** The owner/occupier of a property has the duty to warn a licensee/social guest of hidden dangers unknown to the latter.

■ **PROCEDURAL BASIS**

Appeal in action for recovery of damages for personal injuries from directed verdict.

■ **FACTS**

Barmore (P) was a guest at Elmore's (D), when the latter's 47-year-old son attacked Barmore (P) with a steak knife. Barmore (P) and Elmore (D) were both officers of a Masonic lodge, and Barmore's (P) visit was for the purpose of discussing lodge business. Elmore's (D) attempts to restrain the son were unsuccessful, and the son followed Barmore (P) outside the house, stabbing Barmore (D) in the chest. Barmore (P) sued Elmore (P) for injuries suffered, claiming that Elmore (D) was negligent in failing to warn Barmore (P) of the dangerous condition on the property. The trial court directed a verdict in favor of Elmore (D). Barmore (P) appeals.

■ **ISSUE**

Does the owner/occupier of a property have the duty to warn a licensee/social guest of hidden dangers unknown to the latter?

■ **DECISION AND RATIONALE**

(Lindberg, J.) Yes. The owner/occupier of a property has the duty to warn a licensee/social guest of hidden dangers unknown to the latter. The extent of a homeowner's duty is based on whether the injured party is an invitee or a licensee at time the party was on the owner's property. An invitee is one who enters upon the property of another in furtherance of the owner's business. A licensee or a social guest is one who enters the premises by the owner's permission, but is there as a social guest or the licensee's own purposes such as companionship, diversion, or entertainment. The licensee generally takes the owner's property as he finds it. The owner only owes him the duty to warn of hidden dangers which are unknown to the licensee, but known to the owner. On the other hand, the owner owes the invitee the duty to exercise reasonable care in keeping the premises reasonably safe. In this case, although the plaintiff was there to pay his dues to the Masonic lodge, the benefit of his service went to the organization, and not to the defendant himself. Thus, the plaintiff is a licensee. While the defendant failed to warn the plaintiff of the danger on the premises, the evidence shows that the defendant did not know or have reason to know of the son's tendency to commit a criminal act toward the plaintiff. The defendant knew that the son had mental problems and that he had been involved in violent incidents ten years before this incident. However, the length of time which had passed did not give the defendant any reason to know that the son would behave in a violent manner on the occasion in question. (Affirmed.)

Analysis:

Once again, the duty owed by a landowner/occupier to individuals who are on the property depends mainly on the status of those individuals. So far we have seen that the landowner does not owe trespassers any duty of care unless the owner knows or should know of the trespasser's presence. This duty differs from that owed to a licensee and an invitee. A licensee is one who enters the owner's premises for his own benefit. This benefit could include companionship or even entertainment. The landowner owes the licensee the duty to warn against hidden dangers which are known or should be known to the owner. The landowner's duty to an invitee is more vigilant. An invitee is one who enters upon the premises to further the owner's business. To an invitee, the owner owes the duty to exercise reasonable care to keep the premises reasonably safe. This means that the owner not only has to reasonably inspect the premises for dangerous conditions, but also reasonably remove the conditions so as to make the premises safe. In discussing the duty of landowners, it is usually the condition of the land which gives rise to liability. This case seems to imply that it is also the condition of the individuals on the land which give rise to liability. Is this really correct?

■ CASE VOCABULARY

INVITEE: One who enters another person's property in furtherance of that person's business.

LICENSEE: One to whom a license has been granted; in property, one whose presence on the property is not invited but tolerated. A person who is neither a customer, nor a servant, nor a trespasser, and does not stand in any contractual relation with the owner of the premises, and is permitted expressly or impliedly to go thereon for his own interest, convenience, or gratification.

Campbell v. Weathers

(Patron) v. *(Store Owner)*

153 Kan. 316, 111 P.2d 72 (1941)

AN INVITEE IS ONE WHO IS EXPRESSLY OR IMPLIEDLY INVITED ONTO THE PROPERTY OF ANOTHER IN ORDER TO FURTHER THE PARTY'S ECONOMIC INTEREST

■ **INSTANT FACTS** Campbell (P) sued Weathers (D), a store owner, for injuries suffered when in Weathers' store.

■ **BLACK LETTER RULE** An individual, entering a place of business open to the public, need not make a purchase in order to be considered an invitee.

■ **PROCEDURAL BASIS**

Appeal from order sustaining demurrer in action for recovery of damages for personal injury.

■ **FACTS**

Campbell (P) entered Weathers' (D) lunch counter and cigar store, looked around for twenty minutes without making a purchase, and then went to the back of the store to use the restroom. There, Campbell (P) stepped into a trap and was injured. Campbell (P) sued Weathers (D) for the injuries suffered. The evidence indicated that Campbell (P) had been a customer of Weathers (D) for a number of years, had shopped at the store, and used the restroom many times in the past. The trial court sustained Weathers' (D) demurrer to the evidence. Campbell (P) appeals.

■ **ISSUE**

Must an individual, entering a place of business open to the public, make a purchase in order to be considered an invitee?

■ **DECISION AND RATIONALE**

(Wedell, J.) No. An individual, entering a place of business open to the public, need not make a purchase in order to be considered an invitee. Weathers' (D) business was open to the public and Campbell (P) had been a customer there for many years. Additionally, Weathers' (D) employees conceded that the restroom was not regarded as private and was used by other customers as well. One cannot subscribe to the view that a regular customer is not an invitee to use the restrooms provided by a restaurant because the customer had not actually made a purchase. While a customer entering a store may not have intended to make a purchase, he may nevertheless become interested later or on some future occasion. An invitee is one who enters upon the property of another to further the economic interest of the other. Thus, if one goes into a store with the view to make a purchase, either then or at a future time, he is considered an invitee. (Reversed.)

Analysis:

We have seen so far that an invitee is one who enters upon the premises of another to further an economic benefit or interest to the other. Thus, a person at a clothing store or other similar business is considered an invitee. The issue illustrated by this case is whether one needs to make a purchase in

---

order be an invitee? The answer is no. As long as one enters the premises with the intention of making a purchase then, or in the future, that individual is considered an invitee.

Whelan v. Van Natta

(Injured Customer) v. *(Store Owner)*

382 S.W.2d 205 (Ky.App.1964)

AN INVITEE WHO GOES OUTSIDE OF THE AREA OF HIS INVITATION BECOMES A LICENSEE OR A TRESPASSER DEPENDING ON WHETHER HE GOES THERE WITH OR WITHOUT CONSENT

■ **INSTANT FACTS** Whelan (P), a customer at Van Natta's (D) store, sued the latter for injuries sustained when Whetan (P) fell in the stairwell in the back of the store.

■ **BLACK LETTER RULE** An invitee ceases to be an invitee after the expiration of a reasonable time within which to accomplish the purpose for which he is invited to enter or remain.

■ **PROCEDURAL BASIS**

Appeal in action for negligence for recovery of damages for personal injuries.

■ **FACTS**

Whelan (P) entered Van Natta's (D) store and purchased cigarettes. Prior to leaving the store, Whelan (P) asked Van Natta (D) for empty boxes, and the latter told Whelan (D) he could find them in the back of the store. There, Whelan (P) fell into an unseen staircase and was injured. The evidence pointed out that Van Natta (D) did not warn Whelan (P) of the staircase, and that the lights in the back of the store may have been off. The trial court entered judgment in favor of Van Natta (D). Whelan (P) appeals.

■ **ISSUE**

Does an invitee cease to be an invitee after the expiration of a reasonable time within which to accomplish the purpose for which he is invited to enter or remain?

■ **DECISION AND RATIONALE**

(Montgomery, J.) Yes. An invitee ceases to be an invitee after the expiration of a reasonable time within which to accomplish the purpose for which he is invited to enter or remain. In this case Whelan (P) contends he entered the store on business and therefore had the status of an invitee, even when he fell in the back of the store and was injured. The possessor of land is only subject to liability to the invitee for harm sustained while he is on the land within the scope and area of his invitation. Upon the expiration of this status the invitee becomes a trespasser or a licensee depending on whether he is there with consent or without. Thus, one who goes into a shop is an invitee while within the area and scope of the invitation, but he is a licensee if the shopkeeper allows him to go to the bathroom or to make a call. (Affirmed.)

Analysis:

This case deals with the change in status of an individual who is on a landowner's property. The status of the individual is very important because as you know it defines the liability of the landowner/occupier. According to this case, one is an invitee as long as he/she stays within the scope of the invitation as

---

well as within the physical area of invitation. Thus, the plaintiff who went to the back of the store ceased to be an invitee and became a licensee, because he was there with the consent of the shop owner, and was there for the furtherance of his own purposes.

Rowland v. Christian

(Social Guest) v. *(Homeowner)*

69 Cal.2d 108, 4443 P.2d 561, 70 Cal.Rptr. 97 (1968)

CALIFORNIA SUPREME COURT REJECTS THE COMMON LAW CATEGORIES OF INVITEE, LICENSEE, AND TRESPASSER AS A MEASURE OF LANDOWNER'S DUTY TO OTHERS

■ **INSTANT FACTS** Rowland (P) sued Christian (D) for injuries sustained when the handle of the faucet in Christian's (D) home broke.

■ **BLACK LETTER RULE** An owner/occupier owes the duty to warn others of known dangerous conditions which are known to the owner/occupier or to repair the conditions in order to prevent the risk of unreasonable harm to others.

■ **PROCEDURAL BASIS**

Appeal from summary judgment in negligence action for recovery of damages for personal injuries.

■ **FACTS**

A guest at Christian's (D) home, Rowland (P) asked to use the bathroom. Rowland (P) was injured when the cold water faucet in the bathroom broke, causing severe damages to her nerves and tendons. Rowland (P) sued Christian (D) for injuries sustained. The evidence showed that Christian (D) was aware of the dangerous condition of the faucet but did not warn Rowland (P) about it. The trial court granted judgment in favor of Christian (D) on the ground that Rowland (P) was a licensee to whom Christian (P) did not owe the duty to warn against dangerous conditions. Rowland appeals.

■ **ISSUE**

Does an owner/occupier owe the duty to warn others of known dangerous conditions or repair the conditions in order to prevent the risk of unreasonable harm to others?

■ **DECISION AND RATIONALE**

(Peters, J.) Yes. An owner/occupier owes the duty to warn others of known dangerous conditions which are on the land or repair the conditions in order to prevent the risk of unreasonable harm to others. The common law distinctions between licensees, invitees, and trespassers have their origin in feudalism. These classifications have caused confusion and conflict. Whatever their historical justifications, these distinctions are not necessary in modern society. A man's life or limb does not become less worthy under the law because he is on the land of another without permission, or with permission but without a business purpose. Reasonable people do not vary their conduct based on such matters. Such common law distinctions obscure rather than clarify the proper consideration which should govern the question of duty owed to others. In this case the defendant knew that the faucet was defective, that the defect was not obvious, and the defendant had complained to the manager about the defective faucet. However, the defendant neither remedied nor warned the plaintiff of the danger. Where the owner/occupier is aware of a concealed dangerous condition and does not repair it or warn others, the jury could conclude that the owner/occupier is negligent. A guest should be warned of such conditions so that he will have the same opportunity as the owner/occupier to protect himself against unreasonable risk of injury. (Reversed.)

■ DISSENT

(Burke, J.)   The common law distinctions between trespassers, licensees, and invitees provide a workable approach to problems involving duties of owners/occupiers because they determine whether any duty is owed, and if so, how much.   The approach chosen by the majority will require a case-by-case analysis of each situation and opens the door to limitless liability despite the circumstances motivating a plaintiff in entering the owner's property.

Analysis:

In this case, the California Supreme Court does away with the common law distinctions drawn between trespassers, licensees, and invitees.   The Supreme Court holds that where a dangerous condition is concealed, and the owner/occupier is aware of it, the latter must either repair the condition or warn others of the danger.   This, according to the court, should be the rule regardless of the status of the individual.   Many states have followed the reasoning in *Rowland*, and many other courts have sought middle ground by rejecting the distinctions between licensees and invitees.   However, still over 20 states adhere to the three categories in determining the liability of landowners/occupiers.

Borders v. Roseberry

(Guest of Tenant) v. *(Landlord)*

216 Kan. 486, 532 P.2d 1366 (1975)

GENERALLY, A TENANT, NOT THE LANDLORD, HAS THE DUTY OF MAINTAINING THE PREMISES IN REASONABLY SAFE CONDITION IN ORDER TO PROTECT THOSE WHO COME UPON THE PROPERTY

■ **INSTANT FACTS** Borders (P), a guest at the home of one of Roseberry's (D) tenants, fell and sued Roseberry (D) for the injuries suffered.

■ **BLACK LETTER RULE** A landlord does not, as a matter of law, owe a duty of care to a social guest of his tenant to remedy known dangerous conditions.

■ PROCEDURAL BASIS

Appeal in negligence for recovery of damages for personal injuries.

■ FACTS

Borders (P), while a social guest at Roseberry's (D) tenant's apartment, fell on the icy steps and was injured. Borders (P) sued Roseberry (D), the landlord, for the injuries suffered. The trial court ruled in favor of Roseberry (D). Borders (P) appeals on the ground that the trial court committed reversible error in holding that the landlord as a matter of law owes no duty to the social guests of a tenant for known conditions on the premises.

■ ISSUE

Does a landlord, as a matter of law, owe a duty of care to a social guest of his tenant to remedy known dangerous conditions?

■ DECISION AND RATIONALE

(Prager, J.) No. A landlord does not, as a matter of law, owe a duty of care to a social guest of his tenant to remedy known dangerous conditions. Traditionally, it is the tenant's duty, as a person in possession of the property, to keep the premises in reasonably safe condition to protect persons who come on the property. This rule, however, has six exceptions: 1) The landlord is liable for undisclosed dangerous conditions known to the landlord/lessor, and unknown to the lessee. 2) The landlord/lessee is liable for conditions dangerous to persons outside of the premises (such as those traveling on public roads adjacent to the premises). 3) The landlord/lessor is liable when the premises are leased for the admission of the public. 4) The landlord/lessor is liable where parts of the premises are retained in the lessor's control which the lessee is entitled to use. These areas may include common passageways which do not belong to the tenant and are under the control and possession of the landlord. 5) The landlord/lessor is liable where he/she contracts to repair. 6) Finally, the landlord/lessor is liable where he/she has been negligent in making repairs. This exception applies where the tenant does not know that the purported repairs have not been made or that they have been made negligently. In the instant case, the tenant had full knowledge that the steps were in icy condition. It appears that the landlord could easily assume that the tenant would warn the guests about the condition. The facts of the case do not establish liability on the part of the landlord based on negligent repairs made by him. The plaintiff does not cite any authority to suggest that a landlord is liable for dangerous conditions which are known to the tenant. (Affirmed.)

Analysis:

In general when a party leases property from a landlord, he/she is under the duty to make the property safe for the protection of those who come upon it. Thus, in general, it is the lessee, and not the lessor/landlord who is liable for injuries sustained by guests of the tenants as a result of dangerous conditions on the property. This general rule has six clear exceptions (as pointed out by the case): 1) The lessor is liable for concealed dangerous conditions of which the lessee does not have knowledge. Note that the landlord is under a duty to disclose all such conditions to the lessee, if a reasonable lessee would not know of the conditions. 2) The landlord is liable for dangerous conditions to people outside the property. We do not want landlords to escape liability to others by simply renting the property to another party. 3) The landlord is liable when the premises are used by the general public. Here, the landlord is under the duty to reasonably inspect and repair the premises before possession is transferred to the lessee. 4) The landlord is liable for areas which are under his control, and which the lessee is entitled to use. The simplest example is the common passageway which is used by all the tenants. Since the passageway does not belong to the tenants and it is under the control of the landlord, the latter is in the best position to keep it in reasonably safe condition. 5) The landlord is liable when he/she contracts to repair a condition. Although this action was originally based on a contract between two parties, the rule has expanded to allow others to sue the landlord where they have suffered personal injury as a result of the landlord's breach of contract with the tenant. 6) The landlord is liable for injuries resulting as a consequence of negligent repairs undertaken by him/her. This rule means that if the landlord decides to repair something (even if there is no contractual basis for the repair), he/she had better repair it well; otherwise he/she will be held liable if there are any injuries as a result of his/her negligent repair.

Pagelsdorf v. Safeco Ins. Co. of America

(Tenant's Guest) v. *(Landlord's Insurance)*

91 Wis.2d 734, 284 N.W.2d 55 (1979)

THE SUPREME COURT OF WISCONSIN ABANDONS THE GENERAL RULE OF NON-LIABILITY OF LANDLORDS AND HOLDS THAT A LANDLORD MUST EXERCISE ORDINARY CARE TOWARD HIS TENANT AND OTHERS ON THE PREMISES WITH PERMISSION

■ **INSTANT FACTS** Pagelsdorf (P) sued Safeco Insurance Co. (D) ("Safeco") for injuries suffered when Pagelsdorf (D) was injured by a defective balcony railing.

■ **BLACK LETTER RULE** A landlord owes a tenant, or other individuals on the property with the tenant's permission, the duty to exercise ordinary care in maintaining the premises in safe condition.

■ **PROCEDURAL BASIS**

Appeal from dismissal of complaint in action in negligence for recovery of damages for personal injury.

■ **FACTS**

Pagelsdorf (P) was helping Blattner, a tenant of landlord Mahnke, move some furniture, when Pagelsdorf (P) leaned against a defective balcony railing which collapsed. Pagelsdorf (P) then brought an action against Safeco Insurance Co. ("Safeco") (D), Mahnke's insurance company, for the injuries that Pagelsdorf sustained from the fall. The trial court categorized Pagelsdorf (P) as the licensee of Mahnke, and the jury found that the landlord had no knowledge of the defective condition of the railing. Consequently, the court entered a judgment dismissing Pagelsdorf's (P) complaint. Pagelsdorf (P) appeals to determine the liability of a landlord to a tenant's invitee.

■ **ISSUE**

Does a landlord owe a tenant, or other individuals on the property with the tenant's permission, the duty to exercise ordinary care in maintaining the premises in safe condition?

■ **DECISION AND RATIONALE**

(Callow, J.) Yes. A landlord owes a tenant, or other individuals on the property with the tenant's permission, the duty to exercise ordinary care in maintaining the premises in safe condition. Under the traditional rules, when a property was leased, the landlord was not liable for injuries to his tenants and their visitors as a result of defective conditions on the property. Although there are exceptions to this rule, none of the exceptions apply to the facts of this case. Thus, following the traditional rules, Mahnke owes no duty to Pagelsdorf (P). A better policy, however, would be to abandon the general rule of non-liability of landlords and, instead, to hold them under a duty to exercise reasonable care in the maintenance of the premises. Whatever the justification for the general non-liability rule may have been, there is no longer a reason to excempt landlords from a duty of exercising reasonable care to prevent foreseeable harm. Thus, a landlord's conduct should be measured based on negligence principles. Additionally, in *Antoniewicz v. Reszcynski* this court abolished the common law distinctions between licensees and invitees. Abandonment of such distinctions concerning a landowner/occupier's duty toward his visitors, compel this court to abolish the landlord's immunity for injury to his tenants and their visitors. This court is not persuaded that the landlord's release of possession and control of a property lead to non-liability of the landlord. Tort law policies dictate that one is liable for injuries which result from foreseeably creating unreasonable risk of injury to others. Additionally, the modern day lease is regarded as a contract and not a conveyance of property which releases the landlord of all liability. Thus, this court rules that a landlord owes his tenant, or anyone on the premises with the tenant's consent, a duty to exercise ordinary care. This rule should be applied retrospectively. (Reversed and Remanded.)

Analysis:

Notice that in the previous case, *Borders v. Roseberry*, the court followed the traditional common law rules limiting the liability of landlords. There were a few exceptions to this rule which mostly imposed liability on the landlord where the dangerous conditions were concealed but known to the landlord. In this case the court completely does away with the non-liability rule regarding landlords. The court instead resorts to the general principles of negligence in order to measure the conduct of the landlord. Thus, we are back to the old rule: A landlord owes the tenant and others who are on the premises with the permission of the tenant, the duty to exercise reasonable care to prevent unreasonable risk of harm to them. Once again, the jury will have to take all the facts of the case into consideration and determine whether or not, in light of the circumstances, the conduct of the landlord was reasonable.

■ CASE VOCABULARY

LICENSEE: One whose presence on the property is not invited but tolerated; a person who is neither a customer, nor a servant, nor a trespasser, and does not stand in any contractual relation with the owner of the premises, and is permitted expressly or impliedly to go thereon for his own interest, convenience, or gratification.

Kline v. 1500 Massachusetts Ave. Apartment Corp.

(Lessee) v. *(Lessor)*

141 U.S.App.D.C. 370, 439 F.2d 477 (D.C.Cir.1970)

LANDLORDS MAY HAVE A DUTY TO PROTECT THEIR TENANTS FROM THE CRIMINAL ACTS OF THIRD PARTIES

■ **INSTANT FACTS** Kline (P), criminally assaulted and robbed in the hallway of Kline's (P) residence, sued 1500 Massachusetts Ave. Apartment Corp. (D) ("the landlord") for injuries sustained.

■ **BLACK LETTER RULE** A landlord has the duty to take reasonable precautions to protect tenants from foreseeable criminal acts of third parties.

■ **PROCEDURAL BASIS**

Appeal in action in negligence for recovery of damages for personal injuries.

■ **FACTS**

Kline (P) was criminally assaulted and robbed in the hallway of the apartment building where Kline (P) resided. Having sustained serious injuries, Kline (P) sought recovery against 1500 Massachusetts Ave. Apartment Corp. ("the landlord") (D), the landlord of the building. The evidence showed that although a doorman was hired, the entrances to the building were left unattended and that the landlord (D) had notice of the increasing number of criminal acts perpetrated against the tenants of the building. The District Court ruled in favor of the landlord (D) on the ground that as a matter of law there was no duty on the part of the landlord to protect the tenants against criminal activity by third parties. Kline (P) appeals.

■ **ISSUE**

Does a landlord have the duty to take reasonable precautions to protect tenants from foreseeable criminal acts of third parties.

■ **DECISION AND RATIONALE**

(Wilkey, J.) Yes. A landlord has the duty to take reasonable precautions to protect tenants from foreseeable criminal acts of third parties. In this jurisdiction certain duties are assigned to the landlord because of his control over certain areas which are shared by all tenants within a property, such as lobbies, hallways, and staircases. This duty belongs to the landlord because of his control of such areas, which makes him the only person who has the power to make the necessary repairs or to provide the necessary protection. The same rationale applies to criminal acts committed by third parties against tenants in a property. Traditionally, a private person does not have the duty to protect others against criminal acts of third parties. The reasons for this rule include the fact that the intentional tort is a superseding cause of harm to another, problems with determining foreseeability of intentional criminal acts, vagueness of the standard and economic consequences of the imposition of such duty on the landlord. However, such reasoning is not applicable to a landlord-tenant relationship in multiple-unit dwelling houses. Although the landlord is not the insurer of the tenants' safety, where the landlord had notice of the criminal assaults in the area within the landlord's control, and where the landlord has reason to expect similar crimes in the future, and where he has the exclusive power to take preventive measures, it is not unfair to impose upon him the duty to protect his tenants. Innkeepers have the duty to exercise reasonable care to protect their guests from harm by third parties. This rule is based on the innkeeper's supervision, care, or control of the premises, or on the contract between the guests and the innkeepers, whereby some courts hold that the guests entrust the innkeeper with their comfort and safety. The same duties have been implied in other relationships, such as employer-employee, landowner-invitee, carrier-passenger, and hospital-patient. In all these relationships the theory of liability is that since the ability of one of the parties for his own protection is limited through his submission to the control of the other, a duty should be imposed on the party who controls to take reasonable precautions to protect the other from criminal harm by third parties. This decision, however, does not imply that the landlord is the insurer of the tenants' safety. The landlord should simply take reasonable measures to protect the tenants from criminal acts of other parties. Additionally, the landlord is justified in spreading the cost of such protection to the tenants. (Reversed and Remanded.)

Analysis:

So far we have dealt with the duties of a landowner/occupier to parties who are categorized as invitees, licensees, and trespassers. We have also seen that some courts have set aside the above-referenced categorization and have simply resorted to the rules of negligence (i.e., foreseeability, duty, reasonable conduct, etc.). In this case, however, we see changes in the duties of a landlord to his/her tenants. Specifically, does the landlord have the duty to protect tenants and their guests from intentional criminal acts of third parties? It seems that this court, too, is relying on general principles of negligence by holding that a landlord must take reasonable measures to protect the tenants. The court's rationale, however, is that since the landlord has the exclusive control and power in certain areas of the building, he/she is in a better position to protect his/her tenants.

■ CASE VOCABULARY

SUPERSEDING CAUSE: An intervening cause which is so substantially responsible for the ultimate injury that it acts to cut off the liability of preceding actors regardless of whether their prior negligence was or was not a substantial factor in bringing about the injury.

CHAPTER TEN

Damages

Anderson v. Sears, Roebuck & Co.

Instant Facts: Sears, Roebuck & Co. (D) ("Sears") manufactured a malfunctioning heater which caused extensive injury to Helen Britain (P), an infant.

Black Letter Rule: A trial court may review a jury's award of damages to determine whether it exceeds the maximum amount which the jury could reasonably award.

Richardson v. Chapman

Instant Facts: Two girls were injured when a semi-truck driver rear-ended their car while they were stopped at a red stoplight.

Black Letter Rule: An award of damages will be deemed excessive if it falls outside the range of fair and reasonable compensation or results from passion or prejudice, or if it is so large that it shocks the judicial conscience.

Montgomery Ward & Co., Inc. v. Anderson

Instant Facts: Anderson (P) was badly injured in a fall while she was shopping at Montgomery Ward's (D).

Black Letter Rule: Gratuitous or discounted medical services are a collateral source not to be considered in assessing the damages due a personal-injury plaintiff.

Zimmerman v. Ausland

Instant Facts: Zimmerman (P) sought recovery from Ausland (D) for claimed permanent injury damages suffered as a result of Ausland's (D) negligence.

Black Letter Rule: A person may not recover damages for permanent injury if the permanency could have been avoided by treatment and a reasonable person under the same circumstances would undergo the treatment.

Cheatham v. Pohle

Instant Facts: After recovering punitive damages against Pohle (D), Cheatham (P) challenged a state statute allocating seventy-five percent of the damages to a state fund.

Black Letter Rule: Punitive damages are quasi-criminal in nature and serve to deter and punish wrongful activity.

State Farm Mutual Automobile Ins. Co. v. Campbell

Instant Facts: After State Farm (D) failed to settle claims against Campbell (P) for its policy limits and altered information to lessen his culpability, a jury awarded Campbell $1 million in compensatory damages and $145 million in punitive damages.

Black Letter Rule: In evaluating the appropriateness of a punitive damages award, a court must weight the reprehensibility of the defendant's conduct, the disparity between the actual harm caused and the amount of the punitive damages awarded, and the difference between the punitive damages awarded and the civil penalties imposed under state law.

Anderson v. Sears, Roebuck & Co.

(Parents of Injured Child) v. *(Manufacturer of Heater)*

377 F.Supp. 136 (E.D.La.1974)

THE MAXIMUM RECOVERY RULE DIRECTS A TRIAL JUDGE TO DETERMINE WHETHER A JURY'S AWARD OF DAMAGES EXCEEDS THE AMOUNT WHICH THE JURY COULD REASONABLY AWARD

■ **INSTANT FACTS** Sears, Roebuck & Co. (D) ("Sears") manufactured a malfunctioning heater which caused extensive injury to Helen Britain (P), an infant.

■ **BLACK LETTER RULE** A trial court may review a jury's award of damages to determine whether it exceeds the maximum amount which the jury could reasonably award.

■ **PROCEDURAL BASIS**

Motion for a remittitur of jury award of damages.

■ **FACTS**

Helen Britain (P), an infant, was severely injured when, due to a malfunctioning heater manufactured by Sears, Roebuck & Co. ("Sears") (D), Britain's (P) house caught on fire. Britain suffered third degree burns on over 40% of her body and had to undergo major operations, including a skin graft. The evidence in the case showed that Britain (P) also suffered mental and emotional trauma. Additionally, the evidence pointed out that Britain (P) will suffer from future physical and mental pain due to the injuries suffered and that Britain (P) would incur future medical expenses in large sums. The jury, finding Sears (D) negligent in the manufacture of the heater, awarded a sum of $2,000,000 to Britain (P) in damages. Sears (D) moves for a remittitur of the verdict.

■ **ISSUE**

May a trial court review a jury's award of damages to determine whether it exceeds the maximum amount which the jury could reasonably award?

■ **DECISION AND RATIONALE**

(Cassibry, J.) Yes. A trial court may review a jury's award of damages to determine whether it exceeds the maximum amount which the jury could reasonably award. In this case there are five elements of damages: 1) past physical and mental pain, 2) future physical and mental pain, 3) future medical expenses, 4) loss of earning capacity, and 5) permanent disability and disfigurement. The facts indicate that Britain (P) suffered third degree burns all over her body, and that she underwent several operations including skin grafts, and operations to reduce her deformities and scarring. The undisputed testimony also points to the negative effect of this event on Britain's mental health and psyche. She suffers from bedwetting, nightmares, speech withdrawals, and other problems which have resulted from the effect of the event. The jury award of $600,000 is not unreasonable for past physical and mental pain. In terms of future physical and mental pain, the evidence points out that the scarring and pulling of the skin, during the growth of Britain (P) will cause severe pain, and will cripple her motions in varying degrees. The evidence also points out that she is recommended to undergo 27 future operations, extending over Britain's (P) adult life. Additionally, throughout her life it is reasonable to expect that she will be deprived of a normal social life, and will be subject to rejection and stares, which will have a severe effect on her mental health. Thus, an award of $750,000 for such damages is not unreasonable. An award of $250,000 is not unreasonable for future medical expenses because the evidence points to Britain's (P) need for medical guidance, treatments, surgery, counseling, recommended operations, and other necessary medical help. Furthermore, based on the evidence of Britain's (P) physical, mental, and emotional disability, a jury could reasonably conclude that Britain (P) will not be able to earn a living for herself for the rest of her life. Thus, an award of up to $330,000 was not unreasonable for loss of earning capacity. A long list of Britain's permanent injuries, such as permanent loss of the normal use of her legs, permanent impairment of left fingers, and permanent destruction of 40% of her skin, would allow an award of up to $1,100,000 for permanent disability and disfigurement. Thus, given these figures, the jury's award was not unreasonable. Also, this court does not believe, as the defendants contend, that the presence of Britain (D) in the court, or the presentation of photographs of her injuries were prejudicial to the defendant. (Motion for remittitur denied.)

Analysis:

This case illustrates the common compensatory damages in a personal injury case. Generally, the damages are divided into several categories: 1) past physical and mental pain, 2) future physical and mental pain, 3) future medical expenses, 4) loss of earning capacity, and 5) permanent disability and disfigurement. Notice that past and future medical expenses, and loss of earning capacity are mainly economic losses which can be fairly easily measured. However, past and future mental pain, and damages for permanent disfigurement are those losses which are non-economic, therefore, more difficult to assess. Once the plaintiff has proven that the defendant owed a duty to the plaintiff, and that he/she breached that duty, resulting in injury to the plaintiff, the latter must then spend time on the proof of the amount of damages. As we have seen in these cases, there are several broad categories of damages: nominal, compensatory, and punitive. An example of the compensatory damages was seen in this case. Punitive or exemplary damages are awarded not to compensate the victim for the actual injury, but to punish the defendants. These damages will be discussed in more detail in later cases.

■ CASE VOCABULARY

REMITTITUR: This is the procedural process by which the verdict of a jury is diminished by subtraction. The term generally is used to describe any reduction made by the court without the consent of the jury.

Richardson v. Chapman

(Injured Car Driver) v. *(Semi Driver)*

175 Ill.2d 98, 676 N.E.2d 621 (1997)

AN APPELLATE COURT HAS THE RIGHT TO REDUCE AN EXCESSIVE JURY AWARD

■ **INSTANT FACTS** Two girls were injured when a semi-truck driver rear-ended their car while they were stopped at a red stoplight.

■ **BLACK LETTER RULE** An award of damages will be deemed excessive if it fails outside the range of fair and reasonable compensation or results from passion or prejudice, or if it is so large that it shocks the judicial conscience.

■ **PROCEDURAL BASIS**

Appeal from appellate court's affirming of the jury's award of damages to plaintiffs after the trial court directed a verdict in favor of the plaintiffs on the question of liability.

■ **FACTS**

Richardson (P) was the driver of a car with McGregor (P) as a passenger. The two girls were stopped at a red traffic light when they were hit from behind by a semi-truck driven by Chapman (D) [please pass the No-Doze]. Richardson (P) incurred a fracture of the fifth cervical vertebra, which severely damaged her spinal cord and resulted in incomplete quadriplegia. She underwent surgery to stabilize her spine so that she would be able to support her head. The surgery did not repair the damage to her spinal cord; no treatment existed that could have done so. She also received many facial injuries, not all of which were able to be repaired. Richardson (P) is at risk for several serious health complications as a result of her physical condition, and she requires the assistance of others in all aspects of her daily life. Richardson was awarded a total of $22,358,814 in damages; $258,814 for past medical care, $11,000,000 for future medical care, $900,000 for past and future lost earnings, $3,500,000 for disability, $2,100,000 for disfigurement, and $4,600,000 for pain and suffering. McGregor (P) received a laceration on her forehead, which eventually healed with minimal scarring. She was off work for about two weeks after being treated and released from the hospital on the day of the accident. McGregor (P) testified that she suffers from nightmares about the accident. She was awarded a total of $102,215; $1,615 for past medical expenses, $600 for lost earnings, and $100,000 for pain and suffering.

■ **ISSUE**

Should damage awards be considered excessive, and hence lowered, when there is a tremendous disparity between the trial testimony and the jury's eventual award?

■ **DECISION AND RATIONALE**

(Miller, J.) Yes. An award of damages will be deemed excessive if it falls outside the range of fair and reasonable compensation or results from passion or prejudice, or if it is so large that it shocks the judicial conscience. Chapman (D) first challenged the method of calculation the economist Richardson (P) used to determine the present value of Richardson's (P) future economic losses. Professor Linke calculated both "upper bound" and "lower bound" figures; the difference between the two numbers was based on different assumptions concerning future growth rates and interest rates. We conclude that the approach Professor Linke used was a reasonable one; by using a differential between the two rates, he did not have to make a prediction of future growth and inflation rates. He did not adopt a method which would undercompensate or overcompensate Richardson (P). Chapman (D) next contended that the damages awarded to both Richardson (P) and McGregor (P) are excessive. The jury awarded Richardson nearly $1.5 million more than the larger of the two figures supplied by Professor Linke. We agree that the trier of fact enjoys a certain degree of leeway in awarding compensation for future medical costs, however given the disparity between the trial testimony and the jury's eventual award, we will not attribute the entire difference between those sums simply to miscellaneous costs Richardson (P) is likely to incur in the future. We conclude that it is appropriate, by way of remittitur, to reduce by $1 million the differential between the award for Richardson's (P) future medical expenses and the higher figure presented in the testimony. This adjustment allows Richardson (P) recovery for uncertain future costs, yet it is not so large that it represents a departure from the trial testimony. We do not agree with Chapman (D), however, that the remainder of the award is duplicative or excessive. The record shows that Richardson suffered devastating, disabling injuries as a consequence of the accident. We cannot say that the present award to Richardson (P) is the result of passion or prejudice, or that it shocks conscience. Thus we decline to modify that portion of Richardson's (P) award. We do believe, however, that the award to McGregor (P) of $100,000 for pain and suffering is excessive, as McGregor (P) was not seriously injured in the accident. We conclude a more appropriate figure for pain and suffering would be $50,000 and, by way of remittitur, we accordingly reduce the judgment entered in favor of McGregor to $52,215. For the reasons stated, the judgment of the appellate court is affirmed in part, reversed in part, and vacated in part, and the judgment of the circuit court is affirmed in part, reversed in part, and vacated in part.

■ CONCURRENCE AND DISSENT

(McMorrow, J.) I concur in the opinion of my colleagues in all but one respect: I do not agree that it is proper to order a remittitur of the jury's damage awards to Richardson (P) and McGregor (P). In so holding, the majority usurps the jury's function and substitutes its own judgment regarding what is reasonable and fairly supported. The majority's application of remittitur in this case thereby operates as an arbitrary limitation on the jury's ability to assess the evidence.

Analysis:

This is a very inconsistent opinion. In one sentence the court states that the determination of damages is a question "reserved to the trier of fact, and a reviewing court will not lightly substitute its opinion for the judgment rendered in the trial court." Yet in the next sentence, the court does exactly that, and reduces the awards the jury felt were reasonable under the facts presented to them. The court pronounces that it is "the jury's function to consider the credibility of the witnesses and to determine an appropriate award of damages," and then proceeds to discount the jury's opinion. Reducing a $22 million verdict by $1 hardly seems to have any meaning. Moreover, the court found that the verdict for McGregor (P) was excessive, but that verdict was decided by the same jury; doesn't this suggest that the jury was acting out of passion? If the verdict is excessive, it seems more appropriate for the court to remand to a different jury for a re-evaluation of damages. Instead, the appellate court (but not the trial court) simply lowers damages a little. Of the curious matters in the opinion is the fact that there is no discussion of the trial court's disposition of the remittitur question.

■ CASE VOCABULARY

REMITTITUR: The court's decreasing of an excessive jury award.

Montgomery Ward & Co., Inc. v. Anderson

(Department Store) v. *(Injured Shopper)*
334 Ark. 561, 976 S.W.2d 382 (1998)

A DISCOUNT ON A HOSPITAL BILL CANNOT BE CONSIDERED BY A JURY BECAUSE IT IS A COLLATERAL SOURCE

■ **INSTANT FACTS** Anderson (P) was badly injured in a fall while she was shopping at Montgomery Ward's (D).

■ **BLACK LETTER RULE** Gratuitous or discounted medical services are a collateral source not to be considered in assessing the damages due a personal-injury plaintiff.

■ **PROCEDURAL BASIS**

Appeal from trial court's denial of the defendant's motion in limine and motion for a new trial.

■ **FACTS**

Anderson (P) was badly injured in a fall while shopping at Montgomery Ward's (D) [Fall into Fall Sale?]. The personnel at the Montgomery Ward (D) store sent Anderson (P) to the hospital to be treated. Anderson (P) had surgical and other medical services totaling $24,512.45. Anderson (P) had reached an agreement with the hospital for her services to be discounted fifty percent. Montgomery Ward (D) moved in limine to prohibit Anderson (P) from presenting the total amount billed by the hospital, and asked that Anderson's (P) evidence be limited to the actual amount she would be responsible to pay. Anderson (P) asserted that the collateral-source rule would prohibit Montgomery Ward (D) from introducing evidence of the discount. The trial court excluded the evidence.

■ **ISSUE**

Is the forgiveness of a debt for medical services a collateral source to be sheltered by the collateral-source rule?

■ **DECISION AND RATIONALE**

(Newbern, J.) Yes. Gratuitous or discounted medical services are a collateral source not to be considered in assessing the damages due a personal-injury plaintiff. We have held that the collateral-source rule applies unless the evidence of the benefits from the collateral source is relevant for a purpose other than the mitigation of damages. Despite the result that a double recovery occurs, the rationale behind the rule is that the claimant should benefit from the collateral source recovery rather than the tortfeasor. We recognize four situations in which the rule does not apply. They are cases in which a collateral source of recovery may be introduced (1) to rebut the plaintiff's testimony that he was compelled by financial necessity to return to work prematurely or to forego additional medical care; (2) to show that the plaintiff had attributed his condition to some other cause, such as sickness; (3) to impeach the plaintiff's testimony that he had paid his medical expenses himself; (4) to show that the plaintiff had actually continued to work instead of being out of worked, as claimed. This Court has also allowed evidence of collateral sources when the plaintiff opens the door to his financial condition. We find that none of the exceptions apply to the facts at hand, and no testimony by Anderson (P) invoked any exception. We are persuaded by cases holding that gratuitous medical services do fall under the collateral-source rule, and choose to adopt the rule that such services are not to be considered in assessing the damages due a personal-injury plaintiff. Accordingly, we hold that the Trial Court did not err by excluding evidence of the hospital's discount as a collateral source. Affirmed.

Analysis:

The Court alludes to the idea that a plaintiff may recover double when the collateral source rule is applied. This may happen in some cases, however that is not the usual case. Health insurance contracts and government programs providing benefits typically provide that the insured must pay back benefits provided from the proceeds of a judgment or settlement with a tortfeasor. Additionally, over half the states have modified the common law collateral-source rule by statute; half of these provide that the information concerning the collateral source is admissible in evidence without indicating what the jury is to do with that information. Others specify that the award is to be reduced by the amount of the collateral source. While double recovery doesn't seem like the ideal solution, it is easier to justify than reducing the tortfeasor's burden. It seems that the better solution is to reimburse the source of the gratuitous or discounted services, so that the plaintiff receives everything he is deserving of yet the tortfeasor is not let off the hook. A troubling aspect of this case is that a discount does not come from some other source; it is just a reduction of charges. These days hospital bills are often inflated in anticipation of the fact that the charges may need to be reduced. If the foregoing happened in this case, the tortfeasor was effectively overcharged.

■ CASE VOCABULARY

COLLATERAL-SOURCE RULE: If an injured plaintiff receives compensation from a source, independent of the defendant, the payment should not be deducted from the damages he would receive from the defendant.

MOTION IN LIMINE: Motion made out of the presence of the jury to exclude objectionable evidence.

Zimmerman v. Ausland

(Injured Party) v. *(Negligent Driver)*
266 Or. 427, 513 P.2d 1167 (1973)

EVERY TORT VICTIM HAS THE DUTY TO TAKE REASONABLE MEASURES TO MITIGATE DAMAGES FOR INJURIES WHICH ARE CAUSED BY THE TORTFEASOR

■ **INSTANT FACTS** Zimmerman (P) sought recovery from Ausland (D) for claimed permanent injury damages suffered as a result of Ausland's (D) negligence.

■ **BLACK LETTER RULE** A person may not recover damages for permanent injury if the permanency could have been avoided by treatment and a reasonable person under the same circumstances would undergo the treatment.

■ PROCEDURAL BASIS

Appeal in action for negligence from award of damages.

■ FACTS

Zimmerman (P) suffered injury to the knee (torn cartilage) as a result of an automobile accident caused by Ausland's (D) negligence. A jury verdict awarded Zimmerman (P) $7,500 in damages, which included damages for permanent injury to the knee which prevented Zimmerman (P) from engaging in strenuous physical activities. At the trial, Ausland's (D) expert testified that had Zimmerman (P) undergone treatment, the injury would not have been permanent. Zimmerman (P), however, had not undergone the treatment and did not indicate a desire to do so in the future. Ausland (D) appeals, contending that the trial court erred in instructing the jury on whether the plaintiff sustained permanent injury, and on Zimmerman's (P) life expectancy.

■ ISSUE

May a person recover damages for permanent injury if the permanency could have been avoided by treatment, and a reasonable person under the same circumstances would undergo the treatment?

■ DECISION AND RATIONALE

(Tongue, J.) No. A person may not recover damages for permanent injury if the permanency could have been avoided by treatment, and a reasonable person under the same circumstances would undergo the treatment. Ausland (D) did not request instructions regarding mitigation of damages. However, if the court finds that as a matter of law the plaintiff unreasonably failed to mitigate damages, the plaintiff will not be entitled to damages for permanent injury. If a plaintiff's failure to obtain treatment is not unreasonable under the circumstances, the plaintiff may recover damages for such injury. The factors which determine whether the plaintiff was reasonable in failing to mitigate include the risk involved in the treatment, the probability of success, and the money or effort required. No case holds that a plaintiff with a torn cartilage must submit to surgery or be barred, as a matter of law, from recovery of damages for permanent injury. Additionally, in the instant case, the facts were not so clear and conclusive as to require the plaintiff to submit to surgery. Thus, the question is not one for the court to decide as a matter of law. The defendant, however, was entitled to introduce evidence of these questions and submit them to the jury with the proper instructions. From the record it appears that testimony offered by the plaintiff, if believed by the jury, could lead the jury to find that the plaintiff did suffer permanent injury. (Affirmed.)

Analysis:

In every tort case the plaintiff has the duty to mitigate damages. This is a rule which does not allow the plaintiff a recovery for damages which the plaintiff could have reasonably avoided by reasonable conduct after the injury has occurred. However, in order to take advantage of this doctrine, the defendant must show that the plaintiff's conduct in failing to mitigate damages was unreasonable. Normally, this is a question which will be submitted to the jury, the latter must weigh the circumstances, and the evidence offered by the defendant and the plaintiff in order to determine if the plaintiff's conduct was unreasonable. In some cases, however, the court may decide the issue as a matter of law if there is enough evidence and precedence regarding failure to mitigate that no reasonable jury would conclude otherwise.

■ CASE VOCABULARY

MITIGATION OF DAMAGES: A requirement that one injured by reason of another's tort or breach of contract exercise reasonable diligence and ordinary care to avoid aggravating the injury or increasing the damages. The term also refers to the defendant's request to the court for a reduction of damages owed to the plaintiff, a request that the defendant justifies by reason of some evidence that shows the plaintiff not entitled to the full amount that might otherwise be awarded to him.

Cheatham v. Pohle

(Ex–Wife) v. *(Ex–Husband)*

789 N.E.2d 467 (Ind.2003)

A PERCENTAGE OF A PUNITIVE DAMAGES AWARD MAY LAWFULLY GO TO THE STATE

The State will take 75% of your award. And we'll keep the evidence too!

stus.com

■ **INSTANT FACTS** After recovering punitive damages against Pohle (D), Cheatham (P) challenged a state statute allocating seventy-five percent of the damages to a state fund.

■ **BLACK LETTER RULE** Punitive damages are quasi-criminal in nature and serve to deter and punish wrongful activity.

■ **PROCEDURAL BASIS**

Appeal to challenge a state statute allocating seventy-five percent of all punitive damages awards to a state fund.

■ **FACTS**

After Cheatham (P) and Pohle (D) divorced, Pohle (D) retained several promiscuous photographs of Cheatham (D) and publicly posted fliers containing the photographs, Cheatham's name and work number, and other information around the small community in which they live. Cheatham (P) sued for invasion of privacy and intentional infliction of emotional distress. The jury awarded her $100,000 in compensatory damages and $100,000 in punitive damages. By state statute, however, seventy-five percent of the punitive damages award was payable to the Indiana Violent Crime Victims' Compensation Fund. Cheatham (P) contended that the statute violated the Indiana and U.S. Constitutions by taking her property without just compensation.

■ **ISSUE**

Does a state statute allocating a portion of any punitive damages award to the state violate the Takings Clause of the U.S. and Indiana Constitutions?

■ **DECISION AND RATIONALE**

(Boehm, J.) No. Punitive damages are not intended to make the plaintiff whole or value the plaintiff's injuries. Instead, punitive damages are quasi-criminal in nature and serve to deter and punish wrongful activity. Accordingly, just as with criminal sanctions, state legislatures have broad discretion in regulating punitive damages awards. Under the Constitution, private parties have no vested interest or property right in punitive damages, so states can eliminate them entirely should they so choose.

Punitive damages are considerably different than compensatory damages. While compensatory damages are awarded based on the value of a plaintiff's injuries, punitive damages awards must be made upon consideration of the defendant's financial condition and based on clear and convincing evidence, to serve their purposes. However, unlike compensatory damages, the jury is not obligated to award punitive damages even if the facts warrant them. Accordingly, because here state law defines the plaintiff's property rights as twenty-five percent of any punitive damages award, the allocation to the state fund is not a taking of the plaintiff's property. Cheatham's (P) interest in compensatory damages does not similarly create an interest in the punitive damages award. Affirmed.

Analysis:

In *Kirk v. Denver Publishing Co.*, 818 P.2d 262 (Colo. 1991), the Colorado Supreme Court declared the state's apportionment statute unconstitutional under the takings clause. There, however, the state exemplary damages statute explicitly provided that the state had no interest in exemplary damages awards, bestowing on the plaintiff all property rights in such awards. The Colorado legislature has since repealed that portion of the statute.

■ CASE VOCABULARY

PUNITIVE DAMAGES: Damages awarded in addition to actual damages when the defendant acted with recklessness, malice, or deceit.

TAKING: The government's actual or effective acquisition of private property either by ousting the owner and claiming title or by destroying the property or severely impairing its utility.

TAKINGS CLAUSE: The Fifth Amendment provision that prohibits the government from taking private property for public use without fairly compensating the owner.

State Farm Mutual Automobile Ins. Co. v. Campbell

(Insurance Company) v. *(Insured)*

538 U.S. 408, 123 S.Ct. 1513, 155 L.Ed.2d 585 (2003)

PUNITIVE DAMAGES MAY BE REDUCED IF EXCESSIVE

■ **INSTANT FACTS** After State Farm (D) failed to settle claims against Campbell (P) for its policy limits and altered information to lessen his culpability, a jury awarded Campbell $1 million in compensatory damages and $145 million in punitive damages.

■ **BLACK LETTER RULE** In evaluating the appropriateness of a punitive damages award, a court must weight the reprehensibility of the defendant's conduct, the disparity between the actual harm caused and the amount of the punitive damages awarded, and the difference between the punitive damages awarded and the civil penalties imposed under state law.

■ **PROCEDURAL BASIS**

Certiorari to review the excessiveness of a punitive damages verdict.

■ **FACTS**

Campbell (P) held an automobile policy with State Farm Mutual Automobile Insurance Co. (D). While traveling in Utah, Campbell (P) decided to pass six vans traveling slowly in front of him. As Campbell (P) was driving in the wrong direction, Ospital was forced onto the shoulder to avoid a head-on collision. In the process, Ospital lost control of his vehicle, collided with a vehicle driven by Slusher, and died. Slusher was permanently disabled as a result of the accident. An investigation determined that Campbell's (P) unsafe pass caused Ospital's death and Slusher's injuries. Nonetheless, State Farm (D) decided to contest liability and declined offers from Ospital's estate and Slusher to settle both claims for its total policy limit of $50,000. At trial, a jury found Campbell (P) liable for the accident and returned a verdict for $185,849. State Farm (D) refused to pay the verdict in excess of its $50,000 policy limits and refused to post the supersedeas bond required for Campbell's (P) appeal. Campbell (P) subsequently obtained independent counsel and appealed the verdict. During the appeal, Campbell (P) agreed to pursue a bad faith action against State Farm (D) in exchange for an agreement by Ospital's estate and Slusher not to seek satisfaction of the judgment against Campbell (P). Ospital's estate and Slusher agreed to accept ninety percent of any proceeds received from State Farm (D) in the bad faith suit.

The Utah Supreme Court denied Campbell's (P) appeal from the wrongful death judgment, and State Farm (D) subsequently agreed to pay the full amount of the judgment against him. Campbell (P) then commenced his bad faith suit, alleging State Farm's (D) refusal to accept the settlement offer was a product of a national scheme to control the amount of claims paid. Campbell (D) offered evidence of State Farm's (D) business practices throughout the country over a twenty-year period, although little pertained to payment of third-party automobile claims similar to that asserted by Campbell (D). A jury awarded Campbell $2.6 million in compensatory damages and $145 million in punitive damages. After the compensatory damages award was reduced to $1 million and the punitive damages reduced to $25 million, both parties appealed to the Utah Supreme Court, which reinstated the punitive damages award.

■ ISSUE

When compensatory damages are $1 million, is an award of $145 million in punitive damages against a defendant excessive in violation of the Due Process Clause of the Fourteenth Amendment?

■ DECISION AND RATIONALE

(Kennedy, J.) Yes. Unlike compensatory damages, which serve to compensate an injured person for the wrongful conduct of another, punitive damages are aimed at deterrence and retribution against the wrongdoer. Because punitive damages serve a purpose similar to criminal sanctions, but without the procedural protections accompanying criminal punishment, a court must weigh the reprehensibility of the defendant's conduct, the disparity between the actual harm caused and the amount of the punitive damages awarded, and the difference between the punitive damages awarded and the civil penalties imposed under state law. Weighing these factors, the jury's $145 million punitive damages award was excessive.

First, State Farm's (D) conduct cannot be considered so reprehensible as to justify the award. In gauging a defendant's conduct, a court should consider whether the harm caused was physical rather than economic, whether the defendant acted with reckless disregard for the health and safety of others, whether the plaintiff was financially vulnerable, whether the conduct involved a repetitive pattern or an isolated incident, and whether the conduct was intentional. Here, while State Farm's (D) handling of Campbell's (P) insurance claims is not laudable, its conduct does not justify such an excessive punitive damages award. Rather than focusing on the particular conduct at issue in the case, the award focuses on State Farm's (D) nationwide handling of claims. A state court, however, has no authority to punish a defendant for conduct that occurred outside its territorial limits and involving parties who were directly affected by the out-of-state conduct. A defendant's dissimilar conduct, bearing no relation to the harm involved in a particular lawsuit, may not be taken into account when determining punitive damages. Due process does not permit a court to award a party punitive damages merely because the defendant may have caused some harm to others who were not proper parties to the litigation.

Second, although there is no bright-line ratio between the amount of punitive damages and the harm caused to a plaintiff, an award 145 times the actual harm suffered is excessive. Generally, anything over a single-digit ratio calls for close judicial scrutiny. Likewise, as the compensatory damages award increases, the appropriate proportion to the punitive damages award decreases, since a larger ratio is unnecessary to serve the purposes of deterrence and retribution. Here, the 145:1 ratio between the punitive award and the compensatory award is unreasonable given the $1 million compensatory damages award for plaintiff's emotional distress.

Finally, the $145 million punitive damages award is grossly in excess of the maximum $10,000 civil penalty imposed for fraud under Utah law. Applying this factor, too, the punitive damages award is excessive.

Because a punitive award more closely approximating the compensatory award would be an adequate and rational punishment for the defendant's conduct, the award is excessive. Reversed and remanded.

Analysis:

The Court's fascination with the appropriate ratio between the compensatory damages and punitive damages is interesting. If punitive damages serve a separate and distinct purpose from compensatory damages, why should the amount of compensatory damages affect the amount of punitive damages? If a defendant commits intentional conduct worthy of punishment, should it matter whether the compensatory damages were substantial?

■ CASE VOCABULARY

BAD FAITH: Dishonesty of belief or purpose.

COMPENSATORY DAMAGES: Damages sufficient in amount to indemnify the injured person for the loss suffered.

PUNITIVE DAMAGES: Damages awarded in addition to actual damages when the defendant acted with recklessness, malice, or deceit.

SUPERSEDEAS BOND: A bond that suspends a judgment creditor's power to levy execution, usually pending appeal.

CHAPTER ELEVEN

Wrongful Death and Survival

Moragne v. States Marine Lines, Inc.

Instant Facts: Moragne (P), whose husband was killed while on a vessel owned by State Marine Lines (D) ("States"), sues the latter for the wrongful death of her deceased husband.

Black Letter Rule: Maritime law should allow a cause of action for wrongful death.

Selders v. Armentrout

Instant Facts: Selders (P) brought wrongful death action against Armentrout (D) for the death of Selders' (P) three minor children.

Black Letter Rule: The measure of damages for the wrongful death of a minor child should include loss of society, comfort, and companionship of the child.

Murphy v. Martin Oil Co.

Instant Facts: Murphy (P), the spouse of the decedent, brought action against Martin Oil Co. (D) ("Martin") for negligently causing the death of the decedent.

Black Letter Rule: The spouse of a decedent may maintain an action for the loss of property, loss of wages, and pain and suffering of the decedent during the interval between the injury and death.

Moragne v. States Marine Lines, Inc.

(Widow of Deceased) v. *(Vessel Owner)*

398 U.S. 375, 90 S.Ct. 1772, 26 L.Ed.2d 339 (1970)

THE SUPREME COURT OF THE UNITED STATES REJECTS THE PRECEDENCE WHICH DID NOT ALLOW RECOVERY FOR WRONGFUL DEATH IN MARITIME CASES

■ **INSTANT FACTS** Moragne (P), whose husband was killed while on a vessel owned by State Marine Lines (D) ("States"), sues the latter for the wrongful death of her deceased husband.

■ **BLACK LETTER RULE** Maritime law should allow a cause of action for wrongful death.

■ **PROCEDURAL BASIS**

Grant of certiorari for ruling on availability of wrongful death as a cause of action under maritime law.

■ **FACTS**

Moragne (P), whose husband was killed while on States' (D) vessel, brought a wrongful death action against the latter to recover damages for the death of her deceased husband. Relying on the case of *The Harrisburg*, the state court where the case was filed refused to acknowledge Moragne's (P) cause of action, indicating that under that case, maritime law does not allow a cause of action for wrongful death. The Supreme Court of the United States grated certiorari to review the issue.

■ **ISSUE**

Should maritime law allow a cause of action for wrongful death?

■ **DECISION AND RATIONALE**

(Harlan, J.) Yes. Maritime law should allow a cause of action for wrongful death. The law in *The Harrisburg* stems from traditional common law doctrine of felony-merger which stemmed from English Law. Under that doctrine, the common law did not allow civil recovery for an act which constituted a tort and a felony. The tort was viewed as an offense against the Crown, and it was determined that after criminal punishment and forfeiture of property to the Crown, nothing would remain for the felon on which to base a civil action. At that time, all killings, negligent or intentional, were felonies, and as such there could be no cause of action for wrongful death. However, the justification which existed in England never existed in the United States. Punishment for felonies did not include forfeiture of property, and as such, it cannot bar a subsequent civil suit. Despite this reasoning, most American courts adopted the English rule. Other commentators support the doctrine on the basis of another common law rule which indicated that a personal cause of action in tort did not survive the death of the victim of the tort. However, this principle only applies to victim's own personal claims, such as pain and suffering, and has no relevance to wrongful death actions. Today every state in the United States has a wrongful death statute. Based on such statutes, it appears that there is no public policy against allowing recovery for wrongful death. In this case Congress, by its failure to enact a specific wrongful death statute, did not intend to prevent recovery in this area. Furthermore, the doctrine of stare decisis does not preclude a change in the law. However, one aspect of a wrongful death claim which lacks precision is in the determination of the beneficiaries who can bring such a claim against the tortfeasors. Both the Death on the High Seas Act and the numerous state statutes can be of guidance on this issue.

This court, however, will not resolve this issue now and leaves it for further litigation in the lower courts. The Supreme Court of the United States hereby overrules *The Harrisburg* and holds that an action for wrongful death does lie under general maritime law for death caused by a violation of maritime duties. (Reversed and Remanded.)

Analysis:

As this case suggests, under the common law of England, if a tort victim dies before recovery from the tortfeasor, the victim's rights die with him. Additionally, relatives of a victim who died due to the negligence of another had no cause of action against the defendant. As the instant case suggests, most American states have now changed these rules, especially the last one. Today in most states the relatives of a victim who died due to the negligence of a party do have a wrongful death cause of action against the tortfeasor. These statutes are known as Wrongful Death Statutes and usually describe the individuals who have a claim under this cause of action. Almost all states consider the lawful spouse of the decedent and the children as beneficiaries who could bring this cause of action. Most cases hold that stepchildren are not considered beneficiaries. In many jurisdictions, illegitimate children are not considered as beneficiaries unless the wrongful death statute of the jurisdiction allows them to be. Note, however, that there is much controversy on this matter from the constitutional stand point of denial of equal protection. In *Levy v. Louisiana* the Supreme Court held that Louisiana's statute excluding illegitimate children was a denial of the children's equal protection rights.

■ CASE VOCABULARY

WRONGFUL DEATH STATUTES: Statutes that create a cause of action for any wrongful act, neglect, or default that causes death; the action may be brought by the executor or administrator of the decedent's estate or by his surviving family and is intended to compensate the family for the loss of economic benefits that it would have had in the form of support, services, or contributions had the decedent lived.

Selders v. Armentrout

(*Decedent's Parents*) v. (*Tortfeasor*)

190 Neb. 275, 207 N.W.2d 686 (1973) N.W.2d 686

ACCORDING TO THE SUPREME COURT OF NEBRASKA, THE MEASURE OF DAMAGES FOR THE WRONGFUL DEATH OF A MINOR CHILD SHOULD INCLUDE PECUNIARY LOSSES AS WELL AS LOSS OF SOCIETY, COMFORT, AND COMPANIONSHIP

■ **INSTANT FACTS** Selders (P) brought wrongful death action against Armentrout (D) for the death of Selders' (P) three minor children.

■ **BLACK LETTER RULE** The measure of damages for the wrongful death of a minor child should include loss of society, comfort, and companionship of the child.

■ **PROCEDURAL BASIS**

Appeal from award of damages in wrongful death action.

■ **FACTS**

The Selders (P) brought a wrongful death action against Armentrout (D) for the wrongful death of their three minor children. The trial court's instructions to the jury limited the measure of damages to medical and funeral expenses and the monetary value of the contributions and services which the Selders (P) could have reasonably expected to receive from the children, less the reasonable cost to the parents for supporting the children. The Selders (P) appeal.

■ **ISSUE**

Should the measure of damages for the wrongful death of a minor child include loss of society, comfort, and companionship of the child?

■ **DECISION AND RATIONALE**

(McCown, J.) Yes. The measure of damages for the wrongful death of a minor child should include loss of society, comfort, and companionship of the child. Under the common law, recovery for the death of a minor child was limited to the loss of pecuniary benefits. This rule finds its source in the days when children were viewed as economic assets to the parents because they worked at an early age. Thus, a child's earnings and services could be established, and the pecuniary loss was the measure of damages for the parents. Any other measure of damages was deemed speculative. Today, however, all evidence of damages reflect upon the future life of the decedent had he not died. Thus, by nature such damages are speculative. Limiting the measure of damages to the child's economic value less the expenses spent for educating and rising the child would in fact give a negative value to the child, and only in rare cases will the death of a child result in monetary gain. This court has allowed recovery for the loss of society, comfort and companionship for the wrongful death of a spouse. There is no reason for treating damages for the wrongful death of a child more strictly. This holding overrules prior decisions of this and other lower courts which are in conflict with it. (Judgment as to damages reversed and remanded.)

■ **DISSENT**

(White, C.J.) This opinion, after 50 years of settled law, throws opens the claim for death of minor children to a sympathy contest.

Analysis:

Now that we know most states have Wrongful Death Statutes, we need to know what kind of damages are recoverable under this action. This case deals with what parents can recover for the death of their children. Clearly, there are the actual expenses, such as medical and funeral expenses. There are also pecuniary or economic losses which can be measured by the reasonable value of the child's services less the expense of rearing and educating the child. As the instant case points out, such a measure would usually come to a negative figure because minor children usually provide no economic benefit to their parents. This court extends the measure of damages to include the loss of society, comfort, and companionship of the child to the parents. Such loss is almost always included in the measure of damages in the wrongful death of a parent or a spouse. However, as in this jurisdiction, there are a number of courts which do not allow such recovery for the death of a minor child.

■ CASE VOCABULARY

PECUNIARY: Relating to money and monetary affairs. Many wrongful death statutes limit recovery to pecuniary loss, i.e., a loss of money or of something which can be translated into an economic loss. The loss of affections which parents suffer by the negligent death of a child is not such a loss, whereas the loss of actual or anticipated financial support by the deceased child is pecuniary.

Murphy v. Martin Oil Co.

(Decedent's Spouse) v. *(Tortfeasor)*

56 Ill.2d 423, 308 N.E.2d 583 (1974)

SURVIVAL STATUTES PRESERVE FOR THE DECEDENT'S ESTATE CERTAIN CAUSES OF ACTION WHICH COULD BE BROUGHT AGAINST A TORTFEASOR HAD THE DECEDENT NOT DIED

■ **INSTANT FACTS** Murphy (P), the spouse of the decedent, brought action against Martin Oil Co. (D) ("Martin") for negligently causing the death of the decedent.

■ **BLACK LETTER RULE** The spouse of a decedent may maintain an action for the loss of property, loss of wages, and pain and suffering of the decedent during the interval between the injury and death.

■ **PROCEDURAL BASIS**

Appeal in negligence for recovery of damages for wrongful death based on Wrongful Death and Survival Statutes.

■ **FACTS**

Murphy's (P) husband, who was injured due to a fire on Martin Oil's ("Martin's") (D) property, died nine days after suffering the injuries. Murphy (P) brought action against Martin (D) for negligently causing the decedent's death. Count one of Murphy's (P) action was based on the state's Wrongful Death Statute, and the second count was under the state's Survival Statute under which Murphy (P) asked for recovery of damages for the decedent's mental, and physical suffering, for loss of wages during the nine-day period, and for loss of the decedent's clothing worn at the time of the injury. The trial court dismissed the second count, while the appellate court affirmed it in part, rejecting Murphy's (P) action for the pain and suffering of the decedent. Both Murphy (P) and Martin (D) appeal.

■ **ISSUE**

May the spouse of a decedent maintain an action for the loss of property, loss of wages, and pain and suffering of the decedent during the interval between the injury and death?

■ **DECISION AND RATIONALE**

(Ward, J.) Yes. The spouse of a decedent may maintain an action for the loss of property, loss of wages, and pain and suffering of the decedent during the interval between the injury and death. This state's Survival Statute lists actions which survive a decedent including actions of replevin, actions to recover damages for an injury to the person (except in libel and slander), and actions for recovery of damages to personal and real property. Considering the combination of Wrongful Death and Survival Statutes for the first time, the court in *Holton v. Daly* held that Wrongful Death Act was the sole remedy when a tortious injury resulted in death, and that the Survival Statute allowed survival of a cause of action only when the injured party died from a cause other than that which caused the injuries. Thus, an action for personal injuries could not survive if the death of the party resulted from the conduct which caused the injury. However, in the past 70 years most jurisdictions allow an action for personal injuries and a wrongful death action even though the decedent's death resulted from the conduct which caused the decedent's injuries. Most of these jurisdiction allow recovery for the decedent's pain and suffering.

It is the opinion of this court that remedies available under *Holton* are incomplete. It does not allow for recovery of pain and suffering and the medical expenses that the injured party may have suffered before death. Also, the tortfeasor will have to pay only for part of the damage that he caused. (Judgment affirmed in part, reversed in part.)

Analysis:

This case answers the question of whether an action for personal injuries may be maintained on behalf of a person who has died. Under the old common law rules, personal tort actions, such as actions for recovery of damages for personal injuries, died with the death of the plaintiff or the defendant. This is where survival statutes come into play. They generally list the causes of action which survive the decedent. These actions are usually for injury to all tangible property. In a majority of jurisdiction, personal injury actions also survive. The instant case is an example of such a jurisdiction. On the other hand, hardly any states allow the survival of intangible personal rights, such as defamation (libel and slander) and intentional infliction of emotional distress. Thus, Survival Statutes allow a beneficiary of the decedent to maintain a cause of action on behalf of the decedent for a wrong suffered while the decedent was alive. Wrongful Death Statutes, on the other hand, allow a beneficiary or relative of the decedent to recover damages on his/her own behalf for the loss caused to the beneficiary for the decedent's death. As mentioned in previous cases, such loss includes the pecuniary or economic support the decedent would have provided for the beneficiary had the decedent not died. It also includes recovery for loss of society, comfort, and companionship.

■ CASE VOCABULARY

SURVIVAL STATUTE: A statute which preserves for a decedent's estate a cause of action for infliction of pain and suffering and related damages suffered up to the moment of death by the decedent. Such a statute is to be contrasted with a wrongful death act, which views causing one's death not as a tort to the decedent himself/herself, but as a wrong with respect to the family, and which gives the decedent's immediate family a cause of action for losses occasioned by his/her death, such as loss of wages and lost companionship.

CHAPTER TWELVE

Defenses

Butterfield v. Forrester

Instant Facts: Butterfield (P) sued Forrester for the injuries suffered when Butterfield (P) fell over an obstruction on the road created by Forrester (D).

Black Letter Rule: An injured plaintiff may not recover damages against a negligent defendant if the plaintiff did not exercise reasonable care to avoid the injury.

Davies v. Mann

Instant Facts: Davies (P) sued Mann (P) for negligently running over Davies' (P) mule with a wagon.

Black Letter Rule: A negligent defendant, claiming contributory negligence on the part of the plaintiff, may not escape liability if the defendant had the last chance to prevent the injury had he/she not been negligent.

McIntyre v. Balentine

Instant Facts: McIntyre (P) sued Balentine (D) for personal injuries suffered as a result of an automobile accident with Balentine (D).

Black Letter Rule: The doctrine of contributory negligence should be replaced by a system of comparative fault to allow the plaintiff, whose negligence is less than the defendant, to recover damages which are reduced in proportion to the plaintiff's percentage of fault.

Seigneur v. National Fitness Institute, Inc.

Instant Facts: After executing a membership agreement releasing National Fitness Institute, Inc. (D) of all liability for negligence, Seigneur (P) sued for vicarious liability and negligence after she was injured during a fitness evaluation.

Black Letter Rule: An exculpatory clause is enforceable if it clearly and specifically indicates the intent to release the defendant from liability for personal injuries caused by the defendant's negligence.

Rush v. Commercial Realty Co.

Instant Facts: A lady was injured when she fell through the trap door of a privy that the lady knew to be defective.

Black Letter Rule: A person does not voluntarily accept a risk when no reasonable alternatives exist.

Blackburn v. Dorta

Instant Facts: [No facts provided]

Black Letter Rule: Implied assumption of risk is subsumed by the doctrine of comparative negligence.

Teeters v. Currey

Instant Facts: A woman sued her doctor for negligently performing a tubal ligation when she discovered, two years after the surgery, that she was pregnant.

Black Letter Rule: A cause of action for malpractice does not accrue, and the statute of limitations does not begin to run, until the injured party discovers or should have discovered the injury.

Freehe v. Freehe

Instant Facts: A husband sued his wife for injuries caused by her tractor, and she defended on grounds of interspousal immunity.

Black Letter Rule: Spouses are not immune from liability in personal injury cases.

Renko v. Mclean

Instant Facts: Daughter sued her mother for injuries sustained in a car accident which was caused by the mother's negligent driving.

Black Letter Rule: There is no exception to the parent-child immunity doctrine for injuries sustained in motor tort cases occurring during the child's minority.

Abernathy v. Sisters of St. Mary's

Instant Facts: A patient at a hospital run by a charitable organization sued for negligence, and the hospital claimed charitable immunity from liability.

Black Letter Rule: Nongovernmental charitable institutions are liable for their own negligence and the negligence of their employees.

Ayala v. Philadelphia Board of Public Education

Instant Facts: A student who was injured in shop class sued the school district, which claimed governmental immunity.

Black Letter Rule: Governmental entities are not immune from tort liability.

Riss v. New York

Instant Facts: A woman, who was injured by an attacker after police ignored her pleas for help, sues the police for the failure to provide adequate protection.

Black Letter Rule: Cities are immune from liability for the negligent failure to provide adequate police protection.

Delong v. Erie County

Instant Facts: A woman was stabbed to death while waiting for the police to respond to her 911 emergency call.

Black Letter Rule: Municipalities are not immune from liability when they voluntarily assume a duty to provide police protection for a particular individual.

Deuser v. Vecera

Instant Facts: A drunk man was killed by a car after park rangers threw him out of the park for being disorderly.

Black Letter Rule: Discretionary conduct of government agents acting within the scope of their authority are protected by the discretionary function exception to the Federal Torts Claims Act.

Butterfield v. Forrester

(Injured Party) v. *(Tortfeasor)*

11 East 59, 103 Eng.Rep. 926 (1809)

AT COMMON LAW CONTRIBUTORY NEGLIGENCE OF THE PLAINTIFF WOULD ACT AS A COMPLETE BAR TO RECOVERY BY THE PLAINTIFF

■ **INSTANT FACTS** Butterfield (P) sued Forrester for the injuries suffered when Butterfield (P) fell over an obstruction on the road placed there by Forrester (D).

■ **BLACK LETTER RULE** An injured plaintiff may not recover damages against a negligent defendant if the plaintiff did not exercise reasonable care to avoid the injury.

■ **PROCEDURAL BASIS**

Appeal in action for negligence.

■ **FACTS**

While on a horse, Butterfield (P) fell over an obstruction which Forrester (D) had placed in the road. Butterfield (P) sued Forrester (D) for the injuries suffered as a result of the fall. The evidence at the trial indicated that Forrester (D), while repairing his home on the roadside, had placed a pole on a part of the road while leaving another part free for passage. The evidence also suggested that the pole was discernible from 100 yards away, and that Butterfield (P) could have seen it, had he not been riding too fast. The trial judge instructed the jury that if an individual riding with reasonable care could have avoided the pole, and if the jury found that Butterfield (P) was not riding with ordinary care, the verdict should be in favor of Forrester (D). The jury found for Forrester (D). Butterfield (P) appeals on the ground that the jury instructions were erroneous.

■ **ISSUE**

May an injured plaintiff recover damages against a negligent defendant, when the plaintiff did not exercise reasonable care to avoid the injury?

■ **DECISION AND RATIONALE**

(Bayley, J.) No. An injured plaintiff may not recover damages against a negligent defendant if the plaintiff did not exercise reasonable care to avoid the injury. In this case, had the plaintiff exercised ordinary care, and not ridden as fast as he did, he could have avoided the injury. Thus, the accident is the plaintiff's own fault.

■ **CONCURRENCE**

(Ellenborough, C.J.) One may not recover damages for injuries caused by the negligence of another, if he could avoid the injury by using reasonable care and caution. In this case, the plaintiff could have recovered only if the obstruction was the defendant's fault, and if the plaintiff has exercised reasonable care on his own part.

Analysis:

We were superficially introduced to the concept of contributory negligence in some of the prior cases. Contributory negligence is a defense. This means that the defendant, by showing that the plaintiff was contributorily liable, may escape liability, even though the defendant's negligent conduct caused the plaintiff's injury. Thus, the defense of contributory negligence only comes into play after the plaintiff has completed his/her prima facie case, has proven all the elements of negligence, and has proven that the defendant's negligence was a cause for the plaintiff's injury. At this point, the defendant may escape liability by proving that the plaintiff could have avoided the injury had the plaintiff exercised reasonable care (i.e., had the plaintiff not been negligent). Thus, the defendant has the burden of proving that the plaintiff was negligent. Note that in many jurisdictions, such as the one in this case, contributory negligence bars the plaintiff from any recovery from the defendant. There are, however, jurisdictions where contributory negligence of the plaintiff only reduces the plaintiff's recovery and does not act as a complete bar to it. We will discuss that approach to contributory negligence in more detail in the next few cases.

■ CASE VOCABULARY

CONTRIBUTORY NEGLIGENCE: Conduct on the part of the plaintiff that falls below the standard to which he should conform for his own protection, and which is a legally contributing cause in addition to the negligence of the defendant in bringing about the plaintiff's harm. At common law, any amount of contributory negligence barred recovery by the plaintiff.

Davies v. Mann

(Mule Owner) v. *(Wagon Rider)*
10 M. & W. 547, 152 Eng.Rep. 588 (1842)

A PARTY WHO HAS THE LAST CHANCE TO AVOID INJURY TO ANOTHER, BUT NEGLIGENTLY FAILS TO DO SO, IS LIABLE FOR DAMAGES TO THE OTHER, EVEN IF THE OTHER PARTY WAS INITIALLY NEGLIGENT

■ **INSTANT FACTS** Davies (P) sued Mann (P) for negligently running over Davies' (P) mule with a wagon.

■ **BLACK LETTER RULE** A negligent defendant, claiming contributory negligence on the part of the plaintiff, may not escape liability if the defendant had the last chance to prevent the injury had he/she not been negligent.

■ **PROCEDURAL BASIS**

Motion for a new trial in action for negligence for recovery of damages.

■ **FACTS**

Davies (P) tied the feet of the mule that Davies (P) owned, allowing it to graze at the sides of a public road. Meanwhile, Mann's (D) wagon sped down the road, running down the mule and killing it. Davies (P) sued Mann (D) for recovery of damages. The trial court ordered the jury that even if the act of Davies (P) in tying the mule on the road was illegal or negligent, Mann (D) is still liable if Mann's (D) negligence was the proximate cause of the mule's death. Additionally, the jury was instructed to find for Davies (P) if Mann (D) could have avoided the accident by the exercise of ordinary care. The jury found for Davies (P). Mann (D) moves for a new trial on the ground that the jury instructions were erroneous.

■ **ISSUE**

May a defendant, claiming contributory negligence on the part of the plaintiff, escape liability, even though the defendant had the last chance to prevent the injury had he/she acted reasonably?

■ **DECISION AND RATIONALE**

(Lord Abinger, C.B.) No. A negligent defendant, claiming contributory negligence on the part of the plaintiff, may not escape liability if the defendant had the last chance to prevent the injury had he/she not been negligent. In this case, whether or not the plaintiff was negligent in placing the mule on the road made no difference because the defendant could have avoided injuring the mule by exercising proper care. Since the defendant did not do so, the defendant is liable for the injury even though the mule may have been improperly there.

■ **CONCURRENCE**

(Parke) Even if the mule was improperly on the road, the defendant was negligent because it did not ride the wagon at proper speed.

Analysis:

This case is very similar to the previous case, *Butterfield v. Forrester*. However, it appears that their results are opposite of one another. Yet, they are not. In Butterfield, the person who has created the obstruction was the defendant, and in Davies the person creating the obstruction is the plaintiff. In the first case, the plaintiff was not allowed recovery, while in the second case he was. Thus, it appears that the person whose negligence was first in time is not the one who is liable. This concept is defined as the Last Clear Chance Doctrine. That is the person who is closer to the time of injury, or the person who had the last clear opportunity to avoid the harm and did not, due to negligent conduct, is the person who is liable. In *Butterfield*, even though the defendant had created the obstruction, the plaintiff had the last chance to avoid injury, but did not because his conduct was negligent. In *Davies*, the plaintiff was the first negligent party, however the defendant had the last chance to avoid the injury, and again, he did not, due to negligent conduct. Where the plaintiff had the last chance to prevent the injury but failed to do so, the plaintiff is contributorily negligent. However, where the defendant had the last chance, the defendant is liable based on the Last Clear Chance doctrine. In other words, the Last Clear Chance doctrine is almost a rebuttal for a plaintiff who is accused of contributory negligence. Imagine that the plaintiff sued the defendant in negligence and proves all elements of negligence. The defendant then uses the defense of contributory negligence, and proves that the plaintiff was negligent. At this point, the plaintiff cannot recover damages. However, if the plaintiff can prove that the defendant had the last clear chance to prevent the injury or damage, but negligently failed to do so, the plaintiff is the winner.

■ CASE VOCABULARY

LAST CLEAR CHANCE DOCTRINE: A doctrine in some jurisdictions that a defendant may be liable for the injury he caused even though the plaintiff was contributorily negligent, if the defendant could have avoided the injury to the plaintiff by exercising ordinary care.

McIntyre v. Balentine

(Negligent Truck Driver) v. *(Negligent Tractor Driver)*

833 S.W.2d 52 (Tenn.1992)

THE DOCTRINE OF COMPARATIVE FAULT IS DESIGNED TO ALLOCATE RESPONSIBILITY FOR DAMAGES INCURRED BETWEEN THE PLAINTIFF AND THE DEFENDANT BASED ON THE RELATIVE NEGLIGENCE OF THE TWO PARTIES

■ **INSTANT FACTS** McIntyre (P) sued Balentine (D) for personal injuries suffered as a result of an automobile accident with Balentine (D).

■ **BLACK LETTER RULE** The doctrine of contributory negligence should be replaced by a system of comparative fault to allow the plaintiff, whose negligence is less than the defendant, to recover damages which are reduced in proportion to the plaintiff's percentage of fault.

■ **PROCEDURAL BASIS**

Appeal in action from recovery of damages for personal injuries.

■ **FACTS**

McIntyre (P) and Balentine (D) had an accident while driving their vehicles. McIntyre (P) brought action against Balentine (D) for the personal injuries suffered. Balentine (D) defended on the ground that McIntyre (P) was contributorily negligent because of driving while intoxicated. The evidence at the trial showed that McIntyre's (P) blood-alcohol level was .17 percent. Other evidence suggested that Balentine (D) was driving at an excessive speed. The jury finding both equally at fault ruled in favor of Balentine (D). McIntyre (P) appealed on the ground that the trial court erred in failing to instruct the jury on the doctrine of comparative negligence, and in instructing the jury that a blood-alcohol level greater than .10 percent created an inference of negligence. The Court of Appeals affirmed, holding that comparative negligence was not the law in Tennessee, and that the presumption of intoxication was admissible evidence. McIntyre (P) appeals requesting the court to decide whether to adopt a system of comparative fault in Tennessee.

■ **ISSUE**

Should the doctrine of contributory negligence be replaced by a system of comparative fault to allow the plaintiff, whose negligence is less than the defendant, to recover damages which are reduced in proportion to the plaintiff's percentage of fault?

■ **DECISION AND RATIONALE**

(Drowota, J.) Yes. The doctrine of contributory negligence should be replaced by a system of comparative fault to allow the plaintiff, whose negligence is less than the defendant, to recover damages which are reduced in proportion to the plaintiff's percentage of fault. Under the doctrine of contributory negligence, which is followed in this state, a plaintiff who is negligent is completely barred from recovery of damages from a negligent defendant. Some of the suggested justifications for this rule are that the plaintiff should be penalized for his misconduct, the plaintiff should be deterred from injuring himself, and that the plaintiff's negligence supersedes the defendant's such that the latter's negligence is no longer the proximate cause of the plaintiff's damages. Exceptions to this rule include situations where the conduct of the defendant was intentional or grossly negligent, where the defendant had the last clear chance to prevent the injury, and where the plaintiff's negligence was "remote." However, many jurisdictions have adopted, judicially or legislatively, the doctrine of comparative fault, allowing the plaintiff to recover damages in an amount which is reduced in proportion to the plaintiff's percentage of fault. This court, too, will abandon the doctrine of contributory negligence and replace it with comparative fault. There are two forms of comparative fault systems: "pure" and "modified." Under pure comparative negligence, the plaintiff's damages are reduced in proportion to the percentage of negligence attributed to him. This is true even if the plaintiff's negligence exceeds that of the defendant. Under modified comparative negligence, however, the plaintiff may recover damages, but only if the plaintiff's negligence either 1) does not exceed 50 percent (50% jurisdictions), or 2) is less than the defendant's negligence (49% jurisdictions). This court will adopt the modified version because a party should not be able to recover in tort even though he may be 80, or 90 percent at fault. This court will adopt the 49% rule because while it ameliorates the harshness of an all-or-nothing system, it is comparable to a fault-based tort system. Thus, in all trials where the issue of comparative fault is before the jury, the latter should be instructed on the effect of its finding as to the percentage of negligence between the plaintiff and the defendant. In the instant case, although the jury found that the plaintiff and the defendant were "equally" at fault, since the jury was not properly instructed on determining percentages of fault, and how they affect liability, the equal apportionment cannot be a basis for final determination of the case. This decision has an effect on many legal principles: 1) It makes the doctrines of remote negligence and last clear chance obsolete. 2) Where there is more than one tortfeasor, the plaintiff may recover so long as his percentage of negligence is less than the combined negligence of all tortfeasors. 3) This holding renders the doctrine of joint and several liability obsolete. 4) Defendants will be allowed to testify and prove the negligence of third parties, and the jury will be instructed to determine the percentage, if any, of the non-party's negligence. As to plaintiff's second point on appeal, there is no error in admission of evidence of intoxication in a civil case. (Reversed in part and remanded.)

Analysis:

While the doctrine of contributory negligence bars any recovery to the negligent plaintiff, the doctrine of comparative negligence allows the plaintiff to recover damages which are reduced according to the plaintiff's percentage of negligence. As the court indicates, there are at least three types of comparative negligence systems: 1) *Pure.* Under this system, the plaintiff may recover damages which are reduced based on the plaintiff's percentage of negligence. Thus, plaintiff's recovery is strictly proportional to the percentage of negligence regardless of how big or how small this percentage may be. 2) *Modified.* This system allows the plaintiff to recover damages which are reduced based on the plaintiff's percentage of fault so long as the plaintiff's negligence does not exceed a certain percentage. Some modified comparative negligence jurisdictions require the plaintiff's negligence to be 49% or less (less than the defendant's), while other jurisdictions allow recovery where the plaintiff's negligence is no larger than 50% (equal to the defendant's negligence).

■ CASE VOCABULARY

COMPARATIVE NEGLIGENCE: The allocation of responsibility for damages incurred between the plaintiff and defendant, based on the negligence of the two; the reduction of the damages to be recovered by the negligent plaintiff in proportion to his fault.

Seigneur v. National Fitness Institute, Inc.

(Health Club Member) v. (Fitness Facility)

132 Md.App. 271, 752 A.2d 631 (Spec.Ct.App.2000)

AN EXCULPATORY CLAUSE IN A HEALTH CLUB MEMBERSHIP AGREEMENT IS VALID AND ENFORCEABLE

■ **INSTANT FACTS** After executing a membership agreement releasing National Fitness Institute, Inc. (D) of all liability for negligence, Seigneur (P) sued for vicarious liability and negligence after she was injured during a fitness evaluation.

■ **BLACK LETTER RULE** An exculpatory clause is enforceable if it clearly and specifically indicates the intent to release the defendant from liability for personal injuries caused by the defendant's negligence.

■ **PROCEDURAL BASIS**

Trial court consideration of the defendant's motion to dismiss.

■ **FACTS**

Seigneur (P) injured her right shoulder while undergoing a fitness evaluation at the National Fitness Institute, Inc. (D). In her membership contract, Seigneur (P) disclosed a history of back problems and released National Fitness (D) from all liability for injuries caused by its employees' negligence during her use of the facility. Seigneur (P) sued National Fitness (D) for vicarious liability due to its employee's negligence during her initial evaluation and for negligence in failing to properly hire and train the employee. National Fitness (D) filed a motion to dismiss, which the court treated as a motion for summary judgment, arguing that the release clause of the membership contract was valid and enforceable. In response, Seigneur (P) argued the membership agreement was an adhesion contract and that the release was void as a matter of public policy.

■ **ISSUE**

Is an exculpatory clause in a form membership agreement enforceable?

■ **DECISION AND RATIONALE**

(Salmon, J.) Yes. An exculpatory clause is enforceable if it "clearly and specifically indicates the intent to release the defendant from liability for personal injuries caused by the defendant's negligence." Here, there is no evidence that the contract was a product of fraud, mistake, or undue influence. The language is unambiguous, clearly indicating that the defendant is insulated from liability for active or passive negligence. Accordingly, the clause is valid.

Generally, when parties freely agree to an unambiguous contractual provision, the provision is not void as against public policy. However, when the party protected by the clause engages in intentional, reckless, wanton, or grossly negligent conduct, the bargaining power between the parties is so grossly unequal as to put the other party at an unfair disadvantage, or the contract involves a public interest, public policy may render the contract unenforceable.

Here, Seigneur (P) contends that the membership agreement was an adhesion contract involving grossly disparate bargaining power between the parties. "To possess a decisive bargaining advantage over a customer, the service offered must usually be deemed essential in nature." While health clubs are important to many people, the services offered are not a practical necessity such that one may not freely decline the terms of the contract. The defendant has no special legal relationship to the plaintiff such that it must accept the plaintiff. Nor is the plaintiff compelled by need to accept the terms offered in the defendant's membership agreement. There are numerous other fitness facilities in the plaintiff's area from which she could have selected. Similarly, the plaintiff could have purchased her own fitness equipment for private use in her home. She had significant bargaining power with the defendant.

Likewise, the membership contract does not involve a matter of public interest. While reliance on defined factors to determine whether a public interest is involved is arbitrary, exculpatory clauses in transactions involving the performance of a public obligation or of high importance to the public good are generally unenforceable. Here, no such public interest is involved. Affirmed.

Analysis:

While a court is more likely to find disproportionate bargaining power when the service offered is more important to the consumer, courts generally will enforce contractual provisions when the consumer has various options available to him. For instance, when goods or services—even those of an essential nature—are offered by business competitors in an area, a consumer has the option to purchase from a vendor other than the one with the exculpatory agreement. Only when the goods or services involved are sufficiently necessary to a consumer and the consumer is left without meaningful options will a contractual clause generally be struck down.

■ CASE VOCABULARY

ADHESION CONTRACT: A standard-form contract prepared by one party, to be signed by the party in a weaker position, usually a consumer, who has little choice about the terms.

ASSUMPTION OF THE RISK: The act or an instance of a prospective plaintiff's taking on the risk of loss, injury, or damage.

EXCULPATORY CLAUSE: A contractual provision relieving a party from any liability resulting from a negligent or wrongful act.

RELEASE: Liberation from an obligation, duty, or demand; the act of giving up a right or claim to the person against whom it could have been enforced.

Rush v. Commercial Realty Co.

(Tenant) v. *(Landlord)*

7 N.J.Misc. 337, 145 A. 476 (1929)

RISK IS NOT ASSUMED WHEN A PERSON HAS NO REASONABLE ALTERNATIVE BUT TO ENCOUNTER A KNOWN DANGER

■ **INSTANT FACTS** A lady was injured when she fell through the trap door of a privy that the lady knew to be defective.

■ **BLACK LETTER RULE** A person does not voluntarily accept a risk when no reasonable alternatives exist.

■ **PROCEDURAL BASIS**

Appeal from denial of motions for nonsuit and directed verdict in action for damages for negligence.

■ **FACTS**

Mrs. Rush (P) was a tenant of a house controlled by Commercial Realty Co. (CRC) (D). CRC (D) provided a detached privy. Mrs. Rush (P) used the privy and fell through a trap door in the floor. She descended nine feet into the pit at the bottom of the privy and had to be extricated with a ladder. Mrs. Rush (P) sued for her injuries. CRC (D) moved for nonsuit and a directed verdict on the grounds that Mrs. Rush (P) assumed the risk of injury. The trial court denied the motions, and CRC (D) appeals.

■ **ISSUE**

Where a person has no choice but to encounter a known risk, is the person's conduct voluntary for purposes of implied assumption of the risk?

■ **DECISION AND RATIONALE**

(Per Curiam) No. Where a person has no choice but to encounter a known risk, the person's conduct is not voluntary for purposes of implied assumption of the risk. In this case, CRC (D) had the duty to maintain the privy, and a defective condition caused the accident. Mrs. Rush (P) had no choice, when impelled by the calls of nature, but to use the privy. She was not required to go elsewhere to find another restroom. Thus, Mrs. Rush (P) did not *voluntarily* encounter a known risk. She may have been contributorily negligent, but that is a question for the jury to decide. Affirmed.

Analysis:

In order for a defendant to be relieved of liability based on implied assumption of risk, the plaintiff must have voluntarily assumed the risk. This case illustrates that the concept of "voluntary" can be given wide latitude by courts. Was Mrs. Rush (P) necessarily compelled to use the defective privy? The facts indicated that she knew of the defective condition, and yet she chose to use the restroom and encounter the risk. The court could have just as easily held that, even though Mrs. Rush (P) may have had a strong need to use the restroom, she nevertheless voluntarily chose to use that particular defective privy. However, the case law dealing with the "voluntary" element is generally in accord with this opinion. Where a person is left with no reasonable alternative but to encounter the risk, the conduct is not voluntary. Similarly, where a defendant's improper conduct leaves a plaintiff with a choice of two evils, this is considered a species of duress which destroys the plaintiff's freedom of choice.

■ CASE VOCABULARY

PRIVY: A restroom.

Blackburn v. Dorta

(Not Stated) v. *(Not Stated)*
348 So.2d 287 (Fla.1977)

THE DOCTRINE OF COMPARATIVE NEGLIGENCE ABROGATES IMPLIED ASSUMPTION OF RISK

■ **INSTANT FACTS** [No facts provided]

■ **BLACK LETTER RULE** Implied assumption of risk is subsumed by the doctrine of comparative negligence.

■ **PROCEDURAL BASIS**

Consolidation of three cases under conflict certiorari jurisdiction.

■ **FACTS**

[No facts provided. Court analyzes the viability of the assumption of risk doctrine.]

■ **ISSUE**

Is the doctrine of implied assumption of risk still viable as an absolute bar to recovery subsequent to the adoption of the rule of comparative negligence?

■ **DECISION AND RATIONALE**

(Sundberg, J.) No. The doctrine of implied assumption of risk is not still viable as an absolute bar to recovery subsequent to the adoption of the rule of comparative negligence. The doctrine of implied assumption of risk is not favored, and there is a strong shift toward abrogating the defense. Assumption of risk serves no purpose which is not subsumed either by the doctrine of contributory negligence or the common law concept of duty. In order to understand this, it is necessary to analyze the various types of implied assumption of risk. First, it must be divided into the categories of primary or secondary. *Primary assumption of risk* is simply another way of saying that the defendant was not negligent, either because he owed no duty or did not breach a duty. For example, where a passenger rides in a train, he primarily assumes the risk that the train may lurch and jerk, but he does not primarily assume the risk of extraordinary lurches. It makes more sense to look at this from the defendant's perspective. A defendant train operator is under no duty to prevent usual jerks, but he may be liable for unusual lurching and jerking. Having dispensed with primary assumption of risk, we move on to secondary assumption, an affirmative defense. *Secondary assumption of risk* can be divided into reasonable (pure) assumption, and unreasonable (qualified) assumption. Where a father rushes into a burning building to save his infant child, he is barred from recovery for his injuries because he voluntarily exposed himself to a known risk. Although the father's conduct was reasonable, he is nevertheless barred. This is an unfair doctrine, unsupported by law or justice. If, on the other hand, the father rushed into the building to retrieve his favorite hat, his conduct would be unreasonable. His conduct could be characterized as secondary qualified implied assumption of risk [now that's a catchy phrase!] or simply as contributory negligence. There is no sound rationale for retaining this subset of assumption of risk in light of our modern doctrine of comparative negligence. Furthermore, in the situation where the father rescued his infant, it is more equitable to allow him partial recovery based on comparative negligence than to deny recovery based on assumption of risk.

Analysis:

This opinion essentially presents a hornbook discussion of the abrogation of the doctrine of implied assumption of risk. Based on the court's analysis, it makes sense that the doctrine of comparative negligence should subsume implied assumption of risk. Assumption of risk can bar recovery to plaintiffs in cases of genuine hardship (such as the father rescuing his infant from the burning building), whereas comparative negligence allows some recovery. Of course, express assumption of risk is still valid; however, this is really a contractual concept, largely outside of the law of torts. This opinion is well-written and well-reasoned, but at least one of the examples can be questioned. Where the father rushed to save his infant from the flames, courts could easily hold (and some in similar situations have held) that the father's conduct was not voluntary. Faced with no reasonable alternatives, he had no choice but to save his child. Based on this analysis, assumption of risk would not be available as a defense to a landlord who negligently allowed the building to burn. All in all, however, it is probably wise to eliminate the doctrine and allow comparative negligence principles to apportion liability.

■ CASE VOCABULARY

ABROGATE: To do away with, repeal, or cancel.

PUISSANT: Powerful.

SALIENT: Prominent.

SUBSUME: Classify within a larger category.

Teeters v. Currey

(Patient) v. *(Doctor)*

518 S.W.2d 512 (Tenn.1974)

STATUTE OF LIMITATIONS MAY BE TOLLED UNTIL THE PLAINTIFF DISCOVERS THAT SHE HAS BEEN INVOLVED

■ **INSTANT FACTS** A woman sued her doctor for negligently performing a tubal ligation when she discovered, two years after the surgery, that she was pregnant.

■ **BLACK LETTER RULE** A cause of action for malpractice does not accrue, and the statute of limitations does not begin to run, until the injured party discovers or should have discovered the injury.

■ **PROCEDURAL BASIS**

Appeal from defense verdict in action for damages for medical malpractice.

■ **FACTS**

Teeters (P) gave birth to a child in June 1970. Following delivery, medical complications forced Dr. Currey (D) to perform a tubal ligation on Teeters (P) in order to avoid future pregnancies. In December 1972, Teeters (P) was hospitalized and the doctor discovered that she was pregnant. Following delivery of a premature child, with severe complications, another tubal ligation was performed on Teeters (P). Plaintiff sued Dr. Currey (D) for malpractice in November 1973, alleging that he was negligent in performing the original tubal ligation. Dr. Currey (D) defended based upon the one-year statute of limitations for malpractice suits. The trial court granted a verdict for Dr. Currey (D). Teeters (P) appealed, arguing that, for purposes of the statute, her cause of action accrued when she discovered the malpractice.

■ **ISSUE**

Does the statute of limitations for malpractice begin to run only when the negligent injury was, or should have been, discovered?

■ **DECISION AND RATIONALE**

(Henry, J.) Yes. The statute of limitations for malpractice begins to run only when the negligent injury was, or should have been, discovered. Pursuant to Tennessee law, an action for malpractice must be brought within one year of accrual. Traditionally Tennessee courts have held that a cause of action accrues immediately upon the infliction or occurrence of an injury. Thus, in malpractice cases, an action must have been brought within one year of the surgery or other malpractice causing an injury. The majority of jurisdictions have limited the harsh effects of such a statute of limitations by adopting the "discovery doctrine." Under this doctrine, the statute does not begin to run until the negligent injury was, or should have been, discovered. We adopt this rule in those cases where medical malpractice is alleged to have occurred through the negligent performance of surgical procedures. The statute of limitations begins to run only when the patient discovers, or in the exercise of reasonable care should have discovered, the resulting injury. In the instant case, Teeters' (P) cause of action accrued when she discovered that she was pregnant. This occurred in December 1972, and her action was brought in November 1993. Thus, her action was timely. Reversed and remanded.

Analysis:

As the opinion indicates, statutes of limitations are designed to promote stability and finality and to avoid the burdens inherent in defending antiquated claims. The discovery rule upends this policy rationale, however, allowing claims to be brought within a limited time after an injured party discovers (or should have discovered) the injury. Many jurisdictions have adopted and expanded the discovery rule to cover a variety of latent injuries, from medical and attorney malpractice to construction defects. As a result, professionals often cannot rest secure in the knowledge that they will not be sued for past wrongs. A plaintiff can always argue that she did not discover the injury until a certain date, and defendants face the difficult task of trying to disprove this or to show that a reasonable person would have discovered the injury sooner. Of course, if a discovery doctrine is not applied, parties who had no reason to suspect negligence would be barred from suing if the latent injury surfaced too late. This result is too harsh for most legislatures to stomach. It is also important to note that many jurisdictions employ various tolling doctrines to stop a statute of limitations from running. Common reasons for tolling include an injured party who has not reached the age of majority or who is incompetent. In addition, statutes of limitation may be equitably tolled where, for example, a defendant fraudulently conceals the presence of a cause of action.

■ CASE VOCABULARY

TOLL: To bar, defeat, take away; to show facts which remove the bar of the statute of limitations

TUBAL LIGATION: A surgical procedure by which the fallopian tubes are cut in order to prevent future pregnancies.

Freehe v. Freehe

(Husband) v. *(Wife)*

81 Wash.2d 183, 500 P.2d 771 (1972)

COURT ABOLISHES INTERSPOUSAL IMMUNITY

■ **INSTANT FACTS** A husband sued his wife for injuries caused by her tractor, and she defended on grounds of interspousal immunity.

■ **BLACK LETTER RULE** Spouses are not immune from liability in personal injury cases.

■ PROCEDURAL BASIS

Appeal from grant of summary judgment in action for damages for negligence.

■ FACTS

Clifford Freehe (P) sued his wife for injuries allegedly sustained due to Mrs. Freehe's (D) negligent maintenance of a tractor that she owned, and due to her alleged failure to warn of the tractor's unsafe condition. The injuries occurred on a farm that was the separate property of Mrs. Freehe (D). Mr. Freehe (P) had no interest in the farm and was not an employee of Mrs. Freehe (D). The trial court granted Mrs. Freehe's (D) motion for summary judgment based on interspousal tort immunity. Mr. Freehe (P) appeals.

■ ISSUE

Are spouses immune from tort liability to each other?

■ DECISION AND RATIONALE

(Neill, A.J.) No. Spouses are not immune from tort liability to each other. The common law rule of interspousal immunity was based on the supposed legal unity of man and wife. In antiquity, a wife was considered the chattel of her husband. The husband had the right to all of her choses in action, and he was liable for all torts of his wife. Under this common law framework, interspousal immunity made sense, because it would be meaningless for a husband to be liable to himself for the torts of his wife or to be entitled to the chose in action for his own torts. However, spouses are no longer liable for the separate debts of the other, and modern realities do not comport with the traditional "supposed unity" of husband and wife. Several arguments are nevertheless asserted for maintaining interspousal immunity in modern times. First, it is argued that allowing a married person to sue his spouse would destroy the peace and tranquility of the home. We disagree. If a peaceful home environment exists, spouses will likely not sue each other and risk the consequences. Alternatively, if the relationship is already in turmoil, interspousal immunity would probably cause only more problems. Second, it is argued that an injured spouse already has an adequate remedy through criminal and divorce laws. In addition to the likelihood for destroying the peace and tranquility of a home, criminal and divorce laws do not actually compensate the injured spouse for the damage done. Third, it is argued that permitting litigation between spouses would flood the courts with trivial matrimonial disputes. This has not materialized in other jurisdictions, and courts could apply typical doctrines like consent and assumption of risk to weed out these cases. Finally, proponents of interspousal immunity suggest that permitting suits between spouses would encourage collusion and fraud where one or both spouses are insured.

Courts must deal with this problem, when and if it occurs, just as they deal with any other collusion. Tortfeasors should not be immunized from liability in a whole class of cases because of the possibility of fraud, or because of any of the other arguments offered in support of interspousal immunity. Reversed and remanded.

Analysis:

Immunities, which completely bar suits against the immunized person, are being rapidly abrogated in most jurisdictions. This case adequately describes the history and rationale for marital immunity in personal injury cases. However, the opinion fails to address the difficult issues that arise when interspousal immunity is abolished. For example, what duty of care does one spouse owe the other for such day-to-day activities as preparing meals? How should the duty of care be established, since there would be no common law precedent immediately following the repeal of the interspousal immunity? Should a wife be able to sue her husband if she acquires something as trivial as food poisoning? Or what if she acquires something far more serious, like the HIV virus, from her husband? Perhaps the questions are mainly academic, or perhaps they are important only in conjunction with a divorce proceeding. After all, how many marriages would continue after one spouse sued the other? Regardless, the topic provides an interesting look into the development and evolution of common law.

■ CASE VOCABULARY

CHATTEL: An article of personal property.

CHOSE IN ACTION: The right to bring a cause of action.

Renko v. McLean

(Injured Child) v. *(Mother)*
346 Md. 464, 697 A.2d 468 (1997)

CHILD NOT PERMITTED TO SUE MOTHER FOR INJURIES CAUSED BY CAR ACCIDENT

■ **INSTANT FACTS** Daughter sued her mother for injuries sustained in a car accident which was caused by the mother's negligent driving.

■ **BLACK LETTER RULE** There is no exception to the parent-child immunity doctrine for injuries sustained in motor tort cases occurring during the child's minority.

■ **PROCEDURAL BASIS**

Appeal from the trial court's granting of the McLean's (D) motion to dismiss.

■ **FACTS**

When Renko (P) was seventeen years old, she suffered serious injuries when her mother, McLean (D), negligently drove their car into the rear of another vehicle [now see, I *told* you not to play with the radio while driving!]. Following her eighteenth birthday, Renko (P) filed suit against her mother, McLean (D), for negligence. McLean (D) filed a motion to dismiss based on parent-child immunity [child cannot sue parent], and Renko (P) asked the court to recognize an exception to the parent-child immunity doctrine [exceptions to apply to motor vehicle accidents occuring during her minority]. The court declined to do so, and entered judgment for McLean (D). Renko (P) appealed.

■ **ISSUE**

Is there an exception to the parent-child immunity doctrine for injuries sustained in motor tort cases occurring during the child's minority?

■ **DECISION AND RATIONALE**

(Karwacki, J.) No. The parent-child immunity doctrine grew out of an abiding belief that barring tort actions between parents and their minor children served the compelling public interest in preserving, under normal circumstances, the internal harmony and integrity of the family unit and parental authority in the parent-child relationship. The doctrine also serves to prevent fraud and collusion among family members to the detriment of third parties, and the threat that intrafamilial litigation will deplete family resources. Circumstance sometimes severs the doctrine from its rationale and reason, however that in no way detracts from our fundamental belief that the parent-child immunity rule is still essential to the maintenance of discipline and to the stability of family harmony. We have thus continued to hold that today's parent-child relationship, as recognized by this court and the Legislature, furnishes no compelling reason to abrogate the rule. Renko (P) nonetheless mounts a three-pronged attack upon the parent-child immunity doctrine. She asserts that (1) adult children should be allowed to maintain actions against their parents for injuries occurring during their minority; (2) no contemporary justification exists to apply the doctrine to the facts of the case sub judice in light of compulsory motor vehicle liability insurance; and (3) any such application is violative of the Maryland Declaration of Rights and of the Fourteenth Amendment of the Constitution. We have permitted suits between parents and their minor children in limited circumstances. First, when a child has suffered cruel or unusually malicious conduct at the hands of a parent, and second, a child may sue a parent's business partner for negligence committed in the operation of the partnership. If we were to allow a child to file suit once she reaches the age of majority, the parent-child immunity doctrine would serve not as a bar to actions between parent and child, but rather as an obstacle easily overcome by the passage of time. We refuse to create an exception that would effectively negate the rule and open courthouse doors to every conceivable dispute between parent and child. Other jurisdictions have found persuasive arguments calling for the abolition of the parent-child immunity doctrine in motor tort cases, however we still believe that the argument for abrogation suffers from several infirmities. Unlike a true adversarial proceeding, an insurer is forced in to the position of attempting to defend a suit that its insured has every incentive to lose. Additionally, many families carry medical insurance which would necessarily compensate the child for injuries and injury-related expenses. Further recovery for pain and suffering and other noneconomic damages might potentially saddle a family with a judgment it cannot afford to pay because it exceeds available insurance. As to Renko's (P) final argument, that the application is violative of the Maryland Declaration of Rights and of the Fourteenth Amendment, we find these assertions to be meritless. Thus we remain convinced that the parent-child immunity rule is still in the best interests of both children and parents to retain. Judgment affirmed, with costs.

Analysis:

The decision in this case was correct, however the court perhaps places too much emphasis on "preserving family harmony" as the main justification behind the immunity rule. The reasoning based upon monetary considerations appears to be the more sound argument against departing from the rule. As the court points out, liability insurance places the insurance company in a losing situation; and in some cases the existence of insurance will not help at all. A better departure would be to allow suits to be brought if the child is fully emancipated from the parent. Then, financial considerations would be the same as if the parties were not related.

■ CASE VOCABULARY

CASE SUB JUDICE: The case currently before the court.

DE FACTO: In fact, actual.

EMANCIPATED CHILD: Child is free of parental controls.

Abernathy v. Sisters of St. Mary's

(Patient) v. *(Hospital Operator)*
446 S.W.2d 599 (Mo.1969)

MISSOURI ABROGATES THE DOCTRINE OF CHARITABLE IMMUNITY

■ **INSTANT FACTS** A patient at a hospital run by a charitable organization sued for negligence, and the hospital claimed charitable immunity from liability.

■ **BLACK LETTER RULE** Nongovernmental charitable institutions are liable for their own negligence and the negligence of their employees.

■ **PROCEDURAL BASIS**

Appeal from granting of motion for summary judgment dismissing action for damages for negligence.

■ **FACTS**

Abernathy (P), a patient at a hospital operated by the Sisters of St. Mary's (D), alleged that a hospital employee negligently failed to assist Abernathy (P) as he moved from his hospital bed to the bathroom. Abernathy (P) fell and suffered injuries, and he brought suit against the Sisters (D) for $35,000 in damages. The Sisters (D) moved for summary judgment, arguing that the hospital was a religious, nonprofit corporation and charitable institution and, therefore, is immune from tort liability. The trial court sustained the motion, and Abernathy (P) appeals.

■ **ISSUE**

Is a nongovernmental charitable institution immune from liability for negligence?

■ **DECISION AND RATIONALE**

(Henley, J.) No. A nongovernmental charitable institution is not immune from liability for negligence. The doctrine of charitable immunity was adopted by this state in 1907. The court ruled that it was better that an individual suffer injury without compensation than risk the probability that the public would be deprived of the benefits of the charity. The rationale was justifiable at that time in order to encourage and protect charities. However, charity today is big business. Charities are often large-scale corporations, and donors receive tax deductions for their donations. It makes sense that modern corporations should pay their own way. In addition, liability insurance is available to charities, and most carry such insurance. Furthermore, there has been no indication in states without charitable immunity that donations have been discouraged or that charities have collapsed as a result. Charitable immunity fosters neglect and irresponsibility, while liability promotes care and caution. Two principal arguments have been raised in support of charitable immunity. The "implied waiver" theory states that persons who accept the benefits of a charity implicitly agree that they will not sue the charity for torts. This theory is a mere fiction. It is impossible to say, for example, that unconscious or insane hospital patients implicitly waive all liability against a charitable hospital. Because the theory cannot be applied evenly to all persons, the theory is unsound. Second, the "trust fund" theory says that funds given to charities for charitable purposes cannot be used to pay judgments. This theory confuses liability with the right to satisfaction of a judgment. Regardless of whether charitable donations should be used to pay judgments, charities should not be exempt from liability for their torts. We therefore hold that, in this case and all future cases, a nongovernmental charitable institution is liable for its own negligence and for the negligence of its agents and employees acting within the scope of their employment. Reversed and remanded.

Analysis:

This case exemplifies the difficult balancing of public policy issues that courts face. Charitable institutions are vital aspects of society, and they should perhaps be immune from liability if they would otherwise be forced to close their doors. However, common sense and the reality of modern society dictate that charities can still survive without immunity. Perhaps the strongest argument in support of the abrogation of charitable immunity is the fact that charities can purchase liability insurance. Insurance serves to spread the costs of tort liability throughout society, whether the insured is a for-profit corporation or benevolent charity. Of course, donors might be upset that their money is going towards insurance rather than directly aiding the needy. But the realities of modern society make this a necessity, and it is a small price to pay in comparison to the alternative, i.e., injured persons who cannot be compensated for their losses. The opinion can be questioned on at least one level. In rejecting the theory of implied waiver, the court concludes that, because the theory cannot be applied alike to all persons, it is invalid. However, the law of torts is replete with instances of treating incompetent persons differently. The implied waiver theory might well be valid for all but those incompetent persons who cannot possibly have implicitly consented to charitable immunity. Unlike Missouri, some jurisdictions have declined to abolish charitable immunity entirely. For example, charitable immunity may still be claimed for some non-hospital religious organizations, or the immunity may be limited only to the direct beneficiaries of the charity. In addition, charitable immunity has been retained in some jurisdictions to the extent that liability insurance is not available to fully cover losses.

■ CASE VOCABULARY

AMICI CURIAE: Friends of the court; interested non-parties who file briefs in support of some aspect of a case.

Ayala v. Philadelphia Board of Public Education

(*Student*) v. (*School District*)

453 Pa. 584, 305 A.2d 877 (1973)

PENNSYLVANIA ABROGATES THE DOCTRINE OF GOVERNMENTAL IMMUNITY

■ **INSTANT FACTS** A student who was injured in shop class sued the school district, which claimed governmental immunity.

■ **BLACK LETTER RULE** Governmental entities are not immune from tort liability.

■ **PROCEDURAL BASIS**

Allocatur of per curiam order sustaining objections based on governmental immunity to action for damages for negligence.

■ **FACTS**

William Ayala, Jr. (P) was injured when his arm was caught in a shredding machine in the upholstery class of a Philadelphia public school. Ayala's (P) arm had to be amputated, and he sued for his injuries. Ayala (P) alleged that the school district was negligent in failing to supervise the upholstery class, in supplying the machinery without a proper safety device, in maintaining the machine in a dangerous condition, and in failing to warn the children of the dangerous condition. The Philadelphia Board of Public Education (D) interposed preliminary objections, asserting the defense of governmental immunity. The objections were sustained and an order in the Board's (D) favor was entered. Ayala (P) appeals.

■ **ISSUE**

Are governmental entities immune from tort liability?

■ **DECISION AND RATIONALE**

(Roberts, J.) No. Governmental entities are not immune from tort liability. The historical roots of the governmental immunity doctrine are rooted in an old English case, in which the court expressed the fear that without governmental immunity there would be an infinity of actions. In addition, the court noted the absence of a fund from which any judgments could be satisfied. The court ruled that it was better that an individual sustain an injury than that the public should suffer an inconvenience. Other courts have traced the rationale for governmental immunity to the old maxim that "the King can do no wrong." Under English law, since a King could not himself commit a tort, he could likewise not be liable for the torts of any of his officers. In modern society, governmental immunity can no longer be justified. The entire burden of damages should not be imposed against an individual who suffers injuries. Rather, the damages should be distributed among the entire community. We reject the justification that excessive litigation would result, as there is little empirical support for this theory. In addition, we question the rationale that governments lack funds from which claims could be paid. Governments possess and spend funds in a myriad of ways, and there is no reason that payment of tort judgments should not be a valid use of public funds. In addition, public insurance is available to spread the losses throughout society. Moreover, governmental immunity has the effect of encouraging laxness. Exposure of the government to liability will have the effect of increasing governmental care and concern for the welfare of those who might be injured. Reversed and remanded.

Analysis:

This opinion echoes the analyses of prior cases and again demonstrates the general abrogation of doctrines of immunity. As in prior cases, the widespread availability of insurance militates against any "trust fund" justification. In general, the cases indicate that it is far better to spread the losses throughout society rather than to deny recovery to an injured individual. Unlike other immunities, however, governmental immunity had a strong basis in English common law. The origin of governmental immunity is that a King could do no wrong, and that liability of the King or his officers would contradict his sovereignty. As with many old English doctrines, the rationale makes little sense in modern society. Even the United States federal government, our closest analogy to the King, is not immune from all liability. Specifically, the Federal Tort Claims Act of 1946 waived the sovereign immunity of the federal government under certain circumstances. The case at hand involves a school district, which is a municipal corporation. These entities have the dual character of governments and corporations. The absence of constitutional provisions requiring these entities to consent to suit have made it much easier to create exceptions to the rule of governmental immunity.

■ CASE VOCABULARY

ALLOCATUR: The allowance of a writ for review of an order.

PER CURIAM: By the court; an opinion issued by the entire court rather than just one judge.

DeLong v. Erie County

(911 Dialer) v. (911 Operator)
89 A.D.2d 376, 455 N.Y.S.2d 887 (Sup.Ct.1982)

MUNICIPALITIES ARE NOT IMMUNE WHEN THEY VOLUNTARILY ASSUME A DUTY TO PROTECT A PARTICULAR INDIVIDUAL

■ **INSTANT FACTS** A woman was stabbed to death while waiting for the police to respond to her 911 emergency call.

■ **BLACK LETTER RULE** Municipalities are not immune from liability when they voluntarily assume a duty to provide police protection for a particular individual.

■ **PROCEDURAL BASIS**

Appeal of verdict for damages for negligence.

■ **FACTS**

Amalia DeLong (P) and her family lived in a suburb of Buffalo that was served by the 911 emergency telephone system. An agency of Erie County and the Buffalo Police Department operated the service. One morning, DeLong (P) called 911 and told the complaint writer that a burglar was breaking into her house. The complaint writer said that help would be sent right away. However, the complaint writer wrote down the incorrect address for DeLong (P). In addition, the complaint writer failed to follow proper procedures. For example, he did not ask the name of the caller, he did not determine the exact location of the call, and he did not follow up on the call when he received the report of "no such address." The call was treated as a fake. DeLong (P) was found stabbed to death in her home. DeLong's (P) successors sued Erie County (D) for negligence. The jury awarded $200,000 for pain and suffering, and Erie County (D) appeals.

■ **ISSUE**

Where a municipality has assumed a duty to a particular person, is it nevertheless subject to governmental immunity?

■ **DECISION AND RATIONALE**

(Hancock, J.) No. Where a municipality has assumed a duty to a particular person, it is not subject to immunity. This case is distinguishable from *Riss v. New York* [cities are immune from liability for the negligent failure to provide adequate police protection]. In *Riss*, there was no special relationship between the police and the victim which gave rise to a special duty. The *Riss* court noted that, where the police undertake responsibilities to particular members of the public, the municipality may lose its governmental immunity. In the case at hand, DeLong (P) was induced to rely on an immediate response to her plea for help. This was not a mere failure to furnish police protection, but rather a case where Erie County (D) voluntarily assumed a duty. Erie County (D) was required to perform this duty in a non-negligent manner, which it failed to do. Erie County (D) argued that it would not be liable unless the police conduct in some way increased DeLong's (P) risk. We find that her reliance on the complaint writer's assurance did increase her risk by causing her to remain defenseless in the home rather than fleeing outside to safety. Affirmed.

Analysis:

Following the tragic holding in *Riss*, this case reassures the skeptical reader that there is some justice left in the field of governmental immunity. In some ways, however, Ms. Riss's situation was even more sympathetic than Mrs. DeLong (P). As the opinion notes, DeLong (P) had the opportunity to save herself by fleeing the house; Riss had no such opportunity. Nevertheless, the holding is sound. The police and county voluntarily assumed some duty by establishing a 911 service and by assuring DeLong (P) that help would be on the way. They should not be able to hide behind the shield of governmental immunity, but rather should be responsible for the failure to perform their duty of care.

Deuser v. Vecera

(Family of Drunk Park Visitor) v. *(Park Rangers)*
139 F.3d 1190 (8th Cir.1998)

THE DISCRETIONARY FUNCTION EXCEPTION TO THE FEDERAL TORTS CLAIMS ACT SHIELDS THE GOVERNMENT FROM LIABILITY WHEN GOVERNMENT AGENTS EXERCISE DISCRETION IN THE PERFORMANCE OF THEIR DUTIES

■ **INSTANT FACTS** A drunk man was killed by a car after park rangers threw him out of the park for being disorderly.

■ **BLACK LETTER RULE** Discretionary conduct of government agents acting within the scope of their authority are protected by the discretionary function exception to the Federal Torts Claims Act.

■ **PROCEDURAL BASIS**

Appeal from the trial court's dismissal of wrongful death action.

■ **FACTS**

Deuser (P) was at a fair on the Fourth of July. He was grabbing women's buttocks, which was not appreciated by the recipients [boy, no sense of humor!]. He was given a warning by the park rangers (D), and they continued to monitor his behavior. Deuser (P) was next seen urinating in public, and the rangers (D) arrested him [when you gotta go...]. Deuser (P) continued to be argumentative with the rangers (D), and rude to female park visitors. The chief ranger decided to turn Deuser over to the city police, however they were unable or unwilling to process Deuser's (P) arrest due to an overwhelming workload. The rangers (D) and police decided to release Deuser (P) away from the park so he would not return to the fair that evening. He was freed in a parking lot somewhere in the city, with no money and no transportation [take that, buddy!]. Deuser (P) then wandered onto an interstate highway and was struck and killed by a car. His blood alcohol level was 0.214 at the time of his death, well above the legal limit for intoxication.

■ **ISSUE**

Does the discretionary function exception [claims based upon discretionary conduct] shield the park rangers and the United States from liability for a wrongful death action under the Federal Tort Claims Act?

■ **DECISION AND RATIONALE**

(Bowman, C.J.) Yes. The Federal Tort Claims Act (FTCA) was enacted by Congress to waive sovereign immunity on behalf of the United States. This amenability to suit is not without exception, however, and the discretionary function exception is what is relevant here. This exception is statutory and shields the government from civil liability for claims based upon the exercise or performance of a discretionary function or duty on the part of a federal agency or an employee of the Government, whether or not the discretion involved be abused. To determine whether the discretionary function exception applies here to protect the park rangers (D) and the United States from suit, we must first consider whether the actions taken by the rangers (D) were discretionary, that is, a matter of choice. If the rangers (D) had a policy they were to follow in releasing Deuser (P), then there is no discretion in the conduct for the exception to protect. The rangers (D) have both Standard Operating Procedures as well as a Fair Operations Handbook to provide rules and guidance in the enforcement of laws. It would be impossible to put into a handbook every possible scenario a ranger might encounter, and then to decide in advance whether an arrest should be made and, once made, under what circumstances an arrest could be terminated. The rangers (D) had discretion to decide when and whether to make an arrest, so they also had discretion to terminate an arrest without charging the suspect. We therefore hold that terminating Deuser's (P) arrest, that is, releasing him without charging him with a crime, was a discretionary function reserved to the judgment of the rangers (D). The second part of our inquiry is to decide whether the kind of judgment involved in terminating Deuser's (P) arrest is of the kind that the discretionary function exception was designed to shield. To be protected, the rangers' (D) conduct must be grounded in the social, economic, or political goals of the handbook's discretionary enforcement guidelines. We believe that all three of these goals were the basis for the actions taken by the rangers (D), and as such, their conduct was a classic example of a permissible exercise of policy judgment. Clearly, the decision to remove Deuser (P) from the park served the social goals of protecting innumerable other fairgoers and ensuring that their enjoyment of the festivities was not diminished by the obnoxious and offensive behavior of a fellow attendee. The economic goal served by releasing Deuser (P) without charging him was to preserve already scarce law enforcement resources, and the political goal was that of having all law enforcement agencies involved working together, as opposed to defining "territories" to be defended. The rangers (D) acted properly to preserve that cooperation by releasing Deuser (P) as the local police requested. Thus we hold that the discretionary conduct of the park rangers (D) is a permissible exercise of policy judgment which is protected by the discretionary function exception. The judgment of the District Court is affirmed.

Analysis:

An important part of this rule, which the court really just brushes right over, is that the exception shields the government employee from liability for discretionary conduct, whether or not the discretion involved was abused. It could be argued that the park rangers (D) acted incorrectly when they decided to release Deuser (P) where they did. Further, were the rangers (D) justified in releasing Deuser (P) if his blood alcohol content exceeded the legal limit? Apparently it just doesn't matter. It seems that even when the government acts improperly it is excused. A better rule would be for there to be a possibility for liability if the employee acted either negligently or improperly in exercising his discretionary duty. It must be noted that even if a claimant is unsuccessful under the FTCA, it may still be possible to obtain relief by private bill. This is a very difficult and involved process, however, and wouldn't be the ideal choice.

CHAPTER THIRTEEN

Vicarious Liability

Bussard v. Minimed, Inc.

Instant Facts: Bussard (P) was rear-ended by a Minimed, Inc. (D) employee while she was traveling home after leaving work early because of illness, and Bussard (P) sued the employer.

Black Letter Rule: Under the doctrine of respondeat superior, an employer is ordinarily liable for the injuries its employees cause to others in the course of their work, whether or not the employer had control over the employee.

O'Shea v. Welch

Instant Facts: While traveling on business, Welch (D) struck O'Shea's (P) car during an impromptu service station stop.

Black Letter Rule: Under the slight deviation rule, a detour that involves a complete abandonment of the employment relationship relieves an employer of vicarious liability.

Murrell v. Goertz

Instant Facts: Goertz (D), a delivery boy for Oklahoma Publishing (D), struck Murrell (P) after having an argument with her.

Black Letter Rule: Employer is not liable for the torts of his independent contractor.

Maloney v. Rath

Instant Facts: Rath's (D) car collided with Maloney's (D) car because Evanchik negligently repaired Rath's (D) brakes.

Black Letter Rule: A motorist cannot delegate her duty to keep her brakes in working order to an independent contractor.

Popejoy v. Steinle

Instant Facts: While Connie Steinle (D) was taking her daughter and niece to purchase a calf for the daughter to raise on the ranch, Steinle negligently collided with Popejoy (P).

Black Letter Rule: A defendant is not vicariously liable for the negligence of another under a theory of joint venture unless the joint venture was motivated by profit.

Shuck v. Means

Instant Facts: Hertz (D) leased a rental car to Codling. Codling permitted Means (D) to drive this car. Means (D) negligently collided with and injured Shuck (P).

Black Letter Rule: A car rental agency is liable for the negligence of an individual who drives its rental car, even though it did not rent the car to that individual.

Smalich v. Westfall

Instant Facts: Smalich (P) was killed as a passenger in her own car when Westfall (D), the operator, negligently smashed her car into Blank's (D) car.

Black Letter Rule: Contributory negligence may not be imputed to a passenger riding in her own automobile without the finding of either a master-servant relationship or a finding of joint enterprise.

Bussard v. Minimed, Inc.

(*Accident Victim*) v. (*Employer*)

129 Cal.Rptr.2d 675, 105 Cal.App.4th 798 (2003)

AN EMPLOYER IS LIABLE FOR AN ACCIDENT CAUSED BY ITS EMPLOYEE AFTER EXPOSURE TO FUMES AT WORK

Bosses shouldn't let employees drive under the influence of flea fumes.

stus.com

■ **INSTANT FACTS** Bussard (P) was rear-ended by a Minimed, Inc. (D) employee while she was traveling home after leaving work early because of illness, and Bussard (P) sued the employer.

■ **BLACK LETTER RULE** Under the doctrine of respondeat superior, an employer is ordinarily liable for the injuries its employees cause to others in the course of their work, whether or not the employer had control over the employee.

■ **PROCEDURAL BASIS**

Appeal to review a trial court decision granting summary judgment to the defendant.

■ **FACTS**

Minimed, Inc. (D) hired a pest control company to spray its office building for fleas. The next day, nine employees, including Irma Hernandez (D), fell ill while at work. After alerting two supervisors that she felt ill, Hernandez (D) decided to leave work early. On her way home, Hernandez rear-ended Bussard (P). Hernandez told police she felt dizzy and lightheaded before the accident. Bussard (P) sued Hernandez (D) for negligence and Minimed (D) under the theory of respondeat superior, alleging Hernandez (D) was acting within the scope of her employment at the time of the accident. Minimed (D) moved for summary judgment, arguing that the "going and coming" rule established that Hernandez (D) was not within the scope of her employment while commuting home. The court granted the summary judgment motion.

■ **ISSUE**

Is an employee traveling home after suffering exposure to pesticide fumes at work in the course of employment so that her employer may be liable for injuries caused by her negligence?

■ **DECISION AND RATIONALE**

(Rubin, J.) Yes. "Under the doctrine of respondeat superior, an employer is ordinarily liable for the injuries its employees cause others in the course of their work," whether or not the employer itself had control over the employee. While employee acts necessary to the comfort, convenience, health, and welfare of the employee while at work fall within the course of employment, traveling to and from work does not. Known as the "going-and-coming rule," the employment relationship is suspended while the employee is away from work for purely personal reasons and without rendering services to the employer. However, when the employee endangers others during her commute and the danger is related to work, the going-and-coming rule does not apply.

Whether a danger is related to work is determined by whether the danger was inherent in or caused by the work and the dangerous consequences are foreseeable. For instance, when an employee consumes alcohol on work premises, the consequences are not so "unusual or startling" to make them unforeseeable. Here, Hernandez (D) suffered pesticide exposure while at work, impairing her ability to drive. The possibility of an accident after hours of exposure to pesticide fumes, leaving Hernandez (D) ill, is not so startling or unusual to bar the application of respondeat superior. Hernandez's (D) illness was created by her presence at work, making her job a contributing factor to her negligence. Vicarious liability does not require active negligence on the part of Minimed (D), so long as its employee was negligent and her work contributed to her negligence. Reversed.

Analysis:

As suggested by the opinion, the exception to the going-and-coming rule at issue here generally involves an employee who consumes alcohol while at work with the employer's knowledge, such as at a company party. An exception also applies to employees required to work unreasonably long shifts, resulting in sleepiness and fatigue. Regardless of the cause, when the employer reasonably should know that an employee is unfit to drive because of a workplace condition, vicarious liability will apply.

■ CASE VOCABULARY

GOING–AND–COMING RULE: The principle that torts committed by an employee while commuting to or from work are generally outside the scope of employment.

RESPONDEAT SUPERIOR: The doctrine holding an employer or principal liable for the employee's or agent's wrongful acts committed within the scope of employment or agency.

SCOPE OF EMPLOYMENT: The range of reasonable and foreseeable activities that an employee engages in while carrying out the employer's business.

VICARIOUS LIABILITY: Liability that a supervisory party (such as an employer) bears for the actionable conduct of a subordinate or associate (such as an employee) because of the relationship between the two parties.

O'Shea v. Welch

(Motorist) v. *(Osco Manager)*

350 F.3d 1101 (10th Cir.2003)

AN EMPLOYER MAY BE VICARIOUSLY LIABLE EVEN WHEN THE EMPLOYEE TAKES A SHORT SIDE–TRIP

■ **INSTANT FACTS** While traveling on business, Welch (D) struck O'Shea's (P) car during an impromptu service station stop.

■ **BLACK LETTER RULE** Under the slight deviation rule, a detour that involves a complete abandonment of the employment relationship relieves an employer of vicarious liability.

■ PROCEDURAL BASIS

Appeal to review a trial court decision granting summary judgment to the defendant.

■ FACTS

Welch (D) was driving from the Osco store he managed to the Osco District Office to deliver football tickets to Osco managers. Along the way, Welch (D) decided to pull into a service station for an estimate; he struck O'Shea's (P) car as he entered the station. O'Shea sued Welch (D) for negligence and Osco (D) for vicarious liability. On a motion for summary judgment, the court concluded that no reasonable jury could find that Welch (D) was acting within the scope of employment during the service station stop and entered judgment for Osco (D).

■ ISSUE

Is an employer relieved of vicarious liability by a short deviation from an employee's business trip to tend to maintenance of the employer's vehicle?

■ DECISION AND RATIONALE

(McKay, J.) No. Under the slight deviation rule, a detour that involves a complete abandonment of the employment relationship relieves an employer of vicarious liability, but here there was no such abandonment. It is true that "an employer is only liable for injuries caused by an employee acting within the scope of his employment." To be within the scope of employment, an employee must be performing actions for which he was employed or anything incidental to his employment. The conduct need not be specifically authorized or forbidden by the employer, but merely foreseeable from the nature of his employment. In cases like this, it must be determined whether the employee's actions constitute a detour, which may be conducted within the scope of employment, or a frolic, which involves a complete abandonment of the employment relationship. When the employee abandons his employer's business for his own personal reasons, the employment relationship is severed and the employer is not liable for the employee's actions. Personal acts not far removed from the employer's business, however, are considered incidental to the employment relationship. This determination must be left to the jury.

Upon consideration of the employee's intent in this case, the nature, time, and place of the deviation, the time consumed by the deviation, the work for which the employee was hired, the incidental acts reasonably expected by the employer, and the freedom allowed the employee in performing his job responsibilities, Welch (D) was within the scope of his employment. Welch (D) intended to stop for a maintenance inspection on a car used for Osco's (D) purposes. It occurred within minutes and feet of his direct business route and on the roadway before entering the service station. Further, the jury could conclude that, as a manager, Welch (D) had the freedom to attend to personal needs throughout the day, and that Osco (D) may have expected such maintenance stops to occur while on company business. Assuming that Welch (D) was within the scope of employment en route to the District Office, the jury could reasonably conclude that his stop was merely a slight deviation, remaining within the scope of his employment. Reversed and remanded for trial.

Analysis:

The line between a frolic and a detour can be a close one. Because personal business and employer business can be conducted at the same time, not all liability arising out of personal affairs will fall outside the scope of employment. The determination must be made by a jury on the basis of the facts.

■ CASE VOCABULARY

SCOPE OF EMPLOYMENT: The range of reasonable and foreseeable activities that an employee engages in while carrying out the employer's business.

VICARIOUS LIABILITY: Liability that a supervisory party (such as an employer) bears for the actionable conduct of a subordinate or associate (such as an employee) because of the relationship between the two parties.

Murrell v. Goertz

(Injured) v. *(Employee)*
597 P.2d 1223 (Okl.App.1979)

NEWSPAPER NOT RESPONSIBLE FOR DELIVERY BOY WHO STRUCK CUSTOMER

■ **INSTANT FACTS** Goertz (D), a delivery boy for Oklahoma Publishing (D), struck Murrell (P) after having an argument with her.

■ **BLACK LETTER RULE** Employer is not liable for the torts of his independent contractor.

■ **PROCEDURAL BASIS**

Appeal from grant of summary judgment in action for damages for intentional tort and imputed intentional tort.

■ **FACTS**

Westbrook, not a party to this action, was an independent newspaper distributor for Oklahoma Publishing (D). He employed Goertz (D) as an employee to deliver newspapers. However, Oklahoma Publishing (D) had no knowledge of Goertz's (D) employment in this capacity. When Goertz delivered the morning newspaper to Murrell (P), an argument occurred, whereupon Murrell (P) slapped Goertz (D). Goertz (D) retaliated by striking Murrell (P), resulting in a hospital stay and pain and suffering.

■ **ISSUE**

Is an employer liable for the torts of an independent contractor?

■ **DECISION AND RATIONALE**

(Reynolds) No. It is well settled that a company is not liable for the torts of his independent contractor. If a company does not have the right to control the physical details of the work of a worker, the worker is an independent contractor and not an employee. In this case, Oklahoma Publishing (D) did not have the right to control the work of Goertz (D) because he was an employee of Westbrook. In fact, Oklahoma Publishing (D) did not even know of Goertz's (D) existence. Thus, Goertz (D) was an independent contractor and not an employee of Oklahoma Publishing (D) and Oklahoma Publishing (D) is not liable for his torts. Judgment affirmed.

Analysis:

This case marks the outer limits of the doctrine of respondeat superior: An "employer" is not liable for the torts of his independent contractor. An independent contractor is a worker who independently completes a task for the "employer," and is not under the direct control and supervision of "employer." Is this line of demarcation fair? After all, from plaintiff's viewpoint, he has still suffered injury, and he suffered injury because the "employer" hired the tortfeasor, whether the tortfeasor is classified as an employee or an independent contractor. Moreover, an "employer" is still in the best position to spread the costs of injury. The answer may simply be that it is unfair to hold an "employer" liable for the torts of an independent contractor because an "employer" has no control over the acts of independent contractor and thus can do nothing to prevent the injury.

■ **CASE VOCABULARY**

INDEPENDENT CONTRACTOR: A person who works for employer to complete a task but is not under the direct control and supervision of "employer."

Maloney v. Rath

(Injured) v. *(Employer)*

69 Cal.2d 442, 71 Cal.Rptr. 897, 445 P.2d 513 (1968)

A MOTORIST IS RESPONSIBLE FOR A MECHANIC'S NEGLIGENCE

■ **INSTANT FACTS** Rath's (D) car collided with Maloney's (D) car because Evanchik negligently repaired Rath's (D) brakes.

■ **BLACK LETTER RULE** A motorist cannot delegate her duty to keep her brakes in working order to an independent contractor.

■ PROCEDURAL BASIS

Appeal from judgment for defendant in action for damages for imputed negligence.

■ FACTS

Rath (D) hired Evanchik to repair her brakes; he negligently repaired them. Three months afterwards, the brakes failed and Rath (D) collided with Maloney (P). Maloney (P) seeks to hold Rath (D) liable for Evanchik's negligence under a theory of respondeat superior.

■ ISSUE

Can a motorist delegate her duty to keep her brakes in working order to an independent contractor?

■ DECISION AND RATIONALE

(Traynor) No. As an initial matter, we note that some duties of care may not be delegated to third parties. In such cases, if a third party is injured because of the negligence of an independent contractor, that third party may hold the "employer" directly liable because his duty of care was nondelegable to an independent contractor. Nondelegable duties include: (i) the duty of a general contractor to construct a building safely, (ii) the duty of landowners to maintain their lands in a safe condition and (iii) the duty of employers and suppliers to comply with the Labor Code. Of more relevance to this case, the Restatement provides that (i) one who carries on an activity that presents a grave risk of serious bodily harm may not delegate his duty of care to an independent contractor and (ii) one who is under duty by statute to provide safeguards for the safety of others may not delegate his duty of care to an independent contractor. In this case, Rath (D) was driving an automobile, which certainly presents a grave risk of serious bodily harm. Moreover, Rath (D) was required by the Vehicle Code to keep her car brakes in good working order. Thus, Rath's (D) duty to keep her brakes in good working order was nondelegable to Evanchik. Judgment reversed.

Analysis:

In this case, the court broadens the doctrine of respondeat superior by limiting the independent contractor defense. Recall in *Murrell* that the court there was attempting limit the doctrine of respondeat superior, perhaps because the "employer" had no control over the activities of the independent contractor and thus was not in a position to prevent the injury. Did Rath (D) in this case have the ability to prevent the accident? Unless she has had training in brake repair, she probably was unqualified to assess the quality of the mechanic's work, and thus was not in a position to prevent the injury. Yet she is still held liable. Perhaps the court fails to recognize the independent contractor defense because Rath (D) is in a better position to mitigate the costs of such accidents by purchasing automobile insurance.

■ CASE VOCABULARY

NONDELEGEGABLE DUTY: A duty of care which may not be delegated to a third party because of public policy considerations.

Popejoy v. Steinle

(*Injured*) v. (*Member of Enterprise*)

820 P.2d 545 (Wyo.1991)

FAMILY TRIP TO PURCHASE A CALF IS NOT A JOINT VENTURE OR ENTERPRISE

■ **INSTANT FACTS** While Connie Steinle (D) was taking her daughter and niece to purchase a calf for the daughter to raise on the ranch, Steinle negligently collided with Popejoy (P).

■ **BLACK LETTER RULE** A defendant is not vicariously liable for the negligence of another under a theory of joint venture unless the joint venture was motivated by profit.

■ **PROCEDURAL BASIS**

Appeal from grant of summary judgment in action for damages for imputed negligence.

■ **FACTS**

While Connie Steinle (D) was taking her daughter and niece to purchase a calf for the daughter to raise on the ranch, the truck Steinle was driving negligently collided with Popejoy's (P) vehicle. Connie Steinle (D) died as a result of the accident. Fifteen months after the accident, Popejoy (P) began experiencing serious pain in his back and required surgery. After Popejoy (P) unsuccessfully attempted to reopen Connie Steinle's estate, which had been closed, he filed a claim against the representative of William Steinle (D), who had died in the interim. Popejoy (P) seeks to impute Connie Steinle's (D) negligence to William Steinle (D), arguing that he is vicariously liable for her negligence because her "business trip" to pick up the daughter's calf was part of a joint venture with William (D).

■ **ISSUE**

Is a defendant vicariously liable for the negligence of another under a theory of joint venture if the joint venture was not motivated by profit?

■ **DECISION AND RATIONALE**

(Golden, J.) No. First, given the facts of this case, there is no relevant distinction between joint enterprise and joint venture. The restatement gives the following four elements of joint enterprise: (i) an agreement among the members of the group; (ii) a common purpose; (iii) a community of pecuniary interest; and (iv) an equal right of control of the enterprise. In *Holiday v. Bannister* [hunter father is liable under joint enterprise theory for negligence of hunter son who accidentally shot and killed another hunter] we emphasized the importance of the profit motive. We emphasized this element because it is not appropriate to import the commercial concept of joint venture into social settings. In this case, it is clear that Connie Steinle (D) was not in a joint venture or enterprise with William Steinle (D). First, there is ample evidence that Connie Steinle (D) was going to purchase the calf as a pet for her daughter. Second, although it is true that the daughter's calf and other pets were often sold, the proceeds from such sale did not go to the account of Connie Steinle (D) and William Steinle (D), but to the account of the daughter. In sum, Connie Steinle (D) and William Steinle (D) were not in a joint venture because there was no profit motive to their actions. Thus, William Steinle (D) cannot be vicariously liable for the negligence of Connie Steinle (D).

Analysis:

This case introduces the concept of joint venture as a basis for vicarious liability. It picks up where the doctrine of respondeat superior leaves off. Under the doctrine of respondeat superior, an employer is responsible for the negligence of his employee committed within the scope of employment. If there is not an employer/employee relationship but a partner relationship, respondeat superior does not apply. Rather, in partner relationships, there is vicarious liability if the two partners had a profit motive. But why is this the case? The test for vicarious liability in employer/employee contexts is control, not profit motive. The answer may ??e in the simple reality that in business partnerships, no one person controls another, rather, it is in fact a partnership of equals. The joint venture doctrine simply recognizes this reality and adjusts the test for liability accordingly, in this case the court also states that it is improper to impose vicarious liability because this relationship was a social relationship. But recall that with the family automobile statutes, parents are held liable vicariously for the negligence of their children and other permittees. Why should there be liability in one social setting but not the other? The answer may simply be that courts and legislatures wish to discourage a parent from handing over the keys to a teenager. Law school exams often ask the writer to distinguish between (i) the employer/employee relationship, (ii) the independent contractor/principal relationship and (iii) the joint venture/social relationship.

■ CASE VOCABULARY

JOINT VENTURE/ENTERPRISE: An (i) agreement (ii) carried out by a group (iii) for profit (iv) with each member of the group having equal right of control.

Shuck v. Means

(Injured) v. *(Sub-Bailee)*

302 Minn. 93, 226 N.W.2d 285 (1974)

HERTZ LIABLE FOR DAMAGE CAUSED BY ONE OF ITS RENTAL CARS

■ **INSTANT FACTS** Hertz (D) leased a rental car to Codling. Codling permitted Means (D) to drive this car. Means (D) negligently collided with and injured Shuck (P).

■ **BLACK LETTER RULE** A car rental agency is liable for the negligence of an individual who drives its rental car, even though it did not rent the car to that individual.

■ PROCEDURAL BASIS

Appeal from judgment for plaintiff in action for damages for imputed negligence.

■ FACTS

Hertz (D) leased a rental car to Codling. Codling permitted Means (D) to drive this car. Means (D) negligently collided with and injured Shuck (P). Means was uninsured at the time of the accident.

■ ISSUE

Is a car rental agency liable for the negligence of an individual who drives its rental car but to whom it did not rent the car?

■ DECISION AND RATIONALE

(Kelly, J.) Yes. We start with the statute which provides, generally, that an owner of an automobile is liable for the negligence of an operator of the automobile if the owner gave permission to the operator. This statute is to be interpreted liberally to give injured individuals an avenue of recourse against automobile owners, and to encourage automobile owners to obtain insurance. This court has interpreted this statute to impose liability on an owner when a subpermittee negligently caused damage. This interpretation is based on the belief that permission, as used by statute, refers to permission given by the owner for use of the car, not use of the car by a particular individual. Moreover, we held that an owner is liable for a subpermittee's negligence even if the owner explicitly forbade the operation by the subpermittee. In this case, it is clear that Hertz (D) gave permission for the use of its vehicle. This single fact makes Hertz (D) liable for Means' (D) negligence. It does not matter that it did not give permission Judgment affirmed.

Analysis:

In this case the court finds liability not based upon an employment relationship, but based upon a bailment. A bailor entrusts a car to bailee, the bailee loans it to a sub-bailee, the sub-bailee causes damage, and the bailor is liable. This case and cases like it clearly attempt to force the owner to obtain insurance, because insurance is the easiest method to shift the cost to someone who is most able to bear it, in the case of automobiles, this seems especially fair. But how far does this bailment theory go? If I loan my bat to a pinch hitter, and the pinch hitter decides to hit the pitcher with the bat during a ball field brawl, am I liable for the damages? Clearly I cannot insure for such types of intentional torts. This is perhaps the reason why legislatures have not legislated for vicarious liability for other types of bailments.

Smalich v. Westfall

(Injured passenger) v. *(Negligent driver)*
440 Pa. 409, 269 A.2d 476 (1970)

PASSENGER-OWNER-PLAINTIFF NOT VICARIOUSLY CONTRIBUTORILY NEGLIGENT IN CAR ACCI-DENT TRAGEDY

■ **INSTANT FACTS** Smalich (P) was killed as a passenger in her own car when Westfall (D), the operator, negligently smashed her car into Blank's (D) car.

■ **BLACK LETTER RULE** Contributory negligence may not be imputed to a passenger riding in her own automobile without the finding of either a master-servant relationship or a finding of joint enterprise.

■ **PROCEDURAL BASIS**

Appeal from reversal of judgment in action for damages for negligence.

■ **FACTS**

Smalich (P) was killed as a passenger in her own car when Westfall (D), the operator, negligently smashed her car into Blank's (D) car. Blank (D) and Westfall (D) defended by arguing that Smalich (P) was barred from recovery because, as the owner of the negligently driven automobile, Westfall's (D) negligence was imputed to her.

■ **ISSUE**

May contributory negligence of a driver be imputed to a passenger riding in her own automobile without a finding of either a master-servant relationship or of joint enterprise between the driver and the passenger?

■ **DECISION AND RATIONALE**

(Eagen) No. We first state the general rule: A driver's negligence will not be imputed to a passenger unless the relationship between them is such that the passenger would be vicariously liable as a defendant for the driver's negligence. And a passenger will only be vicariously liable for the negligence of a driver when there is either a master-servant relationship or a finding of joint enterprise. In the ordinary situation such as this, we doubt that the owner-passenger has the right and ability to control the actions of the negligent driver. It seems that the more reasonable mutual understanding is that the driver will use reasonable care, retaining control, yet subject to the duty of obedience to the owner-passenger as to such things as destination. And this is exactly what happened in this case. Smalich (P) gave control of the vehicle to Westfall (D). Thus, negligence could not have been imputed to her, and therefore she cannot be barred from recovery by imputed contributory negligence. Judgment reversed.

■ **CONCURRENCE**

(Roberts) I concur only in the result reached by the court because the court continues to place too much emphasis on the physical control that a master may exert over a servant. In the real world, a passenger can never safely exercise operational control of a vehicle. Moreover, unlike imputing negligence to an defendant owner-passenger, there is no policy justification for imputing contributory negligence to a plaintiff owner-passenger.

Analysis:

This case highlights the policy rationale for imputed negligence by looking at contributory negligence. Recall that in cases like *Lundberg* and *Fruit,* the injured party was neither the operator, passenger nor owner, but a third party. In those cases, courts often imputed liability to the car owner or employee out of a desire to find a financially responsible defendant. Here, however, imputing contributory negligence to a plaintiff obviates the need to find a financially responsible defendant because it prevents recovery by the plaintiff. The plaintiff is left injured, perhaps ruined for life, without any recourse to any defendant, let alone a financially responsible defendant. And all of this without being negligent. Thus, in these cases, contributory negligence may not be imputed as a defense.

CHAPTER FOURTEEN

Strict Liability

Rylands v. Fletcher

Instant Facts: Fletcher (D) built a water reservoir which busted and flooded Rylands' (P) coal mine.

Black Letter Rule: A person carrying on an abnormally dangerous activity is absolutely liable for any damage caused by that activity, even though he was not negligent.

Miller v. Civil Constructors, Inc.

Instant Facts: After Miller (P) was struck by a stray bullet fired from the defendant's gravel pit, he filed suit alleging strict liability.

Black Letter Rule: A defendant is liable when he damages another by a thing or activity unduly dangerous and inappropriate to the place where it is maintained, in the light of the character of that place and its surroundings.

Indiana Harbor Belt R.R. Co. v. American Cyanamid Co.

Instant Facts: American Cyanamid (D) loaded a railway car with toxic chemicals. At Indiana Harbor's (P) railroad yard, these chemicals leaked, causing Indiana Harbor (P) to incur cleanup charges.

Black Letter Rule: The manufacture and shipping (as opposed to carrying) of toxic chemicals is not abnormally dangerous.

Foster v. Preston Mill Co.

Instant Facts: Blasting operations by Preston Mill Co. (D) frightened a mink owned by Foster (P), causing the mink to eat her kittens.

Black Letter Rule: A person carrying on an abnormally dangerous activity is not strictly liable for damage which is not within the scope of danger created by that activity.

Golden v. Amory

Instant Facts: Amory (D) operated a dike and an hydroelectric plant. A hurricane caused the Chicopee river to overflow and cause damage to Amory's (P) real estate.

Black Letter Rule: A person carrying on an abnormally dangerous activity is not absolutely liable if damage caused by that activity was precipitated by an act of God.

Sandy v. Bushey

Instant Facts: Sandy's (P) horse was on Bushey's (D) property. When Sandy (P) went to feed his horse, Bushey's (D) horse kicked Sandy (P), causing injury.

Black Letter Rule: The owner of an animal known to the owner to be vicious is strictly liable for damage caused by the animal. Contributory negligence is not a defense to strict liability.

Rylands v. Fletcher

(Injured) v. *(Tortfeasor)*

(1868) L.R. 3 H.L. 330

EVEN WITHOUT FAULT, DEFENDANTS MUST PAY FOR DAMAGE CAUSED BY ABNORMALLY DAN-
GEROUS ACTIVITIES

■ **INSTANT FACTS** Fletcher (D) built a water reservoir which burst and flooded Rylands' (P) coal mine.

■ **BLACK LETTER RULE** A person carrying on an abnormally dangerous activity is absolutely liable for any damage caused by that activity, even though he was not negligent.

■ **PROCEDURAL BASIS**

Appeal from reversal of judgment in complaint for damages for damage caused by a bursting reservoir.

■ **FACTS**

Fletcher (D) wanted to build a water reservoir. Rylands (P) owned a coal mine composed of two parts, the old part and the new part. The new part, which Rylands (P) worked on a regular basis, was not underneath the land where Fletcher (D) was to build his water reservoir. However, the old part was underneath this area. When Fletcher (D) decided to build his reservoir on this area, he was without fault. When the contractors and engineers were excavating the bed for the reservoir, they found certain shafts relating to Rylands' (P) old mine, but they negligently disregarded these shafts, although no fault was attributable to Fletcher (D). Soon after the reservoir was constructed, it burst downward and flooded Rylands' (P) mine.

■ **ISSUE**

Is a person carrying on an abnormally dangerous activity absolutely liable for any damage caused by that activity, even though he was not negligent?

■ **DECISION AND RATIONALE**

(Blackburn) Yes. The basic rule of negligence is that a plaintiff must bear the costs of any damage caused by the defendant unless the plaintiff can show that the damage was caused by defendant's fault or negligence. Thus, every defendant has the obligation to take due care in his daily life. In this case, we must decide what obligation rests on a person who brings abnormally dangerous activities onto his land. Everyone agrees that such a person must at all times exercise due care. If he is not negligent, but the abnormally dangerous activity causes damage anyway, he must still pay, because he brought something onto his land which was not naturally there. This is the law in other instances as well. For example, if cattle escapes a farmer's premises and eats the grass of a neighbor, the farmer is liable, even if he exercised due care, because he brought something onto his land which was not naturally there, namely, cattle. Here, Fletcher (D) built a reservoir on his land, something which was not naturally there. Thus, he is absolutely liable for the damage caused to Rylands (P). Judgment reversed.

■ **DISSENT**

(Cairns) Fletcher (D) should not be liable for the damage caused to Rylands' (P) mine because Fletcher (D) was using his land in an ordinary and customary fashion. Rylands (P) knows that the laws of nature

---

sometimes cause reservoirs to burst such as happened here, so he could have constructed a barrier to protect himself.

Analysis:

This case establishes the rule of strict liability for damage caused by a defendant carrying on abnormally dangerous activity on his land. Note that this rule substitutes only for the fault element of tort liability. All of the other elements, such as causation, remain in place. Moreover, this rule operates only in the absence of fault. If the defendant is at fault, he is liable without regard to the rule of strict liability. And if the plaintiff is negligent, then the rules of contributory or comparative negligence operate, even though defendant may have been carrying on an abnormally dangerous activity.

■ CASE VOCABULARY

ABNORMALLY DANGEROUS ACTIVITY: Any activity where: (1) the risk of harm is great, (2) the harm which could materialize is great, (3) any damage could not have been prevented with the exercise of due care, (4) the activity was not one of common usage, (5) the activity was inappropriate to the place in which it took place and (6) the value to the community of the activity is not great compare to the unavoidable risk.

STRICT LIABILITY: Liability without fault.

VIS MAJOR: An act of God.

Miller v. Civil Constructors, Inc.

(Injured Plaintiff) v. *(Landowner)*

272 Ill.App.3d 263, 651 N.E.2d 239 (1995)

DISCHARGING FIREARMS IS NOT AN ULTRAHAZARDOUS ACTIVITY

■ **INSTANT FACTS** After Miller (P) was struck by a stray bullet fired from the defendant's gravel pit, he filed suit alleging strict liability.

■ **BLACK LETTER RULE** A defendant is liable when he damages another by a thing or activity unduly dangerous and inappropriate to the place where it is maintained, in the light of the character of that place and its surroundings.

■ **PROCEDURAL BASIS**

Appeal to review a decision of a county circuit court dismissing counts in the plaintiff's complaint.

■ **FACTS**

Miller (P) sued Civil Constructors, Inc. (D) after he was struck by a stray bullet that ricocheted during firearm practice in the defendant's gravel pit. Miller's (P) complaint alleged strict liability in that his injuries arose from an ultrahazardous activity for which the defendant was liable because of its control over the gravel pit or its discharge of the firearms. The county circuit court dismissed Miller's (P) strict liability counts.

■ **ISSUE**

Is the use of firearms an ultrahazardous activity, triggering strict liability?

■ **DECISION AND RATIONALE**

(Bowman, J.) No. Strict liability is derived from the English rule set forth in *Rylands v. Fletcher* (1868), L.R. 3 H.L. 330. Under the *Rylands* rule, "the defendant will be liable when he damages another by a thing or activity unduly dangerous and inappropriate to the place where it is maintained, in the light of the character of that place and its surroundings." Under this rule, strict liability is imposed by classing the activity as ultrahazardous, regardless of the level of care exercised by the landowner.

The *Rylands* rule has been incorporated in the Restatement (Second) of Torts. To determine whether an activity is ultrahazardous, § 520 of the Restatement directs a court to determine the "existence of a high degree of risk of some harm to the person, land or chattel of others," the "likelihood that the harm that results from it will be great," the "inability to eliminate the risk by the exercise of reasonable care," the "extent to which the activity is not a matter of common usage," the "inappropriateness of the activity to the place where it is carried on," and the "extent to which its value to the community is outweighed by its dangerous activities." While not all factors must weigh against the defendant, the court must establish that the risk is so substantial that strict liability is warranted although ordinary care is exercised.

Taking these factors into account, the use of firearms is not ultrahazardous. The risk of harm from discharging a firearm can virtually be eliminated with ordinary care; the harm caused from firearms comes from their misuse rather than their inherent nature. Also, in this instance, the activity occurred in a firing range, and no evidence suggests the gravel pit was an inappropriate location for firearm usage.

Finally, target practice has some social use to the community when performed by law enforcement officers, demonstrating it is not ultrahazardous. Affirmed.

Analysis:

By establishing a set of factors for determining whether an activity is ultrahazardous, the Restatement implicitly acknowledged that what may be dangerous in one set of circumstances may be sufficiently safe under different circumstances. The focus, therefore, appears to be more on the environment surrounding the activity than the nature of the activity itself.

■ CASE VOCABULARY

STRICT LIABILITY: Liability that does not depend on actual negligence or intent to harm, but that is based on the breach of an absolute duty to make something safe.

Indiana Harbor Belt R.R. Co. v. American Cyanamid Co.

(Injured) v. *(Tortfeasor)*

916 F.2d 1174 (7th Cir.1990)

MANUFACTURING AND SHIPPING TOXIC CHEMICALS IS NOT ABNORMALLY DANGEROUS

■ **INSTANT FACTS** American Cyanamid (D) loaded a railway car with toxic chemicals. At Indiana Harbor's (P) railroad yard, these chemicals leaked, causing Indiana Harbor (P) to incur cleanup charges.

■ **BLACK LETTER RULE** The manufacture and shipping (as opposed to carrying) of toxic chemicals is not abnormally dangerous.

■ **PROCEDURAL BASIS**

Appeal from judgment in action for damages.

■ **FACTS**

American Cyanamid (D) loaded a railway car with Acrylonitrile, a toxic chemical, to ship to its New Jersey plant. The car stopped at Indiana Harbor's (P) railroad yard for purposes of switching to another train. While parked in Indiana Harbor's (P) yard, the car began to leak, and 4,000 of the 20,000 gallons spilled. Concerned that there was contamination of the soil, the Illinois Department of Environmental Protection ordered Indiana Harbor (P) to take decontamination measures costing $981,022.75. Indiana Harbor (P) is sung American Cyanamid (D) for this amount.

■ **ISSUE**

Is the manufacture and shipping (as opposed to carrying) of toxic chemicals an abnormally dangerous activity?

■ **DECISION AND RATIONALE**

(Posner) No. Since this is a diversity case, Illinois law governs. The parties agree that the Illinois Supreme Court would look to the restatement for guidance in resolving this novel issue. According to the restatement, an abnormally dangerous activity meets the following criteria: (1) the risk of harm is great, (2) the harm that would occur if the risk materialized is great, (3) such accidents could not be prevented by the exercise of due care, (4) the activity is not a matter of common usage, (5) the activity is inappropriate to the place in which it occurs and (6) the value to the community of the activity does not outweigh the unavoidable risk. The restatement imposes strict liability in any case that meets this test because the common law doctrine of negligence is inadequate in such cases. For example, the negligence doctrine is inadequate to deter accidents if due care will not prevent such accidents. In such cases, defendants will cause accidents, but will not be made to pay for the accidents or will have no incentive to avoid the accidents. The elements of the restatement test are designed to mitigate this by imposing strict liability on defendants who, for example, fail to move such activities to less populated or more appropriate areas (element no. 5). We now look to the facts of this case. First, the district court ruled that manufacturing and shipping Acrylonitrile is abnormally dangerous merely because it was on a certain list of hazardous materials. This is too broad a definition because it would make shippers and carriers of many chemicals strictly liable. Moreover, there is no reason why a negligence test will not work here—due care would have prevented this accident. Put another way, it was not the inherent dangerousness of Acrylonitrile that caused this accident, but someone's negligence which caused a leak. Plaintiff argues that there should be strict liability because the potential harm was great—what if all 20,000 gallons were spilled? But for an activity to be deemed to be abnormally dangerous, we must examine all factors of the restatement test, and plaintiff's argument overlooks the fact that shipping chemicals is very valuable to the community. Thus, manufacturing Acrylonitrile is not abnormally dangerous. Judgment reversed.

Analysis:

Compare this case to *Rylands v. Fletcher* and other cases involving dangerous substances. In those cases, there was liability because there was indeed an abnormally dangerous activity: the abnormally dangerous activity was storage of dangerous substances or chemicals. In this case, Indiana Harbor (P) attempted to hold American Cyanamid (D) liable not for the dangerous activity of storage of Acrylonitrile, but for the manufacturer of Acrylonitrile. The manufacture of Acrylonitrile may be an abnormally dangerous activity (which the court did not decide), but American Cyanamid (D) was not manufacturing Acrylonitrile when this accident occurred. And hauling Acrylonitrile may be an abnormally dangerous activity, but American Cyanamid (D) was not the hauler in this case.

■ CASE VOCABULARY

CARRIER: A person or entity who hauls a product to an intermediate or final destination.

MANUFACTURER: A person or entity who creates a product for sale.

SHIPPER: A person or entity who prepares a product for hauling.

Foster v. Preston Mill Co.

(Injured) v. *(Tortfeasor)*

44 Wash.2d 440, 268 P.2d 645 (1954)

BLASTING CAUSES MINK TO EAT HER KITTENS, BUT NO LIABILITY

■ **INSTANT FACTS** Blasting operations by Preston Mill Co. (D) frightened a mink owned by Foster (P), causing the mink to eat her kittens.

■ **BLACK LETTER RULE** A person carrying on an abnormally dangerous activity is not strictly liable for damage which is not within the scope of danger created by that activity.

■ **PROCEDURAL BASIS**

Appeal from judgment in complaint for damages for damage caused blasting operations.

■ **FACTS**

Preston Mill Co. (D) was conducting blasting operations. These operations frightened a mother mink owned by Foster (P). Consequently, the mother mink killed her kittens, causing Foster (P) $1,958.68 in damages.

■ **ISSUE**

Is a person carrying on an abnormally dangerous activity strictly liable for damage which is not within the scope of danger created by that activity?

■ **DECISION AND RATIONALE**

(Hamley) No. We agree with the authorities and the restatement which state that a person, in carrying on an abnormally dangerous activity, is strictly liable for any damages which lie within the scope of the danger created by the activity. This is the rule because there must be some reasonable bounds to the liability imposed by strict liability. Applying this rule to the present case, we find no liability. What makes blasting an abnormally dangerous activity is the possibility of damage from flying debris or air concussions, not the possibility of a mink killing her kittens. Judgment reversed.

Analysis:

This case limits liability, in cases of abnormally dangerous activity, to damages which lie within the scope of what makes the activity dangerous. This limit is placed on the doctrine of strict liability because one of the goals of strict liability is to deter abnormally dangerous activities only when the value of such activities is outweighed by the reasonable interests of the community. Here, however, the court was simply unwilling to consider the raising of nervous mink as outweighing the useful social activity of blasting. In other words, scaring mink is not what makes blasting abnormally dangerous.

■ **CASE VOCABULARY**

ULTRAHAZARDOUS: An abnormally dangerous activity.

Golden v. Amory

(*Injured*) v. (*Tortfeasor*)

329 Mass. 484, 109 N.E.2d 131 (1952)

DIKE BURSTS, BUT NO STRICT LIABILITY BECAUSE RIVER OVERFLOW CAUSED BY ACT OF GOD

■ **INSTANT FACTS** Amory (D) operated a dike and an hydroelectric plant. A hurricane caused the Chicopee river to overflow and cause damage to Amory's (P) real estate.

■ **BLACK LETTER RULE** A person carrying on an abnormally dangerous activity is not absolutely liable if damage caused by that activity was precipitated by an act of God.

■ PROCEDURAL BASIS

Appeal from directed verdict in action for damages for damage caused by an overflowing river near a dike.

■ FACTS

Amory (D) operated a dike and an hydroelectric plant. Because of the presence of the dike and the plant, a hurricane which caused the Chicopee river to overflow caused damage to Amory's (P) real estate.

■ ISSUE

Is a person carrying on an abnormally dangerous activity absolutely liable if damage caused by that activity was precipitated by an act of God?

■ DECISION AND RATIONALE

(Lummus) No. The basic rule announced in *Rylands v. Fletcher* is that a defendant is liable for damages caused by an abnormally dangerous activity that he brings onto his land. However, the rule of *Rylands v. Fletcher* does not apply when an intervening act of God precipitates the damage. In this case, although it is true that Amory (D) was operating a dike and a hydroelectric plant, which are abnormally dangerous activities, there is no liability because a hurricane, which is an act of God, precipitated the damage. Judgment affirmed.

Analysis:

To understand why there is no liability when there is an intervening act of God, reconsider the case of *Foster v. Preston Mill Co.* In that case there was no liability because the damage caused to the mink was not within the scope of the danger created by the blasting. Likewise in this case, there is no liability because an overflowing river is not within the scope of danger created by a dike. Rather, what makes the operation of a dike an abnormally dangerous activity is the possibility of the dike bursting. A dike presents danger of overflow only when there is an intervening act of God.

■ **CASE VOCABULARY**

VIS MAJOR: Act of God.

Sandy v. Bushey

(Injured) v. *(Tortfeasor)*
124 Me. 320, 128 A. 513 (1925)

OWNER LIABLE FOR DAMAGE CAUSED BY KICKING HORSE

■ **INSTANT FACTS** Sandy's (P) horse was on Bushey's (D) property. When Sandy (P) went to feed his horse, Bushey's (D) horse kicked Sandy (P), causing injury.

■ **BLACK LETTER RULE** The owner of an animal known to the owner to be vicious is strictly liable for damage caused by the animal. Contributory negligence is not a defense to strict liability.

■ **PROCEDURAL BASIS**

Appeal from judgment in action for damages for injury caused by vicious animal.

■ **FACTS**

Sandy's (P) horse was on Bushey's (D) property. Bushey (D) had his own horse on his property, and his horse was known to him to be vicious. When Sandy (P) went to feed his horse, Bushey's (D) horse approached in a threatening manner. Sandy (P) drove the horse away, but the horse returned and kicked him, causing injury.

■ **ISSUE**

(1) Is the owner of an animal known to be vicious, strictly liable for damage caused by the animal? (2) Is contributory negligence a defense to strict liability?

■ **DECISION AND RATIONALE**

(Sturgis) (1) Yes. At common law, there was no liability for injury caused by a domestic animal if the animal was in a place where it had a right to be. However, there was strict liability if the animal caused damage and was known by the owner to be vicious. This is the rule of law in Maine. In this case, the facts disclose that Bushey's (D) horse was known to Bushey (D) to be vicious. (2) No. Bushey (D) tries to escape liability by arguing that he should not be liable because Sandy (P) was contributorily negligent. We reject this argument. Although some states prevent recovery where an injury has been caused by an animal and where the plaintiff has been contributorily negligent, those states use the theory of negligence for cases involving animals. This does not apply in this state because we use strict liability in cases involving animals. Thus, in this state, to escape liability, the defendant must show that the plaintiff actively put himself in a position to bring the injury upon himself. That was not the case here. In fact, Sandy (P) attempted to lead Bushey's (D) horse away. And because Bushey (D) knew that the horse was vicious, he is strictly liable for the damage caused to Sandy (P). Judgment affirmed.

Analysis:

An owner of an animal known to be vicious is strictly liable for all damage caused by the animal. To understand why this should be, reconsider the elements of abnormally dangerous activities enunciated in *Indiana Harbor Belt R.R. Co. v. American Cyanamid Co.*: (1) the risk of harm is great, (2) the harm

---

that would occur if the risk materialized is great, (3) such accidents could not be prevented by the exercise of due care, (4) the activity is not a matter of common usage, (5) the activity is inappropriate to the place in which it occurs and (6) the value to the community of the activity does not outweigh the unavoidable risk. The fifth element is at work here: vicious animals have no place near humans. Thus, the rule of strict liability, with the absence of contributory negligence as a defense, creates an incentive for the owners of animals known to be vicious to keep such animals away from humans.

■ **CASE VOCABULARY**

VICIOUS ANIMAL: An animal known to the owner to have violent tendencies.

CHAPTER FIFTEEN

Products Liability

MacPherson v. Buick Motor Co.

Instant Facts: MacPherson (P) was injured when he was thrown from his car after one of the wheels, made of defective wood, crumbled and the car collapsed.

Black Letter Rule: When there is an element of probable danger with a product, the manufacturer is under a duty to make it carefully.

Baxter v. Ford Motor Co.

Instant Facts: Baxter (P) sued Ford (D) when the windshield of his Model A Ford shattered despite Ford's (D) express warranty to the contrary.

Black Letter Rule: The breach of an express warranty is actionable in tort, even absent privity of contract, if a purchaser of ordinary experience and reasonable prudence could not have discovered the defect.

Henningsen v. Bloomfield Motors, Inc.

Instant Facts: An automobile purchaser sued the dealer and manufacturer for breach of an implied warranty of merchantability, although the express contractual terms of the sale disclaimed all implied warranties.

Black Letter Rule: A contract of adhesion does not trump statutory implied warranties of merchantability.

Greenman v. Yuba Power Products, Inc.

STRICT LIABILITY SURFACES AS BASIS FOR PRODUCTS LIABILITY RECOVERY

Instant Facts: A woodworker sued, under theories of negligence and breach of warranty, for injuries caused by a defective power lathe.

Black Letter Rule: Manufacturers are strictly liable for injuries caused by defective products if the user does not know of the defects.

Rix v. General Motors Corp.

Instant Facts: An injured driver sued a manufacturer for defectively designing and/or manufacturing a truck, which caused injury when its brake system failed and it rear-ended the injured party's vehicle.

Black Letter Rule: Sellers are strictly liable for manufacturing defects that reach the consumer without substantial change in the defective condition.

Prentis v. Yale Mfg. Co.

Instant Facts: A forklift operator who was injured when operating the handle sues for an alleged design defect, the failure of the manufacturer to install a seat on the forklift.

Black Letter Rule: Design defect cases should be judged under a negligence test, weighing the risks of injury against the costs of safer designs.

O'Brien v. Muskin Corp.

Instant Facts: A young man who dove into a shallow above-ground pool sued the manufacturer for designing the pool with a slippery bottom, and for failure to warn of the inherent danger.

Black Letter Rule: A plaintiff must make a prima facie showing of a defective product, based on the risk-utility analysis.

Anderson v. Owens–Corning Fiberglas Corp.

Instant Facts: An electrician sued an insulation manufacturer for failure to warn of the risks of asbestos exposure.

Black Letter Rule: Evidence that a particular risk was neither known nor knowable by the application of scientific knowledge available at the time of manufacture and/or distribution provides a defense to warnings defect cases.

Friedman v. General Motors Corp.

Instant Facts: A driver sued the automobile manufacturer for injuries when his automobile started and went out of control after he turned the ignition switch when the indicator was in the "drive" position.

Black Letter Rule: Circumstantial evidence of defects may be used to make a prima facie case.

Daly v. General Motors Corp.

Instant Facts: A driver who was intoxicated and not wearing a seat belt was killed when an allegedly defective door latch gave way.

Black Letter Rule: Comparative fault principles can be applied to strict products liability actions.

Ford Motor Co. v. Matthews

Instant Facts: A tractor operator was killed when the defective safety switch allowed the tractor to be started in gear.

Black Letter Rule: Manufacturers are liable for reasonably foreseeable, albeit abnormal, uses of their products.

Medtronic, Inc. v. Lohr

Instant Facts: Lohr (P) was implanted with a pacemaker which was faulty and failed, resulting in a "complete heart block" which required emergency surgery.

Black Letter Rule: The Medical Device Amendments of 1976, a federal statute, does not preempt a state common-law negligence action against the manufacturer of an allegedly defective medical device.

Peterson v. Lou Bachrodt Chevrolet Co.

Instant Facts: The father of two children injured in an automobile accident sued the used car dealer for strict products liability because the used car was sold without adequate brakes.

Black Letter Rule: A remote retailer, who outside of the original producing and marketing chain, is not subject to strict products liability.

Hector v. Cedars–Sinai Medical Ctr.

Instant Facts: A patient sued the hospital for allowing a defective pacemaker to be inserted into the patient.

Black Letter Rule: Providers of medical services are not subject to strict products liability.

MacPherson v. Buick Motor Co.

(Car Buyer) v. *(Auto Manufacturer)*
217 N.Y. 382, 111 N.E. 1050 (1916)

AUTO MANUFACTURER HELD LIABLE TO PURCHASER OF DEFECTIVE VEHICLE

■ **INSTANT FACTS** MacPherson (P) was injured when he was thrown from his car after one of the wheels, made of defective wood, crumbled and the car collapsed.

■ **BLACK LETTER RULE** When there is an element of probable danger with a product, the manufacturer is under a duty to make it carefully.

PRIVITY OF CONTRACT: The relationship between the parties to a contract that is necessary to maintain an action on that contract.

■ PROCEDURAL BASIS

Appeal from the judgment of the Appellate Division, affirming a judgment of the Supreme Court for the plaintiff.

■ FACTS

Buick Motor Co. (D) made a new automobile using parts it purchased from its various suppliers. Buick neglected to inspect and perform safety tests on the automobile before it was sold to a retail dealer [what could go wrong with a new car?]. MacPherson (P) then bought this car from the dealer. While MacPherson (P) was driving the car, one of the wheels, which was made of defective wood, crumbled into fragments [darn termites]. The car collapsed and MacPherson (P) was thrown out and injured. There was evidence that the defects could have been discovered if Buick (D) had performed a reasonable inspection.

■ ISSUE

Does a manufacturer owe a duty of care and vigilance to anyone other than the immediate purchaser of a product?

■ DECISION AND RATIONALE

(Cardozo, J.) Yes. We hold that if the nature of a thing is such that it is reasonably certain to place life and limb in peril when negligently made, it is then a thing of danger. If there is added knowledge that the thing will be used by persons other than the purchaser, then the manufacturer of this thing is under a duty to make it carefully. There must be knowledge of a danger, not merely possible, but probable. It is possible to use almost anything in a way that will make it dangerous if defective. That is not enough to charge the manufacturer with a duty independent of his contract. Whether a thing is dangerous may be sometimes a question for the court and sometimes a question for the jury. It is also possible that even knowledge of the danger and of the use will not always be enough. The proximity or remoteness of the relation is also a factor to be considered. We are dealing now with the liability of the manufacturer of the finished product, who puts it on the market to be used without inspection. If he is negligent, where danger is foreseen, liability will follow. We think Buick Motor Co. (D) was not absolved from a duty of inspection because it bought the wheels from a reputable manufacturer. It was not merely a dealer in automobiles; it was responsible for the finished product. It was not at liberty to put

---

the finished product on the market without subjecting the component parts to ordinary and simple tests. The obligation to inspect must vary with the nature of the thing to be inspected. The more probable the danger, the greater the need of caution. The judgment should be affirmed with costs.

Analysis:

In *MacPherson*, the court left it to the jury to decide whether Buick (D) should have foreseen that the car, if negligently constructed, would become dangerous. If danger was to be expected as reasonably certain, there was a duty of vigilance. It seems abundantly reasonable that a jury would find that a car could be a dangerous thing. Automobiles are dangerous things even when constructed *correctly*; the peril to life and limb is inherent. Perhaps a manufacturer should be held accountable if it is responsible for turning a thing which has so much potential for danger into a thing which is probable to cause harm. Buick (D) argued that it only owed a duty to the immediate purchaser. This argument was upheld, as the immediate purchaser was a dealer. The dealer is not the user of the product, but merely a middleman for the transfer of the product. Thus the peril to the dealer is really nonexistent.

■ CASE VOCABULARY

DUTY OF CARE: One must avoid negligent injury to others.

Baxter v. Ford Motor Co.

(*Automobile Purchaser*) v. (*Automobile Manufacturer*)

168 Wash. 456, 12 P.2d 409 (1932)

NO PRIVITY REQUIRED FOR RECOVERY BASED ON BREACH OF EXPRESS WARRANTY

■ **INSTANT FACTS** Baxter (P) sued Ford (D) when the windshield of his Model A Ford shattered despite Ford's (D) express warranty to the contrary.

■ **BLACK LETTER RULE** The breach of an express warranty is actionable in tort, even absent privity of contract, if a purchaser of ordinary experience and reasonable prudence could not have discovered the defect.

■ **PROCEDURAL BASIS**

Appeal from directed verdict denying tort recovery to injured party for breach of express warranty.

■ **FACTS**

Baxter (P) purchased a Model A Ford from St. John Motors (D), who had acquired the automobile from Ford Motor Co. (D). Ford's (D) catalogues, given to Baxter (P) by St. John (D) prior to sale, represented that the car had a shatter-proof glass windshield which would not shatter under the hardest impact. However, Baxter (P) was injured when, while driving his Model A, a pebble struck and shattered the window, causing glass to fly into Baxter's (P) eyes. Baxter (P) lost sight in his left eye, and his right eye was injured. The trial court refused to admit evidence of Ford's (D) printed warranty. The court took the case from the jury and entered judgment for St. John (D) and Ford (D). Baxter (P) appealed.

■ **ISSUE**

Can a tort action be maintained for breach of an express warranty, even when there is no privity of contract between the injured party and the warranting party?

■ **DECISION AND RATIONALE**

(Herman, J.) Yes. A tort action can be maintained for breach of an express warranty, even when there is no privity of contract between the injured party and the warranting party. Baxter (P) reasonably relied upon Ford's (D) printed warranty. He was not in a position to discover by reasonable investigation whether shatter-proof glass was used in the windshield. It has been held that, under such circumstances, a manufacturer may be liable to a consumer, even though the consumer purchased the product from a third person. In *Mazetti v. Armour & Co.*, this court held that a restaurant keeper could recover damage to his business when a customer was served defective canned food manufactured by the defendant. The case at bar is analogous. The *Mazetti* rule does not rest upon contractual obligations, but rather on the principle that the original act of delivering the product is wrong when, because a product lacks certain qualities that the manufacturer had warranted, the article is not safe for ordinary use. The lack of these qualities must not be readily detectable by a person of ordinary experience and reasonable prudence. The traditional doctrine of caveat emptor does not apply in some modern situations where, as here, it would be unjust to apply the rule to permit manufacturers from making false representations and escape liability to those not in privity of contract. We hold that

---

Ford's (D) printed material was improperly excluded from evidence. It was for the jury to determine whether Ford's (D) failure to properly equip the windshield was the proximate cause of Baxter's (P) injury. Reversed with respect to Ford (D). Affirmed as to St. John (D).

Analysis:

This case presents an excellent analysis of the concept of express warranties as a basis for recovery in tort based on products liability. Notice that the topic of warranties overlaps both tort and contract law. An action for breach of contract can be maintained for violation of an express or implied warranty, but typically only by those in privity of contract. Because Baxter (P) did not purchase the automobile directly from Ford (D), Baxter (P) could not sue for breach of contract. However, this opinion notes that it would be unfair for Ford (D) to escape liability for its false representations simply because there was no direct relationship between it and Baxter (P). Ford clearly was in the wrong here. It published a catalogue that contained false information, and Baxter (P) was justified in relying thereon, since Baxter (P) was not in a position to discover the defect himself. Once again, public policy determinations drive the court's opinion. Note also that the distributor, St. John (D), was absolved from liability. St. John (D) made no express warranties, and apparently the court did not feel that St. John (D) should be liable under an implied warranty theory, even though it was in privity with Baxter (P). Not surprisingly, the second trial resulted in a verdict in favor of Baxter (P), which was upheld on appeal. Ford (D) argued on appeal that it should not be liable, since there was no way to make a better windshield. Indeed, if Ford (D) had never made false representations, this evidence probably would have resulted in a judgment in Ford's (D) favor. However, as the opinion notes, Ford (D) should not have represented the windshield to be safe unless Ford (D) was certain that it was safe.

■ CASE VOCABULARY

CAVEAT EMPTOR: Buyer beware; a traditional doctrine that the purchaser of goods has no recourse against the seller for defects.

PRIVITY OF CONTRACT: A relationship between persons who contract, such as between a buyer and seller of goods, that imposes duties and liabilities upon the contracting parties.

Henningsen v. Bloomfield Motors, Inc.

(Auto Purchaser) v. *(Auto Dealer)*

32 N.J. 358, 161 A.2d 69 (1960)

IMPLIED WARRANTIES OF MERCHANTABILITY SURVIVE EXPRESS CONTRACTUAL PROVISIONS TO THE CONTRARY

■ **INSTANT FACTS** An automobile purchaser sued the dealer and manufacturer for breach of an implied warranty of merchantability, although the express contractual terms of the sale disclaimed all implied warranties.

■ **BLACK LETTER RULE** A contract of adhesion does not trump statutory implied warranties of merchantability.

■ **PROCEDURAL BASIS**

Certification to New Jersey Supreme Court of appeal of judgment awarding damages for breach of implied warranty of merchantability.

■ **FACTS**

Mr. Henningsen purchased a car from Bloomfield Motors Inc. (D), a retail dealer. The car had been manufactured by Chrysler Corporation (D). Mr. Henningsen gave the car to his wife for Christmas. Mrs. Henningsen (P) was badly injured a few years later when the steering gear failed and the car turned right into a wall. When he purchased the car, Mr. Henningsen signed a contract without reading the fine print. The fine print contained a "warranty" clause which disclaimed all implied warranties and which granted an express warranty for all defects within 90 days or 4000 miles, whichever came first. Mrs. Henningsen (P) sued Bloomfield (D) and Chrysler (D). The trial court dismissed her negligence counts but ruled for Mrs. Henningsen (P) based on the implied warranty of merchantability. Bloomfield (D) and Chrysler (D) appealed.

■ **ISSUE**

Does a contract of adhesion trump statutory implied warranties of merchantability?

■ **DECISION AND RATIONALE**

(Francis, J.) No. A contract of adhesion does not trump statutory implied warranties of merchantability. In order to ameliorate the harsh effects of the doctrine of caveat emptor, most states have imposed an implied warranty of merchantability on all sales transactions. This warranty simply means that the thing sold must be reasonably fit for the general purpose for which it is manufactured and sold. The warranty extends to all foreseeable users of the product, not merely those in privity of contract with the seller. In order to avoid the implied warranty obligations, many manufacturers, including Chrysler (D) and all other automobile manufacturers, include an express warranty provision which disclaims all statutory implied warranties. We must determine what effect to give this express warranty. Under traditional principles of freedom of contract, the law allows parties to contract away obligations. However, in the auto sales context, the fine-print disclaimer of implied warranties is a contract of adhesion. It is a standardized form contract, and the purchaser has no opportunity to bargain for different terms. He must "take it or leave it," and he cannot shop around to different dealers because all of them use the same standard contract. Because the purchaser and seller occupy grossly inequal bargaining positions, we feel that justice must trump the principle of freedom of contract. Chrysler's (D) attempted disclaimer of an implied warranty of merchantability is so inimical to the public good as to compel an adjudication of its invalidity. Affirmed.

Analysis:

This opinion notes several conflicting interests and principles which the court must weigh. First, the traditional principle of caveat emptor faces the modern doctrine of implied warranties of merchantability. The court has little difficulty in holding that modern commercial transactions require protection for purchasers. An implied warranty of merchantability is imposed in all auto sales transactions in order to protect the buyer. Second, the requirement of privity of contract is weighed against an implied warranty. The court notes that, in modern sales transactions, a warranty safeguards all consumers of a product, not merely those in direct contractual privity with the seller. Third, the principle of freedom of contract is weighed against this implied warranty. Freedom of contract is one of the fundamental tenets of the law. Parties should be free to contract for any provisions, and generally parties are bound by the terms of their contract. However, an important exception exists when a contract is one of adhesion. Contracts of adhesion typically involve terms in fine print, written by a powerful seller to limit liabilities or impose responsibilities upon an unsuspecting buyer. No bargaining occurs for these terms, and indeed the buyer is in no position to bargain. If the buyer attempts to change the terms of the contract, the seller simply will not complete the transaction. In order for a contract to be considered "adhesive" or "unconscionable," the buyer usually has nowhere else to go. As in the case at bar, all sellers of a particular type of goods may include similar terms in their adhesive contracts. Weighing all of these factors, a court may rule that the express contractual terms are invalid, notwithstanding the principle of freedom of contract.

■ CASE VOCABULARY

CONTRACT OF ADHESION: A contract between parties of unequal bargaining position, where the buyer must "take it or leave it."

IMPLIED WARRANTY OF MERCHANTABILITY: A warranty that means that the thing sold must be reasonably fit for the general purpose for which it is manufactured and sold.

Greenman v. Yuba Power Products, Inc.

(Purchaser) v. *(Manufacturer)*

59 Cal.2d 57, 27 Cal.Rptr. 697, 377 P.2d 897 (1963)

STRICT LIABILITY SURFACES AS BASIS FOR PRODUCTS LIABILITY RECOVERY

■ **INSTANT FACTS** A woodworker sued, under theories of negligence and breach of warranty, for injuries caused by a defective power lathe.

■ **BLACK LETTER RULE** Manufacturers are strictly liable for injuries caused by defective products if the user does not know of the defects.

■ PROCEDURAL BASIS

Appeal from denial of motion for new trial following verdict for damages for injuries caused by defective product.

■ FACTS

Greenman (P) saw a demonstration of a Shopsmith (a combination power tool that could be used as a saw, drill and lathe), and he studied a brochure prepared by the manufacturer, Yuba Power Products Inc. (D). Greenman's (P) wife gave him a Shopsmith for Christmas. While properly using the Shopsmith to lathe a piece of wood, Greenman (P) was injured when the wood flew out of the machine and struck him. Almost a year later, Greenman (P) sued Yuba Power (D) and the retailer based on breach of implied and express warranty and negligence theories. Evidence at trial showed that the Shopsmith was defectively designed and constructed. The jury returned a verdict in favor of the retailer but against Yuba Power (D) based on a negligence and/or breach of express warranty theory. The court denied Yuba Power's (D) motion for a new trial and entered judgment on the verdict. Yuba Power (D) appealed.

■ ISSUE

Is a manufacturer strictly liable when an article he places on the market, knowing that it is to be used without inspection for defects, proves to have a defect that causes injury?

■ DECISION AND RATIONALE

(Traynor, J.) Yes. A manufacturer is strictly liable when an article he places on the market, knowing that it is to be used without inspection for defects, proves to have a defect that causes injury. Yuba Power (D) argued that Greenman (P) was barred from recovery because he did not provide notice of the defect to Yuba Power (D) within a reasonable time after the injury, as required by section 1769 of the Civil Code. We hold that section 1769 does not apply to actions by injured consumers against manufacturers with whom they have not dealt. Greenman's (P) action for breach of the express warranties contained in the brochure is not barred. Moreover, Greenman (P) was not required to establish that Yuba Power (D) even made an express warranty. This action is not governed by the contract law of express warranties, but rather by the tort law of products liability. Yuba Power (D) would be strictly liable if the Shopsmith caused injury and if Yuba Power (D) knew that the Shopsmith was to be used without inspection for defects. The purpose of such liability is to insure that the costs of injuries resulting from defective products are borne by the manufacturers who out such products on the market. Greenman (P) was not required to prove any breach of warranty. He proved that he was injured while using the Shopsmith in a way it was intended to be used as a result of a defect in design and manufacture, of which Greenman (P) was not aware, that made the Shopsmith unsafe for its intended use.

Analysis:

This case greatly simplifies the law of products liability. Rather than resting on the pseudo-contractual theories of express or implied warranties, the court adopts a strict liability approach. Regardless of whether any express warranty was made, and regardless of whether the law should impose an implied warranty of merchantability, a manufacturer is liable under a certain set of circumstances. Strict products liability requires four elements: (1) a defective product; (2) use of the product in the manner it was intended to be used; (3) injury as a result; and (4) knowledge by the manufacturer that the product was to be used without inspection for defects. The first three elements make a good deal of sense, but the fourth element poses potential problems. In the instant action, the court does not even discuss whether Yuba Power (D) knew that the Shopsmith was to be used without inspection for defects. In addition, the court rephrases this element in the final sentence of the opinion, stating only that the user must not have had actual knowledge of the defect. Perhaps this element is largely overlooked. But why doesn't the law require a purchaser to make at least a brief inspection before using a potentially dangerous product? Wouldn't a reasonable consumer check to make sure that the Shopsmith was securely constructed before using it? Perhaps the fourth element should be changed to impose liability only for defects that could not have been discovered by a reasonable inspection.

■ CASE VOCABULARY

STRICT LIABILITY: Liability imposed, without any proof of wrongdoing, if certain threshold conditions are met.

Rix v. General Motors Corp.

(Driver) v. *(Truck Manufacturer)*

222 Mont. 318, 723 P.2d 195 (1986)

SELLERS FACE STRICT LIABILITY FOR SELLING PRODUCTS IN DEFECTIVE CONDITION UNREASONABLY DANGEROUS TO CONSUMERS

■ **INSTANT FACTS** An injured driver sued a manufacturer for defectively designing and/or manufacturing a truck, which caused injury when its brake system failed and it rear-ended the injured party's vehicle.

■ **BLACK LETTER RULE** Sellers are strictly liable for manufacturing defects that reach the consumer without substantial change in the defective condition.

■ **PROCEDURAL BASIS**

Appeal from jury verdict for manufacturer for action for design and/or manufacturing defect.

■ **FACTS**

Michael Rix (P) was injured when his pickup was rear-ended by a new General Motors Corporation (D) two-ton truck, which had been equipped with a water tank after sale. Rix (P) sued GMC (D) on a theory of strict liability. The parties stipulated that the accident occurred because of brake failure caused by a brake tube dislodging from a booster unit. Rix (P) argued that there was a manufacturing defect in the tube when it left the assembly line. Rix (P) also argued that the brake system was defectively designed. According to Rix (P), a truck of this size should have been equipped with a dual braking system in order to provide extra braking power. GMC (D) contended that the tube was defective because it had been altered after it left the GMC (D) assembly line. Further, GMC (D) maintained that the single braking system was not unreasonably dangerous, and that the accident would have occurred even if a dual braking system was present. Rix (P) appealed a jury verdict for GMC (D), arguing that the jury was not properly instructed on the law of manufacturing defects.

■ **ISSUE**

Is a manufacturer strictly liable if it sells a product in defective condition unreasonably dangerous and it causes injury?

■ **DECISION AND RATIONALE**

(Weber, J.) Yes. A manufacturer is strictly liable if it sells a product in defective condition unreasonably dangerous to the consumer and it causes injury. The product must be defective at the time it was sold, and it must have been expected to and must actually reach the consumer without substantial change in the defective condition. Manufacturing defects are imperfections that inevitably occur in a small percentage of products of a given design as a natural result of the fallibility of the manufacturing process. It is of no concern whether the intended design was safe or not. As long as the above-stated test is met, a manufacturer is strictly liable. We conclude that the jury was properly instructed regarding manufacturing defects. Reversed and remanded.

Analysis:

This case exemplifies the modern approach to products liability. Note that Rix (P) did not purchase the vehicle from GMC (D). Products liability suits are often based on some alleged defect, either in manufacturing, design, or improper instructions and warnings. In the case at hand, Rix (P) argued alternative theories of recovery. First, Rix (P) maintained that the particular GMC (D) truck had a manufacturing defect. Even if GMC (D) had taken all possible care in designing the braking system for its truck, and even if this braking system was the best of all possible systems, GMC (D) can still face liability if the truck at issue left the assembly line with some deviation from the intended design. Notice that liability is imposed even if GMC (D) was not negligent. However, it may be argued that any manufacturing defect actually is a negligent act by the manufacturer, i.e., by allowing a product to be offered for sale when its construction departed from the rest of the products made by the manufacturer. Of course, a manufacturer can escape liability by proving that the defect was caused at some later point, after the consumer had taken control of the product. Thus, it is not surprising that Rix (P) also alleged a design defect. GMC (D) could be liable for the design defect even if Rix's (P) own actions caused the defective braking system, provided Rix (P) could prove that a reasonable truck manufacturer should foresee the risks of such a defect and should provide a backup braking system. GMC's (D) defense of the design defect claim would likely rest on proof that the brakes would have failed even if GMC (D) had employed a dual braking system. Most manufacturing defect suits also involve some allegation of a design defect as a backup theory of recovery. Finally, note the important general requirement for products liability based on defects: the product must have been sold in a defective condition unreasonably dangerous to the consumer.

■ CASE VOCABULARY

DESIGN DEFECT: An imperfection that occurs when the foreseeable risks of harm posed by a product could have been reduced by the adoption of a reasonable alternative design.

MANUFACTURING DEFECT: An imperfection that occurs when a specific product deviates from the manufacturer's intended design.

Prentis v. Yale Mfg. Co.

(Forklift Operator) v. *(Manufacturer)*

421 Mich. 670, 365 N.W.2d 176 (1984)

COURT APPLIES NEGLIGENCE APPROACH TO DESIGN DEFECT CASES

■ **INSTANT FACTS** A forklift operator who was injured when operating the handle sues for an alleged design defect, the failure of the manufacturer to install a seat on the forklift.

■ **BLACK LETTER RULE** Design defect cases should be judged under a negligence test, weighing the risks of injury against the costs of safer designs.

■ **PROCEDURAL BASIS**

Review of reversal of verdict for damages in design defect action.

■ **FACTS**

Prentis (P), a foreman in a automobile dealership's parts department, utilized a battery-powered forklift to lift an engine into a truck's cargo bed. The Yale Manufacturing (D) forklift was a stand-up variety, rather than a riding machine with a seat, and it was operated by lifting its handle up and down. When the machine experienced a power surge, Prentis (P) lost his footing and fell to the ground. The force of the fall alone caused multiple fractures to Prentis's (P) hip. Prentis (P) sued for an alleged design defect, arguing that Yale (D) should have provided a seat or platform for the operator of the forklift. The trial judge refused to instruct the jury on breach of warranty. Rather, the judge instructed the jury on a single theory of negligent design. The Court of Appeal reversed, holding that both instructions should have been given.

■ **ISSUE**

Should a negligence test apply to products liability actions predicated upon defective design?

■ **DECISION AND RATIONALE**

(Boyle, J.) Yes. A negligence test should apply to products liability actions predicated upon defective design. Courts have never gone so far as to make sellers absolute insurers of the safety of their products. Plaintiffs have always been required to prove that the product was defective. In manufacturing defect cases it is easy to determine whether a product is defective, since the condition of the product must be evaluated only against the manufacturer's own production standards. However, a strict liability test for determining whether a product's design is "defective" has proved problematic. In design defect cases, it is confusing to force juries to focus on the condition of a product rather than on the reasonableness of the manufacturer's conduct. Thus, we adopt a pure negligence, risk-utility test in products liability cases predicated upon defective design. This approach follows the Model Uniform Product Liability Act, and its rationale is sound. First, design defects result from deliberate decisions on the part of manufacturers, and plaintiffs should be able to learn about these facts. Second, a negligence standard would encourage the design of safer products by rewarding careful manufacturers. Third, a high threshold of fault is required in design defect cases, since a verdict for the plaintiff is a determination that the entire product line is defective. Fourth, the negligence standard promotes fairness, since a careful manufacturer should not bear the burden of paying for losses caused by a negligent seller. Our negligence theory is indistinguishable from a breach of implied warranty theory. Both involve identical evidence and require proof that the manufacturer failed to exercise reasonable care in the adoption of a safe plan of design, in light of any reasonably foreseeable use of the product. Thus, the trial judge's refusal to instruct on the breach of warranty was not reversible error. The judgment of the Court of Appeals is reversed and the judgment of the trial court is reinstated.

Analysis:

Just when the strict liability approach to defectively designed products was beginning to make sense, this case abandons that approach and substitutes a negligence standard. The difference is primarily one of semantics, however, since even the former strict liability approach required a determination of reasonableness. Furthermore, the negligence approach allows juries to focus on the manufacturer's conduct, rather than requiring a clear definition of the term "defective" and a focus on the condition of the product. Manufacturers can now escape liability in design defect cases if they can show that their conduct was reasonably safe, in light of the potential risks and the costs of safer alternatives. Judge Learned Hand's risk-utility approach surfaces once again! While this opinion does not apply the balancing approach to the facts at hand, it is not difficult to figure out what the approach requires. Basically, a jury must determine whether a product is as safe as it *should* be, considering the various costs and risks involved. The benefits of this approach are described in detail in the opinion, with the ultimate result being both fairness and the promotion of safer products.

■ CASE VOCABULARY

RISK-UTILITY ANALYSIS: A balancing of the risk of injury versus the costs of alternative designs.

O'Brien v. Muskin Corp.

(Diver) v. *(Pool Manufacturer)*

94 N.J. 169, 463 A.2d 298 (1983)

COURT EXPLAINS FACTORS TO CONSIDER IN RISK-UTILITY ANALYSIS FOR PRODUCT DEFECTS

■ **INSTANT FACTS** A young man who dove into a shallow above-ground pool sued the manufacturer for designing the pool with a slippery bottom, and for failure to warn of the inherent danger.

■ **BLACK LETTER RULE** A plaintiff must make a prima facie showing of a defective product, based on the risk-utility analysis.

■ **PROCEDURAL BASIS**

Review of reversal of judgment for defendants in action for damages for defective product.

■ **FACTS**

Gary O'Brien (P) was injured when he dove head-first into an above-ground swimming pool at his neighbor's house. The swimming pool was four feet deep, and the outer wall of the pool bore a decal that warned "DO NOT DIVE" in ½" high letters. O'Brien (P) dove either from a platform by the pool or from the roof of an adjacent eight-foot high garage. When O'Brien's (P) hands hit the bottom of the pool and contacted the vinyl bottom, his hands slid apart and his head struck the bottom. O'Brien (P) sued Muskin Corp. (D), the pool manufacturer, for a design defect (the slippery vinyl surface) and the lack of adequate warnings. The trial court did not allow the jury to consider whether manufacturing the pool with a vinyl liner constituted a design defect. Rather, the jury was allowed to consider only the adequacy of the warning. The appellate division reversed a judgment for Muskin (D), and O'Brien (P) appealed.

■ **ISSUE**

Does a plaintiff bear the burden of proving a design defect based on a risk-utility analysis?

■ **DECISION AND RATIONALE**

(Pollock, J.) Yes. The plaintiff bears the burden of proving a design defect based on a risk-utility analysis. Products liability cases predicated on a defective design or inadequate warning turn on the duty of the manufacturer to foreseeable users. Manufacturers have a duty not to place defective products on the market, and manufacturers are strictly liable for breaching this duty. A number of tests exist for determining whether a product is defective. One standard, the consumer expectations test, recognizes that the failure of a product to perform safely may be viewed as a violation of the reasonable expectations of a consumer. This standard does not apply to the instant action, however, because the pool fulfilled its function as a place to swim. Another test, the risk-utility analysis, is more appropriate for determining whether the pool was defective when used for diving. Factors relevant to the risk-utility analysis include the following: the usefulness and desirability of the product; the likelihood that the product will cause injury; the availability of a safer substitute product; the manufacturer's ability to eliminate the unsafe character of the product, and the associated costs; the user's ability to avoid danger by the exercise of reasonable care; the user's anticipated awareness of the inherent dangers and their avoidability; and the feasibility, on the part of the manufacturer, of spreading the loss by price-setting or through liability insurance. The ultimate burden is on the plaintiff to establish a prima facie case of defect with reference to the above-stated factors. The defendant may offer proof, in defense, through state-of-the-art evidence. Evidence that the manufacturer designed the product with state-of-the-art technology and materials, together with other evidence relevant to the risk-utility analysis, may support a judgment for the defendant. In the case at bar, the trial court should have permitted the jury to consider whether, because of the dimensions of the pool and the slipperiness of the bottom, the risks of injury so outweighed the utility of the product as to constitute a defect. Affirmed and remanded.

Analysis:

Overall, the case serves primarily to reiterate the factors previously delineated for the risk-utility analysis. The plaintiff must, of course, establish a prima facie case of liability based on the risk-utility test. What result should the trial court reach on remand in this case? In all likelihood, Muskin (D) should prevail. A reasonable user of the pool would know that a four-foot pool is unsafe for diving. Reasonable users can easily avoid injury by exercising care and not diving into the pool, or by executing shallow dives only. In addition, it would be very difficult for a manufacturer to eliminate the unsafe character of the pool. Although O'Brien (P) argued that the vinyl bottom caused his injuries, a more sensible result is that the shallow nature of the pool itself caused the injuries. Furthermore, it seems very difficult for Muskin (D) to eliminate the dangers. Muskin (D) could have installed a padded bottom, or a sticky surface, but even these characteristics could cause injury to a high diver. The opinion also mentions the consumer-expectations test. In many jurisdictions a reasonable consumer's expectations is simply one factor in the risk-utility analysis. In addition, the opinion references the "state-of-the-art" defense. A manufacturer may defend a design defect case by proving that the best scientific technology that was economically feasible was used in the product. Muskin (D) apparently established evidence that would support this defense, even in the unlikely event that O'Brien (P) could make his prima facie showing. Finally, note that manufacturers are potentially liable to any foreseeable users. Even though O'Brien (P) was an uninvited guest, and even though he had no connection to the purchase of the pool, he could still recover damages for his injuries if he prevails on the risk-utility analysis.

■ CASE VOCABULARY

CONSUMER-EXPECTATIONS TEST: A test for product defects based on the reasonable expectations of the consumer.

Anderson v. Owens–Corning Fiberglas Corp.

(*Electrician*) v. (*Insulation Manufacturer*)

53 Cal.3d 987, 281 Cal.Rptr. 528, 810 P.2d 549 (1991)

STATE-OF-THE-ART DEFENSE IS AVAILABLE IN FAILURE-TO-WARN ACTION

■ **INSTANT FACTS** An electrician sued an insulation manufacturer for failure to warn of the risks of asbestos exposure.

■ **BLACK LETTER RULE** Evidence that a particular risk was neither known nor knowable by the application of scientific knowledge available at the time of manufacture and/or distribution provides a defense to warnings defect cases.

■ **PROCEDURAL BASIS**

Review of appeal of verdict for manufacturer in action for failure to warn.

■ **FACTS**

Anderson (P) contracted asbestosis and other lung ailments through exposure to asbestos products while working as an electrician at a naval shipyard for 35 years. Anderson (P) encountered the asbestos while working in the vicinity of others who were removing and installing asbestos products aboard ships. Anderson (P) sued Owens-Corning Fiberglas Corp. (D) under a products liability theory, based upon Owens-Coming's (D) failure to warn of the risk of harm from asbestos exposure. The trial court allowed state-of-the-art evidence of the known and knowable risks of asbestos at the time Owens-Coming (D) distributed their insulation products. The trial court granted a new trial following a verdict for Owens-Corning (D). On appeal, the parties argued the admissibility of state-of-the-art evidence in a failure to warn case.

■ **ISSUE**

Is "state-of-the-art" evidence admissible in an action based upon a warnings defect?

■ **DECISION AND RATIONALE**

(Panelli, J.) Yes. Evidence of the state of the art is admissible in an action based upon an alleged failure to warn. State-of-the-art evidence is relevant to the issue of whether a particular risk was known or knowable by the application of scientific knowledge available at the time of manufacture and/or distribution. Knowledge or knowability must be an element of a cause of action for failure to warn in a products liability action. Exclusion of evidence of knowledge or knowability would make a manufacturer the virtual insurer of its products' safety. Strict liability was never intended to impose absolute liability upon manufacturers in this fashion. Anderson (P) argued that the knowability requirement and admission of state-of-the-art evidence improperly infuse negligence concepts into strict liability cases. However, many prior decisions have incorporated negligence principles into the strict liability analysis. In addition, warnings defects necessarily relate to a failure extraneous to the product itself. A failure to warn cannot be evaluated without reference to the conduct of a manufacturer. Failure to warn in strict liability differs markedly from failure to warn in the negligence context. Strict liability imposes a much lower hurdle for plaintiffs. They must only prove that the manufacturer ignored what was generally known or knowable in the scientific community about a product. There is no requirement to show that the manufacturer was unreasonable, as in a negligence action. Affirmed.

Analysis:

This case reaffirms that evidence of state of the art—i.e., evidence that a particular risk was either known or knowable in the scientific community at the time of manufacture and/or distribution—is relevant to cases based upon warnings defects. This evidence may provide a defense for a manufacturer. In brief, a manufacturer is not the absolute insurer of its products. The manufacturer should not be required to warn of defects that were not known or scientifically knowable. Apparently, the possibility of disease from asbestos exposure was one such defect. Manufacturers are still held to a high standard. They must analyze all known scientific data and must warn if any of the data shows risks from their products. Further, the "knowable" standard seems to impose some greater duty for a manufacturer to conduct its own tests. Here is the one area where the opinion may be questioned. The opinion asserts that failure to warn in the strict liability context is an easier claim to prove than failure to warn based upon a negligence theory. Indeed, if Owens-Corning's (D) own testing showed that the asbestos was safe, and if this result was contrary to that of others in the scientific community, then Owens-Corning (D) could still be liable under strict liability but not under negligence. However, what if the hypothetical were reversed? What if Owens-Corning's (D) testing showed asbestos to be dangerous, but the scientific community found no such risks? Would Owens-Corning (D) be liable for a failure to warn under negligence, but not strict liability, principles?

■ CASE VOCABULARY

ASBESTOSIS: A lung ailment caused by prolonged exposure to asbestos.

Friedman v. General Motors Corp.

(Driver) v. *(Automobile Manufacturer)*

43 Ohio St.2d 209, 331 N.E.2d 702 (1975)

CIRCUMSTANTIAL EVIDENCE MAY BE USED TO MAKE A PRIMA FACIE CASE OF PRODUCTS LIABILITY

■ **INSTANT FACTS** A driver sued the automobile manufacturer for injuries when his automobile started and went out of control after he turned the ignition switch when the indicator was in the "drive" position.

■ **BLACK LETTER RULE** Circumstantial evidence of defects may be used to make a prima facie case.

■ **PROCEDURAL BASIS**

Review of appellate decision overturning directed verdict against injured party in products liability action.

■ **FACTS**

Morton Friedman (P) alleged that his 17-month-old Oldsmobile Toronado was defective. Friedman (P) turned the ignition key while the gearshift was in the "drive" position. Although Friedman (P) did not expect the vehicle to start [why did he turn the key in the first place?], it leaped forward and caused Friedman (P) to lose control, injuring himself and his family. Friedman (P) sued General Motors (D), the manufacturer. Friedman (P) produced various circumstantial evidence in an attempt to show that the car was defective. The trial court granted GM's (D) motion for directed verdict on the ground that Friedman (D) had not proved that the vehicle was defective. The Court of Appeals reversed the judge's decision, ruling that reasonable minds could differ on the evidence presented. The Ohio Supreme Court granted review.

■ **ISSUE**

May a plaintiff utilize circumstantial evidence in order to make a prima facie case of a defective product?

■ **DECISION AND RATIONALE**

(Brown, J.) Yes. A plaintiff may utilize circumstantial evidence in order to make a prima facie case of a defective product. In the case at hand, Friedman (P) was required to prove that the automobile was defective, that the defect existed at the time the car left the factory, and that the defect was the proximate cause of injury. These elements may be proven by circumstantial evidence, where a preponderance of the evidence establishes that the accident was caused by a defect and not other possibilities. Friedman (P) did make a prima facie case based on circumstantial evidence. A jury could have found that the transmission linkages were created by the manufacturer and not some person after delivery. In addition, the jury might have inferred that the car started in Drive because the indicator registered in Drive after the accident. Further, the testimony of eyewitnesses and experts might have led the jury to conclude that the car accelerated immediately to 30 miles per hour upon ignition. Finally, the record clearly established that the Oldsmobile could not have started unless the transmission contacts were misaligned, since the car could not start unless the actual contacts in the neutral start switch were in Neutral or Park position. Viewing the evidence in a light most favorable to Friedman (P), we rule that a reasonable jury could have concluded that GM (D) was guilty of manufacturing a defective automobile. Affirmed.

■ DISSENT

(Stem, J.) Friedman (P) failed to make a prima facie case that the car was defective. In some cases, the defective nature of a product can be shown in a fashion similar to res ipsa loquitur, i.e., that the accident could not have occurred absent some defect. For example, a soda bottle does not ordinarily explode without a defect. However, a car can crash without a defect, because driver error may cause an accident. Friedman (P) could have proven that the indicator and transmission linkages were malaligned by several types of evidence. Friedman (P) could have introduced direct evidence by an expert, or direct evidence by testimony of the injured parties or eyewitnesses, that the most likely probable cause was a defect. In addition, Friedman (P) could have negated the existence of other potential causes that would not be attributable to GM (D). Finally, evidence of the actual condition of the product after the accident may be sufficient to allow a jury to infer that the product was defective. However, Friedman (P) produced evidence only that something unusual happened in the case, and that one possible explanation of that happening is a defect. Friedman (P) produced no expert testimony that the defect probably existed at the time the car was manufactured, and common experience does not permit any such inference. I would uphold the trial court's grant of directed verdict.

Analysis:

This case details the various types of evidence, whether circumstantial or direct, and whether by eyewitness or expert testimony, that can establish a defect. Unfortunately, the actual evidence produced by Friedman (P) is not described in sufficient detail to determine what is required to make a prima facie showing of a defective automobile. The most important lesson is that circumstantial evidence can be used to prove a defect. Indeed, circumstantial evidence is often the only available method of proof in products liability cases. For example, Friedman (P) could not prove that the transmission linkages and start contacts in his vehicle were actually misaligned when they left the manufacturer. There is no videotape to resort to, and interviews of people who made the vehicle (assuming they could even remember building the precise car in question) would prove fruitless. A plaintiff is left to prove that it is more probable than not that the accident was caused by a defect. But perhaps Friedman's (P) own error was the proximate cause of the accident. The notes following the case do provide a good summary. A plaintiff must show that the product was in fact manufactured by the defendant; that the product actually caused the injury; that the product was defective and proximately caused the injury, with no intervening causes (e.g., operator error); and that the defect existed when the product was sold. For some defects, the mere fact that a product went wrong may give rise to an inference that the product was defective and that the defect existed when it left the manufacturer. These are typically cases where some intervening cause could not have caused the injury.

■ CASE VOCABULARY

RES IPSA LOQUITUR: A doctrine in negligence cases when an accident "speaks for itself" and the mere occurrence proves that someone was negligent.

Daly v. General Motors Corp.

(Driver's Successor) v. *(Automobile Manufacturer)*

20 Cal.3d 725, 575 P.2d 1162 (1978)

COMPARATIVE FAULT PROVIDES A DEFENSE TO STRICT PRODUCTS LIABILITY

■ **INSTANT FACTS** A driver who was intoxicated and not wearing a seat belt was killed when an allegedly defective door latch gave way.

■ **BLACK LETTER RULE** Comparative fault principles can be applied to strict products liability actions.

■ **PROCEDURAL BASIS**

Appeal from verdict for defendant in action for injuries based on strict products liability.

■ **FACTS**

Daly (P) sued for the death of the driver of an Opel automobile, which was manufactured by General Motors Corp. (D). The driver was thrown from the automobile in an accident because of an alleged defect in the door latch. There was evidence that the driver did not use the seat belt and that he was intoxicated. General Motors (D) defended on the ground that recovery should be barred by the doctrine of contributory negligence or comparative fault. The jury found for GM (D). Daly (P) appealed.

■ **ISSUE**

Do comparative negligence principles apply to actions founded on strict products liability?

■ **DECISION AND RATIONALE**

(Richardson, J.) Yes. Comparative negligence principles apply to actions founded on strict products liability. Strict products liability is not absolute liability. We have previously held that a manufacturer is not liable when the injury results from an unforeseeable use of its product, and that a plaintiff's negligence is a complete defense when it comprises assumption of the risk. This case, however, involves comparative negligence rather than unforeseeable use or assumption of the risk. The driver was, according to GM (D), to some degree at fault for failing to wear a seat belt and for driving while intoxicated. The doctrine of comparative fault has not heretofore been applied to actions for strict products liability. Other courts have said that the application of the negligence defense of comparative fault to strict liability actions is like mixing oil and water, like apples and oranges. We are not inclined to decide this case based on such semantics and the precise definitional treatment of legal concepts. The most important goal is the attainment of a just and equitable result. Strict liability has been imposed against manufacturers in order to relieve injured consumers from problems in proof inherent in pursuing negligence remedies, and has been used to place the burden of loss on the manufacturer rather than powerless consumers. However, comparative fault will still protect the defenseless consumer. It will reduce an injured party's recovery only to the extent that his own lack of reasonable care contributed to his injury. In addition, plaintiffs will still be relieved from the difficult negligence standards of proof. Furthermore, comparative fault will not diminish a manufacturer's incentive to produce safe products, since manufacturers will not produce defective products on the slim chance that they can prove the injured party was comparatively at fault. In applying comparative fault principles, we abolish the defenses of contributory negligence and assumption of risk, which completely bar recovery if they are shown to have existed in any degree. Rather, an injured party who is comparatively at fault can still recover, with the recovery reduced in proportion to the amount of fault. Reversed.

Analysis:

This case raises a very difficult policy debate in the law of strict products liability. The concept of strict liability is typically antithetical to comparative fault principles, since strict liability does not require negligence and since comparative fault is a defense to negligence. However, the majority's rationale is sound. Assume that GM's (D) Opel was manufactured with a defective door latch. A driver injured by the defect, due to no fault of his own, should surely be able to recover by proving the defect existed at the time of manufacture. However, it is unfair to allow a person to recover in full when his own actions contributed to his injury. What if the latch would break loose and cause injury only if the driver was not wearing a seat belt, or was driving in such a dangerous fashion (perhaps due to intoxication) that he put undue strain on the latch. In these situations, the driver's conduct would actually contribute to the creation of the "defect." Viewed from this perspective, perhaps the doctrine of comparative fault only applies to determining whether a defect actually existed. If the driver's conduct contributed to his injury, then perhaps the latch was not defective at all under normal circumstances.

■ CASE VOCABULARY

ADROIT: Skillful under pressure.

AMICI CURIAE: Friends of the court; non-parties who submit legal briefs in a particular case to assist in the court's ruling.

ANOMALY: Departure from the norm.

FELICITOUS: Yielding great pleasure.

SYLLOGISM: A form of deductive reasoning.

Ford Motor Co. v. Matthews

(Tractor Manufacturer) v. *(Tractor Operator)*

291 So.2d 169 (Miss.1974)

MANUFACTURERS ARE LIABLE FOR ABNORMAL USES OF PRODUCTS THAT ARE REASONABLY FORESEEABLE

■ **INSTANT FACTS** A tractor operator was killed when the defective safety switch allowed the tractor to be started in gear.

■ **BLACK LETTER RULE** Manufacturers are liable for reasonably foreseeable, albeit abnormal, uses of their products.

■ **PROCEDURAL BASIS**

Appeal from judgment for damages based on strict products liability.

■ **FACTS**

Earnest Matthews (P) was killed as a result of being run over by his tractor. Matthews (P) was standing beside his tractor when he started it. The tractor was in gear at the time, even though the tractor was equipped with a starter safety switch designed to prevent the tractor from being started in gear. Matthews' (P) administratrix sued under strict products liability, contending that a plunger connected to the safety switch was defective and allowed the tractor to be started in gear. Ford (D) appealed a jury verdict for $74,272.65 for Matthews (P).

■ **ISSUE**

May a manufacturer be liable for injuries caused by reasonably foreseeable uses of its products?

■ **DECISION AND RATIONALE**

(Rodgers, J.) Yes. A manufacturer may be liable for injuries caused by reasonably foreseeable uses of its products. Ford (D) relies on a comment to the Restatement (Second) of Torts section 402A, which states that sellers are not liable for injuries resulting from abnormal handling of a product. However, the cases cited by Ford (D) are ones in which there was no defect, or where the defect played no part in the causation of the accident. In the case at bar, the failure of the safety switch to prevent the tractor from starting in gear was a cause of the accident. This was not such a misuse of the product as to relieve Ford (D) from liability. Indeed, manufacturers are not liable for injuries resulting from abnormal use of a product if such use was not reasonably foreseeable. However, manufacturers have a duty to foresee certain unintended uses of their products. It could be foreseen by Ford (D) that a tractor operator might carelessly start a tractor without first making sure that it was not in gear. Thus, even if Matthews (P) was negligent, such negligence was reasonably foreseeable and is not a bar to an action based on strict liability resulting from a defective tractor. Affirmed.

Analysis:

This case presents a different approach to comparative negligence and products liability. Rather than reducing the injured party's recovery due to his own comparative fault, as in *Daly v. General Motors*

Corp. [comparative fault principles apply to strict products liability], this court focuses solely on the scope of the manufacturer's duty. A manufacturer must undertake to determine the possible abnormal uses of its product. Indeed, Ford (D) apparently did just this, since it installed a safety switch to prevent starting the tractor while in gear. Matthews (P) injury was exactly the type of occurrence that Ford (D) foresaw in installing this switch. Thus, the case is fairly straightforward. The court treats foreseeability as a defense (i.e., no liability for actions not reasonably foreseeable), but it could easily be viewed as an issue of duty. Perhaps the court does not address the "duty" concept because it rings of negligence rather than strict liability.

Medtronic, Inc. v. Lohr

(Pacemaker Manufacturer) v. *(Pacemaker Patient)*

518 U.S. 470, 116 S.Ct. 2240, 135 L.Ed.2d 700 (1996)

STATE COMMON-LAW NEGLIGENCE ACTION NOT PREEMPTED BY FEDERAL STATUTE

■ **INSTANT FACTS** Lohr (P) was implanted with a pacemaker which was faulty and failed, resulting in a "complete heart block" which required emergency surgery.

■ **BLACK LETTER RULE** The Medical Device Amendments of 1976, a federal statute, does not preempt a state common-law negligence action against the manufacturer of an allegedly defective medical device.

■ PROCEDURAL BASIS

Appeal from Circuit Court's affirming in part and reversing in part of the trial court's decision granting Medtronic's (D) motion to dismiss.

■ FACTS

Lohr (P) was implanted with a Medtronic (D) pacemaker. She was dependent on the pacemaker for the proper functioning of her heart. Three years after the implantation, the pacemaker failed [shocking!]. This allegedly resulted in a "complete heart block," which required emergency surgery. Lohr's (P) physician stated that a defect in the lead was the likely cause of the failure. Lohr (P) filed suit in state court, alleging negligence and strict liability. The negligence count alleged a breach of Medtronic's (D) "duty to use reasonable care in the design, manufacture, assembly, and sale of the subject pacemaker." This claim included the use of defective materials in the lead and a failure to warn of the tendency of the pacemaker to fail, despite knowledge of other earlier failures [no witnesses, eh?]. The strict liability count alleged the pacemaker was defective and unreasonably dangerous at the time of its sale. A third count alleging breach of warranty was dismissed for failure to state a claim. Medtronic (D) removed the case to federal court and filed a motion to dismiss arguing that federal law [MDA of 1976] preempted the state common law claims.

■ ISSUE

Is a state common-law negligence action against the manufacturer of an allegedly defective medical device preempted by the Medical Device Amendments of 1976, a federal statute?

■ DECISION AND RATIONALE

(Stevens, J.) No. Congress enacted the Medical Device Amendments of 1976 (MDA) to provide for the safety and effectiveness of medical devices intended for human use. We are presented with the task of interpreting a statutory provision that expressly preempts state law. While the preemptive language of the statute means that we need not go beyond that language to determine whether Congress intended the MDA to preempt at least some state law, we must nonetheless identify the domain expressly preempted by that language. In all preemption cases, and particularly in those in which Congress has legislated in a field which the States have traditionally occupied, we start with the assumption that the historic police powers of the States were not to be superseded by the Federal Act unless that was the clear and manifest purpose of Congress. Additionally, the purpose of Congress is the ultimate touch-stone in every preemption case. As a result, any understanding of the scope of a preemption statute must rest primarily on a fair understanding of congressional purpose. This intent is discerned from the language of the preemption statute and the statutory framework surrounding it, as well as from the structure and purpose of the statute as a whole. Medtronic (D) argues that the statute effectively precludes state courts from affording state consumers any protection from injuries resulting from a defective medical device. It is, to say the least, difficult to believe that Congress would remove all means for judicial recourse for those injured by illegal conduct, and it would take language much plainer than the text of the MDA to convince us that Congress intended that result. The legislative history of the statute also confirms our understanding that the MDA simply was not intended to preempt most, let alone all, general common-law duties enforced by damages actions. The Lohrs (P) argue that their complaint should survive a reasonable evaluation of the preemptive scope of the MDA. First, the Lohrs (P) assert that their claims were not preempted because the statutory pre-market notification process imposes no "requirement" on the design of Medtronic's (D) pacemaker. Second, they suggest that even if the FDA's general regulation rules are "requirements" that preempt different state requirements, the MDA does not preempt state rules that merely duplicate some or all of those federal requirements. Finally, they argue that because the state's general rules imposing common-law duties upon Medtronic (D) do not impose a requirement "with respect to a device," they do not conflict with the FDA's general rules and are therefore not preempted. Preemption must occur only where a particular state requirement threatens to interfere with a specific federal interest. State requirements must be "with respect to" medical devices and "different from, or in addition to," federal requirements. The statute and regulations, therefore, require a careful comparison between the allegedly preempting federal requirement and the allegedly preempted state requirement to determine whether they fall within the intended preemptive scope of the statute and regulations. Such a comparison mandates a conclusion that the Lohrs' (P) common law claims are not preempted by the federal requirements. The general obligations of the manufacturer to use due care and to inform purchasers of risks therefore escape preemption not because the source of the duty is a judge-made common-law rule, but rather because their generality leaves them outside the category of requirements that the MDA envisioned to be "with respect to" specific devices such as pacemakers. As a result, none of the Lohrs' (P) claims based on allegedly defective manufacturing or labeling are preempted by the MDA. Accordingly, the judgment of the Court of Appeals is reversed insofar as it held that any of the claims were preempted and affirmed insofar as it rejected the preemption defense. The cases are remanded for further proceedings.

Analysis:

This was a very close decision, as the court split 4–4 on the issues and the fifth vote necessary to support the court's holding that the Lohrs' (P) claims were not preempted came from a justice who agreed with the dissent in most other regards. When the courts must determine whether a claim is to be preempted, because Congress' intent is not clear, there must be a case by case analysis, as the statutes themselves vary, and because some claims under a given statute may be preempted while others are not. When the intent of Congress is clear, however, it must be noted that the courts have no choice. The state law is preempted by the federal law, and the manufacturer need only comply with the federal statute and regulations. This is a highly contested area of law, and as the results show, there really is not a consensus of opinion. It seems possible that no decision will be safe from reconsideration in this arena!

■ CASE VOCABULARY

PREEMPTION: Judicial doctrine asserting that federal legislation has supremacy over state legislation on the same matter.

POLICE POWERS: Power of state governments to impose upon private rights in order to protect the public interests.

Peterson v. Lou Bachrodt Chevrolet Co.

(Father of Victims) v. *(Used Car Dealer)*

61 Ill.2d 17, 329 N.E.2d 785 (1975)

REMOTE RETAILERS CAN ESCAPE CLAIMS FOR STRICT PRODUCTS LIABILITY

■ **INSTANT FACTS** The father of two children injured in an automobile accident sued the used car dealer for strict products liability because the used car was sold without adequate brakes.

■ **BLACK LETTER RULE** A remote retailer, who outside of the original producing and marketing chain, is not subject to strict products liability.

■ **PROCEDURAL BASIS**

Review of appeal reversing dismissal of cause of action for strict products liability.

■ **FACTS**

Two young children, Maradean and Mark Peterson, were struck by a 1965 Chevrolet on September 3, 1971. Maradean died from her injuries, and one of Mark's legs had to be amputated. James Peterson (P), the children's father, sued the driver of the used car, its owners, and the used car dealer, Lou Bachrodt Chevrolet Company (D). Bachrodt Chevrolet (D) had sold the used car on June 11, 1971. One of Peterson's (P) claims was for strict products liability against Bachrodt Chevrolet (D). Peterson (P) alleged that, at the time the automobile left Bachrodt Chevrolet's (D) control, the car was defective and not reasonably safe for driving because the braking systems were missing several integral pieces. Bachrodt Chevrolet (D) defended on the ground that it was not liable under a strict products liability theory. The circuit court dismissed the products liability count, the appellate court reversed, and the Illinois Supreme Court granted review.

■ **ISSUE**

Is a remote retailer, who is outside of the original producing and marketing chain, subject to strict products liability?

■ **DECISION AND RATIONALE**

(Schaefer, J.) No. A remote retailer, who is outside of the original producing and marketing chain, is not subject to strict products liability. We have previously imposed strict products liability upon wholesalers through whose warehouse a packaged product passed unopened. Imposition of liability upon wholesalers, and upon some retailers, is justified if their position in the marketing process enables them to exert pressure on the manufacturer to enhance the safety of the product. Innocent wholesalers and retailers are subject to indemnity from the party who is ultimately responsible, i.e., the manufacturer. In the case at hand, there is no allegation that the defects existed when the product left the control of the manufacturer. Nor is there any allegation that the defects were created by the used car dealer. We decline to make used car dealers the insurer against defects which had come into existence after the chain of distribution was completed. Appellate court reversed; circuit court affirmed.

■ **DISSENT**

(Goldenhersh, J.) As the majority states, the rationale underlying the application of strict liability is that those who have created the risk and reaped the profit by placing a product in the stream of commerce

---

should be liable. This policy consideration applies with equal compulsion to all elements in the distribution system. Where a defect is discoverable upon reasonable inspection, a used car dealer who places the defective product in the stream of commerce should be subject to strict products liability.

Analysis:

Is it fair to hold every entity in the chain of distribution to the rigorous strict products liability standard? According to the majority in this case, the answer is no. The entire decision rests on a policy argument. This court feels that the main goal of products liability is to ensure the manufacture and distribution of safe products. Only those distributors who are in some position to exert pressure upon manufacturers to create safe products are subject to strict products liability. And apparently a lowly used car dealer is in no such position, since he probably purchased the vehicle from a prior consumer and not from anyone in the distribution chain. The majority's position can be seriously questioned. After all, didn't the used car dealer place an unreasonably dangerous product in the stream of commerce? What incentive is there for the used car dealer to sell safe products? Of course, Bachrodt Chevrolet (D) could still be liable under a negligence theory if it breached the standard of care of a typical used car dealer. But as we have seen, proof of this negligence cause of action is much more difficult than proof of strict products liability. As one of the notes indicates, a dealer is ordinarily not negligent for failing to open a sealed container and inspect its contents. Perhaps a used car dealer would similarly escape liability for failing to make sure the car it sold had working brakes! Finally, most used cars are sold "as is" or with very limited warranties. If strict liability were imposed, the "as is" warning would be meaningless.

■ CASE VOCABULARY

ARGUENDO: For the sake of argument.

Hector v. Cedars–Sinai Medical Ctr.

(Patient) v. *(Hospital)*

180 Cal.App.3d 493, 225 Cal.Rptr. 595 (1986)

SERVICE PROVIDERS ARE IMMUNE FROM STRICT PRODUCTS LIABILITY

■ **INSTANT FACTS** A patient sued the hospital for allowing a de-fective pacemaker to be inserted into the patient.

■ **BLACK LETTER RULE** Providers of medical services are not subject to strict products liability.

■ **PROCEDURAL BASIS**

Appeal from order granting motion for partial summary judgment that dismissed claim for strict products liability.

■ **FACTS**

Frances Hector (P) was implanted with a defective pacemaker at Cedars-Sinai Medical Center (D). Hector (P) sued Cedars-Sinai (D) for negligence, strict liability and breach of warranty. Cedars-Sinai (D) moved for partial summary judgment on the strict liability and breach of warranty causes of action. Cedars-Sinai (D) maintained that it was not liable because it was not a part of the producing and marketing enterprise; rather, Cedars-Sinai (D) simply provided medical services to Hector (P). The trial court granted the motion. Hector (P) appealed, contending the court erred in finding Cedars-Sinai (D) was exempt from strict products liability.

■ **ISSUE**

Is a provider of medical services subject to strict products liability?

■ **DECISION AND RATIONALE**

(Spencer, J.) No. A provider of medical services is not subject to strict products liability. Strict liability has been extended to retailers who are engaged in the business of distributing goods to the public, but only where they play an integral part in the overall production and marketing enterprise. Courts have declined to apply strict liability to a dentist whose drill, with a latent defect, caused injury, to a doctor who prescribed a drug which produced untoward results, and to a hospital that provided a blood transfusion. Hospitals are not ordinarily engaged in the business of selling any of the products or equipment it uses in providing such services. Cedars-Sinai (D) does not routinely stock pacemakers, nor is it in the business of recommending, selling, distributing or testing pacemakers. The essence of the relationship between Hector (P) and Cedars-Sinai (D) was the provision of professional medical services. Cedars-Sinai (D) was not a seller of the pacemaker, and it is not subject to strict liability. Furthermore, policy considerations would not be served by imposing liability on Cedars-Sinai (D). Strict liability is imposed to insure that the costs of injuries are borne by the manufacturers rather than powerless consumers. Cedars-Sinai (D) is in no position to urge the manufacturer of the pacemaker to make a safer product. If liability were imposed upon Cedars-Sinai (D), it would have to distribute the risks and costs among the public, resulting in higher costs for health care. We conclude that Cedars-Sinai (D) is not engaged in the business of selling pacemakers, but is a provider of medical services which included the provision of a pacemaker implanted in Hector (P). Affirmed.

Analysis:

Most courts have declined to extend strict liability to services. However, in this case Cedars-Sinai (D) did, in a literal sense, "supply" the pacemaker to Hector (P). Wasn't Cedars-Sinai (D) the last link in the distribution chain from the manufacturer to the patient? Perhaps so, but the court does not find this literal, semantic approach persuasive. Cedars-Sinai (D) did not select the pacemaker; the doctor did. Perhaps the hospital could pressure the doctor to select a safe pacemaker, and in turn have the doctor exert pressure on the manufacturer of an unsafe pacemaker. In a service transaction, there is no real ability to spread the risk of loss on consumers of the services, since there is no mass production and distribution system to attack. Even where the service transaction involves an incidental sale of a product, there is generally no strict liability. Note that Cedars–Sinai (D) and the doctor remain under a duty to exercise reasonable care in providing services to Hector (P). Although Hector (P) apparently felt that he could not prove this negligence action, since he dismissed it prior to the appeal, the negligence claim remains available against service providers.

CHAPTER SIXTEEN

Nuisance

Philadelphia Electric Company v. Hercules, Inc.

Instant Facts: Philadelphia Electric Company ("PECO") (P) was forced to remedy the toxic waste seeping from its property and into the Delaware River, and PECO (P) sued the seller, alleging that the seller had caused the situation.

Black Letter Rule: Actions for private nuisance can typically be brought only by neighboring landowners, and actions for public nuisance can be brought by members of the public whose general rights have been interfered with.

Morgan v. High Penn Oil Co.

Instant Facts: Morgan (P) sued High Penn Oil Co. (D) for nuisance resulting from the refinery's noxious fumes entering Morgan's (P) land.

Black Letter Rule: Intentional interferences which cause nuisance are actionable even if the party causing the nuisance is not negligent.

Carpenter v. The Double R Cattle Company, Inc.

Instant Facts: Carpenter (P) sued the owners of a nearby cattle feedlot, alleging that the odor and pollution caused by the feedlot constituted actionable nuisance.

Black Letter Rule: In Idaho, where a serious nuisance may be allowed to continue because the utility of the activity causing the nuisance is great, the injured party is not entitled to compensation for the interference.

Winget v. Winn–Dixie Stores, Inc.

Instant Facts: A residential landowner sued for damages and abatement of an alleged nuisance caused by the location and operation of a neighboring grocery store.

Black Letter Rule: Even lawfully zoned businesses may constitute a nuisance if they are operated so as to unreasonably interfere with the health or comfort of neighbors.

Boomer v. Atlantic Cement Co., Inc.

Instant Facts: A land owner sought an injunction and damages for the air pollution emitted from a neighboring cement plant, and the trial court denied the injunction while allowing continuing actions for damages.

Black Letter Rule: A continuing nuisance may be remedied by the payment of permanent damages, allowing the interfering activity to continue.

Spur Industries, Inc. v. Del E. Webb Development Co.

Instant Facts: Del Webb (P) developed a residential community in close proximity to a cattle feedlot, and Webb (P) seeks to permanently enjoin the operation of the feedlot.

Black Letter Rule: Although a party that "comes to a nuisance" may nevertheless be entitled to an injunction, he may be required to indemnify the enjoined party for the damages suffered as a result.

Philadelphia Electric Company v. Hercules, Inc.

(Vendee) v. *(Vendor)*

762 F.2d 303 (3d Cir.1985)

CAVEAT EMPTOR PRECLUDES REMOTE VENDEES FROM SUING FOR PRIVATE OR PUBLIC NUISANCE RESULTING FROM CONDITIONS ON THE LAND THEY PURCHASED

■ **INSTANT FACTS** Philadelphia Electric Company ("PECO") (P) was forced to remedy the toxic waste seeping from its property and into the Delaware River, and PECO (P) sued the seller, alleging that the seller had caused the situation.

■ **BLACK LETTER RULE** Actions for private nuisance can typically be brought only by neighboring landowners, and actions for public nuisance can be brought by members of the public whose general rights have been interfered with.

■ **PROCEDURAL BASIS**

Appeal from verdict granting damages and injunction for public and private nuisance.

■ **FACTS**

This case involves property previously owned by the Pennsylvania Industrial Chemical Corporation ("PICCO"), which was sold to Gould in 1971 and then sold to Philadelphia Electric Co. ("PECO") (P) in 1974. Several years later, a Pennsylvania state agency discovered that toxic materials similar to those once produced by PICCO were seeping out of the property and into the Delaware River. PECO (P) was forced to eliminate the pollution at a cost of $400,000. PECO (P) sued Hercules, Inc. (D), the successor to PICCO, to recover the damages and to enjoin any further pollution. PECO's (P) suit was based on theories of public and private nuisance. The district court awarded damages and the injunction in favor of PECO (P). Hercules (D) appeals.

■ **ISSUE**

(1) May a seller of real property be liable to a purchaser for private nuisance? (2) Does a party have standing to bring a claim for public nuisance when the party suffers no particular damage in the exercise of a right common to the general public?

■ **DECISION AND RATIONALE**

(Higginbotham, J.) (1) No. A seller of real property is not liable to a purchaser of the property for private nuisance. A private nuisance is a nontrespassory invasion of another's interest in the private use and enjoyment of land. Hercules (D) did not interfere with PECO's (P) use and enjoyment of the land. Even if we assume that PICCO created a private nuisance by allowing toxic materials to eventually seep into the Delaware River, PICCO's successor (Hercules (D)) is not liable to PECO (P) for the nuisance. The principle of caveat emptor applies to this situation. PECO (P) had a full opportunity to inspect the condition of the land prior to purchase. Caveat emptor thus shifts the risks of the sale to the purchaser, and we must assume that the price of the land was appropriately discounted to reflect the toxic condition. Although Hercules (D) could be liable for private nuisance to neighboring land owners, who had no such opportunity to inspect the toxic condition of the land, Hercules (D) is not

---

liable to PECO (P), a remote purchaser of the land. (2) No. A party has no standing to bring a claim for public nuisance when the party suffers no particular damage in the exercise of a right common to the general public. An action for public nuisance is a low-grade criminal offense, in which a party interfering with a public right may be liable. Assuming that Hercules (D) caused a public nuisance by allowing toxic materials to seep into the Delaware River, PECO (P) nevertheless does not have standing to sue for the public nuisance. In order to recover damages for public nuisance, a party must suffer a kind of harm different from that suffered by other members of the general public. PECO (P) suffered no such harm, since the right interfered with by Hercules' (D) actions was the right to "pure water." PECO (P) did not suffer damage as a result of the pollution to the Delaware River. Rather, the condition on PECO's (P) land was the *cause* of the damage to the general public. As the purchaser of PICCO's land, PECO had no cause of action against PICCO's successor, Hercules (D), for private or public nuisance. The injunction is accordingly vacated and the judgment for damages is reversed.

Analysis:

This case does an excellent job in setting forth the elements of public and private nuisance, and in describing who has standing to bring an action for each form of nuisance. Note that a private nuisance is an interference with another's use and enjoyment of their land. Typically only neighboring landowners have standing to sue for private nuisance. Thus, if an adjoining landowner suffered damages from the toxic seepage coming from the property previously owned by PICCO, it could sue PICCO for damages even though PICCO had sold the property. But subsequent owners of the property do not have standing to sue. The case discusses the public policy behind this holding, since the principle of caveat emptor allocates the risks of property defects on vendees. The opinion notes that in some situations, such as where the vendor has fraudulently concealed the condition of land, the vendee may sue. PECO (P) could (and probably did) argue that Hercules (D) fraudulently concealed the toxic condition of the land by failing to disclose these important details; however, PECO (P) would have to overcome the large "caveat emptor" hurdle, since PECO (P) had the duty to investigate the condition of the land prior to purchase. Note also that the doctrine of public nuisance is quite distinct— indeed, almost unrelated—to private nuisance. Public nuisance protects members of the general public who are harmed by some unreasonable interference with their rights. And even where a public nuisance exists, only members of the public who suffer some harm different from that suffered by other members of the public have standing to sue. In most situations, only the state can bring an action to remedy a public nuisance. Finally, note that Hercules (D) is not generally protected from all liability arising out of the toxic seepage. Hercules (D) could be liable to neighboring landowners in private nuisance, or to users of the Delaware River in public nuisance. However, only these people, or the state government agency, have standing to sue. PECO (P) comes out on the short end, failing to heed close attention to the powerful doctrine of caveat emptor.

■ CASE VOCABULARY

CAVEAT EMPTOR: "Buyer beware," a legal theory protecting a vendor from liability arising out of the sale of real property or goods.

PRIVATE NUISANCE: A nontrespassory invasion of another's interest in the private use and enjoyment of land.

PUBLIC NUISANCE: An unreasonable interference with a right common to the general public.

RIPARIAN: Relating to rivers or, in some situations, other bodies of water.

STANDING: The right to bring an action.

VENDEE: The purchaser of property.

VENDOR: The seller of property.

Morgan v. High Penn Oil Co.

(Landowner) v. *(Oil Refining Company)*
238 N.C. 185, 77 S.E.2d 682 (1953)

NEGLIGENCE IS NOT REQUIRED TO ESTABLISH A CAUSE OF ACTION FOR PRIVATE NUISANCE

■ **INSTANT FACTS** Morgan (P) sued High Penn Oil Co. (D) for nuisance resulting from the refinery's noxious fumes entering Morgan's (P) land.

■ **BLACK LETTER RULE** Intentional interferences which cause nuisance are actionable even if the party causing the nuisance is not negligent.

■ PROCEDURAL BASIS

Appeal from disallowance of motion for compulsory nonsuit and verdict for damages and injunction for nuisance.

■ FACTS

Morgan (P) owned a tract of land on which he had a dwelling, a restaurant, and accommodations for 32 trailers. High Penn Oil Co. (D) owned an adjoining tract on which it operated an oil refinery. Morgan (P) complained that on several occasions the refinery emitted nauseating gases which invaded Morgan's (P) land and rendered persons of ordinary sensitiveness uncomfortable and sick. High Penn (D) failed to end its atmospheric pollution after Morgan (P) demanded that it be abated. Morgan (P) then sued to recover temporary damages and to obtain an injunction to abate the private nuisance. The trial court, finding that there was a nuisance, entered a judgment in favor of Morgan (P) for $2,500 and enjoined High Penn (D) from continuing the nuisance. High Penn (D) appeals, contending that the trial court was in error in disallowing High Penn's (D) motion for a compulsory nonsuit. On appeal, High Penn (D) argues that it was lawfully and non-negligently operating the refinery, and therefore that it could not be liable for nuisance.

■ ISSUE

Is negligence required to establish a cause of action for private nuisance?

■ DECISION AND RATIONALE

(Ervin, J.) No. Negligence is not required to establish a cause of action for private nuisance. Private nuisance is a field of tort liability that includes nuisances *per se*, or at law, and *per accidens*, or in fact. Nuisances *per se* consist of a nuisance at all times and under any circumstances, regardless of location or surroundings. Because High Penn's (D) oil refinery is a lawful enterprise, it cannot constitute negligence *per se*. However, High Penn (D) is incorrect in asserting that its refinery cannot become a nuisance *per accidens* unless it is constructed or operated in a negligent manner. Nuisances *per accidens* become nuisances by reason of their location or the manner in which they are operated. The invasion which subjects a person or company to liability for nuisance may be either intentional or unintentional. An invasion of another's interest in the use and enjoyment of land is intentional when the person causing the nuisance acts for the purpose of causing it, or knows that it is resulting from his conduct, or knows that it is substantially certain to result from his conduct. Negligence is not an element of liability. In the case at hand, High Penn (D) intentionally and unreasonably caused noxious gases and odors to escape onto Morgan's (P) property. The fumes impaired in a substantial manner

Morgan's (P) use and enjoyment of his land. Thus, High Penn (D) is liable for intentional private nuisance *per accidens*, and an injunction and damages are the appropriate remedy. New trial ordered, however, because of improper jury instructions.

Analysis:

This case does a good job of setting forth the various types of tortious conduct giving rise to liability for private nuisance. When a person's actions cause substantial interference with another's use and enjoyment of land, the actor may be liable for intentional private nuisance if the person intended to cause the interference, or if he knew that the interference would certainly or probably result from his conduct. According to this court, it makes no difference that the actor was not negligent in causing the interference. However, one word by the court throws this holding into an unstable light. The court noted that High Penn (D) was liable because it "Intentionally and *unreasonably*" caused noxious gases and odors to escape onto Morgan's (P) land. Why would the court even mention the word "unreasonably" if negligence was a non-issue? Typically, the reasonableness of a litigant's conduct is important only in reference to negligence theories of liability. The court seems to be saying that High Penn (D) was, indeed, negligent in causing the nuisance. What if High Penn (D) intended to cause the fumes to leave its refinery, but this action was reasonable under the circumstances? Is the court saying that the refinery's actions could never be reasonable? Or, is the court stating that High Penn (D) operated the refinery in a manner that was unreasonable, compared to other oil refineries in the same circumstances?

■ CASE VOCABULARY

ABATE: To cause something to end or cease.

COMPULSORY NONSUIT: A judgment which must be entered against a plaintiff who fails to prove his case.

NUISANCE PER ACCIDENS: A form of private nuisance which only becomes actionable by reason of its location, or by reason of the manner in which they are constructed, maintained or operated.

NUISANCE PER SE: A form of private nuisance consisting of an act, occupation or structure which is a nuisance at all times and under any circumstances.

TEMPORARY DAMAGES: Damages allowed for occasional wrongs which are abatable.

Carpenter v. The Double R Cattle Company, Inc.

(Landowner) v. *(Cattle Rancher)*

108 Idaho 602, 701 P.2d 222 (1985)

THE DOCTRINE OF CONTINUING NUISANCE ALLOWS THE NUISANCE TO CONTINUE, BUT AGGRIEVED LANDOWNERS NEED NOT BE COMPENSATED FOR THEIR INJURIES

■ **INSTANT FACTS** Carpenter (P) sued the owners of a nearby cattle feedlot, alleging that the odor and pollution caused by the feedlot constituted actionable nuisance.

■ **BLACK LETTER RULE** In Idaho, where a serious nuisance may be allowed to continue because the utility of the activity causing the nuisance is great, the injured party is not entitled to compensation for the interference.

■ **FACTS**

Carpenter (P) was a homeowner in Idaho living near a cattle feedlot operated by The Double R Cattle Company, Inc. (D). Carpenter (P) alleged that the Double R (D) feedlot, which had been expanded to accommodate the feeding of approximately 9,000 cattle, caused noxious odors, the pollution of river and ground water, insect infection, dust and noise. The trial court found that the feedlot did not constitute a nuisance. Carpenter (P) appealed, and the Court of Appeals reversed on the ground that the trial court failed to give a jury instruction that the injured party could be compensated for the nuisance while allowing the harmful activity to continue. The Idaho Supreme Court granted Double R's (D) petition for review.

■ **ISSUE**

(1) Should the interests of the community and the utility of the conduct at issue be considered in determining the existence of a nuisance? (2) Should compensation be given to persons suffering from a continuing nuisance, allowing the interference to continue?

■ **DECISION AND RATIONALE**

(Bakes, J.) (1) Yes. The interests of the community, including the utility of the conduct, should be considered in determining the existence of a nuisance. The State of Idaho is sparsely populated and its economy depends largely upon the benefits of agriculture. To refuse to consider the utility of certain agricultural conduct when ruling on nuisance liability would place an unreasonable burden on the agriculture industry. (2) No. Compensation need not be given to persons suffering from a continuing nuisance. Section 826(b) of the Restatement (Second) of Torts allows for the finding of a continuing nuisance, and the payment of compensation to the injured parties, even though the gravity of the harm is outweighed by the utility of the conduct. Although this would allow the business to continue and would compensate the injured parties for interference with land, we feel that this would unreasonably burden the person causing the nuisance. Thus, Double R (D) need not compensate Carpenter (P), and the cattle feedlot can continue. The trial court did not err in refusing to give an instruction based on Section 826(b) of the Restatement, which does not represent the law of Idaho. Affirmed.

■ **DISSENT**

(Bistline, J.) I agree that the interests of the community should be considered in determining the existence of a nuisance. However, I strongly disagree that the aggrieved party should not be compensated for continuing nuisances. While it may be desirable to have a serious nuisance continue because the utility of the operation causing the nuisance is great, those impacted by the serious nuisance deserve some compensation for the invasion they suffer. The majority suggests that part of the cost of agriculture should be borne by the unfortunate few who live in the immediate vicinity of a nuisance-producing facility. I feel that the agricultural interests should pay for any nuisance caused, and that this should be considered part of the external cost of operating a feedlot in Idaho.

Analysis:

This case touches upon a number of important topics related to nuisance. First, the court notes that, in determining whether a nuisance exists, the utility of the allegedly harmful conduct must be balanced against the serious nature of the nuisance. Both the majority and the dissent agree that activity causing a serious interference with use and enjoyment of land may nevertheless not be actionable if the conduct is of great utility and great interest to the community. Thus, in Idaho, where agriculture and cattle ranching is an important community interest, persons suffering from pollution may have no remedy. Second, even when this balancing approach results in a finding that the nuisance should be allowed to continue, the injured party may have the right to compensation. This topic, often called "continuing nuisance," is where the majority and dissent diverge. If the activity causing the nuisance is important enough to be allowed to continue, should the injured party be required to suffer the consequences, or should the person causing the nuisance bear some of the financial burden? The dissent makes a very persuasive argument in reaching the latter conclusion. Shouldn't the costs of compensating adjoining landowners for nuisance be included as an external cost of operating a feedlot? It seems reasonable that feedlot owners not be allowed to intentionally interfere with another person's use and enjoyment of their land without reasonable compensation. Nevertheless, the majority of the Idaho Supreme Court disagreed.

■ CASE VOCABULARY

DICTUM: A mere observation in an opinion that is not necessarily essential to resolving the issue at hand.

■ PROCEDURAL BASIS

Review of reversal of verdict declining to award damages for nuisance.

Winget v. Winn–Dixie Stores, Inc.

(Homeowner) v. *(Grocery Store)*
242 S.C. 152, 130 S.E.2d 363 (1963)

COMPLIANCE WITH ZONING REGULATIONS DOES NOT NECESSARILY ABSOLVE BUSINESSES FROM LIABILITY FOR NUISANCE

■ **INSTANT FACTS** A residential landowner sued for damages and abatement of an alleged nuisance caused by the location and operation of a neighboring grocery store.

■ **BLACK LETTER RULE** Even lawfully zoned businesses may constitute a nuisance if they are operated so as to unreasonably interfere with the health or comfort of neighbors.

■ **PROCEDURAL BASIS**

Appeal from judgment for damages and denial of motion for new trial for action for damages and injunction for nuisance.

■ **FACTS**

Winget (P), who owned a home in South Carolina, brought an action for damages and a permanent injunction against Winn-Dixie Stores, Inc. (D), the owner of a recently-constructed grocery store located adjacent to Winget's (P) residence. Winget (P) alleged that the grocery store constituted a nuisance because of both its location and the manner of its operation. Specifically, Winget (P) claimed that the store attracted crowds of people, automobiles which caused traffic and fumes, and trash trucks and street sweepers at late hours. In addition, Winget (P) entered evidence that Winn-Dixie (D) erected fans which blew against the trees on Winget's (P) property, that floodlights from the store cast a bright glare over his property, and that noxious odors, paper and trash from the store invaded Winget's (P) property. Winn-Dixie (D) moved for a directed verdict. The trial court ruled that there was no evidence to sustain the allegations that the store was a nuisance because of its location. However, the trial court submitted to the jury the issue of nuisance in the operation of the store. In order to prove damages, evidence was entered that the grocery store caused Winget's (P) property to depreciate by $4,000 in value. The jury awarded $5,000 of damages to Winget (P), but the judge denied injunctive relief. Winn-Dixie (D) appeals.

■ **ISSUE**

(1) Does the operation of a lawful business in a properly zoned area constitute a nuisance by reason of location? (2) Do interferences that are not normal incidents of operating a business give rise to damages for nuisance?

■ **DECISION AND RATIONALE**

(Lewis, J.) (1) No. The operation of a lawful business in a properly zoned area does not constitute a nuisance by reason of its location. Where every statutory requirement is met in establishing a business, locating the business in the area in question is not a nuisance. In the case at hand, Winn-Dixie (D) properly located its store in an area zoned for retail business, and the mere location does not constitute a nuisance. (2) Yes. Interferences that are not normal incidents of operating a business may give rise to damages for nuisance. Lawfully zoned businesses may not unreasonably interfere with the health or comfort of their neighbors. In the case at hand, there is a conflict between the rights of residential landowners and a retail grocer. The crowds of customers, automobile traffic, trash trucks and street sweepers do not form the basis for a finding of nuisance, because each of them are natural consequences of the operation of the supermarket. However, the evidence of interferences onto Winget's (P) property itself, including the wind from the fans, the floodlights, the noxious odors, and the trash, all give rise to a reasonable inference that such acts were not normal incidents of the operation of the business. Thus, the trial judge properly denied Winn-Dixie's (D) motion for directed verdict and properly allowed the determination to be made by the jury. However, Winn-Dixie's (D) motion for a new trial should be granted because the trial court erred in admitting evidence of depreciation in market value of the property. Because the location of the supermarket did not, in itself, constitute a nuisance, damages are not properly calculated by the diminution in property value. Only damages that may have resulted from Winn-Dixie's *operation* of the supermarket should have been considered. In the case at hand, the judge should not have allowed testimony regarding the market-value depreciation of Winget's (P) property. Reversed and remanded.

Analysis:

This case logically divides the nuisance analysis into two components; nuisance by virtue of location, and nuisance according to manner of operation. Where a business complies with the zoning ordinances, a strong presumption arises that the business does not constitute a nuisance by virtue of its location. Indeed, a primary purpose of zoning laws is to authorize specific activities within a certain area. Thus, Winget (P) should have known that his house was located in an area zoned for retail businesses such as a grocery store. If the zoning ordinances were in effect before Winget (P) purchased the house, he cannot rightfully complain about the location of the business. On the other hand, if the zoning ordinances were enacted after Winget (P) purchased the house, he should have lobbied the local Zoning Board at that time. Nevertheless, the mere fact that a business is zoned for a particular area does not mean that the manner of *operation* of the business cannot constitute a nuisance. Winn-Dixie (D) had an obligation not to operate its grocery store so as to unreasonably interfere with the health or comfort of the neighbors. However, as Winget (P) learned, it seems very difficult to prove unreasonable interference. Evidence was offered that the store caused a number of annoying interferences, including traffic and noise. Only those interferences which directly touched Winget's (P) property—the fans, floodlights, odors and trash—were potentially actionable. Further- more, these activities could not be enjoined merely because they caused a diminution in Winget's (P) property value. Winget (P) would have to prove that such consequences of the grocery store were unreasonable, based on the traditional balancing analysis.

■ CASE VOCABULARY

ZONING ORDINANCE: A local statute that prescribes the types of activity that can occur within a certain region.

Boomer v. Atlantic Cement Co., Inc.

(Land Owner) v. *(Cement Manufacturer)*

26 N.Y.2d 219, 257 N.E.2d 870, 309 N.Y.S.2d 312 (1970)

COURTS SHOULD RESOLVE NUISANCE DISPUTES BETWEEN THE PARTIES RATHER THAN AT-
TEMPT TO ELIMINATE PERVASIVE PROBLEMS SUCH AS AIR POLLUTION, GENERALLY

■ **INSTANT FACTS** A land owner sought an injunction and damages for the air pollution emitted from a neighboring cement plant, and the trial court denied the injunction while allowing continuing actions for damages.

■ **BLACK LETTER RULE** A continuing nuisance may be remedied by the payment of permanent damages, allowing the interfering activity to continue.

■ **PROCEDURAL BASIS**

Appeal from judgment denying an injunction but allowing continued actions for damages for nuisance.

■ **FACTS**

Boomer (P), a private land owner, brought an action for damages and an injunction against Atlantic Cement Co., Inc. (D), operators of a large cement plant that allegedly injured neighbors by emitting dirt, smoke and vibrations. The trial court found that Atlantic Cement (D) was causing a nuisance, but the court declined to impose a permanent injunction. The effect of this ruling was that Atlantic Cement (D) could continue to pollute the environment, but that Boomer (P) could maintain successive actions for damages for as long as it continued suffering damages from Atlantic Cement's (D) activities. Atlantic Cement (D) appealed the availability of continuing actions for nuisance.

■ **ISSUE**

Must an injunction be granted where a nuisance results in substantial continuing damage?

■ **DECISION AND RATIONALE**

(Bergan, J.) No. An injunction is not necessarily required, even where a nuisance results in substantial continuing damage. In arriving at this conclusion, we overrule long-established and consistently-followed precedent. However, our decision is equitable in terms of the large disparity in economic consequences of the nuisance and of the injunction. In prior cases, we held that an injunction should be granted even though it would be of slight advantage to the injured party and would cause great loss to the enjoined party. This harsh result can be avoided by following one of two alternatives. One option would be to grant the injunction against Atlantic Cement (D) but postpone its effect for, say, 18 months. If Atlantic Cement (D) failed to abate the nuisance during this time by using improved methods of cement manufacturing, a permanent injunction would be entered. The problem with this option is its dependence on research and technological advances which are beyond the control of Atlantic Cement (D). There is a very real possibility that the cement industry would not find a solution to the pollution problems within the time period, and irreparable harm to Atlantic Cement (D) would result. A second option is more reasonable, as it redresses the economic losses suffered by Boomer (P) without unjustly harming Atlantic Cement (D). Under this option, which we now adopt, the injunction will be granted until Atlantic Cement (D) pays permanent damages to Boomer (P) which would compensate Boomer (P) for the total present and future economic loss to his property caused by Atlantic Cement's (D) operations. This option limits the relief to the particular parties before us, and it does not involve the court in attempting to achieve public objectives that are beyond the scope of the court's function. In addition, the requirement to pay damages may spur Atlantic Cement (D) and other manufacturers to pursue research into improved techniques. Furthermore, the damages award is consistent with the "servitude" imposed onto Boomer's (P) land by Atlantic Cement's (D) nuisance. Finally, the damages award is consistent with the notion that there can be but one recovery for permanent and unabatable nuisance; the award would preclude future recovery by Boomer (P). Reversed and remitted for injunction which shall be vacated upon payment of such permanent damages as shall be determined by the lower court.

■ DISSENT

(Jasen, J.) I see grave dangers in refusing to grant an injunction where a nuisance results in substantial continuing damage. The majority opinion provides no incentive for Atlantic Cement (D) to rectify its pollution, because once the damages are paid there is no incentive for the manufacturer to abate its air pollution. The inverse condemnation allowed by the trial court should only be permitted when the public is served by the impairment of private property. However, in the instant action the public does not benefit from the continued existence of the cement company. It is impermissible to impose a servitude upon Boomer's (P) land without the consent of the private property owner.

Analysis:

This case touches on so many diverse topics that it could probably, by itself, form the entire basis for a chapter on nuisance. First, it is interesting to compare this case to *Carpenter v. The Double R Cattle Company, Inc.* [where a serious nuisance may be allowed to continue because the utility of the activity causing the nuisance is great, the injured party is not entitled to compensation for the interference]. Both cases involve a balancing of the equities when determining whether an injunction should be granted. Since the utility of the interfering activities was great in both cases, in relation to the degree of harm caused, both courts held that an injunction was improper. However, in the instant case, the interference was deemed to be so substantial that compensation was warranted for the private land owner. Perhaps another alternative—based on the theory of continuing nuisance—would have been a better alternative. Under this approach, the land owner would receive compensation on an ongoing basis for as long as the nuisance continued. This would serve the three goals of compensating the private party for the wrong, of providing an incentive to the manufacturer to abate the nuisance, and of allowing the useful manufacturing to continue if the business was willing to pay continuing damages. It is unclear why the court did not even address this alternative. Second, it is interesting to examine the public policy issues surrounding this opinion. The New York Court of Appeals obviously feels uncomfortable with establishing a judicial mandate that would resolve the problem of air pollution in all circumstances. Rather, the Court addresses only the situation at hand. However, this Court was subsequently criticized by the legislature for failing to take a stronger stand against pollution. In the wake of this holding, the Clean Air Act was passed by the United States Congress, forcing industries to eliminate air pollution. Ten years later, the Comprehensive Environmental Response, Compensation and Liability Act (CERCLA) was enacted in order to remedy the widespread problems of pollution. As the New York Court of Appeals had intended, it appears that the legislature, rather than the judiciary, is more equipped to deal with the overarching problems of pollution in modern society.

■ CASE VOCABULARY

INVERSE CONDEMNATION: The impairment of private property that causes the property to lose much of its value, for which compensation must be paid to the owner.

Spur Industries, Inc. v. Del E. Webb Development Co.

(Feedlot Operator) v. *(Residential Developer)*

108 Ariz. 178, 494 P.2d 700 (1972)

A PARTY WHO "COMES TO A NUISANCE" MAY BE ENTITLED TO AN INJUNCTION BUT MAY BE OBLIGATED TO PAY DAMAGES TO THE DEFENDANT

■ **INSTANT FACTS** Del Webb (P) developed a residential community in close proximity to a cattle feedlot, and Webb (P) seeks to permanently enjoin the operation of the feedlot.

■ **BLACK LETTER RULE** Although a party that "comes to a nuisance" may nevertheless be entitled to an injunction, he may be required to indemnify the enjoined party for the damages suffered as a result.

■ **PROCEDURAL BASIS**

Appeal and cross-appeal from judgment for permanent injunction for public and private nuisance.

■ **FACTS**

Spur Industries, Inc. ("Spur") (D) and its predecessors had operated a cattle feedlot in a rural suburb of Phoenix since before 1950. In 1959, Del E. Webb Development Co. ("Webb") (P) began to develop Sun City, a residential real estate development designed primarily for senior citizens. Sun City expanded rapidly and by 1967 was within 500 feet of the feedlot. At that time, Webb (P) brought suit to permanently enjoin Spur (D) from operating the feedlot. Webb (P) alleged that over 1,300 lots in Sun City were unfit for development because of the flies and odor coming from the feedlot [for those with a strong stomach, the opinion describes in detail the quantities of manure produced by the 30,000 cattle!]. Webb (P) sued under theories of public and private nuisance. The evidence at trial proved that, because of the odors and flies, many citizens of Sun City were unable to enjoy the outdoor living which had been advertised. The trial court granted the permanent injunction. Spur (D) appeals the injunction, and Webb (P) cross-appeals.

■ **ISSUE**

(1) Is a party barred from recovery for either a public or private nuisance by the sole fact that he "comes to the nuisance" by purchasing or developing adjoining property? (2) If the party is granted a permanent injunction, may he be required to indemnify the business that has been enjoined?

■ **DECISION AND RATIONALE**

(Cameron, J.) (1) No. A party is not barred from recovery for either a public or private nuisance by the sole fact that he "comes to the nuisance" by purchasing or developing adjoining property. Spur's (D) feedlot was originally a lawful business, and it became a nuisance only by reason of Webb's (P) massive residential development. Nevertheless, Spur (D) may be enjoined from operating the feedlot, which substantially interfered with the use and enjoyment of many people's land. Were Webb (P) the only party injured, we would apply the doctrine of "coming to the nuisance" to bar the relief requested. A landowner who builds in agricultural areas must be prepared to accept the disadvantages of the location. However, because of the damage caused by the feedlot to so many people who had been encouraged to purchase homes in Sun City, we feel that the permanent injunction is warranted. The judgment of the trial court permanently enjoining the operation of the feedlot is affirmed. (2) Yes. If the party who has "come to the nuisance" is granted a permanent injunction, he may nevertheless be required to indemnify the business that has been enjoined. In the case at hand, Webb (P) must pay Spur (D) for the reasonable cost of relocating or shutting down the feedlot. Spur (D) has been forced to cease its operations not because of any wrongdoing on the part of Spur (D), but because of the legitimate interests of the public. If Spur (D) had originally located the feedlot near the outskirts of Sun City, Spur (D) would have to suffer the costs of abating the nuisance. However, Spur's (D) feedlot was there first, and Webb (P) voluntarily developed Sun City in close proximity. Webb (P) is liable because Webb (P) is the source of the damage that Spur (D) will suffer in shutting down his operations. Webb (P) brought people to the nuisance to the foreseeable detriment of Spur (D). Thus, this matter is remanded to the trial court for a determination of the damages suffered by Spur (D) as a direct result of granting the injunction. Reversed in part and remanded.

Analysis:

This case focuses on the doctrine of "coming to the nuisance," with some interesting twists. At its most basic level, the doctrine bars injunctive or compensatory relief to parties who voluntarily bring themselves or their residences into the path of a nuisance. But as in all nuisance cases, courts must balance the equities of the situation. Although Webb (P) was primarily responsible for developing Sun City in close proximity to Spur's (D) feedlot, Webb (P) is entitled to the injunction solely because so many innocent purchasers in Sun City were harmed by the odors and flies from the feedlot. It may be argued that the purchasers of the individual lots in Sun City should have been aware of the feedlot, and hence that each of them "came to the nuisance" and should not be allowed to recover. However, the court feels justified in balancing the equities in favor of these small landowners. It is interesting to note that the landowners are not held liable in any way for forcing Spur (D) to shut down and relocate its cattle operation. Only Webb (P), the developer of Sun City, is required to indemnify Spur (D). Once again, equity prevails in this holding. Webb (P) made the original choice to build Sun City near the feedlot, and Webb (P) surely profited greatly from the development. It seems reasonable to require Webb (P) to bear the costs of his actions, even if these costs arose only because he chose to bring an action to enjoin the operation of the feedlot. Note especially that this indemnity requirement is limited to situations where a developer has, with foreseeability, brought into a previously agricultural area the population which necessitates the granting of an injunction against a lawful business.

■ CASE VOCABULARY

COMING TO THE NUISANCE: A doctrine by which a party that brings himself into a situation where he suffers from nuisance may be barred from recovery.

CROSS-APPEAL: An action by an appellee against the appellant, analogous to a counterclaim brought in response to a complaint.

INDEMNITY: The equitable compensation or reimbursement of a party for losses suffered at the hands of the party who is primarily responsible for the losses.

CHAPTER SEVENTEEN

Defamation

Belli v. Orlando Daily Newspapers, Inc.

Instant Facts: Melvin Belli (P) brings an action for defamation against a newspaper that published a false account of Belli's (P) expense reporting.

Black Letter Rule: Where the defamatory nature of a statement is ambiguous, the trier of fact must determine whether the statement meets the definition of defamation.

Grant v. Reader's Digest Ass'n

Instant Facts: Grant (P) sued Reader's Digest (D) for publishing a false statement that Grant (P) was a legislative agent for the Communist Party.

Black Letter Rule: A statement may be defamatory if it injures a person's reputation in the minds of some people, even if these people are not "right-thinking."

Kilian v. Doubleday & Co., Inc.

Instant Facts: Kilian (P), a Colonel in World War II, sued Doubleday & Co., Inc. (D) for publishing a false account of acts of cruel and unusual punishment allegedly inflicted by Kilian (P).

Black Letter Rule: Although substantial truth is an absolute defense to defamation, the court should not instruct the jury as to the defense if no evidence is presented in support.

Neiman–Marcus v. Lait

Instant Facts: Three groups of Neiman–Marcus (P) employees, and the corporation itself, sued Lait (D) for defamatory statements relating to the sexual activities and sexual preferences of the employees.

Black Letter Rule: Where a publication libels some but not all people in a designated small group, a cause of action exists in individual members of the group.

Bindrim v. Mitchell

Instant Facts: Paul Bindrim (P), a psychologist who conducted nude therapy, sued one of his patients who had written a "fictional" account criticizing this type of therapy.

Black Letter Rule: A fictional publication may be libelous if a reasonable person, reading the book, would understand that the fictional character was, in fact, a real person acting as described.

Shor v. Billingsley

Instant Facts: Shor (P) sued Billingsley (D) for libel for an ad-libbed statement televised to a nationwide audience.

Black Letter Rule: A defamatory remark on a televised program can constitute the publication of libel.

Terwilliger v. Wands

Instant Facts: Wands (P) sued for physical problems and the inability to work resulting from Terwilliger's (D) statements that implied Wands (P) was an adulterer.

Black Letter Rule: In an action for slander, the plaintiff must prove special damages that were the immediate consequence of the words, such as an injury to reputation that prevents the plaintiff from receiving that which would otherwise be conferred upon him.

Economopoulos v. A.G. Pollard Co.

Instant Facts: A shopper, George Economopoulos (P), sued when two clerks, one speaking English and one speaking Greek, alleged that he had stolen handkerchiefs.

Black Letter Rule: A statement must be published, i.e., communicated to someone other than the person defamed, in order to be considered defamatory.

Carafano v. Metrosplash.Com, Inc.

Instant Facts: After an unknown user posted a personal profile of Carafano (P) on Matchmaker.com, Carafano (P) sued the website host.

Black Letter Rule: A provider or user of an interactive web-based service is not considered the publisher or speaker of any information provided by another information provider.

Ogden v. Association Of The United States Army

Instant Facts: Ogden (D) sued for libel nearly four years after the book containing the statement was published.

Black Letter Rule: The publication of a book gives rise to only one cause of action for libel, which accrues at the time of the original publication.

New York Times Co. v. Sullivan

Instant Facts: Sullivan (P), the Commissioner in charge of the Montgomery Police Department, sued the New York Times (D) for publishing a defamatory advertisement regarding the police department's treatment of black students.

Black Letter Rule: A false statement about the official conduct of public officials is defamatory only if made with actual malice.

St. Amant v. Thompson

Instant Facts: Thompson (P), a deputy sheriff, sued St. Amant (D) for televised statements that falsely charged Thompson (P) with criminal conduct.

Black Letter Rule: Reckless disregard, for purposes of the actual malice standard, requires a high degree of actual awareness of the probable falsity of a statement.

Harte–Hanks Communications, Inc. v. Connaughton

Instant Facts: Connaughton (P) sued Harte–Hanks Communications, Inc. (D) for defamation after it published an article quoting a person who accused Connaughton (P) of "dirty tricks" and bribery during his political campaign.

Black Letter Rule: A public figure may not recover damages for a defamatory falsehood without clear and convincing proof that the false statement was made with actual malice.

Gertz v. Robert Welch, Inc.

Instant Facts: Gertz (P), a private attorney involved in a high-publicity case, sued the publisher of American Opinion for damages for libel.

Black Letter Rule: States may adopt lesser standards than actual malice for defamation cases brought by private figures, but actual malice must be proven in order to recover punitive damages.

Dun & Bradstreet, Inc. v. Greenmoss Builders Inc.

Instant Facts: Greenmoss Builders (P) sued for false statements contained on credit reports issued by Dun & Bradstreet (D).

Black Letter Rule: Defamatory statements regarding purely private issues are subject to punitive damages without the requirement of proving actual malice.

Philadelphia Newspapers, Inc. v. Hepps

Instant Facts: Hepps (D) sued Philadelphia Newspapers, Inc. (D) for libel arising out of stories imputing organized criminal behavior.

Black Letter Rule: Where a public figure publishes defamatory statements of public concern, a defamed private party must prove that the statements are false.

Milkovich v. Lorain Journal Co.

Instant Facts: Michael Milkovich (P) sued a newspaper for libel, and the newspaper contended that the writer's statement that Milkovich (P) perjured himself was a pure statement of opinion.

Black Letter Rule: Where a statement of opinion reasonably implies false and defamatory facts, liability may be imposed.

Sindorf v. Jacron Sales Co., Inc.

Instant Facts: Sindorf (P) sued Jacron Sales Co. (D), his former employer, for allegedly defamatory statements made to Sindorf's (P) new employer.

Black Letter Rule: Qualified privileges protect persons speaking in their own self-interest, but the communications must be published in a reasonable manner and for a proper purpose.

Belli v. Orlando Daily Newspapers, Inc.

(Famous Attorney) v. *(Newspaper)*

389 F.2d 579 (5th Cir.1967), cert. denied 393 U.S. 825 (1968)

IF THE DEFAMATORY NATURE OF A STATEMENT IS AMBIGUOUS, THE JURY HAS THE FINAL SAY

■ **INSTANT FACTS** Melvin Belli (P) brings an action for defamation against a newspaper that published a false account of Belli's (P) expense reporting.

■ **BLACK LETTER RULE** Where the defamatory nature of a statement is ambiguous, the trier of fact must determine whether the statement meets the definition of defamation.

■ **PROCEDURAL BASIS**

Appeal from dismissal of complaint for damages for libel and slander.

■ **FACTS**

In 1955, Melvin Belli (P), an attorney of national prominence, agreed to serve as a member on one of the panels at the Florida Bar Association's annual convention. Belli (P) served on the panel with the understanding that the Florida Bar would pay for the hotel tab for Belli (P) and his wife. Nine years later, Jean Yothers published an article in the Orlando Evening Star, repeating a story that she had been told by an attorney in Florida. The article stated that Belli (P) had charged hundreds of dollars of clothing to his hotel room pursuant to his "plan" to "take" the Florida Bar, and that the Florida Bar was forced to pay for the entire tab. In fact, Belli (P) had not charged any purchases to the hotel room. Belli (P) sued Orlando Daily Newspapers, Inc. (D) for damages for libel and slander arising out of the defamation. The district court dismissed Belli's (P) complaint, relying on the erroneous assumption that whether a statement is defamatory per se is for the court to decide. Belli (P) appealed on the ground that a jury must determine whether the publication was capable of having a defamatory interpretation.

■ **ISSUE**

If a statement is open to two meanings, one defamatory and one not, is it for the jury to determine whether the defamatory sense was the one conveyed?

■ **DECISION AND RATIONALE**

(Wisdom, J.) Yes. If a statement is open to two meanings, one defamatory and one not, it is for the jury to determine whether the defamatory sense was the one conveyed. In Florida, a written statement constitutes libel per se if it is (a) false, (b) unprivileged, and (c) exposes a person to distrust, hatred, contempt, ridicule, or obloquy, or (d) has the tendency to injure a person in his personal, social, official, or business relations or life. The court must initially determine whether the words are capable of more than one interpretation. If the statement is unambiguous, then the court may say whether the statement was defamatory. On the other hand, if the common reader of the publication could interpret the statement in more than one way, and if at least one of the interpretations is defamatory, then the jury must determine whether the statement was in fact defamatory. In the case *sub judice*, Yothers' statement was capable of being interpreted as saying that Belli (P) tricked and deceived the Florida Bar out of hundreds of dollars. We think that the statement does carry a defamatory meaning. On the other hand, as Orlando Daily Newspapers, Inc. (D) has (just barely) shown, the article may be reasonably interpreted as non-defamatory. It is impractical to depend upon in-court testimony of recipients of the newspaper for determining whether the publication is defamatory. The jury must determine whether Belli (P) has been defamed, i.e., been lowered in the esteem of those to which the idea was published. Reversed and remanded.

Analysis:

This case is the first of several in this chapter that discuss the common law of defamation. As will be seen in later cases, the modern approach to defamation focuses on First Amendment rights and differs widely from the common law. This case provides an excellent summary of the multifaceted common-law definition of defamation. First, a statement must actually be false in order to be defamatory. Second, no privilege must exist as a defense to the false statement. Third, the statement must either expose a person to some sort of disgrace, or it must tend to injure a person in his occupation. After providing this definition, the main focus of the opinion is on the varying roles of the judge and jury in a defamation action. Pursuant to common law, the court must determine whether the statement, on its face, is unambiguously defamatory or non-defamatory. If the statement could go either way, then a question of fact exists for the jury: Would the publication itself be understood by the common reader as exposing a person to disgrace or injuring a person in his occupation? Apparently a judge cannot answer this question and, as the opinion notes, it would be insufficient merely for a judge to make the determination based on the testimony of a few witnesses who read the publication. While this logic may be questioned, the opinion affirms the general notion that the role of the jury is to decide all factual disputes.

■ CASE VOCABULARY

LIBEL: Defamation published by some means, typically in print but also by pictures or signs.

OBLOQUY: Reprehension or disgrace.

PER SE: In itself; taken in isolation.

SLANDER: Defamation that is spoken rather than published.

SUB JUDICE: Before this court.

Grant v. Reader's Digest Ass'n

(Lawyer) v. *(Publisher)*
151 F.2d 733 (2d Cir.1945)

THE DEFAMATORY NATURE OF A STATEMENT DOES NOT DEPEND ON HOW "RIGHT-MINDED" PEOPLE WOULD INTERPRET THE STATEMENT

■ **INSTANT FACTS** Grant (P) sued Reader's Digest (D) for publishing a false statement that Grant (P) was a legislative agent for the Communist Party.

■ **BLACK LETTER RULE** A statement may be defamatory if it injures a person's reputation in the minds of some people, even if these people are not "right-thinking."

■ **PROCEDURAL BASIS**

Appeal from judgment dismissing action for damages for libel.

■ **FACTS**

Reader's Digest Ass'n (D) published, in a periodical read by the general public, a false statement that Grant (P) was a representative of the Communist Party. Grant, a Massachusetts attorney, sued for libel. The district court dismissed the complaint for failure to state a cause of action. The court ruled that the statement would not expose Grant (P) to hatred, contempt, scorn, obloquy or shame among "right-thinking" people. Grant (P) appeals.

■ **ISSUE**

Should the defamatory nature of a statement be determined in reference to how "right-thinking" people would understand the statement?

■ **DECISION AND RATIONALE**

(L. Hand, J.) No. The defamatory nature of a statement should not be determined in reference to how "right-thinking" people would understand the statement. Rather, a statement may be defamatory provided that there would be *some* people in whom the statement would arouse hatred, contempt, scorn and the like. It may or may not be libelous in New York to write that a lawyer has acted as an agent of the Communist Party. Whether or not this statement damaged the reputation of Grant (P) to a sufficient degree to be considered libelous is for the jury to decide. And in making their determination, the jurors are not limited to determining how "right-minded" people would feel about the statement. For example, the imputation of extreme poverty may be actionable, even though no right-minded person would shun or condemn a person simply because he is poor. Because the district court erred in imposing the "right-minded" standard, the court's decision is reversed and remanded.

Analysis:

In order to be actionable, a false statement must injure a person's reputation in some way. Some torts, such as battery and conversion, have a readily apparent injury. On the other hand, for the tort of defamation, the primary focus is on whether any injury occurred at all. Because the essence of defamation is an injury to a person's reputation, an obvious question arises: In whose opinion must the person's reputation have been damaged? Obviously, a person's reputation is an ethereal and malleable concept existing solely in the minds of others. Whether a false statement about a person arouses feelings of hatred, contempt, scorn, obloquy or shame depends on the listener or reader. However, a court cannot possibly poll every person that heard or read the statement and determine their feelings. The court must, therefore, adopt some standard by which to judge the injurious nature of the false statement. In *Belli v. Orlando Daily Newspapers, Inc.* [where the defamatory nature of a statement is ambiguous, the trier of fact must determine whether the statement meets the definition of defamation] the "common reader" standard was enunciated. The case at hand adopts an even more plaintiff-friendly approach. If *some* readers would feel that Grant (P) should be condemned or scorned for an affiliation with the Communist Party, then Grant (P) may recover for the false statement.

■ **CASE VOCABULARY**

INNUENDO: The indirect meaning of words; in an pleading for libel, an allegation by the plaintiff of the particular defamatory meaning conveyed by the words.

ODIUM: The condition of being the target of scorn or contempt.

Kilian v. Doubleday & Co., Inc.

(Colonel) v. *(Publisher)*

367 Pa. 117, 79 A.2d 657 (1951)

AT COMMON LAW, TRUTH WAS AN AFFIRMATIVE DEFENSE TO DEFAMATION CLAIMS

■ **INSTANT FACTS** Kilian (P), a Colonel in World War II, sued Doubleday & Co., Inc. (D) for publishing a false account of acts of cruel and unusual punishment allegedly inflicted by Kilian (P).

■ **BLACK LETTER RULE** Although substantial truth is an absolute defense to defamation, the court should not instruct the jury as to the defense if no evidence is presented in support.

■ PROCEDURAL BASIS

Appeal from denial of motion for new trial following jury verdict for defendant in action for libel.

■ FACTS

Joseph O'Connell, a disabled veteran of World War II, was a student in a class at the American University in Washington. As an assignment for the course, O'Connell wrote an account of incidents that allegedly occurred at the Lichfield Camp in England shortly after O'Connell was injured during the Normandy invasion. This story and several other essays from the class were published in a book by Doubleday & Co., Inc. (D). O'Connell's essay recounted stories that he had heard at Lichfield. However, in order to make his essay more interesting, O'Connell wrote in the first person, as if he had actually witnessed and experienced the events of which he wrote. Many of these events involved Colonel Kilian (P), the commanding officer at Lichfield. Among other things, O'Connell wrote that Kilian (P) was dictatorial and imposed cruel and unusual punishment on the soldiers. O'Connell described these events in graphic detail. In addition, O'Connell's teacher appended a footnote to the end of the story which stated that Kilian (P) was convicted of permitting cruel and unusual punishment. The story failed to mention that Kilian (P) was acquitted of authorizing, causing, or knowingly permitting such punishment. At trial, Doubleday (D) asserted as an affirmative defense that the story was a true and accurate account. However, neither O'Connell nor any other witnesses at trial could substantiate the truthfulness of the story. The trial court submitted an instruction to the jury that, if the jurors found the story to be substantially true, then Doubleday (D) would not be liable. The jury rendered a verdict for Doubleday (D). Kilian (P) challenged the jury instruction and appeals the refusal of the trial court to grant a new trial.

■ ISSUE

Where evidence does not support a finding that an allegedly defamatory statement is substantially true, may the court instruct the jury that substantial truthfulness is an absolute defense to defamation?

■ DECISION AND RATIONALE

(Stem, J.) No. Where evidence does not support a finding that an allegedly defamatory statement is substantially true, the court may not instruct the jury that substantial truthfulness is an absolute defense to defamation. If O'Connell's account of the events at Lichfield and of Kilian's (P) subsequent conviction was true, or even substantially true, then Doubleday (D) would face no liability for publishing the story. Truth is an absolute defense to defamation. However, none of the witnesses at trial were able to substantiate the specific defamatory accounts made about Kilian's (P) activities at Lichfield. Furthermore, even though it was true that Kilian (P) had been convicted of permitting cruel and unusual punishment, the innuendo created by this statement and the preceding accounts is false and defamatory. Doubleday (D) published the footnote that recounted this conviction without stating that Kilian (P) had been acquitted of the far more serious allegations that had been said or implied in the article. In doing so, Doubleday (D) was essentially corroborating the accounts of cruel punishment at Kilian's (P) hands. Because Kilian (P) had been acquitted of these more-serious allegations, and because no witnesses at trial could substantiate their occurrence, there was no evidence showing that the innuendo was substantially true. Thus, the court should not have submitted to the jury the question whether the publication was substantially true. Reversed and new trial awarded.

Analysis:

This fairly complicated opinion states a very simple and important concept in the common law of defamation. Truth or substantial truth is an absolute defense. However, at common law, the defendant had the burden of proving this defense. Thus, the common law raised a presumption of the falsity of all statements that were defamatory. In the case at hand, both published statements and innuendo are at issue Doubleday (D) failed to establish that the published statements were true, and thus it could not claim the affirmative defense. However, the footnote regarding Kilian's (P) conviction was true. Nevertheless, according to the court, the *innuendo* created by this statement was defamatory. Furthermore, the innuendo, that the conviction for a lesser charge corroborated all of the accounts in the story, was not proven to be true by Doubleday (D). It is interesting to note that even "substantial truth" is an absolute defense. If some evidence exists that the statement, while not word-for-word accurate, is substantially true, then the trial court may instruct the jury accordingly. Thus, this case again reflects the roles of both the judge and the jury in a defamation action. As a final note, it is important to realize that the presumption of falsity has been abandoned by recent decisions. As will be seen in *Philadelphia Newspapers v. Hepps*, a defendant does not always have the burden of proving truth as an affirmative defense. Rather, the burden often rests on the plaintiff to prove the falsity of the statement.

Neiman–Marcus v. Lait

(Department Store) v. *(Author)*
13 F.R.D. 311 (S.D.N.Y.1952)

COURTS ALLOW INDIVIDUALS TO SUE FOR GROUP DEFAMATION IF THE GROUP IS SUFFICIENTLY SMALL

■ **INSTANT FACTS** Three groups of Neiman-Marcus (P) employees, and the corporation itself, sued Lait (D) for defamatory statements relating to the sexual activities and sexual preferences of the employees.

■ **BLACK LETTER RULE** Where a publication libels some but not all people in a designated small group, a cause of action exists in individual members of the group.

■ **PROCEDURAL BASIS**

Motion to dismiss claims for damages for libel.

■ **FACTS**

Lait (D) authored a book entitled "U.S.A. Confidential" that contained several defamatory references to employees of Neiman-Marcus (P). Specifically, the book stated that several Neiman (P) models were call girls; that the Neiman (P) salesgirls were also call girls who were more fun and who charged substantially less than the models; and that many of the Neiman (P) designers were "faggots" and that most of the salesmen were "fairies." The plaintiffs sued in the following groups: (1) all nine models for Neiman (P); (2) fifteen of the twenty-five salesmen; (3) thirty of 382 saleswomen; and (4) the corporation itself. Lait (D) brought a motion to dismiss the claims of each group of plaintiffs.

■ **ISSUE**

Where a publication libels some but not all people in a designated small group, does a cause of action exist in individual members of the group?

■ **DECISION AND RATIONALE**

(Kaufman, J.) Yes. Where a publication libels some but not all people in a designated small group, a cause of action exists in individual members of the group. It is widely accepted that where the group or class libeled is large, no member can sue even though the language used includes all members. Conversely, where the group or class libeled is small, and each and every member of the class is referred to, then any individual member can sue. However, conflict arises when the publication libels some or less than all of a designated small group. We address this issue by examining each group of plaintiffs in the instant action. First, the plaintiff salesmen do have a cause of action. Accordingly, Lait's (D) motion to dismiss the salesmen for failure to state a claim upon which relief can be granted is denied. Second, the plaintiff saleswomen do not have a cause of action. The group of saleswomen is large, consisting of 382 members. In addition, Lait's (D) statement does not refer to some ascertained member of the class. Furthermore, no reasonable man would take Lait (D) seriously and conclude a reference to any individual saleswoman. The thirty saleswomen fail to allege that any of them specifically were defamed. Accordingly, Lait's (D) motion to dismiss their cause of action is granted.

The entire complaint is dismissed with leave to file separate complaints as to the salesmen, models, and the corporation.

Analysis:

This case presents an initial glance into the topic of group defamation. The general rules regarding standing to sue for group defamation are fairly logical. First, if a publication defames a large group (e.g., "All Irish-Americans are drunkards"), no member of the group has standing to sue. If standing were granted to any member, the courts could become clogged with lawsuits. And even if standing were only allowed in a class action, thereby reducing the multiplicity of lawsuits, it is doubtful that any particular member of the class would be injured significantly enough to necessitate a remedy in the courts. Second, if the publication defames each member of a small class, then any member of the class can sue. It is up to the court to determine whether the class is small enough to allow standing for individual members. In the case at hand, Lait's (D) statements defamed the entire group of 382 saleswomen. The court held that this group was too large to justify standing for any individual member. Although the court's reasoning is questionable—that no reasonable man would take Lait's (D) comments seriously—it seems logical that none of the individual saleswomen would be significantly injured by the defamation. Third, the law of group libel is complicated when a publication defames some but not all of a small group. Lait (D) defamed *some* salesmen by stating that "most of the sales staff are fairies." Unfortunately, this case excerpt does not include the court's rationale for holding that any and all of the twenty-five salesmen could maintain a cause of action. Presumably this scenario is treated as if the publication defamed each member of the class. Apparently, because the group of salesmen was small enough, any of them could sue and claim that the statement referred to them [and that it was false, i.e., that they were not "fairies"]. Finally, it is important to note that Neiman-Marcus (P) itself could maintain a cause of action for libel. Even though a corporation has no reputation in a personal sense, it certainly can be damaged by statements that cast aspersion upon its business character.

Bindrim v. Mitchell

(Psychologist) v. *(Novelist)*
92 Cal.App.3d 61, 155 Cal.Rptr. 29 (1979)

AUTHORS CANNOT HIDE BEHIND THE SHIELD OF "FICTION" IN ORDER TO DEFAME REAL PERSONS

■ **INSTANT FACTS** Paul Bindrim (P), a psychologist who conducted nude therapy, sued one of his patients who had written a "fictional" account criticizing this type of therapy.

■ **BLACK LETTER RULE** A fictional publication may be libelous if a reasonable person, reading the book, would understand that the fictional character was, in fact, a real person acting as described.

■ **PROCEDURAL BASIS**

Appeal from verdict for damages for libel and from motion for new trial conditioned on remittitur.

■ **FACTS**

Paul Bindrim (P), a Ph.D. and psychologist, conducted "nude marathon" group therapy. Gwen Davis Mitchell (D), a novelist, attended Bindrim's (P) nude-therapy weekend. Mitchell (D) contracted not to write anything regarding the workshop. However, shortly after the weekend, Mitchell (D) contracted with Doubleday (D) and published a novel called *Touching* based on the nude-therapy technique. The novel's principal character was Dr. Simon Herford, a fictional psychiatrist who, although significantly different in appearance from Bindrim (P), conducted nude therapy in the same manner as Bindrim (P). The novel was critical of nude therapy. Bindrim (P) sued Mitchell (D) and Doubleday (D) for libel. The jury awarded substantial damages to Bindrim (P). The court granted a new trial conditioned on Bindrim's (P) acceptance of a remittitur. Bindrim (P), Mitchell (D), and Doubleday (D) all appealed.

■ **ISSUE**

May a fictional story be defamatory if typical readers would reasonably understand the story to be about a specific real person?

■ **DECISION AND RATIONALE**

(Kingsley, J.) Yes. A fictional story may be defamatory if typical readers would reasonably understand the story to be about a specific real person. Mitchell (D) and Doubleday (D) contend on appeal that Bindrim (P) failed to show that Bindrim (P) was identified as the character Dr. Herford. Mitchell (D) and Doubleday (D) rely in part on *Wheeler v. Dell Publishing Co.* [a reasonable person who was in the position to identify a real person with the fictional character would not reasonably identify the real person and equate the two]. However, the character in *Wheeler* was very different from the real-life individual. Conversely, in the case at hand, several witnesses who read Mitchell's (D) novel identified Bindrim (P) as the fictional character. The similarities between the two are clear. Although Dr. Herford had a different physical description than Bindrim (P), Herford practiced nearly identical nude therapy as Bindrim (P). A reasonable person reading *Touching* would understand that Herford was, in actual fact, Bindrim (P) acting as described. Thus, the judgment is affirmed, although it is modified as to damages.

■ CONCURRENCE

(Jefferson, J.) The dissent maintains that the jury was erroneously instructed regarding the law to apply in the instant action. According to the dissent, an instruction given to the jury stated that only one person was required to have understood the actual defamatory meaning of the novel. I believe, however, that if one person reasonably understood the defamatory character of the language used, it describes what readers generally would reasonably understand. Thus, the jury instruction was not improper.

■ DISSENT

(Files, J.) Mitchell's (D) novel describes a fictitious therapist who is conspicuously different from Bindrim (P) in name, physical appearance, personality and profession. Indeed, the only similarity between the two was the practice of nude therapy. Furthermore, even if the fictional criticism of nude therapy may be interpreted as libel against one practitioner, the evidence does not support a verdict in favor of Bindrim (P). This is because Mitchell (D) and Doubleday (D) submitted an erroneous jury instruction [discussed above]. The chief vice of the majority opinion is that it chills authors and publishers from criticizing an occupational practice, inviting litigation on the theory that "when you criticize my occupation, you libel me."

Analysis:

On the surface, it might appear that fictional accounts should never be the basis for defamation. Fictional novels are, by definition, false. They do not refer to any particular person or account. However, the facts of this case indicate that even "fictional" accounts often reflect or recount real-life experiences. A novelist should not be free to hide under the guise of fiction and defame a real person simply by changing the person's name or description. The evidence shows that Mitchell (D) changed the name and appearance of the main character not to protect the innocent, but in an attempt to protect Mitchell (D) herself from liability. This case raises a number of interesting points. First, as in previous cases, the standard for libel rests in the understanding of a reasonable person reading the published material. Although the concurrence argues that only one person need to have "reasonably" understood the book as referring to Bindrim (P), the test enunciated by the majority seems to require something more. By presenting three witnesses who identified Bindrim (P) with the fictional character, Mitchell (D) and Doubleday (D) presented evidence that several persons reached this conclusion. From this evidence, the jury concluded that the identification was, in fact, reasonable. The second interesting side note is merely dicta. As the majority states, the requirement of a "publication" for libel purposes requires only publication to one person other than the person who was defamed.

■ CASE VOCABULARY

MULCTING: Fining or otherwise censuring.

REMITTITUR: The process by which an excessive verdict is reduced, pursuant to the judge's orders.

TRADUCED: Attacked in a defamatory manner.

Shor v. Billingsley

(Defamed Party) v. *(Television Commentator)*
4 Misc.2d 857, 158 N.Y.S.2d 476 (1956)

SPOKEN WORDS THAT ARE TELEVISED MAY BE CONSIDERED LIBELOUS AND NOT MERELY SLANDEROUS

■ **INSTANT FACTS** Shor (P) sued Billingsley (D) for libel for an ad-libbed statement televised to a nationwide audience.

■ **BLACK LETTER RULE** A defamatory remark on a televised program can constitute the publication of libel.

■ **PROCEDURAL BASIS**

Motion to dismiss causes of action for libel.

■ **FACTS**

On a nationwide television show, one person [assume it was Billingsley (D)] ad-libbed that Shor owed significant amounts of money. Shor (P) brought an action for defamation [apparently for libel, although the opinion does not specify]. Billingsley (D) brought a motion to dismiss on the ground that the remark was spoken, and thus could not form the basis for a cause of action for libel.

■ **ISSUE**

Can a defamatory remark on a televised program constitute the publication of libel?

■ **DECISION AND RATIONALE**

(Hecht, J.) Yes. A defamatory remark on a televised program can constitute the publication of libel. Our appellate courts have held that the utterance of defamatory remarks, read from a script into a microphone and broadcast, constitute the publication of libel. The fact that Billingsley's (D) comments were ad-libbed, and not read from a script, does not change anything. Radio reaches a vast audience, and the broadcast of scandalous utterances is as potentially harmful as a publication by writing. Even though radio broadcasts lack the same durability as written libel, they nevertheless have equal capacity to damage a reputation. Because damage is the basis for common-law defamation, defamation by radio should be actionable as libel [meaning that no "special damages" need to be shown, as in the case of slander]. Accordingly, the motion to dismiss is denied.

Analysis:

In order to understand this opinion, it is necessary to realize that, at common law, damages for slander could typically be obtained only by proving "special damages," i.e., actual harm suffered by the plaintiff. Libel, on the other hand, was actionable without this heightened standard of proof. In this framework, it is of primary importance to characterize the defamatory remarks as libelous or slanderous. At one level, the distinction is straightforward: defamatory remarks that are spoken may constitute slander, and published written statements may constitute libel. However, the distinction is blurred in the modern era of radio and television. This opinion takes a logical approach to dealing with the new media. A radio or television broadcast has the potential to reach as large an audience [and probably even larger] as does a written publication. Thus, a defamed person can be harmed even more by a broadcast than by a written publication. Therefore, statements on broadcasts can constitute libel [whether the statements are ad-libbed or read from a script], which is easier to prove than slander.

Terwilliger v. Wands

(Speaker) v. (Alleged Adulterer)

17 N.Y. 54, 72 Am.Dec. 420 (1858)

ACTUAL DAMAGE TO REPUTATION AND RESULTING PECUNIARY LOSS MUST BE PROVEN TO MEET THE SPECIAL DAMAGES REQUIREMENT FOR SLANDER

■ **INSTANT FACTS** Wands (P) sued for physical problems and the inability to work resulting from Terwilliger's (D) statements that implied Wands (P) was an adulterer.

■ **BLACK LETTER RULE** In an action for slander, the plaintiff must prove special damages that were the immediate consequence of the words, such as an injury to reputation that prevents the plaintiff from receiving that which would otherwise be conferred upon him.

■ PROCEDURAL BASIS

Appeal from motion for nonsuit for action for damages for slander.

■ FACTS

Terwilliger (D) made several statements to a third person regarding Wands (P). Specifically, Terwilliger (D) stated that Wands (P) went to Mrs. Fuller's house in order to have intercourse with Mrs. Fuller, and that Wands (P) did all that he could to keep Mrs. Fuller's husband in the penitentiary so he could have free access to Mrs. Fuller's house. Wands (P) sued Terwilliger (D) for slander. The only damages proved at trial were that Wands (P) suffered sickness and was unable to work after hearing the reports circulated by Terwilliger (D). Terwilliger (D) moved for nonsuit on the ground that the damages proven by Wands (P) were insufficient to sustain the action for slander.

■ ISSUE

In an action for slander, must the plaintiff prove special damages that were the natural, immediate and legal consequence of the words?

■ DECISION AND RATIONALE

(Strong, J.) Yes. In an action for slander, the plaintiff must prove special damages that were the natural, immediate and legal consequence of the words. The only exception to this rule is in cases of slander per se. The defamation at issue does not fall into a category of slander per se, which are words that have a natural and immediate tendency to produce injury. Thus, Wands (P) must aver some particular damage to his reputation, and he must prove that he was prevented by the slander from receiving that which would otherwise be conferred upon him. However, Wands (P) presented only evidence of his physical sickness. He did not prove that anybody who heard the remarks actually treated Wands (P) differently. Thus, Wands' (P) sickness must be attributed to the *apprehension* of a loss of character, since no *actual* loss of reputation was proven. Because no loss of character was proven, Wands (P) cannot recover for slander.

Analysis:

This case illustrates the difficult standard of proof in order to recover for slander at common law. Unless the defamatory language constitutes slander per se [such as the imputation of a crime, loathsome disease, incompetence in a profession, or female unchastity], special damages must be proven. This court defines special damages as those which prevent a person from receiving that which would otherwise be conferred upon him. In other words, special damages must be actual damages to a person's reputation which result in harm at the hands of others. This typically required proof of pecuniary loss. In the case at hand, Wands' (P) damages were limited to his own feelings of sickness in apprehension of a damaged reputation. Wands (P) needed to prove that his reputation was *actually* damaged and that he suffered financial loss as a result. If Wands (P) had done so, he could have recovered additional damages for his mental distress and humiliation. Notice the outdated and absurd double-standard in the common law categorization of slander per se. At common law, the mere imputation that a woman was unchaste was considered slander per se. A woman defamed in this manner could recover even if she proved no special harm to her reputation. However, a man so defamed could not recover without proving actual reputational damage. And even if the defamation alleged that the man was an adulterer, as in the instant action, the statement was not considered slander per se.

■ CASE VOCABULARY

PROSTRATED: Reduced to a helpless or exhausted state.

Economopoulos v. A.G. Pollard Co.

(*Shopper*) v. (*Retail Store*)

218 Mass. 294, 105 N.E. 896 (1914)

STATEMENTS WHICH ARE NOT HEARD OR CANNOT BE UNDERSTOOD BY AT LEAST ONE OTHER PERSON ARE NOT ACTIONABLE AS DEFAMATION

■ **INSTANT FACTS** A shopper, George Economopoulos (P), sued when two clerks, one speaking English and one speaking Greek, alleged that he had stolen handkerchiefs.

■ **BLACK LETTER RULE** A statement must be published, i.e., communicated to someone other than the person defamed, in order to be considered defamatory.

■ PROCEDURAL BASIS

Exceptions to trial court verdict for defendant in action for slander.

■ FACTS

George Economopoulos (P) was shopping at a retail store owned by A.G. Pollard Company (D). Carrier, a clerk working for Pollard (D), stated in English to Economopoulos (P), a Greek [as if the name didn't give it away!], that he had stolen a handkerchief. The evidence showed that no other persons heard this statement. In addition, Miralos, another clerk of Pollard (P), repeated the allegedly defamatory statement in Greek. The evidence showed that only a floor worker [who presumably did not understand Greek] heard this latter statement. Economopoulos (P) sued for the allegedly defamatory statements. The trial court entered a verdict for Pollard (D), and Economopoulos (P) brings exceptions.

■ ISSUE

Must a false statement be heard and understood by a third person in order to be considered defamatory?

■ DECISION AND RATIONALE

(Loring, J.) Yes. A false statement must be heard and understood by a third person in order to be considered defamatory. In the instant action, there was no evidence that anyone other than Economopoulos (P) was present when Carrier accused Economopoulos (P) of the theft in English. Furthermore, there was no evidence that anyone besides Economopoulos (P) understood the words communicated by Miralos in Greek. Exceptions overruled.

Analysis:

Because damage to character is the basis for defamation, a written or spoken statement is actionable as defamation only if it is "published." This term is somewhat misleading. Publication does not mean that the statement must be in writing or in print. In order for a statement to have been "published," It must only have been communicated in some manner to someone other than the person defamed. Thus, a spoken statement is not slanderous, even when made in the presence of other people, if those other people do not understand the statement. As the notes following the case indicate, the publication requirement is subject to a number of various interpretations. Words spoken to a stenographer, for example, may or may not be considered "communicated" for purposes of the publication requirement. Furthermore, the words must have been either intentionally or negligently published. Thus, where a third party improperly opens a letter addressed to a plaintiff, there is generally no publication. However, where the defendant knows or should know that a third person would open the mail (e.g., a secretary), then the publication requirement might be met. Thus, the publication requirement is yet another highly litigated element of the torts of libel and slander. Both courts and juries have a role in determining whether publication actually occurred.

■ CASE VOCABULARY

EXCEPTIONS: A formal objection to a verdict—analogous to an appeal—or to an action of the trial court which is contended to have been improper.

Carafano v. Metrosplash.Com, Inc.

(Actress) v. *(Online Dating Service Host)*

339 F.3d 1119 (9th Cir.2003)

A WEBSITE HOST IS NOT LIABLE FOR FALSE INFORMATION POSTED BY A VISITOR

■ **INSTANT FACTS** After an unknown user posted a personal profile of Carafano (P) on Matchmaker.com, Carafano (P) sued the website host.

■ **BLACK LETTER RULE** A provider or user of an interactive web-based service is not considered the publisher or speaker of any information provided by another information provider.

■ **PROCEDURAL BASIS**

On appeal to review a district court's entry of summary judgment for the defendant.

■ **FACTS**

Metrosplash.com, Inc. (D) hosts an online dating service entitled Matchmaker.com. To use its service, users are asked to complete a questionnaire, which is used to generate a personal profile. An unknown user posted a sexually suggestive profile for Carafano (P), an actress, without her consent. The profile contained pictures of Carafano (P), and e-mails to the account received responses containing her home address and telephone number. After Carafano (P) received sexually explicit messages and faxes threatening her son, she contacted the police. Carafano's (P) representative contacted the defendant, and the profile was deleted. Carafano (P) sued the defendant in state court for invasion of privacy, misappropriation of the right of publicity, defamation, and negligence. After the action was removed to federal court, summary judgment was granted for the defendant, but the court held that the defendant was not immune from liability under 47 U.S.C. § 230(c)(1). Both parties appealed.

■ **ISSUE**

Is a computer matchmaking service legally responsible for false content in a dating profile provided by someone posing as another?

■ **DECISION AND RATIONALE**

(Thomas, J.) No. Under 47 U.S.C. § 230(c)(1), "[n]o provider or user of an interactive computer service shall be treated as the publisher or speaker of any information provided by another information content provider." This section affords Internet providers immunity from suit related to content published over the Internet and treats them differently than publishers of print media. The statute was designed to promote the free exchange of information over the Internet and to encourage voluntary monitoring of offensive or obscene material. Due to the policies underlying the statute, courts have applied it broadly to all interactive computer services that are not also the information content provider.

Here, although the defendant provided the questionnaire from which the profile was created, all information was provided completely by the user. Matchmaker.com (D) is not the information content provider, nor is Matchmaker.com (D) a developer of the underlying information by its categorization of user responses. The information Matchmaker.com (D) collects is designed to provide its users with features necessary to enhance the value of the website. As such, it facilitates the free exchange of information within the intent of the immunity statute. Matchmaker.com (D) is not an information content provider. Affirmed.

Analysis:

Carafano represents one of the challenges the Internet has brought to American jurisprudence. By enacting the Communications Decency Act, Congress sought to protect website hosts from liability for content displayed on their sites by others. In so doing, Congress distinguished the host from publishers of traditional print media. This distinction is necessary because of the ease of entering a website and anonymously posting information without the host's knowledge, unlike with newspapers and magazines.

■ CASE VOCABULARY

DEFAMATION: The act of harming the reputation of another by making a false statement to a third person.

INVASION OF PRIVACY: An unjustified exploitation of one's personality or intrusion into one's personal activity, actionable under tort law and sometimes under constitutional law.

RIGHT OF PUBLICITY: The right to control the use of one's own name, picture, or likeness and to prevent another from using it for commercial benefit without one's consent.

Ogden v. Association of the United States Army

(*Subject of Book*) v. (*Publisher*)
177 F.Supp. 498 (D.C.Cir.1959)

THE PUBLICATION OF A BOOK CREATES ONLY A SINGLE CAUSE OF ACTION FOR LIBEL, WHICH ACCRUES AT THE TIME OF PUBLICATION

■ **INSTANT FACTS** Ogden (D) sued for libel nearly four years after the book containing the statement was published.

■ **BLACK LETTER RULE** The publication of a book gives rise to only one cause of action for libel, which accrues at the time of the original publication.

■ **PROCEDURAL BASIS**

Motion by defendant for summary judgment in action for libel.

■ **FACTS**

Although the facts stated in the opinion are sparse, it can be inferred that the Association of the United States Army (D) published a defamatory statement regarding Ogden (P). The statement was made in a book published in November, 1955. Ogden (P) filed suit in June, 1959, a few years after the one-year statute of limitations for defamation had run. Ogden (P) alleged that the subsequent sales of the book constituted separate "publications" and thus separate causes of action for purposes of the statute of limitations. The Association of the United States Army (D) moved for summary judgment based on the statute of limitations.

■ **ISSUE**

Does every sale of an allegedly defamatory book constitute a "publication" and create a separate cause of action for libel?

■ **DECISION AND RATIONALE**

(Holtzoff, J.) No. Every sale of an allegedly defamatory book does not constitute a "publication" and create a separate cause of action for libel. Rather, the publication of a book gives rise to only one cause of action for libel, which accrues at the time of the original publication. Thus, this court follows the modern "single publication rule" which has been adopted by most jurisdictions. At English common law, every sale or delivery of a libelous matter constituted a new publication, and therefore a new cause of action accrued on each occasion. However, under modern conditions, the English rule would give rise to an unnecessary multiplicity of suits and would undermine the policy rationale behind the statute of limitations. The extent and frequency of publication is a factor to be considered in awarding damages, but it has no bearing on whether a valid cause of action still exists or whether it has been barred by the statute of limitations. The Association of the United States Army's (D) motion for summary judgment is granted.

Analysis:

This case illustrates the difficult balancing that courts must occasionally undertake when applying statutes of limitations. The central purpose of a statute of limitations is to provide repose for potentially liable parties. At some point, claims should be considered stale and no liability should attach to actions in the distant past. In the case at hand, if the English rule was followed, or if no statute of limitations existed, then a party who published a defamatory statement tens or hundreds of years in the past could be liable each time the book was sold or distributed. Putting aside the difficulty of suing deceased or nonexistent parties, this could give rise to a huge number of lawsuits from a single book. However, the court must balance the rights of the defamed party. Suppose a book was originally published and circulated only to a small audience, but ten years later was marketed throughout the entire country. In this situation, any defamatory statement in the book would probably be much more harmful to the defamed person's character than at the time of original publication. And what happens when a book is reprinted in a different language, or a new and revised edition is published? In these situations, courts would have to determine whether to strictly apply the single publication rule or to modify it in the interests of justice.

New York Times Co. v. Sullivan

(*Newspaper Publisher*) v. (*Commissioner*)
376 U.S. 254, 84 S.Ct. 710 (1964)

FALSE STATEMENTS ABOUT PUBLIC OFFICIALS ARE DEFAMATORY ONLY IF MADE WITH ACTUAL MALICE

■ **INSTANT FACTS** Sullivan (P), the Commissioner in charge of the Montgomery Police Department, sued the New York Times (D) for publishing a defamatory advertisement regarding the police department's treatment of black students.

■ **BLACK LETTER RULE** A false statement about the official conduct of public officials is defamatory only if made with actual malice.

■ **PROCEDURAL BASIS**

Writ of certiorari reviewing order affirming verdict for damages for libel.

■ **FACTS**

In March, 1960, the New York Times Co. (D) published an advertisement that had been written and paid for by a number of black activists in Alabama. The advertisement described the wide-spread nonviolent demonstrations that were being conducted by black students in support of the black movement and in support of Dr. Martin Luther King, Jr. In addition, the ad recounted the "wave of terror" being waged against the black students by the Montgomery Police Department. For example, the ad stated that Montgomery police forcefully expelled several black students who had sung "My Country, 'Tis of Thee" on the State Capitol steps. L.B. Sullivan (P) was an elected Commissioner of Montgomery, Alabama, whose responsibilities included supervising the Montgomery Police Department. Although he was not mentioned by name, Sullivan (P) alleged that the statements were defamatory to the extent that they attributed misconduct to him as the Montgomery Commissioner who supervised the Police Department. Sullivan (P) sued the New York Times and four individual black activists who had signed the advertisement. At trial, evidence was entered proving that the article was not an accurate description of what had occurred in Montgomery. A jury in Montgomery County awarded $500,000 against the New York Times (D) and the individuals, holding that the advertisement contained statements "of and concerning" Sullivan (P), and that the ad was written and published with actual malice. The New York Times (D) and the others appealed, citing the constitutional protection of freedom of speech. The Supreme Court of Alabama affirmed the verdict, and the United States Supreme Court granted certiorari.

■ **ISSUE**

Must a public official prove that statements were made with actual malice in order to recover damages for libel relating to his official conduct?

■ **DECISION AND RATIONALE**

(Brennan, J.) Yes. A public official must prove that statements were made with actual malice in order to recover damages for libel relating to his official conduct. In the case at hand, it is uncontroverted that several of the allegedly defamatory statements were not accurate descriptions of the events which occurred in Montgomery. For example, the students were not expelled for singing on the steps of the

State Capitol, and the police did not engage in the "wave of terror" to the extent alleged in the ad. Because the statements were false, and pursuant to Alabama law, the trial judge submitted the case to the jury under instructions that the statements were libelous per se. Thus, the New York Times (D) and the individuals would be liable if the jury found that the statements were "of and concerning" Sullivan (P). The New York Times (D) and the individuals could escape liability only if they could prove that the statements were true. Pursuant to Alabama law, the constitutional privilege of free speech depended only on the truth of the facts upon which the statements were based. This rule of law undermines the constitutional protections of free speech. The nation has a profound commitment to the principle that debate on public issues should be uninhibited, robust and wide-open. Furthermore, the people should be free to discuss the character and qualifications of elected officials. These constitutional guarantees require a federal rule that prohibits a public official from recovering damages for a defamatory falsehood relating to his official conduct unless he proves that the statement was made with "actual malice," i.e., with knowledge that it was false or with reckless disregard of whether it was false or not. In the case at hand, Sullivan (P) failed to prove with convincing clarity that the individuals or the New York Times (D) published the advertisement with actual malice. Witnesses for the Times (D) stated that they thought the advertisement was substantially correct, and there is no evidence that the Times (D) was anything more than negligent in failing to discover the misstatements. Furthermore, we find no evidence supporting the jury's finding that the statements were "of and concerning" Sullivan (P). Sullivan (P) was not named in the advertisement, and the statements do not make even an oblique reference to Sullivan (P) as an individual. Impersonal criticisms of government should not be transmuted into personal criticisms of the officials of whom the government is composed. Reversed and remanded.

Analysis:

This case is one of the leading opinions regarding the constitutional protections of free speech, and it is perhaps the most important decision regarding the tort of defamation. Nevertheless, it is important to realize at the outset how limited the holding is. The requirement for proof of actual malice applies only to criticisms of *public officials* relating to their *official conduct.* The opinion is replete with philosophical, public policy rationale that substantiates the Court's holding. In brief, the Court emphasizes the principle that debate on public issues should not be inhibited by a strict requirement that any factual assertions regarding public officials must be absolutely true. A rule to the contrary could lead to self-censorship, as speakers would have to be certain that their statements were not in any way erroneous. On the other hand, it does seem somewhat unfair to Sullivan (P) to allow widespread publication of false, defamatory, and damaging statements that have a likelihood of permanently shaping public opinion regarding the Montgomery Police Department. But the Court does reach a valid point in finding that the advertisement was not "of and concerning" Sullivan (P). If Sullivan had been named in the advertisement, his case would be more persuasive. However, even in this situation, Sullivan (P) could not recover, as he failed to show that the publication was made with actual malice.

■ CASE VOCABULARY

ACTUAL MALICE: Knowledge that a statement was false, or reckless disregard of the truthfulness of a statement.

St. Amant v. Thompson

(*Television Commentator*) v. (*Deputy Sheriff*)

390 U.S. 727, 88 S.Ct. 1323 (1968)

SUPREME COURT DECLINES TO IMPOSE DUTY TO INVESTIGATE THE REASONABLENESS OF STATEMENTS ABOUT PUBLIC OFFICIALS

■ **INSTANT FACTS** Thompson (P), a deputy sheriff, sued St. Amant (D) for televised statements that falsely charged Thompson (P) with criminal conduct.

■ **BLACK LETTER RULE** Reckless disregard, for purposes of the actual malice standard, requires a high degree of actual awareness of the probable falsity of a statement.

■ **PROCEDURAL BASIS**

Writ of certiorari reviewing reversal of appellate court's reversing of judgment for damages for defamation.

■ **FACTS**

In a televised political speech, St. Amant (D) repeated statements that falsely charged Thompson (P), a deputy sheriff, with criminal conduct. Thompson (P) sued St. Amant (D) for defamation. The trial court found that Thompson (P) sustained his burden of proving that St. Amant (D) had acted with actual malice, and the judge awarded damages for Thompson (P). Following the decision, the Supreme Court rendered its holding in *New York Times v. Sullivan* [a false statement about the official conduct of public officials is defamatory only if made with actual malice]. The trial court reconsidered its holding in light of the *New York Times* standard, but the judge ruled that its ruling should stand, and it denied St. Amant's (D) motion for new trial. A state appellate court reversed the judgment, finding that St. Amant (D) had not acted with actual malice. The Louisiana Supreme Court reversed again, finding that Thompson (P) did meet his burden of proving that St. Amant (D) acted in "reckless disregard" of the truth, even though St. Amant (D) had no personal knowledge of Thompson's (P) activities. The United States Supreme Court granted certiorari.

■ **ISSUE**

For purposes of actual malice, should a "reasonably prudent person" standard be utilized?

■ **DECISION AND RATIONALE**

(White, J.) No. For purposes of actual malice, a "reasonably prudent person" standard should not be utilized. Reckless conduct is not measured by whether a reasonably prudent man would have published the statement or would have investigated the statement before publication. Rather, the party bringing the defamation action must prove that the publisher of the statement did in fact act with recklessness. Accepting as a given that St. Amant's (D) statements were false, and that Thompson (P) was a "public official," we nevertheless find that Thompson (P) failed to prove that St. Amant (D) was reckless in quoting the false statements on television. St. Amant (D) did not have a high degree of awareness of the probable falsity of his statements. It may be said that this test for "recklessness" puts a premium on ignorance and encourages the irresponsible publisher not to inquire. While this may be true, we feel that the stake of the people in the conduct of public officials is so great that neither the defense of truth nor the standard of ordinary care would protect against self-censorship and thus adequately implement First Amendment policies. It is essential that the First Amendment protect some erroneous publications as well as true ones. Of course, St. Amant (D) cannot escape liability merely by testifying that he published with a belief that the statements were true. The trier of fact must determine whether St. Amant (D) made the publication in good faith. Because the Louisiana Supreme Court misunderstood the actual malice standard, we reverse and remand for a determination of St. Amant's (D) good faith.

Analysis:

This case further explains and defines the "actual malice" standard of *New York Times v. Sullivan* [a false statement about the official conduct of public officials is defamatory only if made with actual malice]. Actual malice requires either knowledge of falsity or recklessness with respect to the truthfulness of the statement. Thompson (P) attempted to prove that St. Amant (D) was reckless in failing to investigate whether or not the statements about Thompson's (P) criminal conduct were true. However, the Supreme Court makes clear that the mere failure to investigate does not constitute reckless disregard. Thus, there is no duty for a publisher to investigate the truthfulness of his publications regarding public officials in their official capacity. As long as the speaker has no reasonable grounds to believe the statements might be false, he is free from liability for statements. The logic of this holding is somewhat questionable. Is it not possible to protect the First Amendment policies and still require some reasonable investigation prior to publication? This small burden on the speaker seems slight in comparison to the potentially large harm to the public official from a defamatory statement. Furthermore, the test applied by the Court is highly subjective in nature, as it requires the finder of fact to determine the actual mental state of the speaker. Perhaps an objective test, as mentioned by Justice White in the notes following the case, would be better.

■ CASE VOCABULARY

RECKLESS DISREGARD: A high degree of actual awareness of the probable falsity of a statement.

Harte–Hanks Communications, Inc. v. Connaughton

(Publisher) v. *(Politician)*

491 U.S. 657, 109 S.Ct. 2678 (1989)

DELIBERATE AVOIDANCE OF THE TRUTH IN A PUBLISHED STATEMENT MAY ESTABLISH ACTUAL MALICE

■ **INSTANT FACTS** Connaughton (P) sued Harte–Hanks Communications, Inc. (D) for defamation after it published an article quoting a person who accused Connaughton (P) of "dirty tricks" and bribery during his political campaign.

■ **BLACK LETTER RULE** A public figure may not recover damages for a defamatory falsehood without clear and convincing proof that the false statement was made with actual malice.

■ PROCEDURAL BASIS

Certiorari to review a decision of the court of appeals affirming a judgment for the plaintiff.

■ FACTS

When Connaughton (P) was running for election as a judge in Ohio, Harte–Hanks Communications, Inc. (D) published an article in a local newspaper concerning the bribery trial of the incumbent's Director of Court Services. In the article, Harte–Hanks (D) quoted a grand jury witness as saying that Connaughton (P) used "dirty tricks" and offered her jobs and a trip for her help in the bribery investigation. Connaughton (P) lost the election and sued the publisher for defamation. After hearing the evidence, the jury was instructed on the elements of public figure libel and found unanimously that the article was false based on a preponderance of the evidence, and that there was clear and convincing proof that the article was published with actual malice. Connaughton (P) was awarded $200,000 in compensatory and punitive damages. The court of appeals affirmed without making an independent evaluation of the credibility of conflicting oral testimony underlying the finding of actual malice. The defendant sought a writ of certiorari.

■ ISSUE

Did the court of appeals err in affirming the trial court's finding of actual malice when there was conflicting oral testimony on that issue?

■ DECISION AND RATIONALE

(Stevens, J.) No. A public figure may not recover damages for a defamatory falsehood without clear and convincing proof that the false statement was made with actual malice. Actual malice is established by a finding that the statement was made with knowledge that it was false or with reckless disregard for its untruthfulness. Judges have the constitutional duty to "exercise independent judgment and determine whether the record establishes actual malice with convincing clarity."

The defendant claims that the court of appeals erred in applying a less severe standard by requiring only "highly unreasonable conduct constituting an extreme departure from the standards of investigation and reporting ordinarily adhered to by responsible publishers." In its opinion, the court of appeals concluded that the defendant was motivated by its desire to re-elect the incumbent and gain a competitive advantage over its local newspaper competitors, departing from professional standards to do so. These motives, however, cannot support a finding of actual malice. Actual malice is not established by showing ill will in the ordinary sense, but rather by knowingly publishing a false statement or recklessly publishing a statement without due regard for its truthfulness. Reckless disregard requires a high degree of awareness of the statement's probable falsity. While the defendant's state of mind is relevant, its motive is not.

The appellant also contends that the court of appeals gave undue weight to the jury's findings rather than conducting an independent evaluation of the evidence. Judicial consideration of the evidence as a matter of law is particularly necessary in a defamation case because of the important First Amendment issues at play. Courts must carefully consider the evidence to determine whether the published statements are constitutionally protected or cross the threshold into actionable defamation. This is particularly true when the statements are political in nature, since such statements often inspire "rough and personal" debate. Although the democratic process encourages the open and frank exchange of ideas during political elections, this value does not license the press to publish statements about public officials with knowledge of their falsity or with reckless disregard for their truthfulness. To establish reckless disregard, it is insufficient to show a deviation from accepted standards; nor does a failure to investigate the truthfulness of a statement establish reckless disregard. Instead, there must be evidence of a high degree of awareness of the probable falsity of the statement.

Although on appeal the court must review the credibility determinations of the trier of fact using a clear and convincing standard, the court must examine the statements made and the evidence offered to independently determine whether actual malice has been established. While the court of appeals determined upon examining the facts that the jury could have reasonably found actual malice, actual malice can be established on less speculative grounds. Upon examining the jury's responses to special interrogatories, it follows that the jury indeed rejected certain testimony concerning the defendant's state of mind. Affording due weight to the jury's credibility determinations, it is likely that the defendant's decision not to acquire knowledge of the facts reported constituted a purposeful avoidance of the truth of the facts. While a failure to investigate does not establish actual malice, a deliberate choice not to investigate amounts to reckless disregard for the truth. Affirmed.

Analysis:

Deliberate avoidance is a difficult concept to apply. At what point and to what extent must a publisher investigate a statement to ensure its truthfulness? Especially with sensational journalism, many fact statements may sound too outlandish to be true, yet if the publisher believes the veracity of its source, may it merely accept its source's credibility? These difficult questions must be considered by courts in determining whether reckless disregard for the truth exists in public official defamation suits.

■ CASE VOCABULARY

ACTUAL MALICE: Knowledge (by the person who utters or publishes a defamatory statement) that a statement is false, or reckless disregard about whether the statement is true.

Gertz v. Robert Welch, Inc.

(Attorney) v. *(Publisher)*

418 U.S. 323, 94 S.Ct. 2997 (1974)

STATES MAY ADOPT LOWER STANDARDS FOR DEFAMATION AGAINST PRIVATE INDIVIDUALS

■ **INSTANT FACTS** Gertz (P), a private attorney involved in a high-publicity case, sued the publisher of American Opinion for damages for libel.

■ **BLACK LETTER RULE** States may adopt lesser standards than actual malice for defamation cases brought by private figures, but actual malice must be proven in order to recover punitive damages.

■ PROCEDURAL BASIS

Writ of certiorari reviewing affirmation of judgment notwithstanding the verdict against party bringing claim for damages for libel.

■ FACTS

Elmer Gertz (P) was hired as an attorney to institute a civil action against Nuccio, a Chicago policeman who was convicted of murder. Robert Welch, Inc. (D) published American Opinion, a monthly publication of the John Birch Society. In American Opinion, Welch (D) published an article on the murder trial of Nuccio. The article portrayed Gertz (P) as an architect of the "frame-up" against the Chicago Police Department, and it labeled Gertz (P) as a "Leninist" and a "Communist-fronter." These allegations and others contained in the article were false, and the managing editor of American Opinion made no effort to substantiate the charges against Gertz (P). Gertz (P) sued for damages for libel in District Court. The District Court initially denied Welch's (D) motion to dismiss and awarded $50,000 to Gertz (P). However, the District Court later concluded that the *New York Times* malice standard applied to Gertz (P). Accordingly, a judgment for Welch (D) was entered notwithstanding the verdict. This judgment was affirmed by the Court of Appeals. The Supreme Court granted certiorari.

■ ISSUE

(1) May States define appropriate standards for the publication of defamatory falsehoods against private figures, even if the standards are less demanding than the *New York Times* malice standard?
(2) May States permit recovery of punitive damages when liability is not based on actual malice?

■ DECISION AND RATIONALE

(Powell, J.) (1) Yes. States may define appropriate standards for the publication of defamatory falsehoods against private figures, even if the standards are less demanding than the *New York Times* malice standard. States have a legitimate interest in compensating individuals for harm inflicted by defamatory falsehoods. In order to avoid the problems with ad hod resolutions of each case, broad rules may be established. Private individuals are more vulnerable to injury than public officials or public figures. They lack effective opportunities for rebuttal of false statements, and they are more deserving of recovery, since private individuals have not voluntarily exposed themselves to increased risk of injury from defamatory falsehoods. Thus, so long as States do not impose strict liability for defamation, they are free to define the appropriate standard of liability for publishers of defamatory falsehoods that injure a private individual. (2) No. States may not permit the recovery of punitive damages when liability is not based on actual malice. In reconciling State interests with the competing interest grounded in the First Amendment, we hold that the remedies for defamatory falsehood must reach no farther than necessary to protect the legitimate interests involved. The legitimate interests of private individuals in recovering damages for defamation extend to only compensation for actual injury. Finally, in the case at hand, we disagree with Welch's (D) contention that Gertz (P) should be considered a "de facto public official." Although in some cases a private individual may achieve such general fame or notoriety in the community as to be considered public figures, Gertz (P) did not voluntarily inject himself into a particular public controversy in the facts at hand. Reversed and remanded for proper application of the standard for private figures and proper determination of damages.

Analysis:

This opinion raises three important points regarding defamation actions brought by private individuals. First, private individuals can recover without showing that the defamatory statement was made with actual *New York Times* malice. The Court describes the convincing and compelling policy rationale for its holding. Second, punitive damages are inappropriate unless actual malice is proven. Although the opinion does not fully explain this holding, it seems sensible that a publisher should not be punished (by an award of punitive damages) unless he acted with a high degree of culpability and malice. Third, even private individuals may be considered "limited purpose" public figures for purposes of defamation actions. This typically occurs when the private person voluntarily injects himself or is drawn into a particular public controversy. If an individual achieves fame or notoriety with respect to a certain controversy, then that individual presumably has effective opportunities for rebuttal (by, for example, going to the press). Moreover, the limited purpose public figure, by voluntarily choosing to enter a certain controversy, is somewhat less deserving of protection than a purely private individual. Finally, note that this holding merely asserts what States are free to do. States can adopt any standard they choose for private defamation, except a strict liability standard. Presumably, therefore, States can utilize the actual malice standard of *New York Times*, as this opinion did not assert to the contrary.

■ CASE VOCABULARY

AD HOC: For a special limited purpose.

NORMATIVE: Pertaining to correct behavior.

Dun & Bradstreet, Inc. v. Greenmoss Builders, Inc.

(Credit Service) v. *(Construction Company)*

472 U.S. 749, 105 S.Ct. 2939 (1985)

SPEECH ON MATTERS OF PRIVATE CONCERN IS LESS DESERVING OF FIRST AMENDMENT PROTECTION THAN PUBLIC SPEECH

■ **INSTANT FACTS** Greenmoss Builders (P) sued for false statements contained on credit reports issued by Dun & Bradstreet (D).

■ **BLACK LETTER RULE** Defamatory statements regarding purely private issues are subject to punitive damages without the requirement of proving actual malice.

■ **PROCEDURAL BASIS**

Writ of certiorari reviewing affirmation of verdict for compensatory and punitive damages for libel.

■ **FACTS**

Dun & Bradstreet (D), a credit-rating service, supplied confidential credit reports regarding Greenmoss Builders (P) to five subscribers. The credit reports erroneously indicated that Greenmoss (P) had filed a voluntary petition for bankruptcy. Dun & Bradstreet's (D) error resulted from its use of a 17-year-old student who checked Vermont bankruptcy filings, and from Dun & Bradstreet's (D) failure to make routine checks for accuracy. Greenmoss (P) sued for libel and obtained a verdict for $50,000 in compensatory damages and $300,000 in punitives. The trial court granted Dun & Bradstreet's (D) motion for new trial. Greenmoss (P) appealed to the Vermont Supreme Court, which reversed and reinstated the verdict on the ground that the constitutional requirements regarding defamation did not apply to suits against a non-media defendant. The United States Supreme Court granted certiorari.

■ **ISSUE**

In a defamation action involving matters of private concern, must actual malice be proven in order to recover punitive damages?

■ **DECISION AND RATIONALE**

(Powell, J.) No. In a defamation action involving matters of private concern, actual malice need not be proven in order to recover punitive damages. In reaching this conclusion, we must balance the State's interest in compensating private individuals for injury to their reputation against the First Amendment interest in protecting this type of expression. Speech on matters of purely private concern is of less First Amendment concern than speech on matters of public concern. The State's interest in awarding punitive damages is substantial relative to the incidental effect that punitive damages may have on speech of less constitutional interest. This State interest supports awards of punitive damages absent a showing of actual malice. The only remaining issue in the case at hand is whether Dun & Bradstreet's (D) credit report involved a matter of public concern. Because the credit report was solely in the interest of Dun & Bradstreet (D) and its business audience, Dun & Bradstreet's (D) credit report concerns no public issue. The credit report was clearly false and damaging to Greenmoss's (P) business reputation, and thus Dun & Bradstreet's (D) constitutional interest in free speech warrants no special protection. In addition, Dun & Bradstreet's (D) free speech is unlikely to be deterred by incidental state regulation. Thus, we affirm the holding of the Vermont Supreme Court, although for different reasons than those relied upon by that Court.

■ DISSENT

(Brennan, J.) We believe that the First Amendment requires restraints on punitive damage awards for the expression at issue. There must be some showing of fault in order to recover punitive damages. The majority departs too far from the holding in *Gertz* [States may adopt lesser standards than actual malice for defamation cases brought by private figures, but actual malice must be proven in order to recover punitive damages]. *Gertz* was intended to reach any false statements, whether or not they implicate a matter of public importance. In addition, we feel that the credit report at issue involves a matter of sufficient public concern to require the protections of *Gertz*. Thus, Greenmoss (P) should have recovered punitive damages only if it could show actual malice.

Analysis:

This case considers the issue of First Amendment protections of free speech when the speaker is not a member of the media. Does it make sense to give speech on matters of public concern more protection from punitive damages than speech on private issues? The majority applies a balancing test that appears to be logical, yet its efficacy can be questioned. According to the majority, speech on matters of private concern is less deserving of First Amendment protection. The rationale is that the nature of private information militates against its production and dissemination being "chilled" by punitive damages liability. But wouldn't private companies, in light of this holding, be wary to make any statement about a private individual, knowing that potentially huge punitive damages could be imposed? Perhaps the majority is short-sighted in concluding that private companies would continue to provide services such as credit reports in light of their potential for heightened liability. Finally, note that the holding does not grant media defendants any more protection than non-media defendants. The scope of this opinion deals only with the nature of the publication—whether it is of public or private concern—and not on the status of the speaker.

■ CASE VOCABULARY

PUBLIC CONCERN: Speech that, based on its content, form, and context, is of general interest to the public at large.

Philadelphia Newspapers, Inc. v. Hepps

(Newspaper Publisher) v. (Controlling Stockholder)

475 U.S. 767, 106 S.Ct. 1558 (1986)

THE FIRST AMENDMENT PROTECTS THE SPEECH OF PUBLIC FIGURES SO LONG AS THE SPEECH CANNOT BE PROVEN TO BE FALSE

■ **INSTANT FACTS** Hepps (D) sued Philadelphia Newspapers, Inc. (D) for libel arising out of stories imputing organized criminal behavior.

■ **BLACK LETTER RULE** Where a public figure publishes defamatory statements of public concern, a defamed private party must prove that the statements are false.

■ **PROCEDURAL BASIS**

Writ of certiorari reviewing affirmation of verdict in action for damages for libel.

■ **FACTS**

Philadelphia Newspapers, Inc. (D) published a series of articles which charged that Maurice Hepps (P) and the corporation he controlled, General Programming, Inc. ("GPI"), had links to organized crime and used the ties to influence the governmental process. Hepps (P) and GPI (P) sued Philadelphia Newspapers (D) in state court for libel. Pursuant to Pennsylvania common law, the trial court required Philadelphia Newspapers (D) to prove the truth of the statements in order to escape liability. The jury rendered a verdict for Philadelphia Newspapers (D), and the Pennsylvania Supreme Court affirmed on appeal, holding that the imposition on a speaker of the burden to prove truth did not unconstitutionally inhibit free debate. The United States Supreme Court granted certiorari.

■ **ISSUE**

Where a public figure publishes defamatory statements of public concern, must a defamed private party prove that the statements are false?

■ **DECISION AND RATIONALE**

(O'Connor, J.) Yes. Where a public figure publishes defamatory statements of public concern, a defamed private party must prove that the statements are false. At common law, and pursuant to the law of Pennsylvania, the speaker was required to bear the burden of proving the truth of the statements in order to escape liability. We believe, conversely, that the constitution requires a defamed private party to bear this burden of proving falsity, as well as fault, before recovering damages. The common-law presumption that speech is false cannot stand when a plaintiff seeks damages against a media defendant for speech of public concern. This common-law approach is too restrictive and has a definite "chilling" effect on free speech. Our approach, while imposing a large burden on the defamed party, may result in the protection of false speech, but it accomplishes the greater goal of protecting speech that matters. We note that this burden on the defamed party is not much greater than the common-law requirement to show fault. As a practical matter, a publisher's fault in failing to adequately investigate the truth of published statements will generally encompass evidence of the falsity of the matters asserted. Reversed and remanded.

■ **DISSENT**

(Stevens, J.) The majority is overly protective of free speech on matters of public concern. Our precedents do not require a private individual to bear the risk that he cannot prove the falsity of a defamatory statement. The State has a great interest in protecting the private individual's good name. This defamed individual already must meet the heavy burden of proving fault in the publication of the statements. Society has a compelling need to redress libelous utterances. A public party, such as a newspaper, should not be given an absolute license to defame by means of statements that cannot be disproven. As long as publishers are protected by the requirement that the plaintiff has the burden of proving fault, there is little danger of deterring *true* speech.

Analysis:

This case asserts a powerful rule of law, imposing the burden of proving falsity on the private individual who claims to have been defamed by a public entity. Although both the majority and dissent raise valid points, the holding can be criticized. In most situations, the private individual would not have the financial resources necessary to compete with a powerful public entity like Philadelphia Newspapers (D). In addition, it is logically very difficult to "prove a negative," i.e., that a statement is not true. Furthermore, the majority's justification on grounds of preventing speech from being "chilled" is questionable. Would a newspaper really cease to publish statements if it knew that it might be later forced to prove the truthfulness of the material it published? And even if the newspaper was somewhat deterred from publishing articles of questionable truth, isn't it very important to protect private individuals from false, defamatory statements? On the other hand, newspapers every day publish stories relating to a large number of private individuals. Perhaps the news media would cease to exist if it could be liable to each individual merely by a showing that the publisher failed to exercise due care in investigating the truthfulness of its statements. All in all, the results of this holding are clearly evident every time a person visits a grocery store checkout counter. Tabloids like the National Enquirer have no need to worry about all of the ludicrous stories they publish, since they are shielded by the Supreme Court's interpretation of the First Amendment.

■ **CASE VOCABULARY**

ASSAYING: Analyzing or evaluating.

PERNICIOUS: Harmful, ruinous or fatal.

TAUTOLOGICALLY: Relating to a needless repetition.

VILIFY: To utter slanderous and abusive statements.

Milkovich v. Lorain Journal Co.

(Wrestling Coach) v. *(Newspaper Owner)*

497 U.S. 1, 110 S.Ct. 2695 (1990)

SUPREME COURT ABOLISHES IMMUNITY FOR DEFAMATORY STATEMENTS COUCHED AS OPINIONS

■ **INSTANT FACTS** Michael Milkovich (P) sued a newspaper for libel, and the newspaper contended that the writer's statement that Milkovich (P) perjured himself was a pure statement of opinion.

■ **BLACK LETTER RULE** Where a statement of opinion reasonably implies false and defamatory facts, liability may be imposed.

■ PROCEDURAL BASIS

Writ of certiorari reviewing affirmation of grant of summary judgment dismissing action for damages for libel.

■ FACTS

In 1974, the wrestling team from a high school in Maple Heights, Ohio, was involved in an altercation at a wrestling match in which several people were injured. The coach of Maple Heights, Michael Milkovich (P), and the Superintendent, H. Don Scott, testified about the events at a hearing before the Ohio High School Athletic Association (OHSAA). After OHSAA placed the team on probation, a group of wrestlers and parents sued in Ohio state court for an order restraining the ruling. Milkovich (P) and Scott again testified, and the state court overturned OHSAA's probation. The day after the court rendered its decision, J. Theodore Diadiun (D) wrote a newspaper article in the News-Herald, a paper owned by Lorain Journal Co. (D). The article began with a large headline that read "TD [Diadiun (D)] Says," and it went on to allege that Milkovich (P) and Scott had lied under oath in order to get out of a jam [OHSAA had them in a headlock]. Milkovich (P) sued Diadiun (D) and Lorain Journal (D) for libel, and the trial court granted summary judgment against Milkovich (P). The Ohio Court of Appeals affirmed, based on the Ohio Supreme Court's ruling in a libel case brought by Scott involving the same facts. In *Scott,* the Ohio Supreme Court concluded that, based on the "totality of circumstances," the article was "constitutionally protected opinion." Milkovich (P) appealed to the Ohio Supreme Court, which dismissed the appeal based on its holding in *Scott.* The United States Supreme Court granted certiorari.

■ ISSUE

Do statements of opinion enjoy special constitutional protections and immunity from liability for defamation?

■ DECISION AND RATIONALE

(Rehnquist, J.) No. Statements of opinion do not enjoy special constitutional protections and immunity from liability for defamation. Rather, statements of opinion are treated as any other statement for purposes of defamation actions. Where a statement of opinion reasonably implies false and defamatory facts, liability attaches based on the standards of proof previously enunciated by the Supreme Court. In the case at hand, where Diadiun's (D) statement was on a matter of public concern involving a public figure, Milkovich (P) must prove that the statement was made with actual malice. At common law, defamatory communications were actionable whether they were deemed to be statements of fact or opinion. However, the privilege of "fair comment" eventually eroded this common-law rule, providing legal immunity for the honest expression of opinion on matters of legitimate public interest. Nevertheless, this privilege of fair comment extended only to expressions of pure opinion, not false statements of fact. But it is essential to recognize that expressions of opinion may often imply an assertion of objective fact. For example, the statement that "In my opinion John Jones is a liar" implies a knowledge of facts which lead to the conclusion that John Jones told an untruth. Such a statement can cause as much damage to reputation as the factual averment that "John Jones is a liar." A writer should not be able to escape liability simply by using the words "in my opinion." Furthermore, our prior holdings on defamatory communications and the heightened burdens of proof adequately protect the uninhibited, robust debate on public issues. Thus, an additional separate constitutional privilege for opinion is not required in order to ensure the freedom of expression guaranteed by the First Amendment. Returning to the instant case, we hold that a reasonable factfinder could conclude that Diadiun's (D) statements imply an assertion that Milkovich (P) perjured himself. In addition, the connotation of perjury is sufficiently factual to be susceptible of being proved true or false. Our holding recognizes and preserves society's strong interest in preventing and redressing attacks on reputation, whether the attacks are classified as fact or opinion. Reversed and remanded.

Analysis:

A writer certainly should not be allowed to destroy a person's reputation merely by categorizing his statement as opinion rather than a statement of fact. Based on this simple idea, the Court essentially abolishes any special constitutional privilege for statements of opinion that are factual in nature. Only pure statements of opinion, such as "Milkovich (P) is a terrible coach," are protected by the "fair comment" privilege. In order to reach this conclusion, the Court engages in an extensive and difficult balancing test. On one hand, the First Amendment protections must be safeguarded in order to assure a robust debate on matters of public concern. On the other hand, the rights of individuals to be free from false and malicious attacks on their reputation must be protected. Nearly all of the Supreme Court's holdings we have read hinge upon this balancing test. Because both sides of the balance are very compelling, the Court could have easily held that the First Amendment protections should prevail over the rights of individuals to be free from defamation. However, the First Amendment safeguards retain significant force by virtue of the difficult standard of proof that public figures must bear when proving defamation by a media defendant. It is nevertheless easy to see the can of worms opened by this holding. Newspapers contain thousands of statements every day that can be construed as opinion-based. The Court leaves it up to juries to determine whether defamatory statements of opinion are really so rooted in fact, or at least imply assertions of fact, that they may result in defamation liability. Although a precise test is not enunciated by the Court, presumably analyses like the D.C. Circuit's "totality of the circumstances" test are plausible so long as every effort is made to classify opinion statements as factually-based and, therefore, potentially defamatory.

■ CASE VOCABULARY

INTER ALIA: Among other things.

Sindorf v. Jacron Sales Co., Inc.

(Salesman) v. *(Former Employer)*
27 Md.App. 53, 341 A.2d 856 (1975)

CONDITIONAL PRIVILEGES PROTECT STATEMENTS MADE FOR THE DECLARANT'S SELF-INTER-EST, IF THEY ARE PUBLISHED IN A REASONABLE MANNER AND FOR A PROPER PURPOSE

■ **INSTANT FACTS** Sindorf (P) sued Jacron Sales Co. (D), his former employer, for allegedly defamatory statements made to Sindorf's (P) new employer.

■ **BLACK LETTER RULE** Qualified privileges protect persons speaking in their own self-interest, but the communications must be published in a reasonable manner and for a proper purpose.

■ FACTS

Sindorf (P) worked as a salesman for the Pennsylvania division of Jacron Sales Co. (D). Sindorf (P) resigned amidst a dispute with the company. Jacron (D) contended that Sindorf (P) was selling to people without adequately checking their credit ratings, and Jacron (D) allegedly withheld some commissions due to Sindorf (P) until Jacron (D) received payment for all of the sales. In turn, Sindorf (P) kept some of his inventory as partial payment for commissions owed to him. Sindorf (P) then went to work for Tool Box Corporation. Bob Fridkis, the president of the Virginia branch of Jacron (D), called the president of Tool Box to see whether Sindorf (P) had started working for Tool Box before leaving Jacron (D). Fridkis told Tool Box that they had better watch their stock carefully, and Fridkis made other derogatory comments about Sindorf (P). Sindorf (P) sued for defamation. The trial court held that Fridkis' conversation was constitutionally privileged and not made with malice, and it granted Jacron's (D) motion for directed verdict. Sindorf (P) appeals.

■ ISSUE

(1) Does a qualified privilege exist that protects communications made by a former employer about a former employee to a new employer? (2) In order for qualified privileges to serve as defenses to defamation, must the communications be published in a reasonable manner and for a proper purpose?

■ DECISION AND RATIONALE

(Orth, J.) (1) Yes. A qualified privilege exists that protects communications made by a former employer about a former employee to a new employer. Qualified privileges typically occur in situations where a person discharges some duty in matters where his own interest is concerned. Maryland common law dictates that a defamatory publication is conditionally privileged where the communicating party and the recipient have a mutual interest in the subject matter, or some duty with respect thereto. Thus, where a former employer communicates with a new or prospective employer about a former employee, a conditional privilege arises from a discharge of duty owed by the former employer to the new or prospective employer. Thus, the trial court did not err in holding as a matter of law that Fridkis, and therefore Jacron (D), had a conditional privilege to communicate defamatory statements about Sindorf (P) to Tool Box. (2) Yes. In order for qualified privileges to serve as defenses to defamation, the communications must be published in a reasonable manner and for a proper purpose. The statements must not be published to any person other than those whose hearing is reasonably believed to be necessary for the furtherance of their interest. The speaker must establish the reasonableness of the publication. Certain factors to be considered include the speaker's reasonable belief in the truth of his statements, the nature of the language used, and whether the statements were solicited and made to proper parties. In the case at hand, Fridkis' statements were volunteered. Furthermore, Fridkis incorrectly told Tool Box that Sindorf (P) had been fired, when in fact he had resigned. We believe that a reasonable person could conclude that Fridkis' statement was an effort to pressure Sindorf (P) into returning the inventory which he was holding. We cannot find that Jacron (D), through Fridkis, did not abuse the privilege to defame by use of the communication for an improper purpose. Thus, the question of malice should have gone to the jury, and the trial judge erred in granting the motion for directed verdict. Reversed and remanded.

Analysis:

It may be somewhat surprising that certain defamatory statements are acceptable if they are made for the self-interest of the speaker and the listener. In the case at hand, a former employer could have been privileged to utter false statements to a new employer about a former employee, presumably because both employers had significant interests in the communication. However, the harsh effect of this common-law rule is militated by the "conditional" nature of the privilege. In order to be protected, the defamatory statements must not be made for an improper motive. Furthermore, the speaker must have a reasonable belief in the truth of his statements. Fortunately for Sindorf (P), the fact that Fridkis uttered his statements on his own volition, and not on request from Tool Box, helped to establish that the statements were not as a matter of law exempt from liability. In addition, the statements were not clearly truthful in Fridkis' own mind. Thus, the jury should have determined whether the privilege applied. As the notes following this case indicate, a wide variety of conditional privileges exist. These privileges generally require some overriding interest that outweighs the harm done to the defamed party. But it is important to realize that the defamation must be innocent and not malicious, i.e., the speaker must have a reasonable belief in the truthfulness of his statements.

■ CASE VOCABULARY

DEFEASIBLE: Subject to revocation upon the occurrence of a certain event or condition.

VEL NON: Or not.

CHAPTER EIGHTEEN

Privacy

Joe Dickerson & Associates, Llc v. Dittmar

Instant Facts: Dittmar (P) sued Joe Dickerson & Associates (D) after Dickerson (D) published her name and picture in a newsletter.

Black Letter Rule: To establish a cause of action for invasion of privacy by appropriation of one's name and likeness, the plaintiff must demonstrate that the defendant used her name or likeness, that the use of her name or likeness was for the defendant's own benefit, damages, and causation.

Sanders v. American Broadcasting Cos., Inc., et al.

Instant Facts: Lescht (D), a reporter for the American Broadcasting Co. (D), secretly recorded conversations with Sanders (P) at his workplace.

Black Letter Rule: In a workplace to which the general public does not have unfettered access, employees enjoy a limited, but legitimate, expectation that their conversations and other interactions will not be secretly recorded, even though those conversations may not be completely private from coworkers.

Hall v. Post

Instant Facts: Hall (P) sued Post (D) for publishing two truthful articles about her adoption and subsequent reunion with her natural parents.

Black Letter Rule: Liability for the public disclosure of private facts requires that the matter publicized is of a kind that would be highly offensive to a reasonable person and is not of legitimate concern to the public.

Cantrell v. Forest City Publishing Co.

Instant Facts: Margaret Cantrell (P) and her children sued for the publication of a newspaper article depicting their family as living in abject poverty.

Black Letter Rule: Actual malice must be proven in order to recover under a "false light" theory.

Hustler Magazine v. Falwell

Instant Facts: Jerry Falwell (P) sued Hustler Magazine (D) for intentional infliction of emotional distress for publishing a parody of Falwell (P) engaged in incestuous acts with his mother.

Black Letter Rule: In order to recover for intentional infliction of emotional distress, public figures must show that a false statement of fact was made with actual malice.

Joe Dickerson & Associates, LLC v. Dittmar

(Private Investigator) v. *(Bond Thief)*

34 P.3d 995 (Colo.2001) (en banc)

A PLAINTIFF NEED NOT PROVE THE *VALUE* OF HER IDENTITY TO RECOVER FOR APPROPRIATION OF HER NAME OR LIKENESS

■ **INSTANT FACTS** Dittmar (P) sued Joe Dickerson & Associates (D) after Dickerson (D) published her name and picture in a newsletter.

■ **BLACK LETTER RULE** To establish a cause of action for invasion of privacy by appropriation of one's name and likeness, the plaintiff must demonstrate that the defendant used her name or likeness, that the use of her name or likeness was for the defendant's own benefit, damages, and causation.

■ **PROCEDURAL BASIS**

On appeal to review a decision of the Colorado Court of Appeals reversing a trial court's grant of summary judgment for the defendant.

■ **FACTS**

Joe Dickerson & Associates (D) was hired during a child custody dispute to investigate Dittmar (P). During the investigation, Dickerson (D) discovered that Dittmar (P) had stolen certain bearer bonds; it reported her to the police, and she was convicted. In a free newsletter published and distributed to law enforcement officials, law firms, and others, Dickerson (D) discussed Dittmar's (P) case as an example of his success, using Dittmar's (P) name and photograph in the article and on the newsletter's cover. Dittmar (P) sued Dickerson (D) for defamation, outrageous conduct, and invasion of privacy by appropriation of her name and likeness. The trial court granted Dickerson's (D) motion for summary judgment, deciding that Colorado law did not recognize the invasion of privacy claim. The trial court further concluded that even if the claim was cognizable, Dittmar (P) failed to demonstrate that her name and likeness had any value. On appeal, the court of appeals agreed that Dittmar's (P) identity required certain value to be protected, but reversed because issues of fact existed concerning the purpose of the publication and the benefit Dickerson (D) derived from it. Dickerson (D) appealed.

■ **ISSUE**

When a plaintiff is damaged by the invasion of her privacy by appropriation of her name and likeness, must she demonstrate the value of her name and likeness?

■ **DECISION AND RATIONALE**

(Bender, J.) No. A plaintiff's privacy is invaded when a defendant appropriates her name or likeness for the defendant's own benefit. While the plaintiff can recover damages for personal injuries, such as emotional distress, there is uncertainty whether the plaintiff may recover pecuniary losses for the appropriation itself. Unlike other privacy torts, some courts and commentators view one's identity as a property right, compensable by the commercial value of the plaintiff's identity. The Restatement (Second) of Torts § 652C has incorporated this view: "The value of a plaintiff's name is not appropriated by mere mention of it, or by reference to it in connection with legitimate mention of his public activities; nor is the value of his likeness when it is published for purposes other than taking advantage of his reputation, prestige, or other value . . ., for purposes of publicity." Other courts distinguish between mental damages and pecuniary damages by taking the "right to publicity" action outside the "right to privacy" arena, acknowledging that the right to publicity is a commercial right, not one of privacy.

Colorado law recognizes the tort of invasion of privacy by appropriation of an individual's name or likeness. To establish a cause of action, the Colorado Civil Jury Instructions state that a plaintiff must demonstrate that (1) the defendant used her name or likeness, (2) the defendant sought to take advantage of the plaintiff's reputation, status, or other value of her likeness, (3) the use of her name or likeness was for defendant's own benefit, (4) damages, and (5) causation.

Here, the dispute centers on the second element. Some courts have interpreted this requirement to mean that the plaintiff's identity must have some pre-existing commercial value to establish the tort. This approach, however, considers the plaintiff's identity a property right, discounting her claim for emotional distress. When the plaintiff claims personal, not pecuniary, damages, the market value of her identity is unrelated to whether she has suffered emotional distress. Accordingly, the second element proposed in the jury instructions is not adopted and is not a requirement of the tort. Applying the remaining elements here, Dittmar (P) produced sufficient facts to establish her claim. Summary judgment should have been denied on this ground.

However, summary judgment was appropriate because the article about Dittmar (P) was a matter of legitimate public concern, protected by the First Amendment. In appropriation cases, the First Amendment affords a privilege to use another's name or likeness if it reasonably relates to a publication concerning a matter that is newsworthy or of legitimate public concern. Where the appropriation is used for primarily commercial reasons, however, rather than for communicating news, the privilege does not attach. Here, the defendant's newsletter is primarily noncommercial because it relates to a matter of public concern. It recounted his investigation, detection, and subsequent conviction of Dittmar's (P) crime, and the fact that Dickerson (D) operated the newsletter for profit does not render the article commercial. Because the article was truthful and a matter of legitimate public concern, it is privileged under the First Amendment. Affirmed.

Analysis:

In many cases like this, the plaintiff may also have a cause of action for negligent or intentional infliction of emotional distress. To establish a cause of action for intentional infliction of emotional distress, a Colorado plaintiff must generally demonstrate conduct "so outrageous in character and so extreme in degree as to go beyond all possible bounds of decency and to be regarded as atrocious and utterly intolerable in a civilized community." The court here appears to reduce this requirement to recover for emotional distress in privacy cases.

■ CASE VOCABULARY

COMMERCIAL SPEECH: Communication (such as advertising and marketing) that involves only the commercial interests of the speaker and the audience, and is therefore afforded lesser First Amendment protection than social, political, or religious speech.

INVASION OF PRIVACY: An unjustified exploitation of one's personality or intrusion into one's personal activity, actionable under tort law and sometimes under constitutional law.

Sanders v. American Broadcasting Cos., Inc., et al.

(Telepsychic) v. *(Broadcast Company)*

20 Cal.4th 907, 978 P.2d 67, 85 Cal.Rptr.2d 909 (1999)

A *COMPLETE* EXPECTATION OF PRIVACY IS NOT REQUIRED TO SUSTAIN A CLAIM FOR COMMON LAW INTRUSION

■ **INSTANT FACTS** Lescht (D), a reporter for the American Broadcasting Co. (D), secretly recorded conversations with Sanders (P) at his workplace.

■ **BLACK LETTER RULE** In a workplace to which the general public does not have unfettered access, employees enjoy a limited, but legitimate, expectation that their conversations and other interactions will not be secretly recorded, even though those conversations may not be completely private from coworkers.

■ **PROCEDURAL BASIS**

On appeal to review a decision of the California Court of Appeals reversing a verdict for the plaintiff.

■ **FACTS**

Lescht (D), a reporter for the American Broadcasting Co., Inc., (D) went undercover as a telepsychic with the Psychic Marketing Group. While undercover, Lescht (D) wore a hidden video camera and recorded conversations with Sanders (P), another telepsychic, that occurred in their cubicles, where coworkers could overhear them. Sanders (P) sued Lescht (D) and ABC (D) for common law invasion of privacy by intrusion and violations of California Penal Code § 632. After the jury concluded that the conversations occurred in a place where they could easily be overheard by coworkers, the trial court directed judgment for the defendants on the § 632 cause of action. The trial court denied the defendants' motion for summary judgment on the common law claims, however, and the jury entered a verdict for Sanders (P). On appeal, the California Court of Appeals reversed, finding that Sanders (P) could not have a reasonable expectation of privacy in his workplace conversations because such conversations could be overheard by others, precluding his common law claims. Sanders (P) appealed.

■ **ISSUE**

Does an employee have a reasonable expectation of privacy with regard to communications that can be overheard by coworkers?

■ **DECISION AND RATIONALE**

(Werdegar, J.) Yes. "In an office or other workplace to which the general public does not have unfettered access, employees may enjoy a limited, but legitimate, expectation that their conversations and other interactions will not be secretly videotaped by undercover television reporters, even though those conversations may not have been completely private from the participants' coworkers." Whether the reasonable expectation of privacy exists depends, however, on the nature of the conduct and the surrounding circumstances. A cause of action for intrusion requires an intrusion into a private place, conversation, or matter in a manner highly offensive to a reasonable person. When the intrusion occurs in a public place, capable of observation by others, there is no reasonable expectation of privacy. In other words, to establish the cause of action, the plaintiff must demonstrate an objectively reasonable expectation of solitude or seclusion in the place, conversation, or matter.

But this expectation need not be absolute or complete to establish the claim. Instead, when the plaintiff expects that his conversations may be overheard by only a limited group of people, his expectation of privacy may be established. Similarly, although the plaintiff may have no reasonable expectation of confidentiality of a conversation with another, he may still have an expectation that he will not be secretly recorded and that his firsthand conversations will not be disseminated to others. One who entertains a conversation with another bears the risk that the conversation will be repeated to others, but not that it will be recorded and broadcast to everyone.

Accordingly, even though a person lacks a complete expectation of privacy in his workplace because his conversations can be overheard by a limited number of coworkers, he nevertheless has a limited expectation of privacy protecting him against a reporter's covert recording of his conversations. This expectation of privacy is sufficient to establish common law invasion of privacy. Reversed and remanded.

Analysis:

The United States Supreme Court has not yet considered whether an employee has a reasonable expectation of privacy in his or her workplace. While many jurisdictions agree with the California Supreme Court that a limited expectation of privacy exists, others do not recognize the invasion of privacy tort in such circumstances. Those jurisdictions largely reason that any damages caused by the intrusion are adequately compensable under a cause of action for trespass, relieving the need for an additional cause of action.

■ CASE VOCABULARY

INTRUSION: In an action for invasion of privacy, a highly offensive invasion of another person's seclusion or private life.

Hall v. Post

(*Article Subject*) v. (*Reporter*)
323 N.C. 259, 372 S.E.2d 711 (1988)

TRUTHFUL PUBLIC DISCLOSURE OF PRIVATE FACTS IS NOT AN INVASION OF PRIVACY

■ **INSTANT FACTS** Hall (P) sued Post (D) for publishing two truthful articles about her adoption and subsequent reunion with her natural parents.

■ **BLACK LETTER RULE** Liability for the public disclosure of private facts requires that the matter publicized is of a kind that would be highly offensive to a reasonable person and is not of legitimate concern to the public.

■ **PROCEDURAL BASIS**

On appeal to review a decision of the North Carolina Court of Appeals

■ **FACTS**

Hall (P) and her adoptive mother sued Post (D) based on two articles published in the Salisbury Post. The first article chronicled the search of Hall's (P) birth mother for the daughter she had placed for adoption with her babysitter seventeen years earlier. After the article was published, Hall's birth mother learned the identity of her child. A second article recounted the discovery of Hall's (P) identity and her reunion with her birth mother. The plaintiffs claimed to have suffered emotional and mental distress as a result of the articles and that they were forced to leave their home because of the public attention. Although the facts in the articles were true, the plaintiffs sued Post (D) for invasion of privacy.

■ **ISSUE**

Are claims for tortious invasion of privacy by truthful public disclosure of private facts cognizable under North Carolina law?

■ **DECISION AND RATIONALE**

(Mitchell, J.) No. The general right of privacy encompasses, among others, the public disclosure of private facts about the plaintiff. Liability under this right of privacy requires that "the matter publicized is of a kind that (a) would be highly offensive to a reasonable person, and (b) is not of legitimate concern to the public." In determining the public interest involved, a court must take into account the customs and conventions of the community to draw the line between the giving of information to which the public is entitled and sensational prying into private lives for its own sake.

Although North Carolina acknowledges a general right of privacy, invasion of privacy arising from publicity that places the plaintiff in a false light is not a cognizable claim because it often duplicates or overlaps with other claims. So, too, are claims arising from the publication of private, but true, facts not cognizable. Such claims are constitutionally suspect, asking the defendant's constitutional right to free speech to yield to the plaintiff's state-law right of privacy. Furthermore, any violation of the right of privacy based on the publication of truthful statements, just like false light claims, often duplicates relief already available under the torts of intentional infliction of emotional distress, trespass, or intrusive invasion of privacy. Because the recognition of the privacy tort at issue risks confrontation with the First

---

Amendment with little benefit to plaintiffs, the publication of truthful private facts is not a cognizable tort under North Carolina law. Reversed.

■ CONCURRENCE

(Frye, J.) The tension between the First Amendment and the privacy tort is an insufficient basis not to recognize a legitimate claim of public disclosure of private facts about a non-public figure by a media defendant. Unlike public figures, private citizens have a strong interest in protecting their most intimate facts, and the media may not publicize them without any accountability. Although the Supreme Court has not decided whether the private facts tort is constitutionally protected, the tension between state law and the First Amendment can be resolved by examining the public interest in the information publicized as a matter of law. Charging the court to determine the level of public interest eliminates the fear that the jury will become ex post facto public sensors. If the court determines that a reasonable person would consider the information within the public interest, the publication would be privileged. The Restatement (Second) of Torts provides that "[t]he line is to be drawn when the publicity ceases to be the giving of information to which the public is entitled, and becomes a morbid and sensational prying into private lives for its own sake, with which a reasonable member of the public, with decent standards, would say that he had no concern." Applying this standard, a reasonable juror here could not conclude that the articles are the morbid and sensational prying into Hall's (P) private life. The story of adoption and subsequent reunion carries a legitimate public interest. While the majority should recognize the private facts tort, the evidence in this case is insufficient to sustain a claim.

Analysis:

The tension between state rights of privacy and the First Amendment has long existed. Most, if not all, cases of media publication invoke the First Amendment right of the press. By refusing to recognize the right of privacy action, the court took the unprecedented step of placing the First Amendment above plaintiffs' privacy rights in nearly every case. Before this case, neither the United States Supreme Court nor any other state court had taken such a drastic stance.

■ CASE VOCABULARY

RIGHT OF PRIVACY: The right to personal autonomy. The right of a person and the person's property to be free from unwarranted public scrutiny or exposure.

Cantrell v. Forest City Publishing Co.

(Widow and Children) v. *(Publisher)*

419 U.S. 245, 95 S.Ct. 465 (1974)

ACTUAL MALICE MUST BE SHOWN TO RECOVER FOR FALSE LIGHT IN THE PUBLIC EYE

■ **INSTANT FACTS** Margaret Cantrell (P) and her children sued for the publication of a newspaper article depicting their family as living in abject poverty.

■ **BLACK LETTER RULE** Actual malice must be proven in order to recover under a "false light" theory.

■ **PROCEDURAL BASIS**

Writ of certiorari reviewing reversal of verdict for compensatory damages for false light.

■ **FACTS**

In 1967, Melvin Cantrell was one of 43 people who died when a bridge collapsed. Forest City Publishing Co. (D) published two stories focusing on the impact of Mr. Cantrell's death on the Cantrell family. For the second story, a reporter and photographer visited the Cantrell's home, taking several pictures and interviewing the Cantrell children. Margaret Cantrell (P) was not home at the time. The article focused on the family's abject poverty, including pictures and text of the poor living conditions. Mrs. Cantrell (P) and her children (P) sued for damages. They alleged that the story was inaccurate and portrayed the family in a false light, which made the Cantrells (P) the subject of ridicule and caused mental distress, shame and humiliation. Forest City Publishing (D) conceded that the story contained a number of inaccuracies regarding Mrs. Cantrell (P) and the conditions of the family residence. The District Court instructed the jury that liability could be imposed only if it concluded that Forest City Publishing (D) had actual knowledge of the falsity or reckless disregard of the truth. The District Judge also struck the demand for punitive damages, finding that the evidence did not show legal malice. The jury returned a verdict awarding compulsory damages for Mrs. Cantrell (P) and William Cantrell (P). The Court of Appeals reversed, holding that the requisite malice was not shown. The Supreme Court granted certiorari.

■ **ISSUE**

In order to recover for "false light," must knowledge of falsity or reckless disregard of the truth be proven?

■ **DECISION AND RATIONALE**

(Stewart, J.) Yes. In order to recover for "false light," *New York Times* malice—i.e., knowledge of falsity or reckless disregard of the truth—must be proven. The Court of Appeals held that such knowledge or recklessness had not been shown, interpreting the District Judge's striking of punitive damages as a finding that there was no evidence of knowledge of falsity or reckless disregard of the truth. However, the actual malice required for a false light action is very different from the common-law standard of malice generally required to support an award of punitive damages. In order to recover punitives, the Cantrells (P) would have to show some personal ill-will or wanton disregard of the Cantrells' (P) rights. This malice standard would focus on Forest City Publishing's (D) attitude toward the Cantrells' (P) privacy, not towards the truth or falsity of the material published. We conclude, contrary to the appellate court, that the District Judge was referring to the punitive standard of malice, not the actual malice standard of *New York Times*. Furthermore, in denying Forest City Publishing's (D) motion for a new trial, the District Judge necessarily and correctly found that the evidence was sufficient to support a finding that Forest City Publishing (D) had published knowing or reckless falsehoods. The knowledge of the reporter and photographer are imputed to Forest City Publishing (D), who is vicariously liable under the theory of *respondeat superior* for portraying the Cantrells (P) in a false light. Reversed and remanded with directions to enter a judgment affirming the District Court's judgment.

Analysis:

This case essentially restates the requirements for a cause of action for false light, the fourth branch of privacy torts examined in this chapter. The main import of the case is the requirement that actual malice, as defined in *New York Times Co. v. Sullivan*, be proven in order to recover damages. Thus, a publisher may be liable for knowingly or recklessly publishing falsities. Note that the false light need not necessarily be a defamatory one, although it very often is. Thus, actions for defamation and false light may be brought concurrently. However, false light typically requires that the publication must be offensive to a reasonable person. In addition, defamation differs from false light in that the former protects a person's reputation, whereas the latter protects a person's interest in being left alone. But realize that the privileges available in defamation actions, including those regarding public figures, are also available in false light actions. Finally, note that the tort of false light is very similar to that for intentional infliction of emotional distress.

■ CASE VOCABULARY

RESPONDEAT SUPERIOR: A theory of liability in which an employer can be held vicariously liable for the torts of its employees.

Hustler Magazine v. Falwell

(Publisher) v. *(Minister)*

485 U.S. 46, 108 S.Ct. 876 (1988)

ACTUAL MALICE STANDARD APPLIES TO ACTIONS FOR EMOTIONAL DISTRESS AS WELL AS FALSE LIGHT

■ **INSTANT FACTS** Jerry Falwell (P) sued Hustler Magazine (D) for intentional infliction of emotional distress for publishing a parody of Falwell (P) engaged in incestuous acts with his mother.

■ **BLACK LETTER RULE** In order to recover for intentional infliction of emotional distress, public figures must show that a false statement of fact was made with actual malice.

■ **PROCEDURAL BASIS**

Writ of certiorari reviewing affirmation of verdict for damages for intentional infliction of emotional distress.

■ **FACTS**

Hustler Magazine (D) published a parody of Reverend Jerry Falwell (P). The drawing and text stated that Falwell's (P) "first time" was during a drunken incestuous rendezvous with his mother in an outhouse. Beneath the parody, in small print, is a disclaimer stating "ad parody—not to be taken seriously." Falwell (P) sued for invasion of privacy, libel, and intentional infliction of emotional distress. The District Court directed a verdict for Hustler (D) on the privacy claim, and the jury awarded Falwell (P) $200,000 in damages for the intentional infliction of emotional distress claim. The Court of Appeals affirmed, rejecting Hustler's (D) argument that *New York Times* actual malice must be proven before emotional damages can be recovered. Hustler (D) also claimed that because the jury found that the parody did not describe actual events about Falwell (P), the parody was an opinion that was protected by the First Amendment. The Court of Appeals held that this was irrelevant on the issue of whether the conduct was sufficiently outrageous to allow recovery for intentional infliction of emotional distress. The Supreme Court granted certiorari.

■ **ISSUE**

Must actual malice be proven in order for a public figure to recover for intentional infliction of emotional distress?

■ **DECISION AND RATIONALE**

(Rehnquist, J.) Yes. Actual malice must be proven in order for a public figure to recover for intentional infliction of emotional distress. Falwell (P) argues that the State's interest in protecting public figures from emotional distress is sufficient to deny First Amendment protection for the speech at issue. We disagree. The First Amendment recognizes the fundamental importance of the free flow of ideas on matters of public interest, and this is bound to produce speech that is critical of public figures. While the First Amendment does not protect *any* type of speech about public figures, these figures must meet a high burden in order to recover. The mere presence of a bad motive, or of the "outrageous" nature of the speech, is not sufficient to recover for intentional infliction of emotional distress. Rather, public figures must prove that the publication contains a false statement of fact which was made with actual malice. In the case at hand, Falwell (P) was a public figure. The jury already found that the caricature did not contain a statement of fact. Thus, Falwell (P) cannot recover. Reversed.

■ CONCURRENCE

(White, J.) I see little reason for the majority's reference to *New York Times v. Sullivan.* However, I agree with the holding because the jury did find that the ad contained no assertion of fact.

Analysis:

After reading this case, you may be wondering why it appeared in a chapter on privacy torts. Good question. The case does present an excellent application of the tort of intentional infliction of emotional distress in the context of public figures. However, the case barely mentions privacy at all. Perhaps the placement of the case can be better understood by reviewing the notes immediately preceding it. The tort of false light requires some intentional or reckless publication of material that places a person in a false light in the eyes of the public. This standard is nearly identical to that laid down by the Supreme Court in the instant action. In fact, the two torts seem virtually indistinguishable. Both involve the same overriding constitutional restraints, requiring actual malice to be proven.

CHAPTER NINETEEN

Civil Rights

Ashby v. White

Instant Facts: Ashby (P) sued when a public official denied Ashby (P) from exercising his right to vote.

Black Letter Rule: An action may be brought for the infringement of a civil right even where no pecuniary or other tangible damage results.

Camp v. Gregory

Instant Facts: A sixteen year old ward of the Department of Children and Family Services (DCFS) was shot and killed two blocks from his Aunt/caretaker's house.

Black Letter Rule: A public official who has deprived someone of his constitutional rights may nonetheless enjoy immunity from an action for civil damages if his actions were objectively reasonable.

Memphis Community School Dist. v. Stachura

Instant Facts: Stachura (P) sued when he was suspended from his teaching job for showing sexually explicit movies to 7th graders.

Black Letter Rule: Section 1983 damages cannot be measured by the jury's determination of the abstract importance of the constitutional right infringed.

Ashby v. White

(Burgess) v. *(Public Official)*

2 Ld.Raym.938 (Court of King's Bench, 1702) (House of Lords, 1706)

EVERY CIVIL RIGHT NECESSITATES A REMEDY

■ **INSTANT FACTS** Ashby (P) sued when a public official denied Ashby (P) from exercising his right to vote.

■ **BLACK LETTER RULE** An action may be brought for the infringement of a civil right even where no pecuniary or other tangible damage results.

■ **PROCEDURAL BASIS**

Action on case for violation of a civil right.

■ **FACTS**

Although the facts are somewhat unclear, it appears that this action was brought by a man (say Ashby (P)) who was hindered in the exercise of his right to vote. Ashby (P), a free burgess of a corporation, had an undoubted right to vote in a Parliamentary election. However, an election official refused to allow Ashby (P) to vote. The person for whom Ashby (P) desired to vote was elected notwithstanding the absence of Ashby's vote. Ashby (P) sued for infringement of his right to vote.

■ **ISSUE**

May an action be brought for the infringement of a civil right even where no pecuniary or other tangible damage results?

■ **DECISION AND RATIONALE**

(Holt, J.) Yes. An action may be brought for the infringement of a civil right even where no pecuniary or other tangible damage results. In the case at hand, Ashby (P) was prevented, by a public official, from exercising his right to vote. If Ashby (P) has a right to vote, he must have a means to vindicate and maintain it, and a remedy if he is injured in the exercise of the right. With every right comes a remedy. The majority of this Court holds that Ashby (P) cannot maintain an action because he suffered no hurt or damage. However, surely every injury to a right imports a damage, whether or not pecuniary. Even though this may occasion a multiplicity of lawsuits, it is necessary in order to protect individual rights. In my opinion, the judgment should be for Ashby (P).

Analysis:

This case is an excellent introduction to the concept that tort actions may be maintained for violations of individual civil rights. Ashby (P) possessed the fundamental civil right to vote, a right which was hindered by a public official. Chief Justice Holt's opinion is replete with oft-quoted passages, i.e., "it is a vain thing to imagine a right without a remedy." Where a right to vote exists, remedies must be available for the infringement of that right, even if no pecuniary damage is suffered. Note that, upon further review, the House of Lords agreed, granting damages in favor of Ashby (P). However, where no pecuniary harm occurs, it is obviously difficult to determine the appropriate measure of damages. For this reason, in modern American jurisprudence, the violation of civil rights is handled by statute rather than common law actions. These statutes provide a way for an individual to assert rights against the government. The U.S. Code, in particular, provides broad authority for anyone to sue for the deprivation of constitutional civil rights by every person acting "under color of statute, ordinance, regulation, custom or usage of any State or Territory." 42 U.S.C.A. § 1983. This "every person" language was later clarified to include state officers such as policemen. However, in certain situations, governmental immunities are available for civil rights violators.

■ CASE VOCABULARY

BURGESS: An inhabitant of an English borough who is entitled to vote.

FARTHING: One-quarter of an English penny.

Camp v. Gregory

(Dead Child's Aunt) v. *(DCFS Caseworker)*
67 F.3d 1286 (7th Cir.1995)

QUALIFIED IMMUNITY PROTECTS STATE'S CASEWORKER FROM LIABILITY FOR VIOLATING WARD'S CONSTITUTIONAL RIGHTS

■ **INSTANT FACTS** A sixteen-year-old ward of the Department of Children and Family Services (DCFS) was shot and killed two blocks from his Aunt/caretaker's house.

■ **BLACK LETTER RULE** A public official who has deprived someone of his constitutional rights may nonetheless enjoy immunity from an action for civil damages if his actions were objectively reasonable.

■ **PROCEDURAL BASIS**

Appeal from the district court's dismissal of the case.

■ **FACTS**

Camp's (P) nephew, Anthony Young, was shot and killed two blocks from Camp's (P) home. At the time of his death, Anthony was sixteen years old, and a ward of the Department of Children and Family Services (DCFS). Camp (P) was originally Anthony's guardian, after his mother's medical condition rendered her unable to care for him. Camp (P) felt she was unable to provide the type of environment necessary to ensure Anthony's well-being, however, so she sought appointment of another guardian. DCFS was appointed as Anthony's guardian by the state court, and Gregory (D) was assigned to be Young's caseworker. A DCFS referral form recommended a highly structured and supervised environment for Anthony, yet Gregory (D) chose to return Anthony to Camp's (P) care. Gregory (D) subsequently neglected to make any referrals or applications for appropriate educational or guidance programs, despite numerous requests from Camp (P). Camp (P) wrote Gregory (D) a letter advising him that Anthony was not attending school, was placing himself in dangerous situations, and that Camp (P) could not ensure Anthony's safety. Gregory (D) failed to follow up on Anthony's progress and, three months later, Anthony died while still under his aunt's (P) care. It is unclear the exact circumstances of Anthony's death, however there was evidence presented that it was perhaps the result of a gang-related incident. Camp (P) claims that Gregory (D) denied Anthony substantive due process by failing to ensure that he was placed in a safe living environment.

■ **ISSUE**

Can the government be held responsible for the death of a child if the child is a ward of the State?

■ **DECISION AND RATIONALE**

(Rovner, C.J.) Yes. A public official who has deprived someone of his constitutional rights may be held liable, but may nonetheless enjoy immunity from an action of civil damages if his actions were objectively reasonable. Camp (P) maintains that her nephew's (Anthony's) death resulted directly from Gregory's (D) failure to arrange for Anthony to be placed in an appropriate environment and to be given the types of services he required to ensure his safety and well-being. Our focus in this case is first to decide whether DCFS (and thus Gregory) (D), by virtue of being appointed Anthony's guardian, acquired any duty to protect Anthony, and whether that duty would extend to dangers beyond the household in which DCFS and Gregory (D) placed Anthony. Gregory (D) argues that under *DeShaney v. Winnebago County Dep't of Social Services*, 489 U.S. 189 (1989) (due process did not require the state to protect a child from the abuse he suffered at the hands of his father), he bore no duty to protect Anthony from a danger neither he nor the state played any role in creating. We believe the fact that the DCFS (D) had been made Anthony's guardian represents a key point of distinction from *DeShaney*, however. At that juncture, whether the DCFS (D) had a duty to intervene on Anthony's behalf was moot; it had already assumed a role that made it constitutionally liable (at least to some extent) for Anthony's well-being. *DeShaney* does not preclude liability when the state, as guardian of the child, places that child in an environment where harm results. We believe that a child placed in the guardianship of the state has a due process right not to be placed by the state with a custodian who the state knows will fail to exercise the requisite degree of supervision over the child. This is precisely the right that Camp (P) alleges Gregory (D) denied to Anthony, and it is this denial which resulted in Anthony's death. Gregory (D) maintains nonetheless that he could not have violated Anthony's liberty interest because he did nothing to interfere with Anthony's ability to avoid or extricate himself from dangerous situations or with Camp's (P) ability to help him do so. This argument is misplaced, however, because even that assumption does not detract from the affirmative duty to intervene on Anthony's behalf which sprang from the DCFS (D) being made his guardian. Whether Gregory's (D) duty extended to dangers outside of the household to which he had returned Anthony is a more difficult question. If a DCFS caseworker places a child in a foster home where he knows the child will likely suffer abuse, he can be held liable. But to place on the caseworker a duty to evaluate and protect a child from dangers outside of the household is a great step beyond that. Even so, a parent does not relinquish all responsibility once a child leaves the house. Parents are not the insurers of their children's conduct, but when they fail to exercise a reasonable degree of supervision, they can be held liable for their omissions. Commensurate with the parental obligation to supervise a child's activities outside the home is a duty on the part of the state not to place one of its charges with an adult that it knows will not or cannot exercise that responsibility. Thus, we believe that when a DCFS caseworker places a child in a home knowing that his caretaker cannot provide reasonable supervision, and the failure to provide that degree of supervision and care results in injury to the child outside of the home, it might be appropriate, depending upon the facts culminating in the injury, for the caseworker to be held liable for a deprivation of liberty. However, the injury suffered by the child must, we believe, be one reasonably foreseeable to the official. A caseworker who is aware that the caretaker he selects will not supervise the child appropriately may not be able to foresee the particular injury that will result from the lack of supervision. If that is the case, then it would be inappropriate to impose liability on the caseworker. Finally, we stress that there must be a sufficient causal link between the failure to provide reasonable supervision and the injury. Because the complaint does not detail the particular circumstances of Anthony's death, we cannot say one way or another whether this case would fit the criteria we have articulated. However, a public official who has deprived someone of his constitutional right may nonetheless enjoy immunity from an award of damages if his actions were objectively reasonable. Although we believe that Camp's (P) complaint alleged facts sufficient to state a claim for the deprivation of Anthony's liberty in violation of his Fourteenth Amendment right to substantive due process, we also conclude that Gregory (D) is entitled to qualified immunity. Affirmed.

Analysis:

This decision's basic holding is that, if a public official's conduct does not violate a clearly established statutory or constitutional right of which a reasonable person would have known, he is immune from an action for civil damages. Carrying this case one step further, what does it mean to say that the injury must be reasonably foreseeable to the official? If the child lives in a gang area, perhaps just by stepping outside, the child can be killed. On the other hand, if the child is left with someone that the official knows cannot care for the child, isn't it true that, by definition, it means that the child is likely to be injured? Can it be argued that the DCFS was so busy and there was such a shortage of foster families that the official had no choice but to place the child with Young?   If such conduct was objectively reasonable, no liability attaches.

■ CASE VOCABULARY

QUALIFIED IMMUNITY: If a public official has acted reasonably, he is immune from an award of civil damages for depriving someone of his constitutional rights.

Memphis Community School Dist. v. Stachura

(School District) v. *(Teacher)*

477 U.S. 299, 106 S.Ct. 2537 (1986)

DAMAGES FOR CIVIL RIGHTS VIOLATIONS MUST COMPENSATE SOME CONSTITUTIONAL DEPRIVATION

■ **INSTANT FACTS** Stachura (P) sued when he was suspended from his teaching job for showing sexually explicit movies to 7th graders.

■ **BLACK LETTER RULE** Section 1983 damages cannot be measured by the jury's determination of the abstract importance of the constitutional right infringed.

■ **PROCEDURAL BASIS**

Writ of certiorari reviewing affirmation of award of compensatory and punitive damages for civil rights violation.

■ **FACTS**

Stachura (P), a teacher in the Memphis Community School District (D), was suspended for allegedly showing sexually explicit movies to his 7th grade life science class. Stachura (P) sued under 42 U.S.C. § 1983, alleging that the suspension deprived him of liberty and property without due process and violated his First Amendment right to academic freedom. The District Court authorized the jury to award (1) compensatory damages for the injury to Stachura (P), (2) punitive damages, and (3) damages based on the jury's perception of the "importance" of the constitutional rights that were violated. The jury awarded compensatory and punitive damages. The Court of Appeals affirmed, and the Supreme Court granted certiorari.

■ **ISSUE**

Can § 1983 damages be measured by the jury's determination of the abstract importance of the constitutional right infringed?

■ **DECISION AND RATIONALE**

(Powell, J.) No. Section 1983 damages cannot be measured by the jury's determination of the abstract importance of the constitutional right infringed. Damages for civil rights violations are designed to provide compensation for injury caused, including out-of-pocket loss as well as impairment of reputation, personal humiliation, and mental anguish. We agree with the holding in *Carey v. Piphus* [the basic purpose of § 1983 damages is to compensate persons for injuries that are caused by the deprivation of constitutional rights]. Thus, the jurors should not have been instructed to consider the abstract value of the constitutional rights infringed. Such damages are an unwieldy tool for ensuring compliance with the Constitution. Reversed and remanded, as the submission of the third standard for damages was in error.

■ **CONCURRENCE**

(Marshall, J.) The majority's opinion is incorrect if it can be read to suggest that § 1983 damages must be based on some common-law damages formulation. We have repeatedly held that the injury to a

First Amendment-protected interest could constitute an injury apart from typical common-law injuries, provided the damages were reasonably quantifiable.

Analysis:

The fairly complicated majority opinion can be boiled down to one narrow holding. Jurors should not be allowed to award damages based on some subjective view of the importance of the constitutional rights infringed. Nevertheless, the majority certainly seems to be stating that some actual compensable injury must be suffered in order to recover damages for § 1983. This appears in direct contrast with *Ashby v. White* [an action may be brought for the infringement of a civil right even where no pecuniary or other tangible damage results]. Nevertheless, the majority does discuss the role of presumed damages, which may be awarded for an injury that is likely to have occurred but difficult to establish. Thus, this case may be squared with the fundamental holding in *Ashby* as long as the damages do not necessarily have to compensate the injured party for some specific pecuniary loss.

■ **CASE VOCABULARY**

PRESUMED DAMAGES: Damages awarded for an actual injury that is difficult to establish and quantify.

CHAPTER TWENTY

Misuse of Legal Procedure

Texas Skaggs, Inc. v. Graves

Instant Facts: Sharon Graves (P) sued for malicious prosecution after she was absolved of liability on criminal charges for intentionally bouncing two checks to Texas Skaggs, Inc. (D).

Black Letter Rule: The elements of malicious prosecution are the following: (1) A criminal prosecution instituted or continued by the defendant against the plaintiff; (2) Termination of the prosecution in favor of the accused; (3) Absence of probable cause for the proceeding; (4) Malice; and (5) Damages.

Friedman v. Dozorc

Instant Facts: A surgeon brings an action for negligence, abuse of process, and malicious prosecution of civil proceedings against an attorney who filed a malpractice claim on behalf of his client.

Black Letter Rule: While attorneys owe no duty to their client's adversary, they may be liable for wrongful institution of civil proceedings if a special injury can be proven by the adversary.

Grainger v. Hill

Instant Facts: Hill (D) improperly prosecuted and imprisoned Grainger (P) in order to force Grainger (P) to relinquish his vessel, and Grainger (P) sues for this improper use of legal process.

Black Letter Rule: Former proceedings need not be terminated in order to bring action for abuse of process.

Texas Skaggs, Inc. v. Graves

(Grocery Store) v. *(Customer)*

582 S.W.2d 863 (Tex.Civ.App.1979)

IMPROPERLY ACCUSED INDIVIDUALS MAY RECOVER DAMAGES FOR MALICIOUS PROSECUTION

■ **INSTANT FACTS** Sharon Graves (P) sued for malicious prosecution after she was absolved of liability on criminal charges for intentionally bouncing two checks to Texas Skaggs, Inc. (D).

■ **BLACK LETTER RULE** The elements of malicious prosecution are the following: (1) A criminal prosecution instituted or continued by the defendant against the plaintiff; (2) Termination of the prosecution in favor of the accused; (3) Absence of probable cause for the proceeding; (4) Malice; and (5) Damages

---

■ **PROCEDURAL BASIS**

Appeal from jury verdict for damages for malicious prosecution.

■ **FACTS**

Sharon Graves (P), a former employee of Texas Skaggs, Inc. ("Skaggs") (D), wrote two checks totaling $34.70 to purchase groceries at a Skaggs (D) store. Although she did not know it at the time, Graves' (P) checking account had insufficient funds to cover the checks. As soon as she found out that the checks had bounced, Graves (P) immediately purchased a money order and mailed it to Skaggs (D) to cover the checks. Nevertheless, a Skaggs (D) manager filed an affidavit for a warrant for Graves' (P) arrest under the Arkansas Hot Check Law. A week later, when Graves (P) was again shopping in the store, a Skaggs (D) manager summoned the police to arrest Graves (P). Graves (P) was later released and the checks were returned to her because the checks had, in fact, been paid. However, a Skaggs (D) employee informed police that he wanted Graves (P) prosecuted anyway. A municipal judge dismissed the criminal proceeding when the "hot checks" could not be produced. Graves (P) filed an action for malicious prosecution, and the jury awarded $20,000 in damages to Graves (P). Skaggs (D) appeals.

■ **ISSUE**

May an action for malicious prosecution be maintained after the criminal proceeding terminated in dismissal rather than acquittal?

■ **DECISION AND RATIONALE**

(Ray, J.) Yes. An action for malicious prosecution can be maintained even when the criminal proceeding terminated in dismissal rather than acquittal. Five elements must be proven in order to recover for malicious prosecution: (1) A criminal prosecution instituted or continued by the defendant against the plaintiff; (2) Termination of the prosecution in favor of the accused; (3) Absence of probable cause for the proceeding; (4) Malice; and (5) Damages. In the case at hand, a criminal prosecution was initiated by Skaggs (D). Furthermore, the evidence shows that Skaggs (D) lacked probable cause to continue the prosecution. A lack of probable cause exists when a reasonable person would know that the accused was not guilty of the crime, or when a person with special knowledge of the facts actually knew that the accused was not guilty. Skaggs (D) knew, or should have known, that Graves (P) did not write the checks with the intent to defraud, as must be proven in order to convict Graves (P) under the Hot Check Law. After all, Graves (P) immediately made restitution after learning that the checks had bounced. The police had released Graves (P) after learning this fact, but Skaggs (D) demanded that the prosecution continue nonetheless. In addition, the evidence shows malice on behalf of Skaggs (D). Lack of probable cause itself gives rise to an inference of malice; moreover, the facts of this case show that Skaggs (D) prosecuted Graves (P) with improper motives. Furthermore, Graves (P) was certainly damaged. Not only was she publicly humiliated at the store, but she also was not hired by several prospective employers because of her arrest record. Finally, we find that the criminal proceedings did, in fact, terminate in favor of Graves (P). Although the case was dismissed, we conclude that Graves (P) likely would have secured an acquittal had the prosecution continued through trial. In addition, we hold that an abandonment of proceedings where the prosecution has become impossible constitutes a termination in favor of the accused. Although Skaggs (D) could have defended against this element by proving that Graves (P) was, in fact, guilty of the charges, the evidence does not support the defense in this case. Affirmed.

Analysis:

This case sets out the five elements typically required in order to recover for malicious prosecution. Note that the tort of malicious prosecution is one branch of the general tort of misuse of legal procedure. Malicious prosecution involves the misuse of criminal actions, whereas other sub-torts (such as wrongful civil proceedings or abuse of process) involve separate issues. The opinion and the notes following the case present an excellent analysis of the five elements and of defenses to the tort of malicious prosecution. First, note that the "institution of criminal proceedings" requirement may be met by an indictment or arrest. But since most prosecuting officials are immune from any tort liability for their prosecutions, the malicious prosecution action must be typically brought against some private citizen (or company, in this case) that made the initial accusation. Second, the "termination in favor of the accused" requirement does not necessarily require an acquittal. A dismissal, failure to prosecute for lack of evidence, *nolle prosequi*, or quashing of an indictment is sufficient. However, an indecisive termination, or the impossibility of bringing the accused to trial, does not meet the second prong. In addition, a defense is available if the evidence shows that the accused was, in fact, guilty of the charge. It is important to remember that the burden of proof for guilt in a civil proceeding is only "preponderance." Third, the "lack of probable cause" standard implicates both an objective (reasonable person) and subjective standard, as discussed in the opinion. Even if no probable cause existed, if the private prosecutor had reasonable grounds to bring the charges, based on a mistake of fact or a mistake of law, he may successfully defend against a malicious prosecution action. Fourth, the "malice" requirement does not necessarily mean hatred or ill-will, but rather any improper purpose in bringing the prosecution (i.e., any purpose other than the desire to bring the accused to justice). Finally, the "damages" requirement is satisfied by harm to reputation, humiliation, mental suffering, or any other injury that may give rise to damages in a civil action.

■ CASE VOCABULARY

ACQUITTAL: A finding of not guilty entered in favor of an accused.

ARREST WARRANT: A court order that commands law enforcement to arrest an accused.

NOLLE PROSEQUI: A voluntary withdrawal of criminal charges against an accused.

Friedman v. Dozorc

(Doctor) v. *(Attorney)*

412 Mich. 1, 312 N.W.2d 585 (1981)

SPECIAL INJURY REQUIRED IN ORDER TO HOLD ATTORNEY LIABLE FOR MALICIOUS PROSECUTION OF CIVIL ACTION

■ **INSTANT FACTS** A surgeon brings an action for negligence, abuse of process, and malicious prosecution of civil proceedings against an attorney who filed a malpractice claim on behalf of his client.

■ **BLACK LETTER RULE** While attorneys owe no duty to their client's adversary, they may be liable for wrongful institution of civil proceedings if a special injury can be proven by the adversary.

■ **FACTS**

In 1970, Leona Serafin entered Outer Drive Hospital, and Dr. Friedman recommended the surgical removal of a kidney stone. Five days later, Ms. Serafin died from a rare, incurable blood disease that was discovered during the surgery. The administrator of Ms. Serafin's estate, represented by attorneys Dozorc and Golden, filed a malpractice action against Dr. Friedman, the hospital, and other doctors. Following a directed verdict in his favor, Dr. Friedman (P) commenced the instant action for negligence, abuse of process and malicious prosecution against attorney Dozorc (D). Dr. Friedman (P) argued that an attorney who institutes a civil action owes a duty to his client's adversary to conduct an adequate investigation and have a good-faith basis for asserting the action on behalf of his client. The trial court granted summary judgment for Dozorc (D), finding that no such duty exists and that the elements for the other causes of action were not met. The Court of Appeals affirmed the dismissal of the negligence and abuse of process claims, but it reversed the dismissal of Dr. Friedman's (P) cause of action for malicious prosecution. Dr. Friedman (P) appeals this portion of the Court of Appeals' holding. Dozorc (D) cross-appeals the portion of the decision reversing the dismissal of the cause of action for malicious prosecution.

■ **ISSUE**

(1) Does an attorney owe an actionable duty to his client's adversary to conduct a reasonable investigation and have a good-faith belief that his client has a tenable claim? (2) Is a special injury an essential element of the tort cause of action for malicious prosecution of civil proceedings?

■ **DECISION AND RATIONALE**

(Levin, J.) (1) No. An attorney does not owe an actionable duty to his client's adversary to conduct a reasonable investigation and have a good-faith belief that his client has a tenable claim. While an attorney may have such a duty to his client, we decline to extend the duty to protect his client's adversary, because such a duty would be inconsistent with the basic precepts of the adversary system. This conflict between the adversary's interests and the client's interests, and the attorney's concern for being sued for negligence, would seriously hamper the attorney-client relationship. With respect to Dr. Friedman's (P) abuse of process claim, we note that a plaintiff must plead and prove (a) an ulterior purpose and (b) an act in the use of process which is improper. Plaintiff failed to allege the second element, and thus summary judgment is proper and this claim was correctly dismissed. Affirmed. (2)

Yes. A special injury remains an essential element of the tort cause of action for malicious prosecution of civil proceedings. This tort, arising out of English common law, traditionally has required one of the following three categories of damage: (a) injury to one's fame; (b) injury to one's person or liberty; or (c) injury to one's property. Although many American jurisdictions have departed from this requirement, we find that Michigan has not significantly departed from the English rule. Because Dr. Friedman (P) failed to allege special injury, we reverse the decision of the Court of Appeals and affirm the trial court's grant of summary judgment in favor of Dozorc (D). Reversed.

Analysis:

This weighty opinion addresses a number of issues related to an attorney's liability for the institution of civil proceedings on behalf of his client. First, it is important to note that general negligence principles do not apply to this situation. As this holding makes clear, an attorney owes no duty to his client's adversary to make sure his client's claims are brought in good faith. However, an attorney may still be liable under two specific and distinct torts: abuse of process and malicious prosecution of civil proceedings. The basic elements of the tort of malicious prosecution are essentially identical in the civil and criminal settings, i.e., prior proceedings terminated in favor of the present plaintiff, absence of probable cause, malice, and damages. In order to have probable cause for bringing a civil action, an attorney must make a reasonable investigation of legal authority and must thereafter retain an honest belief that the claim is tenable. Thus, this element is similar to the duty issue in the negligence context. However, notice that an additional element—special injury to the prior defendant's fame, person, liberty, or property—must be proven in Michigan and other states that adhere to the old English rules. This opinion devotes extensive analysis to the merits of retaining the special injury requirement. Finally, the court concludes with a public policy argument that, without a special injury requirement, the pendulum of the adversarial system would swing too far in a defendant's favor. The cure for an excess of litigation, according to the Court, is not more litigation.

■ CASE VOCABULARY

ABUSE OF PROCESS: Tort imposing liability for using a legal process for an end other than that which it was designated to accomplish.

AMICI: Friends of the court; persons or entities who file briefs on appeal even though they are not parties to the proceedings.

Grainger v. Hill

(Ship Owner) v. *(Mortgagee)*

4 Bing .N.C. 212, 132 Eng. Rep.769 (Court of Common Pleas, 1838)

ENGLISH COURT CREATES TORT TO FILL GAP IN THE LAW OF MISUSE OF LEGAL PROCEDURE

■ **INSTANT FACTS** Hill (D) improperly prosecuted and imprisoned Grainger (P) in order to force Grainger (P) to relinquish his vessel, and Grainger (P) sues for this improper use of legal process.

■ **BLACK LETTER RULE** Former proceedings need not be terminated in order to bring action for abuse of process.

■ **PROCEDURAL BASIS**

Application for nonsuit following verdict for abuse of process.

■ **FACTS**

Grainger (P) was the owner of a ship which he mortgaged to Hill (D). The mortgage allowed Grainger (P) to retain command of the ship and conduct voyages. However, in order to force Grainger (P) into relinquishing control of the ship, Hill (D) threatened to arrest Grainger (P) unless Grainger (P) paid the mortgage. Grainger (P) refused to pay, as the mortgage was not yet due. Hill (D) instituted legal proceedings against Grainger (P), knowing that Grainger (P) could not provide bail. Hill (D) kept Grainger (P) imprisoned until Grainger (P) was forced to relinquish the vessel. Grainger (P) lost several voyages as a result. Grainger (P) brought an action for abuse of process. Hill (D) filed a motion for nonsuit, alleging that the suit commenced by Hill (D) had not terminated.

■ **ISSUE**

Must a legal proceeding have been decided in favor of the accused in order for the accused to sue for abuse of process?

■ **DECISION AND RATIONALE**

(Tindal, J.) No. A legal proceeding need not be finally decided in favor of the accused in order for the accused to sue for abuse of process. Indeed, in an action for malicious prosecution, it is necessary to show that a previous proceeding has terminated, and that there was no probable cause for the previous proceeding. However, this action by Grainger (P) is for abuse of process. Grainger (P) alleges that Hill (D) brought this action in order to extort property from Grainger (P). Such an action does not require the termination of previous proceedings or a lack of probable cause. Application for nonsuit denied.

Analysis:

Although the facts of this case are a bit confusing, the holding is simple. A party should not be entitled to bring legal proceedings for improper ends. For this reason, the court creates a new cause of action—abuse of process. Although Grainger (P) could not have sued for malicious prosecution—since Grainger's (P) criminal case was not yet terminated—Grainger (P) should have some recourse for this blatant attempt by Hill (D) to extort Grainger's (P) vessel. Thus, abuse of process is a separate and

---

distinct tort from malicious prosecution Both torts have the common element of an improper purpose in the use of legal process, but all that must be proven for the abuse of process tort is that a party used legal proceedings for an ulterior, improper purpose. It is not necessary to prove that the proceedings were brought with actual malice, such as spite or ill will. The most common example of this tort is, as in the instant action, when a legal proceeding is brought to extort money or property. Note that it is the extortion itself, rather than the mere issuance of or formal use of the process, which constitutes the tort.

■ CASE VOCABULARY

CAPIAS: A writ requiring an officer to take a named defendant into custody, similar to a modern-day indictment.

CHAPTER TWENTY-ONE

Misrepresentation

Swinton v. Whitinsville Savings Bank

Instant Facts: Neil Swinton (P) brought an action for misrepresentation against the seller of a house, Whitinsville Savings Bank (D), which allegedly failed to disclose the termite-infested state of the house at the time of sale.

Black Letter Rule: Unless a fiduciary relationship exists between parties to a transaction, concealment of a material fact does not give rise to the tort of misrepresentation.

Griffith v. Byers Constr. Co. of Kansas, Inc.

Instant Facts: Griffith (P), the purchaser of residential real estate, sued the developer Byers Construction Company (D) for failing to disclose the defective soil condition of the property.

Black Letter Rule: In certain contexts, including residential real estate development, a party with knowledge has a duty to disclose material defects to parties who may be expected to act in reliance on the knowledgeable party's nondisclosure.

Derry v. Peek

Instant Facts: Derry (P), an investor in a tram company, sued for misrepresentation when a material statement in the prospectus turned out to be false.

Black Letter Rule: A speaker who honestly believes a statement to be true, even if the belief is negligent or unreasonable, is not liable for misrepresentation.

International Products Co. v. Erie R.R. Co.

Instant Facts: International Products Co. ("IPC") (P), relying on a false statement by Erie R.R. Co. (D), insured goods for one location when the goods were actually stored in another, and thus IPC could not recover when the goods were destroyed by fire.

Black Letter Rule: The American Rule imposes liability for negligent false statements that induce reliance, based on a case-by-case determination.

Winter v. G.P. Putnam's Sons

Instant Facts: Winter (P) became seriously ill after picking and eating wild mushrooms learned about in a reference book.

Black Letter Rule: Products liability law does not include the ideas and expression in a book and a publisher has no duty to investigate the accuracy of the contents of the books it publishes.

Hanberry v. Hearst Corp.

Instant Facts: A woman sued the publisher of Good Housekeeping magazine for misrepresentation after she slipped and fell wearing shoes that the magazine had recommended.

Black Letter Rule: A publisher may be liable for endorsing a product which proves to be defective and causes an injury to a consumer.

Richard v. A. Waldman and Sons, Inc.

Instant Facts: Relying on an innocent misrepresentation by a real estate developer, Richard (P) purchased a house and later discovered that he was trespassing on his neighbor's land.

Black Letter Rule: Liability may be imposed for an innocent misrepresentation if the declarant had a duty to speak the truth.

Credit Alliance Corp. v. Arthur Andersen & Co.

Instant Facts: Two separate lenders, who were not in contractual privity with accountants, attempt to impose liability on the accountants for misrepresentations made in financial statements upon which the lenders relied.

Black Letter Rule: Where privity exists from a contractual relationship or its equivalent, accountants may be held liable to third parties who rely on misrepresentations.

Citizens State Bank v. Timm, Schmidt & Co.

Instant Facts: Citizens State Bank (P) made loans in reliance on financial statements prepared by Timm, Schmidt & Co. (D), and, although not in contractual privity with Timm (D), Citizens (P) sues for damages incurred as a result.

Black Letter Rule: The absence of contractual privity does not preclude actions against accountants by persons who rely on negligently prepared financial statements.

Ultramares Corporation v. Touche

Instant Facts: Ultramares (P) relied on accountant Touche's (D) written certification that Fred Stern & Co. was audited correctly, and Ultramares (P) sued for fraudulent misrepresentation after it incurred damages as a result of the reliance.

Black Letter Rule: An accountant may be liable to third persons, not in privity with the accountant, for fraudulent misrepresentations in financial statements.

Williams v. Rank & Son Buick, Inc.

Instant Facts: After purchasing a car in reliance on a false statement that the car had air conditioning, Williams (P) sues for damages when he discovers the falsity.

Black Letter Rule: A person cannot recover for an obviously false misrepresentation, and the obviousness of the falsity should be judged by examining the intelligence of the person and the relationship between the parties.

Saxby v. Southern Land Co.

Instant Facts: A buyer sued the seller of land for misrepresentations regarding the quantity of timber on the land and the suitability of the land for potato farming.

Black Letter Rule: Statements of opinion do not give rise to liability for misrepresentation.

Vulcan Metals Co. v. Simmons Mfg. Co.

Instant Facts: The Vulcan Metals Company (P) sued Simmons Manufacturing Company (D) for alleged misrepresentations made in connection with the sale of vacuum cleaner machinery.

Black Letter Rule: Statements of opinion made in conjunction with the sale of goods rarely give rise to an action for misrepresentation.

Sorenson v. Gardner

Instant Facts: A home buyer sued the seller for allegedly misrepresenting that the house complied with all minimum code requirements.

Black Letter Rule: Liability may be imposed for a false representation as to a matter of law in a business transaction, provided the representation concerns the legal effect of facts not disclosed or otherwise known to the recipient.

McElrath v. Electric Investment Co.

Instant Facts: Electric Investment Co. ("EIC") (D), the lessor of a summer vacation hotel, allegedly misrepresented the occurrence of certain future events.

Black Letter Rule: Predictions as to future events are not actionable unless the speaker knows certain facts which would prevent the event from occurring.

Burgdorfer v. Thielemann

Instant Facts: Burgdorfer (P) alleges that he was fraudulently induced, by Thielemann's (D) misstatement of his future intention, to exchange two notes and a mortgage.

Black Letter Rule: Where a speaker does not actually intend to do a future event, his statement to the contrary may constitute grounds for fraudulent misrepresentation.

Hinkle v. Rockville Motor Co., Inc.

Instant Facts: Hinkle (P), an automobile purchaser, sued the dealer upon discovering that, despite the dealer's representation to the contrary, the car was not new at the time of sale.

Black Letter Rule: Depending on the circumstances, a party may be able to recover either "benefit of the bargain" or "out of pocket" measure of damages for misrepresentation.

Swinton v. Whitinsville Savings Bank

(Buyer) v. *(Seller)*

311 Mass. 677, 42 N.E.2d 808 (1942)

SELLERS ARE UNDER NO DUTY TO DISCLOSE HIDDEN DEFECTS IN THE PRODUCT FOR SALE

■ **INSTANT FACTS** Neil Swinton (P) brought an action for misrepresentation against the seller of a house, Whitinsville Savings Bank (D), which allegedly failed to disclose the termite-infested state of the house at the time of sale.

■ **BLACK LETTER RULE** Unless a fiduciary relationship exists between parties to a transaction, concealment of a material fact does not give rise to the tort of misrepresentation.

■ **PROCEDURAL BASIS**

Appeal from order upholding demurrer to complaint.

■ **FACTS**

Neil W. Swinton (P) purchased a house from Whitinsville Savings Bank ("Bank") (D). Two years later, Swinton (P) discovered that the house was infested with termites, and Swinton (P) was forced to repair the termite damage at a great expense [or open up his own termite zoo and start charging admission!]. Swinton (P) sued the Bank (D) for misrepresentation, alleging that the house was infested at the time of purchase, that the Bank (D) knew the house was infested, and that the Bank (D) fraudulently concealed the true condition of the house from Swinton (P). The Bank (D) demurred to the complaint, and the demurrer was sustained. Swinton (P) appeals the ruling.

■ **ISSUE**

Absent some special relationship between the parties, is mere concealment of material facts sufficient to impose liability for misrepresentation?

■ **DECISION AND RATIONALE**

(Qua, J.) No. Absent some special relationship between the parties, mere concealment or nondisclosure of material facts is insufficient to impose liability for misrepresentation. Swinton (P) alleged no false statement by the Bank (D) and presented no facts that the Bank (D) prevented Swinton (P) from acquiring information as to the condition of the house. Moreover, there was no fiduciary relationship between the parties, and the Bank (D) had no duty to reveal any hidden defects in the house. Swinton (P) and the Bank (D) made a business deal at arms length. If the Bank (D) was liable for its nondisclosure, then any party who failed to disclose any hidden defect which materially reduces the value of a house would be liable. In addition, any buyer who failed to disclose virtues which actually made the house worth more than the selling price would also be liable. Although Swinton's (P) attempt at holding the Bank (D) liable possesses a certain moral appeal, we follow the general rule of nonliability for bare nondisclosure of defects in the sale of a house. Affirmed.

Analysis:

This case evidences a return to the less litigious past, in which the law imposed no duty on sellers to reveal latent defects in the property for sale. The common law doctrine of *caveat emptor* was in force,

---

and buyers were required to inspect houses and accept any potential defects at their own risk. While this doctrine put a premium on a buyer's individual responsibility, it shielded morally reprehensible sellers and allowed them to take advantage of unsuspecting purchasers. In modem times, therefore, numerous exceptions have developed to the general rule of no liability for tacit nondisclosure. For example, where a seller does make some assertions as to the quality of a house, he must disclose enough to prevent his words from being misleading. In addition, where a fiduciary relationship exists between the parties, the law imposes a duty to disclose all material facts, thus preventing a party from taking advantage of a blindly trusting buyer. In addition, modern cases have modified the harsh common law rule by allowing parties to rescind a contract in cases of nondisclosure or even mutual mistake. Nevertheless, the general common law rule still applies in many situations, and absent some special relationship there is no tortious liability for mere nondisclosure.

■ CASE VOCABULARY

CONCEALMENT: The nondisclosure of some information.

DEMURRER: An attack on a complaint stating that, even if the facts of the complaint are accepted as true, the complaint nevertheless fails to state a valid cause of action.

FIDUCIARY RELATIONSHIP: A special relationship of trust and confidence between parties, such as a doctor-patient or attorney-client relationship, which imposes certain legal duties.

Griffith v. Byers Constr. Co. of Kansas, Inc.

(Homebuyer) v. *(Developer)*

212 Kan. 65, 510 P.2d 198 (1973)

COURTS ERODE THE COMMON LAW RULE BY REQUIRING DISCLOSURE OF MATERIAL FACTS TO PARTIES WHO MAY BE EXPECTED TO ACT IN RELIANCE

■ **INSTANT FACTS** Griffith (P), the purchaser of residential real estate, sued the developer Byers Construction Company (D) for failing to disclose the defective soil condition of the property.

■ **BLACK LETTER RULE** In certain contexts, including residential real estate development, a party with knowledge has a duty to disclose material defects to parties who may be expected to act in reliance on the knowledgeable party's nondisclosure.

■ PROCEDURAL BASIS

Appeal from order granting summary judgment in favor of developer in action by buyer for damages for breach of implied warranty and fraud.

■ FACTS

Griffith (P) and others purchased homes which had been constructed on an abandoned oil field, and the soil contained high concentrations of saline. Byers Construction Company (D) developed this property and had knowledge of the soil conditions, yet Byers (D) failed to disclose the conditions to Griffith (P). Griffith (P) and other purchasers sued Byers (D) for breaching the implied warranty of fitness and for fraudulent concealment. Griffith (P) alleged that Byers (D) graded and developed the area in such a manner that it was impossible for Griffith (P) to discover the soil conditions, and that plants were unable to grow in the soil. Byers (D) contended that as a matter of law no claims for fraud could be maintained because of a lack of privity between the developer and the home purchasers. From an order granting summary judgment in favor of Byers (D), Griffith (P) appeals.

■ ISSUE

May a developer be liable for concealing facts from a home purchaser whom the developer expects to act in reliance?

■ DECISION AND RATIONALE

Yes. A developer may be liable for concealing facts from a home purchaser whom the developer expects to act in reliance. In general, when there is some relationship between the parties or when the customs in the trade dictate that material facts should be disclosed, the party with knowledge has a duty to disclose. In relation to the building trade, the rule stated in *Jenkins v. McCormick* [where a vendor has knowledge of a latent defect, failure to disclose the defect constitutes actionable fraud] can be extended to fit the facts of this case. Although Byers (D) was not a vendor of the property, and hence not in direct privity with the purchasers, Griffith (P) was within the class of persons whom Byers (D) intended and had reason to expect would purchase and build their homes. Thus, the failure of Byers (D) to disclose the defective soil condition to Griffith (P) could constitute actionable fraudulent concealment. In addition, the fraudulent concealment was material, since a reasonable homebuyer would attach importance to the soil condition. However, a real estate developer does not implicitly warrant the fertility of the soil of the lots he develops. Thus, the order of summary judgment is affirmed as to those claims based on implied warranty but reversed as to the claims based on fraud. Reversed in part and remanded.

Analysis:

This case reveals the modern approach to fraudulent concealment, exemplifying the numerous exceptions to the common law rule that imposed no duty to disclose defects. Courts have determined that, in the residential real estate context, sellers or land developers have a duty to disclose material, latent defects. Thus, even if there is no fiduciary relationship between the parties, a seller or developer may be liable for nondisclosure. Notice that the buyer could have sued the seller directly without any potential privity concerns, but perhaps the seller had insufficient funds to pay the judgment or perhaps the seller had no actual knowledge of the soil defects. Does the common law rule still have any effect in the modern context, where courts seem to impose duties to disclose in many situations? At the very least, the rule of nonliability for mere concealment has been significantly eroded by modern courts. As is the case with many torts, modern courts shy away from imposing a burden on purchasers to investigate thoroughly the condition of buildings and land prior to purchase. Perhaps the purchasers should be required to investigate more fully. Nevertheless, purchasers are protected, and somewhat paradoxically the purchasers do not even have a duty to disclose special information that enhances the value of the property. All in all, this decision and the modern law regarding liability for fraudulent nondisclosure reflect general public policy considerations to protect relatively unsophisticated purchasers from being taken advantage of by corrupt sellers and developers.

■ CASE VOCABULARY

LATENT DEFECT: A hidden fault which cannot be discovered by the exercise of reasonable care.

PRIVITY: A relationship between parties, including two contracting parties, which allows one party to sue the other.

Derry v. Peek

(Shareholder) v. *(Chairman)*
14 App.Cas. 337 (House of Lords, 1889)

ENGLISH LAW IMPOSED NO LIABILITY FOR NEGLIGENT MISREPRESENTATIONS

■ **INSTANT FACTS** Derry (P), an investor in a tram company, sued for misrepresentation when a material statement in the prospectus turned out to be false.

■ **BLACK LETTER RULE** A speaker who honestly believes a statement to be true, even if the belief is negligent or unreasonable, is not liable for misrepresentation.

■ **PROCEDURAL BASIS**

Appeal from judgment reversing dismissal of action for damages for deceit.

■ **FACTS**

Sir Henry William Peek (P) purchased shares of stock in the Plymouth, Devonport and District Tramways Company (the "Company"). Peek (P) relied on a prospectus that stated that the Company could legally use steam or mechanical power, instead of horses, in operating its tram. The prospectus indicated that the use of steam or mechanical power would give the Company a distinct advantage over other trams. After Peek (P) made the investment, the Board of Trade consented to the Company using steam or mechanical power only on limited portions of its tramway. The directors of the Company refused to consent to the company opening under such conditions, and as a result the Company was wound up [and Peek (P) was steamed up!]. Peek (P) sued William Derry (D), the chairman, and four directors of the Company for deceit. Justice Stirling dismissed the action, holding that the Company's belief in its rights stated in the prospectus was not unreasonable and that their conduct was not reckless. On appeal, Stirling's judgment was reversed on the ground that the statements in the prospectus were made without any reasonable grounds for believing them. Derry (D) and the others appeal to the House of Lords.

■ **ISSUE**

Is negligence alone a sufficient ground for imposing liability for deceit?

■ **DECISION AND RATIONALE**

(Herschell, L.) No. Under English law, negligence is not a sufficient ground for imposing liability for deceit. It should be noted that this common law action for deceit differs significantly from an action brought to obtain rescission of a contract. Whereas any misrepresentation, whether negligent or intentional, is sufficient to rescind a contract, this is not the case for the tort of deceit. In order to prove fraud and establish liability for deceit, it must be shown that the false representation was made (1) knowingly, or (2) without belief in its truth, or (3) recklessly, careless whether it be true or false. In fact, the first and third grounds are really just instances of the second, for one who makes a knowingly false statement or who recklessly makes such a statement can harbor no honest belief in its truth. Moreover, the motive of the person uttering the statement is immaterial. So long as the person has an honest belief in the truth of the statement, no liability will attach. Of course, courts face a difficult task in determining what the speaker actually believed. Courts must determine whether a reasonable man, situated as the defendant, might well believe what they state they did believe. Reversed.

Analysis:

This is the leading early case in establishing the basis for liability for misrepresentation. In short, the House of Lords excluded from the action of deceit any innocent or negligent misrepresentation. Thus, there is no general duty to use care when making statements, even if others are likely to act in reliance. Liability attaches only when the speaker had no honest belief in the truth of a statement, including cases in which the speaker knowingly or carelessly uttered a false statement. Although this is a leading case, many American courts flatly refuse to accept it, or have devised exceptions which essentially undermine the holding. Indeed, the House of Lords may have taken an overly favorable approach to the Company. Perhaps it is more reasonable to require corporations to more fully investigate the claims made in their prospectuses. Although the Company in this case may indeed have believed that it would have the right to use steam or mechanical power, it appears that the issue was never fully investigated.

■ CASE VOCABULARY

RESCISSION: A tool used to cancel a contract that is based on fraud, mistake, or duress.

International Products Co. v. Erie R.R. Co.

(Importer) v. *(Shipping Company)*
244 N.Y. 331, 155 N.E. 662 (1927)

THE AMERICAN RULE IS THAT A NEGLIGENT MISREPRESENTATION MAY BE A BASIS FOR LIABILITY

■ **INSTANT FACTS** International Products Co. ("IPC") (P), relying on a false statement by Erie R.R. Co. (D), insured goods for one location when the goods were actually stored in another, and thus IPC could not recover when the goods were destroyed by fire.

■ **BLACK LETTER RULE** The American Rule imposes liability for negligent false statements that induce reliance, based on a case-by-case determination.

■ PROCEDURAL BASIS

Appeal from affirmation of directed verdict for recovery of damages for misrepresentation.

■ FACTS

International Products Co. ("IPC") (P) was expecting a valuable shipment of goods to be delivered and stored at a dock. Desiring to insure the goods once they reached the dock, IPC (P) asked Erie R.R. Co. (D) where the goods would be stored. Erie (D) informed IPC (P) that the goods were stored at Dock F, and IPC (P) obtained insurance in reliance on this statement. However, the goods were actually stored at Dock D. When the goods were destroyed by fire, the insurance company refused to pay, and IPC (P) sued Erie (D) to recover its damages. The trial court directed a verdict for IPC (P), and the Appellate Division affirmed. Erie (D) appeals.

■ ISSUE

May liability be imposed for negligently false statements that induce reliance?

■ DECISION AND RATIONALE

(Andrews, J.) Yes. Pursuant to the American Rule, liability may be imposed for negligently false statements that induce reliance. The old English law of *Derry v. Peek* [negligence is not a sufficient ground for imposing liability for deceit] has been criticized by American courts. The English Rule imposes no general duty to use any care whatever in making statements. American courts have more liberally construed the law of deceit in order to enforce what conscience, fair dealing, and the usages of business require. Thus, in some situations a negligent statement may be the basis for recovery of damages. Liability in such cases arises when there is a duty, which requires the following: (1) knowledge that the information is required for a serious purpose; (2) knowledge that the listener intends to rely upon the statement; and (3) an injury occurring because of the reliance. Each case must be decided on the peculiar facts presented. In the instant action, Erie (D) had a duty to speak with care. Erie (D) negligently answered IPC's (P) question without an adequate basis for belief, and IPC (P) relied thereon to its detriment. Even though the statement was not made to further Erie's (D) own purposes, this fact is immaterial. Affirmed.

Analysis:

This cases represents a significant departure from the somewhat harsh English Rule regarding nonliability for negligent misrepresentations. Basically the New York court has adopted a case-by-case approach, in which liability will be imposed if it appears morally correct to do so. Of course, this approach also has its drawbacks, including extensive litigation and court costs required to determine the liability for misrepresentations in each individual case. But nearly all modern tort law, and especially the law of negligence, requires such an approach. Courts essentially must determine whether a party had the duty to fully investigate its statements, or at least to avoid negligent and careless responses, prior to imposing liability for negligent misrepresentation. And duties do not necessarily attach only in fiduciary situations, such as a doctor-patient relationship. American courts, as represented by this case, are thus moving towards a strict liability standard for misrepresentation. The moral of this story is that, especially in business situations, a speaker must be fairly sure his words are truthful if he decides to speak at all.

■ **CASE VOCABULARY**

BAILEE: A person who takes responsibility for storing goods, and who typically is later responsible for delivering the goods.

Winter v. G.P. Putnam's Sons

(Mushroom Eaters) v. *(Book Publisher)*

938 F.2d 1033 (9th Cir.1991)

IDEAS AND EXPRESSIONS CONTAINED IN BOOKS CANNOT BE THE BASIS FOR A LAWSUIT

■ **INSTANT FACTS** Winter (P) became seriously ill after picking and eating wild mushrooms learned about in a reference book.

■ **BLACK LETTER RULE** Products liability law does not include the ideas and expression in a book, and a publisher has no duty to investigate the accuracy of the contents of the books it publishes.

■ **PROCEDURAL BASIS**

Appeal from the decision of the district court granting summary judgment for Putnam (D).

■ **FACTS**

Winters (P) bought a book entitled "The Encyclopedia of Mushrooms," a reference guide containing information on the habitat, collection, and cooking of mushrooms. This book was published by Putnam (D), an American book publisher, which purchased copies of the book from the British publisher and distributed the finished product in the United States. Putnam (D) neither wrote nor edited the book. Winters (P) bought this book to help in the collection and preparation of wild mushrooms for eating. Winters (P) relied on descriptions in the book in determining which mushrooms were safe to eat. After cooking and eating the harvest, Winters (P) became critically ill and required liver transplants. It is alleged that the book contained erroneous and misleading information concerning the identification of the most deadly species of mushrooms.

■ **ISSUE**

Is the information contained in a book a "product" for purposes of products liability law, and can a publisher be held liable for failure to investigate the accuracy of the text it publishes?

■ **DECISION AND RATIONALE**

(Sneed, C.J.) No. Products liability law does not include the ideas and expressions in a book, and a publisher has no duty to investigate the accuracy of the contents of the books it publishes. The language of products liability law is geared to tangible items, and the purposes served are also focused on the tangible world and do not take into consideration the unique characteristics of ideas and expression. The threat of financial responsibility for our words and ideas in the absence of fault or a special undertaking or responsibility could seriously inhibit those who wish to share thoughts and theories, and this is an unacceptable and disturbing prospect. As a result, we decline to expand products liability law to embrace the ideas and expressions in a book. Winter (P) also urges this court that Putnam (D) had a duty to investigate the accuracy of The Encyclopedia of Mushrooms' contents. We conclude that Putnam (D) has no duty to investigate the accuracy of the books it publishes. A publisher may, of course, assume such a burden, but there is nothing inherent in the role of publisher or the surrounding legal doctrines to suggest that such a duty should be imposed on publishers. Were we tempted to create this duty, the gentle tug of the First Amendment and the values embodied therein would remind us of the social costs. Finally, Winter (P) asks us to find that a publisher should be

---

required to give a warning that the information in the book is not complete and that a consumer may not fully rely on it, or that this publisher has not investigated the text and cannot guarantee its accuracy. A publisher would not know what, if any, warnings were required without engaging in a detailed analysis of the factual contents of the book, and this is exactly what we have said it has no duty to do. Additionally, such a warning is unnecessary given that *no* publisher has a duty as a guarantor. For these reasons, the decision of the district court is affirmed.

Analysis:

In this case, Winter (P) argued that the book should be analogized to aeronautical charts because both contain representations of natural features and both are intended to be used while engaging in a dangerous activity. Several jurisdictions have held that such charts are to be considered products for the purposes of products liability law. The court does a good job of twisting the definitions of the two items so as not to arrive at the same conclusion for Putnam's (D) book. The court says that an aeronautical chart is used to guide an individual who requires certain knowledge of natural features, much like a compass. In contrast, The Encyclopedia of Mushrooms is more like a book on how to *use* a chart or compass, the "product," and consists of pure thought and expression. It seems as though the court made a policy decision up front, and then worked to fashion a legal justification to fit the purpose.

■ CASE VOCABULARY

PRODUCT LIABILITY: Injury or damage cause by a defective product.

Hanberry v. Hearst Corp.

(Buyer) v. *(Magazine Publisher)*
276 Cal.App.2d 680, 81 Cal.Rptr. 519 (1969)

PUBLISHERS MAY BE LIABLE FOR NEGLIGENTLY MISREPRESENTING THE QUALITY OF PRODUCTS REVIEWED

■ **INSTANT FACTS** A woman sued the publisher of *Good Housekeeping* magazine for misrepresentation after she slipped and fell wearing shoes that the magazine had recommended.

■ **BLACK LETTER RULE** A publisher may be liable for endorsing a product which proves to be defective and causes an injury to a consumer.

■ **PROCEDURAL BASIS**

Appeal from judgment of dismissal of action for damages for injury caused by reliance on negligent misrepresentation.

■ **FACTS**

Hanberry (P) purchased a pair of Handal shoes from Akron. Hanberry (P) suffered severe physical injuries when she wore the shoes on vinyl flooring and slipped and fell. Hanberry (P) sued Handal and Akron for the allegedly defective shoes. Hanberry (P) also sued Hearst Corporation (D), publishers of *Good Housekeeping*, for negligently reviewing and giving a *Good Housekeeping* seal of approval to the shoes [apparently the shoes were not tested on super-slippery vinyl flooring!]. *Good Housekeeping* guaranteed the quality of any goods to which it granted a seal of approval. Hanberry (P) alleged that Hearst (D) was careless and negligent in reviewing the shoes, and that she purchased the shoes without testing them, relying on the *Good Housekeeping* recommendation. Hearst (D) demurred to this action for negligent misrepresentation, and the court dismissed the claims against Hearst (D). Hanberry (P) appeals.

■ **ISSUE**

May a publisher be liable for endorsing a product to a purchaser who buys the product in reliance on the representation and is injured?

■ **DECISION AND RATIONALE**

(Ault, A.J.) Yes. A publisher may be liable for endorsing a product to a purchaser who buys the product in reliance on the representation and is injured. If Hearst (D) did, indeed, fail to adequately test the shoes in order to reveal their dangerous propensity, then Hearst (D) violated a duty of care to Hanberry (P) and may be held liable for the misrepresentation. Hearst (D) alleges that the review was merely a statement of opinion and, therefore, not actionable. However, Hearst (D) stood in a far superior position to Hanberry (P). Hearst (D) represented to the public that it possessed superior knowledge and special information concerning the shoes, and under such circumstances Hearst (D) may be liable for negligent representations of either fact or opinion. Whether or not the slippery nature of the shoes was a matter of common knowledge, as Hearst (D) argues, is a question to be determined by the trier of fact at trial. We are not prepared at this stage to hold that, as a matter of law, liability will not attach based on recommendations of the defectively designed shoe. Reversed.

Analysis:

This case further highlights the insignificance of the distinction between statements of fact and opinion in actions in imposing liability for misrepresentation. Whether *Good Housekeeping's* recommendation was merely an opinion or a statement of fact is inconsequential. Rather, according to the court, the focus should be on the relative positions of the parties. Hanberry (P) is portrayed as a naive buyer who blindly relied on *Good Housekeeping's* seal of approval. But shouldn't Hanberry (P) have some responsibility to test the shoes before purchase? Is it fair to impose liability on Hearst (D) for its review, when Hanberry (P) could have at least tried the shoes on and examined them for herself? Nevertheless, the somewhat harsh holding in this case must be viewed in the proper light. The court is not saying that Hearst (D) is liable for the defective condition of any product it recommends. Rather, it is simply holding that, at the pleadings stage, it is improper to relieve Hearst (D) of all liability for a statement, which the trier of fact might determine to be materially misleading.

Richard v. A. Waldman and Sons, Inc.

(Purchaser) v. *(Real Estate Developer)*

155 Conn. 343, 232 A.2d 307 (1967)

INNOCENT MISREPRESENTATIONS ARE ACTIONABLE WHEN THE DECLARANT HAS A DUTY TO SPEAK TRUTHFULLY

■ **INSTANT FACTS** Relying on an innocent misrepresentation by a real estate developer, Richard (P) purchased a house and later discovered that he was trespassing on his neighbor's land.

■ **BLACK LETTER RULE** Liability may be imposed for an innocent misrepresentation if the declarant had a duty to speak the truth.

■ **PROCEDURAL BASIS**

Appeal from judgment for damages for false representations in connection with sale of land.

■ **FACTS**

Richard (P) purchased a house from A. Waldman and Sons, Inc. (D). Richard (P) had relied on a plot plan prepared by a land surveyor, and delivered by Waldman (D), which indicated that the house complied with zoning regulations. Several months later, Waldman (D) discovered that the southeast comer of the house was only 1.8 feet from the boundary of the lot. As a result, Richard (P) was actually trespassing on his neighbor's lot every time he left his back door, and the house failed to comply with zoning regulations. Richard (P) sued for misrepresentation. Waldman (D) contended that, at most, there was an innocent misrepresentation of fact. Richard (P) obtained a judgment for damages at trial, and Waldman (D) appeals.

■ **ISSUE**

May an innocent misrepresentation be actionable if the declarant has the means of knowing, or ought to know, or has the duty of knowing the truth?

■ **DECISION AND RATIONALE**

(Cotter, A.J.) Yes. An innocent misrepresentation may be actionable if the declarant has the means of knowing, or ought to know, or has the duty of knowing the truth. Waldman (D), a developer of residential real estate, had special means of knowledge regarding zoning compliance, and Richard (P) was entitled to rely thereon. Richard (P) need not show that Waldman (D) actually knew that the representations contained in the plot plan were false. The plan was in the nature of a warranty, and Richard (P) can recover damages for the difference between the actual value of the property and the value of the property had it been as represented. Affirmed.

Analysis:

Once again, this case demonstrates that liability for negligent misrepresentations is determined on a case-by-case basis. Much like the law of negligence, liability may be imposed on a declarant who had the duty to know the truth of his representations but who failed to tell the truth. The cases essentially balance the equities of the situation. If one party should have superior knowledge, based on that party's position or experience, then he may be required to guarantee the truth of the facts he asserts. This case may be compared with *Winter v. G.P. Putnam's Sons* [publishers have no duty to guarantee the information contained in their books], in which the court imposed no liability for innocent misrepresentations contained in an encyclopedia. Whereas a publisher is responsible only for transferring an author's exact words and ideas into print, a residential real estate developer must be correct in stating that a house complies with zoning requirements. Prior common law imposed only a duty to bargain honestly in a business transaction. However, liability now attaches in some situations even if one party makes a completely innocent misrepresentation. Courts in these states must now make a policy decision in each case and determine whether a party with a greater ability to determine the truth should be liable for misrepresentations. It should be noted that this case represents a minority approach; in most states, no liability is imposed for innocent misrepresentations. On the other hand, statutes in the majority of states now provide for strict liability for certain statements made in commercial transactions.

■ CASE VOCABULARY

PLOT PLAN: A description of the land being conveyed in a real estate transaction, including a description of the boundaries of the land.

Credit Alliance Corp. v. Arthur Andersen & Co.

(Lender) v. *(Accountant)*

65 N.Y.2d 536, 483 N.E.2d 110, 493 N.Y.S.2d 435 (1985)

ACCOUNTANTS FACE LIABILITY FOR MISREPRESENTATIONS IN AUDITED FINANCIAL STATEMENTS MADE FOR THE INTENDED BENEFIT OF THIRD PARTIES

■ **INSTANT FACTS** Two separate lenders, who were not in contractual privity with accountants, attempt to impose liability on the accountants for misrepresentations made in financial statements upon which the lenders relied.

■ **BLACK LETTER RULE** Where privity exists from a contractual relationship or its equivalent, accountants may be held liable to third parties who rely on misrepresentations.

■ **PROCEDURAL BASIS**

Appeals from two rulings on motions to dismiss actions for negligent misrepresentation.

■ **FACTS**

This opinion addresses two appeals with a critical issue in common, i.e., the liability of an accountant who prepared financial statements to a contracting party, on which statements a third party lender relied in providing credit. In *Credit Alliance Corp. v. Arthur Andersen & Co.*, Arthur Andersen (D) was an accountant who provided audited financial statements pursuant to a contract with L.B. Smith, Inc. Smith used the statements to obtain credit from Credit Alliance (P). Credit Alliance (P) alleged that the statements were inaccurate because of failure to use the proper auditing standards, and Credit Alliance (P) sued Andersen (D) for damages sustained in reliance on the statements. The trial court denied Andersen's (D) motion to dismiss, and the appellate court affirmed. Andersen (D) appeals. In the other case, *European Am. Bank & Trust Co. v. Strauhs & Kaye*, Strahs & Kaye ("S & K") (D) was an accountant who also provided audited financial statements under contract with Majestic Electro. A party not in privity to the contract, European American Bank ("EAB") (P) relied on the statements and provided loans to Majestic. EAB (P) sued S & K (D) for seriously exaggerating Majestic's assets, resulting in damages to EAB (P) when Majestic went bankrupt. The trial court granted S & K's (D) motion to dismiss, the appellate division reversed, and S & K (D) appeals.

■ **ISSUE**

May an accountant be held liable to a third party who relies upon negligently prepared financial reports?

■ **DECISION AND RATIONALE**

(Jasen, J.) Yes. An accountant may be held liable to a third party who relies upon negligently prepared financial reports, but only if the relationship between the accountant and the third party was so close as to approach that of contractual privity. Our holding and resolution of the two appeals in dispute hinges on the application of the following two seminal cases: *Ultramares Corp. v. Touche* [accounting firm not liable to party having no contractual privity with accountants for misrepresentations in financial statement] and *Glanzer v. Shepard* [liability may attach in the absence of contractual privity when information is directly transferred to the noncontracting third party who relies thereon]. The primary difference between the two cases involves the relationship between the declarant and the third

---

party. In *Ultramares*, the accountants prepared financial statements solely for their client, and the client gave one of the statements to a lender who relied on the information contained in the statement. In *Glanzer*, the declarant furnished one copy of a weight certificate to the contracting party, the seller of goods, and another copy directly to the noncontracting buyer. Because the end aim of the transaction was a transmission of the weigher's findings to the buyer, we held that a sufficient degree of privity existed to impose liability even in the absence of a contract between the weigher and the buyer. Based on these holdings, certain criteria may be gleaned for the appeals before us. Accountants may be held liable to noncontracting parties who rely to their detriment on inaccurate financial reports if: (1) the accountants were aware of the purposes the statements would be used for; (2) a known third party was intended to rely on the statements; and (3) there was some conduct on the part of the accountants linking them to the third party. In *Credit Alliance*, there was not a relationship sufficiently approaching privity to impose liability on Andersen (D), because no claim was made that Andersen (D) was employed to prepare reports with the purpose of helping Smith obtain credit. Accordingly, the *Credit Alliance* causes of action are dismissed and the appellate division's order is reversed. In *European American*, on the other hand, S & K (D) was well aware that the goal of the audits of Majestic was to provide EAB (P) with financial information. Thus, the order of the appellate division in *European American* is affirmed.

Analysis:

This factually complicated case illustrates the difficulty with courts adopting a case-by-case analysis to the topic of negligent misrepresentation. The court could have saved itself a lot of trouble if it simply held that accountants are never liable to noncontracting third parties. However, in the interests of justice, the New York high court has determined that liability may be imposed when there is a relationship so close as to approach contractual privity. But does the court really adopt a distinction without a difference? Does it matter that Andersen (D) had no direct knowledge of the party who was intended to rely on the financial statements, and that S & K (D) had such knowledge? Whenever an accountant is employed to prepare financial statements, they should probably know that the statements will be used for some purpose. Shouldn't liability always be imposed, therefore, for negligently prepared audits? It is important to note, as stated in the opinion, the downside of imposing liability upon all accountants in this situation. Faced with the threat of liability to every person who reads a financial statement, accountants might well go out of business or charge nearly inaccessible fees in order to protect themselves. This case essentially adopts a third-party beneficiary analysis found in contract law. If the third party who benefits from a contract was the intended beneficiary of the contract, then certain duties and liabilities attach to the contracting parties. Only where the third party is known or intended to benefit from the contract is liability imposed.

■ CASE VOCABULARY

PRIVITY: A relationship between parties to a contract entitling the parties to sue each other for breaches or negligence.

Citizens State Bank v. Timm, Schmidt & Co.

(Lender) v. *(Accountant)*

113 Wis.2d 376, 335 N.W.2d 361 (1983)

WISCONSIN COURT ALLOWS RECOVERY FOR DISTANT THIRD PARTIES WHO RELY ON AUDITED FINANCIAL STATEMENTS

■ **INSTANT FACTS** Citizens State Bank (P) made loans in reliance on financial statements prepared by Timm, Schmidt & Co. (D), and, although not in contractual privity with Timm (D), Citizens (P) sues for damages incurred as a result.

■ **BLACK LETTER RULE** The absence of contractual privity does not preclude actions against accountants by persons who rely on negligently prepared financial statements.

■ **PROCEDURAL BASIS**

Appeal from grant of motion for summary judgment dismissing action for damages for misrepresentation.

■ **FACTS**

Timm, Schmidt & Co. ("Timm") (D), an accounting firm, prepared financial statements for Clintonville Fire Apparatus, Inc, (CFA). Relying on these statements, Citizens State Bank ("Citizens") (P) loaned $380,000 to CFA. [Doesn't the scenario sound familiar?] Timm (D) subsequently discovered mistakes in its statements, and Security called all of CFA's loans due upon learning of the mistakes. CFA went into receivership and was dissolved, and Citizens (P) was unpaid for over $150,000 of the loans. Citizens (P) sued Timm (D) for that amount. Timm (D) moved for summary judgment, contending that it had no knowledge that CFA intended to obtain loans from Citizens (P). The trial court granted Timm's (D) motion, and the appellate court affirmed. Citizens (P) appeals.

■ **ISSUE**

May accountants be held liable for the negligent preparation of an audit report to a third party not in privity who relies on the report?

■ **DECISION AND RATIONALE**

(Day, J.) Yes. Accountants may be held liable for the negligent preparation of an audit report to a third party not in privity who relies on the report. We depart somewhat from the long-accepted New York principle of *Ultramares Corp. v. Touche* [accounting firm not liable to party having no contractual privity with accountants for misrepresentations in financial statement]. In this state, privity is not required for liability, and it is not necessary that the accountant actually know the person who is intended to rely upon the financial statement. It is hoped that this holding will make accountants more careful in preparing financial statements. Furthermore, without such a holding the third parties who rely on the statements would not be protected. Our holding is consistent with general negligence law, in which a tortfeasor is liable for all foreseeable consequences of his act except as those consequences are limited by policy factors. We have previously set out a number of public policy reasons for not imposing liability despite a finding of negligence, including the fact that the injury is too remote from the negligence, or that allowance of recovery would place an unreasonable burden on the tortfeasor or

---

would open the way for fraudulent claims. These public policy exceptions should be applied at trial, not on a motion for summary judgment. Furthermore, Timm (D) failed to establish that it was entitled to summary judgment as a matter of law. Reversed and remanded.

Analysis:

As the notes following this case indicate, this case and *Credit Alliance v. Arthur Andersen* [where privity exists from a contractual relationship or its equivalent, accountants may be held liable to third parties who rely on misrepresentations] represent opposite of the spectrum of auditor's liability for negligent misrepresentations. The holding places a great burden on accountants, who may be liable to very remote third persons who rely on information contained in audited financial statements. Making a public policy determination of its own, the court notes that accountants can spread their risks through liability insurance. If third-party creditors could not justifiably rely on audited statements, the cost of credit to the general public would increase. Apparently the court feels obliged to protect the general public over professionals. While the opinion notes that public policy grounds may exempt even negligent tortfeasors from liability, it is unlikely that accountants or other professionals could benefit from these exemptions in Wisconsin, Perhaps the court's holding would make professionals, including attorneys and accountants, more careful in the execution of their responsibilities. Whether or not this goal is justifiable must be determined by each court in each state that tackles the tricky issue of liability for innocent misrepresentations to third parties.

Ultramares Corporation v. Touche

(Third Person) v. *(Accountant)*
255 N.Y. 170, 174 N.E. 441 (1931)

COURTS ALLOW WIDE CIRCLE OF NONCONTRACTING THIRD PERSONS TO RECOVER FOR FRAUDULENT MISREPRESENTATIONS OF ACCOUNTANTS

■ **INSTANT FACTS** Ultramares (P) relied on accountant Touche's (D) written certification that Fred Stem & Co. was audited correctly, and Ultramares (P) sued for fraudulent misrepresentation after it incurred damages as a result of the reliance.

■ **BLACK LETTER RULE** An accountant may be liable to third persons, not in privity with the accountant, for fraudulent misrepresentations in financial statements.

■ **PROCEDURAL BASIS**

Appeal from order dismissing action for damages for fraudulent misrepresentation.

■ **FACTS**

Although part of this holding has been summarized in prior cases in the chapter, this portion of the opinion focuses on the alleged fraud of Touche, Nivens (D), an accountant who audited Fred Stern & Co. Touche (D) certified that the financial statement presented a true and correct view of Fred Stern's financial condition. Ultramares (P) apparently relied on the audited statements, which apparently overlooked a fictitious $706,000 item in the accounts receivable. While not in contractual privity with Touche (D), Ultramares (P) sued Touche (D) for fraudulent misrepresentation in preparing the audited statement. Ultramares (P) alleged that Touche (D) failed to adequately inspect and verify the accounts receivable entry. Although not specifically stated, Ultramares (P) apparently appeals from a judgment in favor of Touche (D) on the fraud cause of action.

■ **ISSUE**

May an accountant be liable to third persons for fraudulent misrepresentations in financial statements?

■ **DECISION AND RATIONALE**

(Cardozo, C.J.) Yes. An accountant may be liable to third persons, not in privity with the accountant, for fraudulent misrepresentations in financial statements. Touche (D) certified as a fact that it had properly audited Fred Stern & Co., and yet the facts indicate that the accountants performing the audit failed to verify the $706,000 entry in the accounts receivable by referring to books other than the general ledger. If the accountants had looked, they would have found irregularities so unusual as to have called for further investigation. This gross negligence on the part of Touche (D) is sufficient to sustain an inference of fraud. Reversed.

Analysis:

At first glance, it appears that an advanced accounting degree is necessary in order to fully understand the alleged wrongs committed by Touche (D). The opinion is made even more difficult to understand by its insufficient description of the factual basis of the claim. Nevertheless, this case presents an important and fairly straightforward holding regarding liability for fraudulent misrepresentations. Even where an accountant is held not liable to third parties, absent a relationship of privity, for negligent misrepresentations, the accountant may still be liable for fraud if it affirmatively represents that the audited statements are correct. But doesn't an accountant always make such a representation, at least implicitly, when performing an audit? Perhaps so, but the accountant should not attest to the accuracy of its audit without being fairly certain that it performed the audit correctly. Thus, liability to noncontracting third persons is imposed in cases of fraud more liberally than in cases of mere negligence. This appears to be a sound rule, but as the notes following the opinion indicate, many courts have held exactly the opposite. Several courts draw a circle of liability for fraudulent misrepresentation that is even more narrow than for negligent misrepresentation.

■ CASE VOCABULARY

ACCOUNTS RECEIVABLE: Income expected to be received by a company, including money due and owing to the company.

BALANCE SHEET: A report on which a company tracks its assets and liabilities:

GENERAL LEDGER: A set of books prepared by a company that describes all of the inflows and outflows to and from the company.

Williams v. Rank & Son Buick, Inc.

(Buyer) v. *(Car Dealer)*

44 Wis.2d 239, 170 N.W.2d 807 (1969)

RECOVERY FOR MISREPRESENTATION REQUIRES JUSTIFIABLE RELIANCE UNDER ALL OF THE CIRCUMSTANCES

■ **INSTANT FACTS** After purchasing a car in reliance on a false statement that the car had air conditioning, Williams (P) sues for damages when he discovers the falsity.

■ **BLACK LETTER RULE** A person cannot recover for an obviously false misrepresentation, and the obviousness of the falsity should be judged by examining the intelligence of the person and the relationship between the parties.

■ **PROCEDURAL BASIS**

Appeal from judgment for damages for fraudulent misrepresentation.

■ **FACTS**

Williams (P) went to Rank & Son Buick, Inc. (D) and looked at a used automobile for purchase. Williams (P) alleged that Rank & Son's (D) salesman fraudulently misrepresented that the automobile had air conditioning. [How strange that a used car dealer would lie about the condition of a car!] Contending that he purchased the car in reliance on the misrepresentation, Williams (P) sued Rank & Son (D) for damages resulting when he discovered the car did not have air conditioning. The trial court granted a judgment for $150 in favor of Williams (P). Rank & Son (D) appeals.

■ **ISSUE**

May a party recover for relying on an obviously false statement?

■ **DECISION AND RATIONALE**

(Hanley, J.) No. A party may not recover for relying on an obviously false statement. In order to obtain recovery for false representations, a party must prove that he justifiably relied on the representations. It is impossible to justifiably rely on a statement that is obviously false. The main issue is obviousness of the falsity, i.e., whether the statement's falsity can be detected by ordinary observation. This must be determined in light of the intelligence and experience of the misled individual and in view of the relationship between the parties. In the instant case, no factors negated the opportunity for Williams (P) to have inspected the obviousness of the statement's falsity. Although Rank & Son's (D) salesman did make a false statement, Williams (P) was intelligent enough to have tested the ventilation system of the automobile prior to purchase. Furthermore, there was no fiduciary relationship between the parties, and Rank & Son (D) made no effort to interfere with Williams' (P) investigation of the car. Had Williams (P) reasonably inspected the car, by merely flipping a knob, he would have determined that the car did not have air conditioning. Thus, as a matter of law, Williams (P) was not justified in relying on the oral representations of the salesman. Reversed.

■ DISSENT

(Wilkie, J.)   The representation made by the salesman was not so obviously false that Williams (P) had no legal right to rely on it.   Merely by finding that Williams (P) relied on the statement, the court necessarily found that Williams (P) had a right to rely thereon.

Analysis:

Before any recovery can be obtained for fraudulent misrepresentation, a plaintiff must prove that he justifiably relied on the fraud.   This case examines the requirements for justifiable reliance.   The opinion notes that, as a matter of law, a party cannot justifiably rely on a statement that is obviously false.   Of course, the inevitable question arises: obviously false to whom?   According to this court, the obvious false nature must be judged as to the party himself.   In light of his intelligence and experience and in light of the relationship between the parties.   The holding can be questioned, since it is very difficult to determine whether an individual should have been smart enough to discover the falsity of a statement. What if the purchaser had never driven in an automobile and had no idea how air conditioning worked? In addition, in the context of purchasing a car, many otherwise intelligent people may blindly rely on a dealer's statements.   Should the dealer have more responsibility, as a matter of public policy, for intentionally misleading a purchaser?   On the other hand, the opinion may be praised for not allowing an intelligent car buyer to seize upon an otherwise harmless error and exact damages from a dealer.   In sum, it probably makes sense to impose some duty on a buyer to reasonably inspect a vehicle and to rely on his own observations over the fraudulent misrepresentations of a sleazy salesperson.   Perhaps as a matter of law purchasers should *never* be entitled to rely on *any* statement made by a used car dealer, since many such statements are false or at least exaggerated!   The justifiability of reliance necessarily must be determined on a case-by-case basis, and the notes following the case present several good examples of reliance in various situations.

■ CASE VOCABULARY

ACUMEN: Insight, shrewdness, or expertise.

VITIATES: Impairs, reduces, or revokes.

Saxby v. Southern Land Co.

(Buyer) v. *(Seller)*

109 Va. 196, 63 S.E. 423 (1909)

RELIANCE ON MERE STATEMENTS OF OPINION IS NOT JUSTIFIED

■ **INSTANT FACTS** A buyer sued the seller of land for misrepresentations regarding the quantity of timber on the land and the suitability of the land for potato farming.

■ **BLACK LETTER RULE** Statements of opinion do not give rise to liability for misrepresentation.

■ **PROCEDURAL BASIS**

Appeal from order sustaining demurrer to complaint for damages for misrepresentation.

■ **FACTS**

In connection with the sale of a farm to Saxby (P), Southern Land Co. (D) represented that the farm contained at least 130 acres of non-burned pine timber. In reality, the land contained only 60 acres of non-burned timber. In addition, Southern (D) misrepresented that the timber would sell for $4 per cord, and that the land would yield 100 bushels of potatoes per acre. Saxby (P) sued for these misrepresentations. Southern (D) demurred to the complaint, contending that the representations were merely statements of opinion and that Saxby (P) was not justified in relying thereon. From an order sustaining the demurrer, Saxby (P) appeals.

■ **ISSUE**

Does a misstatement of opinion give rise to liability for misrepresentation?

■ **DECISION AND RATIONALE**

(Harrison, J.) No. A misstatement of opinion does not give rise to liability for misrepresentation. Statements of opinion do not ordinarily deceive or mislead, and in any event an individual is not justified in relying on mere opinions. The facts indicate that Southern (D) was not asserting a fact in stating the number of acres of pine. The statements were sufficiently indefinite to have required Saxby (P) to inquire further. In addition, the predictions about the selling price of wood and the potential potato production were not assertions of fact. All of Southern's (D) statements were merely trade talk. Thus, the order sustaining the demurrer must be affirmed.

Analysis:

This case states the general rule that statements of opinion are not a basis for liability. The court imposes a duty on Saxby (P), the buyer, to investigate Southern's (D) opinion statements rather than simply relying on them. However, it is obviously difficult to determine whether a representation is a statement of opinion or fact. It could be argued that Southern (D), who had superior knowledge regarding the property, was making factual assertions regarding the amount of timber on the farm. Thus, as other cases have held, the distinction between statements of fact and of opinion is not very helpful. Essentially, liability hinges on whether someone like Saxby (P) may justifiably rely on the statements. Perhaps the general rule makes sense only if all statements of opinion are defined as those on which someone should not justifiably rely, whereas statements of fact are defined as those on which reliance gives rise to liability. As the remainder of cases in this section demonstrate, the general rule regarding statements of opinion no longer carries much weight.

■ CASE VOCABULARY

CORD: A measure of an amount of cut timber, equal to 128 cubic feet.

POLE: A unit of area which equals one square rod.

ROD: A unit of measure which equals 30.25 square yards.

Vulcan Metals Co. v. Simmons Mfg. Co.

(Buyer) v. *(Seller)*

248 Fed. 853 (2d Cir.1918)

SELLERS MAY ENGAGE IN "PUFFING" WITHOUT BEING LIABLE FOR MISREPRESENTATION

■ **INSTANT FACTS** The Vulcan Metals Company (P) sued Simmons Manufacturing Company (D) for alleged misrepresentations made in connection with the sale of vacuum cleaner machinery.

■ **BLACK LETTER RULE** Statements of opinion made in conjunction with the sale of goods rarely give rise to an action for misrepresentation.

■ **PROCEDURAL BASIS**

Appeal from directed verdict denying claim for damages for misrepresentation.

■ **FACTS**

The Vulcan Metals Company (P) purchased machinery and patents for the manufacture of vacuum cleaners from the Simmons Manufacturing Company (D). In connection with the sale, Simmons (D) allegedly opined that the vacuum cleaner was absolutely perfect, affordable, simple to use, and that it would last a lifetime. Simmons (D) also stated that the vacuum cleaner had never been sold to the public. Vulcan (P) sued Simmons (D) for deceit, claiming that this puffery was a misrepresentation. Simmons (D) brought a separate suit against Vulcan (P) to collect on notes given for the purchase price, and Vulcan (P) counterclaimed for the same misrepresentations. The trial court directed a verdict for Simmons (D) on each action, and Vulcan (P) appeals.

■ **ISSUE**

May a seller be liable for statements of opinion and "puffery" made in conjunction with the sale of machinery to another manufacturer?

■ **DECISION AND RATIONALE**

(Learned Hand, J.) No. A seller is not liable for statements of opinion and "puffery" made in conjunction with the sale of machinery to another manufacturer. It is of little concern whether these statements are considered statements of fact or of opinion. The primary focus should be on the relative bargaining positions of the parties. Where parties stand on equal footing, such as a chemist stating an opinion to another chemist, the parties are on equal footing to independently weigh the merits of any statement. There are some statements in a bargaining process which no sensible man would take seriously. In the case at bar, since Vulcan (P) was allowed full opportunity to inspect the quality of the vacuum cleaner, the parties stood on equal footing. Simmons' (D) representations were not to be taken literally by Vulcan (P), and Vulcan (P) has no right to treat Simmons' (D) "puffing" as material in Vulcan's (P) determination to buy the machinery. With respect to the representation that the vacuum had never been sold on the market, however, Simmons (D) may be liable. A reasonable jury could conclude that these factual statements were deceitful, based on the fact that vacuums had been sold in several states. Therefore, we reverse the trial court's ruling and order a new trial on the action for deceit.

Analysis:

This case essentially turns on the justifiability of Vulcan's (P) reliance on Simmons' (D) statements. Whether Simmons' (D) statements are considered opinions or factual assertions is relevant only insofar as it affects whether Vulcan's (P) reliance was justified. Judge Hand concludes that Vulcan (P) did not justifiably rely on Simmons' (D) statements about the virtues of the vacuum cleaner, since Vulcan (P) had an adequate opportunity to inspect the cleaners for itself. But is it really true that Vulcan (P) stood on equal footing with Simmons (D) in this respect? Indeed, it appears that Vulcan (P) was not nearly as experienced as Simmons (D) with regards to the quality of the machines. Perhaps Judge Hand too abruptly dismissed Vulcan's (P) claim of reliance on these statements. Alternatively, perhaps there really is some significance to the difference between statements of opinion and statements of fact, in that a buyer is never justified in relying on mere opinions. This conclusion is further bolstered by Judge Hand's approach to Simmons' (D) statements that the cleaner had not been sold on the market. This was a definite factual averment by Simmons (D), and the fact that a reasonable jury could conclude that the statement was incorrect ultimately led to a reversal of the directed verdict.

■ CASE VOCABULARY

ALLAY: To ease or alleviate.

PUFFING: Making exaggerated assertions of opinion, typically in connection with the sale of goods, in order to induce a prospective buyer to purchase the goods.

Sorensen v. Gardner

(Buyer) v. *(Seller)*

215 Or. 255, 334 P.2d 471 (1959)

COURT RESTRICTS POTENTIAL LIABILITY FOR MISSTATEMENTS OF LAW

■ **INSTANT FACTS** A home buyer sued the seller for allegedly misrepresenting that the house complied with all minimum code requirements.

■ **BLACK LETTER RULE** Liability may be imposed for a false representation as to a matter of law in a business transaction, provided the representation concerns the legal effect of facts not disclosed or otherwise known to the recipient.

■ PROCEDURAL BASIS

Appeal from judgment denying directed verdict and granting damages for deceit.

■ FACTS

Sorenson (P) purchased a house from Gardner (D). Alleging that Gardner (D) falsely represented that the house was constructed in a workmanlike manner and met all code requirements, Sorenson (P) sued Gardner (D) for deceit. At trial, evidence was produced showing that certain code requirements with respect to electric wiring, plumbing, and sewage were not met. The trial court granted a judgment for $2000 for Sorenson (P). Gardner (D) appeals.

■ ISSUE

May liability be imposed for a false representation as to a matter of law in a business transaction?

■ DECISION AND RATIONALE

(Lusk, J.) Yes. Liability may be imposed for a false representation as to a matter of law in a business transaction, provided the representation concerns the legal effect of facts not disclosed or otherwise known to the recipient. Thus, the antiquated general rule that no cause of action exists for misrepresentations of law is not entirely correct. Liability may attach to misrepresentations of fact. Likewise, a speaker may be liable for making a misrepresentation of law that concerns facts not disclosed or not otherwise known to the recipient, because such a statement implies that there are sufficient facts to back up the statement. In the case at hand, Gardner (D) represented that the house complied with the minimum code requirements. There was evidence that Sorenson (P) did not know the facts regarding compliance with the code. Thus, Gardner (D) is not entitled to a directed verdict because Sorenson (P) was ignorant of the facts. Reversed, however, and new trial ordered on the grounds of error in instructing the jury as to the measure of damages.

Analysis:

The central theme of this case is that there is no longer much significance in differentiating between false statements of law and other false statements. If the misrepresentation is merely a pure statement of law, then it is analogous to a statement of opinion and no liability attaches. The reason for this general rule, according to commentators, is that every man is presumed to know the law, and hence a recipient cannot claim justifiable reliance on a misstatement of law. This Court follows the Restatement approach concerning statements of the legal consequences of certain facts. If the facts are known by both parties, then there can be no liability for any statement of law regarding those facts. Thus, if Sorenson (P) had known the true state of the wiring and sewage systems of the house, Gardner (D) would not have been liable for stating that the wiring and sewage complied with the codes, since Sorenson (P) is presumed to know the codes and could not justifiably rely on such a statement. However, Gardner's (D) statements in the present case are actionable because Sorenson (P) did not know the true facts underlying those statements. In short, this case essentially eliminates the distinction between statements of law and statements of fact. A statement of law, like any other statement, may be intended and understood as either one of fact or one of opinion. Liability may attach to the former but not the latter.

■ CASE VOCABULARY

DECEIT: Another name for the cause of action based on fraudulent misrepresentation.

McElrath v. Electric Investment Co.

(Lessee) v. *(Lessor)*
114 Minn. 358, 131 N.W. 380 (1911)

PREDICTIONS AS TO FUTURE EVENTS MAY BE ACTIONABLE IF THEY INVOLVE FACTUAL MISREP-RESENTATIONS

■ **INSTANT FACTS** Electric Investment Co. ("EIC") (D), the lessor of a summer vacation hotel, allegedly misrepresented the occurrence of certain future events.

■ **BLACK LETTER RULE** Predictions as to future events are not actionable unless the speaker knows certain facts which would prevent the event from occurring.

■ **PROCEDURAL BASIS**

Appeal from order overruling general demurrer to complaint for damages for fraudulent misrepresentation.

■ **FACTS**

Electric Investment Co. ("EIC") (D), the owner of hotel property in Antlers Park, leased the property to McElrath (P). McElrath (P) intended to operate the property as a summer resort. EIC (D) made the following three predictions to McElrath (P): (1) that an electric railroad would soon be completed that would run electric cars to Antlers Park during the summer; (2) that EIC (D) would make Antlers Park an important summer resort for Minneapolis residents; and (3) that McElrath (P) would make at least $1500 per year running the hotel. McElrath (P) sued, claiming the representations were fraudulent. Contending that the false representations were not actionable because there were merely predictions of future intentions, EIC (D) demurred to the complaint. The trial court overruled the general demurrer, and EIC (D) appeals.

■ **ISSUE**

Do predictions of future intentions, which create in the recipient the belief that the predictions are a fact, constitute grounds for a misrepresentation action?

■ **DECISION AND RATIONALE**

(Brown, J.) Yes. Predictions of future intentions, which create in the recipient the belief that the predictions are a fact, may constitute grounds for a misrepresentation action. This is an exception to the general rule that false representations must be of existing facts in order to be actionable. In making the representations regarding the electric railroad, EIC (D) intended to create in McElrath (P) the belief that the railroad would actually go to Antlers Park. Thus, McElrath (P) was justified in relying on the representations, and if the representations were in fact false then McElrath (P) may recover damages for EIC's (D) fraud. With respect to the other two representations, however, we find that McElrath (P) did not state facts sufficient to constitute an action for misrepresentation. The statement regarding the future summer resort status of Antlers Park, and the prediction of future income, rested wholly in conjecture and speculation. The intended outcomes were out of the control of EIC (D), and McElrath (P) had equal notice of the circumstances surrounding the representations. Affirmed.

Analysis:

This case sets forth the subtle and often difficult distinctions between actionable and non-actionable predictions as to future events. In general, predictions are regarded as statements of opinion, and reliance on such statements is not justifiable. However, statements as to future events always carry an implied representation that the speaker does not know any facts which will prevent the event from occurring. Thus, for example, if EIC (D) knew that the railroad would not go to Antlers Park, then McElrath (P) could sue for the representation to the contrary. The Court holds that EIC (D) did know such facts, and that EIC (D) nevertheless intended to make McElrath (P) believe to the contrary. It makes sense that such declarations should be actionable, since they are essentially false factual statements. On the other hand, it can be argued that no one can ever *know* that a future event will certainly *not* occur. EIC (D) could have contended that, although it was not confident that the electric railway would run to Antlers Park, it did not know this for sure and thus was not making a fraudulent misrepresentation.

■ CASE VOCABULARY

GENERAL DEMURRER: A pleading that simply states, without explaining the specific nature of the objection, that the facts alleged in the complaint do not constitute a cause of action.

Burgdorfer v. Thielemann

(Mortgage Holder) v. *(Property Owner)*
153 Or. 354, 55 P.2d 1122 (1936)

FRAUDULENT MISSTATEMENTS OF FUTURE INTENTION ARE ACTIONABLE

■ **INSTANT FACTS** Burgdorfer (P) alleges that he was fraudulently induced, by Thielemann's (D) misstatement of his future intention, to exchange two notes and a mortgage.

■ **BLACK LETTER RULE** Where a speaker does not actually intend to do a future event, his statement to the contrary may constitute grounds for fraudulent misrepresentation.

■ **PROCEDURAL BASIS**

Appeal from judgment for damages for deceit.

■ **FACTS**

Charles Burgdorfer (P) alleged that Carl Thielemann (D) fraudulently induced Burgdorfer (P) to exchange $2,323 in notes and a mortgage for two lots. Burgdorfer (P) contended that Thielemann (D) promised that he would pay a $500 mortgage on one of the new lots, and that Thielemann (D) never actually intended to do so. The trial court granted a judgment for Burgdorfer (P). Thielemann (D) appeals, arguing that the trial court committed error by permitting Burgdorfer (P) to testify as to the statement. Thielemann (D) contends that the statute of frauds prohibits such testimony, since the oral promise to pay the $500 mortgage could not be performed in one year.

■ **ISSUE**

Where a speaker does not actually intend to do a future event, is a statement to the contrary actionable?

■ **DECISION AND RATIONALE**

(Kelly, J.) Yes. Where a speaker does not actually intend to do a future event, his statement to the contrary may constitute grounds for fraudulent misrepresentation. To profess an intend to do or not do something, when a party intends to the contrary, is a clear case of fraud. The state of a person's mind, and his future intentions, is a fact. Thus, a misrepresentation as to the state of the person's mind is a misstatement of fact. In the case at hand, we find that Thielemann (D) never intended to pay the $500 mortgage. Burgdorfer (P) was justified in relying on Thielemann's (D) statement to the contrary. Furthermore, the statute of frauds provides no defense to Thielemann (D), and Burgdorfer (P) may testify as to the statement. The purpose of the testimony was not to establish the agreement, but rather to prove fraud. Affirmed.

Analysis:

This case is relevant only to the extent that it states the general rule regarding statements of future intention. It makes sense that a speaker, who makes a representation of future intent that he knows is false, should be held accountable for such obvious fraud. The tricky part, as noted in the opinion, is

---

determining what the speaker's true intentions were. Thielemann (D) could of course have argued that he actually intended to pay the $500 mortgage, and it would be difficult to disprove this allegation. However, facts must have existed which assured the trial court that Thielemann (D) never actually had such an intention. Note that the holding essentially boils down to the same determination we have seen throughout the chapter, i.e., whether the statement was an assertion of fact or of opinion. The court makes an interesting point in noting that the state of a person's mind is "as much a fact as the state of his digestion." Finally, in order to fully understand the case, it is necessary to review the statute of frauds. In general, the statute of frauds prohibits testimony regarding an oral contract that cannot possibly be performed within one year, if that testimony is offered to establish the existence or non-existence of the agreement. Thus, if Burgdorfer (P) was suing for a breach of contract, he could not have entered the evidence of Thielemann's (D) statement; however, since Burgdorfer (P) was suing for fraud, the statute of frauds is [somewhat ironically] not applicable. Actions for deceit have other advantages over actions for breach of the promise itself. They avoid certain defenses that may be raised to breach of contract, including the parol evidence rule, failure of consideration, the statute of limitations, illegality, and incapacity.

■ CASE VOCABULARY

ASSIGNMENT OF ERROR: An assertion by an appellant that certain actions of the trial court were improper as a matter of law.

Hinkle v. Rockville Motor Co., Inc.

(Buyer) v. *(Auto Dealer)*
262 Md. 502, 278 A.2d 42 (App.1971)

PARTIES MAY RECOVER DAMAGES FOR MISREPRESENTATION UNDER EITHER OF TWO METHODS OF DAMAGES CALCULATION

■ **INSTANT FACTS** Hinkle (P), an automobile purchaser, sued the dealer upon discovering that, despite the dealer's representation to the contrary, the car was not new at the time of sale.

■ **BLACK LETTER RULE** Depending on the circumstances, a party may be able to recover either "benefit of the bargain" or "out of pocket" measure of damages for misrepresentation.

■ **PROCEDURAL BASIS**

Appeal from directed verdict in favor of defendant in action for damages for misrepresentation.

■ **FACTS**

Donald Hinkle (P) purchased a 1969 Ford Galaxie from Rockville Motor Company, Inc. (D). Although Rockville (D) had allegedly represented that the car was new, Hinkle (P) subsequently discovered that the car had over 2,000 miles on it. Hinkle (P) also discovered that the car had been involved in an accident, and that the front and rear portions had been welded together after being severed in the accident. Alleging that Rockville (D) fraudulently concealed the true state of the car, Hinkle (P) sought $100,000 in damages for the deceit. At the close of Hinkle's (P) case, Rockville (D) moved for a directed verdict on grounds that Hinkle (P) failed to produce evidence of the actual value of the automobile. Notwithstanding the fact that Hinkle (P) had produced expert testimony that the car could be returned to new condition for $800, the trial court granted Rockville's (D) motion. Hinkle (P) appeals.

■ **ISSUE**

May a party recover "benefit of the bargain" damages in an action for deceit?

■ **DECISION AND RATIONALE**

(Barnes, J.) Yes. A party may recover "benefit of the bargain" damages in an action for deceit. The benefit of the bargain theory allows a party to be compensated based on the difference between the value of property as represented and the actual value of the property. This is in contrast to the other typical tort measure of damages, in which a party can recover only his "out of pocket" losses. A review of several courts and commentators reveals that either the benefit of the bargain or the out-of-pocket theory may be applied to actions for deceit. Hinkle (P) provided evidence in regard to the cost of necessary repairs, demonstrating the existence of damages and providing an adequate measure upon which damages could be predicated. Thus, the trial court erred in directing a verdict against Hinkle (P) for failing to produce such evidence. Reversed and remanded.

Analysis:

At the outset, it is important to note that a party can recover for misrepresentation only if he has relied on the misrepresentation to his detriment, i.e., suffered losses as a result. Although this case presents a much-needed overview of the two different damages theories commonly applied, the opinion can be criticized for sloppy drafting and for incorrectly stating one of the theories. An example would have assisted the reader in differentiating the two theories. Assume Hinkle (P) had purchased the car for $11,000, receiving what he thought was a great deal because a new Galaxie would have been worth $15,000. Suppose further that the actual value of the Galaxie in its state of disrepair was $10,000. Under an "out of pocket" theory, Hinkle (P) could recover only $1,000, the difference between the purchase price and the actual value [and *not* the difference between the value as represented and the actual value, as the court incorrectly states]. Under a "benefit of the bargain" analysis, on the other hand, Hinkle (P) could recover $5,000, the difference between the value of a new Galaxie and the actual value of the car he purchased. Thus, the benefit of the bargain theory generally allows parties to recover greater damages. It is interesting to note that Hinkle's (P) damages under either theory would be nowhere near the $100,000 he seeks in this case. Unless some tort other than deceit was alleged, Hinkle (P) could recover at most the benefit of the bargain measure of damages. Note, however, that if Hinkle (P) had been injured as a result of the defective automobile, he could recover all of his consequential damages [to compensate him for his injuries] resulting from the misrepresentation. Also note that the typical tort measure of damages is merely out-of-pocket loss, since tort remedies are designed only to compensate for the harm actually suffered.

■ **CASE VOCABULARY**

BENEFIT OF THE BARGAIN: A theory of damages in which a party can recover the difference between the value as represented and the actual value.

OUT OF POCKET: A theory of damages in which a party can only recover the difference between the price paid and the actual value.

CHAPTER TWENTY-TWO

Interference With Advantageous Relationships

Ratcliffe v. Evans

Instant Facts: Ratcliffe (P), a boiler maker, sued Evans (D), a newspaper publisher, for publishing statements indicating that Ratcliffe (P) was no longer doing business after his father died.

Black Letter Rule: Evidence of general damages, such as a general decline in business, may be sufficient to sustain an action for injurious falsehood.

Horning v. Hardy

Instant Facts: The Hardys (P) caused the sale of a house from the Hornings (D) to a buyer to be rescinded by falsely stating that the Hornings (D) did not actually own the land.

Black Letter Rule: A qualified privilege exists to protect purported interests in property, even if an injuriously false statement is published.

Testing Systems, Inc. v. Magnaflux Corp.

Instant Facts: Testing Systems, Inc. (P) sued a competitor for trade libel after the competitor made unfavorable, allegedly false factual assertions regarding the poor quality of TSI's (P) products.

Black Letter Rule: A competitor is not privileged to make false factual statements which unfavorably compare a competitor's product to their own.

Lumley v. Gye

Instant Facts: Gye (D) enticed employee to quit working for Lumley (P), and to come to work for him.

Black Letter Rule: It is a tort to knowingly cause an individual to break her contract.

Bacon v. St. Paul Union Stockyards Co.

Instant Facts: A livestock dealer was prevented from conducting his business by a stockyard owner.

Black Letter Rule: The wrongful interference with a party's ability to carry out a contract is actionable in tort.

Della Penna v. Toyota Motor Sales, U.S.A., Inc.

Instant Facts: Auto wholesaler which bought cars for export suffered extreme business and economic losses when the auto distributor inserted "no export" clauses in its dealership agreements.

Black Letter Rule: A plaintiff seeking to recover for an alleged interference with economic relations must plead and prove as part of its case-in-chief that the defendant not only knowingly interfered with the plaintiff's expectancy, but engaged in conduct that was wrongful by some legal measure other than the fact of interference itself.

Adler, Barish, Daniels, Levin, and Creskoff v. Epstein

Instant Facts: Epstein (D), former law associate at Adler, Barish, Daniels, Levin, and Creskoff (P), attempted to get clients of Adler (P) to switch to his law firm by sending them a change of counsel form to sign.

Black Letter Rule: It is tortious interference with contractual relations for a former law associate to recruit clients of his old firm by doing anything more than notifying the clients that he has formed his own practice.

Brimelow v. Casson

Instant Facts: Brimelow (P) owned a traveling revue, but he paid the chorus girls very poorly. In an effort to increase the chorus girls' wages, Casson (D) induced the owners of the theaters to break contracts with Brimelow (P).

Black Letter Rule: Interference with contractual relations is not improper if it is done for the public interest.

Harmon v. Harmon

Instant Facts: R. Harmon (P) was to inherit some property from his mother upon her death. H & V Harmon (D) induced the mother to give this very same property to them before she died via inter vivos transfer.

Black Letter Rule: It is tortious to interfere with a potential inheritance by unduly influencing the testatrix to transfer property to a third person prior to her death.

Neibuhr v. Gage

Instant Facts: By threatening that he would falsely tell the police that Neibuhr (P) was guilty of grand larceny, Gage (D) induced Neibuhr (P) to sell stock to him.

Black Letter Rule: Duress based on misrepresentation is a tort.

Freeman & Mills, Inc. v. Belcher Oil Company

Instant Facts: Belcher Oil (D) refused to pay its accountant, Freeman & Mills' (P), bill after attorneys for Belcher (D) hired Freeman(P) for accounting services to assist in ongoing litigation.

Black Letter Rule: There is no tort cause of action based on a defendant's bad faith denial of the existence of a contract between the parties.

Nash v. Baker

Instant Facts: Baker (D) seduced away Nash's (P) husband and father.

Black Letter Rule: Intentional interference with paternal relations is not a tort.

Ratcliffe v. Evans

(*Boiler Maker*) v. (*Publisher*)

2 Q.B. 524 (1892)

PROOF OF A GENERAL LOSS IN BUSINESS IS SUFFICIENT TO MAINTAIN AN ACTION FOR INJURIOUS FALSEHOOD

■ **INSTANT FACTS** Ratcliffe (P), a boiler maker, sued Evans (D), a newspaper publisher, for publishing statements indicating that Ratcliffe (P) was no longer doing business after his father died.

■ **BLACK LETTER RULE** Evidence of general damages, such as a general decline in business, may be sufficient to sustain an action for injurious falsehood.

■ **PROCEDURAL BASIS**

Appeal from verdict for damages for injurious falsehood.

■ **FACTS**

Ratcliffe (P) and his father conducted business as an engineer and boiler maker under the name Ratcliffe & Sons. After the father died, Ratcliffe (P) continued the business. However, Evans (D), a newspaper publisher, published a statement that Ratcliffe (P) had ceased to carry on business and that the firm no longer existed. Ratcliffe (P) sued Evans (D) for the allegedly false and malicious publication. The jury, finding that the writing was a false statement purposely made to cause damage to Ratcliffe (P), entered a verdict for Ratcliffe (P). The only proof of damages at trial consisted of evidence of general loss of business. Evans (D) appeals, contending that Ratcliffe (P) was required to prove specific rather than general damages.

■ **ISSUE**

Is evidence of general damages sufficient to sustain an action for injurious falsehood?

■ **DECISION AND RATIONALE**

(Bowen, J.) Yes. Evidence of general damages is sufficient to sustain an action for injurious falsehood. The action for written or oral falsehoods, maliciously published to cause damage, is analogous to an action for slander of title. Actual damage must be shown in order to maintain such an action. In contrast, in the case of personal libel, general damages are presumed. In the instant action, evidence of general damages must be admitted and may be sufficient to sustain the action. To refuse to admit this evidence would involve an absolute denial of justice and of redress for the intentionally false and injurious statements.

Analysis:

The notes following this case describe the general nature of the tort of injurious falsehood, also known as trade libel or slander of title. In general, injurious falsehood is a tort covering all false and malicious statements resulting in pecuniary loss. Thus, this tort can be distinguished from defamation, which involves false statements about a person which do not necessarily cause pecuniary loss. The elements required to sustain a cause of action for injurious falsehood are typically the following: (1) a false statement intended to cause pecuniary loss; (2) published to a third person; (3) "malice" in the publication; and (4) resulting in special damage in the form of pecuniary loss. This English case sheds some light onto the fourth element, giving it a very broad interpretation. Some pecuniary loss must be shown, but according to this case it is not necessary to prove specific losses. Rather, general evidence of loss of business is sufficient. Thus, Ratcliffe (P) need not show that he actually lost certain customers, but only that he suffered some reduction in business. The requirement of special damages essentially means that personal elements of damage, such as emotional distress, are not sufficient to sustain the action. In brief, the modern tendency is to require the plaintiff to be specific only when it is reasonable for him to do so. If it is not reasonable, then evidence of general decline in business is enough to maintain the action.

■ CASE VOCABULARY

ACTION ON THE CASE: The common-law term for a general class of suits for damages.

ASSIZES: A common-law court consisting of a group of persons commissioned by the King to try cases.

GENERAL DAMAGES: Damages implied at law to have necessarily resulted from a certain wrong, without reference to the special circumstances of the injured party.

NEGATIVED: Disproved.

SLANDER OF TITLE: A false and malicious statement relating to a person's title to property.

SPECIAL DAMAGES: Damages which actually result from a certain wrong, depending on the special circumstances of the injured party.

Horning v. Hardy

(Property Developer) v. *(Purported Land Owner)*
36 Md.App. 419, 373 A.2d 1273 (1977)

QUALIFIED PRIVILEGES SERVE AS DEFENSES TO INJURIOUS FALSEHOODS

■ **INSTANT FACTS** The Hardys (P) caused the sale of a house from the Hornings (D) to a buyer to be rescinded by falsely stating that the Hornings (D) did not actually own the land.

■ **BLACK LETTER RULE** A qualified privilege exists to protect purported interests in property, even if an injuriously false statement is published.

■ **PROCEDURAL BASIS**

Appeal from verdict dismissing claim for trespass and ejectment and dismissing counterclaim for damages for injurious falsehood.

■ **FACTS**

The Hardys (P) sued the Hornings (D) for trespass and ejectment, alleging that the Hornings (D) were developing certain property that the Hardys (P) owned without the Hardys' (P) permission. The Hornings (D) had developed one house and were in the process of closing the sale, but on the morning of the closing date, the Hardys' (P) attorney told the buyers that the Hardys (P) were the actual owners of the property. The buyers rescinded the sale, and the house went unsold. The Hornings (D) thus filed a counterclaim for slander of title and interference with contract. The trial court ruled against the claim, finding that the Hardys (P) had failed to establish that they owned the property. The court also ruled against the counterclaim, finding that the Hardys (P) were privileged to make the statement—that they actually owned the property—to the buyers.

■ **ISSUE**

Does a qualified privilege exist to protect property ownership, serving as a defense to an action for injurious falsehood?

■ **DECISION AND RATIONALE**

(Liss, J.) Yes. A qualified privilege exists to protect property ownership, serving as a defense to an action for injurious falsehood. Injurious falsehood may consist of the publication of a statement derogatory to someone's title to property, calculated to prevent others from dealing with the property owner. The statement must be made with malice, which means one of the following: (1) the declarant acts, motivated by spite; (2) the declarant acts to harm the interests of another; or (3) the declarant knows that what he says is false, regardless of motive. The facts of this case show an injurious falsehood made by the Hardys (P), since they were not actually the owners of the property and since they falsely claimed to the Hornings' (D) potential buyer that they were the owners. However, a qualified privilege precludes liability for this injurious falsehood. If a person has a present, existing economic interest to protect, such as the ownership of property, he is privileged to prevent performance of a contract which threatens his property ownership. This privilege is justified, because if the person fails to inform the intending buyer of the actual ownership, he may be barred from later asserting an adverse claim against the purchaser. A showing of actual malice may cause the purported owner to

---

forfeit the qualified privilege. However, the mere failure to investigate the ownership of the land does not constitute actual malice and does not cause the Hardys (P) to forfeit their privilege in the instant action. Thus, we hold that the Hardys (P) did not abuse their conditional privilege. Affirmed.

Analysis:

This factually complicated case can be distilled to make it easier to understand. Essentially, the Hardys (P) thought that they owned certain land that was going to be improperly sold by the Hornings (D). The Hardys (P) have the privilege of protecting their purported interest in the land by telling the buyers that the Hornings (D) did not own the land. Even if the Hardys' (P) statement proved to be false—which it did, according to the trial court—they are not liable for making the statement. This opinion presents a good summary of the policy reasons underlying the qualified privilege. If the Hardys (P) never informed the buyer of their purported ownership, and if the sale actually went through, then the Hardys (P) could later be estopped from asserting any adverse claim. Note, however, that the privilege is not absolute. The Hardys (P) would not be justified in maliciously asserting that they owned the land, if they knew fully well, or if they were reckless in failing to investigate, that they owned the land. The declarant will also be liable if there is excessive publication to persons to whom it is not reasonably necessary to reach. All in all, the same privileges that apply to personal defamation actions apply to injurious falsehoods.

■ CASE VOCABULARY

CONSTITUTIONAL PRIVILEGE: A privilege guaranteed by the First Amendment allowing declarants to make misstatements of fact without liability in certain situations.

EJECTMENT: A common-law action for the recovery of possession of land and for damages for wrongful intrusion onto land.

SLANDER OF GOODS: A false statement made in disparagement of a person's title to personal property.

TRADE LIBEL: A common-law cause of action analogous to slander of goods.

Testing Systems, Inc. v. Magnaflux Corp.

(Manufacturer) v. *(Competitor)*

251 F.Supp. 286 (E.D.Pa.1966)

DISTRICT COURT LIMITS THE EXTENT TO WHICH COMPETITORS CAN DISPARAGE THE QUALITY OF A RIVAL PRODUCT

■ **INSTANT FACTS** Testing Systems, Inc. (P) sued a competitor for trade libel after the competitor made unfavorable, allegedly false factual assertions regarding the poor quality of TSI's (P) products.

■ **BLACK LETTER RULE** A competitor is not privileged to make false factual statements which unfavorably compare a competitor's product to their own.

■ **PROCEDURAL BASIS**

Motion to dismiss action for damages for trade libel.

■ **FACTS**

Testing Systems, Inc. ("TSI") (P) and Magnaflux Corp. (D) were competitors engaged in the manufacture of devices to test commercial materials. Magnaflux (D) allegedly circulated a false report to TSI's (P) customers. The report stated that the U.S. government had tested TSI's (P) product and found it only 40% as effective as Magnaflux's (D) testing systems. In addition, at a manufacturer's convention, Magnaflux (D) allegedly stated to TSI's (P) customers that TSI's (P) devices were no good. TSI (P) sued for trade libel. Magnaflux (D) moved to dismiss the action, contending that Magnaflux (D) was merely making an unfavorable comparison of TSI's (P) product. Such unfavorable comparisons, according to Magnaflux (D), are protected from injurious falsehood liability.

■ **ISSUE**

Is a company absolutely privileged to make unfavorable comparisons of fact regarding a competitor's product?

■ **DECISION AND RATIONALE**

(Lord, J.) No. A company is not absolutely privileged to make unfavorable comparisons of fact regarding a competitor's product. Ordinarily, no liability is imposed for statements which unfavorably compare a competitor's product to the product of the declarant. The rationale for this general rule is the near impossibility of a trial court in ascertaining the truth or falsity of such comparisons. In addition, the general rule recognizes the importance of protecting a tradesman's right of free speech, and the necessity of allowing the public to learn the relative merits of particular products. Thus, statements of opinion which disparage a competitor's product, in comparison to the declarant's product, are privileged from liability for trade libel. However, false assertions of fact made in an unfavorable comparison may be actionable. In the instant action, if Magnaflux (D) indeed made a false factual statement by declaring that the U.S. government had found Magnaflux's (D) products to be 60% more effective than TSI's (P), then Magnaflux (D) cannot escape liability. Magnaflux (D) gave added authenticity to its statements by invoking the reputation of the U.S. government. Hence, Magnaflux's (D) statements may be actionable, and the claim should not be dismissed.

Analysis:

This case raises a number of interesting points regarding injurious falsehoods among competitors. Note first the peculiar nature of the general rule. Whereas a manufacturer's naked opinions regarding the poor quality of a competitor's product may be actionable if they meet the general test for injurious falsehood, the same statements are not ordinarily actionable if they are made in the context of comparing the competitor's product to the declarant's. However, liability may be imposed for unfavorable factual assertions. The Court's reasoning may be questioned on this issue, since statements of opinion are arguably as damaging as statements of fact. Nevertheless, the holding is analogous to the fact/opinion distinction discussed in the chapter on misrepresentation. In summary, the law protects business "puffery" and allows, consistent with the constitutional guarantee of free speech, disparaging comparisons regarding a competitor's products. But this privilege ceases to exist at a certain level of culpability, especially when the statements take the form of factual assertions, and in particular when these assertions are based on false authentications by third parties like the U.S. government.

■ CASE VOCABULARY

TRADE DISPARAGEMENT: Another name for the cause of action for trade libel, a specialized form of injurious falsehood which relates to statements regarding a company or its products.

Lumley v. Gye

(Employer) v. *(Employee Seducer)*

(1853) 118 Eng.Rep. 749

COURT RULES THAT COMPANY CANNOT LURE AWAY RIVAL'S EMPLOYEES

■ **INSTANT FACTS** Gye (D) enticed employee to quit working for Lumley (P), and to come to work for him.

■ **BLACK LETTER RULE** It is a tort to knowingly cause an individual to break her contract.

■ **PROCEDURAL BASIS**

Appeal from granting of demurrer in complaint for damages for interference with a contractual relationship.

■ **FACTS**

Wagner, an opera singer, was under contract to perform for Lumley's (P) theater. She agreed by contract not to perform elsewhere during the tenure of her contract. Gye (D) knew that Wagner was bound by this contract, but nevertheless enticed Wagner to refuse to perform.

■ **ISSUE**

Is it a tort to knowingly cause an individual to break her contract?

■ **DECISION AND RATIONALE**

(Erle) Yes. First, it is clear that it is a tort for a third party to interfere with an employment relationship, and to induce the employee to quit. This case is no different, since it likewise involves inducing a party to break her contract. Moreover, the fact this contract involves the theater, and not trade, manufactures or household service, is no basis for distinction. In this case, Gye (D) knew that Wagner was employed by Lumley (P). He also knew that Wagner agreed not to perform elsewhere. But notwithstanding, Dye (D) still induced Wagner to refuse to perform for Lumley (P). Judgment reversed.

Analysis:

The tort of interference with contractual relations is in tension with the contract principle of efficient breach. On the one hand, the tort of interference with contractual relations aims to encourage performance of contracts, or at least to prevent others from discouraging contractual performance. On the other hand, the contract principle of efficient breach reasons that parties to a contract should be free to breach (and pay damages) and re-contract if more favorable opportunities arise, because this freedom allows resources to be allocated to their most valuable use. The line is drawn at two places. First, it is not a tort if the third party does not know that the breacher is bound by a contract. Second, a third party may hire a contract breacher even if he knows of the contract, so long as he does not induce the breach. In other words, the decision to breach must rest solely on the breacher.

Bacon v. St. Paul Union Stockyards Co.

(Livestock Dealer) v. *(Stockyards)*
161 Minn. 522, 201 N.W. 326 (1924)

WRONGFUL INTERFERENCE WITH A PERSON'S ABILITY TO PERFORM A CONTRACT IS ACTIONABLE IN TORT

■ **INSTANT FACTS** A livestock dealer was prevented from conducting his business by a stockyard owner.

■ **BLACK LETTER RULE** The wrongful interference with a party's ability to carry out a contract is actionable in tort.

■ **PROCEDURAL BASIS**

Appeal from order sustaining demurrer to cause of action for wrongful interference with contractual relations.

■ **FACTS**

Bacon (P) was employed by the Drover Livestock Commission Co. and was engaged in buying and selling livestock [probably pigs!] in the St. Paul Union Stockyards. Bacon (P) sued for the tort of wrongful interference with contract. Bacon (P) alleged that St. Paul Union Stockyards Co. (D) prevented him from carrying on his occupation by excluding Bacon (P) from the stockyards and by forbidding any person or corporation from dealing with him in the stockyards. St. Paul (D) demurred to the complaint. The trial court, holding that the facts stated did not give rise to a cause of action, sustained the demurrer. Bacon (P) appeals.

■ **ISSUE**

Is interference with a contract of employment actionable in tort?

■ **DECISION AND RATIONALE**

(Per Curiam) Yes. Interference with a contract of employment is actionable in tort. In the case at hand, Bacon (P) was engaged in the steady employment of dealing livestock in the St. Paul Union Stockyards. It appears from the complaint that St. Paul (D) wrongfully, willfully, and unlawfully prevented him from continuing in that employment, causing Bacon (P) to breach his employment contract. If these allegations are true, they constitute a violation of Bacon's (P) rights and may constitute the tort of wrongful interference with contract. While St. Paul (D) may have had valid reasons for its actions, such reasons do not appear on the face of the complaint. Therefore, St. Paul's (D) demurrer must be denied. Reversed.

Analysis:

This case briefly illustrates the tort of wrongful interference with contract. In general, the tort involves an intentional and improper interference with the plaintiff's rights under a contract with another person, causing the plaintiff to lose a right under the contract. The elements of this tort can be gleaned from the brief opinion. First, there must be an existing contractual relationship. Bacon (P) had a contract with the Drover Livestock Commission Co. to deal livestock in the St. Paul Union Stockyards. Second, there must be some intentional, improper act of interference with the contract. If the allegations are true, St. Paul (D) intentionally prevented Bacon (P) from carrying out his contract. Third, the interference must cause the affected party to breach his contract or must make the contract rights more costly or less valuable. Bacon (P) apparently would have been forced to breach his contract if he were not allowed to deal livestock at the St. Paul Union Stockyards. This tort, part of a larger body of tort law aimed at protecting economic relationships, traces its origins back to ancient Rome. The ability of parties to freely contract and to carry out their contracts is of central importance in any advanced economic society, and it makes sense that parties should not be unreasonably prevented from doing their business.

Della Penna v. Toyota Motor Sales, U.S.A., Inc.

(Auto Wholesaler) v. (Auto Distributor)

11 Cal.4th 376, 902 P.2d 740 (1995)

TO SUPPORT A CLAIM FOR ECONOMIC INTERFERENCE, ONE MUST SHOW MORE THAN INTER-
FERENCE ALONE

■ **INSTANT FACTS** Auto wholesaler which bought cars for export suffered extreme business and economic losses when the auto distributor inserted "no export" clauses in its dealership agreements.

■ **BLACK LETTER RULE** A plaintiff seeking to recover for an alleged interference with economic relations must plead and prove as part of its case-in-chief that the defendant not only knowingly interfered with the plaintiff's expectancy, but engaged in conduct that was wrongful by some legal measure other than the fact of interference itself.

■ PROCEDURAL BASIS

Appeal from the Court of Appeal's judgment which reversed the trial court's jury verdict for the defendant.

■ FACTS

Della Penna (P) was an automobile wholesaler doing a profitable business purchasing Lexus automobiles at near retail price and exporting them to Japan for resale. Concerned that the reexport of the Lexus models to Japan would jeopardize Toyota's (D) American market, as production and availability of the Lexus in America is limited, Toyota (D) inserted in its dealership agreements a "no export" clause. This clause provided that the dealers were authorized to sell the Lexus only to customers in the United States, and not for resale or use outside the United States. Toyota (D) compiled a list of "offenders" (dealers and others believed to be involved with the Lexus foreign resale market), which it distributed to American Lexus dealers [ooh, renegades!]. They were warned that doing business with the "offenders" could lead to sanctions, from reducing a dealer's allocation to possible reevaluation of the dealer's franchise agreement. As a result, Della Penna's (P) sources began to dry up, and eventually all his sources declined to sell the Lexus automobiles to him [who's afraid of the big bad wolf?]. Della Penna (P) then filed suit against Toyota (D), alleging both state antitrust claims and interference with his economic relationship with Lexus retail dealers. The antitrust claim was dismissed, but the tort cause of action went to the jury. The trial court modified the standard jury instructions, over objections of Della Penna (P), to require that the interference by Toyota (D) be proven by Della Penna (P) to have been "wrongful." The jury returned a verdict for Toyota (D). The Court of Appeals reversed that judgment, stating that the modified instruction was erroneous, and ordered a new trial.

■ ISSUE

In an interference with economic relations cause of action, must the plaintiff prove the defendant's conduct was wrongful by some measure other than just an interference with the plaintiff's interest itself?

■ DECISION AND RATIONALE

(Arabian, J.) Yes. A plaintiff seeking to recover for an alleged interference with economic relations must plead and prove as part of its case-in-chief that the defendant not only knowingly interfered with the plaintiff's expectancy, but engaged in conduct that was wrongful by some legal measure other than the fact of interference itself. The "interference torts" have origins as far back as the Roman law, and the development of these torts through the mid-19th century English common law lead to the pleading and burden of proof requirement that the plaintiff merely had to show the defendant's conscious act and plaintiff's economic injury to establish the defendant's liability. However, this prima facie approach to the economic interference tort requires too little of the plaintiff, and much criticism ensued. Recognizing the force of the criticisms, the state courts began to redefine the elements and burdens surrounding the tort. In Top Serv. Body Shop, Inc. v. Allstate Ins. Co., 283 Or. 201, 582 P.2d 1365 (1978) (*Top Service*), the Oregon Supreme Court held that a claim of interference with economic relations is made out when interference resulting in injury to another is wrongful by some measure beyond the fact of the interference itself. The defendant's liability may arise from improper motives or from the use of improper means. Over the past decade or so, close to a majority of the high courts of American jurisdictions have imported into the economic relations tort variations on the *Top Service* line of reasoning, explicitly approving a rule that requires the plaintiff in such a suit to plead and prove the alleged interference was either "wrongful," "improper," "illegal," "independently tortious" or some variant on these formulations. In searching for a means to recast the elements of the economic relations tort and allocate the associated burdens of proof, we are guided by an overmastering concern articulated by high courts of other jurisdictions and legal commentators: the need to draw and enforce a sharpened distinction between claims for the tortious disruption of an existing contract and claims that a prospective contractual or economic relationship has been interfered with by the defendant. Our courts should, in short, firmly distinguish the two kinds of business contexts, bringing a greater solicitude to those relationships that have ripened into agreements, while recognizing that relationships short of the above subsist in a zone where the rewards and risks of competition are dominant. Beyond that we need not tread today. It is sufficient to dispose of the issue before us in this case by holding that a plaintiff seeking to recover for alleged interference with economic relations has the burden of pleading and proving that the defendant's interference was wrongful by some legal measure beyond the fact of interference itself. The judgment of the Court of Appeal is reversed and the cause is remanded with directions to affirm the judgment of the trial court.

■ CONCURRENCE

(Mosk, J.) On many points, I agree with the majority's discussion of the tort of intentional interference with prospective economic advantage and Della Penna's (P) claim against Toyota (D) asserting such a cause of action. On two major points, however, I am compelled to state my disagreement. First, I would not adopt the "standard" of "wrongfulness." That term is ambiguous and should probably be avoided. Second, if I were to adopt such a "standard," I would not allow it to remain undefined. Any definition of the "standard" should avoid suggesting that the interfering party's motive might be material for present purposes. The focus on this issue is inappropriate.

Analysis:

The court did a good job of incorporating the views of several jurisdictions, the Restatement of Torts, the Court of Appeal, and leading academic authorities to redress the balance between providing a remedy for predatory economic behavior and keeping legitimate business competition beyond litigative bounds. By accepting and adopting the rulings that require proof of a wrongful act as a component of the cause of action, and allocating the burden of proving it to the plaintiff, the court goes against its own prior rulings to the contrary. The court was humble enough to recognize that its present rule was insufficient and required reexamination, and wise enough to adopt the widely accepted and applied views of burden allocation in interference tort cases. The law is not static and must change with the changing needs and views of society. The only reasonable choice in this case was reformulation, and the court was successful in that regard.

■ CASE VOCABULARY

ANTITRUST STATUTE: Promotes free competition, cannot restrain competitors.

INTERFERENCE WITH ECONOMIC RELATIONS: Purposely and wrongfully restricting another's business.

Adler, Barish, Daniels, Levin, and Creskoff v. Epstein

(Contractee) v. *(Interferer)*
482 Pa. 416, 393 A.2d 1175 (1978)

COURT LIMITS TACTICS THAT FORMER LAW ASSOCIATES MAY EMPLOY IN LURING AWAY CLIENTS FROM OLD FIRM

■ **INSTANT FACTS** Epstein (D), former law associate at Adler, Barish, Daniels, Levin, and Creskoff (P), attempted to get clients of Adler (P) to switch to his law firm by sending them a change of counsel form to sign.

■ **BLACK LETTER RULE** It is tortious interference with contractual relations for a former law associate to recruit clients of his old firm by doing anything more than notifying the clients that he has formed his own practice.

■ **PROCEDURAL BASIS**

Appeal from reversal of judgment in complaint for damages for tortious interference with contractual relations.

■ **FACTS**

Epstein (D) was an associate at the law firm of Adler, Barish, Daniels, Levin and Creskoff (Adler) (D). When Epstein (D) ended his employment there, he sought to lure away clients from Adler (P) to his own newly established practice. Epstein (D) called the clients, met them in person, and sent them form letters which the clients could use to discharge Adler (P). All the clients had to do was sign this discharge form, and mail it back to Epstein (D) in a pre-addressed stamped envelope, which Epstein (D) provided.

■ **ISSUE**

Is it constitutional for a state to impose tort liability on an attorney who encourages clients of his former firm to switch to his newly founded firm?

■ **DECISION AND RATIONALE**

(Roberts, J.) Yes. As a starting point, we note that the Supreme Court in *Virginia Pharmacy Board v. Virginia Consumer Council* [issue of whether a statute which prohibited advertisement of prescription drugs violated the First Amendment] ruled that speech which proposes a commercial transaction is protected by the First Amendment. Likewise, a state cannot impose a blanket prohibition on legal advertisements. But after *Ohralik v. Ohio State Bar Association* [issue of whether an attorney can go to hospital to propose a "commercial transaction" to person who was recently injured], states can regulate the commercial transactions that attorneys engage in with clients. Thus, this state can use the tort of interference with contractual relations to regulate the recruitment of clients by attorneys. We turn to the test for tortious interference with contractual relations. There is liability if an individual improperly interferes with the performance of a contract between another and a third party. In determining whether the interference was improper, we consider (1) the nature of the actor's conduct; (2) the actor's motive; (3) the interests of the other with which the actor's conduct interferes; (4) the interests sought to be advanced by the actor; (5) the social interests in protecting the freedom of action of the actor and the contractual interests of the others; (6) the proximity and remoteness of the actor's conduct to the interference; and (7) the relations between the parties. In this case, Epstein's (D) intentional interference was improper because (1) it violated state rules for recruitment of clients; (2) it presented the possibility that the clients would be unduly influenced; (3) it unfairly injured Adler (P) because it was relying on the future revenues which would be generated by these clients; (4) the circumstances surrounding Epstein's (D) departure unduly suggested that the clients leave Adler (P); and (5) clients may suffer from such sharp practices in the long run. Judgment reversed.

Analysis:

Two aspects of this case are worth noting. First, this case exemplifies that the touchstone of many cases involving interference with contractual relations is the issue of whether or not the interference was improper. This inquiry is important because in the modern commercial marketplace, competitors, by the very nature of competition, interfere with the contractual relations of their competitors. Yet, we don't want to discourage that kind of activity. Thus, ordinary competition is not improper interference with contractual relations. The second point worth noting is that this case again highlights the importance of First Amendment law in these types of "speaking" torts. Recall that the First Amendment made an appearance in the context of libel and slander law.

■ CASE VOCABULARY

COMMERCIAL TRANSACTION: A transaction which does not involve personal relations or animus, but merely business considerations.

IMPROPER INTERFERENCE WITH CONTRACTUAL RELATIONS: Interference with contractual relations that is so egregious that it rises to the level of a tort.

Brimelow v. Casson

(Contractee) v. *(Interferer)*

[1923] 1 Ch. 302

COURT RULES THAT LABOR ADVOCATES MAY INTERFERE WITH MUSICAL COMPANY CONTRACTS TO INCREASE WAGES

■ **INSTANT FACTS** Brimelow (P) owned a traveling revue, but he paid the chorus girls very poorly. In an effort to increase the chorus girls' wages, Casson (D) induced the owners of the theaters to break contracts with Brimelow (P).

■ **BLACK LETTER RULE** Interference with contractual relations is not improper if it is done for the public interest.

■ **PROCEDURAL BASIS**

Action for damages for intentional interference with contractual relations.

■ **FACTS**

Brimelow (P) owned a traveling revue, but he paid the chorus girls very poorly. Because of their low wages, the girls were very poor and were forced into prostitution. Appalled by this, Casson (D), who was secretary of the Actor's Association, persuaded the owners of the theaters with which Brimelow (P) had contracts to cancel the contract and not to enter into future contracts until higher wages were paid.

■ **ISSUE**

Is interference with contractual relations improper if it is done for the public interest?

■ **DECISION AND RATIONALE**

(Russell) No. It is clear in this case that there was intentional interference with current and future contractual relations. But we must decide whether this conduct was improper. We conclude that the conduct was not improper and that it was privileged because it was done for the public good. Action dismissed.

Analysis:

Note again how this case demonstrates the friction between interference with economic relations and commerce. In particular, notice how this case reallocates the bargaining power between employer and employee. On the one hand, employees are more likely now to earn higher wages. On the other hand, there is likely to be more unemployment, since employers will now not be able to hire as many of these more expensive employees.

Harmon v. Harmon

(Legatee) v. *(Defrauder)*

404 A.2d 1020 (Me.1979)

COURT RULES THAT IT IS TORTIOUS TO INDUCE A TESTIMONY TO CIRCUMVENT HER WILL

■ **INSTANT FACTS** R. Harmon (P) was to inherit some property from his mother upon her death. H & V Harmon (D) induced the mother to give this very same property to them before she died via inter vivos transfer.

■ **BLACK LETTER RULE** It is tortious to interfere with a potential inheritance by unduly influencing the testatrix to transfer property to a third person prior to her death.

■ **PROCEDURAL BASIS**

Appeal from demurrer in action for damages for interference with potential inheritance.

■ **FACTS**

R. Harmon (P) was to inherit some property from his mother upon her death. In an effort to get this property before it was "too late," H & V Harmon (D) employed fraud and undue influence to induce the mother, who was in ill health and old age, to transfer this property to them via inter vivos transfer. By her most recent will and statements, the mother made it clear that she originally intended half of this property to go to R. Harmon (P).

■ **ISSUE**

Is it tortious to interfere with a potential inheritance by unduly influencing the testatrix to transfer property to a third person prior to her death?

■ **DECISION AND RATIONALE**

(Nichols, J.) Yes. In *Cyr v. Cote* [issue of whether it is tortious to effectively disinherit legatee by inducing legatee to make inter vivos transfer] we recognized that even a mere expectancy of an inheritance is something that the law will protect. We will protect this interest even though it is possible that the testatrix would change her will without the undue influence of a third party. We do this because it is the possibility that the law protects. We are sure that this is correct when we look to the area of contracts, where there too the law protects prospective economic relations. Even Prosser and the Restatement agree. As a final example, a beneficiary under a life insurance policy can claim against a third person if that person somehow damages the beneficiary's interest in the life insurance policy, even though his interest is a mere expectancy. Thus, we conclude that it is a tort for a person to interfere with a gift or transfer that would have likely been received by another. In the case of a legatee who is thus injured, he may bring the action before the testatrix dies, because witnesses and evidence are more likely to be available. Judgment reversed.

Analysis:

This case exemplifies the law of torts reaching beyond commercial transactions to the realm of "private" transactions. Note how there is no contract, or even prospective contract, involved (a will is not a contract because only one party is needed to make it). This facet of this tort tends to make its application almost unlimited. Is there tort liability if you convince your mother that your sister needs clothes for her birthday, rather than the new car that your mother planned to buy her? Not only does this court extend the tort into the realm of private transactions, but it also allows for recovery for a mere "expectancy." In practice, it is very hard to value an expectancy, so damages in this area are likely to be disproportionate at times.

■ CASE VOCABULARY

INTER VIVOS TRANSFER: A transfer of property prior to death.

LEGATEE: One who is entitled to take under a will.

TESTATRIX: A female who leaves property in a will.

TESTATOR: A male who leaves property in a will.

INHERITANCE: The very property that is left in a will.

Neibuhr v. Gage

(Person Under Duress) v. *(Person Applying Pressure)*
108 N.W. 884 (Minn.1906)

COURT RULES THAT DURESS, LIKE DECEIT, IS A TORT

■ **INSTANT FACTS** By threatening that he would falsely tell the police that Neibuhr (P) was guilty of grand larceny, Gage (D) induced Neibuhr (P) to sell stock to him.

■ **BLACK LETTER RULE** Duress based on misrepresentation is a tort.

■ **PROCEDURAL BASIS**

Appeal from dismissal of verdict in action to recover damages for tort of duress based on misrepresentation.

■ **FACTS**

Neibuhr (P) possessed shares of stock in Gage, Hayden & Co. Gage (D) threatened that he would falsely tell the police that Neibuhr (P) was guilty of grand larceny unless Neibuhr (P) transferred his shares of the stock to Gage (D). Neibuhr (P) alleged that he was innocent of grand larceny, but claimed that Gage (D) threatened that he would produce false testimony against Neibuhr (P). Under this threat of immediate arrest, Neibuhr (P) transferred the shares of stock.

■ **ISSUE**

Is duress based on misrepresentation a tort?

■ **DECISION AND RATIONALE**

(Elliot) Yes. First, we note that there is no difference between deceit, which is a tort, and duress based on misrepresentation. This is because fraud based on misrepresentation takes some form of deception, just as the tort of deceit does. Because duress based on misrepresentation is very similar to deceit, we hold that it is a tort. Moreover, the fact that an inured person may also seek the contract remedy of rescission does not preclude him from a tort remedy. It is not for the defendant to determine the choice of remedy. In this case, Gage (P) threatened that he would falsely tell the police that Neibuhr (P) was guilty of grand larceny. Under threat of immediate arrest, Neibuhr (P) transferred the shares of stock. Thus, Gage (D) committed the tort of duress based on misrepresentation. Judgment reversed.

Analysis:

In this odd case, the Supreme Court of Minnesota held that duress, which is typically asserted in order to justify rescission of a contract, may itself be an independent tort. Certainly duress, which takes the form of blackmail in this case, can injure a party by causing him to relinquish some property interest. This duress itself may be actionable, but there is a better way to analyze the situation. In taking Neibuhr's (P) stock, Gage (D) may have committed a tort of intentional interference with property—more specifically, the tort of conversion. Consent is a defense to the tort of conversion. Thus, if Gage (D)

---

could show that Neibuhr (P) consented to the property transfer, Gage (D) would not be liable for conversion. Neibuhr (P) could argue that his consent was invalid because it was obtained by duress. Yielding to a threat, against a party's will, is in fact no consent at all. Thus, rather than asserting a novel theory of recovery, it would have made more sense for Neibuhr (P) to allege that Gage (D) converted Neibuhr's (P) stock, and that Neibuhr (P) consented only because he was under duress. The presence of duress would invalidate Neibuhr's (P) consent and allow him to recover.

■ CASE VOCABULARY

DURESS: The threat of force directed against a person or his property, which can operate to justify rescission of a contract or to invalidate the apparent consent of the threatened party.

Freeman & Mills, Inc. v. Belcher Oil Company

(Accounting Firm) v. *(Delinquent Client)*

11 Cal.4th 85, 44 Cal.Rptr.2d 420, 900 P.2d 669 (1995)

BAD FAITH DENIAL OF A CONTRACT'S EXISTENCE IS NOT A CAUSE OF ACTION UNDER TORT LAW

■ **INSTANT FACTS** Belcher Oil (D) refused to pay its accountant, Freeman & Mills' (P), bill after attorneys for Belcher (D) hired Freeman(P) for accounting services to assist in ongoing litigation.

■ **BLACK LETTER RULE** There is no tort cause of action based on a defendant's bad faith denial of the existence of a contract between the parties.

■ **PROCEDURAL BASIS**

Appeal from the Court of Appeal's decision which reversed the trial court's judgment for the plaintiff and remanded the case for retrial.

■ **FACTS**

Belcher Oil (D) hired a law firm, Morgan, Lewis & Bockius (Morgan), to represent Belcher (D) in a lawsuit. Belcher's general counsel (Dunker) signed a letter of understanding with a Morgan partner (Smaltz), stating that Belcher (D) would pay all costs incurred on its behalf, including fees for accountants. Smaltz then hired Freeman & Mills (P) to provide a financial analysis and litigation support for Belcher (D) in the lawsuit. About one month later, Dunker left Belcher (D) and was replaced by Bowman. The next month, Bowman became dissatisfied with Morgan's efforts and the lawyers were discharged [moves quickly!]. Bowman asked Morgan for a summary of all work performed by Freeman & Mills (P), and, at the same time, directed Smaltz to have Freeman & Mills (P) stop their work for Belcher (D). The total amounted to $77,538.13, and Freeman & Mills (P) billed Morgan accordingly. Payment was never made, so Freeman & Mills (P) then billed Belcher (D) directly, and, for about a year, sent monthly statements and regularly called Belcher (D) about the bill, but no payment was forthcoming. Belcher (D) complained that it had not been consulted about the extent of Freeman & Mills' (P) services, and suggested that Freeman & Mills (P) look to Morgan for payment due. Freeman & Mills (P) finally filed suit against Belcher (D), alleging causes of action for breach of contract, "bad faith denial of contract," and quantum meruit. The jury found for Freeman & Mills (P), and awarded $25,000 in compensatory damages, and $477,538.13 in punitive damages. Three post-trial motions were filed, resulting in a "corrected" judgment of $131,614.93 in compensatory damages, and $400,000 in punitive damages. The Court of Appeals found there was no justification for a tort theory of recovery, and as such reversed the judgment of the trial court and remanded the case for retrial limited to the issue of damages under Freeman & Mills' (P) breach of contract cause of action.

■ **ISSUE**

May a party to a contract recover in tort for another party's bad faith denial of the contract's existence?

■ **DECISION AND RATIONALE**

(Lucas, C.J.) No. We granted review in this case to resolve some of the widespread confusion that has arisen regarding the application of our opinion in Seaman's Direct Buying Service, Inc. v. Standard

---

Oil Co. 36 Cal. 3d 752, 206 Cal. Rptr. 354, 686 P.2d 1158 (1984) (*Seaman's*). We held in that case that a tort cause of action might lie "when, in addition to breaching the contract, [defendant] seeks to shield itself from liability by denying, in bad faith and without probable cause, that the contract exists." We have concluded that the *Seaman's* court incorrectly recognized a tort cause of action based on the defendant's bad faith denial of the existence of a contract between the parties and, after careful review, we have determined that our *Seaman's* holding should be overruled. Much confusion and conflict has arisen regarding the scope and application of our *Seaman's* holding, but confusion and conflict alone might not justify a decision to abrogate *Seaman's*. Many of the pertinent Court of Appeal decisions recognize compelling policy reasons supporting the preclusion of tort remedies for contractual breaches outside the insurance context. Some of these reasons include (1) the different objectives underlying the remedies for tort and contract breach, (2) the importance of predictability in assuring commercial stability in contractual dealings, (3) the potential for converting every contract breach into a tort, with accompanying punitive damage recovery, and (4) the preference for legislative action in affording appropriate remedies. The foregoing policy considerations fully support our decision to overrule *Seaman's* rather than attempt to clarify its uncertain boundaries. Even if we were unimpressed by the nearly unanimous criticism leveled at *Seaman's,* on reconsideration the analytical defects in the opinion have become apparent. It seems anomalous to characterize as "tortious" the bad faith denial of the existence of a contract, while treating as "contractual" the bad faith denial of liability or responsibility under an acknowledged contract. Thus, we overrule *Seaman's* and hold that the judgment of the Court of Appeal, reversing the trial court's judgment in Freeman & Mills' (P) favor and remanding the case for a retrial limited to the issue of damages under Freeman & Mills' (P) breach of contract cause of action, and for judgment in favor of Belcher Oil (D) on Freeman & Mills' (P) bad faith denial of contract cause of action, is affirmed.

Analysis:

The holding in the *Seaman's* case has been widely criticized by legal scholars, has caused considerable confusion among lower courts, and has been rejected by the courts in several other jurisdictions. As the court correctly points out, to include bad faith denials of liability within *Seaman's* scope could potentially convert every contract breach into a tort, which is simply an untenable result. The court's decision in this case effectively serves to keep contract breach actions in the contract law arena, a result which is reasonable and promotes better policy.

■ CASE VOCABULARY

BIFURCATED TRIAL: Guilt and punishment, or liability and damages, or punitive damages and general damages, etc. are decided in two separate trials.

PER CURIAM: A decision in a case in which the author of the opinion is not identified, it is simply credited "to the court."

QUANTUM MERUIT: Allows recovery for a contract implied in law, based upon principles of natural justice and equity, for reasonable value.

Nash v. Baker

(Wife/Children) v. *(Home Interferer)*
522 P.2d 1335 (Okl.App.1974)

COURT RULES THAT TEMPTRESS IS NOT LIABLE FOR LURING AWAY FATHER AND HUSBAND

■ **INSTANT FACTS** Baker (D) seduced away Nash's (P) husband and father.

■ **BLACK LETTER RULE** Intentional interference with paternal relations is not a tort.

■ **PROCEDURAL BASIS**

Appeal from demurrer in action for damages for intentional interference with paternal relations.

■ **FACTS**

Marian Nash (P) was married to James Nash, and they had five children. Baker (D) lured away James Nash with the promise of a finer home, sexual charms, and other inducements. Marian Nash (P) brought an action on her own behalf for loss of affection. The jury found for Baker (D) on this action. Marian Nash (P) also sued on behalf of her children for loss of paternal relations. The trial court dismissed that complaint, and Nash (P) now appeals.

■ **ISSUE**

Is intentional interference with paternal relations a tort?

■ **DECISION AND RATIONALE**

(Romang) No. Although spouses had an action for loss of affection at common law, children did not have the right to sue for loss of paternal affections. Moreover, we are not inclined to create such an action for the benefit of such children because the modern trend is towards increased divorce, "no fault" divorce, and an increase in the number of children whose parents are divorced. Therefore, Nash (P) has no cause of action against Baker (D). Judgment affirmed.

Analysis:

Note again the tendency of the law to expand. The law of torts is concerned with more than just property and contract interests, but also relational interests. Potentially, this tort has no boundaries. For example, does a wife have an action against another woman because that woman merely talked to her husband and made the wife jealous? Do mere boyfriends have standing to bring such actions?

■ **CASE VOCABULARY**

ADULTERY: Sexual intercourse with a married person by a person other than the married person's spouse.

ALIENATION OF AFFECTIONS: The intentional causing of one to lose affection for another, usually spouse.

CRIMINAL INTERCOURSE: Adultery.

LOSS OF CONSORTIUM: Loss of fellowship and friendship between husband and wife.

CHAPTER TWENTY-THREE

Torts in the Age of Statutes

Burnette v. Wahl

Instant Facts: Wahl (D), mother of the five Burnette (D) children, failed to support, nurture and care for the children.

Black Letter Rule: It is no tort for a parent to fail to support, nurture and care for her children.

Nearing v. Weaver

Instant Facts: An abused wife sued police officers for failure to enforce a restraining order she had against her husband.

Black Letter Rule: The defenses of official discretion and official immunity do not preclude potential liability for resulting harm to the intended beneficiary of a judicial order when the police knowingly fail to enforce the order.

Bivens v. Six Unknown Named Agents Of Federal Bureau Of Narcotics

Instant Facts: Agents (D) searched Bivens' (P) home in violation of the Fourth Amendment.

Black Letter Rule: There is a cause of action in federal court for searches by government agents done in violation of the Fourth Amendment.

Alexander v. Sandoval

Instant Facts: Sandoval (P) sued Alexander (D), as director of the Alabama Department of Public Safety, over its policy of administering drivers' license examinations in English only.

Black Letter Rule: Agency regulations cannot create a private cause of action when the authorizing legislation did not so intend.

DeFalco v. Bernas

Instant Facts: DeFalco (P) sued Bernas (D) and other defendants for acts of extortion associated with the withholding of approvals necessary for the development of real property.

Black Letter Rule: To establish a violation of 18 U.S.C. § 1962(c), a plaintiff must show that the defendant, through the commission of two or more acts constituting a pattern of racketeering activity, directly or indirectly participated in an enterprise, the activities of which affected interstate or foreign commerce.

Pulliam v. Coastal Emergency Svcs.

Instant Facts: A woman's family sued the hospital for malpractice after she was misdiagnosed with influenza and subsequently died from bacterial pneumonia and bacteremia.

Black Letter Rule: The medical malpractice cap does not violate any constitutional guarantees and as such will be upheld.

Burnette v. Wahl

(Abandoned Child) v. *(Mother)*
284 Or. 705, 588 P.2d 1105 (1978)

COURT RULES THAT IT IS NOT A TORT FOR MOTHER TO ABANDON CHILDREN

■ **INSTANT FACTS** Wahl (D), mother of the five Burnette (D) children, failed to support, nurture and care for the children.

■ **BLACK LETTER RULE** It is no tort for a parent to fail to support, nurture and care for her children.

■ **PROCEDURAL BASIS**

Appeal from demurrer in action for damages by children against mother for failure to support, nurture and care for the children.

■ **FACTS**

Wahl (D) failed to support, nurture and care for her five children, named Burnette (P). In addition, she abandoned the children, as the children are now in the custody of the state. Finally, Wahl (D) left the Burnette (P) children unattended for long periods of time, and refused to financially support the children. These actions have caused emotional and psychological injury to the Burnette (P) children, although they suffered no physical harm.

■ **ISSUE**

Is it a tort for a parent to fail to support, nurture and care for her children?

■ **DECISION AND RATIONALE**

(Holman) No. First, we note that this claim against a parent, which is based on emotional injury, is different from claims against a parent based on physical injury, where we have allowed recovery. Next, we proceed to analyze some of the relevant statutes in this area of child protection, to see if the statutes can provide the basis for this cause of action. Oregon Code § 418 allows aggrieved children to get support payments. But we must determine if the statutes support tort damages for psychological injury. Upon close examination, the statutes provide broad measures to protect children, such as support actions and criminal sanctions. However, the statutes do not establish a tort action for damages for emotional injury. The legislature explicitly created causes of action in other fields, such as tort actions for unlawful discrimination. Here, however, the legislature created no such action. Moreover, there is no such action at common law. Thus, if this action is to exist, this court must create it. We should not create this cause of action if there is any chance that this would interfere with the total legislative scheme. In this case, it is possible that the creation of an action against parents for emotional injury due to neglect would conflict with other legislative policies, such as the policy of reuniting abandoned children with their parents. Also, this cause of action might interfere with other policies, such as state actions to permanently divest parents of custody. Finally, the courts are not institutionally equipped to address this area of social concern. It is best to leave this problem to the legislature. As another argument, Burnette (P) contends that there should be an action here because Wahl (D) intentionally abandoned the children. This basis for creating an action is inapplicable in the context of parent child relations, because it would interfere in other areas that we do not allow recovery for. For example, it would create an action for children of divorced parents, who intentionally inflict emotional injury. As a final argument, Burnette (P) contends that the common law tort of alienation of affection is applicable. We disagree because the tort is only available for one spouse against another. In any event this tort has been abolished by the legislature. Consequently, the Burnette (P) children fail to state a cause of action. Judgment affirmed.

■ CONCURRENCE

(Tongue) Although immunity between family members for torts causing physical injuries has been abolished, there should still be immunity between family members for emotional injury.

■ CONCURRENCE AND DISSENT

(Lent) I agree with the result in this case because Burnette (P) has not alleged that Wahl (D) intentionally inflicted the emotional injury. I disagree with the reasoning of the majority. I believe that Wahl (D) should pay damages so as to defray some of the social costs that the state incurs in caring for the Burnette (P) children whom she has abandoned.

■ DISSENT

(Linde) I think that there should be a tort for a parent to fail to support, nurture and care for her children. First, mere silence on the part of the legislature does not mean that they didn't want to create an action. In the past, when the legislature has not expressly created an action, we have created a cause of action for the plaintiff who belongs to the class which the statute intended to protect. For example, we did this in *Davis v. Billy's Con-Teena* (issue of whether there was a tort action available to minor children and others, when alcohol was sold to minor children in violation of law). These causes of action are not a pronouncement of new common law, because unlike common law, the cause of action in these types of actions fall when the underlying statutes fall. Turning to this case, the fact that it is a crime to abandon a child weighs in favor of allowing a tort action. Next, I disagree that a creation of an action for failure to support, nurture and care for one's children will interfere with policy of reuniting families. In this case, the plaintiff has alleged that Wahl (D) has abandoned the Burnette (P) children. In these circumstances, nothing will reunite this family. It is unlikely that the legislature intended this, since the legislature did provide for state prosecution. Finally, we provide children with a cause of action for physical injury, and given this, there is no reason why there shouldn't be a cause of action for emotional injury.

Analysis:

This case is an example of a court unwilling to further extend the law of torts. Although many courts allow recovery against parents by children for physical injury, and some courts allow recovery by one spouse against a third person for emotional damage due to alienation of affections, this court was unwilling to extend an action for emotional injury caused by a parent against children. However, it is difficult to determine whether or not the rule in this case promotes or discourages family harmony. Does it encourage parents to neglect their children? Should the court be involved in family relations?

■ CASE VOCABULARY

LEGISLATIVE PURPOSE: The underlying goals which the legislature hopes to promote in passing a certain statute.

STATUTORY SCHEME: The overall policy goals of a collection of statutes.

Nearing v. Weaver

(*Abused Wife*) v. (*Police Officers*)
295 Or. 702, 670 P.2d 137 (1983)

COPS CAN BE HELD LIABLE FOR FAILURE TO ENFORCE RESTRAINING ORDER

■ **INSTANT FACTS** An abused wife sued police officers for failure to enforce a restraining order she had against her husband.

■ **BLACK LETTER RULE** The defenses of official discretion and official immunity do not preclude potential liability for resulting harm to the intended beneficiary of a judicial order when the police knowingly fail to enforce the order.

■ **PROCEDURAL BASIS**

Appeal from the circuit court's summary judgment for defendants, affirmed by the Court of Appeals.

■ **FACTS**

Nearing (P) was separated from her husband in November 1979. Almost six months later, the husband entered Nearing's (P) home without permission and assaulted her. Nearing called the police and Weaver (D) was one of the officers to respond. Nearing's (P) husband was arrested and charged with assault. The circuit court issued a restraining order for Nearing (P) against her husband, and it was served upon him. A copy of the order and proof of service were delivered to the police department. The next month, Nearing's (P) husband twice again entered her home without permission, first damaging the premises, and then attempting to remove the children. Nearing (P) again called Officer Weaver (D), and asked him to arrest her husband for violating the restraining order. Weaver (D) did not arrest him, however, as he did not actually see the husband on the premises. [She did it herself, right?] Nearing's (P) husband returned to her home three more times that month, seeking entry, assaulting Nearing's (P) friend, and damaging a van. Weaver (D) told Nearing (P) that her husband would be arrested, however no action was ever taken. [So many criminals, so little time.] Two days later, Nearing's (P) husband called her and threatened to kill her friend, and a few days after that the husband again assaulted Nearing's (P) friend outside her home. Nearing (P) claims that, as a result of the officers' (D) failure to enforce the restraining order issued against her husband, she and her children have suffered severe emotional distress and psychological impairment. The police officers (D) denied the allegations, and pleaded the affirmative defenses of immunity and discretion. The circuit court granted summary judgment for the officers (D), and that judgment was affirmed by the Court of Appeals.

■ **ISSUE**

Are officers who knowingly fail to enforce a judicial order potentially liable for resulting harm to the psychic and physical health of the intended beneficiaries of the order?

■ **DECISION AND RATIONALE**

(Linde, J.) Yes. Police officers who knowingly fail to enforce a judicial order are potentially liable for resulting harm to the psychic and physical health of the intended beneficiaries of the judicial order. Weaver (D) contends that the law does not allow recovery on the theory of negligent infliction of emotional distress, however the law does allow recovery when the defendant's conduct infringes some legal right of the plaintiff, independent of an ordinary tort claim for negligence. The duty Weaver (D) is alleged to have neglected is not simply an ordinary common law duty of due care to avoid predictable harm to another, it is a specific duty imposed by statute for the benefit of individuals previously identified by a judicial order. The order clearly gave rise to a duty of Weaver's (D) toward Nearing (P). Weaver (D) also argues that the police officers are immune from liability due to the fact that they were engaged in a discretionary function or duty. Discretion, as we have previously stated, exists only insofar as an officer has been delegated responsibility for value judgments and policy choices among competing goals and priorities. There is no discretion of that kind in enforcing restraining orders, and the circuit court erred in denying Nearing's (P) motion to strike this defense. Weaver (D) also claims official immunity under the Oregon statutes. That section, however, provides immunity for making good faith arrests, not for failing to do so. To invert that text as Weaver (D) proposes, would fly in the face of the legislative purpose of the statute, thus this affirmative defense raised by Weaver (D) should also have been stricken. The dissent raises several issues which we must also address. The dissent asserts that we "overrule" two cases in which the court declined to find defendants liable for injury resulting from conduct contrary to statutes. Neither case was cited by Weaver (D), however, and neither case holds that statutory duties never give rise to civil liability unless the legislature makes that intention explicit. That conclusion must be reached for different statutes on a case-by-case basis. The dissent also states that this decision creates "strict" liability. We have, however, made it clear that the liability is not absolute; there may be defenses. The dissent asserts that the plaintiffs did not make a claim based on the statute, however Nearing's (P) argument to the circuit did indeed cover both a common law and a statutory theory. Finally, the dissent simply opposes tort liability for injuries caused by disregard of the statute on policy grounds, because it may cost local governments money. That argument can be made against all claims under the Tort Claims Act, yet the act was nevertheless enacted. That policy decision was made by the legislature; it is not a new policy choice to be made in this case. Additionally, there is in fact no liability if the statute is actually followed. When compliance with the statute, unless prevented by good cause, will avoid exposure to liability, the argument that there should be no liability because of the potential expense, actually is an argument for a privilege not to comply with the statute. But that policy choice, like the policy of the Tort Claims Act, also has been settled by the legislature. In this case, there was a specific duty toward the Nearings (P), thus the decision of the Court of Appeals affirming the summary judgment must be reversed and the case remanded to the circuit court for further proceedings.

■ DISSENT

(Peterson, J.) I must dissent for several reasons. The majority has created a strict liability tort against public bodies and their police employees which is inconsistent with a number of recent decisions of this court, which it overrules without a passing glance. The ability of public bodies to perform their duties may depend upon availability of resources and demands of other mandated duties, and we should tread warily before holding them liable without fault for damages arising from their failure to perform the duty imposed. The Nearing's (P) theory of recovery has always been negligence, and on its own, the majority has converted the case to one of strict liability. If stare decisis has any residual life, we must follow the past cases and reject the creation of a new, strict liability tort based upon violation of a statute.

Analysis:

This case is important because it explicitly sets forth a standard whereby public officials can be held liable for their tortious conduct, and the usual defenses of discretionary immunity and official immunity will not afford absolute protection. What would be a defense under the statute is still a defense to civil liability, however failure to act as the statute provides will create the potential for liability. The failure of the police to respond as is statutorily required will not be excused as discretionary. The express purpose of the statute in this case was to negate any discretion on the officers' part, and this conclusion does not depend on the facts in each individual case. The court does an excellent job of distinguishing the previously decided cases which the dissent attempts to claim are overruled by its immediate decision. The court recognizes that the statutes in this case are unique in that the legislative purpose is clearly to protect specific, named individuals for whom the order is issued, not simply to protect the community at large by general law enforcement activity. The court also points out that this decision does not create liability without fault, nor does it mean that the liability is absolute. The governing standard of conduct is set by the statute itself, not this decision.

■ CASE VOCABULARY

AD HOC JUDGMENTS: Judgments made for a specific purpose.

MANDATORY ARREST: Statutory provision requiring the arrest of a party violating a judicial order.

Bivens v. Six Unknown Named Agents of Federal Bureau of Narcotics

(*Homeowner*) v. (*Illegal Searchers*)

403 U.S. 388, 91 S.Ct. 1999 (1971)

COURT RULES THAT IT IS A TORT FOR FEDERAL AGENTS TO SEARCH IN VIOLATION OF THE FOURTH AMENDMENT

■ **INSTANT FACTS** Agents (D) searched Bivens' (P) home in violation of the Fourth Amendment.

■ **BLACK LETTER RULE** There is a cause of action in federal court for searches by government agents done in violation of the Fourth Amendment.

■ **PROCEDURAL BASIS**

Appeal from sustaining of demurrer in action for damages for search in violation of the Fourth Amendment.

■ **FACTS**

Agents (D) searched Bivens' (P) home in violation of the Fourth Amendment. As the Agents (D) searched the home, they handcuffed Bivens (P) in front of his wife and children, and threatened to arrest the entire family. They searched the entire house.

■ **ISSUE**

Is there is a cause of action in federal court for searches by government agents done in violation of the Fourth Amendment?

■ **DECISION AND RATIONALE**

(Brennan, J.) Yes. First, we reject the argument that Bivens' (P) remedy should lie only in state court. We reject this argument because the common law state actions in this area were fashioned to protect one private citizen from another private citizen, and do not adequately deal with the unique problem of a government official searching the home of a private citizen in violation of the Fourth Amendment. For example, the state law of trespass imposes no liability where the homeowner consents to entry. However, when government agents are involved, a homeowner may feel compelled to consent even though he doesn't want to, because the officer appears to have authority. Moreover, federal courts must be open because it is possible that a state may not penalize unreasonable searches and searches without probable cause. This would deprive the Fourth Amendment of force. Thus, where a federally created right has been invaded, the federal courts will fashion appropriate remedies. Finally, we note that Congress has not seen fit to deprive such plaintiffs of an action for damages. In this case, Bivens (P) has alleged that the Agents (D) searched his home in violation of the Fourth Amendment. This is sufficient to survive a demurrer. Judgment reversed.

■ **CONCURRENCE**

(Harlan, J.) The power to authorize damages as a remedy to a violation of the Fourth Amendment is vested by the Constitution in the federal courts as well as Congress. This is because it is undisputed that the federal courts are empowered to enforce equitable remedies (such as the suppression of evidence); it would be anomalous to accord the federal courts equitable remedies while denying to the court the authority to fashion damages as a remedy. While it is true that the courts must first find that damages are "necessary" or "appropriate" before damages will be allowed, I reject the view that the test should be heightened in this context because the federal courts are specially charged with enforcing the Constitution. In this case, I agree that damages are "necessary" or appropriate in this context. I make this conclusion because the federal government is immune from suit. Thus, Bivens (P) must pursue the Agents (D) if he is to have a remedy at all. Moreover, the mere fact that such damages will not deter future lawlessness is not enough to defeat this determination.

■ DISSENT

(Burger, J.) I dissent because nowhere does the Constitution empower the federal courts to grant damages for violation of the Fourth Amendment. Also, Congress has not authorized damages in this context. Separation of powers dictates that it is for Congress to decide whether or not damages should be available for violation of the Fourth Amendment.

■ DISSENT

(Black, J.): Although Congress has created a cause of action against state officials for violation of the Fourth Amendment, it has created no such action against federal officials. Moreover, given the risk of frivolous lawsuits, as well as the fact that the courts are already overloaded with cases, it is unsound to create yet another cause of action.

Analysis:

This case demonstrates that a tort cause of action need not be fashioned solely from the operation of a common law court. Indeed, the United States Supreme Court is certainly not a common law court. Rather, the cause of action in this case was created by the Fourth Amendment. This makes this tort uniquely federal. This is rare, as most torts are matters of state law.

■ CASE VOCABULARY

COMMON-LAW ACTION: Old historical law, based on precedent, originally in England; a civil suit, as distinguished from a proceeding to enforce a penalty; not a criminal prosecution.

FOURTH AMENDMENT: Provision of the U.S. Constitution prohibiting unreasonable searches and searches not supported by probable cause.

PROBABLE CAUSE: That degree of suspicion that evidence of crime is present in a particular place which is required before a search may be undertaken.

Alexander v. Sandoval

(Director of Alabama Department of Public Safety) v. *(Non–English–Speaking Citizen)*

532 U.S. 275, 121 S.Ct. 1511 (2001)

THERE IS NO PRIVATE CAUSE OF ACTION TO ENFORCE AGENCY REGULATIONS UNDER TITLE VI

■ **INSTANT FACTS** Sandoval (P) sued Alexander (D), as director of the Alabama Department of Public Safety, over its policy of administering drivers' license examinations in English only.

■ **BLACK LETTER RULE** Agency regulations cannot create a private cause of action when the authorizing legislation did not so intend.

■ PROCEDURAL BASIS

Certiorari to review a decision of the Eleventh Circuit Court of Appeals affirming a district court injunction.

■ FACTS

Alexander (D) was the director of the Alabama Department of Public Safety, which is subject to Title VI of the Civil Rights Act of 1964 due to its receipt of federal financial assistance. Title VI provides that no person shall be denied participation in or the benefits of any program or activity by reason of his race, color, or national origin, and it authorizes federal agencies to promulgate regulations to carry out its provisions. The Department of Justice (DOJ) promulgated a regulation forbidding recipients of federal funding to "utilize criteria or methods of administration which have the effect of subjecting individuals to discrimination because of their race, color, or national origin." To promote public safety, the Department decided to administer drivers' license examinations in English only. Sandoval (P), a non-English-speaking Alabama citizen, sued in Alabama federal court for discrimination on the basis of his national origin. The district court found that the English-only policy was discriminatory and issued an injunction. On appeal, the Eleventh Circuit Court of Appeals affirmed, deciding that Sandoval (P) had a private cause of action under Title VI. Alexander (D) sought a writ of certiorari.

■ ISSUE

May private individuals sue to enforce disparate-impact regulations promulgated under Title VI of the Civil Rights Act of 1964?

■ DECISION AND RATIONALE

(Scalia, J.) No. Under Title VI, a private citizen may sue to enforce the statute and obtain injunctive relief and damages. A Title VI violation requires intentional discrimination by the federal funding recipient. While the statute proscribes intentional discrimination, the DOJ regulation applies to disparate-impact actions that do not directly discrimination on a protected basis, but rather have the effect of doing so. A private right of action to enforce the former does not create a private right of action to enforce the latter.

Private rights of action must be created by Congress, so the language of Title VI must be examined to determine whether a private right of action to enforce agency regulations was intended. Reviewing the text of the statute, § 601 provides that "no person ... shall ... be subjected to discrimination." Section 602, on the other hand, authorizes federal agencies to "effectuate" the provisions of § 601 through agency regulation. Its language empowers federal agency action to further the provisions of Title VI, but it cannot be read as conferring private rights upon individuals subject to discrimination. The means of enforcement set forth by the statute include limiting federal funding, requesting a funding recipient to cease and desist certain practices, and requesting judicial review, among others. By expressly providing the means of enforcing regulations promulgated under § 602, it must be assumed that Congress intended its remedial scheme to be exhaustive. Without express reference to a private right of action, none can be presumed to be intended. Nor can the language of the regulation itself create a private right of action where Congress chose not to create one by legislation. Without express language of Congressional intent, there is no private cause of action to enforce agency regulations under Title VI. Reversed.

Analysis:

While the Supreme Court foreclosed a private right of action to enforce regulations promulgated under Title VI, there is some debate whether a plaintiff may enforce disparate impact claims under 42 U.S.C. § 1983. Under § 1983, a person may assert a private right of action based on any discriminatory governmental action taken under color of law. While the majority of federal circuits have determined that Title VI regulations may not be enforced through § 1983, the Supreme Court has not yet considered the issue.

■ CASE VOCABULARY

DISCRIMINATION: The effect of a law or established practice that confers privileges on a certain class or that denies privileges to a certain class because of race, age, sex, nationality, religion, or handicap.

DISPARATE IMPACT: The adverse effect of a facially neutral practice (especially an employment practice) that nonetheless discriminates against persons because of their race, sex, national origin, age, or disability and that is not justified by business necessity.

NATIONAL ORIGIN: The country in which a person was born, or from which the person's ancestors came.

DeFalco v. Bernas

(Land Purchaser) v. *(Road Constructor)*

244 F.3d 286 (2d Cir.2001)

RACKETEERING ACTIVITIES WITHOUT PROXIMATE CAUSE DO NOT SUPPORT A RICO CLAIM

■ **INSTANT FACTS** DeFalco (P) sued Bernas (D) and other defendants for acts of extortion associated with the withholding of approvals necessary for the development of real property.

■ **BLACK LETTER RULE** To establish a violation of 18 U.S.C. § 1962(c), a plaintiff must show that the defendant, through the commission of two or more acts constituting a pattern of racketeering activity, directly or indirectly participated in an enterprise, the activities of which affected interstate or foreign commerce.

■ **PROCEDURAL BASIS**

On appeal to consider a decision of the federal district court vacating a verdict for the plaintiffs.

■ **FACTS**

DeFalco (P) bought and proposed to develop land in New York. He sued Bernas (D) and other defendants for acts of extortion associated with the withholding of approvals necessary to develop the land. The defendants were public officials and private individuals who were part of or influenced by the local government. Dirie (D) was the Town Supervisor, responsible for issuing the necessary development approvals for the Town. The Bernas (D) defendants were private individuals who performed road construction and gravel removal on the property.

After the purchase of the land, the defendants threatened and intimidated the plaintiffs to force the plaintiffs to surrender the property and employ certain individuals or risk the withholding of crucial development approvals. For instance, Dirie (D) insisted that DeFalco (P) grant his son a logging contract on the property to secure the necessary approvals from the Planning Board. When DeFalco (P) hired an out-of-state logger, Dirie (D) threatened that his approval would be withheld. Additionally, the Bernas (D) defendants demanded an assignment of the gravel pit located on the property. When DeFalco (P) refused, Bernas (D) threatened to shut down the development. The plaintiffs filed suit in federal court under the Racketeer Influenced and Corrupt Organizations Act (RICO), claiming that the defendants impeded the plaintiffs' real estate activities. The plaintiffs alleged that the defendants engaged in a conspiracy, plan, and scheme to use the local government as a racketeering enterprise to extort money and property. A jury determined that the defendants were a RICO enterprise engaged in a pattern of racketeering and entered a verdict for the plaintiffs. After the district court vacated the award, the plaintiffs appealed.

■ **ISSUE**

Were the defendants a RICO enterprise engaged in a pattern of racketeering in violation of 18 U.S.C. § 1962(c)?

■ DECISION AND RATIONALE

(Underhill, J.) Yes. To establish a violation of 18 U.S.C. § 1962(c), "a plaintiff must establish that a defendant, through the commission of two or more acts constituting a pattern of racketeering activity, directly or indirectly participated in an enterprise, the activities of which affected interstate or foreign commerce." A RICO enterprise "includes any individual, partnership, corporation, association, or other legal entity, and any union or group of individuals associated in fact although not a legal entity." Among the activities constituting "racketeering" are murder, kidnapping, gambling, arson, robbery, bribery, and extortion.

To constitute a RICO enterprise, more than one individual must associate as a common unit for a common purpose, and the enterprise and the individuals must be distinct. Individuals acting within the enterprise are insufficient to establish a RICO enterprise. Here, the evidence was sufficient for a reasonable jury to conclude that the individual defendants were separate from the local government, using their political influence to influence the town's decision-making. That is not to say that a local governmental unit cannot be deemed a RICO enterprise. By including bribery and extortion among the predicate acts of racketeering, the statute indicates an intent to include governmental units as possible RICO enterprises. Here the jury determined that the town was a RICO enterprise, and it concluded that the individual defendants' liability was separate from any enterprise activities.

In order to establish that the RICO enterprise engages in interstate commerce, only a minimal effect on interstate commerce is necessary. Here, one of the allegations complained of is Dirie's (D) demand that the plaintiffs break a contract with an out-of-state logger. Moreover, evidence of the town's ordinary business indicates its impact on interstate commerce. To sustain a violation of the statute, the defendants must also be "employed by or associated with any enterprise ... to conduct or participate, directly or indirectly, in the conduct of such enterprise's affairs through a pattern of racketeering activity." Participation in the enterprise's affairs requires participation in the management or operation of the enterprise. Here, the evidence supports that the individual defendants participated in the town's affairs. Dirie (D) served as a member of the Town Board and the Town Legislature, using his authority to affect the plaintiffs' development. Similarly, a reasonable jury could conclude that the Bernas (D) defendants, who were involved in road construction and gravel removal, participated in the town's affairs. While not public officials, these defendants were "associated with" the town and helped direct town affairs. When these defendants demanded a financial gain from the plaintiffs' development, they threatened to have the development shut down. In response, the defendant tax assessors reassessed the tax value of the plaintiffs' land to increase their property taxes, and Dirie (D) required acquiescence to the Bernas's (D) demands to secure the necessary development approvals. The evidence supports the jury's findings.

Turning to the two predicate acts required to establish a RICO violation, a reasonable jury could find that the defendants engaged in such acts. DeFalco (P) argues that each of the five times he abided by Dirie's (D) orders, he did so under fear of economic loss, sufficient to establish five acts of extortion. Extortion is "the obtaining of property from another, with his consent, induced by wrongful use of actual or threatened force, violence, or fear, or under color of official right." Dirie's (D) demands are sufficient to establish the obtaining of property under threat of economic loss. For the Bernas (D) defendants' extortion to constitute a pattern of racketeering, it must have closed-ended continuity or open-ended continuity. Closed-ended continuity requires predicate acts of sufficient duration to demonstrate racketeering over a substantial period of time. Generally, the predicate acts must span at least two years to meet the closed-ended continuity requirement. Here, the evidence at best suggests that the extortion was committed over a year-and-a-half span. Such a period is insufficient to establish closed-ended continuity. However, the evidence supports that the pattern of racketeering activity satisfies the open-ended continuity requirement. To establish open-ended continuity, "the plaintiff need not show that the predicates extended over a substantial period of time but must show that there was a threat of continuing criminal activity beyond the period during which the predicate acts were performed." When an enterprise engages primarily in unlawful activities, the threat of continuing criminal activity is established. When, however, the enterprise engages in primarily legitimate business, there must be evidence to demonstrate by the nature of the predicate acts themselves that the threat of continuing criminal activity exists. Here, although the defendants' goals were finite, the evidence is sufficient to demonstrate that their demands and extortion would continue indefinitely until they obtained DeFalco's (P) property, establishing open-ended continuity.

Having established a RICO violation, it must also be demonstrated that the violation was the proximate cause of DeFalco's (P) injury. In this instance, De Falco (P) must prove that but for the defendant's racketeering activities, he was otherwise entitled to his development approvals and that no intervening causes would prevent him from selling his lots. Here, the plaintiffs have failed to show a sufficient causal link between the defendants' pattern of racketeering and their injuries. Affirmed.

Analysis:

The RICO statute is one of the most complex statutes in practice. The detailed and precise pleading requirements often result in successful motions to dismiss and summary judgment. Attorneys bringing a RICO claim must do so with extreme care to avoid an early dismissal.

■ CASE VOCABULARY

BRIBERY: The corrupt payment, receipt, or solicitation of a private favor for official action.

EXTORTION: The offense committed by a public official who illegally obtains property under the color of office, especially an official's collection of an unlawful fee.

PROXIMATE CAUSE: A cause that is legally sufficient to result in liability.

PREDICATE ACT: Under RICO, one of two or more related acts of racketeering necessary to establish a pattern.

RACKETEER INFLUENCED AND CORRUPT ORGANIZATIONS ACT: A law designed to attack organized criminal activity and preserve marketplace integrity by investigating, controlling, and prosecuting persons who participate or conspire to participate in racketeering.

RACKETEERING: A system of organized crime traditionally involving the extortion of money from businesses by intimidation, violence, or other illegal methods. A pattern of illegal activity (such as bribery, extortion, fraud, and murder) carried out as part of an enterprise (such as a crime syndicate) that is owned or controlled by those engaged in the illegal activity.

Pulliam v. Coastal Emergency Svcs.

(*Dead Woman's Family*) v. (*Hospital*)

257 Va. 1, 509 S.E.2d 307 (1999)

CONSTITUTIONALITY OF STATUTORY MEDICAL MALPRACTICE CAP UPHELD

■ **INSTANT FACTS** A woman's family sued the hospital for malpractice after she was misdiagnosed with influenza and subsequently died from bacterial pneumonia and bacteremia.

■ **BLACK LETTER RULE** The medical malpractice cap does not violate any constitutional guarantees and as such will be upheld.

■ **PROCEDURAL BASIS**

Appeal from trial court judge's reduction of the jury award to Pulliam (P).

■ **FACTS**

Mrs. Pulliam had been diagnosed with influenza by her private physician. Two days later she presented to a hospital and was seen by a Coastal Emergency Svcs. (D) doctor, Dr. DiGiovanna. An hour after she arrived at the emergency room, she was discharged with a prescription for a muscle relaxant and instructions on influenza and bed rest [who needs instructions on *bed rest*?]. About four hours later, Mrs. Pulliam returned to the emergency room complaining of general weakness [that's helpful]. She underwent another exam by a different physician, and was started on IV fluids and further tests. She was transferred to the ICU, where her condition worsened until her death that evening [oops!]. An autopsy revealed that her cause of death was bacterial pneumonia and bacteremia. Her husband sued Dr. DiGiovanna and Coastal Emergency Svcs. (D) for medical malpractice. The jury returned a verdict of $2,045,000. Pursuant to a statute which limited the amount of recovery in a medical malpractice case, the trial judge reduced the verdict to $1,000,000, and this appeal followed.

■ **ISSUE**

Is a statutory provision which places a monetary cap on recovery in medical malpractice cases constitutional?

■ **DECISION AND RATIONALE**

(Carrico, C.J.) Yes. A statutory provision placing a monetary cap on recovery in medical malpractice cases is constitutional and will be upheld. We adhere to the well-settled principle that *all* actions of the General Assembly are presumed to be constitutional. This Court, therefore, will resolve any reasonable doubt regarding a statute's constitutionality in favor of its validity. We previously upheld the constitutionality of the cap in *Etheridge v. Medical Center Hospitals*, 237 Va. 87, 376 S.E.2d 525 (1989), and when a court of last resort has established a precedent, it will not be treated lightly or ignored in the absence of flagrant error or mistake. Pulliam (P) argues that the cap violates his Seventh Amendment right to a jury trial, however the cap is applied only after a plaintiff has had the benefit of a proper jury trial, thus the constitutional mandate has been satisfied. If it is permissible for a legislature to enact a statute of limitations completely barring recovery in a particular cause of action without impinging upon the right of trial by jury, it should be permissible for the legislature to impose a limitation upon the amount of recovery as well. Pulliam (P) also argues that the cap was impermissible special legislation.

We disagree. If a law is made to apply to a class, and the classification bears a reasonable and substantial relation to the object sought to be accomplished, it will survive a special-laws constitutional challenge. We think that the cap does bear such relation to the General Assembly's objective to protect the public's health, safety, and welfare by insuring the availability of health care providers. Accordingly, we conclude that the medical malpractice cap does not constitute special legislation. Pulliam (P) next argues that the cap effectively takes the property of himself and his son in violation of the constitutional protections against the taking of private property with just compensation. This argument must fail as well, as it is only when a right has accrued or a claim has arisen that it is subject to the protections of the due process clause. Pulliam's (P) cause of action for wrongful death had not accrued at the time the cap was imposed upon recoveries in medical malpractice cases, thus there could be no property interest. Accordingly, we find no violation of the "taking" clauses in this case. Pulliam (P) also argues that the Court should apply an intermediate level of scrutiny, rather than the rational basis test, in our due process and equal protection analysis of the medical malpractice cap. Here, however, no fundamental right or suspect class is affected by application of the cap, therefore the rational basis test is the proper standard to be used. Finally, Pulliam (P) argues that the cap violates the separation of powers doctrine and also invades the province of the judiciary. We have said before, and we adhere to the principle now, that the legislature has the power to provide, modify, or repeal a remedy. Whether the remedy is viewed as a modification of the common law, or as establishing the jurisdiction of the courts in specific cases, clearly it was a proper exercise of legislative power. Thus we find no merit in Pulliam's (P) last argument either. As such, we hold that the statutory cap applies to Coastal Emergency Svcs. (D), and that pre-judgment interest is included in the statutory cap. Affirmed.

■ CONCURRENCE

(Kinser, J.) I agree with the majority's decision and rationale that the medical malpractice cap is constitutional, however I believe that the cap creates an unwarranted injustice in certain situations. Such concerns cannot influence my decision, but I express my views with hope that the General Assembly will adopt a more equitable method by which to ensure the availability of health care.

Analysis:

Compare this case to *William v. Wilson* [a statute which limits the right to punitive damages contrary to common law is unconstitutional]. Damages were up to the jury at common law, so doesn't a statute limiting damages fly in the face of the common law? We will not know from this case because the plaintiff did not raise the issue in the same manner as it was raised in *Williams*. In general, this is another case where the importance of *stare decisis* is made abundantly clear. The weight of past case law made this decision an easy one for the Court. Even in the face of questionable judgment on the legislature's part, the Court stands firm on the principle that it does not pass on the wisdom of a statute, it merely inquires into the question of legislative power. The court clearly outlines each point of Pulliam's (P) claim, and soundly follows substantial precedent to arrive at the conclusion that the statute is indeed constitutional.

■ CASE VOCABULARY

ADDITUR: Increase by the court of an inadequate jury verdict.

REMITTITUR: Reduction by the court of an excessive jury verdict.

SERIATIM: One at a time.

CHAPTER TWENTY–FOUR

Compensation Systems as Substitutes for Tort Law

Blankenship v. Cincinnati Milacron Chemicals, Inc.

Instant Facts: Blankenship (P) was injured on the job while working for Cincinnati (D).

Black Letter Rule: An employee in Ohio may maintain an action against his employer for an intentional tort.

Blankenship v. Cincinnati Milacron Chemicals, Inc.

(Injured Employee) v. *(Employer)*

69 Ohio St.2d 608, 433 N.E.2d 572 (1982)

COURT RULES THAT EMPLOYER IN WORKERS' COMPENSATION STATE MAY NOT INTENTIONALLY INJURE WORKERS AND GET AWAY WITH IT

■ **INSTANT FACTS** Blankenship (P) was injured on the job while working for Cincinnati (D).

■ **BLACK LETTER RULE** An employee in Ohio may maintain an action against his employer for an intentional tort.

■ PROCEDURAL BASIS

Appeal from affirmance of granting of demurrer in action damages for an intentional tort.

■ FACTS

Blankenship (P), along with several other employees, was injured when exposed to chemicals while working at Cincinnati Chemicals (Cincinnati) (D). Blankenship (P) and the employees alleged that Cincinnati (D) knew the conditions could cause injury, yet failed to warn the employees, failed to provide medical examinations as required by law, and failed to notify the appropriate state and federal agencies as required by law. Blankenship (P) and the employees finally alleged that Cincinnati's (D) omissions were intentional, willful and malicious.

■ ISSUE

Can an employee in Ohio maintain an action against his employer for an intentional tort?

■ DECISION AND RATIONALE

(Brown, J.) Yes. The Ohio constitution gives the legislature the authority to provide for a system of workers' compensation. Pursuant to this authority, the legislature has passed a workers' compensation statute. This statute allows employers to contribute to a fund which is used to pay for occupational injuries. Employers who contribute to this fund are immune from any employee suit at common law or by statute if the employee's injury arises out of his employment. However, employers are not immune from suit in cases involving intentional torts because employees do not anticipate that they will face this risk when they decide to work for an employer, and because such intentional torts are not deemed to arise out of employment. Moreover, the policy of the workers' compensation act is that an employer is protected from suit for negligence in exchange for making contributions to the fund, and that an employee relinquishes his common law remedies and accepts lower benefits in exchange for greater assurance of payment if injured. If we bar suit for an intentional tort, these policies will be frustrated, since we will in effect be encouraging employers to intentionally injure employees, which in turn will make the workplace less safe. In this case, Blankenship (P) and the employees have made allegations of an intentional tort. They should be allowed to prove these allegations. Judgment reversed.

■ DISSENT

(Holmes, J.) Actions for intentional tort should only be allowed in cases of actual intent.

■ DISSENT

(Krupansky, J.) Intentional torts should be barred because there is no express exception for such torts in the Workers' Compensation Act.

Analysis:

This case is an example of how tort law is a system of social engineering. First, recall that the traditional system of general negligence encourages individuals to be "careful." Although this approach to tort law encourages care, it results in some injured individuals going without compensation because they can't prove negligence. Note that the workers' compensation system is a hybrid system of strict liability: Every injured person is compensated, but the state, not the employer, pays. Although all who are injured are compensated, this system has the serious drawback that employees are not encouraged to be careful, because the state will pay for all who are injured. This is clearly undesirable. But, in the other direction, employers are also not encouraged to be careful. This case acknowledges that careless employers are protected by workers' compensation. But, employers who cause intentional injury are not protected.

■ CASE VOCABULARY

WORKERS' COMPENSATION: A system of tort compensation, where all who are injured are compensated as a matter of strict liability, and where the state pays.